**Department
of the
Treasury**

**Internal
Revenue
Service**

Your Federal Income Tax

For Individuals

Catalog Number 10311G

For use in preparing
2018 Returns

TAX GUIDE
2018
FOR INDIVIDUALS

Get forms and other information faster and easier at:
- *IRS.gov* (English)
- *IRS.gov/Chinese* (中文)
- *IRS.gov/Russian* (Русский)
- *IRS.gov/Spanish* (Español)
- *IRS.gov/Korean* (한국어)
- *IRS.gov/Vietnamese* (TiếngViệt)

Jan 30, 2019

Department
of the
Treasury

Internal
Revenue
Service

Your Federal Income Tax
For Individuals

Contents

The explanations and examples in this publication reflect the interpretation by the Internal Revenue Service (IRS) of:

- Tax laws enacted by Congress,
- Treasury regulations, and
- Court decisions.

However, the information given does not cover every situation and is not intended to replace the law or change its meaning.

This publication covers some subjects on which a court may have made a decision more favorable to taxpayers than the interpretation by the IRS. Until these differing interpretations are resolved by higher court decisions or in some other way, this publication will continue to present the interpretations by the IRS.

All taxpayers have important rights when working with the IRS. These rights are described in *Your Rights as a Taxpayer* in the back of this publication.

What's New

This section summarizes important tax changes that took effect in 2018. Most of these changes are discussed in more detail throughout this publication.

Future developments. For the latest information about the tax law topics covered in this publication, such as legislation enacted after it was published, go to *IRS.gov/Pub17*.

 At the time this publication went to print, Congress was considering legislation that would do the following.

1. *Provide additional tax relief for those affected by certain 2018 disasters.*

2. *Extend certain tax benefits that expired at the end of 2017 and that currently can't be claimed on your 2018 tax return, such as the deduction for qualified tuition and fees and for mortgage insurance premiums, and the credit for nonbusiness energy property. See chapter 37 for a more complete list.*

3. *Change certain other tax provisions.*

To learn whether this legislation was enacted, resulting in changes that affect your 2018 tax return, go to Recent Developments at IRS.gov/Pub17.

Form 1040 has been redesigned for 2018. The new design uses a "building block" approach. Form 1040, which many taxpayers can file by itself, is supplemented with new Schedules 1 through 6. These additional schedules will be used as needed to complete more complex tax returns. The instructions for the new schedules are at the end of the Instructions for Form 1040. See chapter 1.

Forms 1040A and 1040EZ no longer available. Forms 1040A and 1040EZ aren't available to file your 2018 taxes. If you used one of these forms in the past, you will now file Form 1040. Some 2018 forms and publications that were released in 2017 or early 2018 may still have references to Form 1040A or Form 1040EZ. Please disregard these references. See chapter 1.

Due date of return. File your tax return by April 15, 2019. If you live in Maine or Massachusetts, you have until April 17, 2019, because of the Patriots' Day holiday in those states and the Emancipation Day holiday in the District of Columbia. See chapter 1.

Change in tax rates. For 2018, most tax rates have been reduced. The 2018 tax rates are 10%, 12%, 22%, 24%, 32%, 35%, and 37%.

Standard deduction amount increased. For 2018, the standard deduction amount has been increased for all filers. The amounts are:

- Single or Married filing separately—$12,000.

- Married filing jointly or Qualifying widow(er)—$24,000.

- Head of household—$18,000.

See chapter 21.

Personal exemption suspended. For 2018, you can't claim a personal exemption for yourself, your spouse, or your dependents. See chapter 3.

Increased child tax credit and additional child tax credit. For 2018, the maximum child tax credit has increased to $2,000 per qualifying child, of which $1,400 can be claimed for the additional child tax credit. In addition, the modified adjusted gross income threshold at which the credit begins to phase out has increased to $200,000 ($400,000 if married filing jointly). See chapter 33.

New credit for other dependents. If you have a dependent, you may be able to claim the credit for other dependents. The credit is a nonrefundable credit of up to $500 for each eligible dependent who can't be claimed for the child tax credit. The child tax credit and credit for other dependents are both figured using the Child Tax Credit and Credit for Other Dependents Worksheet and reported on line 12a of Form 1040. See chapter 33.

Social security number (SSN) required for child tax credit. Your child must have an SSN valid for employment issued before the due date of your 2018 return (including extensions) to be claimed as a qualifying child for the child tax credit or additional child tax credit. If your child doesn't qualify you for the child tax credit but has a taxpayer identification number (TIN) issued on or before the due date of your 2018 return (including extensions), you may be able to claim the new credit for other dependents for that child. See chapter 33.

Qualified business income deduction. Beginning in 2018, you may be able to deduct up to 20% of your qualified business income

from your qualified trade or business, plus 20% of your qualified real estate investment trust (REIT) dividends and qualified publicly traded partnership (PTP) income. The deduction can be taken in addition to your standard deduction or itemized deductions. For more information, see chapter 28.

Special rules for eligible gains invested in Qualified Opportunity Funds. If you have an eligible gain, you can invest that gain into a Qualified Opportunity Fund (QO Fund) and elect to defer part or all of the gain that is otherwise includible in income. The gain is deferred until the date you sell or exchange the investment or December 31, 2026, whichever is earlier. You also may be able to permanently exclude gain from the sale or exchange of an investment in a QO Fund if the investment is held for at least 10 years. For information about what types of gains entitle you to elect these special rules, see the Instructions for Schedule D (Form 1040). For information on how to elect to use these special rules, see the Instructions for Form 8949.

Changes to itemized deductions. For 2018, there have been changes to the itemized deductions that can be claimed on Schedule A (Form 1040). These include the following.

- Your overall itemized deductions are no longer limited if your adjusted gross income is over a certain limit.

- Your deduction of state and local income, sales, and property taxes is limited to a combined total deduction of $10,000 ($5,000 if married filing separately). See chapter 23.

- You can no longer deduct job-related expenses or other miscellaneous itemized deductions that were subject to the 2%-of-adjusted-gross-income floor.

- You may be able to deduct mortgage interest only on the first $750,000 ($375,000 if married filing separately) of indebtedness. Higher limitations apply if you're deducting mortgage interest from indebtedness incurred on or before December 15, 2017. Also, you can no longer deduct interest on a home equity loan. See chapter 24.

- You can no longer deduct a personal casualty or theft loss

unless the loss is from a federally declared disaster. See chapter 26.

- Your deduction for most cash or check contributions is now limited to 60% of your adjusted gross income instead of 50%. Certain cash contributions you made for relief efforts for California wildfires are not subject to the 60% limit for cash contributions. See chapter 25.

See chapters 22 through 27 and the Schedule A (Form 1040) instructions for more information about the allowable itemized deductions.

Standard mileage rates. The 2018 rate for business use of your vehicle is 54.5 cents a mile. The 2018 rate for use of your vehicle to get medical care or to move is 18 cents a mile. See Pub. 521, Moving Expenses.

Adoption credit. The adoption credit and the exclusion for employer-provided adoption benefits have both increased to $13,810 per eligible child in 2018. The amount begins to phase out if you have modified adjusted gross income (MAGI) in excess of $207,140 and is completely phased out if your MAGI is $247,140 or more.

Alternative minimum tax (AMT) exemption amount has increased. The exemption amount for the AMT has increased to $70,300 ($109,400 if married filing jointly or qualifying widow(er); $54,700 if married filing separately). The income levels at which the AMT exemption begins to phase out has increased to $500,000 ($1,000,000 if married filing jointly or qualifying widow(er)).

Section 965 deferred foreign income. If you own (directly or indirectly) certain foreign corporations, you may have to include on your return certain deferred foreign income. You may pay the entire amount of tax due with respect to this deferred foreign income this year or elect to pay in eight installments; or in the case of certain stock owned through an S corporation, elect to defer payment until a triggering event occurs. See the instructions for Form 1040, line 11a; Schedule 1 (Form 1040), line 21; Schedule 5 (Form 1040), line 74; Form 965; and Form 965-A for more information.

Global intangible low-taxed income (GILTI) under section

951A. If you're a U.S. shareholder of a controlled foreign corporation, you must include your GILTI in your income. If you own an interest in a domestic pass-through entity that is a U.S. shareholder of a controlled foreign corporation, you may have a GILTI inclusion related to that interest, even if you are not a U.S. shareholder of the controlled foreign corporation. See *IRS.gov/Form8992* and Form 8992 and its instructions for the latest information regarding GILTI and domestic pass-through entities.

Domestic production activities deduction. The domestic production activities deduction has been repealed with limited exceptions. See Form 8903, Domestic Production Activities Deduction, and its instructions; and the Instructions for Schedule 1 (Form 1040), line 36, for more information.

Reminders

Listed below are important reminders and other items that may help you file your 2018 tax return. Many of these items are explained in more detail later in this publication.

Disaster-related tax relief. If you were affected by a disaster in 2016 or 2017, see Pub. 976 for information on how your 2018 taxes may be affected. For information on disaster assistance and emergency relief information for the 2018 tax year, as well as prior years, see *IRS.gov/Disaster*. For information on whether distributions made from your retirement plan in 2018 are qualified 2017 disaster distributions eligible for special tax benefits, see the 2018 Instructions for Form 8915B.

Enter your social security number (SSN). Enter your SSN in the space provided on your tax form. If you filed a joint return for 2017 and are filing a joint return for 2018 with the same spouse, enter your names and SSNs in the same order as on your 2017 return. See chapter 1.

Secure your tax records from identity theft. Identity theft occurs when someone uses your personal information, such as your name, SSN, or other identifying information, without your permission, to commit fraud or other crimes. An identity thief may use your SSN to get a job or may file a tax return using your SSN to receive a refund. For more information about identity theft and how to reduce your risk from it, see chapter 1.

Taxpayer identification numbers. You must provide the taxpayer identification number for each person for whom you claim certain tax benefits. This applies even if the person was born in 2018. Generally, this number is the person's SSN. See chapter 1.

Foreign-source income. If you are a U.S. citizen with income from sources outside the United States (foreign income), you must report all such income on your tax return unless it is exempt by law or a tax treaty. This is true whether you live inside or outside the United States and whether or not you receive a Form W-2 or Form 1099 from the foreign payer. This applies to earned income (such as wages and tips) as well as unearned income (such as interest, dividends, capital gains, pensions, rents, and royalties).

If you live outside the United States, you may be able to exclude part or all of your foreign earned income. For details, see Pub. 54, Tax Guide for U.S. Citizens and Resident Aliens Abroad.

Foreign financial assets. If you had foreign financial assets in 2018, you may have to file Form 8938 with your return. See Form 8938 and its instructions or visit *IRS.gov/Form8938* for details.

Automatic 6-month extension to file tax return. You can get an automatic 6-month extension of time to file your tax return. See chapter 1.

Payment of taxes. You can pay your taxes by making electronic payments online; from a mobile device using the IRS2Go app; or in cash, or by check or money order. Paying electronically is quick, easy, and faster than mailing in a check or money order. See chapter 1.

Faster ways to file your return. The IRS offers fast, accurate ways to file your tax return information without filing a paper tax return. You can use IRS *e-file* (electronic filing). See chapter 1.

Free electronic filing. You may be able to file your 2018 taxes online for free. See chapter 1.

Change of address. If you change your address, notify the IRS. See chapter 1.

Refund on a late-filed return. If you were due a refund but you did not file a return, you generally must file your return within 3 years from the date the return was due (including extensions) to get that refund. See chapter 1.

Frivolous tax returns. The IRS has published a list of positions that are identified as frivolous. The penalty for filing a frivolous tax return is $5,000. See chapter 1.

Filing erroneous claim for refund or credit. You may have to pay a penalty if you file an erroneous claim for refund or credit. See chapter 1.

Secure access. To combat identity fraud, the IRS has upgraded its identity verification process for certain self-help tools on IRS.gov. To find out what types of information new users will need, go to *IRS.gov/SecureAccess*.

Access your online account. You must authenticate your identity. To securely log in to your federal tax account, go to *IRS.gov/Account*. View the amount you owe, review 24 months of payment history, access online payment options, and create or modify an online payment agreement. You can also access your tax records online.

Privacy Act and paperwork reduction information. The IRS Restructuring and Reform Act of 1998, the Privacy Act of 1974, and the Paperwork Reduction Act of 1980 require that when we ask you for information we must first tell you what our legal right is to ask for the information, why we are asking for it, how it will be used, what could happen if we do not receive it, and whether your response is voluntary, required to obtain a benefit, or mandatory under the law. A complete statement on this subject can be found in your tax form instructions.

Preparer *e-file* mandate. Most paid preparers must *e-file* returns they prepare and file. Your preparer may make you aware of this requirement and the options available to you.

Treasury Inspector General for Tax Administration. If you want to confidentially report misconduct, waste, fraud, or abuse by an IRS employee, you can call 1-800-366-4484 (call 1-800-877-8339 if you are deaf, hard of hearing, or have a speech disability, and are using TTY/TDD equipment). You can remain anonymous.

Photographs of missing children. The IRS is a proud partner with the *National Center for Missing & Exploited Children®* *(NCMEC)*. Photographs of missing children selected by the Center may appear in this publication on pages that would otherwise be blank. You can help bring these children home by looking at the photographs and calling 1-800-THE-LOST (1-800-843-5678) if you recognize a child.

Introduction

This publication covers the general rules for filing a federal income tax return. It supplements the information contained in your tax form instructions. It explains the tax law to make sure you pay only the tax you owe and no more.

How this publication is arranged. Pub. 17 closely follows Form 1040, U.S. Individual Income Tax Return, and its six new Schedules 1 through 6. Pub. 17 is divided into six parts. Each part is further divided into chapters, most of which generally discuss one line of the form or one line of one of the six schedules. The introduction at the beginning of each part lists the schedule(s) discussed in that part.

The table of contents inside the front cover, the introduction to each part, and the index in the back of the publication are useful tools to help you find the information you need.

What is in this publication. The publication begins with the rules for filing a tax return. It explains:

1. Who must file a return,

2. When the return is due,

3. How to *e-file* your return, and

4. Other general information.

It will help you identify which filing status you qualify for, whether you can claim any dependents, and whether the income you receive is taxable. The publication goes on to explain the standard deduction, the kinds of expenses you may be able to deduct, and the various kinds of credits you may be able to take to reduce your tax.

Throughout this publication are examples showing how the tax law applies in typical situations. Also throughout this publication are flowcharts and tables that present tax information in an easy-to-understand manner.

Many of the subjects discussed in this publication are discussed in greater detail in other IRS publications. References to those other publications are provided for your information.

Icons. Small graphic symbols, or icons, are used to draw your attention to special information. See Table 1 for an explanation of each icon used in this publication.

What is not covered in this publication. Some material that you may find helpful is not included in this publication but can be found in your tax form instruction booklet. This includes lists of:

- Where to report certain items shown on information documents, and

- Tax Topics you can read at *IRS.gov/TaxTopics*.

If you operate your own business or have other self-employment income, such as from babysitting or selling crafts, see the following publications for more information.

- Pub. 334, Tax Guide for Small Business.

- Pub. 535, Business Expenses.

- Pub. 587, Business Use of Your Home.

Help from the IRS. There are many ways you can get help from the IRS. These are explained under *How To Get Tax Help* at the end of this publication.

Comments and suggestions. We welcome your comments about this publication and your suggestions for future editions.

You can send us comments through *IRS.gov/FormComments*. Or you can write to:

Internal Revenue Service
Tax Forms and Publications
1111 Constitution Ave. NW,
IR-6526
Washington, DC 20224

Although we can't respond individually to each comment received, we do appreciate your feedback and will consider your comments as we revise our tax forms, instructions, and publications.

Ordering forms and publications. Visit *IRS.gov/FormsPubs* to download forms and publications. Otherwise, you can go to *IRS.gov/OrderForms* to order current and prior-year forms and instructions. Your order should arrive within 10 business days.

Tax questions. If you have a tax question not answered by this publication, check IRS.gov and *How To Get Tax Help* at the end of this publication.

IRS mission. Provide America's taxpayers top-quality service by helping them understand and meet their tax responsibilities and enforce the law with integrity and fairness to all.

Table 1. **Legend of Icons**

Icon	Explanation
⚠	Items that may cause you particular problems, or an alert about pending legislation that may be enacted after this publication goes to print.
▣	An Internet site or an email address.
✉	An address you may need.
🗂	Items you should keep in your personal records.
✍	Items you may need to figure or a worksheet you may need to complete and keep for your records.
☎	An important phone number.
TIP	Helpful information you may need.

Part One.

The Income Tax Return

The four chapters in this part provide basic information on the tax system. They take you through the first steps of filling out a tax return. They also provide information about dependents, and discuss recordkeeping requirements, IRS e-file (electronic filing), certain penalties, and the two methods used to pay tax during the year: withholding and estimated tax.

The new Form 1040 schedules that are discussed in these chapters are:

- *Schedule 1, Additional Income and Adjustments to Income.*
- *Schedule 5, Other Payments and Refundable Credits.*
- *Schedule 6, Foreign Address and Third Party Designee.*

1.

Filing Information

What's New

 At the time this publication went to print, Congress was considering legislation that would do the following.

1. Provide additional tax relief for those affected by certain 2018 disasters.

2. Extend certain tax benefits that expired at the end of 2017 and that currently can't be claimed on your 2018 tax return.

3. Change certain other tax provisions.

To learn whether this legislation was enacted resulting in changes that affect your 2018 tax return, go to Recent Developments at IRS.gov/Pub17.

Form 1040 has been redesigned for 2018. The new design uses a "building block" approach. Form 1040, which many taxpayers can file by itself, is supplemented with new Schedules 1 through 6. These additional schedules will be used as needed to complete more complex tax returns.

Forms 1040A and 1040EZ no longer available. Forms 1040A and 1040EZ aren't available to file your 2018 taxes. If you used one of those forms in the past, you will now file Form 1040. Some forms and publications that were released in 2017 or early 2018 (for example Form W-2) may still have references to Form 1040A or 1040EZ. Please disregard these references.

Social security number (SSN) required. Your child must have an SSN valid for employment issued before the due date of your 2018 return (including extensions) to be considered a qualifying child for certain tax benefits on your original or amended 2018 return.

Taxpayer identification number requirements. If you, or your spouse if filing jointly, do not have an SSN (or ITIN) issued on or before the due date of your 2018 return (including extensions), you can't claim certain tax benefits on your original or amended 2018 return.

Due date of return. The due date to file your tax return is April 15, 2019. If you live in Maine or Massachusetts, you have until April 17, 2019, because of the Patriots' Day holiday in those states and the Emancipation Day holiday in the District of Columbia.

Who must file. Generally, the amount of income you can receive before you must file a return has been increased. See Table 1-1, Table 1-2, and Table 1-3 for the specific amounts.

Reminders

File online. Rather than filing a return on paper, you may be able to file electronically using IRS e-file. For more information, see *Why Should I File Electronically*, later.

Access your online account (individual taxpayers only). Go to *IRS.gov/Account* to securely access information about your federal tax account.

- View the amount you owe, pay online, or set up an online payment agreement.

- Access your tax records online.

- Review the past 24 months of your payment history.

- Go to *IRS.gov/SecureAccess* to view the required identity authentication process.

Change of address. If you change your address, you should notify the IRS. You can use Form 8822 to notify the IRS of the change. See *Change of Address*, later, under *What Happens After I File*.

Enter your social security number. You must enter your social security number (SSN) in the spaces provided on your tax return. If you file a joint return, enter the SSNs in the same order as the names.

Direct deposit of refund. Instead of getting a paper check, you may be able to have your refund deposited directly into your account at a bank or other financial institution. See *Direct Deposit* under *Refunds*, later. If you choose direct deposit of your refund, you may be able to split the refund among two or three accounts.

Pay online or by phone. If you owe additional tax, you may be able to pay online or by phone. See *How To Pay*, later.

Installment agreement. If you can't pay the full amount due with your return, you may ask to make monthly installment payments. See *Installment Agreement*, later, under *Amount You Owe*. You may be able to apply online for a payment agreement if you owe federal tax, interest, and penalties.

Automatic 6-month extension. You can get an automatic 6-month extension to file your tax return if, no later than the date your return is due, you file Form 4868. See *Automatic Extension*, later.

Service in combat zone. You are allowed extra time to take care of your tax matters if you are a member of the Armed Forces who served in a combat zone, or if you served in a combat zone in support of the Armed Forces. See *Individuals Serving in Combat Zone*, later, under *When Do I Have To File*.

Adoption taxpayer identification number. If a child has been placed in your home for purposes of legal adoption and you won't be able to get a social security number for the child in time to file your return, you may be able to get an adoption taxpayer identification number (ATIN). For more information, see *Social Security Number (SSN)*, later.

Taxpayer identification number for aliens. If you or your dependent is a nonresident or resident alien who doesn't have and isn't eligible to get a social security number, file Form W-7, Application for IRS Individual Taxpayer Identification Number, with the IRS. For more information, see *Social Security Number (SSN)*, later.

Individual taxpayer identification number (ITIN) renewal. Some ITINs must be renewed. If you haven't used your ITIN on a U.S. tax return at least once in the last 3 years, or if your ITIN has the middle digits 73, 74, 75, 76, 77, 81, or 82 (9NN-73-NNNN), it will expire at the end of 2018 and must be renewed if you need to file a U.S. federal tax return in 2019. You don't need to renew your ITIN if you don't need to file a federal tax return. You can find more information at *IRS.gov/ITIN*.

ITINs with middle digits 70, 71, 72, 78, 79, or 80 that expired in 2016 or 2017 also can be renewed if you need to file a tax return in 2019 and haven't already renewed the ITIN.

Frivolous tax submissions. The IRS has published a list of positions that are identified as frivolous. The penalty for filing a frivolous tax return is $5,000. Also, the $5,000 penalty will apply to other specified frivolous submissions. For more information, see *Civil Penalties*, later.

Introduction

This chapter discusses the following topics.

- Whether you have to file a return.
- How to file electronically.
- How to file for free.
- When, how, and where to file your return.
- What happens if you pay too little or too much tax.
- What records you should keep and how long you should keep them.
- How you can change a return you have already filed.

Do I Have To File a Return?

You must file a federal income tax return if you are a citizen or resident of the United States or a resident of Puerto Rico and you meet the filing requirements for any of the following categories that apply to you.

1. Individuals in general. (There are special rules for surviving spouses, executors, administrators, legal representatives, U.S. citizens and residents living outside the United States, residents of Puerto Rico, and individuals with income from U.S. possessions.)
2. Dependents.
3. Certain children under age 19 or full-time students.
4. Self-employed persons.
5. Aliens.

The filing requirements for each category are explained in this chapter.

The filing requirements apply even if you don't owe tax.

 Even if you don't have to file a return, it may be to your advantage to do so. See Who Should File, *later.*

 File only one federal income tax return for the year regardless of how many jobs you had, how many Forms W-2 you received, or how many states you lived in during the year. Don't file more than one original return for the same year, even if you haven't received your refund or haven't heard from the IRS since you filed.

Individuals—In General

If you are a U.S. citizen or resident, whether you must file a return depends on three factors.

1. Your gross income.
2. Your filing status.
3. Your age.

To find out whether you must file, see Table 1-1, Table 1-2, and Table 1-3. Even if no table shows that you must file, you may need to file to get money back. See *Who Should File,* later.

Gross income. This includes all income you receive in the form of money, goods, property, and services that isn't exempt from tax. It also includes income from sources outside the United States or from the sale of your main home (even if you can exclude all or part of it). Include part of your social security benefits if:

1. You were married, filing a separate return, and you lived with your spouse at any time during 2018; or
2. Half of your social security benefits plus your other gross income and any tax-exempt interest is more than $25,000 ($32,000 if married filing jointly).

If either (1) or (2) applies, see the Instructions for Form 1040 or Pub. 915, Social Security and Equivalent Railroad Retirement Benefits, to figure the social security benefits you must include in gross income.

Common types of income are discussed in *Part Two* of this publication.

Community property states. Community property states include Arizona, California, Idaho, Louisiana, Nevada, New Mexico, Texas, Washington, and Wisconsin. If you and your spouse lived in a community property state, you usually must follow state law to determine what is community property and what is separate income. For details, see Form 8958 and Pub. 555.

Nevada, Washington, and California domestic partners. A registered domestic partner in Nevada, Washington, or California generally must report half the combined community income of the individual and his or her domestic partner. See Pub. 555.

Self-employed individuals. If you are self-employed, your gross income includes the amount on line 7 of Schedule C (Form 1040), Profit or Loss From Business; line 1 of Schedule C-EZ (Form 1040), Net Profit From Business; and line 9 of Schedule F (Form 1040), Profit or Loss From Farming. See *Self-Employed Persons*, later, for more information about your filing requirements.

 If you don't report all of your self-employment income, your social security benefits may be lower when you retire.

Filing status. Your filing status depends on whether you are single or married and on your family situation. Your filing status is determined on the last day of your tax year, which is December 31 for most taxpayers. See chapter 2 for an explanation of each filing status.

Age. If you are 65 or older at the end of the year, you generally can have a higher amount of gross income than other taxpayers before you must file. See Table 1-1. You are considered 65 on the day before your 65th birthday. For example, if your 65th birthday is on January 1, 2019, you are considered 65 for 2018.

Surviving Spouses, Executors, Administrators, and Legal Representatives

You must file a final return for a decedent (a person who died) if both of the following are true.

- You are the surviving spouse, executor, administrator, or legal representative.
- The decedent met the filing requirements at the date of death.

For more information on rules for filing a decedent's final return, see Pub. 559.

U.S. Citizens and Resident Aliens Living Abroad

To determine whether you must file a return, include in your gross income any income you received abroad, including any income you can exclude under the foreign earned income exclusion. For information on special tax rules that may apply to you, see Pub. 54. It is available online and at most U.S. embassies and consulates. See *How To Get Tax Help* in the back of this publication.

Residents of Puerto Rico

If you are a U.S. citizen and also a bona fide resident of Puerto Rico, you generally must file a U.S. income tax return for any year in which you meet the income requirements. This is in addition to any legal requirement you may have to file an income tax return with Puerto Rico.

If you are a bona fide resident of Puerto Rico for the entire year, your U.S. gross income doesn't include income from sources within Puerto Rico. It does, however, include any income you received for your services as an employee of the United States or a U.S. agency. If you receive income from Puerto Rican sources that isn't subject to U.S. tax, you must reduce your standard deduction. As a result, the amount of income you must have before you are required to file a U.S. income tax return is lower than the applicable amount in Table 1-1 or Table 1-2. For more information, see Pub. 570.

Individuals With Income From U.S. Possessions

If you had income from Guam, the Commonwealth of the Northern Mariana Islands, American Samoa, or the U.S. Virgin Islands, special rules may apply when determining whether you must file a U.S. federal income tax return. In addition, you may have to file a return with the individual island government. See Pub. 570 for more information.

Dependents

If you are a dependent (one who meets the dependency tests in chapter 3), see Table 1-2 to find out whether you must file a return. You also must file if your situation is described in Table 1-3.

Responsibility of parent. Generally, a child is responsible for filing his or her own tax return and for paying any tax on the return. If a dependent child must file an income tax return but can't file due to age or any other reason, then a parent, guardian, or other legally responsible person must file it for the child. If the child can't sign the return, the parent or guardian must sign the child's name followed by the words "By (your signature), parent for minor child."

Child's earnings. Amounts a child earns by performing services are included in his or her gross income and not the gross income of the parent. This is true even if under local law the child's parent has the right to the earnings and may actually have received them. But if the child doesn't pay the tax due on this income, the parent is liable for the tax.

Certain Children Under Age 19 or Full-Time Students

If a child's only income is interest and dividends (including capital gain distributions and Alaska Permanent Fund dividends), the child was under age 19 at the end of 2018 or was a full-time student under age 24 at the end of 2018, and certain other conditions are met, a parent can elect to include the child's income on the parent's return. If this election is made, the child doesn't have to file a return. See *Parent's Election To Report Child's Interest and Dividends* in chapter 30.

Self-Employed Persons

You are self-employed if you:

- Carry on a trade or business as a sole proprietor,
- Are an independent contractor,
- Are a member of a partnership, or
- Are in business for yourself in any other way.

Self-employment can include work in addition to your regular full-time business activities, such as certain part-time work you do at home or in addition to your regular job.

You must file a return if your gross income is at least as much as the filing requirement amount for your filing status and age (shown in Table 1-1). Also, you must file Form 1040 and Schedule SE (Form 1040), Self-Employment Tax, if:

1. Your net earnings from self-employment (excluding church employee income) were $400 or more, or

2. You had church employee income of $108.28 or more. (See Table 1-3.)

Table 1-1. 2018 Filing Requirements for Most Taxpayers

IF your filing status is...	AND at the end of 2018 you were...*	THEN file a return if your gross income was at least...**
Single	under 65	$12,000
	65 or older	$13,600
Married filing jointly***	under 65 (both spouses)	$24,000
	65 or older (one spouse)	$25,300
	65 or older (both spouses)	$26,600
Married filing separately	any age	$ 5
Head of household	under 65	$18,000
	65 or older	$19,600
Qualifying widow(er)	under 65	$24,000
	65 or older	$25,300

*   If you were born on January 1, 1954, you are considered to be age 65 at the end of 2018. (If your spouse died in 2018 or if you are preparing a return for someone who died in 2018, see Pub. 501.)

**   Gross income means all income you received in the form of money, goods, property, and services that isn't exempt from tax, including any income from sources outside the United States or from the sale of your main home (even if you can exclude part or all of it). Don't include any social security benefits unless (a) you are married filing a separate return and you lived with your spouse at any time during 2018 or (b) one-half of your social security benefits plus your other gross income and any tax-exempt interest is more than $25,000 ($32,000 if married filing jointly). If (a) or (b) applies, see the Instructions for Form 1040 or Pub. 915 to figure the taxable part of social security benefits you must include in gross income. Gross income includes gains, but not losses, reported on Form 8949 or Schedule D. Gross income from a business means, for example, the amount on Schedule C, line 7, or Schedule F, line 9. But, in figuring gross income, don't reduce your income by any losses, including any loss on Schedule C, line 7, or Schedule F, line 9.

***   If you didn't live with your spouse at the end of 2018 (or on the date your spouse died) and your gross income was at least $5, you must file a return regardless of your age.

Use Schedule SE (Form 1040) to figure your self-employment tax. Self-employment tax is comparable to the social security and Medicare tax withheld from an employee's wages. For more information about this tax, see Pub. 334, Tax Guide for Small Business.

Employees of foreign governments or international organizations. If you are a U.S. citizen who works in the United States for an international organization, a foreign government, or a wholly owned instrumentality of a foreign government, and your employer isn't required to withhold social security and Medicare taxes from your wages, you must include your earnings from services performed in the United States when figuring your net earnings from self-employment.

Ministers. You must include income from services you performed as a minister when figuring your net earnings from self-employment, unless you have an exemption from self-employment tax. This also applies to Christian Science practitioners and members of a religious order who have not taken a vow of poverty. For more information, see Pub. 517.

Aliens

Your status as an alien (resident, nonresident, or dual-status) determines whether and how you must file an income tax return.

The rules used to determine your alien status are discussed in Pub. 519, U.S. Tax Guide for Aliens.

Resident alien. If you are a resident alien for the entire year, you must file a tax return following the same rules that apply to U.S. citizens. Use the forms discussed in this publication.

Nonresident alien. If you are a nonresident alien, the rules and tax forms that apply to you are different from those that apply to U.S. citizens and resident aliens. See Pub. 519 to find out if U.S. income tax laws apply to you and which forms you should file.

Dual-status taxpayer. If you are a resident alien for part of the tax year and a nonresident alien for the rest of the year, you are a dual-status taxpayer. Different rules apply for each part of the year. For information on dual-status taxpayers, see Pub. 519.

Who Should File

Even if you don't have to file, you should file a federal income tax return to get money back if any of the following conditions apply.

1. You had federal income tax withheld or made estimated tax payments.

2. You qualify for the earned income credit. See chapter 35 for more information.

3. You qualify for the additional child tax credit. See chapter 33 for more information.

4. You qualify for the premium tax credit. See chapter 36 for more information.

Table 1-2. 2018 Filing Requirements for Dependents

See chapter 3 to find out if someone can claim you as a dependent.

If your parents (or someone else) can claim you as a dependent, use this table to see if you must file a return. (See Table 1-3 for other situations when you must file.)

In this table, unearned income includes taxable interest, ordinary dividends, and capital gain distributions. It also includes unemployment compensation, taxable social security benefits, pensions, annuities, and distributions of unearned income from a trust. Earned income includes salaries, wages, tips, professional fees, and taxable scholarship and fellowship grants. (See *Scholarships and fellowships* in chapter 12.) Gross income is the total of your earned and unearned income.

Single dependents—Were you **either** age 65 or older or blind?

☐ **No.** You must file a return if **any** of the following apply.
- Your unearned income was more than $1,050.
- Your earned income was more than $12,000.
- Your gross income was more than the **larger** of:
  - $1,050, or
  - Your earned income (up to $11,650) plus $350.

☐ **Yes.** You must file a return if **any** of the following apply.
- Your unearned income was more than $2,650 ($4,250 if 65 or older **and** blind).
- Your earned income was more than $13,600 ($15,200 if 65 or older **and** blind).
- Your gross income was more than the **larger** of:
  - $2,650 ($4,250 if 65 or older **and** blind), or
  - Your earned income (up to $11,650) plus $1,950 ($3,550 if 65 or older **and** blind).

Married dependents—Were you **either** age 65 or older or blind?

☐ **No.** You must file a return if **any** of the following apply.
- Your unearned income was more than $1,050.
- Your earned income was more than $12,000.
- Your gross income was at least $5 and your spouse files a separate return and itemizes deductions.
- Your gross income was more than the **larger** of:
  - $1,050, or
  - Your earned income (up to $11,650) plus $350.

☐ **Yes.** You must file a return if **any** of the following apply.
- Your unearned income was more than $2,350 ($3,650 if 65 or older **and** blind).
- Your earned income was more than $13,300 ($14,600 if 65 or older **and** blind).
- Your gross income was at least $5 and your spouse files a separate return and itemizes deductions.
- Your gross income was more than the **larger** of:
  - $2,350 ($3,650 if 65 or older **and** blind), or
  - Your earned income (up to $11,650) plus $1,650 ($2,950 if 65 or older **and** blind).

5. You qualify for the health coverage tax credit. See chapter 37 for more information.

6. You qualify for the American opportunity credit. See chapter 34 for more information.

7. You qualify for the credit for federal tax on fuels. See chapter 29 for more information.

Form 1040

Use Form 1040 to file your return. Forms 1040A and 1040EZ are not available to file your return in 2018. If you used Form 1040A or 1040EZ in the past, you will use Form 1040 this year. (But also see *Why Should I File Electronically*, later.)

You can use Form 1040 to report all types of income, deductions, and credits.

Why Should I File Electronically?

Electronic Filing

If your adjusted gross income (AGI) is less than a certain amount, you are eligible for *Free File*, a free tax software service offered by IRS partners, to prepare and *e-file* your return for free. If your income is over the amount, you are still eligible for Free File Fillable Forms, an electronic version of IRS paper forms. Table 1-4 lists the free ways to electronically file your return.

 IRS *e-file* uses automation to replace most of the manual steps needed to process paper returns. As a result, the processing of *e-file* returns is faster and more accurate than the processing of paper returns. However, as with a paper return, you are responsible for making sure your return contains accurate information and is filed on time.

If your return is filed with IRS *e-file*, you will receive an acknowledgment that your return was received and accepted. If you owe tax, you can *e-file* and pay electronically. The IRS has processed more than one billion *e-filed* returns safely and securely. Using *e-file* doesn't affect your chances of an IRS examination of your return.

Electronic return signatures. To file your return electronically, you must sign the return electronically using a personal identification number (PIN). If you are filing online, you must use a Self-Select PIN. If you are filing electronically using a tax practitioner, you can use a Self-Select PIN or a Practitioner PIN.

Self-Select PIN. The Self-Select PIN method allows you to create your own PIN. If you are married filing jointly, you and your spouse will each need to create a PIN and enter these PINs as your electronic signatures.

A PIN is any combination of five digits you choose except five zeros. If you use a PIN, there is nothing to sign and nothing to mail—not even your Forms W-2.

To verify your identity, you will be prompted to enter your adjusted gross income (AGI) from your originally filed 2017 federal income tax return, if applicable. Don't use your AGI from an amended return (Form 1040X) or a math error correction made by the IRS. AGI is the amount shown on your 2017 Form 1040, line 38; Form 1040A, line 22; or Form 1040EZ, line 4. If you don't have your 2017 income tax return, you can request a transcript by using our automated self-service tool. Go to *IRS.gov/Transcript*. (If you filed electronically last year, you may use your prior year PIN to verify your identity instead of your prior year AGI. The prior year PIN is the five-digit PIN you used to electronically sign your 2017 return.) You also will be prompted to enter your date of birth.

⚠ **CAUTION** *You can't use the Self-Select PIN method if you are a first-time filer under age 16 at the end of 2018.*

Practitioner PIN. The Practitioner PIN method allows you to authorize your tax practitioner to enter or generate your PIN. The practitioner can provide you with details.

Form 8453. You must send in a paper Form 8453 if you have to attach certain forms or other documents that can't be electronically filed. For details, see Form 8453. For more details, visit *IRS.gov/efile*.

Identity Protection PIN. If the IRS gave you an identity protection personal identification number (IP PIN) because you were a victim of identity theft, enter it in the spaces provided on your tax form. If the IRS hasn't given you this type of number, leave these spaces blank. For more information, see the Instructions for Form 1040.

Power of attorney. If an agent is signing your return for you, a power of attorney (POA) must be filed. Attach the POA to Form 8453 and file it

Table 1-3. **Other Situations When You Must File a 2018 Return**

You must file a return if any of the seven conditions below apply for 2018.

1. You owe any special taxes, including any of the following.
   a. Alternative minimum tax.
   b. Additional tax on a qualified plan, including an individual retirement arrangement (IRA), or other tax-favored account. But if you are filing a return only because you owe this tax, you can file **Form 5329** by itself.
   c. Household employment taxes. But if you are filing a return only because you owe this tax, you can file **Schedule H** by itself.
   d. Social security and Medicare tax on tips you didn't report to your employer or on wages you received from an employer who didn't withhold these taxes.
   e. Write-in taxes, including uncollected social security and Medicare or RRTA tax on tips you reported to your employer or on group-term life insurance and additional taxes on health savings accounts. See the Instructions for Form 1040, Schedule 4, line 62.
   f. Recapture taxes. See the Instructions for Form 1040, line 11a, and Schedule 4, lines 60b and 62.

2. You (or your spouse, if filing jointly) received health savings account, Archer MSA, or Medicare Advantage MSA distributions.
3. You had net earnings from self-employment of at least $400.
4. You had wages of $108.28 or more from a church or qualified church-controlled organization that is exempt from employer social security and Medicare taxes.
5. Advance payments of the premium tax credit were made for you, your spouse, or a dependent who enrolled in coverage through the Marketplace. You or whoever enrolled you should have received Form(s) 1095-A showing the amount of the advance payments.
6. Advance payments of the health coverage tax credit were made for you, your spouse, or a dependent. You or whoever enrolled you should have received Form(s) 1099-H showing the amount of the advance payments.
7. You are required to include amounts in income under section 965 or you have a net tax liability under section 965 that you are paying in installments under section 965(h) or deferred by making an election under section 965(i).

using that form's instructions. See *Signatures*, later, for more information on POAs.

State returns. In most states, you can file an electronic state return simultaneously with your federal return. For more information, check with your local IRS office, state tax agency, tax professional, or the IRS website at *IRS.gov/efile*.

Refunds. You can have a refund check mailed to you, or you can have your refund deposited directly to your checking or savings account or split among two or three accounts. With *e-file*, your refund will be issued faster than if you filed on paper.

As with a paper return, you may not get all of your refund if you owe certain past-due amounts, such as federal tax, state income tax, state unemployment compensation debts, child support, spousal support, or certain other federal nontax debts, such as student loans. See *Offset against debts* under *Refunds*, later.

Refund inquiries. Information about your return generally will be available within 24 hours after the IRS receives your *e-filed* return. See *Refund Information*, later.

Amount you owe. To avoid late-payment penalties and interest, pay your taxes in full by April 15, 2019. If you live in Maine or Massachusetts, you have until April 17, 2019, because of the Patriots' Day holiday in those states and the Emancipation Day holiday in the District of Columbia. See *How To Pay*, later, for information on how to pay the amount you owe.

Table 1-4. **Free Ways To *e-file***

Use Free File for free tax software and free *e-file*.
• IRS partners offer name-brand products for free.
• Many taxpayers are eligible for Free File software.
• Everyone is eligible for Free File Fillable Forms, an electronic version of IRS paper forms.
• Free File software and Free File Fillable Forms are available only at *IRS.gov/FreeFile*.
Use VITA/TCE for free tax help from volunteers and free *e-file*.
• Volunteers prepare your return and *e-file* it for free.
• Some sites also offer do-it-yourself software.
• You are eligible based either on your income or age.
• Sites are located nationwide. Find one near you by visiting *IRS.gov/VITA*.

Using Your Personal Computer

You can file your tax return in a fast, easy, and convenient way using your personal computer. A computer with Internet access and tax preparation software are all you need. Best of all, you can *e-file* from the comfort of your home 24 hours a day, 7 days a week.

IRS approved tax preparation software is available for online use on the Internet, for download from the Internet, and in retail stores. For information, visit *IRS.gov/efile*.

Through Employers and Financial Institutions

Some businesses offer free *e-file* to their employees, members, or customers. Others offer it for a fee. Ask your employer or financial institution if they offer IRS *e-file* as an employee, member, or customer benefit.

Free Help With Your Return

The Volunteer Income Tax Assistance (VITA) program offers free tax help to people who generally make $55,000 or less, persons with disabilities, and limited-English-speaking taxpayers who need help preparing their own tax returns. The Tax Counseling for the Elderly (TCE) program offers free tax help for all taxpayers, particularly those who are 60 years of age and older. TCE volunteers specialize in answering questions about pensions and retirement-related issues unique to seniors.

You can go to IRS.gov to see your options for preparing and filing your return, which include the following.

- **Free File.** Go to *IRS.gov/FreeFile*. See if you qualify to use brand-name software to prepare and *e-file* your federal tax return for free.
- **VITA.** Go to *IRS.gov/VITA*, download the free IRS2Go app, or call 800-906-9887 to find the nearest VITA location for free tax return preparation.
- **TCE.** Go to *IRS.gov/TCE*, download the free IRS2Go app, or call 888-227-7669 to find the nearest TCE location for free tax return preparation.

Using a Tax Professional

Many tax professionals electronically file tax returns for their clients. You may personally enter your PIN or complete Form 8879, IRS *e-file* Signature Authorization, to authorize the tax professional to enter your PIN on your return.

Note. Tax professionals may charge a fee for IRS *e-file*. Fees can vary depending on the professional and the specific services rendered.

When Do I Have To File?

April 15, 2019, is the due date for filing your 2018 income tax return if you use the calendar year. If you live in Maine or Massachusetts, you have until April 17, 2019, because of the Patriots' Day holiday in those states and the Emancipation Day holiday in the District of Columbia. For a quick view of due dates for filing a return with or without an extension of time to file (discussed later), see Table 1-5.

If you use a fiscal year (a year ending on the last day of any month except December, or a 52-53-week year), your income tax return is due by the 15th day of the 4th month after the close of your fiscal year.

When the due date for doing any act for tax purposes—filing a return, paying taxes, etc.—falls on a Saturday, Sunday, or legal holiday, the due date is delayed until the next business day.

Filing paper returns on time. Your paper return is filed on time if it is mailed in an envelope that is properly addressed, has enough postage, and is postmarked by the due date. If you send your return by registered mail, the date of the registration is the postmark date. The registration is evidence that the return was delivered. If you send a return by certified mail and have your receipt postmarked by a postal employee, the date on the receipt is the postmark date. The postmarked certified mail receipt is evidence that the return was delivered.

Private delivery services. If you use a private delivery service designated by the IRS to send your return, the postmark date generally is the date the private delivery service records in

Table 1-5. When To File Your 2018 Return

For U.S. citizens and residents who file returns on a calendar year.

	For Most Taxpayers	For Certain Taxpayers Outside the U.S.
No extension requested	April 15, 2019*	June 15, 2019
Automatic extension	October 15, 2019	October 15, 2019

*The due date is April 17, 2019, if you live in Maine or Massachusetts because of the Patriots' Day holiday in those states and the Emancipation Day holiday in the District of Columbia.

its database or marks on the mailing label. The private delivery service can tell you how to get written proof of this date.

The following are designated private delivery services.

- Federal Express (FedEx): FedEx First Overnight, FedEx Priority Overnight, FedEx Standard Overnight, FedEx 2 Day, FedEx International Next Flight Out, FedEx International Priority, FedEx International First, and FedEx International Economy.
- DHL Express 9:00, DHL Express 10:30, DHL Express 12:00, DHL Express Worldwide, DHL Express Envelope, DHL Import Express 10:30, DHL Import Express 12:00, and DHL Import Express Worldwide.
- United Parcel Service (UPS): UPS Next Day Air Early AM, UPS Next Day Air, UPS Next Day Air Saver, UPS 2nd Day Air, UPS 2nd Day Air A.M., UPS Worldwide Express Plus, and UPS Worldwide Express.

To check for any updates to the list of designated private delivery services, go to *IRS.gov/PDS*. For the IRS mailing addresses to use if you're using a private delivery service, go to *IRS.gov/PDSStreetAddresses*.

The private delivery service can tell you how to get written proof of the mailing date.

Filing electronic returns on time. If you use IRS *e-file*, your return is considered filed on time if the authorized electronic return transmitter postmarks the transmission by the due date. An authorized electronic return transmitter is a participant in the IRS *e-file* program that transmits electronic tax return information directly to the IRS.

The electronic postmark is a record of when the authorized electronic return transmitter received the transmission of your electronically filed return on its host system. The date and time in your time zone controls whether your electronically filed return is timely.

Filing late. If you don't file your return by the due date, you may have to pay a failure-to-file penalty and interest. For more information, see *Penalties*, later. Also see *Interest* under *Amount You Owe*.

If you were due a refund but you didn't file a return, you generally must file within 3 years from the date the return was due (including extensions) to get that refund.

Nonresident alien. If you are a nonresident alien and earn wages subject to U.S. income tax withholding, your 2018 U.S. income tax return (Form 1040NR or Form 1040NR-EZ) is due by:

- April 15, 2019, if you use a calendar year; or

- The 15th day of the 4th month after the end of your fiscal year if you use a fiscal year.

If you don't earn wages subject to U.S. income tax withholding, your return is due by:

- June 15, 2019, if you use a calendar year; or
- The 15th day of the 6th month after the end of your fiscal year, if you use a fiscal year.

See Pub. 519 for more filing information.

Filing for a decedent. If you must file a final income tax return for a taxpayer who died during the year (a decedent), the return is due by the 15th day of the 4th month after the end of the decedent's normal tax year. See Pub. 559.

Extensions of Time To File

You may be able to get an extension of time to file your return. There are three types of situations where you may qualify for an extension.

- Automatic extensions.
- You are outside the United States.
- You are serving in a combat zone.

Automatic Extension

If you can't file your 2018 return by the due date, you may be able to get an automatic 6-month extension of time to file.

Example. If your return is due on April 15, 2019, you will have until October 15, 2019, to file.

 If you don't pay the tax due by the regular due date (April 15 for most taxpayers), you will owe interest. You also may be charged penalties, discussed later.

How to get the automatic extension. You can get the automatic extension by:

1. Using IRS *e-file* (electronic filing), or
2. Filing a paper form.

E-file **options.** There are two ways you can use *e-file* to get an extension of time to file. Complete Form 4868 to use as a worksheet. If you think you may owe tax when you file your return, use *Part II* of the form to estimate your balance due. If you *e-file* Form 4868 to the IRS, don't send a paper Form 4868.

E-file using your personal computer or a tax professional. You can use a tax software package with your personal computer or a tax professional to file Form 4868 electronically.

Free File and Free File Fillable Forms, both available at IRS.gov, allow you to prepare and *e-file* Form 4868 for free. You will need to provide certain information from your 2017 tax return. If you wish to make a payment by direct transfer from your bank account, see *Pay online* under *How To Pay*, later, in this chapter.

E-file and pay by credit or debit card or by direct transfer from your bank account. You can get an extension by paying part or all of your estimate of tax due by using a credit or debit card or by direct transfer from your bank account. You can do this by phone or over the Internet. You don't file Form 4868. See *Pay online* under *How To Pay*, later, in this chapter.

Filing a paper Form 4868. You can get an extension of time to file by filing a paper Form 4868. If you are a fiscal year taxpayer, you must file a paper Form 4868. Mail it to the address shown in the form instructions.

If you want to make a payment with the form, make your check or money order payable to "United States Treasury." Write your SSN, daytime phone number, and "2018 Form 4868" on your check or money order.

When to file. You must request the automatic extension by the due date for your return. You can file your return any time before the 6-month extension period ends.

When you file your return. Enter any payment you made related to the extension of time to file on Schedule 5 (Form 1040), line 71.

Individuals Outside the United States

You are allowed an automatic 2-month extension, without filing Form 4868 (until June 17, 2019, if you use the calendar year), to file your 2018 return and pay any federal income tax due if:

1. You are a U.S. citizen or resident; and

2. On the due date of your return:

   a. You are living outside the United States and Puerto Rico, and your main place of business or post of duty is outside the United States and Puerto Rico; or

   b. You are in military or naval service on duty outside the United States and Puerto Rico.

However, if you pay the tax due after the regular due date (April 15 for most taxpayers), interest will be charged from that date until the date the tax is paid.

If you served in a combat zone or qualified hazardous duty area, you may be eligible for a longer extension of time to file. See *Individuals Serving in Combat Zone*, later, for special rules that apply to you.

Married taxpayers. If you file a joint return, only one spouse has to qualify for this automatic extension. If you and your spouse file separate returns, the automatic extension applies only to the spouse who qualifies.

How to get the extension. To use this automatic extension, you must attach a statement to your return explaining what situation qualified you for the extension. (See the situations listed under (2), earlier.)

Extensions beyond 2 months. If you can't file your return within the automatic 2-month extension period, you may be able to get an additional 4-month extension, for a total of 6 months. File Form 4868 and check the box on line 8.

No further extension. An extension of more than 6 months generally will not be granted. However, if you are outside the United States and meet certain tests, you may be granted a longer extension. For more information, see *When To File and Pay* in Pub. 54.

Individuals Serving in Combat Zone

The deadline for filing your tax return, paying any tax you may owe, and filing a claim for refund is automatically extended if you serve in a combat zone. This applies to members of the Armed Forces, as well as merchant marines serving aboard vessels under the operational control of the Department of Defense, Red Cross personnel, accredited correspondents, and civilians under the direction of the Armed Forces in support of the Armed Forces.

Combat zone. A combat zone is any area the President of the United States designates by executive order as an area in which the U.S. Armed Forces are engaging or have engaged in combat. An area usually becomes a combat zone and ceases to be a combat zone on the dates the President designates by executive order. For purposes of the automatic extension, the term "combat zone" includes the following areas.

1. The Arabian peninsula area, effective January 17, 1991.

2. The Kosovo area, effective March 24, 1999.

3. The Afghanistan area, effective September 19, 2001.

See Pub. 3 for more detailed information on the locations comprising each combat zone. Pub. 3 also has information about other tax benefits available to military personnel serving in a combat zone.

Extension period. The deadline for filing your return, paying any tax due, filing a claim for refund, and taking other actions with the IRS is extended in two steps. First, your deadline is extended for 180 days after the later of:

1. The last day you are in a combat zone or the last day the area qualifies as a combat zone, or

2. The last day of any continuous qualified hospitalization (defined, later) for injury from service in the combat zone.

Second, in addition to the 180 days, your deadline also is extended by the number of days you had left to take action with the IRS when you entered the combat zone. For example, you have 3½ months (January 1 – April 15) to file your tax return. Any days left in this period when you entered the combat zone (or the entire 3½ months if you entered it before the beginning of the year) are added to the 180 days. See *Extension of Deadlines* in Pub. 3 for more information.

The rules on the extension for filing your return also apply when you are deployed outside the United States (away from your permanent duty station) while participating in a designated contingency operation.

Qualified hospitalization. The hospitalization must be the result of an injury received while serving in a combat zone or a contingency operation. Qualified hospitalization means:

- Any hospitalization outside the United States, and

- Up to 5 years of hospitalization in the United States.

See Pub. 3 for more information on qualified hospitalizations.

How Do I Prepare My Return?

This section explains how to get ready to fill in your tax return and when to report your income and expenses. It also explains how to complete certain sections of the form. You may find Table 1-6 helpful when you prepare your paper return.

Table 1-6. Six Steps for Preparing Your Paper Return

1 — Get your records together for income and expenses.
2 — Get the forms, schedules, and publications you need.
3 — Fill in your return.
4 — Check your return to make sure it is correct.
5 — Sign and date your return.
6 — Attach all required forms and schedules.

Electronic returns. For information you may find useful in preparing an electronic return, see *Why Should I File Electronically*, earlier.

Substitute tax forms. You can't use your own version of a tax form unless it meets the requirements explained in Pub. 1167.

Form W-2. If you were an employee, you should receive Form W-2 from your employer. You will need the information from this form to prepare your return. See *Form W-2* under *Credit for Withholding and Estimated Tax for 2018* in chapter 4.

Your employer is required to provide or send Form W-2 to you no later than January 31, 2019. If it is mailed, you should allow adequate time to receive it before contacting your employer. If you still don't get the form by February 15, the IRS can help you by requesting the form from your employer. When you request IRS help, be prepared to provide the following information.

- Your name, address (including ZIP code), and phone number.
- Your SSN.
- Your dates of employment.
- Your employer's name, address (including ZIP code), and phone number.

Form 1099. If you received certain types of income, you may receive a Form 1099. For example, if you received taxable interest of $10 or more, the payer is required to provide or send Form 1099 to you no later than January 31, 2019 (or by February 15, 2019, if furnished by a broker). If it is mailed, you should allow adequate time to receive it before contacting the payer. If you still don't get the form by February 15 (or by March 1, 2019, if furnished by a broker), call the IRS for help.

When Do I Report My Income and Expenses?

You must figure your taxable income on the basis of a tax year. A "tax year" is an annual accounting period used for keeping records and reporting income and expenses. You must account for your income and expenses in a way that clearly shows your taxable income. The way you do this is called an accounting method. This section explains which accounting periods and methods you can use.

Accounting Periods

Most individual tax returns cover a calendar year—the 12 months from January 1 through December 31. If you don't use a calendar year, your accounting period is a fiscal year. A regular fiscal year is a 12-month period that ends on the last day of any month except December. A 52-53-week fiscal year varies from 52 to 53 weeks and always ends on the same day of the week.

You choose your accounting period (tax year) when you file your first income tax return. It can't be longer than 12 months.

More information. For more information on accounting periods, including how to change your accounting period, see Pub. 538.

Accounting Methods

Your accounting method is the way you account for your income and expenses. Most taxpayers use either the cash method or an accrual method. You choose a method when you file your first income tax return. If you want to change your accounting method after that, you generally must get IRS approval. Use Form 3115 to request an accounting method change.

Cash method. If you use this method, report all items of income in the year in which you actually or constructively receive them. Generally, you deduct all expenses in the year you actually pay them. This is the method most individual taxpayers use.

Constructive receipt. Generally, you constructively receive income when it is credited to your account or set apart in any way that makes it available to you. You don't need to have physical possession of it. For example, interest credited to your bank account on December 31, 2018, is taxable income to you in 2018 if you could have withdrawn it in 2018 (even if the amount isn't entered in your records or withdrawn until 2019).

Garnished wages. If your employer uses your wages to pay your debts, or if your wages are attached or garnished, the full amount is constructively received by you. You must include these wages in income for the year you would have received them.

Debts paid for you. If another person cancels or pays your debts (but not as a gift or loan), you have constructively received the amount and generally must include it in your gross income for the year. See *Canceled Debts* in chapter 12 for more information.

Payment to third party. If a third party is paid income from property you own, you have constructively received the income. It is the same as if you had actually received the income and paid it to the third party.

Payment to an agent. Income an agent receives for you is income you constructively received in the year the agent receives it. If you indicate in a contract that your income is to be paid to another person, you must include the amount in your gross income when the other person receives it.

Check received or available. A valid check that was made available to you before the end of the tax year is constructively received by you in that year. A check that was "made available to you" includes a check you have already received, but not cashed or deposited. It also includes, for example, your last paycheck of the year that your employer made available for you to pick up at the office before the end of the year. It is constructively received by you in that year whether or not you pick it up before the end of the year or wait to receive it by mail after the end of the year.

No constructive receipt. There may be facts to show that you didn't constructively receive income.

Example. Alice Johnson, a teacher, agreed to her school board's condition that, in her absence, she would receive only the difference between her regular salary and the salary of a substitute teacher hired by the school board. Therefore, Alice didn't constructively receive the amount by which her salary was reduced to pay the substitute teacher.

Accrual method. If you use an accrual method, you generally report income when you earn it, rather than when you receive it. You generally deduct your expenses when you incur them, rather than when you pay them.

Income paid in advance. An advance payment of income generally is included in gross income in the year you receive it. Your method of accounting doesn't matter as long as the income is available to you. An advance payment may include rent or interest you receive in advance and pay for services you will perform later.

A limited deferral until the next tax year may be allowed for certain advance payments. See Pub. 538 for specific information.

Additional information. For more information on accounting methods, including how to change your accounting method, see Pub. 538.

Social Security Number (SSN)

You must enter your SSN on your return. If you are married, enter the SSNs for both you and your spouse, whether you file jointly or separately.

If you are filing a joint return, include the SSNs in the same order as the names. Use this same order in submitting other forms and documents to the IRS.

 If you, or your spouse if filing jointly, don't have an SSN (or ITIN) issued on or before the due date of your 2018 return (including extensions), you can't claim certain tax benefits on your original or an amended 2018 return.

Check that both the name and SSN on your Form 1040, W-2, and 1099 agree with your social security card. If they don't, certain deductions and credits on your Form 1040 may be reduced or disallowed and you may not receive credit for your social security earnings. If your Form W-2 shows an incorrect SSN or name, notify your employer or the form-issuing agent as soon as possible to make sure your earnings are credited to your social security record. If the name or SSN on your social security card is incorrect, call the SSA at 800-772-1213.

Name change. If you changed your name because of marriage, divorce, etc., be sure to report the change to your local Social Security Administration (SSA) office before filing your return. This prevents delays in processing your return and issuing refunds. It also safeguards your future social security benefits.

Dependent's SSN. You must provide the SSN of each dependent you claim, regardless of the dependent's age. This requirement applies to all dependents (not just your children) claimed on your tax return.

 Your child must have an SSN valid for employment issued before the due date of your 2018 return (including extensions) to be considered a qualifying child for certain tax benefits on your original or amended 2018 return. See chapters 33 and 35.

Exception. If your child was born and died in 2018 and didn't have an SSN, enter "DIED" in column (2) of the *Dependents* section of Form 1040 and include a copy of the child's birth certificate. death certificate. or hospital records. The document must show that the child was born alive.

No SSN. File Form SS-5, Application for a Social Security Card, with your local SSA office to get an SSN for yourself or your dependent. It usually takes about 2 weeks to get an SSN. If you or your dependent isn't eligible for an SSN, see *Individual taxpayer identification number (ITIN)*, later.

If you are a U.S. citizen or resident alien, you must show proof of age, identity, and citizenship or alien status with your Form SS-5. If you are 12 or older and have never been assigned an SSN, you must appear in person with this proof at an SSA office.

Form SS-5 is available at any SSA office, on the Internet at SSA.gov, or by calling 800-772-1213. If you have any questions about which documents you can use as proof of age, identity, or citizenship, contact your SSA office.

If your dependent doesn't have an SSN by the time your return is due, you may want to ask for an extension of time to file, as explained earlier under When Do I Have To File.

If you don't provide a required SSN or if you provide an incorrect SSN, your tax may be increased and any refund may be reduced.

Adoption taxpayer identification number (ATIN). If you are in the process of adopting a child who is a U.S. citizen or resident and can't get an SSN for the child until the adoption is final, you can apply for an ATIN to use instead of an SSN.

File Form W-7A, Application for Taxpayer Identification Number for Pending U.S. Adoptions, with the IRS to get an ATIN if all of the following are true.

- You have a child living with you who was placed in your home for legal adoption.

- You can't get the child's existing SSN even though you have made a reasonable attempt to get it from the birth parents, the placement agency, and other persons.

- You can't get an SSN for the child from the SSA because, for example, the adoption isn't final.

- You are eligible to claim the child as a dependent on your tax return.

After the adoption is final, you must apply for an SSN for the child. You can't continue using the ATIN.

See Form W-7A for more information.

Nonresident alien spouse. If your spouse is a nonresident alien, your spouse must have either an SSN or an ITIN if:

- You file a joint return, or

- Your spouse is filing a separate return.

If your spouse isn't eligible for an SSN, see the following discussion on ITINs.

Individual taxpayer identification number (ITIN). The IRS will issue you an ITIN if you are a nonresident or resident alien and you don't have and aren't eligible to get an SSN. This also applies to an alien spouse or dependent. To apply for an ITIN, file Form W-7 with the IRS. It usually takes about 7 weeks to get an ITIN. Enter the ITIN on your tax return wherever an SSN is requested.

Make sure your ITIN hasn't expired. If you haven't used your ITIN on a U.S. tax return at least once in the last 3 years, or if your ITIN has the middle digits 73, 74, 75, 76, 77, 81, or 82 (9NN-73-NNNN), it will expire at the end of 2018 and must be renewed if you need to file a U.S. federal tax return in 2019. You don't need to renew your ITIN if you don't need to file a federal tax return. You can find more information at IRS.gov/ITIN.

 ITINs with middle digits 70, 71, 72, 78, 79, or 80 that expired in 2016 or 2017 also can be renewed if you need to file a tax return in 2019 and haven't already renewed the ITIN.

 If you are applying for an ITIN for yourself, your spouse, or a dependent in order to file your tax return, attach your completed tax return to your Form W-7. See the Form W-7 instructions for how and where to file.

 You can't e-file a return using an ITIN in the calendar year the ITIN is issued; however, you can e-file returns in the following years.

ITIN for tax use only. An ITIN is for federal tax use only. It doesn't entitle you to social security benefits or change your employment or immigration status under U.S. law.

Penalty for not providing social security number. If you don't include your SSN or the SSN of your spouse or dependent as required, you may have to pay a penalty. See the discussion on Penalties, later, for more information.

SSN on correspondence. If you write to the IRS about your tax account, be sure to include your SSN (and the name and SSN of your spouse, if you filed a joint return) in your correspondence. Because your SSN is used to identify your account, this helps the IRS respond to your correspondence promptly.

Presidential Election Campaign Fund

This fund helps pay for Presidential election campaigns. The fund also helps pay for pediatric medical research. If you want $3 to go to this fund, check the box. If you are filing a joint return, your spouse also can have $3 go to the fund. If you check a box, your tax or refund won't change.

Computations

The following information may be useful in making the return easier to complete.

Rounding off dollars. You can round off cents to whole dollars on your return and schedules. If you do round to whole dollars, you must round all amounts. To round, drop amounts under 50 cents and increase amounts from 50 to 99 cents to the next dollar. For example, $1.39 becomes $1 and $2.50 becomes $3.

If you have to add two or more amounts to figure the amount to enter on a line, include cents when adding the amounts and round off only the total.

Equal amounts. If you are asked to enter the smaller or larger of two equal amounts, enter that amount.

Negative amounts. If you file a paper return and you need to enter a negative amount, put the amount in parentheses rather than using a minus sign. To combine positive and negative amounts, add all the positive amounts together and then subtract the negative amounts.

Attachments

Depending on the form you file and the items reported on your return, you may have to complete additional schedules and forms and attach them to your paper return.

 You may be able to file a paperless return using IRS e-file. There's nothing to attach or mail, not even your Forms W-2. See Why Should I File Electronically, earlier.

Form W-2. Form W-2 is a statement from your employer of wages and other compensation paid to you and taxes withheld from your pay. You should have a Form W-2 from each employer. If you file a paper return, be sure to attach a copy of Form W-2 in the place indicated on your return. For more information, see Form W-2 in chapter 4.

Form 1099-R. If you received a Form 1099-R showing federal income tax withheld, and you file a paper return, attach a copy of that form in the place indicated on your return.

Form 1040. If you file a paper return, attach any forms and schedules behind Form 1040 in order of the "Attachment Sequence Number" shown in the upper right corner of the form or schedule. Then arrange all other statements or attachments in the same order as the forms and schedules they relate to and attach them last. Don't attach items unless required to do so.

Third Party Designee

You can authorize the IRS to discuss your return with your preparer, a friend, family member, or any other person you choose (other than your paid preparer) by checking the "Yes" box in the "Third Party Designee" section of Schedule 6. Also, enter the designee's name, phone number, and any five digits the designee chooses as his or her personal identification number (PIN).

 If you want your paid preparer to be your third party designee, check the "3rd Party Designee" box on page 1 of Form 1040. Do not complete Schedule 6.

If you check the "Yes" box, you, and your spouse if filing a joint return, are authorizing:

1. The IRS to call the designee to answer any questions that arise during the processing of your return, and

2. The designee to:

   a. Give information that is missing from your return to the IRS;

   b. Call the IRS for information about the processing of your return or the status of your refund or payments;

   c. Receive copies of notices or transcripts related to your return, upon request; and

   d. Respond to certain IRS notices about math errors, offsets (see Refunds, later), and return preparation.

The authorization will automatically end no later than the due date (without any extensions) for filing your 2019 tax return. This is April 15, 2020, for most people.

See your form instructions for more information.

Signatures

You must sign and date your return. If you file a joint return, both you and your spouse must sign the return, even if only one of you had income.

 If you file a joint return, both spouses are generally liable for the tax, and the entire tax liability may be assessed against either spouse. See chapter 2.

 If you electronically file your return, you can use an electronic signature to sign your return. See Why Should I File Electronically, earlier.

If you are due a refund, it can't be issued unless you have signed your return.

Enter your occupation. If you file a joint return, enter both your occupation and your spouse's occupation.

When someone can sign for you. You can appoint an agent to sign your return if you are:

1. Unable to sign the return because of disease or injury,

2. Absent from the United States for a continuous period of at least 60 days before the due date for filing your return, or

3. Given permission to do so by the IRS office in your area.

Power of attorney. A return signed by an agent in any of these cases must have a power of attorney (POA) attached that authorizes the agent to sign for you. You can use a POA that states that the agent is granted authority to sign the return, or you can use Form 2848. Part I of Form 2848 must state that the agent is granted authority to sign the return.

Court-appointed, conservator, or other fiduciary. If you are a court-appointed conservator, guardian, or other fiduciary for a mentally or physically incompetent individual who has to file a tax return, sign your name for the individual. File Form 56.

Unable to sign. If the taxpayer is mentally competent but physically unable to sign the return or POA, a valid "signature" is defined under state law. It can be anything that clearly indicates the taxpayer's intent to sign. For example, the taxpayer's "X" with the signatures of two witnesses might be considered a valid signature under a state's law.

Spouse unable to sign. If your spouse is unable to sign for any reason, see *Signing a joint return* in chapter 2.

Child's return. If a child has to file a tax return but can't sign the return, the child's parent, guardian, or another legally responsible person must sign the child's name, followed by the words "By (your signature), parent for minor child."

Paid Preparer

Generally, anyone you pay to prepare, assist in preparing, or review your tax return must sign it and fill in the other blanks, including their Preparer Tax Identification Number (PTIN), in the paid preparer's area of your return.

Many preparers are required to *e-file* the tax returns they prepare. They sign these *e-filed* returns using their tax preparation software. However, you can choose to have your return completed on paper if you prefer. In that case, the paid preparer can sign the paper return manually or use a rubber stamp or mechanical device. The preparer is personally responsible for affixing his or her signature to the return.

If the preparer is self-employed (that is, not employed by any person or business to prepare the return), he or she should check the self-employed box in the *Paid Preparer Use Only* space on the return.

The preparer must give you a copy of your return in addition to the copy filed with the IRS.

If you prepare your own return, leave this area blank. If another person prepares your return and doesn't charge you, that person shouldn't sign your return.

If you have questions about whether a preparer must sign your return, contact any IRS office.

Refunds

When you complete your return, you will determine if you paid more income tax than you owed. If so, you can get a refund of the amount you overpaid or you can choose to apply all or part of the overpayment to your next year's (2019) estimated tax.

 If you choose to have a 2018 overpayment applied to your 2019 estimated tax, you can't change your mind and have any of it refunded to you after the due date (without extensions) of your 2018 return.

Follow the Instructions for Form 1040 to complete the entries to claim your refund and/or to apply your overpayment to your 2019 estimated tax.

 If your refund for 2018 is large, you may want to decrease the amount of income tax withheld from your pay in 2019. See chapter 4 for more information.

DIRECT DEPOSIT *Simple. Safe. Secure.* Instead of getting a paper check, you may be able to have your refund deposited directly into your checking or savings account, including an individual retirement arrangement. Follow the Instructions for Form 1040 to request direct deposit. If the direct deposit can't be done, the IRS will send a check instead.

Don't request a deposit of any part of your refund to an account that isn't in your name. Don't allow your tax preparer to deposit any part of your refund into his or her account. The number of direct deposits to a single account or prepaid debit card is limited to three refunds a year. After this limit is exceeded, paper checks will be sent instead. Learn more at *IRS.gov/Individuals/Direct-Deposit-Limits.*

IRA. You can have your refund (or part of it) directly deposited to a traditional IRA, Roth IRA, or SEP-IRA, but not a SIMPLE IRA. You must establish the IRA at a bank or financial institution before you request direct deposit.

TreasuryDirect®. You can request a deposit of your refund to a TreasuryDirect® online account to buy U.S. Treasury marketable securities and savings bonds. For more information, go to *http://go.usa.gov/3KvcP.*

Split refunds. If you choose direct deposit, you may be able to split the refund and have it deposited among two or three accounts or buy up to $5,000 in paper series I savings bonds. Complete Form 8888 and attach it to your return.

Overpayment less than one dollar. If your overpayment is less than one dollar, you won't get a refund unless you ask for it in writing.

Cashing your refund check. Cash your tax refund check soon after you receive it. Checks expire the last business day of the 12th month of issue.

If your check has expired, you can apply to the IRS to have it reissued.

Refund more or less than expected. If you receive a check for a refund you aren't entitled to, or for an overpayment that should have been credited to estimated tax, don't cash the check. Call the IRS.

If you receive a check for more than the refund you claimed, don't cash the check until you receive a notice explaining the difference.

If your refund check is for less than you claimed, it should be accompanied by a notice explaining the difference. Cashing the check doesn't stop you from claiming an additional amount of refund.

If you didn't receive a notice and you have any questions about the amount of your refund, you should wait 2 weeks. If you still haven't received a notice, call the IRS.

Offset against debts. If you are due a refund but haven't paid certain amounts you owe, all or part of your refund may be used to pay all or part of the past-due amount. This includes past-due federal income tax, other federal debts (such as student loans), state income tax, child and spousal support payments, and state unemployment compensation debt. You will be notified if the refund you claimed has been offset against your debts.

Joint return and injured spouse. When a joint return is filed and only one spouse owes a past-due amount, the other spouse can be considered an injured spouse. An injured spouse should file Form 8379, Injured Spouse Allocation, if both of the following apply and the spouse wants a refund of his or her share of the overpayment shown on the joint return.

1. You aren't legally obligated to pay the past-due amount.

2. You made and reported tax payments (such as federal income tax withheld from your wages or estimated tax payments), or claimed a refundable tax credit (see the credits listed under *Who Should File*, earlier).

Note. If the injured spouse's residence was in a community property state at any time during the tax year, special rules may apply. See the Instructions for Form 8379.

If you haven't filed your joint return and you know that your joint refund will be offset, file Form 8379 with your return. You should receive your refund within 14 weeks from the date the paper return is filed or within 11 weeks from the date the return is filed electronically.

If you filed your joint return and your joint refund was offset, file Form 8379 by itself. When filed after offset, it can take up to 8 weeks to receive your refund. Don't attach the previously filed tax return, but do include copies of all Forms W-2 and W-2G for both spouses and any Forms 1099 that show income tax withheld. The processing of Form 8379 may be delayed if these forms aren't attached, or if the form is incomplete when filed.

A separate Form 8379 must be filed for each tax year to be considered.

 An injured spouse claim is different from an innocent spouse relief request. An injured spouse uses Form 8379 to request the division of the tax overpayment attributed to each spouse. An innocent spouse uses Form 8857, Request for Innocent Spouse Relief, to request relief from joint liability for tax, interest, and penalties on a joint return for items of the other spouse (or former spouse) that were incorrectly reported on the joint return. For information on innocent spouses, see Relief from joint responsibility under Filing a Joint Return in chapter 2.

Amount You Owe

When you complete your return, you will determine if you have paid the full amount of tax that you owe. If you owe additional tax, you should pay it with your return.

 You don't have to pay if the amount you owe is under $1.

If the IRS figures your tax for you, you will receive a bill for any tax that is due. You should pay this bill within 30 days (or by the due date of your return, if later). See *Tax Figured by IRS* in chapter 29.

 If you don't pay your tax when due, you may have to pay a failure-to-pay penalty. See Penalties, later. For more information about your balance due, see Pub. 594.

 If the amount you owe for 2018 is large, you may want to increase the amount of income tax withheld from your pay or make estimated tax payments for 2019. See chapter 4 for more information.

How To Pay

You can pay online, by phone, by mobile device, in cash, or by check or money order. Don't include any estimated tax payment for 2019 in this payment. Instead, make the estimated tax payment separately.

Bad check or payment. The penalty for writing a bad check to the IRS is $25 or 2% of the check, whichever is more. This penalty also applies to other forms of payment if the IRS doesn't receive the funds.

Pay online. Paying online is convenient and secure and helps make sure we get your payments on time.

You can pay online with a direct transfer from your bank account using IRS Direct Pay or the Electronic Federal Tax Payment System, or by debit or credit card.

To pay your taxes online or for more information, go to *IRS.gov/Payments*.

Pay by phone. Paying by phone is another safe and secure method of paying electronically. Use one of the following methods.

* Electronic Federal Tax Payment System (EFTPS).

* Debit or credit card.

To use EFTPS, you must be enrolled either online or have an enrollment form mailed to you. To make a payment using EFTPS, call 800-555-4477 (English) or 800-244-4829 (Español). People who are deaf, hard of hearing, or have a speech disability and have access to TTY/TDD equipment can call 800-733-4829. For more information about EFTPS, go to *IRS.gov/Payments* or *www.EFTPS.gov*.

To pay using a debit or credit card, you can call one of the following service providers. There is a convenience fee charged by these providers that varies by provider, card type, and payment amount.

> Official Payments
> 1-888-UPAY-TAX™ (1-888-872-9829)
> *www.officialpayments.com*
>
> Link2Gov Corporation
> 1-888-PAY-1040™ (1-888-729-1040)
> *www.PAY1040.com*
>
> WorldPay US, Inc.
> 1-844-PAY-TAX-8™ (1-844-729-8298)
> *www.payUSAtax.com*

For the latest details on how to pay by phone, go to *IRS.gov/Payments*.

Pay by mobile device. To pay through your mobile device, download the IRS2Go app.

Pay by cash. Cash is an in-person payment option for individuals provided through retail partners with a maximum of $1,000 per day per transaction. To make a cash payment, you must first be registered online at *www.officialpayments.com*.

Pay by check or money order. Make your check or money order payable to "United States Treasury" for the full amount due. Don't send cash. Don't attach the payment to your return. Show your correct name, address, SSN, daytime phone number, and the tax year and form number on the front of your check or money order. If you are filing a joint return, enter the SSN shown first on your tax return.

Estimated tax payments. Don't include any 2019 estimated tax payment in the payment for

your 2018 income tax return. See chapter 4 for information on how to pay estimated tax.

Interest

Interest is charged on tax you don't pay by the due date of your return. Interest is charged even if you get an extension of time for filing.

 If the IRS figures your tax for you, to avoid interest for late payment, you must pay the bill within 30 days of the date of the bill or by the due date of your return, whichever is later. For information, see Tax Figured by IRS in chapter 29.

Interest on penalties. Interest is charged on the failure-to-file penalty, the accuracy-related penalty, and the fraud penalty from the due date of the return (including extensions) to the date of payment. Interest on other penalties starts on the date of notice and demand, but isn't charged on penalties paid within 21 calendar days from the date of the notice (or within 10 business days if the notice is for $100,000 or more).

Interest due to IRS error or delay. All or part of any interest you were charged can be forgiven if the interest is due to an unreasonable error or delay by an officer or employee of the IRS in performing a ministerial or managerial act.

A ministerial act is a procedural or mechanical act that occurs during the processing of your case. A managerial act includes personnel transfers and extended personnel training. A decision concerning the proper application of federal tax law isn't a ministerial or managerial act.

The interest can be forgiven only if you aren't responsible in any important way for the error or delay and the IRS has notified you in writing of the deficiency or payment. For more information, see Pub. 556.

Interest and certain penalties also may be suspended for a limited period if you filed your return by the due date (including extensions) and the IRS doesn't provide you with a notice specifically stating your liability and the basis for it before the close of the 36-month period beginning on the later of:

* The date the return is filed, or

* The due date of the return without regard to extensions.

For more information, see Pub. 556.

Installment Agreement

If you can't pay the full amount due with your return, you can ask to make monthly installment payments for the full or a partial amount. However, you will be charged interest and may be charged a late payment penalty on the tax not paid by the date your return is due, even if your request to pay in installments is granted. If your request is granted, you also must pay a fee. To limit the interest and penalty charges, pay as much of the tax as possible with your return. But before requesting an installment agreement, you should consider other less costly alternatives, such as a bank loan or credit card payment.

To apply for an installment agreement online, go to *IRS.gov/OPA*. You also can use Form 9465.

In addition to paying by check or money order, you can use a credit or debit card or direct payment from your bank account to make installment agreement payments. See *How To Pay*, earlier.

Gift To Reduce Debt Held by the Public

 You can make a contribution (gift) to reduce debt held by the public. If you wish to do so, make a separate check payable to "Bureau of the Fiscal Service."

Send your check to:

Bureau of the Fiscal Service
ATTN: Department G
P.O. Box 2188
Parkersburg, WV 26106-2188

Or, enclose your separate check in the envelope with your income tax return. Don't add this gift to any tax you owe.

For information on making this type of gift online, go to *www.treasurydirect.gov* and click on "How To Make a Contribution to Reduce the Debt."

You may be able to deduct this gift as a charitable contribution on next year's tax return if you itemize your deductions on Schedule A (Form 1040).

Name and Address

After you have completed your return, fill in your name and address in the appropriate area of Form 1040.

 You must include your SSN in the correct place on your tax return.

P.O. box. If your post office doesn't deliver mail to your street address and you have a P.O. box, enter your P.O. box number on the line for your present home address instead of your street address.

Foreign address. If your address is outside the United States or its possessions or territories, enter the city name on the appropriate line of your Form 1040. Don't enter any other information on that line, but also complete the applicable lines on Schedule 6 listing:

1. Foreign country name,

2. Foreign province/state/county, and

3. Foreign postal code.

Follow the country's practice for entering the postal code and the name of the province, county, or state. Attach Schedule 6 to your return.

Where Do I File?

After you complete your return, you must send it to the IRS. You can mail it or you may be able to

file it electronically. See *Why Should I File Electronically*, earlier.

Mailing your paper return. Mail your paper return to the address shown in the Instructions for Form 1040.

What Happens After I File?

After you send your return to the IRS, you may have some questions. This section discusses concerns you may have about recordkeeping, your refund, and what to do if you move.

What Records Should I Keep?

This part discusses why you should keep records, what kinds of records you should keep, and how long you should keep them.

 You must keep records so that you can prepare a complete and accurate income tax return. The law doesn't require any special form of records. However, you should keep all receipts, canceled checks or other proof of payment, and any other records to support any deductions or credits you claim.

If you file a claim for refund, you must be able to prove by your records that you have overpaid your tax.

This part doesn't discuss the records you should keep when operating a business. For information on business records, see Pub. 583, Starting a Business and Keeping Records.

Why Keep Records?

Good records help you:

- **Identify sources of income.** Your records can identify the sources of your income to help you separate business from nonbusiness income and taxable from nontaxable income.

- **Keep track of expenses.** You can use your records to identify expenses for which you can claim a deduction. This helps you determine if you can itemize deductions on your tax return.

- **Keep track of the basis of property.** You need to keep records that show the basis of your property. This includes the original cost or other basis of the property and any improvements you made.

- **Prepare tax returns.** You need records to prepare your tax return.

- **Support items reported on tax returns.** The IRS may question an item on your return. Your records will help you explain any item and arrive at the correct tax. If you can't produce the correct documents, you may have to pay additional tax and be subject to penalties.

Kinds of Records To Keep

The IRS doesn't require you to keep your records in a particular way. Keep them in a

manner that allows you and the IRS to determine your correct tax.

You can use your checkbook to keep a record of your income and expenses. You also need to keep documents, such as receipts and sales slips, that can help prove a deduction.

In this section you will find guidance about basic records that everyone should keep. The section also provides guidance about specific records you should keep for certain items.

Electronic records. All requirements that apply to hard copy books and records also apply to electronic storage systems that maintain tax books and records. When you replace hard copy books and records, you must maintain the electronic storage systems for as long as they are material to the administration of tax law.

For details on electronic storage system requirements, see Revenue Procedure 97-22, which is on page 9 of Internal Revenue Bulletin 1997-13 at *IRS.gov/pub/irs-irbs/irb97-13.pdf*.

Copies of tax returns. You should keep copies of your tax returns as part of your tax records. They can help you prepare future tax returns, and you will need them if you file an amended return or are audited. Copies of your returns and other records can be helpful to your survivor or the executor or administrator of your estate.

If necessary, you can request a copy of a return and all attachments (including Form W-2) from the IRS by using Form 4506. There is a charge for a copy of a return. For information on the cost and where to file, see the Instructions for Form 4506.

If you just need information from your return, you can order a transcript in one of the following ways.

- Go to *IRS.gov/Transcript*.

- Call 800-908-9946.

- Use Form 4506-T or Form 4506T-EZ.

There is no fee for a transcript. For more information, see Form 4506-T.

Basic Records

Basic records are documents that everybody should keep. These are the records that prove your income and expenses. If you own a home or investments, your basic records should contain documents related to those items.

Income. Your basic records prove the amounts you report as income on your tax return. Your income may include wages, dividends, interest, and partnership or S corporation distributions. Your records also can prove that certain amounts aren't taxable, such as tax-exempt interest.

Note. If you receive a Form W-2, keep Copy C until you begin receiving social security benefits. This will help protect your benefits in case there is a question about your work record or earnings in a particular year.

Expenses. Your basic records prove the expenses for which you claim a deduction (or credit) on your tax return. Your deductions may include alimony, charitable contributions, mortgage interest, and real estate taxes. You also may have child care expenses for which you can claim a credit.

Home. Your basic records should enable you to determine the basis or adjusted basis of your home. You need this information to determine if you have a gain or loss when you sell your home or to figure depreciation if you use part of your home for business purposes or for rent. Your records should show the purchase price, settlement or closing costs, and the cost of any improvements. They also may show any casualty losses deducted and insurance reimbursements for casualty losses.

For detailed information on basis, including which settlement or closing costs are included in the basis of your home, see chapter 13.

When you sell your home, your records should show the sales price and any selling expenses, such as commissions. For information on selling your home, see chapter 15.

Investments. Your basic records should enable you to determine your basis in an investment and whether you have a gain or loss when you sell it. Investments include stocks, bonds, and mutual funds. Your records should show the purchase price, sales price, and commissions. They also may show any reinvested dividends, stock splits and dividends, load charges, and original issue discount (OID).

For information on stocks, bonds, and mutual funds, see chapters 8, 13, 14, and 16.

Proof of Payment

One of your basic records is proof of payment. You should keep these records to support certain amounts shown on your tax return. Proof of payment alone isn't proof that the item claimed on your return is allowable. You also should keep other documents that will help prove that the item is allowable.

Generally, you prove payment with a cash receipt, financial account statement, credit card statement, canceled check, or substitute check. If you make payments in cash, you should get a dated and signed receipt showing the amount and the reason for the payment.

If you make payments using your bank account, you may be able to prove payment with an account statement.

Account statements. You may be able to prove payment with a legible financial account statement prepared by your bank or other financial institution.

Pay statements. You may have deductible expenses withheld from your paycheck, such as union dues or medical insurance premiums. You should keep your year-end or final pay statements as proof of payment of these expenses.

How Long To Keep Records

You must keep your records as long as they may be needed for the administration of any provision of the Internal Revenue Code. Generally, this means you must keep records that support items shown on your return until the period of limitations for that return runs out.

The period of limitations is the period of time in which you can amend your return to claim a credit or refund or the IRS can assess additional tax. Table 1-7 contains the periods of limitations that apply to income tax returns. Unless otherwise stated, the years refer to the period beginning after the return was filed. Returns filed before the due date are treated as being filed on the due date.

Table 1-7. **Period of Limitations**

IF you...	THEN the period is...
1 File a return and (2), (3), and (4) don't apply to you	3 years
2 Don't report income that you should and it is more than 25% of the gross income shown on your return	6 years
3 File a fraudulent return	No limit
4 Don't file a return	No limit
5 File a claim for credit or refund after you filed your return	The later of 3 years or 2 years after tax was paid
6 File a claim for a loss from worthless securities or bad debt deduction	7 years

Property. Keep records relating to property until the period of limitations expires for the year in which you dispose of the property in a taxable disposition. You must keep these records to figure your basis for computing gain or loss when you sell or otherwise dispose of the property.

Generally, if you received property in a nontaxable exchange, your basis in that property is the same as the basis of the property you gave up. You must keep the records on the old property, as well as the new property, until the period of limitations expires for the year in which you dispose of the new property in a taxable disposition.

Refund Information

You can go online to check the status of your 2018 refund 24 hours after the IRS receives your e-filed return, or 4 weeks after you mail a paper return. If you filed Form 8379 with your return, allow 14 weeks (11 weeks if you filed electronically) before checking your refund status. Be sure to have a copy of your 2018 tax return handy because you will need to know the filing status, the first SSN shown on the return, and the exact whole-dollar amount of the refund. To check on your refund, do one of the following.

- Go to IRS.gov/Refunds.

- Download the free IRS2Go app to your smart phone and use it to check your refund status.

- Call the automated refund hotline at 800-829-1954.

Interest on Refunds

If you are due a refund, you may get interest on it. The interest rates are adjusted quarterly.

If the refund is made within 45 days after the due date of your return, no interest will be paid. If you file your return after the due date (including extensions), no interest will be paid if the refund is made within 45 days after the date you filed. If the refund isn't made within this 45-day period, interest will be paid from the due date of the return or from the date you filed, whichever is later.

Accepting a refund check doesn't change your right to claim an additional refund and interest. File your claim within the period of time that applies. See Amended Returns and Claims for Refund, later. If you don't accept a refund check, no more interest will be paid on the overpayment included in the check.

Interest on erroneous refund. All or part of any interest you were charged on an erroneous refund generally will be forgiven. Any interest charged for the period before demand for repayment was made will be forgiven unless:

1. You, or a person related to you, caused the erroneous refund in any way; or

2. The refund is more than $50,000.

For example, if you claimed a refund of $100 on your return, but the IRS made an error and sent you $1,000, you wouldn't be charged interest for the time you held the $900 difference. You must, however, repay the $900 when the IRS asks.

Change of Address

If you have moved, file your return using your new address.

If you move after you filed your return, you should give the IRS clear and concise notification of your change of address. The notification may be written, electronic, or oral. Send written notification to the Internal Revenue Service Center serving your old address. You can use Form 8822, Change of Address. If you are expecting a refund, also notify the post office serving your old address. This will help in forwarding your check to your new address (unless you chose direct deposit of your refund). For more information, see Revenue Procedure 2010-16, 2010-19 I.R.B. 664, available at IRS.gov/irb/2010-19_IRB/ar07.html.

Be sure to include your SSN (and the name and SSN of your spouse if you filed a joint return) in any correspondence with the IRS.

What If I Made a Mistake?

Errors may delay your refund or result in notices being sent to you. If you discover an error, you can file an amended return or claim for refund.

Amended Returns and Claims for Refund

You should correct your return if, after you have filed it, you find that:

1. You didn't report some income,

2. You claimed deductions or credits you shouldn't have claimed,

3. You didn't claim deductions or credits you could have claimed, or

4. You should have claimed a different filing status. (Once you file a joint return, you can't choose to file separate returns for that year after the due date of the return. However, an executor may be able to make this change for a deceased spouse.)

If you need a copy of your return, see *Copies of tax returns* under *Kinds of Records To Keep*, earlier, in this chapter.

Form 1040X. Use Form 1040X to correct a return you have already filed. An amended tax return can't be filed electronically.

Completing Form 1040X. On Form 1040X, enter your income, deductions, and credits as you originally reported them on your return; the changes you are making; and the corrected amounts. Then figure the tax on the corrected amount of taxable income and the amount you owe or your refund.

If you owe tax, the IRS offers several payment options. See *How To Pay*, earlier. The tax owed won't be subtracted from any amount you had credited to your estimated tax.

If you can't pay the full amount due with your return, you can ask to make monthly installment payments. See *Installment Agreement*, earlier.

If you overpaid tax, you can have all or part of the overpayment refunded to you, or you can apply all or part of it to your estimated tax. If you choose to get a refund, it will be sent separately from any refund shown on your original return.

Filing Form 1040X. When completing Form 1040X, don't forget to show the year of your original return and explain all changes you made. Be sure to attach any forms or schedules needed to explain your changes. Mail your Form 1040X to the Internal Revenue Service Center serving the area where you now live (as shown in the Instructions for Form 1040X). However, if you are filing Form 1040X in response to a notice you received from the IRS, mail it to the address shown on the notice.

File a separate form for each tax year involved.

Time for filing a claim for refund. Generally, you must file your claim for a credit or refund within 3 years after the date you filed your original return or within 2 years after the date you paid the tax, whichever is later. Returns filed before the due date (without regard to extensions) are considered filed on the due date (even if the due date was a Saturday, Sunday, or legal holiday). These time periods are suspended while you are financially disabled, discussed later.

If the last day for claiming a credit or refund is a Saturday, Sunday, or legal holiday, you can file the claim on the next business day.

If you don't file a claim within this period, you may not be entitled to a credit or a refund.

Federally declared disaster. If you were affected by a federally declared disaster, you may have additional time to file your amended return. See Pub. 556 for details.

Protective claim for refund. Generally, a protective claim is a formal claim or amended return for credit or refund normally based on current litigation or expected changes in tax law or other legislation. You file a protective claim when your right to a refund is contingent on future events and may not be determinable until after the statute of limitations expires. A valid protective claim doesn't have to list a particular dollar amount or demand an immediate refund. However, a valid protective claim must:

- Be in writing and signed;

- Include your name, address, SSN or ITIN, and other contact information;

- Identify and describe the contingencies affecting the claim;

- Clearly alert the IRS to the essential nature of the claim; and

- Identify the specific year(s) for which a refund is sought.

Mail your protective claim for refund to the address listed in the Instructions for Form 1040X under *Where To File*.

Generally, the IRS will delay action on the protective claim until the contingency is resolved.

Limit on amount of refund. If you file your claim within 3 years after the date you filed your return, the credit or refund can't be more than the part of the tax paid within the 3-year period (plus any extension of time for filing your return) immediately before you filed the claim. This time period is suspended while you are financially disabled, discussed later.

Tax paid. Payments, including estimated tax payments, made before the due date (without regard to extensions) of the original return are considered paid on the due date. For example, income tax withheld during the year is considered paid on the due date of the return, April 15 for most taxpayers.

Example 1. You made estimated tax payments of $500 and got an automatic extension of time to October 15, 2015, to file your 2014 income tax return. When you filed your return on that date, you paid an additional $200 tax. On October 15, 2018, you filed an amended return and claimed a refund of $700. Because you filed your claim within 3 years after you filed your original return, you can get a refund of up to $700, the tax paid within the 3 years plus the 6-month extension period immediately before you filed the claim.

Example 2. The situation is the same as in *Example 1*, except you filed your return on October 30, 2015, 2 weeks after the extension period ended. You paid an additional $200 on that date. On October 31, 2018, you filed an amended return and claimed a refund of $700. Although you filed your claim within 3 years from the date you filed your original return, the refund

was limited to $200, the tax paid within the 3 years plus the 6-month extension period immediately before you filed the claim. The estimated tax of $500 paid before that period can't be refunded or credited.

If you file a claim more than 3 years after you file your return, the credit or refund can't be more than the tax you paid within the 2 years immediately before you file the claim.

Example. You filed your 2014 tax return on April 15, 2015. You paid taxes of $500. On November 5, 2016, after an examination of your 2014 return, you had to pay an additional tax of $200. On May 12, 2018, you file a claim for a refund of $300. However, because you filed your claim more than 3 years after you filed your return, your refund will be limited to the $200 you paid during the 2 years immediately before you filed your claim.

Financially disabled. The time periods for claiming a refund are suspended for the period in which you are financially disabled. For a joint income tax return, only one spouse has to be financially disabled for the time period to be suspended. You are financially disabled if you are unable to manage your financial affairs because of a medically determinable physical or mental impairment which can be expected to result in death or which has lasted or can be expected to last for a continuous period of not less than 12 months. However, you aren't treated as financially disabled during any period your spouse or any other person is authorized to act on your behalf in financial matters.

To claim that you are financially disabled, you must send in the following written statements with your claim for refund.

1. A statement from your qualified physician that includes:

   a. The name and a description of your physical or mental impairment;

   b. The physician's medical opinion that the impairment prevented you from managing your financial affairs;

   c. The physician's medical opinion that the impairment was or can be expected to result in death, or that its duration has lasted, or can be expected to last, at least 12 months;

   d. The specific time period (to the best of the physician's knowledge); and

   e. The following certification signed by the physician: "I hereby certify that, to the best of my knowledge and belief, the above representations are true, correct, and complete."

2. A statement made by the person signing the claim for credit or refund that no person, including your spouse, was authorized to act on your behalf in financial matters during the period of disability (or the exact dates that a person was authorized to act for you).

Exceptions for special types of refunds. If you file a claim for one of the items in the following list, the dates and limits discussed earlier may not apply. These items, and where to get more information, are as follows.

- Bad debt. See *Nonbusiness Bad Debts* in chapter 14.

- Worthless security. See *Worthless securities* in chapter 14.

- Foreign tax paid or accrued. See Pub. 514.

- Net operating loss carryback. See Pub. 536.

- Carryback of certain business tax credits. See Form 3800.

- Claim based on an agreement with the IRS extending the period for assessment of tax.

Processing claims for refund. Claims are usually processed 8–12 weeks after they are filed. Your claim may be accepted as filed, disallowed, or subject to examination. If a claim is examined, the procedures are the same as in the examination of a tax return.

If your claim is disallowed, you will receive an explanation of why it was disallowed.

Taking your claim to court. You can sue for a refund in court, but you must first file a timely claim with the IRS. If the IRS disallows your claim or doesn't act on your claim within 6 months after you file it, you can then take your claim to court. For information on the burden of proof in a court proceeding, see Pub. 556.

The IRS provides a direct method to move your claim to court if:

- You are filing a claim for a credit or refund based solely on contested income tax or on estate tax or gift tax issues considered in your previously examined returns, and

- You want to take your case to court instead of appealing it within the IRS.

When you file your claim with the IRS, you get the direct method by requesting in writing that your claim be immediately rejected. A notice of claim disallowance will be sent to you.

You have 2 years from the date of mailing of the notice of claim disallowance to file a refund suit in the United States District Court having jurisdiction or in the United States Court of Federal Claims.

Interest on refund. If you receive a refund because of your amended return, interest will be paid on it from the due date of your original return or the date you filed your original return, whichever is later, to the date you filed the amended return. However, if the refund isn't made within 45 days after you file the amended return, interest will be paid up to the date the refund is paid.

Reduced refund. Your refund may be reduced by an additional tax liability that has been assessed against you.

Also, your refund may be reduced by amounts you owe for past-due federal tax, state income tax, state unemployment compensation debts, child support, spousal support, or certain other federal nontax debts, such as student loans. If your spouse owes these debts, see *Offset against debts* under *Refunds*, earlier, for the correct refund procedures to follow.

Effect on state tax liability. If your return is changed for any reason, it may affect your state income tax liability. This includes changes made as a result of an examination of your return by the IRS. Contact your state tax agency for more information.

Penalties

The law provides penalties for failure to file returns or pay taxes as required.

Civil Penalties

If you don't file your return and pay your tax by the due date, you may have to pay a penalty. You also may have to pay a penalty if you substantially understate your tax, understate a reportable transaction, file an erroneous claim for refund or credit, file a frivolous tax submission, or fail to supply your SSN or individual taxpayer identification number. If you provide fraudulent information on your return, you may have to pay a civil fraud penalty.

Filing late. If you don't file your return by the due date (including extensions), you may have to pay a failure-to-file penalty. The penalty is usually 5% for each month or part of a month that a return is late, but not more than 25%. The penalty is based on the tax not paid by the due date (without regard to extensions).

Fraud. If your failure to file is due to fraud, the penalty is 15% for each month or part of a month that your return is late, up to a maximum of 75%.

Return over 60 days late. If you file your return more than 60 days after the due date or extended due date, the minimum penalty is the smaller of $210 or 100% of the unpaid tax.

Exception. You won't have to pay the penalty if you show that you failed to file on time because of reasonable cause and not because of willful neglect.

Paying tax late. You will have to pay a failure-to-pay penalty of 1/2 of 1% (0.50%) of your unpaid taxes for each month, or part of a month, after the due date that the tax isn't paid. This penalty doesn't apply during the automatic 6-month extension of time to file period if you paid at least 90% of your actual tax liability on or before the due date of your return and pay the balance when you file the return.

The monthly rate of the failure-to-pay penalty is half the usual rate (0.25% instead of 0.50%) if an installment agreement is in effect for that month. You must have filed your return by the due date (including extensions) to qualify for this reduced penalty.

If a notice of intent to levy is issued, the rate will increase to 1% at the start of the first month beginning at least 10 days after the day that the notice is issued. If a notice and demand for immediate payment is issued, the rate will increase to 1% at the start of the first month beginning after the day that the notice and demand is issued.

This penalty can't be more than 25% of your unpaid tax. You won't have to pay the penalty if you can show that you had a good reason for not paying your tax on time.

Combined penalties. If both the failure-to-file penalty and the failure-to-pay penalty (discussed earlier) apply in any month, the 5% (or 15%) failure-to-file penalty is reduced by the failure-to-pay penalty. However, if you file your return more than 60 days after the due date or extended due date, the minimum penalty is the smaller of $210 or 100% of the unpaid tax.

Accuracy-related penalty. You may have to pay an accuracy-related penalty if you underpay your tax because:

1. You show negligence or disregard of the rules or regulations,

2. You substantially understate your income tax,

3. You claim tax benefits for a transaction that lacks economic substance, or

4. You fail to disclose a foreign financial asset.

The penalty is equal to 20% of the underpayment. The penalty is 40% of any portion of the underpayment that is attributable to an undisclosed noneconomic substance transaction or an undisclosed foreign financial asset transaction. The penalty won't be figured on any part of an underpayment on which the fraud penalty (discussed later) is charged.

Negligence or disregard. The term "negligence" includes a failure to make a reasonable attempt to comply with the tax law or to exercise ordinary and reasonable care in preparing a return. Negligence also includes failure to keep adequate books and records. You won't have to pay a negligence penalty if you have a reasonable basis for a position you took.

The term "disregard" includes any careless, reckless, or intentional disregard.

Adequate disclosure. You can avoid the penalty for disregard of rules or regulations if you adequately disclose on your return a position that has at least a reasonable basis. See *Disclosure statement*, later.

This exception won't apply to an item that is attributable to a tax shelter. In addition, it won't apply if you fail to keep adequate books and records, or substantiate items properly.

Substantial understatement of income tax. You understate your tax if the tax shown on your return is less than the correct tax. The understatement is substantial if it is more than the larger of 10% of the correct tax or $5,000. However, the amount of the understatement may be reduced to the extent the understatement is due to:

1. Substantial authority, or

2. Adequate disclosure and a reasonable basis.

If an item on your return is attributable to a tax shelter, there is no reduction for an adequate disclosure. However, there is a reduction for a position with substantial authority, but only if you reasonably believed that your tax treatment was more likely than not the proper treatment.

Substantial authority. Whether there is or was substantial authority for the tax treatment of an item depends on the facts and circumstances. Some of the items that may be considered are court opinions, Treasury regulations, revenue rulings, revenue procedures, and notices and announcements issued by the IRS and published in the Internal Revenue Bulletin that involve the same or similar circumstances as yours.

Disclosure statement. To adequately disclose the relevant facts about your tax treatment of an item, use Form 8275. You also must have a reasonable basis for treating the item the way you did.

In cases of substantial understatement only, items that meet the requirements of Revenue Procedure 2018-11 (or later update) are considered adequately disclosed on your return without filing Form 8275.

Use Form 8275-R to disclose items or positions contrary to regulations.

Transaction lacking economic substance. For more information on economic substance, see section 7701(o).

Foreign financial asset. For more information on undisclosed foreign financial assets, see section 6662(j).

Reasonable cause. You won't have to pay a penalty if you show a good reason (reasonable cause) for the way you treated an item. You also must show that you acted in good faith. This doesn't apply to a transaction that lacks economic substance.

Filing erroneous claim for refund or credit. You may have to pay a penalty if you file an erroneous claim for refund or credit. The penalty is equal to 20% of the disallowed amount of the claim, unless you can show a reasonable basis for the way you treated an item. However, any disallowed amount due to a transaction that lacks economic substance won't be treated as having a reasonable basis. The penalty won't be figured on any part of the disallowed amount of the claim that relates to the earned income credit or on which the accuracy-related or fraud penalties are charged.

Frivolous tax submission. You may have to pay a penalty of $5,000 if you file a frivolous tax return or other frivolous submissions. A frivolous tax return is one that doesn't include enough information to figure the correct tax or that contains information clearly showing that the tax you reported is substantially incorrect. For more information on frivolous returns, frivolous submissions, and a list of positions that are identified as frivolous, see Notice 2010-33, 2010-17 I.R.B. 609, available at *IRS.gov/irb/2010-17_IRB/ar13.html*.

You will have to pay the penalty if you filed this kind of return or submission based on a frivolous position or a desire to delay or interfere with the administration of federal tax laws. This includes altering or striking out the preprinted language above the space provided for your signature.

This penalty is added to any other penalty provided by law.

Fraud. If there is any underpayment of tax on your return due to fraud, a penalty of 75% of the underpayment due to fraud will be added to your tax.

Joint return. The fraud penalty on a joint return doesn't apply to a spouse unless some part of the underpayment is due to the fraud of that spouse.

Failure to supply SSN. If you don't include your SSN or the SSN of another person where required on a return, statement, or other document, you will be subject to a penalty of $50 for each failure. You also will be subject to a penalty of $50 if you don't give your SSN to another person when it is required on a return, statement, or other document.

For example, if you have a bank account that earns interest, you must give your SSN to the bank. The number must be shown on the Form 1099-INT or other statement the bank sends you. If you don't give the bank your SSN, you will be subject to the $50 penalty. (You also may be subject to "backup" withholding of income tax. See chapter 4.)

You won't have to pay the penalty if you are able to show that the failure was due to reasonable cause and not willful neglect.

Criminal Penalties

You may be subject to criminal prosecution (brought to trial) for actions such as:

1. Tax evasion;

2. Willful failure to file a return, supply information, or pay any tax due;

3. Fraud and false statements;

4. Preparing and filing a fraudulent return; or

5. Identity theft.

Identity Theft

Identity theft occurs when someone uses your personal information such as your name, SSN, or other identifying information, without your permission, to commit fraud or other crimes. An identity thief may use your SSN to get a job or may file a tax return using your SSN to receive a refund.

To reduce your risk:

- Protect your SSN,

- Ensure your employer is protecting your SSN, and

- Be careful when choosing a tax preparer.

If your tax records are affected by identity theft and you receive a notice from the IRS, respond right away to the name and phone number printed on the IRS notice or letter.

If your SSN has been lost or stolen or you suspect you are a victim of tax-related identity theft, visit *IRS.gov/IdentityTheft* to learn what steps you should take.

For more information, see Pub. 5027.

Victims of identity theft who are experiencing economic harm or a systemic problem, or are seeking help in resolving tax problems that have not been resolved through normal channels, may be eligible for Taxpayer Advocate Service (TAS) assistance. You can reach TAS by calling the National Taxpayer Advocate helpline at 877-777-4778 or TTY/TDD at 800-829-4059. Deaf or hard-of-hearing individuals also can contact the IRS through relay services such as the Federal Relay Service, available at *www.gsa.gov/fedrelay*.

Protect yourself from suspicious emails or phishing schemes. Phishing is the creation and use of email and websites designed to mimic legitimate business emails and websites. The most common form is the act of sending an email to a user falsely claiming to be an established legitimate enterprise in an attempt to scam the user into surrendering private information that will be used for identity theft.

The IRS doesn't initiate contacts with taxpayers via emails. Also, the IRS doesn't request detailed personal information through email or ask taxpayers for the PIN numbers, passwords, or similar secret access information for their credit card, bank, or other financial accounts.

If you receive an unsolicited email claiming to be from the IRS, forward the message to *phishing@irs.gov*. You also may report misuse of the IRS name, logo, forms, or other IRS property to the Treasury Inspector General for Tax Administration toll-free at 800-366-4484. You can forward suspicious emails to the Federal Trade Commission (FTC) at *spam@uce.gov* or report them at *ftc.gov/complaint*. You can contact them at *www.ftc.gov/idtheft* or 877-ID-THEFT (877-438-4338). If you have been a victim of identity theft, see *www.IdentityTheft.gov* or Pub. 5027. People who are deaf, hard of hearing, or have a speech disability and who have access to TTY/TDD equipment can call 866-653-4261.

Go to *IRS.gov/IDProtection* to learn more about identity theft and how to reduce your risk.

2.

Filing Status

What's New

 At the time this publication went to print, Congress was considering legislation that would do the following.

1. Provide additional tax relief for those affected by certain 2018 disasters.

2. Extend certain tax benefits that expired at the end of 2017 and that currently can't be claimed on your 2018 tax return.

3. Change certain other tax provisions.

To learn whether this legislation was enacted, resulting in changes that affect your 2018 tax return, go to Recent Developments at *IRS.gov/Pub17*.

Introduction

This chapter helps you determine which filing status to use. There are five filing statuses.

- Single.

- Married Filing Jointly.

- Married Filing Separately.
- Head of Household.
- Qualifying Widow(er).

 TIP *If more than one filing status applies to you, choose the one that will give you the lowest tax.*

You must determine your filing status before you can determine whether you must file a tax return (chapter 1), your standard deduction (chapter 21), and your tax (chapter 29). You also use your filing status to determine whether you are eligible to claim certain deductions and credits.

Useful Items
You may want to see:

Publication
❑ **501** Dependents, Standard Deduction, and Filing Information

❑ **519** U.S. Tax Guide for Aliens

❑ **555** Community Property

For these and other useful items, go to *IRS.gov/ Forms*.

Marital Status

In general, your filing status depends on whether you are considered unmarried or married.

Unmarried persons. You are considered unmarried for the whole year if, on the last day of your tax year, you are either:

- Unmarried, or
- Legally separated from your spouse under a divorce or separate maintenance decree. State law governs whether you are married or legally separated under a divorce or separate maintenance decree.

Divorced persons. If you are divorced under a final decree by the last day of the year, you are considered unmarried for the whole year.

Divorce and remarriage. If you obtain a divorce for the sole purpose of filing tax returns as unmarried individuals, and at the time of divorce you intend to and do, in fact, remarry each other in the next tax year, you and your spouse must file as married individuals in both years.

Annulled marriages. If you obtain a court decree of annulment, which holds that no valid marriage ever existed, you are considered unmarried even if you filed joint returns for earlier years. File Form 1040X, Amended U.S. Individual Income Tax Return, claiming single or head of household status for all tax years that are affected by the annulment and not closed by the statute of limitations for filing a tax return. Generally, for a credit or refund, you must file Form 1040X within 3 years (including extensions) after the date you filed your original return or within 2 years after the date you paid the tax, whichever is later. If you filed your original return early (for example, March 1), your return is considered filed on the due date (generally April 15). However, if you had an extension to file (for

example, until October 15) but you filed earlier and we received it on July 1, your return is considered filed on July 1.

Head of household or qualifying widow(er). If you are considered unmarried, you may be able to file as head of household or as qualifying widow(er). See *Head of Household* and *Qualifying Widow(er)* to see if you qualify.

Married persons. If you are considered married, you and your spouse can file a joint return or separate returns.

Considered married. You are considered married for the whole year if, on the last day of your tax year, you and your spouse meet any one of the following tests.

1. You are married and living together.

2. You are living together in a common law marriage recognized in the state where you now live or in the state where the common law marriage began.

3. You are married and living apart, but not legally separated under a decree of divorce or separate maintenance.

4. You are separated under an interlocutory (not final) decree of divorce.

Spouse died during the year. If your spouse died during the year, you are considered married for the whole year for filing status purposes.

If you didn't remarry before the end of the tax year, you can file a joint return for yourself and your deceased spouse. For the next 2 years, you may be entitled to the special benefits described later under *Qualifying Widow(er)*.

If you remarried before the end of the tax year, you can file a joint return with your new spouse. Your deceased spouse's filing status is married filing separately for that year.

Married persons living apart. If you live apart from your spouse and meet certain tests, you may be able to file as head of household even if you aren't divorced or legally separated. If you qualify to file as head of household instead of married filing separately, your standard deduction will be higher. Also, your tax may be lower, and you may be able to claim the earned income credit. See *Head of Household*, later.

Single

Your filing status is single if you are considered unmarried and you don't qualify for another filing status. To determine your marital status, see *Marital Status*, earlier.

Widow(er). Your filing status may be single if you were widowed before January 1, 2018, and didn't remarry before the end of 2018. You may, however, be able to use another filing status that will give you a lower tax. See *Head of Household* and *Qualifying Widow(er)*, later, to see if you qualify.

How to file. On Form 1040, show your filing status as single by checking the *Single* box on the *Filing status* line at the top of the form. Use the *Single* column of the Tax Table or Section A of the Tax Computation Worksheet to figure your tax.

Married Filing Jointly

You can choose married filing jointly as your filing status if you are considered married and both you and your spouse agree to file a joint return. On a joint return, you and your spouse report your combined income and deduct your combined allowable expenses. You can file a joint return even if one of you had no income or deductions.

If you and your spouse decide to file a joint return, your tax may be lower than your combined tax for the other filing statuses. Also, your standard deduction (if you don't itemize deductions) may be higher, and you may qualify for tax benefits that don't apply to other filing statuses.

 TIP *If you and your spouse each have income, you may want to figure your tax both on a joint return and on separate returns (using the filing status of married filing separately). You can choose the method that gives the two of you the lower combined tax.*

How to file. On Form 1040, show your filing status as married filing jointly by checking the *Married filing jointly* box on the *Filing Status* line at the top of the form. Use the *Married filing jointly* column of the Tax Table or Section B of the Tax Computation Worksheet to figure your tax.

Spouse died. If your spouse died during the year, you are considered married for the whole year and can choose married filing jointly as your filing status. See *Spouse died during the year* under *Marital Status*, earlier, for more information.

If your spouse died in 2019 before filing a 2018 return, you can choose married filing jointly as your filing status on your 2018 return.

Divorced persons. If you are divorced under a final decree by the last day of the year, you are considered unmarried for the whole year and you can't choose married filing jointly as your filing status.

Filing a Joint Return

Both you and your spouse must include all of your income and deductions on your joint return.

Accounting period. Both of you must use the same accounting period, but you can use different accounting methods. See *Accounting Periods* and *Accounting Methods* in chapter 1.

Joint responsibility. Both of you may be held responsible, jointly and individually, for the tax and any interest or penalty due on your joint return. This means that if one spouse doesn't pay the tax due, the other may have to. Or, if one spouse doesn't report the correct tax, both spouses may be responsible for any additional taxes assessed by the IRS. One spouse may be held responsible for all the tax due even if all the income was earned by the other spouse.

You may want to file separately if:

- You believe your spouse isn't reporting all of his or her income, or

- You don't want to be responsible for any taxes due if your spouse doesn't have enough tax withheld or doesn't pay enough estimated tax.

Divorced taxpayer. You may be held jointly and individually responsible for any tax, interest, and penalties due on a joint return filed before your divorce. This responsibility may apply even if your divorce decree states that your former spouse will be responsible for any amounts due on previously filed joint returns.

Relief from joint responsibility. In some cases, one spouse may be relieved of joint responsibility for tax, interest, and penalties on a joint return for items of the other spouse that were incorrectly reported on the joint return. You can ask for relief no matter how small the liability.

There are three types of relief available.

1. Innocent spouse relief.

2. Separation of liability (available only to joint filers who are divorced, widowed, legally separated, or haven't lived together for the 12 months ending on the date the election for this relief is filed).

3. Equitable relief.

You must file Form 8857, Request for Innocent Spouse Relief, to request relief from joint responsibility. Pub. 971, Innocent Spouse Relief, explains these kinds of relief and who may qualify for them.

Signing a joint return. For a return to be considered a joint return, both spouses generally must sign the return.

Spouse died before signing. If your spouse died before signing the return, the executor or administrator must sign the return for your spouse. If neither you nor anyone else has yet been appointed as executor or administrator, you can sign the return for your spouse and enter "Filing as surviving spouse" in the area where you sign the return.

Spouse away from home. If your spouse is away from home, you should prepare the return, sign it, and send it to your spouse to sign so that it can be filed on time.

Injury or disease prevents signing. If your spouse can't sign because of disease or injury and tells you to sign for him or her, you can sign your spouse's name in the proper space on the return followed by the words "By (your name), Husband (or Wife)." Be sure to sign in the space provided for your signature. Attach a dated statement, signed by you, to the return. The statement should include the form number of the return you are filing, the tax year and the reason your spouse can't sign, and it should state that your spouse has agreed to your signing for him or her.

Signing as guardian of spouse. If you are the guardian of your spouse who is mentally incompetent, you can sign the return for your spouse as guardian.

Spouse in combat zone. You can sign a joint return for your spouse if your spouse can't sign because he or she is serving in a combat zone (such as the Persian Gulf Area, Serbia, Montenegro, Albania, or Afghanistan), even if

you don't have a power of attorney or other statement. Attach a signed statement to your return explaining that your spouse is serving in a combat zone. For more information on special tax rules for persons who are serving in a combat zone, or who are in missing status as a result of serving in a combat zone, see Pub. 3, Armed Forces' Tax Guide.

Other reasons spouse can't sign. If your spouse can't sign the joint return for any other reason, you can sign for your spouse only if you are given a valid power of attorney (a legal document giving you permission to act for your spouse). Attach the power of attorney (or a copy of it) to your tax return. You can use Form 2848, Power of Attorney and Declaration of Representative.

Nonresident alien or dual-status alien. Generally, a married couple can't file a joint return if either one is a nonresident alien at any time during the tax year. However, if one spouse was a nonresident alien or dual-status alien who was married to a U.S. citizen or resident alien at the end of the year, the spouses can choose to file a joint return. If you do file a joint return, you and your spouse are both treated as U.S. residents for the entire tax year. See chapter 1 of Pub. 519.

Married Filing Separately

You can choose married filing separately as your filing status if you are married. This filing status may benefit you if you want to be responsible only for your own tax or if it results in less tax than filing a joint return.

If you and your spouse don't agree to file a joint return, you must use this filing status unless you qualify for head of household status, discussed later.

You may be able to choose head of household filing status if you are considered unmarried because you live apart from your spouse and meet certain tests (explained under _Head of Household_, later). This can apply to you even if you aren't divorced or legally separated. If you qualify to file as head of household, instead of as married filing separately, your tax may be lower, you may be able to claim the earned income credit and certain other benefits, and your standard deduction will be higher. The head of household filing status allows you to choose the standard deduction even if your spouse chooses to itemize deductions. See _Head of Household_, later, for more information.

 You will generally pay more combined tax on separate returns than you would on a joint return for the reasons listed under Special Rules, _later. However, unless you are required to file separately, you should figure your tax both ways (on a joint return and on separate returns). This way you can make sure you are using the filing status that results in the lowest combined tax. When figuring the combined tax of a married couple, you may want to consider state taxes as well as federal taxes._

How to file. If you file a separate return, you generally report only your own income, credits, and deductions.

Select this filing status by checking the _Married filing separately_ box on the _Filing Status_ line at the top of Form 1040. Enter your spouse's full name and SSN or ITIN in the entry space at the far right of the filing status checkboxes (next to _Qualifying Widow(er)_). If your spouse doesn't have and isn't required to have an SSN or ITIN, enter "NRA" in the space for your spouse's SSN. Use the _Married filing separately_ column of the Tax Table or Section C of the Tax Computation Worksheet to figure your tax.

Special Rules

If you choose married filing separately as your filing status, the following special rules apply. Because of these special rules, you usually pay more tax on a separate return than if you use another filing status you qualify for.

1. Your tax rate generally is higher than on a joint return.

2. Your exemption amount for figuring the alternative minimum tax is half that allowed on a joint return.

3. You can't take the credit for child and dependent care expenses in most cases, and the amount you can exclude from income under an employer's dependent care assistance program is limited to $2,500 (instead of $5,000). However, if you are legally separated or living apart from your spouse, you may be able to file a separate return and still take the credit. For more information about these expenses, the credit, and the exclusion, see chapter 31.

4. You can't take the earned income credit.

5. You can't take the exclusion or credit for adoption expenses in most cases.

6. You can't take the education credits (the American opportunity credit and lifetime learning credit), or the deduction for student loan interest.

7. You can't exclude any interest income from qualified U.S. savings bonds you used for higher education expenses.

8. If you lived with your spouse at any time during the tax year:

   a. You can't claim the credit for the elderly or the disabled, and

   b. You must include in income a greater percentage (up to 85%) of any social security or equivalent railroad retirement benefits you received.

9. The following credits and deductions are reduced at income levels half of those for a joint return.

   a. The child tax credit and the credit for other dependents.

   b. The retirement savings contributions credit.

10. Your capital loss deduction limit is $1,500 (instead of $3,000 on a joint return).

11. If your spouse itemizes deductions, you can't claim the standard deduction. If you can claim the standard deduction, your basic standard deduction is half of the amount allowed on a joint return.

 At the time this publication was prepared for printing, Congress was considering legislation that would extend the tuition and fees deduction, which expired at the end of 2017. Even if it is extended, you can't take the deduction if your filing status is married filing separately. To see if it was extended, go to Recent Developments at IRS.gov/Pub17.

Adjusted gross income (AGI) limits. If your AGI on a separate return is lower than it would have been on a joint return, you may be able to deduct a larger amount for certain deductions that are limited by AGI, such as medical expenses.

Individual retirement arrangements (IRAs). You may not be able to deduct all or part of your contributions to a traditional IRA if you or your spouse were covered by an employee retirement plan at work during the year. Your deduction is reduced or eliminated if your income is more than a certain amount. This amount is much lower for married individuals who file separately and lived together at any time during the year. For more information, see *How Much Can You Deduct* in chapter 17.

Rental activity losses. If you actively participated in a passive rental real estate activity that produced a loss, you generally can deduct the loss from your nonpassive income, up to $25,000. This is called a special allowance. However, married persons filing separate returns who lived together at any time during the year can't claim this special allowance. Married persons filing separate returns who lived apart at all times during the year are each allowed a $12,500 maximum special allowance for losses from passive real estate activities. See *Limits on Rental Losses* in chapter 9.

Community property states. If you live in a community property state and file separately, your income may be considered separate income or community income for income tax purposes. Community property states include Arizona, California, Idaho, Louisiana, Nevada, New Mexico, Texas, Washington, and Wisconsin. See Pub. 555.

Joint Return After Separate Returns

You can change your filing status from a separate return to a joint return by filing an amended return using Form 1040X.

You generally can change to a joint return any time within 3 years from the due date of the separate return or returns. This doesn't include any extensions. A separate return includes a return filed by you or your spouse claiming married filing separately, single, or head of household filing status.

Separate Returns After Joint Return

Once you file a joint return, you can't choose to file separate returns for that year after the due date of the return.

Exception. A personal representative for a decedent can change from a joint return elected by the surviving spouse to a separate return for the decedent. The personal representative has 1 year from the due date of the return (including extensions) to make the change. See Pub. 559, Survivors, Executors, and Administrators, for more information on filing a return for a decedent.

Head of Household

You may be able to file as head of household if you meet all the following requirements.

1. You are unmarried or "considered unmarried" on the last day of the year. See *Marital Status*, earlier, and *Considered Unmarried*, later.

2. You paid more than half of the cost of keeping up a home for the year.

3. A qualifying person lived with you in the home for more than half the year (except for temporary absences, such as school). However, if the qualifying person is your dependent parent, he or she doesn't have to live with you. See *Special rule for parent*, later, under *Qualifying Person*.

 If you qualify to file as head of household, your tax rate usually will be lower than the rates for single or married filing separately. You also will receive a higher standard deduction than if you file as single or married filing separately.

How to file. Indicate your choice of this filing status by checking the *Head of Household* box on the *Filing Status* line at the top of Form 1040. If the child who qualifies you for this filing status isn't claimed as your dependent in the *Dependents* section of Form 1040, enter the child's name in the entry space at the far right of the filing status checkboxes (next to *Qualifying Widow(er)*). Use the *Head of a household* column of the Tax Table or Section D of the Tax Computation Worksheet to figure your tax.

Considered Unmarried

To qualify for head of household status, you must be either unmarried or considered unmarried on the last day of the year. You are considered unmarried on the last day of the tax year if you meet all the following tests.

1. You file a separate return. A separate return includes a return claiming married filing separately, single, or head of household filing status.

2. You paid more than half of the cost of keeping up your home for the tax year.

3. Your spouse didn't live in your home during the last 6 months of the tax year. Your spouse is considered to live in your home even if he or she is temporarily absent due

to special circumstances. See *Temporary absences* under *Qualifying Person*, later.

4. Your home was the main home of your child, stepchild, or foster child for more than half the year. (See *Home of qualifying person* under *Qualifying Person*, later, for rules applying to a child's birth, death, or temporary absence during the year.)

5. You must be able to claim the child as a dependent. However, you meet this test if you can't claim the child as a dependent only because the noncustodial parent can claim the child using the rules described in *Children of divorced or separated parents (or parents who live apart)* under *Qualifying Child* in chapter 3, or referred to in *Support Test for Children of Divorced or Separated Parents (or Parents Who Live Apart)* under *Qualifying Relative* in chapter 3. The general rules for claiming a child as a dependent are explained in chapter 3.

 If you were considered married for part of the year and lived in a community property state (listed earlier under Married Filing Separately), special rules may apply in determining your income and expenses. See Pub. 555 for more information.

Nonresident alien spouse. You are considered unmarried for head of household purposes if your spouse was a nonresident alien at any time during the year and you don't choose to treat your nonresident spouse as a resident alien. However, your spouse isn't a qualifying person for head of household purposes. You must have another qualifying person and meet the other tests to be eligible to file as head of household.

Choice to treat spouse as resident. You are considered married if you choose to treat your spouse as a resident alien. See Pub. 519.

Keeping Up a Home

To qualify for head of household status, you must pay more than half of the cost of keeping up a home for the year. You can determine whether you paid more than half of the cost of keeping up a home by using *Worksheet 2-1*.

Costs you include. Include in the cost of keeping up a home expenses, such as rent, mortgage interest, real estate taxes, insurance on the home, repairs, utilities, and food eaten in the home.

Costs you don't include. Don't include the costs of clothing, education, medical treatment, vacations, life insurance, or transportation. Also, don't include the rental value of a home you own or the value of your services or those of a member of your household.

Qualifying Person

See Table 2-1 to see who is a qualifying person. Any person not described in Table 2-1 isn't a qualifying person.

Example 1—Child. Your unmarried son lived with you all year and was 18 years old at

Worksheet 2-1. Cost of Keeping Up a Home

Keep for Your Records

	Amount You Paid	Total Cost
Property taxes	$	$
Mortgage interest expense		
Rent		
Utility charges		
Repairs/Maintenance		
Property insurance		
Food eaten in the home		
Other household expenses		
Totals	$	$
Minus total **amount you paid**		( )
Amount others paid		$

If the total amount you paid is more than the amount others paid, you meet the requirement of paying more than half of the cost of keeping up the home.

the end of the year. He didn't provide more than half of his own support and doesn't meet the tests to be a qualifying child of anyone else. As a result, he is your qualifying child (see *Qualifying Child* in chapter 3) and, because he is single, your qualifying person for you to claim head of household filing status.

Example 2—Child who isn't qualifying person. The facts are the same as in *Example 1*, except your son was 25 years old at the end of the year and his gross income was $5,000. Because he doesn't meet the age test (explained under *Qualifying Child* in chapter 3), your son isn't your qualifying child. Because he doesn't meet the gross income test (explained later under *Qualifying Relative* in chapter 3), he isn't your qualifying relative. As a result, he isn't your qualifying person for head of household purposes.

Example 3—Girlfriend. Your girlfriend lived with you all year. Even though she may be your qualifying relative if the gross income and support tests (explained in chapter 3) are met, she isn't your qualifying person for head of household purposes because she isn't related to you in one of the ways listed under *Relatives who don't have to live with you* in chapter 3. See Table 2-1.

Example 4—Girlfriend's child. The facts are the same as in *Example 3*, except your girlfriend's 10-year-old son also lived with you all year. He isn't your qualifying child and, because he is your girlfriend's qualifying child, he isn't your qualifying relative (see *Not a Qualifying Child Test* in chapter 3). As a result, he isn't your qualifying person for head of household purposes.

Home of qualifying person. Generally, the qualifying person must live with you for more than half the year.

Special rule for parent. If your qualifying person is your father or mother, you may be eligible to file as head of household even if your

father or mother doesn't live with you. However, you must be able to claim your father or mother as a dependent. Also, you must pay more than half of the cost of keeping up a home that was the main home for the entire year for your father or mother.

If you pay more than half of the cost of keeping your parent in a rest home or home for the elderly, that counts as paying more than half of the cost of keeping up your parent's main home.

Death or birth. You may be eligible to file as head of household even if the individual who qualifies you for this filing status is born or dies during the year. If the individual is your qualifying child, the child must have lived with you for more than half the part of the year he or she was alive. If the individual is anyone else, see Pub. 501.

Temporary absences. You and your qualifying person are considered to live together even if one or both of you are temporarily absent from your home due to special circumstances, such as illness, education, business, vacation, military service, or detention in a juvenile facility. It must be reasonable to assume the absent person will return to the home after the temporary absence. You must continue to keep up the home during the absence.

Kidnapped child. You may be eligible to file as head of household even if the child who is your qualifying person has been kidnapped. For more information, see Pub 501.

Qualifying Widow(er)

If your spouse died in 2018, you can use married filing jointly as your filing status for 2018 if you otherwise qualify to use that status. The year of death is the last year for which you can file jointly with your deceased spouse. See *Married Filing Jointly*, earlier.

You may be eligible to use qualifying widow(er) as your filing status for 2 years following the year your spouse died. For example,

if your spouse died in 2017, and you haven't remarried, you may be able to use this filing status for 2018 and 2019.

This filing status entitles you to use joint return tax rates and the highest standard deduction amount (if you don't itemize deductions). It doesn't entitle you to file a joint return.

How to file. Indicate your choice of this filing status by checking the *Qualifying Widower* box on the *Filing Status* line at the top of Form 1040. If the child who qualifies you for this filing status isn't claimed as your dependent in the *Dependents* section of Form 1040, enter the child's name in the entry space at the far right of the filing status checkboxes (next to *Qualifying widow(er)*). Use the *Married filing jointly* column of the Tax Table or Section B of the Tax Computation Worksheet to figure your tax.

Eligibility rules. You are eligible to file your 2018 return as a qualifying widow(er) if you meet all of the following tests.

- You were entitled to file a joint return with your spouse for the year your spouse died. It doesn't matter whether you actually filed a joint return.

- Your spouse died in 2016 or 2017 and you didn't remarry before the end of 2018.

- You have a child or stepchild (not a foster child) whom you can claim as a dependent or could claim as a dependent except that, for 2018:

  a. The child had gross income of $4,150 or more,

  b. The child filed a joint return, or

  c. You could be claimed as a dependent on someone else's return.

  If the child isn't claimed as your dependent in the *Dependents* section on Form 1040, enter the child's name in the entry space at the far right of the filing status checkboxes (next to *Qualifying widow(er)*). If you don't enter the name, it will take us longer to process your return.

- This child lived in your home all year, except for temporary absences. See *Temporary absences*, earlier, under *Head of Household*. There also are exceptions, described later, for a child who was born or died during the year and for a kidnapped child.

- You paid more than half of the cost of keeping up a home for the year. See *Keeping Up a Home*, earlier, under *Head of Household*.

Example. John's wife died in 2016. John hasn't remarried. During 2017 and 2018, he continued to keep up a home for himself and his child, who lives with him and whom he can claim as a dependent. For 2016, he was entitled to file a joint return for himself and his deceased wife. For 2017 and 2018, he can file as qualifying widower. After 2018, he can file as head of household if he qualifies.

Death or birth. You may be eligible to file as a qualifying widow(er) if the child who qualifies you for this filing status is born or dies during the year. You must have provided more than half of the cost of keeping up a home that was

Table 2-1. Who Is a Qualifying Person Qualifying You To File as Head of Household?[1]

Caution. See the text of this chapter for the other requirements you must meet to claim head of household filing status.

IF the person is your . . .	AND . . .	THEN that person is . . .
qualifying child (such as a son, daughter, or grandchild who lived with you more than half the year and meets certain other tests)[2]	he or she is single	a qualifying person, whether or not the child meets the *Citizen or Resident Test*. See chapter 3.
	he or she is married **and** you can claim him or her as a dependent	a qualifying person.
	he or she is married **and** you can't claim him or her as a dependent	not a qualifying person.[3]
qualifying relative[4] who is your father or mother	you can claim him or her as a dependent[5]	a qualifying person.[6]
	you can't claim him or her as a dependent	not a qualifying person.
qualifying relative[4] other than your father or mother (such as a grandparent, brother, or sister who meets certain tests)	he or she lived with you more than half the year, **and** he or she is related to you in one of the ways listed under *Relatives who don't have to live with you* in chapter 3 **and** you can claim him or her as a dependent[5]	a qualifying person.
	he or she didn't live with you more than half the year	not a qualifying person.
	he or she isn't related to you in one of the ways listed under *Relatives who don't have to live with you* in chapter 3 **and** is your qualifying relative only because he or she lived with you all year as a member of your household	not a qualifying person.
	you can't claim him or her as a dependent	not a qualifying person.

[1] A person can't qualify more than one taxpayer to use the head of household filing status for the year.

[2] The term qualifying child is defined in chapter 3. **Note.** If you are a noncustodial parent, the term "qualifying child" for head of household filing status doesn't include a child who is your qualifying child only because of the rules described under *Children of divorced or separated parents (or parents who live apart)* under *Qualifying Child* in chapter 3. If you are the custodial parent and those rules apply, the child generally is your qualifying child for head of household filing status even though the child isn't a qualifying child you can claim as a dependent.

[3] This person is a qualifying person if the only reason you can't claim them as a dependent is that you, or your spouse if filing jointly, can be claimed as a dependent on someone else's return.

[4] The term qualifying relative is defined in chapter 3.

[5] If you can claim a person as a dependent only because of a multiple support agreement, that person isn't a qualifying person. See *Multiple Support Agreement* in chapter 3.

[6] See *Special rule for parent* under *Qualifying Person*, earlier.

---

the child's main home during the entire part of the year he or she was alive.

Kidnapped child. You may be eligible to file as a qualifying widow(er) even if the child who qualifies you for this filing status has been kidnapped. See Pub. 501.

 As mentioned earlier, this filing status is available for only 2 years following the year your spouse died.

3.

Dependents

What's New

 At the time this publication went to print, Congress was considering legislation that would do the following.

1. *Provide additional tax relief for those affected by certain 2018 disasters.*

2. *Extend certain tax benefits that expired at the end of 2017 and that currently can't be claimed on your 2018 tax return.*

3. *Change certain other tax provisions.*

To learn whether this legislation was enacted resulting in changes that affect your 2018 tax return, go to Recent Developments at IRS.gov/Pub17.

Personal exemption suspended. For 2018, you can't claim a personal exemption deduction for yourself, your spouse, or your dependents.

Introduction

This chapter discusses the following topics.

- Dependents—You generally can claim your qualifying child or qualifying relative as a dependent.

- Social security number (SSN) requirement for dependents—You must list the SSN of any person you claim as a dependent.

How to claim dependents. On page 1 of your Form 1040, enter the names of your dependents in the *Dependents* section.

Table 3-1. **Overview of the Rules for Claiming a Dependent**

Caution. This table is only an overview of the rules. For details, see the rest of this chapter.

- You can't claim any dependents if you (or your spouse, if filing jointly) could be claimed as a dependent by another taxpayer.

- You can't claim a married person who files a joint return as a dependent unless that joint return is filed only to claim a refund of withheld income tax or estimated tax paid.

- You can't claim a person as a dependent unless that person is a U.S. citizen, U.S. resident alien, U.S. national, or a resident of Canada or Mexico.[1]

- You can't claim a person as a dependent unless that person is your **qualifying child** or **qualifying relative**.

Tests To Be a Qualifying Child	Tests To Be a Qualifying Relative
1. The child must be your son, daughter, stepchild, foster child, brother, sister, half brother, half sister, stepbrother, stepsister, or a descendant of any of them.	1. The person can't be your qualifying child or the qualifying child of any other taxpayer.
2. The child must be (a) under age 19 at the end of the year and younger than you (or your spouse, if filing jointly), (b) under age 24 at the end of the year, a student, and younger than you (or your spouse, if filing jointly), or (c) any age if permanently and totally disabled.	2. The person either (a) must be related to you in one of the ways listed under _Relatives who don't have to live with you_, or (b) must live with you all year as a member of your household[2] (and your relationship must not violate local law).
3. The child must have lived with you for more than half of the year.[2]	3. The person's gross income for the year must be less than $4,150.[3]
4. The child must not have provided more than half of his or her own support for the year.	4. You must provide more than half of the person's total support for the year.[4]
5. The child must not be filing a joint return for the year (unless that return is filed only to get a refund of income tax withheld or estimated tax paid).	
If the child meets the rules to be a qualifying child of more than one person, only one person can actually treat the child as a qualifying child. See _Qualifying Child of More Than One Person_, later, to find out which person is the person entitled to claim the child as a qualifying child.	

[1] There is an exception for certain adopted children.

[2] There are exceptions for temporary absences, children who were born or died during the year, children of divorced or separated parents (or parents who live apart), and kidnapped children.

[3] There is an exception if the person is disabled and has income from a sheltered workshop.

[4] There are exceptions for multiple support agreements, children of divorced or separated parents (or parents who live apart), and kidnapped children.

Useful Items

You may want to see:

Publication

❏ 501 Dependents, Standard Deduction, and Filing Information

Form (and Instructions)

❏ 2120 Multiple Support Declaration

❏ 8332 Release/Revocation of Release of Claim to Exemption for Child by Custodial Parent

Dependents

The term "dependent" means:

- A qualifying child, or
- A qualifying relative.

The terms qualifying child and qualifying relative are defined later.

All the requirements for claiming a dependent are summarized in Table 3-1.

Housekeepers, maids, or servants. If these people work for you, you can't claim them as dependents.

Child tax credit. You may be entitled to a child tax credit for each qualifying child who was under age 17 at the end of the year if you claimed that child as a dependent. For more information, see chapter 33.

Credit for other dependents. You may be entitled to a credit for other dependents for each qualifying child who isn't a qualifying child for the child tax credit and for each qualifying relative. For more information, see chapter 33.

Exceptions

Even if you have a qualifying child or qualifying relative, you can claim that person as a dependent only if these three tests are met.

1. Dependent taxpayer test.
2. Joint return test.
3. Citizen or resident test.

These three tests are explained in detail here.

Dependent Taxpayer Test

If you can be claimed as a dependent by another person, you can't claim anyone else as a dependent. Even if you have a qualifying child or qualifying relative, you can't claim that person as a dependent.

If you are filing a joint return and your spouse can be claimed as a dependent by someone else, you and your spouse can't claim any dependents on your joint return.

Joint Return Test

You generally can't claim a married person as a dependent if he or she files a joint return.

Exception. You can claim a person as a dependent who files a joint return if that person and his or her spouse file the joint return only to claim a refund of income tax withheld or estimated tax paid.

Example 1—Child files joint return. You supported your 18-year-old daughter, and she lived with you all year while her husband was in the Armed Forces. He earned $25,000 for the year. The couple files a joint return. You can't claim your daughter as a dependent.

Example 2—Child files joint return only as claim for refund of withheld tax. Your 18-year-old son and his 17-year-old wife had $800 of wages from part-time jobs and no other income. They lived with you all year. Neither is required to file a tax return. They don't have a child. Taxes were taken out of their pay so they filed a joint return only to get a refund of the withheld taxes. The exception to the joint return test applies, so you aren't disqualified from claiming each of them as a dependent just because they file a joint return. You can claim each of them as a dependent if all the other tests to do so are met.

Example 3—Child files joint return to claim American opportunity credit. The facts are the same as in *Example 2*, except no taxes were taken out of your son's pay or his wife's pay. However, they file a joint return to claim an American opportunity credit of $124 and get a refund of that amount. Because claiming the American opportunity credit is their reason for filing the return, they aren't filing it only to get a refund of income tax withheld or estimated tax paid. The exception to the joint return test doesn't apply, so you can't claim either of them as a dependent.

Citizen or Resident Test

You generally can't claim a person as a dependent unless that person is a U.S. citizen, U.S. resident alien, U.S. national, or a resident of Canada or Mexico. However, there is an exception for certain adopted children, as explained next.

Exception for adopted child. If you are a U.S. citizen or U.S. national who has legally adopted a child who isn't a U.S. citizen, U.S. resident alien, or U.S. national, this test is met if the child lived with you as a member of your household all year. This exception also applies if the child was lawfully placed with you for legal adoption.

Child's place of residence. Children usually are citizens or residents of the country of their parents.

If you were a U.S. citizen when your child was born, the child may be a U.S. citizen and meet this test even if the other parent was a nonresident alien and the child was born in a foreign country.

Foreign students' place of residence. Foreign students brought to this country under a qualified international education exchange program and placed in American homes for a temporary period generally aren't U.S. residents and don't meet this test. You can't claim them as dependents. However, if you provided a home for a foreign student, you may be able to take a charitable contribution deduction. See *Expenses Paid for Student Living With You* in chapter 25.

U.S. national. A U.S. national is an individual who, although not a U.S. citizen, owes his or her allegiance to the United States. U.S. nationals include American Samoans and Northern Mariana Islanders who chose to become U.S. nationals instead of U.S. citizens.

Qualifying Child

Five tests must be met for a child to be your qualifying child. The five tests are:

1. Relationship,
2. Age,
3. Residency,
4. Support, and
5. Joint return.

These tests are explained next.

 If a child meets the five tests to be the qualifying child of more than one person, there are rules you must use to determine which person can actually treat the child as a qualifying child. See Qualifying Child of More Than One Person, *later.*

Relationship Test

To meet this test, a child must be:

- Your son, daughter, stepchild, foster child, or a descendant (for example, your grandchild) of any of them, or
- Your brother, sister, half brother, half sister, stepbrother, stepsister, or a

descendant (for example, your niece or nephew) of any of them.

Adopted child. An adopted child is always treated as your own child. The term "adopted child" includes a child who was lawfully placed with you for legal adoption.

Foster child. A foster child is an individual who is placed with you by an authorized placement agency or by judgment, decree, or other order of any court of competent jurisdiction.

Age Test

To meet this test, a child must be:

- Under age 19 at the end of the year and younger than you (or your spouse, if filing jointly),
- A student under age 24 at the end of the year and younger than you (or your spouse, if filing jointly), or
- Permanently and totally disabled at any time during the year, regardless of age.

Example. Your son turned 19 on December 10. Unless he was permanently and totally disabled or a student, he doesn't meet the age test because, at the end of the year, he wasn't **under** age 19.

Child must be younger than you or spouse. To be your qualifying child, a child who isn't permanently and totally disabled must be younger than you. However, if you are married filing jointly, the child must be younger than you or your spouse but doesn't have to be younger than both of you.

Example 1—Child not younger than you or spouse. Your 23-year-old brother, who is a student and unmarried, lives with you and your spouse, who provide more than half of his support. He isn't disabled. Both you and your spouse are 21 years old, and you file a joint return. Your brother isn't your qualifying child because he isn't younger than you or your spouse.

Example 2—Child younger than your spouse but not younger than you. The facts are the same as in *Example 1*, except your spouse is 25 years old. Because your brother is younger than your spouse, and you and your spouse are filing a joint return, your brother is your qualifying child, even though he isn't younger than you.

Student defined. To qualify as a student, your child must be, during some part of each of any 5 calendar months of the year:

1. A full-time student at a school that has a regular teaching staff, course of study, and a regularly enrolled student body at the school; or
2. A student taking a full-time, on-farm training course given by a school described in (1), or by a state, county, or local government agency.

The 5 calendar months don't have to be consecutive.

Full-time student. A full-time student is a student who is enrolled for the number of hours or courses the school considers to be full-time attendance.

School defined. A school can be an elementary school; junior or senior high school; college; university; or technical, trade, or mechanical school. However, an on-the-job training course, correspondence school, or school offering courses only through the Internet doesn't count as a school.

Vocational high school students. Students who work on "co-op" jobs in private industry as a part of a school's regular course of classroom and practical training are considered full-time students.

Permanently and totally disabled. Your child is permanently and totally disabled if both of the following apply.

- He or she can't engage in any substantial gainful activity because of a physical or mental condition.
- A doctor determines the condition has lasted or can be expected to last continuously for at least a year or can lead to death.

Residency Test

To meet this test, your child must have lived with you for more than half the year. There are exceptions for temporary absences, children who were born or died during the year, kidnapped children, and children of divorced or separated parents.

Temporary absences. Your child is considered to have lived with you during periods of time when one of you, or both, are temporarily absent due to special circumstances such as:

- Illness,
- Education,
- Business,
- Vacation,
- Military service, or
- Detention in a juvenile facility.

Death or birth of child. A child who was born or died during the year is treated as having lived with you more than half of the year if your home was the child's home more than half of the time he or she was alive during the year. The same is true if the child lived with you more than half the year except for any required hospital stay following birth.

Child born alive. You may be able to claim as a dependent a child born alive during the year, even if the child lived only for a moment. State or local law must treat the child as having been born alive. There must be proof of a live birth shown by an official document, such as a birth certificate. The child must be your qualifying child or qualifying relative, and all the other tests to claim the child as a dependent must be met.

Stillborn child. You can't claim a stillborn child as a dependent.

Kidnapped child. You may be able to treat your child as meeting the residency test even if the child has been kidnapped. See Pub. 501 for details.

Children of divorced or separated parents (or parents who live apart). In most cases, because of the residency test, a child of divorced or separated parents is the qualifying child of the custodial parent. However, the child will be treated as the qualifying child of the noncustodial parent if all four of the following statements are true.

1. The parents:
   a. Are divorced or legally separated under a decree of divorce or separate maintenance;
   b. Are separated under a written separation agreement; or
   c. Lived apart at all times during the last 6 months of the year, whether or not they are or were married.

2. The child received over half of his or her support for the year from the parents.

3. The child is in the custody of one or both parents for more than half of the year.

4. Either of the following statements is true.
   a. The custodial parent signs a written declaration, discussed later, that he or she won't claim the child as a dependent for the year, and the noncustodial parent attaches this written declaration to his or her return. (If the decree or agreement went into effect after 1984 and before 2009, see *Post-1984 and pre-2009 divorce decree or separation agreement*, later. If the decree or agreement went into effect after 2008, see *Post-2008 divorce decree or separation agreement*, later.)
   b. A pre-1985 decree of divorce or separate maintenance or written separation agreement that applies to 2018 states that the noncustodial parent can claim the child as a dependent, the decree or agreement wasn't changed after 1984 to say the noncustodial parent can't claim the child as a dependent, and the noncustodial parent provides at least $600 for the child's support during the year.

If statements (1) through (4) are all true, only the noncustodial parent can:

- Claim the child as a dependent, and
- Claim the child as a qualifying child for the child tax credit or credit for other dependents.

However, this doesn't allow the noncustodial parent to claim head of household filing status, the credit for child and dependent care expenses, the exclusion for dependent care benefits, the earned income credit, or the health coverage tax credit. See *Applying the tiebreaker rules to divorced or separated parents (or parents who live apart)*, later.

Example—Earned income credit. Even if statements (1) through (4) are all true and the custodial parent signs Form 8332 or a substantially similar statement that he or she won't claim the child as a dependent for 2018, this doesn't allow the noncustodial parent to claim the child as a qualifying child for the earned income credit. The custodial parent or another taxpayer, if eligible, can claim the child for the earned income credit.

Custodial parent and noncustodial parent. The custodial parent is the parent with whom the child lived for the greater number of nights during the year. The other parent is the noncustodial parent.

If the parents divorced or separated during the year and the child lived with both parents before the separation, the custodial parent is the one with whom the child lived for the greater number of nights during the rest of the year.

A child is treated as living with a parent for a night if the child sleeps:

- At that parent's home, whether or not the parent is present; or
- In the company of the parent, when the child doesn't sleep at a parent's home (for example, the parent and child are on vacation together).

Equal number of nights. If the child lived with each parent for an equal number of nights during the year, the custodial parent is the parent with the higher adjusted gross income (AGI).

December 31. The night of December 31 is treated as part of the year in which it begins. For example, the night of December 31, 2018, is treated as part of 2018.

Emancipated child. If a child is emancipated under state law, the child is treated as not living with either parent. See *Examples 5* and *6*.

Absences. If a child wasn't with either parent on a particular night (because, for example, the child was staying at a friend's house), the child is treated as living with the parent with whom the child normally would have lived for that night, except for the absence. But if it can't be determined with which parent the child normally would have lived or if the child wouldn't have lived with either parent that night, the child is treated as not living with either parent that night.

Parent works at night. If, due to a parent's nighttime work schedule, a child lives for a greater number of days, but not nights, with the parent who works at night, that parent is treated as the custodial parent. On a school day, the child is treated as living at the primary residence registered with the school.

Example 1—Child lived with one parent for a greater number of nights. You and your child's other parent are divorced. In 2018, your child lived with you 210 nights and with the other parent 155 nights. You are the custodial parent.

Example 2—Child is away at camp. In 2018, your daughter lives with each parent for alternate weeks. In the summer, she spends 6 weeks at summer camp. During the time she is at camp, she is treated as living with you for 3 weeks and with her other parent, your ex-spouse, for 3 weeks because this is how long she would have lived with each parent if she hadn't attended summer camp.

Example 3—Child lived same number of nights with each parent. Your son lived with you 180 nights during the year and lived the same number of nights with his other parent, your ex-spouse. Your AGI is $40,000. Your ex-spouse's AGI is $25,000. You are treated as your son's custodial parent because you have the higher AGI.

Example 4—Child is at parent's home but with other parent. Your son normally lives with you during the week and with his other parent, your ex-spouse, every other weekend. You become ill and are hospitalized. The other parent lives in your home with your son for 10 consecutive days while you are in the hospital. Your son is treated as living with you during this 10-day period because he was living in your home.

Example 5—Child emancipated in May. When your son turned age 18 in May 2018, he became emancipated under the law of the state where he lives. As a result, he isn't considered in the custody of his parents for more than half of the year. The special rule for children of divorced or separated parents doesn't apply.

Example 6—Child emancipated in August. Your daughter lives with you from January 1, 2018, until May 31, 2018, and lives with her other parent, your ex-spouse, from June 1, 2018, through the end of the year. She turns 18 and is emancipated under state law on August 1, 2018. Because she is treated as not living with either parent beginning on August 1, she is treated as living with you the greater number of nights in 2018. You are the custodial parent.

Written declaration. The custodial parent must use either Form 8332 or a similar statement (containing the same information required by the form) to make the written declaration to release a claim to an exemption for a child to the noncustodial parent. Although the exemption amount is zero for tax year 2018, this release allows the noncustodial parent to claim the child tax credit, additional child tax credit, and credit for other dependents, if applicable, for the child. The noncustodial parent must attach a copy of the form or statement to his or her tax return.

The release can be for 1 year, for a number of specified years (for example, alternate years), or for all future years, as specified in the declaration.

Post-1984 and pre-2009 divorce decree or separation agreement. If the divorce decree or separation agreement went into effect after 1984 and before 2009, the noncustodial parent may be able to attach certain pages from the decree or agreement instead of Form 8332. The decree or agreement must state all three of the following.

1. The noncustodial parent can claim the child as a dependent without regard to any condition, such as payment of support.

2. The custodial parent won't claim the child as a dependent for the year.

3. The years for which the noncustodial parent, rather than the custodial parent, can claim the child as a dependent.

The noncustodial parent must attach all of the following pages of the decree or agreement to his or her tax return.

- The cover page (write the other parent's social security number on this page).

- The pages that include all of the information identified in items (1) through (3) above.

- The signature page with the other parent's signature and the date of the agreement.

Post-2008 divorce decree or separation agreement. The noncustodial parent can't attach pages from the decree or agreement instead of Form 8332 if the decree or agreement went into effect after 2008. The custodial parent must sign either Form 8332 or a similar statement whose only purpose is to release the custodial parent's claim to an exemption for a child, and the noncustodial parent must attach a copy to his or her return. The form or statement must release the custodial parent's claim to the child without any conditions. For example, the release must not depend on the noncustodial parent paying support.

 The noncustodial parent must attach the required information even if it was filed with a return in an earlier year.

Revocation of release of claim to an exemption. The custodial parent can revoke a release of claim to an exemption. For the revocation to be effective for 2018, the custodial parent must have given (or made reasonable efforts to give) written notice of the revocation to the noncustodial parent in 2017 or earlier. The custodial parent can use Part III of Form 8332 for this purpose and must attach a copy of the revocation to his or her return for each tax year he or she claims the child as a dependent as a result of the revocation.

Remarried parent. If you remarry, the support provided by your new spouse is treated as provided by you.

Parents who never married. This special rule for divorced or separated parents also applies to parents who never married and who lived apart at all times during the last 6 months of the year.

Support Test (To Be a Qualifying Child)

To meet this test, the child can't have provided more than half of his or her own support for the year.

This test is different from the support test to be a qualifying relative, which is described later. However, to see what is or isn't support, see *Support Test (To Be a Qualifying Relative),* later. If you aren't sure whether a child provided more than half of his or her own support, you may find Worksheet 3-1 helpful.

Example. You provided $4,000 toward your 16-year-old son's support for the year. He has a part-time job and provided $6,000 to his own support. He provided more than half of his own support for the year. He isn't your qualifying child.

Foster care payments and expenses. Payments you receive for the support of a foster child from a child placement agency are considered support provided by the agency. Similarly, payments you receive for the support of a foster child from a state or county are considered support provided by the state or county.

If you aren't in the trade or business of providing foster care and your unreimbursed out-of-pocket expenses in caring for a foster child were mainly to benefit an organization qualified to receive deductible charitable contributions, the expenses are deductible as charitable contributions but aren't considered support you provided. For more information about the deduction for charitable contributions, see chapter 25. If your unreimbursed expenses aren't deductible as charitable contributions, they may qualify as support you provided.

If you are in the trade or business of providing foster care, your unreimbursed expenses aren't considered support provided by you.

Example 1. Lauren, a foster child, lived with Mr. and Mrs. Smith for the last 3 months of the year. The Smiths cared for Lauren because they wanted to adopt her (although she hadn't been placed with them for adoption). They didn't care for her as a trade or business or to benefit the agency that placed her in their home. The Smiths' unreimbursed expenses aren't deductible as charitable contributions but are considered support they provided for Lauren.

Example 2. You provided $3,000 toward your 10-year-old foster child's support for the year. The state government provided $4,000, which is considered support provided by the state, not by the child. See *Support provided by the state (welfare, food stamps, housing, etc.),* later. Your foster child didn't provide more than half of her own support for the year.

Scholarships. A scholarship received by a child who is a student isn't taken into account in determining whether the child provided more than half of his or her own support.

Joint Return Test (To Be a Qualifying Child)

To meet this test, the child can't file a joint return for the year.

Exception. An exception to the joint return test applies if your child and his or her spouse file a joint return only to claim a refund of income tax withheld or estimated tax paid.

Example 1—Child files joint return. You supported your 18-year-old daughter, and she lived with you all year while her husband was in the Armed Forces. He earned $25,000 for the year. The couple files a joint return. Because your daughter and her husband file a joint return, she isn't your qualifying child.

Example 2—Child files joint return only as a claim for refund of withheld tax. Your 18-year-old son and his 17-year-old wife had $800 of wages from part-time jobs and no other income. They lived with you all year. Neither is required to file a tax return. They don't have a child. Taxes were taken out of their pay so they

Funds Belonging to the Person You Supported

1. Enter the total funds belonging to the person you supported, including income received (taxable and nontaxable) and amounts borrowed during the year, plus the amount in savings and other accounts at the beginning of the year. Don't include funds provided by the state; include those amounts on line 23 instead .... 1. _____

2. Enter the amount on line 1 that was used for the person's support .... 2. _____

3. Enter the amount on line 1 that was used for other purposes .... 3. _____

4. Enter the total amount in the person's savings and other accounts at the end of the year ...... 4. _____

5. Add lines 2 through 4. (This amount should equal line 1.) .... 5. _____

Expenses for Entire Household (where the person you supported lived)

6. Lodging (complete line 6a or 6b):
   a. Enter the total rent paid .... 6a. _____
   b. Enter the fair rental value of the home. If the person you supported owned the home, also include this amount in line 21 .... 6b. _____

7. Enter the total food expenses .... 7. _____

8. Enter the total amount of utilities (heat, light, water, etc., not included in line 6a or 6b) .... 8. _____

9. Enter the total amount of repairs (not included in line 6a or 6b) .... 9. _____

10. Enter the total of other expenses. Don't include expenses of maintaining the home, such as mortgage interest, real estate taxes, and insurance .... 10. _____

11. Add lines 6a through 10. These are the total household expenses .... 11. _____

12. Enter total number of persons who lived in the household .... 12. _____

Expenses for the Person You Supported

13. Divide line 11 by line 12. This is the person's share of the household expenses .... 13. _____

14. Enter the person's total clothing expenses .... 14. _____

15. Enter the person's total education expenses .... 15. _____

16. Enter the person's total medical and dental expenses not paid for or reimbursed by insurance .... 16. _____

17. Enter the person's total travel and recreation expenses .... 17. _____

18. Enter the total of the person's other expenses .... 18. _____

19. Add lines 13 through 18. This is the total cost of the person's support for the year .... 19. _____

Did the Person Provide More Than Half of His or Her Own Support?

20. Multiply line 19 by 50% (0.50) .... 20. _____

21. Enter the amount from line 2, plus the amount from line 6b if the person you supported owned the home. This is the amount the person provided for his or her own support .... 21. _____

22. Is line 21 more than line 20?

   ☐ **No.** You meet the support test for this person to be your qualifying child. If this person also meets the other tests to be a qualifying child, stop here; don't complete lines 23–26. Otherwise, go to line 23 and fill out the rest of the worksheet to determine if this person is your qualifying relative.

   ☐ **Yes.** You don't meet the support test for this person to be either your qualifying child or your qualifying relative. **Stop here.**

Did You Provide More Than Half?

23. Enter the amount others provided for the person's support. Include amounts provided by state, local, and other welfare societies or agencies. Don't include any amounts included on line 1 .... 23. _____

24. Add lines 21 and 23 .... 24. _____

25. Subtract line 24 from line 19. This is the amount you provided for the person's support .... 25. _____

26. Is line 25 more than line 20?

   ☐ **Yes.** You meet the support test for this person to be your qualifying relative.

   ☐ **No.** You don't meet the support test for this person to be your qualifying relative. You can't claim this person as a dependent unless you can do so under a multiple support agreement, the support test for children of divorced or separated parents, or the special rule for kidnapped children. See *Multiple Support Agreement* or *Support Test for Children of Divorced or Separated Parents (or Parents Who Live Apart)*, or *Kidnapped child* under *Qualifying Relative*.

filed a joint return only to get a refund of the withheld taxes. The exception to the joint return test applies, so your son may be your qualifying child if all the other tests are met.

Example 3—Child files joint return to claim American opportunity credit. The facts are the same as in *Example 2*, except no taxes were taken out of your son's pay or his wife's pay. However, they file a joint return to claim an American opportunity credit of $124 and get a refund of that amount. Because claiming the American opportunity credit is their reason for filing the return, they aren't filing it only to get a refund of income tax withheld or estimated tax paid. The exception to the joint return test doesn't apply, so your son isn't your qualifying child.

Qualifying Child of More Than One Person

 If your qualifying child isn't a qualifying child of anyone else, this topic doesn't apply to you and you don't need to read about it. This also is true if your qualifying child isn't a qualifying child of anyone else except your spouse with whom you plan to file a joint return.

 If a child is treated as the qualifying child of the noncustodial parent under the rules for children of divorced or separated parents (or parents who live apart) described earlier, see Applying the tiebreaker rules to divorced or separated parents (or parents who live apart), *later.*

Sometimes, a child meets the relationship, age, residency, support, and joint return tests to be a qualifying child of more than one person. Although the child is a qualifying child of each of these persons, only one person can actually treat the child as a qualifying child to take all of the following tax benefits (provided the person is eligible for each benefit).

1. The child tax credit or credit for other dependents.

2. Head of household filing status.

3. The credit for child and dependent care expenses.

4. The exclusion from income for dependent care benefits.

5. The earned income credit.

The other person can't take any of these benefits based on this qualifying child. In other words, you and the other person can't agree to divide these benefits between you.

Tiebreaker rules. To determine which person can treat the child as a qualifying child to claim these five tax benefits, the following tiebreaker rules apply.

- If only one of the persons is the child's parent, the child is treated as the qualifying child of the parent.

- If the parents file a joint return together and can claim the child as a qualifying child, the child is treated as the qualifying child of the parents.

- If the parents don't file a joint return together but both parents claim the child as a qualifying child, the IRS will treat the child as the qualifying child of the parent with whom the child lived for the longer period of time during the year. If the child lived with each parent for the same amount of time, the IRS will treat the child as the qualifying child of the parent who had the higher adjusted gross income (AGI) for the year.

- If no parent can claim the child as a qualifying child, the child is treated as the qualifying child of the person who had the highest AGI for the year.

- If a parent can claim the child as a qualifying child but no parent does so claim the child, the child is treated as the qualifying child of the person who had the highest AGI for the year, but only if that person's AGI is higher than the highest AGI of any of the child's parents who can claim the child.

Subject to these tiebreaker rules, you and the other person may be able to choose which of you claims the child as a qualifying child.

 You may be able to qualify for the earned income credit under the rules for taxpayers without a qualifying child if you have a qualifying child for the earned income credit who is claimed as a qualifying child by another taxpayer. For more information, see Pub. 596.

Example 1—Child lived with parent and grandparent. You and your 3-year-old daughter Jane lived with your mother all year. You are 25 years old, unmarried, and your AGI is $9,000. Your mother's AGI is $15,000. Jane's father didn't live with you or your daughter. You haven't signed Form 8332 (or a similar statement).

Jane is a qualifying child of both you and your mother because she meets the relationship, age, residency, support, and joint return tests for both you and your mother. However, only one of you can claim her. Jane isn't a qualifying child of anyone else, including her father. You agree to let your mother claim Jane. This means your mother can claim Jane as a qualifying child for all of the five tax benefits listed earlier, if she qualifies for each of those benefits (and if you don't claim Jane as a qualifying child for any of those tax benefits).

Example 2—Parent has higher AGI than grandparent. The facts are the same as in *Example 1*, except your AGI is $18,000. Because your mother's AGI isn't higher than yours, she can't claim Jane. Only you can claim Jane.

Example 3—Two persons claim same child. The facts are the same as in *Example 1*, except that you and your mother both claim Jane as a qualifying child. In this case, you, as the child's parent, will be the only one allowed to claim Jane as a qualifying child. The IRS will disallow your mother's claim to the five tax benefits listed earlier based on Jane. However, your mother may qualify for the earned income credit as a taxpayer without a qualifying child.

Example 4—Qualifying children split between two persons. The facts are the same as in *Example 1*, except you also have two other young children who are qualifying children of both you and your mother. Only one of you can claim each child. However, if your mother's AGI is higher than yours, you can allow your mother to claim one or more of the children. For example, if you claim one child, your mother can claim the other two.

Example 5—Taxpayer who is a qualifying child. The facts are the same as in *Example 1*, except you are only 18 years old and didn't provide more than half of your own support for the year. This means you are your mother's qualifying child. If she can claim you as a dependent, then you can't claim your daughter as a dependent because of the *Dependent Taxpayer Test*, explained earlier.

Example 6—Separated parents. You, your husband, and your 10-year-old son lived together until August 1, 2018, when your husband moved out of the household. In August and September, your son lived with you. For the rest of the year, your son lived with your husband, the boy's father. Your son is a qualifying child of both you and your husband because your son lived with each of you for more than half the year and because he met the relationship, age, support, and joint return tests for both of you. At the end of the year, you and your husband still weren't divorced, legally separated, or separated under a written separation agreement, so the rule for children of divorced or separated parents (or parents who live apart) doesn't apply.

You and your husband will file separate returns. Your husband agrees to let you treat your son as a qualifying child. This means, if your husband doesn't claim your son as a qualifying child, you can claim your son as a qualifying child for the child tax credit and exclusion for dependent care benefits (if you qualify for each of those tax benefits). However, you can't claim head of household filing status because you and your husband didn't live apart for the last 6 months of the year. As a result, your filing status is married filing separately, so you can't claim the earned income credit or the credit for child and dependent care expenses.

Example 7—Separated parents claim same child. The facts are the same as in *Example 6*, except that you and your husband both claim your son as a qualifying child. In this case, only your husband will be allowed to treat your son as a qualifying child. This is because, during 2018, the boy lived with him longer than with you. If you claimed the child tax credit for your son, the IRS will disallow your claim to the child tax credit. If you don't have another qualifying child or dependent, the IRS also will disallow your claim to the exclusion for dependent care benefits. In addition, because you and your husband didn't live apart for the last 6 months of the year, your husband can't claim head of household filing status. As a result, his filing status is married filing separately, so he can't claim the earned income credit or the credit for child and dependent care expenses.

Example 8—Unmarried parents. You, your 5-year-old son, and your son's father lived together all year. You and your son's father aren't married. Your son is a qualifying child of both you and his father because he meets the relationship, age, residency, support, and joint return tests for both you and his father. Your AGI is $12,000 and your son's father's AGI is $14,000. Your son's father agrees to let you claim the child as a qualifying child. This means you can claim him as a qualifying child for the child tax credit, head of household filing status, credit for child and dependent care expenses, exclusion for dependent care benefits, and the earned income credit, if you qualify for each of those tax benefits (and if your son's father doesn't claim your son as a qualifying child for any of those tax benefits).

Example 9—Unmarried parents claim same child. The facts are the same as in *Example 8*, except that you and your son's father both claim your son as a qualifying child. In this case, only your son's father will be allowed to treat your son as a qualifying child. This is because his AGI, $14,000, is more than your AGI, $12,000. If you claimed the child tax credit for your son, the IRS will disallow your claim to this credit. If you don't have another qualifying child or dependent, the IRS also will disallow your claim to head of household filing status, the credit for child and dependent care expenses, and the exclusion for dependent care benefits. However, you may be able to claim the earned income credit as a taxpayer without a qualifying child.

Example 10—Child didn't live with a parent. You and your 7-year-old niece, your sister's child, lived with your mother all year. You are 25 years old, and your AGI is $9,300. Your mother's AGI is $15,000. Your niece's parents file jointly, have an AGI of less than $9,000, and don't live with you or their child. Your niece is a qualifying child of both you and your mother because she meets the relationship, age, residency, support, and joint return tests for both you and your mother. However, only your mother can treat her as a qualifying child. This is because your mother's AGI, $15,000, is more than your AGI, $9,300.

Applying the tiebreaker rules to divorced or separated parents (or parents who live apart). If a child is treated as the qualifying child of the noncustodial parent under the rules described earlier for children of divorced or separated parents (or parents who live apart), only the noncustodial parent can claim the child as a dependent and the child tax credit or credit for other dependents for the child. However, only the custodial parent can claim the credit for child and dependent care expenses or the exclusion for dependent care benefits for the child, and only the custodial parent can treat the child as a dependent for the health coverage tax credit. Also, the noncustodial parent can't claim the child as a qualifying child for head of household filing status or the earned income credit. Instead, the custodial parent, if eligible, or other eligible person can claim the child as a qualifying child for those two benefits. If the child is the qualifying child of more than one person for these benefits, then the tiebreaker rules just explained determine whether the cus-

todial parent or another eligible person can treat the child as a qualifying child.

Example 1. You and your 5-year-old son lived all year with your mother, who paid the entire cost of keeping up the home. Your AGI is $10,000. Your mother's AGI is $25,000. Your son's father didn't live with you or your son.

Under the rules explained earlier for children of divorced or separated parents (or parents who live apart), your son is treated as the qualifying child of his father, who can claim the child tax credit for him. Because of this, you can't claim the child tax credit for your son. However, those rules don't allow your son's father to claim your son as a qualifying child for head of household filing status, the credit for child and dependent care expenses, the exclusion for dependent care benefits, the earned income credit, or the health coverage tax credit.

You and your mother didn't have any child care expenses or dependent care benefits, so neither of you can claim the credit for child and dependent care expenses or the exclusion for dependent care benefits. Also, neither of you qualifies for the health coverage tax credit. But the boy is a qualifying child of both you and your mother for head of household filing status and the earned income credit because he meets the relationship, age, residency, support, and joint return tests for both you and your mother. (The support test doesn't apply for the earned income credit.) However, you agree to let your mother claim your son. This means she can claim him for head of household filing status and the earned income credit if she qualifies for each and if you don't claim him as a qualifying child for the earned income credit. (You can't claim head of household filing status because your mother paid the entire cost of keeping up the home.) You may be able to claim the earned income credit as a taxpayer without a qualifying child.

Example 2. The facts are the same as in *Example 1*, except your AGI is $25,000 and your mother's AGI is $21,000. Your mother can't claim your son as a qualifying child for any purpose because her AGI isn't higher than yours.

Example 3. The facts are the same as in *Example 1*, except you and your mother both claim your son as a qualifying child for the earned income credit. Your mother also claims him as a qualifying child for head of household filing status. You, as the child's parent, will be the only one allowed to claim your son as a qualifying child for the earned income credit. The IRS will disallow your mother's claim to head of household filing status unless she has another qualifying child or dependent. Your mother can't claim the earned income credit as a taxpayer without a qualifying child because her AGI is more than $15,270.

Qualifying Relative

Four tests must be met for a person to be your qualifying relative. The four tests are:

1. Not a qualifying child test,
2. Member of household or relationship test,

3. Gross income test, and
4. Support test.

Age. Unlike a qualifying child, a qualifying relative can be any age. There is no age test for a qualifying relative.

Kidnapped child. You may be able to treat a child as your qualifying relative even if the child has been kidnapped. See Pub. 501 for details.

Not a Qualifying Child Test

A child isn't your qualifying relative if the child is your qualifying child or the qualifying child of any other taxpayer.

Example 1. Your 22-year-old daughter, who is a student, lives with you and meets all the tests to be your qualifying child. She isn't your qualifying relative.

Example 2. Your 2-year-old son lives with your parents and meets all the tests to be their qualifying child. He isn't your qualifying relative.

Example 3. Your son lives with you but isn't your qualifying child because he is 30 years old and doesn't meet the age test. He may be your qualifying relative if the gross income test and the support test are met.

Example 4. Your 13-year-old grandson lived with his mother for 3 months, with his uncle for 4 months, and with you for 5 months during the year. He isn't your qualifying child because he doesn't meet the residency test. He may be your qualifying relative if the gross income test and the support test are met.

Child of person not required to file a return. A child isn't the qualifying child of any other taxpayer and so may qualify as your qualifying relative if the child's parent (or other person for whom the child is defined as a qualifying child) isn't required to file an income tax return and either:

- Doesn't file an income tax return, or
- Files a return only to get a refund of income tax withheld or estimated tax paid.

Example 1—Return not required. You support an unrelated friend and her 3-year-old child, who lived with you all year in your home. Your friend has no gross income, isn't required to file a 2018 tax return, and doesn't file a 2018 tax return. Both your friend and her child are your qualifying relatives if the support test is met.

Example 2—Return filed to claim refund. The facts are the same as in *Example 1*, except your friend had wages of $1,500 during the year and had income tax withheld from her wages. She files a return only to get a refund of the income tax withheld and doesn't claim the earned income credit or any other tax credits or deductions. Both your friend and her child are your qualifying relatives if the support test is met.

Example 3—Earned income credit claimed. The facts are the same as in *Example 2*, except your friend had wages of $8,000 during the year and claimed the earned income credit on her return. Your friend's child is the qualifying child of another taxpayer (your friend), so you can't claim your friend's child as your qualifying relative. Also, you can't claim your friend as your qualifying relative because of the gross income test explained later.

Child in Canada or Mexico. You may be able to claim your child as a dependent even if the child lives in Canada or Mexico. If the child doesn't live with you, the child doesn't meet the residency test to be your qualifying child. However, the child may still be your qualifying relative. If the persons the child does live with aren't U.S. citizens and have no U.S. gross income, those persons aren't "taxpayers," so the child isn't the qualifying child of any other taxpayer. If the child isn't the qualifying child of any other taxpayer, the child is your qualifying relative as long as the gross income test and the support test are met.

You can't claim as a dependent a child who lives in a foreign country other than Canada or Mexico, unless the child is a U.S. citizen, U.S. resident alien, or U.S. national. There is an exception for certain adopted children who lived with you all year. See *Citizen or Resident Test,* earlier.

Example. You provide all the support of your children, ages 6, 8, and 12, who live in Mexico with your mother and have no income. You are single and live in the United States. Your mother isn't a U.S. citizen and has no U.S. income, so she isn't a "taxpayer." Your children aren't your qualifying children because they don't meet the residency test. But since they aren't the qualifying children of any other taxpayer, they are your qualifying relatives and you can claim them as dependents. You also may be able to claim your mother as a dependent if the gross income and support tests are met.

Member of Household or Relationship Test

To meet this test, a person must either:

1. Live with you all year as a member of your household, or

2. Be related to you in one of the ways listed under *Relatives who don't have to live with you,* next.

If at any time during the year the person was your spouse, that person can't be your qualifying relative.

Relatives who don't have to live with you. A person related to you in any of the following ways doesn't have to live with you all year as a member of your household to meet this test.

- Your child, stepchild, foster child, or a descendant of any of them (for example, your grandchild). (A legally adopted child is considered your child.)

- Your brother, sister, half brother, half sister, stepbrother, or stepsister.

- Your father, mother, grandparent, or other direct ancestor, but not foster parent.

- Your stepfather or stepmother.

- A son or daughter of your brother or sister.

- A son or daughter of your half brother or half sister.

- A brother or sister of your father or mother.

- Your son-in-law, daughter-in-law, father-in-law, mother-in-law, brother-in-law, or sister-in-law.

Any of these relationships that were established by marriage aren't ended by death or divorce.

Example. You and your wife began supporting your wife's father, a widower, in 2012. Your wife died in 2017. Despite your wife's death, your father-in-law continues to meet this test, even if he doesn't live with you. You can claim him as a dependent if all other tests are met, including the gross income test and support test.

Foster child. A foster child is an individual who is placed with you by an authorized placement agency or by judgment, decree, or other order of any court of competent jurisdiction.

Joint return. If you file a joint return, the person can be related to either you or your spouse. Also, the person doesn't need to be related to the spouse who provides support.

For example, your spouse's uncle who receives more than half of his support from you may be your qualifying relative, even though he doesn't live with you. However, if you and your spouse file separate returns, your spouse's uncle can be your qualifying relative only if he lives with you all year as a member of your household.

Temporary absences. A person is considered to live with you as a member of your household during periods of time when one of you, or both, are temporarily absent due to special circumstances such as:

- Illness,

- Education,

- Business,

- Vacation,

- Military service, or

- Detention in a juvenile facility.

If the person is placed in a nursing home for an indefinite period of time to receive constant medical care, the absence may be considered temporary.

Death or birth. A person who died during the year, but lived with you as a member of your household until death, will meet this test. The same is true for a child who was born during the year and lived with you as a member of your household for the rest of the year. The test also is met if a child lived with you as a member of your household except for any required hospital stay following birth.

If your dependent died during the year and you otherwise qualify to claim that person as a dependent, you can still claim that person as a dependent.

Example. Your mother died on January 15. She met the tests to be your qualifying relative. You can claim her as a dependent.

Local law violated. A person doesn't meet this test if at any time during the year the relationship between you and that person violates local law.

Example. Your girlfriend lived with you as a member of your household all year. However, your relationship with her violated the laws of the state where you live because she was married to someone else. Therefore, she doesn't meet this test and you can't claim her as a dependent.

Adopted child. An adopted child is always treated as your own child. The term "adopted child" includes a child who was lawfully placed with you for legal adoption.

Cousin. Your cousin meets this test only if he or she lives with you all year as a member of your household. A cousin is a descendant of a brother or sister of your father or mother.

Gross Income Test

To meet this test, a person's gross income for the year must be less than $4,150.

Gross income defined. Gross income is all income in the form of money, property, and services that isn't exempt from tax.

In a manufacturing, merchandising, or mining business, gross income is the total net sales minus the cost of goods sold, plus any miscellaneous income from the business.

Gross receipts from rental property are gross income. Don't deduct taxes, repairs, or other expenses to determine the gross income from rental property.

Gross income includes a partner's share of the gross (not a share of the net) partnership income.

Gross income also includes all taxable unemployment compensation, taxable social security benefits, and certain scholarship and fellowship grants. Scholarships received by degree candidates and used for tuition, fees, supplies, books, and equipment required for particular courses generally aren't included in gross income. For more information about scholarships, see chapter 12.

Disabled dependent working at sheltered workshop. For purposes of the gross income test, the gross income of an individual who is permanently and totally disabled at any time during the year doesn't include income for services the individual performs at a sheltered workshop. The availability of medical care at the workshop must be the main reason for the individual's presence there. Also, the income must come solely from activities at the workshop that are incident to this medical care.

A "sheltered workshop" is a school that:

- Provides special instruction or training designed to alleviate the disability of the individual; and

- Is operated by certain tax-exempt organizations, or by a state, a U.S. possession, a political subdivision of a state or possession, the United States, or the District of Columbia.

Permanently and totally disabled has the same meaning here as under *Qualifying Child,* earlier.

Support Test (To Be a Qualifying Relative)

To meet this test, you generally must provide more than half of a person's total support during the calendar year.

However, if two or more persons provide support, but no one person provides more than half of a person's total support, see *Multiple Support Agreement*, later.

How to determine if support test is met. You figure whether you have provided more than half of a person's total support by comparing the amount you contributed to that person's support with the entire amount of support that person received from all sources. This includes support the person provided from his or her own funds.

You may find Worksheet 3-1 helpful in figuring whether you provided more than half of a person's support.

Person's own funds not used for support. A person's own funds aren't support unless they are actually spent for support.

Example. Your mother received $2,400 in social security benefits and $300 in interest. She paid $2,000 for lodging and $400 for recreation. She put $300 in a savings account.

Even though your mother received a total of $2,700 ($2,400 + $300), she spent only $2,400 ($2,000 + $400) for her own support. If you spent more than $2,400 for her support and no other support was received, you have provided more than half of her support.

Child's wages used for own support. You can't include in your contribution to your child's support any support paid for by the child with the child's own wages, even if you paid the wages.

Year support is provided. The year you provide the support is the year you pay for it, even if you do so with borrowed money that you repay in a later year.

If you use a fiscal year to report your income, you must provide more than half of the dependent's support for the calendar year in which your fiscal year begins.

Armed Forces dependency allotments. The part of the allotment contributed by the government and the part taken out of your military pay are both considered provided by you in figuring whether you provide more than half of the support. If your allotment is used to support persons other than those you name, you can claim them as dependents if they otherwise qualify.

Example. You are in the Armed Forces. You authorize an allotment for your widowed mother that she uses to support herself and her sister. If the allotment provides more than half of each person's support, you can claim each of them as a dependent, if they otherwise qualify, even though you authorize the allotment only for your mother.

Tax-exempt military quarters allowances. These allowances are treated the same way as dependency allotments in figuring support. The allotment of pay and the tax-exempt basic allowance for quarters are both considered as provided by you for support.

Tax-exempt income. In figuring a person's total support, include tax-exempt income, savings, and borrowed amounts used to support that person. Tax-exempt income includes certain social security benefits, welfare benefits, nontaxable life insurance proceeds, Armed Forces family allotments, nontaxable pensions, and tax-exempt interest.

Example 1. You provide $4,000 toward your mother's support during the year. She has earned income of $600, nontaxable social security benefits of $4,800, and tax-exempt interest of $200. She uses all these for her support. You can't claim your mother as a dependent because the $4,000 you provide isn't more than half of her total support of $9,600 ($4,000 + $600 + $4,800 + $200).

Example 2. Your niece takes out a student loan of $2,500 and uses it to pay her college tuition. She is personally responsible for the loan. You provide $2,000 toward her total support. You can't claim her as a dependent because you provide less than half of her support.

Social security benefits. If a married couple receives benefits that are paid by one check made out to both of them, half of the total paid is considered to be for the support of each spouse, unless they can show otherwise.

If a child receives social security benefits and uses them toward his or her own support, the benefits are considered as provided by the child.

Support provided by the state (welfare, food stamps, housing, etc.). Benefits provided by the state to a needy person generally are considered support provided by the state. However, payments based on the needs of the recipient won't be considered as used entirely for that person's support if it is shown that part of the payments weren't used for that purpose.

Foster care. Payments you receive for the support of a foster child from a child placement agency are considered support provided by the agency. See *Foster care payments and expenses*, earlier.

Home for the aged. If you make a lump-sum advance payment to a home for the aged to take care of your relative for life and the payment is based on that person's life expectancy, the amount of support you provide each year is the lump-sum payment divided by the relative's life expectancy. The amount of support you provide also includes any other amounts you provided during the year.

Total Support

To figure if you provided more than half of a person's support, you must first determine the total support provided for that person. Total support includes amounts spent to provide food, lodging, clothing, education, medical and dental care, recreation, transportation, and similar necessities.

Generally, the amount of an item of support is the amount of the expense incurred in providing that item. For lodging, the amount of support is the fair rental value of the lodging.

Expenses not directly related to any one member of a household, such as the cost of food for the household, must be divided among the members of the household.

Example 1. Grace Brown, mother of Mary Miller, lives with Frank and Mary Miller and their two children. Grace gets social security benefits of $2,400, which she spends for clothing, transportation, and recreation. Grace has no other income. Frank and Mary's total food expense for the household is $5,200. They pay Grace's medical and drug expenses of $1,200. The fair rental value of the lodging provided for Grace is $1,800 a year, based on the cost of similar rooming facilities. Figure Grace's total support as follows.

Fair rental value of lodging	$1,800
Clothing, transportation, and recreation	2,400
Medical expenses	1,200
Share of food (1/5 of $5,200)	1,040
Total support	**$6,440**

The support Frank and Mary provide, $4,040 ($1,800 lodging + $1,200 medical expenses + $1,040 food), is more than half of Grace's $6,440 total support.

Example 2. Your parents live with you, your spouse, and your two children in a house you own. The fair rental value of your parents' share of the lodging is $2,000 a year ($1,000 each), which includes furnishings and utilities. Your father receives a nontaxable pension of $4,200, which he spends equally between your mother and himself for items of support such as clothing, transportation, and recreation. Your total food expense for the household is $6,000. Your heat and utility bills amount to $1,200. Your mother has hospital and medical expenses of $600, which you pay during the year. Figure your parents' total support as follows:

Support provided	Father	Mother
Fair rental value of lodging	$1,000	$1,000
Pension spent for their support	2,100	2,100
Share of food (1/6 of $6,000)	1,000	1,000
Medical expenses for mother		600
Parents' total support	**$4,100**	**$4,700**

You must apply the support test separately to each parent. You provide $2,000 ($1,000 lodging + $1,000 food) of your father's total support of $4,100 — less than half. You provide $2,600 to your mother ($1,000 lodging + $1,000 food + $600 medical) — more than half of her total support of $4,700. You meet the support test for your mother, but not your father. Heat and utility costs are included in the fair rental value of the lodging, so these aren't considered separately.

Lodging. If you provide a person with lodging, you are considered to provide support equal to the fair rental value of the room, apartment, house, or other shelter in which the person lives. Fair rental value includes a reasonable allowance for the use of furniture and appliances, and for heat and other utilities that are provided.

Fair rental value defined. Fair rental value is the amount you could reasonably expect to receive from a stranger for the same kind of lodging. It is used instead of actual expenses such as taxes, interest, depreciation, paint, insurance, utilities, and the cost of furniture and appliances. In some cases, fair rental value may be equal to the rent paid.

If you provide the total lodging, the amount of support you provide is the fair rental value of the room the person uses, or a share of the fair rental value of the entire dwelling if the person has use of your entire home. If you don't provide the total lodging, the total fair rental value must be divided depending on how much of the total lodging you provide. If you provide only a part and the person supplies the rest, the fair rental value must be divided between both of you according to the amount each provides.

Example. Your parents live rent free in a house you own. It has a fair rental value of $5,400 a year furnished, which includes a fair rental value of $3,600 for the house and $1,800 for the furniture. This doesn't include heat and utilities. The house is completely furnished with furniture belonging to your parents. You pay $600 for their utility bills. Utilities aren't usually included in rent for houses in the area where your parents live. Therefore, you consider the total fair rental value of the lodging to be $6,000 ($3,600 fair rental value of the unfurnished house + $1,800 allowance for the furnishings provided by your parents + $600 cost of utilities) of which you are considered to provide $4,200 ($3,600 + $600).

Person living in his or her own home. The total fair rental value of a person's home that he or she owns is considered support contributed by that person.

Living with someone rent free. If you live with a person rent free in his or her home, you must reduce the amount you provide for support of that person by the fair rental value of lodging he or she provides you.

Property. Property provided as support is measured by its fair market value. Fair market value is the price that property would sell for on the open market. It is the price that would be agreed upon between a willing buyer and a willing seller, with neither being required to act, and both having reasonable knowledge of the relevant facts.

Capital expenses. Capital items, such as furniture, appliances, and cars, bought for a person during the year can be included in total support under certain circumstances.

The following examples show when a capital item is or isn't support.

Example 1. You buy a $200 power lawn mower for your 13-year-old child. The child is given the duty of keeping the lawn trimmed. Because the lawn mower benefits all members of the household, don't include the cost of the lawn mower in the support of your child.

Example 2. You buy a $150 television set as a birthday present for your 12-year-old child. The television set is placed in your child's bedroom. You can include the cost of the television set in the support of your child.

Example 3. You pay $5,000 for a car and register it in your name. You and your 17-year-old daughter use the car equally. Because you own the car and don't give it to your daughter but merely let her use it, don't include the cost of the car in your daughter's total support. However, you can include in your daughter's support your out-of-pocket expenses of operating the car for her benefit.

Example 4. Your 17-year-old son, using personal funds, buys a car for $4,500. You provide the rest of your son's support, $4,000. Because the car is bought and owned by your son, the car's fair market value ($4,500) must be included in his support. Your son has provided more than half of his own total support of $8,500 ($4,500 + $4,000), so he isn't your qualifying child. You didn't provide more than half of his total support, so he isn't your qualifying relative. You can't claim your son as a dependent.

Medical insurance premiums. Medical insurance premiums you pay, including premiums for supplementary Medicare coverage, are included in the support you provide.

Medical insurance benefits. Medical insurance benefits, including basic and supplementary Medicare benefits, aren't part of support.

Tuition payments and allowances under the GI Bill. Amounts veterans receive under the GI Bill for tuition payments and allowances while they attend school are included in total support.

Example. During the year, your son receives $2,200 from the government under the GI Bill. He uses this amount for his education. You provide the rest of his support, $2,000. Because GI benefits are included in total support, your son's total support is $4,200 ($2,200 + $2,000). You haven't provided more than half of his support.

Child care expenses. If you pay someone to provide child or dependent care, you can include these payments in the amount you provided for the support of your child or disabled dependent, even if you claim a credit for the payments. For information on the credit, see chapter 31.

Other support items. Other items may be considered as support depending on the facts in each case.

Don't Include in Total Support

The following items aren't included in total support.

1. Federal, state, and local income taxes paid by persons from their own income.

2. Social security and Medicare taxes paid by persons from their own income.

3. Life insurance premiums.

4. Funeral expenses.

5. Scholarships received by your child if your child is a student.

6. Survivors' and Dependents' Educational Assistance payments used for the support of the child who receives them.

Multiple Support Agreement

Sometimes no one provides more than half of the support of a person. Instead, two or more persons, each of whom would be able to claim the person as a dependent but for the support test, together provide more than half of the person's support.

When this happens, you can agree that any one of you who individually provides more than 10% of the person's support, but only one, can claim the person as a dependent. Each of the others must sign a statement agreeing not to claim the person as a dependent for that year. The person who claims the person as a dependent must keep these signed statements for his or her records. A multiple support declaration identifying each of the others who agreed not to claim the person as a dependent must be attached to the return of the person claiming the person as a dependent. Form 2120 can be used for this purpose.

You can claim someone as a dependent under a multiple support agreement for someone related to you or for someone who lived with you all year as a member of your household.

Example 1. You, your sister, and your two brothers provide the entire support of your mother for the year. You provide 45%, your sister 35%, and your two brothers each provide 10%. Either you or your sister can claim your mother as a dependent. The other must sign a statement agreeing not to claim your mother as a dependent. The one who claims your mother as a dependent must attach Form 2120, or a similar declaration, to his or her return and must keep the statement signed by the other for his or her records. Because neither brother provides more than 10% of the support, neither can claim your mother as a dependent and neither has to sign a statement.

Example 2. You and your brother each provide 20% of your mother's support for the year. The remaining 60% of her support is provided equally by two persons who aren't related to her. She doesn't live with them. Because more than half of her support is provided by persons who can't claim her as a dependent, no one can claim her as a dependent.

Example 3. Your father lives with you and receives 25% of his support from social security, 40% from you, 24% from his brother (your uncle), and 11% from a friend. Either you or your uncle can claim your father as a dependent if the other signs a statement agreeing not to. The one who claims your father as a dependent must attach Form 2120, or a similar declaration, to his return and must keep for his records the signed statement from the one agreeing not to claim your father as a dependent.

Support Test for Children of Divorced or Separated Parents (or Parents Who Live Apart)

In most cases, a child of divorced or separated parents (or parents who live apart) will be a qualifying child of one of the parents. See *Children of divorced or separated parents (or parents who live apart)* under *Qualifying Child*, earlier. However, if the child doesn't meet the requirements to be a qualifying child of either parent, the child may be a qualifying relative of one of the parents. If you think this might apply to you, see Pub. 501.

Social Security Numbers for Dependents

You must show the social security number (SSN) of any dependent you list in the *Dependents* section of your Form 1040.

 If you don't show the dependent's SSN when required, or if you show an incorrect SSN, certain tax benefits may be disallowed.

No SSN. If a person whom you expect to claim as a dependent on your return doesn't have an SSN, either you or that person should apply for an SSN as soon as possible by filing Form SS-5, Application for a Social Security Card, with the Social Security Administration (SSA). You can get Form SS-5 online at *SSA.gov* or at your local SSA office.

It usually takes about 2 weeks to get an SSN once the SSA has all the information it needs. If you don't have a required SSN by the filing due date, you can file Form 4868 for an extension of time to file.

Born and died in 2018. If your child was born and died in 2018, and you don't have an SSN for the child, you may attach a copy of the child's birth certificate, death certificate, or hospital records instead. The document must show the child was born alive. If you do this, enter "DIED" in column (2) of the *Dependents* section of your Form 1040.

Alien or adoptee with no SSN. If your dependent doesn't have and can't get an SSN, you must list the individual taxpayer identification number (ITIN) or adoption taxpayer identification number (ATIN) instead of an SSN.

Taxpayer identification numbers for aliens. If your dependent is a resident or nonresident alien who doesn't have and isn't eligible to get an SSN, your dependent must apply for an individual taxpayer identification number (ITIN). For details on how to apply, see Form W-7, Application for IRS Individual Taxpayer Identification Number.

Taxpayer identification numbers for adoptees. If you have a child who was placed with you by an authorized placement agency, you may be able to claim the child as a dependent. However, if you can't get an SSN or an ITIN for the child, you must get an adoption taxpayer identification number (ATIN) for the child from the IRS. See Form W-7A, Application for

Taxpayer Identification Number for Pending U.S. Adoptions, for details.

4.

Tax Withholding and Estimated Tax

What's New for 2019

 At the time this publication went to print, Congress was considering legislation that would do the following.

1. *Provide additional tax relief for those affected by certain 2018 disasters.*

2. *Extend certain tax benefits that expired at the end of 2017 and that currently can't be claimed on your 2018 tax return.*

3. *Change certain other tax provisions.*

To learn whether this legislation was enacted resulting in changes that affect your 2018 tax return, go to Recent Developments at IRS.gov/ Pub17.

Tax law changes for 2019. When you figure how much income tax you want withheld from your pay and when you figure your estimated tax, consider tax law changes effective in 2019. For more information, see Pub. 505, Tax Withholding and Estimated Tax.

Reminders

Estimated tax safe harbor for higher income taxpayers. If your 2018 adjusted gross income was more than $150,000 ($75,000 if you are married filing a separate return), you must pay the smaller of 90% of your expected tax for 2019 or 110% of the tax shown on your 2018 return to avoid an estimated tax penalty.

Introduction

This chapter discusses how to pay your tax as you earn or receive income during the year. In general, the federal income tax is a pay-as-you-go tax. There are two ways to pay as you go.

- *Withholding.* If you are an employee, your employer probably withholds income tax from your pay. Tax also may be withheld from certain other income, such as pensions, bonuses, commissions, and gambling winnings. The amount withheld is paid to the IRS in your name.

- *Estimated tax.* If you don't pay your tax through withholding, or don't pay enough

tax that way, you may have to pay estimated tax. People who are in business for themselves generally will have to pay their tax this way. Also, you may have to pay estimated tax if you receive income such as dividends, interest, capital gains, rent, and royalties. Estimated tax is used to pay not only income tax, but self-employment tax and alternative minimum tax as well.

This chapter explains these methods. In addition, it also explains the following.

- *Credit for withholding and estimated tax.* When you file your 2018 income tax return, take credit for all the income tax withheld from your salary, wages, pensions, etc., and for the estimated tax you paid for 2018. Also take credit for any excess social security or railroad retirement tax withheld (discussed in chapter 37).

- *Underpayment penalty.* If you didn't pay enough tax during the year, either through withholding or by making estimated tax payments, you may have to pay a penalty. In most cases, the IRS can figure this penalty for you. See *Underpayment Penalty for 2018* at the end of this chapter.

Useful Items

You may want to see:

Publication

❑ **505** Tax Withholding and Estimated Tax

Form (and Instructions)

❑ **W-4** Employee's Withholding Allowance Certificate

❑ **W-4P** Withholding Certificate for Pension or Annuity Payments

❑ **W-4S** Request for Federal Income Tax Withholding From Sick Pay

❑ **W-4V** Voluntary Withholding Request

❑ **1040-ES** Estimated Tax for Individuals

❑ **2210** Underpayment of Estimated Tax by Individuals, Estates, and Trusts

❑ **2210-F** Underpayment of Estimated Tax by Farmers and Fishermen

Tax Withholding for 2019

This section discusses income tax withholding on:

- Salaries and wages,
- Tips,
- Taxable fringe benefits,
- Sick pay,
- Pensions and annuities,
- Gambling winnings,
- Unemployment compensation, and
- Certain federal payments.

This section explains the rules for withholding tax from each of these types of income.

This section also covers backup withholding on interest, dividends, and other payments.

Salaries and Wages

Income tax is withheld from the pay of most employees. Your pay includes your regular pay, bonuses, commissions, and vacation allowances. It also includes reimbursements and other expense allowances paid under a nonaccountable plan. See *Supplemental Wages*, later, for more information about reimbursements and allowances paid under a nonaccountable plan.

If your income is low enough that you won't have to pay income tax for the year, you may be exempt from withholding. This is explained under *Exemption From Withholding*, later.

You can ask your employer to withhold income tax from noncash wages and other wages not subject to withholding. If your employer doesn't agree to withhold tax, or if not enough is withheld, you may have to pay estimated tax, as discussed later under *Estimated Tax for 2019*.

Military retirees. Military retirement pay is treated in the same manner as regular pay for income tax withholding purposes, even though it is treated as a pension or annuity for other tax purposes.

Household workers. If you are a household worker, you can ask your employer to withhold income tax from your pay. A household worker is an employee who performs household work in a private home, local college club, or local fraternity or sorority chapter.

Tax is withheld only if you want it withheld and your employer agrees to withhold it. If you don't have enough income tax withheld, you may have to pay estimated tax, as discussed later under *Estimated Tax for 2019*.

Farmworkers. Generally, income tax is withheld from your cash wages for work on a farm unless your employer does both of these:

- Pays you cash wages of less than $150 during the year, and

- Has expenditures for agricultural labor totaling less than $2,500 during the year.

Differential wage payments. When employees are on leave from employment for military duty, some employers make up the difference between the military pay and civilian pay. Payments to an employee who is on active duty for a period of more than 30 days will be subject to income tax withholding, but not subject to social security, Medicare, or federal unemployment (FUTA) tax withholding. The wages and withholding will be reported on Form W-2, Wage and Tax Statement.

Determining Amount of Tax Withheld Using Form W-4

The amount of income tax your employer withholds from your regular pay depends on two things.

- The amount you earn in each payroll period.

- The information you give your employer on Form W-4.

Form W-4 includes four types of information that your employer will use to figure your withholding.

- Whether to withhold at the single rate or at the lower married rate.

- How many withholding allowances you claim (each allowance reduces the amount withheld).

- Whether you want an additional amount withheld.

- Whether you are claiming an exemption from withholding in 2019. See *Exemption From Withholding*, later.

Note. You must specify a filing status and a number of withholding allowances on Form W-4. You can't specify only a dollar amount of withholding.

New Job

When you start a new job, you must fill out Form W-4 and give it to your employer. Your employer should have copies of the form. If you need to change the information later, you must fill out a new form.

If you work only part of the year (for example, you start working after the beginning of the year), too much tax may be withheld. You may be able to avoid overwithholding if your employer agrees to use the part-year method. See *Part-Year Method* in chapter 1 of Pub. 505 for more information.

Employee also receiving pension income. If you receive pension or annuity income and begin a new job, you will need to file Form W-4 with your new employer. However, you can choose to split your withholding allowances between your pension and job in any manner.

Changing Your Withholding

During the year changes may occur to your marital status, adjustments, deductions, or credits you expect to claim on your tax return. When this happens, you may need to give your employer a new Form W-4 to change your withholding status or your number of allowances.

If the changes reduce the number of allowances you are claiming or changes your marital status from married to single, you must give your employer a new Form W-4 within 10 days.

Generally, you can submit a new Form W-4 whenever you wish to change the number of your withholding allowances for any other reason.

Changing your withholding for 2020. If events in 2019 will decrease the number of your withholding allowances for 2020, you must give your employer a new Form W-4 by December 1, 2019. If the event occurs in December 2019, submit a new Form W-4 within 10 days.

Checking Your Withholding

After you have given your employer a Form W-4, you can check to see whether the amount of tax withheld from your pay is too little or too much. If too much or too little tax is being withheld, you should give your employer a new Form W-4 to change your withholding. You

should try to have your withholding match your actual tax liability. If not enough tax is withheld, you will owe tax at the end of the year and may have to pay interest and a penalty. If too much tax is withheld, you will lose the use of that money until you get your refund. Always check your withholding if there are personal or financial changes in your life or changes in the law that might change your tax liability.

Note. You can't give your employer a payment to cover withholding on salaries and wages for past pay periods or a payment for estimated tax.

Completing Form W-4 and Worksheets

Form W-4 has worksheets to help you figure how many withholding allowances you can claim. The worksheets are for your own records. Don't give them to your employer.

Multiple jobs. If you have income from more than one job at the same time, complete only one set of Form W-4 worksheets. Then split your allowances between the Forms W-4 for each job. You can't claim the same allowances with more than one employer at the same time. You can claim all your allowances with one employer and none with the other(s), or divide them any other way.

Married individuals. If both you and your spouse are employed and expect to file a joint return, figure your withholding allowances using your combined income, adjustments, deductions, and credits. Use only one set of worksheets. You can divide your total allowances any way, but you can't claim an allowance that your spouse also claims.

If you and your spouse expect to file separate returns, figure your allowances using separate worksheets based on your own individual income, adjustments, deductions, and credits.

Alternative method of figuring withholding allowances. You don't have to use the Form W-4 worksheets if you use a more accurate method of figuring the number of withholding allowances. For more information, see *Alternative method of figuring withholding allowances* under *Completing Form W-4 and Worksheets* in Pub. 505, chapter 1.

Personal Allowances Worksheet. Use the Personal Allowances Worksheet on Form W-4 to figure your withholding allowances based on filing status and any special allowances that apply.

Deductions, Adjustments, and Additional Income Worksheet. Use the Deductions, Adjustments, and Additional Income Worksheet on Form W-4 if you plan to itemize your deductions, claim certain adjustments to the income, or have a large amount of nonwage income on your 2019 tax return and you want to reduce your withholding. Also, complete this worksheet when you have changes to these items to see if you need to change your withholding.

Two-Earners/Multiple Jobs Worksheet. You may need to complete the Two-Earners/Multiple Jobs Worksheet on Form W-4 if you have more than one job or are married filing jointly and have a working spouse. Also, on this worksheet you can figure any additional withholding necessary to cover any amount you expect to owe other than income tax, such as self-employment tax.

Getting the Right Amount of Tax Withheld

In most situations, the tax withheld from your pay will be close to the tax you figure on your return if you follow these two rules.

- You accurately complete all the Form W-4 worksheets that apply to you.

- You give your employer a new Form W-4 when changes occur.

But because the worksheets and withholding methods don't account for all possible situations, you may not be getting the right amount withheld. This is most likely to happen in the following situations.

- You are married and both you and your spouse work.

- You have more than one job at a time.

- You have nonwage income, such as interest, dividends, alimony, unemployment compensation, or self-employment income.

- You will owe additional amounts with your return, such as self-employment tax.

- Your withholding is based on obsolete Form W-4 information for a substantial part of the year.

- You work only part of the year.

- You change the number of your withholding allowances during the year.

Cumulative wage method. If you change the number of your withholding allowances during the year, too much or too little tax may have been withheld for the period before you made the change. You may be able to compensate for this if your employer agrees to use the cumulative wage withholding method for the rest of the year. You must ask your employer in writing to use this method.

To be eligible, you must have been paid for the same kind of payroll period (weekly, biweekly, etc.) since the beginning of the year.

Publication 505

To make sure you are getting the right amount of tax withheld, get Pub. 505. It will help you compare the total tax to be withheld during the year with the tax you can expect to figure on your return. It also will help you determine how much, if any, additional withholding is needed each payday to avoid owing tax when you file your return. If you don't have enough tax withheld, you may have to pay estimated tax, as explained under *Estimated Tax for 2019*, later.

 You can use the IRS Withholding Calculator at IRS.gov/W4App, instead of Pub. 505 or the worksheets included with Form W-4, to determine whether you need to have your withholding increased or decreased.

Rules Your Employer Must Follow

It may be helpful for you to know some of the withholding rules your employer must follow. These rules can affect how to fill out your Form W-4 and how to handle problems that may arise.

New Form W-4. When you start a new job, your employer should have you complete a Form W-4. Beginning with your first payday, your employer will use the information you give on the form to figure your withholding.

If you later fill out a new Form W-4, your employer can put it into effect as soon as possible. The deadline for putting it into effect is the start of the first payroll period ending 30 or more days after you turn it in.

No Form W-4. If you don't give your employer a completed Form W-4, your employer must withhold at the highest rate, as if you were single and claimed no withholding allowances.

Repaying withheld tax. If you find you are having too much tax withheld because you didn't claim all the withholding allowances you are entitled to, you should give your employer a new Form W-4. Your employer can't repay any of the tax previously withheld. Instead, claim the full amount withheld when you file your tax return.

However, if your employer has withheld more than the correct amount of tax for the Form W-4 you have in effect, you don't have to fill out a new Form W-4 to have your withholding lowered to the correct amount. Your employer can repay the amount that was withheld incorrectly. If you aren't repaid, your Form W-2 will reflect the full amount actually withheld, which you would claim when you file your tax return.

Exemption From Withholding

If you claim exemption from withholding, your employer won't withhold federal income tax from your wages. The exemption applies only to income tax, not to social security, Medicare, or FUTA tax withholding.

You can claim exemption from withholding for 2019 only if both of the following situations apply.

- For 2018 you had a right to a refund of all federal income tax withheld because you had no tax liability.

- For 2019 you expect a refund of all federal income tax withheld because you expect to have no tax liability.

Students. If you are a student, you aren't automatically exempt. See chapter 1 to find out if you must file a return. If you work only part time or only during the summer, you may qualify for exemption from withholding.

Age 65 or older or blind. If you are 65 or older or blind, use Worksheet 1-1 or 1-2 in chapter 1 of Pub. 505, to help you decide if you qualify for exemption from withholding. Don't use either worksheet if you will itemize deductions, or claim tax credits on your 2019 return. Instead, see *Itemizing deductions or claiming credits* in chapter 1 of Pub. 505.

Claiming exemption from withholding. To claim exemption, you must give your employer

a Form W-4. Don't complete lines 5 and 6. Enter "Exempt" on line 7.

If you claim exemption, but later your situation changes so that you will have to pay income tax after all, you must file a new Form W-4 within 10 days after the change. If you claim exemption in 2019, but you expect to owe income tax for 2020, you must file a new Form W-4 by December 1, 2019.

Your claim of exempt status may be reviewed by the IRS.

An exemption is good for only 1 year. You must give your employer a new Form W-4 by February 15 each year to continue your exemption.

Supplemental Wages

Supplemental wages include bonuses, commissions, overtime pay, vacation allowances, certain sick pay, and expense allowances under certain plans. The payer can figure withholding on supplemental wages using the same method used for your regular wages. However, if these payments are identified separately from your regular wages, your employer or other payer of supplemental wages can withhold income tax from these wages at a flat rate.

Expense allowances. Reimbursements or other expense allowances paid by your employer under a nonaccountable plan are treated as supplemental wages.

Reimbursements or other expense allowances paid under an accountable plan that are more than your proven expenses are treated as paid under a nonaccountable plan if you don't return the excess payments within a reasonable period of time.

For more information about accountable and nonaccountable expense allowance plans, see *Reimbursements* in chapter 20.

Penalties

You may have to pay a penalty of $500 if both of the following apply.

- You make statements or claim withholding allowances on your Form W-4 that reduce the amount of tax withheld.

- You have no reasonable basis for those statements or allowances at the time you prepare your Form W-4.

There is also a criminal penalty for willfully supplying false or fraudulent information on your Form W-4 or for willfully failing to supply information that would increase the amount withheld. The penalty upon conviction can be either a fine of up to $1,000 or imprisonment for up to 1 year, or both.

These penalties will apply if you deliberately and knowingly falsify your Form W-4 in an attempt to reduce or eliminate the proper withholding of taxes. A simple error or an honest mistake won't result in one of these penalties. For example, a person who has tried to figure the number of withholding allowances correctly, but claims seven when the proper number is six, won't be charged a W-4 penalty.

Tips

The tips you receive while working on your job are considered part of your pay. You must include your tips on your tax return on the same line as your regular pay. However, tax isn't withheld directly from tip income, as it is from your regular pay. Nevertheless, your employer will take into account the tips you report when figuring how much to withhold from your regular pay.

See chapter 6 for information on reporting your tips to your employer. For more information on the withholding rules for tip income, see Pub. 531, Reporting Tip Income.

How employer figures amount to withhold. The tips you report to your employer are counted as part of your income for the month you report them. Your employer can figure your withholding in either of two ways.

- By withholding at the regular rate on the sum of your pay plus your reported tips.

- By withholding at the regular rate on your pay plus a percentage of your reported tips.

Not enough pay to cover taxes. If your regular pay isn't enough for your employer to withhold all the tax (including income tax and social security and Medicare taxes (or the equivalent railroad retirement tax)) due on your pay plus your tips, you can give your employer money to cover the shortage. See Giving your employer money for taxes in chapter 6.

Allocated tips. Your employer shouldn't withhold income tax, Medicare tax, social security tax, or railroad retirement tax on any allocated tips. Withholding is based only on your pay plus your reported tips. Your employer should refund to you any incorrectly withheld tax. See Allocated Tips in chapter 6 for more information.

Taxable Fringe Benefits

The value of certain noncash fringe benefits you receive from your employer is considered part of your pay. Your employer generally must withhold income tax on these benefits from your regular pay.

For information on fringe benefits, see Fringe Benefits under Employee Compensation in chapter 5.

Although the value of your personal use of an employer-provided car, truck, or other highway motor vehicle is taxable, your employer can choose not to withhold income tax on that amount. Your employer must notify you if this choice is made.

For more information on withholding on taxable fringe benefits, see chapter 1 of Pub. 505.

Sick Pay

Sick pay is a payment to you to replace your regular wages while you are temporarily absent from work due to sickness or personal injury. To qualify as sick pay, it must be paid under a plan to which your employer is a party.

If you receive sick pay from your employer or an agent of your employer, income tax must be withheld. An agent who doesn't pay regular wages to you may choose to withhold income tax at a flat rate.

However, if you receive sick pay from a third party who isn't acting as an agent of your employer, income tax will be withheld only if you choose to have it withheld. See Form W-4S, later.

If you receive payments under a plan in which your employer doesn't participate (such as an accident or health plan where you paid all the premiums), the payments aren't sick pay and usually aren't taxable.

Union agreements. If you receive sick pay under a collective bargaining agreement between your union and your employer, the agreement may determine the amount of income tax withholding. See your union representative or your employer for more information.

Form W-4S. If you choose to have income tax withheld from sick pay paid by a third party, such as an insurance company, you must fill out Form W-4S. Its instructions contain a worksheet you can use to figure the amount you want withheld. They also explain restrictions that may apply.

Give the completed form to the payer of your sick pay. The payer must withhold according to your directions on the form.

Estimated tax. If you don't request withholding on Form W-4S, or if you don't have enough tax withheld, you may have to make estimated tax payments. If you don't pay enough tax, either through estimated tax or withholding, or a combination of both, you may have to pay a penalty. See Underpayment Penalty for 2018 at the end of this chapter.

Pensions and Annuities

Income tax usually will be withheld from your pension or annuity distributions unless you choose not to have it withheld. This rule applies to distributions from:

- A traditional individual retirement arrangement (IRA);

- A life insurance company under an endowment, annuity, or life insurance contract;

- A pension, annuity, or profit-sharing plan;

- A stock bonus plan; and

- Any other plan that defers the time you receive compensation.

The amount withheld depends on whether you receive payments spread out over more than 1 year (periodic payments), within 1 year (nonperiodic payments), or as an eligible rollover distribution (ERD). Income tax withholding from an ERD is mandatory.

More information. For more information on taxation of annuities and distributions (including ERDs) from qualified retirement plans, see chapter 10. For information on IRAs, see chapter 17. For more information on withholding on pensions and annuities, including a discussion of Form W-4P, see Pensions and Annuities in chapter 1 of Pub. 505.

Gambling Winnings

Income tax is withheld at a flat 24% rate from certain kinds of gambling winnings.

Gambling winnings of more than $5,000 from the following sources are subject to income tax withholding.

- Any sweepstakes; wagering pool, including payments made to winners of poker tournaments; or lottery.

- Any other wager, if the proceeds are at least 300 times the amount of the bet.

It doesn't matter whether your winnings are paid in cash, in property, or as an annuity. Winnings not paid in cash are taken into account at their fair market value.

Exception. Gambling winnings from bingo, keno, and slot machines generally aren't subject to income tax withholding. However, you may need to provide the payer with a social security number to avoid withholding. See Backup withholding on gambling winnings in chapter 1 of Pub. 505. If you receive gambling winnings not subject to withholding, you may need to pay estimated tax. See Estimated Tax for 2019, later.

If you don't pay enough tax, either through withholding or estimated tax, or a combination of both, you may have to pay a penalty. See Underpayment Penalty for 2018 at the end of this chapter.

Form W-2G. If a payer withholds income tax from your gambling winnings, you should receive a Form W-2G, Certain Gambling Winnings, showing the amount you won and the amount withheld. Report the tax withheld on line 16 of Form 1040.

Unemployment Compensation

You can choose to have income tax withheld from unemployment compensation. To make this choice, fill out Form W-4V (or a similar form provided by the payer) and give it to the payer.

All unemployment compensation is taxable. If you don't have income tax withheld, you may have to pay estimated tax. See Estimated Tax for 2019, later.

If you don't pay enough tax, either through withholding or estimated tax, or a combination of both, you may have to pay a penalty. For information, see Underpayment Penalty for 2018 at the end of this chapter.

Federal Payments

You can choose to have income tax withheld from certain federal payments you receive. These payments are the following.

1. Social security benefits.

2. Tier 1 railroad retirement benefits.

3. Commodity credit corporation loans you choose to include in your gross income.

4. Payments under the Agricultural Act of 1949 (7 U.S.C. 1421 et seq.), as amended, or title II of the Disaster Assistance

Act of 1988, that are treated as insurance proceeds and that you receive because:

   a. Your crops were destroyed or damaged by drought, flood, or any other natural disaster; or

   b. You were unable to plant crops because of a natural disaster described in (a).

5. Any other payment under federal law as determined by the Secretary.

To make this choice, fill out Form W-4V (or a similar form provided by the payer) and give it to the payer.

If you don't choose to have income tax withheld, you may have to pay estimated tax. See *Estimated Tax for 2019*, later.

If you don't pay enough tax, either through withholding or estimated tax, or a combination of both, you may have to pay a penalty. For information, see *Underpayment Penalty for 2018* at the end of this chapter.

More information. For more information about the tax treatment of social security and railroad retirement benefits, see chapter 11. Get Pub. 225, Farmer's Tax Guide, for information about the tax treatment of commodity credit corporation loans or crop disaster payments.

Backup Withholding

Banks or other businesses that pay you certain kinds of income must file an information return (Form 1099) with the IRS. The information return shows how much you were paid during the year. It also includes your name and taxpayer identification number (TIN). TINs are explained in chapter 1 under *Social Security Number (SSN)*.

These payments generally aren't subject to withholding. However, "backup" withholding is required in certain situations. Backup withholding can apply to most kinds of payments that are reported on Form 1099.

The payer must withhold at a flat 24% rate in the following situations.

- You don't give the payer your TIN in the required manner.

- The IRS notifies the payer that the TIN you gave is incorrect.

- You are required, but fail, to certify that you aren't subject to backup withholding.

- The IRS notifies the payer to start withholding on interest or dividends because you have underreported interest or dividends on your income tax return. The IRS will do this only after it has mailed you four notices over at least a 210-day period.

Go to *www.irs.gov/businesses/small-businesses-self-employed/backup-withholding* for more information on kinds of payments subject to backup withholding.

Penalties. There are civil and criminal penalties for giving false information to avoid backup withholding. The civil penalty is $500. The criminal penalty, upon conviction, is a fine of up to $1,000 or imprisonment of up to 1 year, or both.

Estimated Tax for 2019

Estimated tax is the method used to pay tax on income that isn't subject to withholding. This includes income from self-employment, interest, dividends, alimony, rent, gains from the sale of assets, prizes, and awards. You also may have to pay estimated tax if the amount of income tax being withheld from your salary, pension, or other income isn't enough.

Estimated tax is used to pay both income tax and self-employment tax, as well as other taxes and amounts reported on your tax return. If you don't pay enough tax, either through withholding or estimated tax, or a combination of both, you may have to pay a penalty. If you don't pay enough by the due date of each payment period (see *When To Pay Estimated Tax*, later), you may be charged a penalty even if you are due a refund when you file your tax return. For information on when the penalty applies, see *Underpayment Penalty for 2018* at the end of this chapter.

Who Doesn't Have To Pay Estimated Tax

If you receive salaries or wages, you can avoid having to pay estimated tax by asking your employer to take more tax out of your earnings. To do this, give a new Form W-4 to your employer. See chapter 1 of Pub. 505.

Estimated tax not required. You don't have to pay estimated tax for 2019 if you meet all three of the following conditions.

- You had no tax liability for 2018.

- You were a U.S. citizen or resident alien for the whole year.

- Your 2018 tax year covered a 12-month period.

You had no tax liability for 2018 if your total tax was zero or you didn't have to file an income tax return. For the definition of "total tax" for 2018, see Pub. 505, chapter 2.

Who Must Pay Estimated Tax

If you owe additional tax for 2018, you may have to pay estimated tax for 2019.

You can use the following general rule as a guide during the year to see if you will have enough withholding, or if you should increase your withholding or make estimated tax payments.

General rule. In most cases, you must pay estimated tax for 2019 if both of the following apply.

1. You expect to owe at least $1,000 in tax for 2019, after subtracting your withholding and refundable credits.

2. You expect your withholding plus your refundable credits to be less than the smaller of:

   a. 90% of the tax to be shown on your 2019 tax return, or

   b. 100% of the tax shown on your 2018 tax return (but see *Special rules for farmers, fishermen, and higher income taxpayers*, later). Your 2018 tax return must cover all 12 months.

 If the result from using the general rule above suggests that you won't have enough withholding, complete the 2019 Estimated Tax Worksheet in Pub. 505 for a more accurate calculation.

Special rules for farmers, fishermen, and higher income taxpayers. If at least two-thirds of your gross income for tax year 2018 or 2019 is from farming or fishing, substitute 66$\frac{2}{3}$% for 90% in (2a) under the *General rule*, earlier. If your AGI for 2018 was more than $150,000 ($75,000 if your filing status for 2019 is married filing a separate return), substitute 110% for 100% in (2b) under *General rule*, earlier. See Figure 4-A and Pub. 505, chapter 2, for more information.

Aliens. Resident and nonresident aliens also may have to pay estimated tax. Resident aliens should follow the rules in this chapter unless noted otherwise. Nonresident aliens should get Form 1040-ES (NR), U.S. Estimated Tax for Nonresident Alien Individuals.

You are an alien if you aren't a citizen or national of the United States. You are a resident alien if you either have a green card or meet the substantial presence test. For more information about the substantial presence test, see Pub. 519, U.S. Tax Guide for Aliens.

Married taxpayers. If you qualify to make joint estimated tax payments, apply the rules discussed here to your joint estimated income.

You and your spouse can make joint estimated tax payments even if you aren't living together.

However, you and your spouse can't make joint estimated tax payments if:

- You are legally separated under a decree of divorce or separate maintenance,

- You and your spouse have different tax years, or

- Either spouse is a nonresident alien (unless that spouse elected to be treated as a resident alien for tax purposes (see chapter 1 of Pub. 519)).

If you don't qualify to make joint estimated tax payments, apply these rules to your separate estimated income. Making joint or separate estimated tax payments won't affect your choice of filing a joint tax return or separate returns for 2019.

2018 separate returns and 2019 joint return. If you plan to file a joint return with your spouse for 2019, but you filed separate returns for 2018, your 2018 tax is the total of the tax shown on your separate returns. You filed a separate return if you filed as single, head of household, or married filing separately.

2018 joint return and 2019 separate returns. If you plan to file a separate return for 2019 but you filed a joint return for 2018, your

Figure 4-A. **Do You Have To Pay Estimated Tax?**

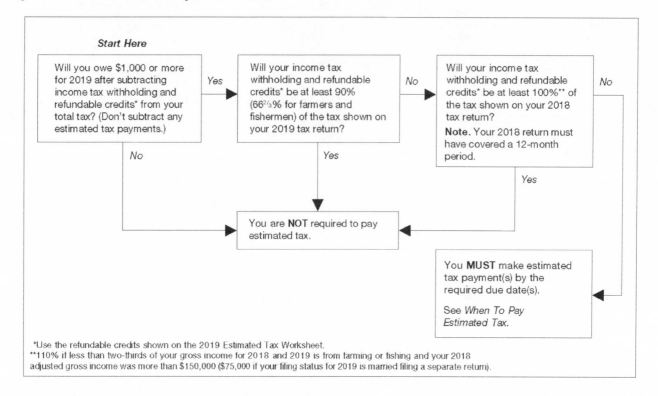

Start Here

Will you owe $1,000 or more for 2019 after subtracting income tax withholding and refundable credits* from your total tax? (Don't subtract any estimated tax payments.) — **Yes** →

Will your income tax withholding and refundable credits* be at least 90% (66²/₃% for farmers and fishermen) of the tax shown on your 2019 tax return? — **No** →

Will your income tax withholding and refundable credits* be at least 100%** of the tax shown on your 2018 tax return? **Note.** Your 2018 return must have covered a 12-month period. — **No** →

No ↓ / **Yes** ↓ / **Yes** ↓

You are **NOT** required to pay estimated tax.

You **MUST** make estimated tax payment(s) by the required due date(s).

See *When To Pay Estimated Tax.*

*Use the refundable credits shown on the 2019 Estimated Tax Worksheet.
**110% if less than two-thirds of your gross income for 2018 and 2019 is from farming or fishing and your 2018 adjusted gross income was more than $150,000 ($75,000 if your filing status for 2019 is married filing a separate return).

2018 tax is your share of the tax on the joint return. You file a separate return if you file as single, head of household, or married filing separately.

To figure your share of the tax on the joint return, first figure the tax both you and your spouse would have paid had you filed separate returns for 2018 using the same filing status as for 2019. Then multiply the tax on the joint return by the following fraction.

$$\frac{\text{The tax you would have paid had you filed a separate return}}{\text{The total tax you and your spouse would have paid had you filed separate returns}}$$

Example. Joe and Heather filed a joint return for 2018 showing taxable income of $48,500 and a tax of $5,442. Of the $48,500 taxable income, $40,100 was Joe's and the rest was Heather's. For 2019, they plan to file married filing separately. Joe figures his share of the tax on the 2018 joint return as follows.

Tax on $40,100 based on a separate return	$4,767
Tax on $8,400 based on a separate return	843
Total	$5,610
Joe's percentage of total ($4,767 ÷ $5,610)	85%
Joe's share of tax on joint return ($5,442 × 85%)	$4,626

How To Figure Estimated Tax

To figure your estimated tax, you must figure your expected adjusted gross income (AGI), taxable income, taxes, deductions, and credits for the year.

When figuring your 2019 estimated tax, it may be helpful to use your income, deductions, and credits for 2018 as a starting point. Use your 2018 federal tax return as a guide. You can use Form 1040-ES and Pub. 505 to figure your estimated tax. Nonresident aliens use Form 1040-ES (NR) and Pub. 505 to figure estimated tax (see chapter 8 of Pub. 519 for more information).

You must make adjustments both for changes in your own situation and for recent changes in the tax law. For a discussion of these changes, visit *IRS.gov*.

For more complete information on how to figure your estimated tax for 2019, see chapter 2 of Pub. 505.

When To Pay Estimated Tax

For estimated tax purposes, the tax year is divided into four payment periods. Each period has a specific payment due date. If you don't pay enough tax by the due date of each payment period, you may be charged a penalty even if you are due a refund when you file your income tax return. The payment periods and due dates for estimated tax payments are shown next.

For the period:	Due date:*
Jan. 1 – March 31	April 15
April 1 – May 31	June 17
June 1 – August 31	Sept. 16
Sept. 1– Dec. 31	Jan. 15, next year

*See *Saturday, Sunday, holiday rule* and *January payment*.

Saturday, Sunday, holiday rule. If the due date for an estimated tax payment falls on a Saturday, Sunday, or legal holiday, the payment will be on time if you make it on the next day that isn't a Saturday, Sunday, or legal holiday.

January payment. If you file your 2019 Form 1040 by January 31, 2020, and pay the rest of the tax you owe, you don't need to make the payment due on January 15, 2020.

Fiscal year taxpayers. If your tax year doesn't start on January 1, see the Form 1040-ES instructions for your payment due dates.

When To Start

You don't have to make estimated tax payments until you have income on which you will owe income tax. If you have income subject to estimated tax during the first payment period, you must make your first payment by the due date for the first payment period. You can pay all your estimated tax at that time, or you can pay it in installments. If you choose to pay in installments, make your first payment by the due date for the first payment period. Make your remaining installment payments by the due dates for the later periods.

No income subject to estimated tax during first period. If you don't have income subject to estimated tax until a later payment period, you must make your first payment by the due date for that period. You can pay your entire estimated tax by the due date for that period or you can pay it in installments by the due date for that period and the due dates for the remaining periods.

Table 4-1 **General Due Dates for Estimated Tax Installment Payments**

If you first have income on which you must pay estimated tax:	Make installments by:*	Make later installments by:*
Before April 1	April 15	June 15 Sept. 15 Jan. 15, next year
April 1–May 31	June 15	Sept. 15 Jan. 15, next year
June 1–Aug. 31	Sept. 15	Jan. 15, next year
After Aug. 31	Jan. 15, next year	(None)

*See _Saturday, Sunday, holiday rule_ and _January payment_.

How much to pay to avoid a penalty. To determine how much you should pay by each payment due date, see _How To Figure Each Payment_ next.

How To Figure Each Payment

You should pay enough estimated tax by the due date of each payment period to avoid a penalty for that period. You can figure your required payment for each period by using either the regular installment method or the annualized income installment method. These methods are described in chapter 2 of Pub. 505. If you don't pay enough during each payment period, you may be charged a penalty even if you are due a refund when you file your tax return.

If the earlier discussion of _No income subject to estimated tax during first period_ or the later discussion of _Change in estimated tax_ applies to you, you may benefit from reading _Annualized Income Installment Method_ in chapter 2 of Pub. 505 for information on how to avoid a penalty.

Underpayment penalty. Under the regular installment method, if your estimated tax payment for any period is less than one-fourth of your estimated tax, you may be charged a penalty for underpayment of estimated tax for that period when you file your tax return. Under the annualized income installment method, your estimated tax payments vary with your income, but the

amount required must be paid each period. See chapter 4 of Pub. 505 for more information.

Change in estimated tax. After you make an estimated tax payment, changes in your income, adjustments, deductions, or credits may make it necessary for you to refigure your estimated tax. Pay the unpaid balance of your amended estimated tax by the next payment due date after the change or in installments by that date and the due dates for the remaining payment periods.

Estimated Tax Payments Not Required

You don't have to pay estimated tax if your withholding in each payment period is at least as much as:

- One-fourth of your required annual payment, or
- Your required annualized income installment for that period.

You also don't have to pay estimated tax if you will pay enough through withholding to keep the amount you owe with your return under $1,000.

How To Pay Estimated Tax

There are several ways to pay estimated tax.

- Credit an overpayment on your 2018 return to your 2019 estimated tax.
- Pay by direct transfer from your bank account, or pay by debit or credit card using a pay-by-phone system or the Internet.
- Send in your payment (check or money order) with a payment voucher from Form 1040-ES.

Credit an Overpayment

If you show an overpayment of tax after completing your Form 1040 for 2018, you can apply part or all of it to your estimated tax for 2019. On line 21 of Form 1040 enter the amount you want credited to your estimated tax rather than refunded. Take the amount you have credited into account when figuring your estimated tax payments.

You can't have any of the amount you credited to your estimated tax refunded to you until you file your tax return for the following year. You also can't use that overpayment in any other way.

Pay Online

The IRS offers an electronic payment option that is right for you. Paying online is convenient, secure, and helps make sure we get your payments on time. To pay your taxes online or for more information, go to _IRS.gov/Payments_. You can pay using any of the following methods.

- **IRS Direct Pay** for online transfers directly from your checking or savings account at no cost to you, go to _IRS.gov/Payments_.
- **Pay by Card.** To pay by debit or credit card, go to _IRS.gov/Payments_. A convenience fee is charged by these service providers.

- **Electronic Funds Withdrawal** (EFW) is an integrated _e-file/_e-pay option offered only when filing your federal taxes electronically using tax preparation software, through a tax professional, or the IRS at _IRS.gov/Payments_.
- **Online Payment Agreement.** If you can't pay in full by the due date of your tax return, you can apply for an online monthly installment agreement at _IRS.gov/ Payments_. Once you complete the online process, you will receive immediate notification of whether your agreement has been approved. A user fee is charged.
- **IRS2GO** is the mobile application of the IRS. You can access Direct Pay or Pay By Card by downloading the application.

Pay by Phone

Paying by phone is another safe and secure method of paying electronically. Use one of the following methods: (**1**) call one of the debit or credit card providers, or (**2**) use the Electronic Federal Tax Payment System (EFTPS).

Debit or credit card. Call one of our service providers. Each charges a fee that varies by provider, card type, and payment amount.

> Link2Gov Corporation
> 1-888-PAY-1040™ (1-888-729-1040)
> _www.PAY1040.com_
>
> WorldPay US, Inc.
> 1-844-PAY-TAX-8™ (1-844-729-8298)
> _www.payUSAtax.com_
>
> Official Payments Corporation
> 1-888-UPAY-TAX™ (1-888-872-9829)
> _www.officialpayments.com_

EFTPS. To use EFTPS, you must be enrolled either online or have an enrollment form mailed to you. To make a payment using EFTPS, call 1-800-555-4477 (English) or 1-800-244-4829 (Español). People who are deaf, hard of hearing, or have a speech disability and who have access to TTY/TDD equipment can call 1-800-733-4829. For more information about EFTPS, go to _IRS.gov/Payments_ or _www.EFTPS.gov_.

Pay by Mobile Device

To pay through your mobile device, download the IRS2Go application.

Pay by Cash

Cash is an in-person payment option for individuals provided through retail partners with a maximum of $1,000 per day per transaction. To make a cash payment, you must first be registered online at _www.officialpayments.com_, our Official Payment provider.

Pay by Check or Money Order Using the Estimated Tax Payment Voucher

Before submitting a payment through the mail using the estimated tax payment voucher, please consider alternative methods. One of our safe, quick, and easy electronic payment options might be right for you.

If you choose to mail in your payment, each payment of estimated tax by check or money order must be accompanied by a payment voucher from Form 1040-ES.

During 2018, if you:

• made at least one estimated tax payment but not by electronic means,

• didn't use software or a paid preparer to prepare or file your return,

then you should receive a copy of the 2019 Form 1040-ES/V.

The enclosed payment vouchers will be preprinted with your name, address, and social security number. Using the preprinted vouchers will speed processing, reduce the chance of error, and help save processing costs.

Use the window envelopes that came with your Form 1040-ES package. If you use your own envelopes, make sure you mail your payment vouchers to the address shown in the Form 1040-ES instructions for the place where you live.

No checks of $100 million or more accepted. The IRS can't accept a single check (including a cashier's check) for amounts of $100,000,000 ($100 million) or more. If you are sending $100 million or more by check, you'll need to spread the payment over two or more checks with each check made out for an amount less than $100 million. This limit does not apply to other methods of payment (such as electronic payments). Please consider a method of payment other than check if the amount of the payment is over $100 million.

Note. These criteria can change without notice. If you don't receive a Form 1040-ES/V package and you are required to make an estimated tax payment, you should go to *IRS.gov/Form1040ES* and print a copy of Form 1040-ES which includes four blank payment vouchers. Complete one of these and make your payment timely to avoid penalties for paying late.

 Don't use the address shown in the Form 1040 instructions for your estimated tax payments.

If you didn't pay estimated tax last year, you can order Form 1040-ES from the IRS (see the inside back cover of this publication) or download it from IRS.gov. Follow the instructions to make sure you use the vouchers correctly.

Joint estimated tax payments. If you file a joint return and are making joint estimated tax payments, enter the names and social security numbers on the payment voucher in the same order as they will appear on the joint return.

Change of address. You must notify the IRS if you are making estimated tax payments and you changed your address during the year. Complete Form 8822, Change of Address, and

mail it to the address shown in the instructions for that form.

Credit for Withholding and Estimated Tax for 2018

When you file your 2018 income tax return, take credit for all the income tax and excess social security or railroad retirement tax withheld from your salary, wages, pensions, etc. Also take credit for the estimated tax you paid for 2018. These credits are subtracted from your total tax. Because these credits are refundable, you should file a return and claim these credits, even if you don't owe tax.

Two or more employers. If you had two or more employers in 2018 and were paid wages of more than $128,400, too much social security or tier 1 railroad retirement tax may have been withheld from your pay. You may be able to claim the excess as a credit against your income tax when you file your return. See *Credit for Excess Social Security Tax or Railroad Retirement Tax Withheld* in chapter 37.

Withholding

If you had income tax withheld during 2018, you should be sent a statement by January 31, 2019, showing your income and the tax withheld. Depending on the source of your income, you should receive:

• Form W-2, Wage and Tax Statement;

• Form W-2G, Certain Gambling Winnings; or

• A form in the 1099 series.

Forms W-2 and W-2G. If you file a paper return, always file Form W-2 with your income tax return. File Form W-2G with your return only if it shows any federal income tax withheld from your winnings.

You should get at least two copies of each form. If you file a paper return, attach one copy to the front of your federal income tax return. Keep one copy for your records. You also should receive copies to file with your state and local returns.

Form W-2

Your employer is required to provide or send Form W-2 to you no later than January 31, 2019. You should receive a separate Form W-2 from each employer you worked for.

If you stopped working before the end of 2018, your employer could have given you your Form W-2 at any time after you stopped working. However, your employer must provide or send it to you by January 31, 2019.

If you ask for the form, your employer must send it to you within 30 days after receiving your written request or within 30 days after your final wage payment, whichever is later.

If you haven't received your Form W-2 by January 31, you should ask your employer for it. If you don't receive it by early February, call the IRS.

Form W-2 shows your total pay and other compensation and the income tax, social security tax, and Medicare tax that was withheld during the year. Include the federal income tax withheld (as shown in box 2 of Form W-2) on line 16 of Form 1040.

In addition, Form W-2 is used to report any taxable sick pay you received and any income tax withheld from your sick pay.

Form W-2G

If you had gambling winnings in 2018, the payer may have withheld income tax. If tax was withheld, the payer will give you a Form W-2G showing the amount you won and the amount of tax withheld.

Report the amounts you won on Schedule 1 (Form 1040). Take credit for the tax withheld on line 16 of Form 1040.

The 1099 Series

Most forms in the 1099 series aren't filed with your return. These forms should be furnished to you by January 31, 2019 (or, for Forms 1099-B, 1099-S, and certain Forms 1099-MISC, by February 15, 2019). Unless instructed to file any of these forms with your return, keep them for your records. There are several different forms in this series, including:

• Form 1099-B, Proceeds From Broker and Barter Exchange Transactions;

• Form 1099-DIV, Dividends and Distributions;

• Form 1099-G, Certain Government Payments;

• Form 1099-INT, Interest Income;

• Form 1099-K, Payment Card and Third Party Network Transactions;

• Form 1099-MISC, Miscellaneous Income;

• Form 1099-OID, Original Issue Discount;

• Form 1099-PATR, Taxable Distributions Received From Cooperatives;

• Form 1099-Q, Payments From Qualified Education Programs;

• Form 1099-R, Distributions From Pensions, Annuities, Retirement or Profit-Sharing Plans, IRAs, Insurance Contracts, etc.;

• Form 1099-S, Proceeds From Real Estate Transactions;

• Form RRB-1099, Payments by the Railroad Retirement Board.

Form 1099-R. Attach Form 1099-R to your paper return if box 4 shows federal income tax withheld. Include the amount withheld in the total on line 16 of Form 1040.

Backup withholding. If you were subject to backup withholding on income you received during 2018, include the amount withheld, as shown on your Form 1099, in the total on line 16 of Form 1040.

Form Not Correct

If you receive a form with incorrect information on it, you should ask the payer for a corrected form. Call the telephone number or write to the address given for the payer on the form. The corrected Form W-2G or Form 1099 you receive will have an "X" in the "CORRECTED" box at the top of the form. A special form, Form W-2c, Corrected Wage and Tax Statement, is used to correct a Form W-2.

In certain situations, you will receive two forms in place of the original incorrect form. This will happen when your taxpayer identification number is wrong or missing, your name and address are wrong, or you received the wrong type of form (for example, a Form 1099-DIV instead of a Form 1099-INT). One new form you receive will be the same incorrect form or have the same incorrect information, but all money amounts will be zero. This form will have an "X" in the "CORRECTED" box at the top of the form. The second new form should have all the correct information, prepared as though it is the original (the "CORRECTED" box won't be checked).

Form Received After Filing

If you file your return and you later receive a form for income that you didn't include on your return, you should report the income and take credit for any income tax withheld by filing Form 1040X, Amended U.S. Individual Income Tax Return.

Separate Returns

If you are married but file a separate return, you can take credit only for the tax withheld from your own income. Don't include any amount withheld from your spouse's income. However, different rules may apply if you live in a community property state.

Community property states are listed in chapter 2. For more information on these rules, and some exceptions, see Pub. 555, Community Property.

Fiscal Years (FYs)

If you file your tax return on the basis of a fiscal year (a 12-month period ending on the last day of any month except December), you must follow special rules to determine your credit for federal income tax withholding. For a discussion of how to take credit for withholding on a fiscal year return, see *Fiscal Years (FYs)* in chapter 3 of Pub. 505.

Estimated Tax

Take credit for all your estimated tax payments for 2018 on Schedule 5 (Form 1040), line 66. Include any overpayment from 2017 that you had credited to your 2018 estimated tax.

Name changed. If you changed your name, and you made estimated tax payments using your old name, attach a brief statement to the front of your paper tax return indicating:

- When you made the payments,
- The amount of each payment,
- Your name when you made the payments, and
- Your social security number.

The statement should cover payments you made jointly with your spouse as well as any you made separately.

Be sure to report the change to the Social Security Administration. This prevents delays in processing your return and issuing any refunds.

Separate Returns

If you and your spouse made separate estimated tax payments for 2018 and you file separate returns, you can take credit only for your own payments.

If you made joint estimated tax payments, you must decide how to divide the payments between your returns. One of you can claim all of the estimated tax paid and the other none, or you can divide it in any other way you agree on. If you can't agree, you must divide the payments in proportion to each spouse's individual tax as shown on your separate returns for 2018.

Divorced Taxpayers

If you made joint estimated tax payments for 2018, and you were divorced during the year, either you or your former spouse can claim all of the joint payments, or you each can claim part of them. If you can't agree on how to divide the payments, you must divide them in proportion to each spouse's individual tax as shown on your separate returns for 2018.

If you claim any of the joint payments on your tax return, enter your former spouse's social security number (SSN) in the space provided on the front of Form 1040. If you divorced and remarried in 2018, enter your present spouse's SSN in that space. Enter your former spouse's SSN followed by "DIV" on the dotted line next to Schedule 5 (Form 1040), line 66.

Underpayment Penalty for 2018

If you didn't pay enough tax, either through withholding or by making timely estimated tax payments, you will have an underpayment of estimated tax and you may have to pay a penalty.

Generally, you won't have to pay a penalty for 2018 if any of the following apply.

- The total of your withholding and estimated tax payments was at least as much as your 2017 tax (or 110% of your 2017 tax if your AGI was more than $150,000, $75,000 if your 2018 filing status is married filing separately) and you paid all required estimated tax payments on time;
- The tax balance due on your 2018 return is no more than 10% of your total 2018 tax, and you paid all required estimated tax payments on time;
- Your total 2018 tax minus your withholding and refundable credits is less than $1,000;
- You didn't have a tax liability for 2017 and your 2017 tax year was 12 months; or
- You didn't have any withholding taxes and your current year tax less any household employment taxes is less than $1,000.

See Pub. 505, chapter 4, for a definition of "total tax" for 2017 and 2018.

Farmers and fishermen. Special rules apply if you are a farmer or fisherman. See *Farmers and Fishermen* in chapter 4 of Pub. 505 for more information.

Waiver of underpayment penalty due to tax reform. The December 22, 2017, enactment of Public Law 115-97, commonly referred to as the "Tax Cuts and Jobs Act" included a broad array of tax changes affecting millions of individual taxpayers. Some taxpayers may have been unable to accurately calculate the amount of their required estimated income tax payments for 2018 and would be liable for a penalty. Therefore, the IRS is providing relief to these taxpayers by waiving the estimated tax penalty in certain circumstances. To qualify for the waiver, the total of your withholding and estimated tax payments made on or before January 15, 2019, must be at least 85% of the tax shown on your 2018 return. See Form 2210 and its instructions for more information on how to determine your eligibility for the waiver and how to request it.

IRS can figure the penalty for you. If you think you owe the penalty but you don't want to figure it yourself when you file your tax return, you may not have to. Generally, the IRS will figure the penalty for you and send you a bill. However, if you think you are able to lower or eliminate your penalty, you must complete Form 2210 or Form 2210-F and attach it to your paper return. See chapter 4 of Pub. 505 for more information.

Part Two.

Income

The eight chapters in this part discuss many kinds of income. They explain which income is and isn't taxed. See Part Three for information on gains and losses you report on the sale or disposition of property.

The new Form 1040 schedules that are discussed in these chapters are:

- *Schedule 1, Additional Income and Adjustments to Income.*
- *Schedule 4, Other Taxes.*
- *Schedule 5, Other Payments and Refundable Credits.*

5.

Wages, Salaries, and Other Earnings

What's New

At the time this publication went to print, Congress was considering legislation that would do the following.

1. *Provide additional tax relief for those affected by certain 2018 disasters.*

2. *Extend certain tax benefits that expired at the end of 2017 and that currently can't be claimed on your 2018 tax return.*

3. *Change certain other tax provisions.*

To learn whether this legislation was enacted, resulting in changes that affect your 2018 tax return, go to Recent Developments at IRS.gov/ Pub17.

Suspension of qualified bicycle commuting reimbursement exclusion. Beginning in 2018, reimbursement you receive from your employer for the purchase, repair, or storage of a bicycle you regularly use for travel between your residence and place of employment must be included in your gross income.

Deferred compensation contribution limit increased. If you participate in a 401(k) plan, 403(b) plan, or the federal government's Thrift Savings Plan, the total annual amount you can contribute is increased to $18,500. This also applies to most 457 plans.

Reminder

Foreign income. If you're a U.S. citizen or resident alien, you must report income from sources outside the United States (foreign income) on your tax return unless it's exempt by U.S. law. This is true whether you reside inside or outside the United States and whether or not you receive a Form W-2, Wage and Tax Statement, or Form 1099 from the foreign payer. This applies to earned income (such as wages and tips) as well as unearned income (such as interest, dividends, capital gains, pensions, rents, and royalties).

If you reside outside the United States, you may be able to exclude part or all of your foreign source earned income. For details, see Pub. 54, Tax Guide for U.S. Citizens and Resident Aliens Abroad.

Introduction

This chapter discusses compensation received for services as an employee, such as wages, salaries, and fringe benefits. The following topics are included.

- Bonuses and awards.
- Special rules for certain employees.
- Sickness and injury benefits.

The chapter explains what income is included and isn't included in the employee's gross income and what's not included.

Useful Items

You may want to see:

Publication

- ❑ **463** Travel, Gift, and Car Expenses
- ❑ **525** Taxable and Nontaxable Income
- ❑ **554** Tax Guide for Seniors
- ❑ **926** Household Employer's Tax Guide
- ❑ **3920** Tax Relief for Victims of Terrorist Attacks

For these and other useful items, go to IRS.gov/ Forms.

Employee Compensation

This section discusses various types of employee compensation, including fringe benefits, retirement plan contributions, stock options, and restricted property.

Form W-2. If you're an employee, you should receive a Form W-2 from your employer showing the pay you received for your services. Include your pay on line 1 of Form 1040, even if you don't receive a Form W-2.

In some instances, your employer isn't required to give you a Form W-2. Your employer isn't required to give you a Form W-2 if you perform household work in your employer's home for less than $2,100 in cash wages during the calendar year and you have no federal income taxes withheld from your wages. Household work is work done in or around an employer's home. Some examples of workers who do household work are:

- Babysitters,
- Caretakers,
- House cleaning workers,
- Domestic workers,
- Drivers,
- Health aides,
- Housekeepers,
- Maids,
- Nannies,
- Private nurses, and
- Yard workers.

See Schedule H (Form 1040), Household Employment Taxes, and its instructions, and Pub. 926 for more information.

If you performed services, other than as an independent contractor, and your employer didn't withhold social security and Medicare taxes from your pay, you must file Form 8919, Uncollected Social Security and Medicare Tax on Wages, with your Form 1040. See Form 8919 and its instructions for more information on how to figure unreported wages and taxes and how to include them on your income tax return.

Childcare providers. If you provide childcare, either in the child's home or in your home or other place of business, the pay you receive must be included in your income. If you aren't an employee, you're probably self-employed and must include payments for your services on Schedule C (Form 1040), Profit or Loss From Business, or Schedule C-EZ (Form 1040), Net Profit From Business. You generally aren't an employee unless you're subject to the will and control of the person who employs you as to what you're to do and how you're to do it.

Babysitting. If you're paid to babysit, even for relatives or neighborhood children, whether on a regular basis or only periodically, the rules for childcare providers apply to you.

Employment tax. Whether you're an employee or self-employed person, your income could be subject to self-employment tax. See the instructions for Schedules C and SE (Form 1040) if you're self-employed. Also see Pub. 926 for more information.

Miscellaneous Compensation

This section discusses different types of employee compensation.

Advance commissions and other earnings. If you receive advance commissions or other amounts for services to be performed in the future and you're a cash-method taxpayer, you must include these amounts in your income in the year you receive them.

If you repay unearned commissions or other amounts in the same year you receive them, reduce the amount included in your income by the repayment. If you repay them in a later tax year, you can deduct the repayment as an itemized deduction on your Schedule A (Form 1040), line 16, or you may be able to take a credit for that year. See *Repayments* in chapter 12.

Allowances and reimbursements. If you receive travel, transportation, or other business expense allowances or reimbursements from your employer, see Pub. 463. If you're reimbursed for moving expenses, see Pub. 521, Moving Expenses.

Back pay awards. If you receive an amount in payment of a settlement or judgment for back pay, you must include the amount of the payment in your income. This includes payments made to you for damages, unpaid life insurance premiums, and unpaid health insurance premiums. They should be reported to you by your employer on Form W-2.

Bonuses and awards. If you receive a bonus or award (cash, goods, services) from your employer, you must include its value in your income. However, if your employer merely promises to pay you a bonus or award at some future time, it isn't taxable until you receive it or it's made available to you.

Employee achievement award. If you receive tangible personal property (other than cash, a gift certificate, or an equivalent item) as an award for length of service or safety achievement, you generally can exclude its value from your income. The amount you can exclude is limited to your employer's cost and can't be more than $1,600 for qualified plan awards or $400 for nonqualified plan awards for all such awards you receive during the year. Your employer can tell you whether your award is a qualified plan award. Your employer must make the award as part of a meaningful presentation, under conditions and circumstances that don't create a significant likelihood of it being disguised pay.

However, the exclusion doesn't apply to the following awards.

- A length-of-service award if you received it for less than 5 years of service or if you received another length-of-service award during the year or the previous 4 years.

- A safety achievement award if you're a manager, administrator, clerical employee, or other professional employee or if more than 10% of eligible employees previously received safety achievement awards during the year.

Example. Ben Green received three employee achievement awards during the year: a nonqualified plan award of a watch valued at $250, two qualified plan awards of a stereo valued at $1,000, and a set of golf clubs valued at $500. Assuming that the requirements for qualified plan awards are otherwise satisfied, each award by itself would be excluded from income. However, because the $1,750 total value of the awards is more than $1,600, Ben must include $150 ($1,750 – $1,600) in his income.

Differential wage payments. This is any payment made to you by an employer for any period during which you're, for a period of more than 30 days, an active duty member of the uniformed services and represents all or a portion of the wages you would have received from the employer during that period. These payments are treated as wages and are subject to income tax withholding, but not FICA or FUTA taxes. The payments are reported as wages on Form W-2.

Government cost-of-living allowances. Most payments received by U.S. Government civilian employees for working abroad are taxable. However, certain cost-of-living allowances are tax free. Pub. 516, U.S. Government Civilian Employees Stationed Abroad, explains the tax treatment of allowances, differentials, and other special pay you receive for employment abroad.

Nonqualified deferred compensation plans. Your employer may report to you the total amount of deferrals for the year under a nonqualified deferred compensation plan on Form W-2, box 12, using code Y. This amount isn't included in your income.

However, if at any time during the tax year, the plan fails to meet certain requirements, or isn't operated under those requirements, all amounts deferred under the plan for the tax year and all preceding tax years to the extent vested and not previously included in income are included in your income for the current year. This amount is included in your wages shown on Form W-2, box 1. It's also shown on Form W-2, box 12, using code Z.

Note received for services. If your employer gives you a secured note as payment for your services, you must include the fair market value (usually the discount value) of the note in your income for the year you receive it. When you later receive payments on the note, a proportionate part of each payment is the recovery of the fair market value that you previously included in your income. Don't include that part again in your income. Include the rest of the payment in your income in the year of payment.

If your employer gives you a nonnegotiable unsecured note as payment for your services, payments on the note that are credited toward the principal amount of the note are compensation income when you receive them.

Severance pay. If you receive a severance payment when your employment with your employer ends or is terminated, you must include this amount in your income.

Accrued leave payment. If you're a federal employee and receive a lump-sum payment for accrued annual leave when you retire or resign, this amount will be included as wages on your Form W-2.

If you resign from one agency and are reemployed by another agency, you may have to repay part of your lump-sum annual leave payment to the second agency. You can reduce gross wages by the amount you repaid in the same tax year in which you received it. Attach to your tax return a copy of the receipt or statement given to you by the agency you repaid to explain the difference between the wages on the return and the wages on your Forms W-2.

Outplacement services. If you choose to accept a reduced amount of severance pay so that you can receive outplacement services (such as training in résumé writing and interview techniques), you must include the unreduced amount of the severance pay in income.

Sick pay. Pay you receive from your employer while you're sick or injured is part of your salary or wages. In addition, you must include in your income sick pay benefits received from any of the following payers.

- A welfare fund.

- A state sickness or disability fund.

- An association of employers or employees.

- An insurance company, if your employer paid for the plan.

However, if you paid the premiums on an accident or health insurance policy yourself, the benefits you receive under the policy aren't taxable. For more information, see Pub. 525.

Social security and Medicare taxes paid by employer. If you and your employer have an agreement that your employer pays your social security and Medicare taxes without deducting them from your gross wages, you must report the amount of tax paid for you as taxable wages on your tax return. The payment also is treated as wages for figuring your social security and Medicare taxes and your social security and Medicare benefits. However, these payments aren't treated as social security and Medicare wages if you're a household worker or a farm worker.

Stock appreciation rights. Don't include a stock appreciation right granted by your employer in income until you exercise (use) the right. When you use the right, you're entitled to a cash payment equal to the fair market value of the corporation's stock on the date of use minus the fair market value on the date the right was granted. You include the cash payment in your income in the year you use the right.

Fringe Benefits

Fringe benefits received in connection with the performance of your services are included in your income as compensation unless you pay fair market value for them or they're specifically excluded by law. Refraining from the performance of services (for example, under a covenant not to compete) is treated as the performance of services for purposes of these rules.

Accounting period. You must use the same accounting period your employer uses to report your taxable noncash fringe benefits. Your employer has the option to report taxable noncash fringe benefits by using either of the following rules.

- The general rule: benefits are reported for a full calendar year (January 1–December 31).
- The special accounting period rule: benefits provided during the last 2 months of the calendar year (or any shorter period) are treated as paid during the following calendar year. For example, each year your employer reports the value of benefits provided during the last 2 months of the prior year and the first 10 months of the current year.

Your employer doesn't have to use the same accounting period for each fringe benefit, but must use the same period for all employees who receive a particular benefit.

You must use the same accounting period that you use to report the benefit to claim an employee business deduction (for use of a car, for example).

Form W-2. Your employer must include all taxable fringe benefits in box 1 of Form W-2 as wages, tips, and other compensation and, if applicable, in boxes 3 and 5 as social security and Medicare wages. Although not required, your employer may include the total value of fringe benefits in box 14 (or on a separate statement). However, if your employer provided you with a vehicle and included 100% of its annual lease value in your income, the employer must separately report this value to you in box 14 (or on a separate statement).

Accident or Health Plan

In most cases, the value of accident or health plan coverage provided to you by your employer isn't included in your income. Benefits you receive from the plan may be taxable, as explained later under *Sickness and Injury Benefits*.

For information on the items covered in this section, other than long-term care coverage, see Pub. 969, Health Savings Accounts and Other Tax-Favored Health Plans.

Long-term care coverage. Contributions by your employer to provide coverage for long-term care services generally aren't included in your income. However, contributions made through a flexible spending or similar arrangement offered by your employer must be included in your income. This amount will be reported as wages in box 1 of your Form W-2.

Contributions you make to the plan are discussed in Pub. 502, Medical and Dental Expenses.

Archer MSA contributions. Contributions by your employer to your Archer MSA generally aren't included in your income. Their total will be reported in box 12 of Form W-2 with code R. You must report this amount on Form 8853, Archer MSAs and Long-Term Care Insurance Contracts. File the form with your return.

Health flexible spending arrangement (health FSA). If your employer provides a health FSA that qualifies as an accident or health plan, the amount of your salary reduction, and reimbursements of your medical care expenses, in most cases, aren't included in your income.

Note. Health FSAs are subject to a limit on salary reduction contributions for plan years beginning after 2012. For tax year 2018, the dollar limitation (as indexed for inflation) on voluntary employee salary reductions for contributions to health FSAs is $2,650.

Health reimbursement arrangement (HRA). If your employer provides an HRA that qualifies as an accident or health plan, coverage and reimbursements of your medical care expenses generally aren't included in your income.

Health savings account (HSA). If you're an eligible individual, you and any other person, including your employer or a family member, can make contributions to your HSA. Contributions, other than employer contributions, are deductible on your return whether or not you itemize deductions. Contributions made by your employer aren't included in your income. Distributions from your HSA that are used to pay qualified medical expenses aren't included in your income. Distributions not used for qualified medical expenses are included in your income. See Pub. 969 for the requirements of an HSA.

Contributions by a partnership to a bona fide partner's HSA aren't contributions by an employer. The contributions are treated as a distribution of money and aren't included in the partner's gross income. Contributions by a partnership to a partner's HSA for services rendered are treated as guaranteed payments that are includible in the partner's gross income. In both situations, the partner can deduct the contribution made to the partner's HSA.

Contributions by an S corporation to a 2% shareholder-employee's HSA for services rendered are treated as guaranteed payments and are includible in the shareholder-employee's gross income. The shareholder-employee can deduct the contribution made to the shareholder-employee's HSA.

Qualified HSA funding distribution. You can make a one-time distribution from your individual retirement account (IRA) to an HSA and you generally won't include any of the distribution in your income.

Adoption Assistance

You may be able to exclude from your income amounts paid or expenses incurred by your employer for qualified adoption expenses in connection with your adoption of an eligible child.

See the Instructions for Form 8839, Qualified Adoption Expenses, for more information.

Adoption benefits are reported by your employer in box 12 of Form W-2 with code T. They also are included as social security and Medicare wages in boxes 3 and 5. However, they aren't included as wages in box 1. To determine the taxable and nontaxable amounts, you must complete Part III of Form 8839. File the form with your return.

De Minimis (Minimal) Benefits

If your employer provides you with a product or service and the cost of it is so small that it would be unreasonable for the employer to account for it, you generally don't include its value in your income. In most cases, don't include in your income the value of discounts at company cafeterias, cab fares home when working overtime, and company picnics.

Holiday gifts. If your employer gives you a turkey, ham, or other item of nominal value at Christmas or other holidays, don't include the value of the gift in your income. However, if your employer gives you cash or a cash equivalent, you must include it in your income.

Educational Assistance

You can exclude from your income up to $5,250 of qualified employer-provided educational assistance. For more information, see Pub. 970, Tax Benefits for Education.

Group-Term Life Insurance

In most cases, the cost of up to $50,000 of group-term life insurance coverage provided to you by your employer (or former employer) isn't included in your income. However, you must include in income the cost of employer-provided insurance that is more than the cost of $50,000 of coverage reduced by any amount you pay toward the purchase of the insurance.

For exceptions, see *Entire cost excluded* and *Entire cost taxed*, later.

If your employer provided more than $50,000 of coverage, the amount included in your income is reported as part of your wages in box 1 of your Form W-2. Also, it's shown separately in box 12 with code C.

Group-term life insurance. This insurance is term life insurance protection (insurance for a fixed period of time) that:

- Provides a general death benefit,
- Is provided to a group of employees,
- Is provided under a policy carried by the employer, and
- Provides an amount of insurance to each employee based on a formula that prevents individual selection.

Permanent benefits. If your group-term life insurance policy includes permanent benefits, such as a paid-up or cash surrender value, you must include in your income, as wages, the cost of the permanent benefits minus the amount you pay for them. Your employer should be able to tell you the amount to include in your income.

Accidental death benefits. Insurance that provides accidental or other death benefits but doesn't provide general death benefits (travel insurance, for example) isn't group-term life insurance.

Former employer. If your former employer provided more than $50,000 of group-term life insurance coverage during the year, the amount included in your income is reported as wages in box 1 of Form W-2. Also, it's shown separately in box 12 with code C. Box 12 also will show the amount of uncollected social security and Medicare taxes on the excess coverage, with codes M and N. You must pay these taxes with your income tax return. Include them on Schedule 4 (Form 1040), line 62, and follow the instructions there.

Two or more employers. Your exclusion for employer-provided group-term life insurance coverage can't exceed the cost of $50,000 of coverage, whether the insurance is provided by a single employer or multiple employers. If two or more employers provide insurance coverage that totals more than $50,000, the amounts reported as wages on your Forms W-2 won't be correct. You must figure how much to include in your income. Reduce the amount you figure by any amount reported with code C in box 12 of your Forms W-2, add the result to the wages reported in box 1, and report the total on your return.

Figuring the taxable cost. Use Worksheet 5-1 to figure the amount to include in your income.

Worksheet 5-1. **Figuring the Cost of Group-Term Life Insurance To Include in Income**
Keep for Your Records

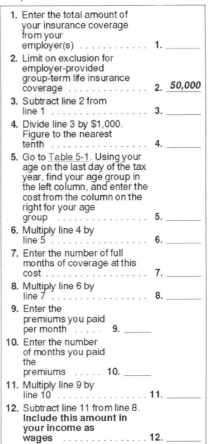

1. Enter the total amount of your insurance coverage from your employer(s)	1. ____
2. Limit on exclusion for employer-provided group-term life insurance coverage	2. _50,000_
3. Subtract line 2 from line 1	3. ____
4. Divide line 3 by $1,000. Figure to the nearest tenth	4. ____
5. Go to Table 5-1. Using your age on the last day of the tax year, find your age group in the left column, and enter the cost from the column on the right for your age group	5. ____
6. Multiply line 4 by line 5	6. ____
7. Enter the number of full months of coverage at this cost	7. ____
8. Multiply line 6 by line 7	8. ____
9. Enter the premiums you paid per month . . . . . 9. ____	
10. Enter the number of months you paid the premiums . . . . . 10. ____	
11. Multiply line 9 by line 10	11. ____
12. Subtract line 11 from line 8. **Include this amount in your income as wages**	12. ____

Table 5-1. **Cost of $1,000 of Group-Term Life Insurance for 1 Month**

Age	Cost
Under 25	$ 0.05
25 through 29	0.06
30 through 34	0.08
35 through 39	0.09
40 through 44	0.10
45 through 49	0.15
50 through 54	0.23
55 through 59	0.43
60 through 64	0.66
65 through 69	1.27
70 and above	2.06

Example. You are 51 years old and work for employers A and B. Both employers provide group-term life insurance coverage for you for the entire year. Your coverage is $35,000 with employer A and $45,000 with employer B. You pay premiums of $4.15 a month under the employer B group plan. You figure the amount to include in your income as shown in Worksheet 5-1. Figuring the Cost of Group-Term Life Insurance To Include in Income—Illustrated next.

Worksheet 5-1. **Figuring the Cost of Group-Term Life Insurance To Include in Income—Illustrated**
Keep for Your Records

1. Enter the total amount of your insurance coverage from your employer(s)	1. _80,000_
2. Limit on exclusion for employer-provided group-term life insurance coverage	2. _50,000_
3. Subtract line 2 from line 1	3. _30,000_
4. Divide line 3 by $1,000. Figure to the nearest tenth	4. _30.0_
5. Go to Table 5-1. Using your age on the last day of the tax year, find your age group in the left column, and enter the cost from the column on the right for your age group	5. _0.23_
6. Multiply line 4 by line 5	6. _6.90_
7. Enter the number of full months of coverage at this cost	7. _12_
8. Multiply line 6 by line 7	8. _82.80_
9. Enter the premiums you paid per month . . . . . 9. _4.15_	
10. Enter the number of months you paid the premiums . . . . . 10. _12_	
11. Multiply line 9 by line 10	11. _49.80_
12. Subtract line 11 from line 8. **Include this amount in your income as wages**	12. _33.00_

Entire cost excluded. You aren't taxed on the cost of group-term life insurance if any of the following circumstances apply.

1. You're permanently and totally disabled and have ended your employment.

2. Your employer is the beneficiary of the policy for the entire period the insurance is in force during the tax year.

3. A charitable organization (defined in chapter 25) to which contributions are deductible is the only beneficiary of the policy for the entire period the insurance is in force during the tax year. (You aren't entitled to a deduction for a charitable contribution for naming a charitable organization as the beneficiary of your policy.)

4. The plan existed on January 1, 1984, and:

   a. You retired before January 2, 1984, and were covered by the plan when you retired, or

   b. You reached age 55 before January 2, 1984, and were employed by the employer or its predecessor in 1983.

Entire cost taxed. You're taxed on the entire cost of group-term life insurance if either of the following circumstances apply.

- The insurance is provided by your employer through a qualified employees' trust, such as a pension trust or a qualified annuity plan.

- You're a key employee and your employer's plan discriminates in favor of key employees.

Retirement Planning Services

Generally, don't include the value of qualified retirement planning services provided to you and your spouse by your employer's qualified retirement plan. Qualified services include retirement planning advice, information about your employer's retirement plan, and information about how the plan may fit into your overall individual retirement income plan. You can't exclude the value of any tax preparation, accounting, legal, or brokerage services provided by your employer.

Transportation

If your employer provides you with a qualified transportation fringe benefit, it can be excluded from your income, up to certain limits. A qualified transportation fringe benefit is:

- Transportation in a commuter highway vehicle (such as a van) between your home and work place,

- A transit pass, or

- Qualified parking.

Cash reimbursement by your employer for these expenses under a bona fide reimbursement arrangement is also excludable. However, cash reimbursement for a transit pass is excludable only if a voucher or similar item that can be exchanged only for a transit pass isn't readily available for direct distribution to you.

Exclusion limit. The exclusion for commuter vehicle transportation and transit pass fringe benefits can't be more than $260 a month.

The exclusion for the qualified parking fringe benefit can't be more than $260 a month.

If the benefits have a value that is more than these limits, the excess must be included in your income.

Commuter highway vehicle. This is a highway vehicle that seats at least six adults (not including the driver). At least 80% of the vehicle's mileage must reasonably be expected to be:

- For transporting employees between their homes and workplace, and

- On trips during which employees occupy at least half of the vehicle's adult seating capacity (not including the driver).

Transit pass. This is any pass, token, farecard, voucher, or similar item entitling a person to ride mass transit (whether public or private) free or at a reduced rate or to ride in a commuter highway vehicle operated by a person in the business of transporting persons for compensation.

Qualified parking. This is parking provided to an employee at or near the employer's place of business. It also includes parking provided on or near a location from which the employee commutes to work by mass transit, in a commuter highway vehicle, or by carpool. It doesn't include parking at or near the employee's home.

Retirement Plan Contributions

Your employer's contributions to a qualified retirement plan for you aren't included in income at the time contributed. (Your employer can tell you whether your retirement plan is qualified.) However, the cost of life insurance coverage included in the plan may have to be included. See *Group-Term Life Insurance*, earlier, under *Fringe Benefits*.

If your employer pays into a nonqualified plan for you, you generally must include the contributions in your income as wages for the tax year in which the contributions are made. However, if your interest in the plan isn't transferable or is subject to a substantial risk of forfeiture (you have a good chance of losing it) at the time of the contribution, you don't have to include the value of your interest in your income until it's transferable or is no longer subject to a substantial risk of forfeiture.

 For information on distributions from retirement plans, see Pub. 575, Pension and Annuity Income (or Pub. 721, Tax Guide to U.S. Civil Service Retirement Benefits, if you're a federal employee or retiree).

Elective deferrals. If you're covered by certain kinds of retirement plans, you can choose to have part of your compensation contributed by your employer to a retirement fund, rather than have it paid to you. The amount you set aside (called an elective deferral) is treated as an employer contribution to a qualified plan. An elective deferral, other than a designated Roth contribution (discussed later), isn't included in wages subject to income tax at the time contributed. Rather, it's subject to income tax when distributed from the plan. However, it's included in wages subject to social security and Medicare taxes at the time contributed.

Elective deferrals include elective contributions to the following retirement plans.

1. Cash or deferred arrangements (section 401(k) plans).

2. The Thrift Savings Plan for federal employees.

3. Salary reduction simplified employee pension plans (SARSEP).

4. Savings incentive match plans for employees (SIMPLE plans).

5. Tax-sheltered annuity plans (section 403(b) plans).

6. Section 501(c)(18)(D) plans.

7. Section 457 plans.

Qualified automatic contribution arrangements. Under a qualified automatic contribution arrangement, your employer can treat you as having elected to have a part of your compensation contributed to a section 401(k) plan. You're to receive written notice of your rights and obligations under the qualified automatic contribution arrangement. The notice must explain:

- Your rights to elect not to have elective contributions made, or to have contributions made at a different percentage; and

- How contributions made will be invested in the absence of any investment decision by you.

You must be given a reasonable period of time after receipt of the notice and before the first elective contribution is made to make an election with respect to the contributions.

Overall limit on deferrals. For 2018, in most cases, you shouldn't have deferred more than a total of $18,500 of contributions to the plans listed in (1) through (3) and (5) above. The limit for SIMPLE plans is $12,500. The limit for section 501(c)(18)(D) plans is the lesser of $7,000 or 25% of your compensation. The limit for section 457 plans is the lesser of your includible compensation or $18,500. Amounts deferred under specific plan limits are part of the overall limit on deferrals.

Designated Roth contributions. Employers with section 401(k) and section 403(b) plans can create qualified Roth contribution programs so that you may elect to have part or all of your elective deferrals to the plan designated as after-tax Roth contributions. Designated Roth contributions are treated as elective deferrals, except that they're included in income at the time contributed.

Excess deferrals. Your employer or plan administrator should apply the proper annual limit when figuring your plan contributions. However, you're responsible for monitoring the total you defer to ensure that the deferrals aren't more than the overall limit.

If you set aside more than the limit, the excess generally must be included in your income for that year, unless you have an excess deferral of a designated Roth contribution. See Pub. 525 for a discussion of the tax treatment of excess deferrals.

Catch-up contributions. You may be allowed catch-up contributions (additional elective deferral) if you're age 50 or older by the end of the tax year.

Stock Options

If you receive a nonstatutory option to buy or sell stock or other property as payment for your services, you usually will have income when you receive the option, when you exercise the option (use it to buy or sell the stock or other property), or when you sell or otherwise dispose of the option. However, if your option is a statutory stock option, you won't have any income until you sell or exchange your stock. Your employer can tell you which kind of option you hold. For more information, see Pub. 525.

Restricted Property

In most cases, if you receive property for your services, you must include its fair market value in your income in the year you receive the property. However, if you receive stock or other property that has certain restrictions that affect its value, you don't include the value of the property in your income until it has substantially vested. (Although you can elect to include the value of the property in your income in the year it's transferred to you.) For more information, see *Restricted Property* in Pub. 525.

Dividends received on restricted stock. Dividends you receive on restricted stock are treated as compensation and not as dividend income. Your employer should include these payments on your Form W-2.

Stock you elected to include in income. Dividends you receive on restricted stock you elected to include in your income in the year transferred are treated the same as any other dividends. Report them on your return as dividends. For a discussion of dividends, see chapter 8.

For information on how to treat dividends reported on both your Form W-2 and Form 1099-DIV, see *Dividends received on restricted stock* in Pub. 525.

Special Rules for Certain Employees

This section deals with special rules for people in certain types of employment: members of the clergy, members of religious orders, people working for foreign employers, military personnel, and volunteers.

Clergy

Generally, if you're a member of the clergy, you must include in your income offerings and fees you receive for marriages, baptisms, funerals, masses, etc., in addition to your salary. If the offering is made to the religious institution, it isn't taxable to you.

If you're a member of a religious organization and you give your outside earnings to the religious organization, you still must include the earnings in your income. However, you may be entitled to a charitable contribution deduction for the amount paid to the organization. See chapter 25.

Pension. A pension or retirement pay for a member of the clergy usually is treated as any other pension or annuity. It must be reported on lines 4a and 4b of Form 1040.

Housing. Special rules for housing apply to members of the clergy. Under these rules, you don't include in your income the rental value of a home (including utilities) or a designated housing allowance provided to you as part of your pay. However, the exclusion can't be more than the reasonable pay for your services. If you pay for the utilities, you can exclude any allowance designated for utility cost, up to your actual cost. The home or allowance must be provided as compensation for your services as an ordained, licensed, or commissioned minister.

However, you must include the rental value of the home or the housing allowance as earnings from self-employment on Schedule SE (Form 1040) if you're subject to the self-employment tax. For more information, see Pub. 517, Social Security and Other Information for Members of the Clergy and Religious Workers.

Members of Religious Orders

If you're a member of a religious order who has taken a vow of poverty, how you treat earnings that you renounce and turn over to the order depends on whether your services are performed for the order.

Services performed for the order. If you're performing the services as an agent of the order in the exercise of duties required by the order, don't include in your income the amounts turned over to the order.

If your order directs you to perform services for another agency of the supervising church or an associated institution, you're considered to be performing the services as an agent of the order. Any wages you earn as an agent of an order that you turn over to the order aren't included in your income.

Example. You're a member of a church order and have taken a vow of poverty. You renounce any claims to your earnings and turn over to the order any salaries or wages you earn. You're a registered nurse, so your order assigns you to work in a hospital that is an associated institution of the church. However, you remain under the general direction and control of the order. You're considered to be an agent of the order and any wages you earn at the hospital that you turn over to your order aren't included in your income.

Services performed outside the order. If you're directed to work outside the order, your services aren't an exercise of duties required by the order unless they meet both of the following requirements.

- They're the kind of services that are ordinarily the duties of members of the order.

- They're part of the duties that you must exercise for, or on behalf of, the religious order as its agent.

If you're an employee of a third party, the services you perform for the third party won't be considered directed or required of you by the order. Amounts you receive for these services are included in your income, even if you have taken a vow of poverty.

Example. Mark Brown is a member of a religious order and has taken a vow of poverty. He renounces all claims to his earnings and turns over his earnings to the order.

Mark is a schoolteacher. He was instructed by the superiors of the order to get a job with a private tax-exempt school. Mark became an employee of the school, and, at his request, the school made the salary payments directly to the order.

Because Mark is an employee of the school, he is performing services for the school rather than as an agent of the order. The wages Mark earns working for the school are included in his income.

Foreign Employer

Special rules apply if you work for a foreign employer.

U.S. citizen. If you're a U.S. citizen who works in the United States for a foreign government, an international organization, a foreign embassy, or any foreign employer, you must include your salary in your income.

Social security and Medicare taxes. You're exempt from social security and Medicare employee taxes if you're employed in the United States by an international organization or a foreign government. However, you must pay self-employment tax on your earnings from services performed in the United States, even though you aren't self-employed. This rule also applies if you're an employee of a qualifying wholly owned instrumentality of a foreign government.

Employees of international organizations or foreign governments. Your compensation for official services to an international organization is exempt from federal income tax if you aren't a citizen of the United States or you're a citizen of the Philippines (whether or not you're a citizen of the United States).

Your compensation for official services to a foreign government is exempt from federal income tax if all of the following are true.

- You aren't a citizen of the United States or you're a citizen of the Philippines (whether or not you're a citizen of the United States).

- Your work is like the work done by employees of the United States in foreign countries.

- The foreign government gives an equal exemption to employees of the United States in its country.

Waiver of alien status. If you're an alien who works for a foreign government or international organization and you file a waiver under section 247(b) of the Immigration and Nationality Act to keep your immigrant status, different rules may apply. See *Foreign Employer* in Pub. 525.

Employment abroad. For information on the tax treatment of income earned abroad, see Pub. 54.

Military

Payments you receive as a member of a military service generally are taxed as wages except for retirement pay, which is taxed as a pension. Allowances generally aren't taxed. For more information on the tax treatment of military allowances and benefits, see Pub. 3, Armed Forces' Tax Guide.

Differential wage payments. Any payments made to you by an employer during the time you're performing service in the uniformed services are treated as compensation. These wages are subject to income tax withholding and are reported on a Form W-2. See the discussion under *Miscellaneous Compensation*, earlier.

Military retirement pay. If your retirement pay is based on age or length of service, it's taxable and must be included in your income as a pension on lines 4a and 4b of Form 1040. Don't include in your income the amount of any reduction in retirement or retainer pay to provide a survivor annuity for your spouse or children under the Retired Serviceman's Family Protection Plan or the Survivor Benefit Plan.

For more detailed discussion of survivor annuities, see chapter 10.

Disability. If you're retired on disability, see *Military and Government Disability Pensions* under *Sickness and Injury Benefits*, later.

Veterans' benefits. Don't include in your income any veterans' benefits paid under any law, regulation, or administrative practice administered by the Department of Veterans Affairs (VA). The following amounts paid to veterans or their families aren't taxable.

- Education, training, and subsistence allowances.

- Disability compensation and pension payments for disabilities paid either to veterans or their families.

- Grants for homes designed for wheelchair living.

- Grants for motor vehicles for veterans who lost their sight or the use of their limbs.

- Veterans' insurance proceeds and dividends paid either to veterans or their beneficiaries, including the proceeds of a veteran's endowment policy paid before death.

- Interest on insurance dividends you leave on deposit with the VA.

- Benefits under a dependent-care assistance program.

- The death gratuity paid to a survivor of a member of the Armed Forces who died after September 10, 2001.

- Payments made under the compensated work therapy program.

- Any bonus payment by a state or political subdivision because of service in a combat zone.

Volunteers

The tax treatment of amounts you receive as a volunteer worker for the Peace Corps or similar agency is covered in the following discussions.

Peace Corps. Living allowances you receive as a Peace Corps volunteer or volunteer leader for housing, utilities, household supplies, food, and clothing are generally exempt from tax.

Taxable allowances. The following allowances, however, must be included in your income and reported as wages.

- Allowances paid to your spouse and minor children while you're a volunteer leader training in the United States.

- Living allowances designated by the Director of the Peace Corps as basic compensation. These are allowances for personal items such as domestic help, laundry and clothing maintenance, entertainment and

recreation, transportation, and other miscellaneous expenses.

- Leave allowances.

- Readjustment allowances or termination payments. These are considered received by you when credited to your account.

Example. Gary Carpenter, a Peace Corps volunteer, gets $175 a month as a readjustment allowance during his period of service, to be paid to him in a lump sum at the end of his tour of duty. Although the allowance isn't available to him until the end of his service, Gary must include it in his income on a monthly basis as it's credited to his account.

Volunteers in Service to America (VISTA). If you're a VISTA volunteer, you must include meal and lodging allowances paid to you in your income as wages.

National Senior Services Corps programs. Don't include in your income amounts you receive for supportive services or reimbursements for out-of-pocket expenses from the following programs.

- Retired Senior Volunteer Program (RSVP).

- Foster Grandparent Program.

- Senior Companion Program.

Service Corps of Retired Executives (SCORE). If you receive amounts for supportive services or reimbursements for out-of-pocket expenses from SCORE, don't include these amounts in gross income.

Volunteer tax counseling. Don't include in your income any reimbursements you receive for transportation, meals, and other expenses you have in training for, or actually providing, volunteer federal income tax counseling for the elderly (TCE).

You can deduct as a charitable contribution your unreimbursed out-of-pocket expenses in taking part in the volunteer income tax assistance (VITA) program. See chapter 25.

Sickness and Injury Benefits

This section discusses sickness and injury benefits, including disability pensions, long-term care insurance contracts, workers' compensation, and other benefits.

In most cases, you must report as income any amount you receive for personal injury or sickness through an accident or health plan that is paid for by your employer. If both you and your employer pay for the plan, only the amount you receive that is due to your employer's payments is reported as income. However, certain payments may not be taxable to you. For information on nontaxable payments, see *Military and Government Disability Pensions* and *Other Sickness and Injury Benefits*, later in this discussion.

TIP *Don't report as income any amounts paid to reimburse you for medical expenses you incurred after the plan was established.*

Cost paid by you. If you pay the entire cost of a health or accident insurance plan, don't include any amounts you receive from the plan for personal injury or sickness as income on your tax return. If your plan reimbursed you for medical expenses you deducted in an earlier year, you may have to include some, or all, of the reimbursement in your income. See *Reimbursement in a later year* in chapter 22.

Cafeteria plans. In most cases, if you're covered by an accident or health insurance plan through a cafeteria plan, and the amount of the insurance premiums wasn't included in your income, you aren't considered to have paid the premiums and you must include any benefits you receive in your income. If the amount of the premiums was included in your income, you're considered to have paid the premiums, and any benefits you receive aren't taxable.

Disability Pensions

If you retired on disability, you must include in income any disability pension you receive under a plan that is paid for by your employer. You must report your taxable disability payments as wages on line 1 of Form 1040 until you reach minimum retirement age. Minimum retirement age generally is the age at which you can first receive a pension or annuity if you're not disabled.

 You may be entitled to a tax credit if you were permanently and totally disabled when you retired. For information on this credit and the definition of permanent and total disability, see chapter 32.

Beginning on the day after you reach minimum retirement age, payments you receive are taxable as a pension or annuity. Report the payments on lines 4a and 4b of Form 1040. The rules for reporting pensions are explained in *How To Report* in chapter 10.

For information on disability payments from a governmental program provided as a substitute for unemployment compensation, see chapter 12.

Retirement and profit-sharing plans. If you receive payments from a retirement or profit-sharing plan that doesn't provide for disability retirement, don't treat the payments as a disability pension. The payments must be reported as a pension or annuity. For more information on pensions, see chapter 10.

Accrued leave payment. If you retire on disability, any lump-sum payment you receive for accrued annual leave is a salary payment. The payment is not a disability payment. Include it in your income in the tax year you receive it.

Military and Government Disability Pensions

Certain military and government disability pensions aren't taxable.

Service-connected disability. You may be able to exclude from income amounts you receive as a pension, annuity, or similar allowance for personal injury or sickness resulting from active service in one of the following government services.

- The armed forces of any country.
- The National Oceanic and Atmospheric Administration.
- The Public Health Service.
- The Foreign Service.

Conditions for exclusion. Don't include the disability payments in your income if any of the following conditions apply.

1. You were entitled to receive a disability payment before September 25, 1975.

2. You were a member of a listed government service or its reserve component, or were under a binding written commitment to become a member, on September 24, 1975.

3. You receive the disability payments for a combat-related injury. This is a personal injury or sickness that:

    a. Results directly from armed conflict;

    b. Takes place while you're engaged in extra-hazardous service;

    c. Takes place under conditions simulating war, including training exercises such as maneuvers; or

    d. Is caused by an instrumentality of war.

4. You would be entitled to receive disability compensation from the Department of Veterans Affairs (VA) if you filed an application for it. Your exclusion under this condition is equal to the amount you would be entitled to receive from the VA.

Pension based on years of service. If you receive a disability pension based on years of service, in most cases you must include it in your income. However, if the pension qualifies for the exclusion for a service-connected disability (discussed earlier), don't include in income the part of your pension that you would have received if the pension had been based on a percentage of disability. You must include the rest of your pension in your income.

Retroactive VA determination. If you retire from the armed services based on years of service and are later given a retroactive service-connected disability rating by the VA, your retirement pay for the retroactive period is excluded from income up to the amount of VA disability benefits you would have been entitled to receive. You can claim a refund of any tax paid on the excludable amount (subject to the statute of limitations) by filing an amended return on Form 1040X for each previous year during the retroactive period. You must include with each Form 1040X a copy of the official VA Determination letter granting the retroactive benefit. The letter must show the amount withheld and the effective date of the benefit.

If you receive a lump-sum disability severance payment and are later awarded VA disability benefits, exclude 100% of the severance benefit from your income. However, you must include in your income any lump-sum readjustment or other nondisability severance payment you received on release from active duty, even

if you're later given a retroactive disability rating by the VA.

Special period of limitation. In most cases, under the period of limitation, a claim for credit or refund must be filed within 3 years from the time a return was filed or 2 years from the time the tax was paid. However, if you receive a retroactive service-connected disability rating determination, the period of limitation is extended by a 1-year period beginning on the date of the determination. This 1-year extended period applies to claims for credit or refund filed after June 17, 2008, and doesn't apply to any tax year that began more than 5 years before the date of the determination.

Terrorist attack or military action. Don't include in your income disability payments you receive for injuries incurred as a direct result of a terrorist attack directed against the United States (or its allies), whether outside or within the United States or from military action. See Pub. 3920 for more information.

Long-Term Care Insurance Contracts

Long-term care insurance contracts in most cases are treated as accident and health insurance contracts. Amounts you receive from them (other than policyholder dividends or premium refunds) in most cases are excludable from income as amounts received for personal injury or sickness. To claim an exclusion for payments made on a per diem or other periodic basis under a long-term care insurance contract, you must file Form 8853 with your return.

A long-term care insurance contract is an insurance contract that only provides coverage for qualified long-term care services. The contract must:

- Be guaranteed renewable;

- Not provide for a cash surrender value or other money that can be paid, assigned, pledged, or borrowed;

- Provide that refunds, other than refunds on the death of the insured or complete surrender or cancellation of the contract, and dividends under the contract, may only be used to reduce future premiums or increase future benefits; and

- In most cases, not pay or reimburse expenses incurred for services or items that would be reimbursed under Medicare, except where Medicare is a secondary payer or the contract makes per diem or other periodic payments without regard to expenses.

Qualified long-term care services. Qualified long-term care services are:

- Necessary diagnostic, preventive, therapeutic, curing, treating, mitigating, and rehabilitative services, and maintenance and personal care services; and

- Required by a chronically ill individual and provided pursuant to a plan of care prescribed by a licensed health care practitioner.

Chronically ill individual. A chronically ill individual is one who has been certified by a li-

censed health care practitioner within the previous 12 months as one of the following.

- An individual who, for at least 90 days, is unable to perform at least two activities of daily living without substantial assistance due to loss of functional capacity. Activities of daily living are eating, toileting, transferring, bathing, dressing, and continence.

- An individual who requires substantial supervision to be protected from threats to health and safety due to severe cognitive impairment.

Limit on exclusion. You generally can exclude from gross income up to $360 a day for 2018. See *Limit on exclusion*, under *Long-Term Care Insurance Contracts*, under *Other Sickness and Injury Benefits* in Pub. 525 for more information.

Workers' Compensation

Amounts you receive as workers' compensation for an occupational sickness or injury are fully exempt from tax if they're paid under a workers' compensation act or a statute in the nature of a workers' compensation act. The exemption also applies to your survivors. The exemption, however, doesn't apply to retirement plan benefits you receive based on your age, length of service, or prior contributions to the plan, even if you retired because of an occupational sickness or injury.

 If part of your workers' compensation reduces your social security or equivalent railroad retirement benefits received, that part is considered social security (or equivalent railroad retirement) benefits and may be taxable. For more information, see Pub. 915, Social Security and Equivalent Railroad Retirement Benefits.

Return to work. If you return to work after qualifying for workers' compensation, salary payments you receive for performing light duties are taxable as wages.

Other Sickness and Injury Benefits

In addition to disability pensions and annuities, you may receive other payments for sickness or injury.

Railroad sick pay. Payments you receive as sick pay under the Railroad Unemployment Insurance Act are taxable and you must include them in your income. However, don't include them in your income if they're for an on-the-job injury.

If you received income because of a disability, see *Disability Pensions*, earlier.

Federal Employees' Compensation Act (FECA). Payments received under this Act for personal injury or sickness, including payments to beneficiaries in case of death, aren't taxable. However, you're taxed on amounts you receive under this Act as continuation of pay for up to 45 days while a claim is being decided. Report this income as wages. Also, pay for sick leave while a claim is being processed is taxable and must be included in your income as wages.

If part of the payments you receive under FECA reduces your social security or equivalent railroad retirement benefits received, that part is considered social security (or equivalent railroad retirement) benefits and may be taxable. See Pub. 554 for more information.

Other compensation. Many other amounts you receive as compensation for sickness or injury aren't taxable. These include the following amounts.

- Compensatory damages you receive for physical injury or physical sickness, whether paid in a lump sum or in periodic payments.

- Benefits you receive under an accident or health insurance policy on which either you paid the premiums or your employer paid the premiums but you had to include them in your income.

- Disability benefits you receive for loss of income or earning capacity as a result of injuries under a no-fault car insurance policy.

- Compensation you receive for permanent loss or loss of use of a part or function of your body, or for your permanent disfigurement. This compensation must be based only on the injury and not on the period of your absence from work. These benefits aren't taxable even if your employer pays for the accident and health plan that provides these benefits.

Reimbursement for medical care. A reimbursement for medical care is generally not taxable. However, it may reduce your medical expense deduction. For more information, see chapter 22.

6.

Tip Income

What's New

At the time this publication went to print, Congress was considering legislation that would do the following.

1. *Provide additional tax relief for those affected by certain 2018 disasters.*

2. *Extend certain tax benefits that expired at the end of 2017 and that currently can't be claimed on your 2018 tax return.*

3. *Change certain other tax provisions.*

To learn whether this legislation was enacted, resulting in changes that affect your 2018 tax

return, go to Recent Developments at *IRS.gov/ Pub17.*

Introduction

This chapter is for employees who receive tips.

All tips you receive are income and are subject to federal income tax. You must include in gross income all tips you receive directly, charged tips paid to you by your employer, and your share of any tips you receive under a tip-splitting or tip-pooling arrangement.

The value of noncash tips, such as tickets, passes, or other items of value, also is income and subject to tax.

Reporting your tip income correctly isn't difficult. You must do three things.

1. Keep a daily tip record.

2. Report tips to your employer.

3. Report all your tips on your income tax return.

This chapter will explain these three things and show you what to do on your tax return if you haven't done the first two. This chapter also will show you how to treat allocated tips.

For information on special tip programs and agreements, see Pub. 531.

Useful Items

You may want to see:

Publication

❑ **531** Reporting Tip Income

❑ **1244** Employee's Daily Record of Tips and Report to Employer

Form (and Instructions)

❑ **4137** Social Security and Medicare Tax on Unreported Tip Income

❑ **4070** Employee's Report of Tips to Employer

For these and other useful items, go to *IRS.gov/ Forms.*

Keeping a Daily Tip Record

Why keep a daily tip record? You must keep a daily tip record so you can:

- Report your tips accurately to your employer,

- Report your tips accurately on your tax return, and

- Prove your tip income if your return is ever questioned.

How to keep a daily tip record. There are two ways to keep a daily tip record. You can either:

- Write information about your tips in a tip diary; or

- Keep copies of documents that show your tips, such as restaurant bills and credit or debit card charge slips.

You should keep your daily tip record with your tax or other personal records. You must keep

your records for as long as they're important for administration of the federal tax law. For information on how long to keep records, see *How Long To Keep Records* in chapter 1.

To help you keep a record or diary of your tips, you can use Form 4070A, Employee's Daily Record of Tips. To get Form 4070A, ask your employer for Pub. 1244, which includes a 1-year supply of Form 4070A or go online to *IRS.gov/Pub1244* for a copy of Pub. 1244. Each day, write in the information asked for on the form.

In addition to the information asked for on Form 4070A, you also need to keep a record of the date and value of any noncash tips you get, such as tickets, passes, or other items of value. Although you don't report these tips to your employer, you must report them on your tax return.

If you don't use Form 4070A, start your records by writing your name, your employer's name, and the name of the business (if it's different from your employer's name). Then, each workday, write the date and the following information.

- Cash tips you get directly from customers or from other employees.

- Tips from credit and debit card charge customers that your employer pays you.

- The value of any noncash tips you get, such as tickets, passes, or other items of value.

- The amount of tips you paid out to other employees through tip pools or tip splitting, or other arrangements, and the names of the employees to whom you paid the tips.

Electronic tip record. You can use an electronic system provided by your employer to record your daily tips. If you do, you must receive and keep a paper copy of this record.

Service charges. Don't write in your tip diary the amount of any service charge that your employer adds to a customer's bill and then pays to you and treats as wages. This is part of your wages, not a tip. See examples below.

Example 1. Good Food Restaurant adds an 18% charge to the bill for parties of six or more customers. Jane's bill for food and beverages for her party of eight includes an amount on the tip line equal to 18% of the charges for food and beverages, and the total includes this amount. Because Jane didn't have an unrestricted right to determine the amount on the "tip line," the 18% charge is considered a service charge. Don't include the 18% charge in your tip diary. Service charges that are paid to you are considered wages, not tips.

Example 2. Good Food Restaurant also includes sample calculations of tip amounts at the bottom of its bills for food and beverages provided to customers. David's bill includes a blank "tip line," with sample tip calculations of 15%, 18%, and 20% of his charges for food and beverages at the bottom of the bill beneath the signature line. Because David is free to enter any amount on the "tip line" or leave it blank, any amount he includes is considered a tip. Include this amount in your tip diary.

Reporting Tips to Your Employer

Why report tips to your employer? You must report tips to your employer so that:

- Your employer can withhold federal income tax and social security, Medicare, Additional Medicare, or railroad retirement taxes;

- Your employer can report the correct amount of your earnings to the Social Security Administration or Railroad Retirement Board (which affects your benefits when you retire or if you become disabled, or your family's benefits if you die); and

- You can avoid the penalty for not reporting tips to your employer (explained later).

What tips to report. Report to your employer only cash, check, and debit and credit card tips you receive.

If your total tips for any 1 month from any one job are less than $20, don't report the tips for that month to that employer.

If you participate in a tip-splitting or tip-pooling arrangement, report only the tips you receive and retain. Don't report to your employer any portion of the tips you receive that you pass on to other employees. However, you must report tips you receive from other employees.

Don't report the value of any noncash tips, such as tickets or passes, to your employer. You don't pay social security, Medicare, Additional Medicare, or railroad retirement taxes on these tips.

How to report. If your employer doesn't give you any other way to report tips, you can use Form 4070. Fill in the information asked for on the form, sign and date the form, and give it to your employer. To get a 1-year supply of the form, ask your employer for Pub. 1244 or go online to *IRS.gov/Pub1244* for a copy of Pub. 1244.

If you don't use Form 4070, give your employer a statement with the following information.

- Your name, address, and social security number.

- Your employer's name, address, and business name (if it's different from your employer's name).

- The month (or the dates of any shorter period) in which you received tips.

- The total tips required to be reported for that period.

You must sign and date the statement. Be sure to keep a copy with your tax or other personal records.

Your employer may require you to report your tips more than once a month. However, the statement can't cover a period of more than 1 calendar month.

Electronic tip statement. Your employer can have you furnish your tip statements electronically.

When to report. Give your report for each month to your employer by the 10th of the next month. If the 10th falls on a Saturday, Sunday, or legal holiday, give your employer the report by the next day that isn't a Saturday, Sunday, or legal holiday.

Example 1. You must report your tips received in October 2019 by November 12, 2019. November 10 is a Sunday and November 11 is a legal holiday (Veterans' Day). November 12 is the next day that is not a Saturday, Sunday, or legal holiday.

Example 2. You must report your tips received in September 2019 by October 10, 2019.

Final report. If your employment ends during the month, you can report your tips when your employment ends.

Penalty for not reporting tips. If you don't report tips to your employer as required, you may be subject to a penalty equal to 50% of the social security, Medicare, and Additional Medicare taxes or railroad retirement tax you owe on the unreported tips. For information about these taxes, see *Reporting social security, Medicare, Additional Medicare, or railroad retirement taxes on tips not reported to your employer* under *Reporting Tips on Your Tax Return,* later. The penalty amount is in addition to the taxes you owe.

You can avoid this penalty if you can show reasonable cause for not reporting the tips to your employer. To do so, attach a statement to your return explaining why you didn't report them.

Giving your employer money for taxes. Your regular pay may not be enough for your employer to withhold all the taxes you owe on your regular pay plus your reported tips. If this happens, you can give your employer money until the close of the calendar year to pay the rest of the taxes.

If you don't give your employer enough money, your employer will apply your regular pay and any money you give in the following order.

1. All taxes on your regular pay.

2. Social security, Medicare, and Additional Medicare taxes or railroad retirement taxes on your reported tips.

3. Federal, state, and local income taxes on your reported tips.

Any taxes that remain unpaid can be collected by your employer from your next paycheck. If withholding taxes remain uncollected at the end of the year, you may be subject to a penalty for underpayment of estimated taxes. See Pub. 505, Tax Withholding and Estimated Tax, for more information.

 Uncollected taxes. You must report on your tax return any social security and Medicare taxes or railroad retirement tax that remained uncollected at the end of 2018. These uncollected taxes will be shown on your 2018 Form W-2. See *Reporting uncollected social security, Medicare, or railroad retirement taxes on tips reported to your employer* under Reporting Tips on Your Tax Return, *later.*

 Your employer may participate in the Tip Rate Determination and Education Program, which was developed to help employees and employers understand and meet their tip reporting responsibilities. See Pub. 531, Reporting Tip Income, for more information.

Reporting Tips on Your Tax Return

How to report tips. Report your tips with your wages on Form 1040, line 1.

What tips to report. You must report all tips you received in 2018 on your tax return, including both cash tips and noncash tips. Any tips you reported to your employer for 2018 are included in the wages shown on your Form W-2, box 1. Add to the amount in box 1 only the tips you didn't report to your employer.

 If you received $20 or more in cash and charge tips in a month and didn't report all of those tips to your employer, see Reporting social security, Medicare, Additional Medicare, or railroad retirement taxes on tips not reported to your employer, *later.*

 If you didn't keep a daily tip record as required and an amount is shown on your Form W-2, box 8, see Allocated Tips, *later.*

If you kept a daily tip record and reported tips to your employer as required under the rules explained earlier, add the following tips to the amount on your Form W-2, box 1.

- Cash and charge tips you received that totaled less than $20 for any month.

- The value of noncash tips, such as tickets, passes, or other items of value.

Example. Ben Smith began working at the Blue Ocean Restaurant (his only employer in 2018) on June 30 and received $10,000 in wages during the year. Ben kept a daily tip record showing that his tips for June were $18 and his tips for the rest of the year totaled $7,000. He wasn't required to report his June tips to his employer, but he reported all of the rest of his tips to his employer as required.

Ben's Form W-2 from Blue Ocean Restaurant shows $17,000 ($10,000 wages plus $7,000 reported tips) in box 1. He adds the $18 unreported tips to that amount and reports $17,018 as wages on his tax return.

Reporting social security, Medicare, Additional Medicare, or railroad retirement taxes on tips not reported to your employer. If you received $20 or more in cash and charge tips in a month from any one job and didn't report all of those tips to your employer, you must report the social security, Medicare, and Additional Medicare taxes on the unreported tips as additional tax on your return. To report these taxes, you must file Form 1040, 1040NR, 1040-PR, or 1040-SS even if you wouldn't otherwise have to file.

Use Form 4137 to figure social security and Medicare taxes and/or Form 8959 to figure Additional Medicare Tax. Enter the taxes on your return as instructed, and attach the completed Form 4137 and/or Form 8959 to your return.

 If you're subject to the Railroad Retirement Tax Act, you can't use Form 4137 to pay railroad retirement tax on unreported tips. To get railroad retirement credit, you must report tips to your employer.

Reporting uncollected social security, Medicare, or railroad retirement taxes on tips reported to your employer. You may have uncollected taxes if your regular pay wasn't enough for your employer to withhold all the taxes you owe and you didn't give your employer enough money to pay the rest of the taxes. For more information, see *Giving your employer money for taxes* under *Reporting Tips to Your Employer,* earlier.

If your employer couldn't collect all the social security and Medicare taxes or railroad retirement tax you owe on tips reported for 2018, the uncollected taxes will be shown on your Form W-2, box 12 (codes A and B). You must report these amounts as additional tax on your return. Unlike the uncollected portion of the regular (1.45%) Medicare tax, the uncollected Additional Medicare Tax isn't reported on your Form W-2.

To report these uncollected taxes, you must file Form 1040, 1040NR, 1040-PR, or 1040-SS even if you wouldn't otherwise have to file. You must report these taxes on Schedule 4 (Form 1040), line 62, or the corresponding line of Form 1040NR, 1040-PR, or 1040-SS. See the instructions for these forms for exact reporting information.

Allocated Tips

If your employer allocated tips to you, they're shown separately on your Form W-2, box 8. They aren't included in box 1 with your wages and reported tips. If box 8 is blank, this discussion doesn't apply to you.

What are allocated tips? These are tips that your employer assigned to you in addition to the tips you reported to your employer for the year. Your employer will have done this only if:

- You worked in an establishment (restaurant, cocktail lounge, or similar business) that must allocate tips to employees; and

- The tips you reported to your employer were less than your share of 8% of food and drink sales.

No income, social security, Medicare, Additional Medicare, or railroad retirement taxes are withheld on allocated tips.

How were your allocated tips figured? The tips allocated to you are your share of an amount figured by subtracting the reported tips of all employees from 8% (or an approved lower rate) of food and drink sales (other than carryout sales and sales with a service charge of 10% or more). Your share of that amount was figured using either a method provided by an employer-employee agreement or a method provided by IRS regulations based on employees' sales or hours worked. For information about the exact allocation method used, ask your employer.

Must you report your allocated tips on your tax return? You must report all tips you received in 2018, including both cash tips and noncash tips, on your tax return. Any tips you reported to your employer for 2018 are included in the wages shown on your Form W-2, box 1. Add to the amount in box 1 only the tips you didn't report to your employer. This should include any allocated tips shown on your Form(s) W-2, box 8, unless you have adequate records to show that you received less tips in the year than the allocated figures.

See *What tips to report* under *Reporting Tips on Your Tax Return,* and *Keeping a Daily Tip Record,* earlier.

How to report allocated tips. Report the amounts shown on your Form(s) W-2, box 1 (wages and tips) and box 8 (allocated tips), as wages on Form 1040, line 1 or Form 1040NR-EZ, line 3.

Because social security, Medicare, and Additional Medicare taxes weren't withheld from the allocated tips, you must report those taxes as additional tax on your return. Complete Form 4137, and include the allocated tips on line 1 of the form. See *Reporting social security, Medicare, Additional Medicare, or railroad retirement taxes on tips not reported to your employer* under *Reporting Tips on Your Tax Return,* earlier.

7.

Interest Income

What's New

 At the time this publication went to print, Congress was considering legislation that would do the following.

1. *Provide additional tax relief for those affected by certain 2018 disasters.*

2. *Extend certain tax benefits that expired at the end of 2017 and that currently can't be claimed on your 2018 tax return.*

3. *Change certain other tax provisions.*

To learn whether this legislation was enacted, resulting in changes that affect your 2018 tax return, go to Recent Developments at IRS.gov/ Pub17.

Reminder

Foreign-source income. If you are a U.S. citizen with interest income from sources outside the United States (foreign income), you must report that income on your tax return unless it is exempt by U.S. law. This is true whether you reside inside or outside the United States and whether or not you receive a Form 1099 from the foreign payer.

Automatic 6-month extension. If you receive your Form 1099 reporting your interest income late and you need more time to file your tax return, you can request a 6-month extension of time to file. See *Automatic Extension* in chapter 1.

Introduction

This chapter discusses the following topics.

- Different types of interest income.

- What interest is taxable and what interest is nontaxable.

- When to report interest income.

- How to report interest income on your tax return.

In general, any interest you receive or that is credited to your account and can be withdrawn is taxable income. Exceptions to this rule are discussed later in this chapter.

You may be able to deduct expenses you have in earning this income on Schedule A (Form 1040) if you itemize your deductions. See *Money borrowed to invest in certificate of deposit,* later, and chapter 27.

Useful Items
You may want to see:

Publication

❏ **537** Installment Sales

❏ **550** Investment Income and Expenses

❏ **1212** Guide to Original Issue Discount (OID) Instruments

Form (and Instructions)

❏ **Schedule A (Form 1040)** Itemized Deductions

❏ **Schedule B (Form 1040)** Interest and Ordinary Dividends

❏ **8615** Tax for Certain Children Who Have Unearned Income

❏ **8814** Parents' Election To Report Child's Interest and Dividends

❏ **8815** Exclusion of Interest From Series EE and I U.S. Savings Bonds Issued After 1989

❏ **8818** Optional Form To Record Redemption of Series EE and I U.S. Savings Bonds Issued After 1989

For these and other useful items, go to *IRS.gov/ Forms.*

General Information

A few items of general interest are covered here.

 Recordkeeping. You should keep a list showing sources of interest income and interest amounts received during the year. Also, keep the forms you receive showing your interest income (Forms 1099-INT, for example) as an important part of your records.

Tax on unearned income of certain children. Part of a child's 2018 unearned income may be taxed at the parent's tax rate. If so, Form 8615, Tax for Certain Children Who Have Unearned Income, must be completed and attached to the child's tax return. If not, Form 8615 isn't required and the child's income is taxed at his or her own tax rate.

Some parents can choose to include the child's interest and dividends on the parent's return. If you can, use Form 8814, Parents' Election To Report Child's Interest and Dividends, for this purpose.

For more information about the tax on unearned income of children and the parents' election, see chapter 30.

Beneficiary of an estate or trust. Interest you receive as a beneficiary of an estate or trust is generally taxable income. You should receive a Schedule K-1 (Form 1041), Beneficiary's Share of Income, Deductions, Credits, etc., from the fiduciary. Your copy of Schedule K-1 (Form 1041) and its instructions will tell you where to report the income on your Form 1040.

Social security number (SSN). You must give your name and SSN or individual taxpayer identification number (ITIN) to any person required by federal tax law to make a return, statement, or other document that relates to you. This includes payers of interest. If you don't give your SSN or ITIN to the payer of interest, you may have to pay a penalty.

SSN for joint account. If the funds in a joint account belong to one person, list that person's name first on the account and give that person's SSN to the payer. (For information on who owns the funds in a joint account, see *Joint accounts,* later.) If the joint account contains combined funds, give the SSN of the person whose name is listed first on the account. This is because only one name and SSN can be shown on Form 1099.

These rules apply to both joint ownership by a married couple and to joint ownership by other individuals. For example, if you open a joint savings account with your child using funds belonging to the child, list the child's name first on the account and give the child's SSN.

Custodian account for your child. If your child is the actual owner of an account that is recorded in your name as custodian for the child, give the child's SSN to the payer. For example, you must give your child's SSN to the payer of interest on an account owned by your child, even though the interest is paid to you as custodian.

Penalty for failure to supply SSN. If you don't give your SSN to the payer of interest, you may have to pay a penalty. See *Failure to supply SSN* under *Penalties* in chapter 1. Backup withholding also may apply.

Backup withholding. Your interest income is generally not subject to regular withholding. However, it may be subject to backup withholding to ensure that income tax is collected on the income. Under backup withholding, the payer of interest must withhold, as income tax, on the amount you are paid, by applying the appropriate withholding rate.

Backup withholding may also be required if the IRS has determined that you underreported your interest or dividend income. For more information, see *Backup Withholding* in chapter 4.

Reporting backup withholding. If backup withholding is deducted from your interest income, the payer must give you a Form 1099-INT for the year indicating the amount withheld. The Form 1099-INT will show any backup withholding as "Federal income tax withheld."

Joint accounts. If two or more persons hold property (such as a savings account or bond) as joint tenants, tenants by the entirety, or tenants in common, each person's share of any interest from the property is determined by local law.

Income from property given to a child. Property you give as a parent to your child under the Model Gifts of Securities to Minors Act, the Uniform Gifts to Minors Act, or any similar law becomes the child's property.

Income from the property is taxable to the child, except that any part used to satisfy a legal obligation to support the child is taxable to the parent or guardian having that legal obligation.

Savings account with parent as trustee. Interest income from a savings account opened for a minor child, but placed in the name and subject to the order of the parents as trustees, is taxable to the child if, under the law of the state in which the child resides, both of the following are true.

- The savings account legally belongs to the child.

- The parents aren't legally permitted to use any of the funds to support the child.

Form 1099-INT. Interest income is generally reported to you on Form 1099-INT, or a similar statement, by banks, savings and loans, and other payers of interest. This form shows you the interest income you received during the year. Keep this form for your records. You don't have to attach it to your tax return.

Report on your tax return the total interest income you receive for the tax year. See the instructions to Form 1099-INT to see whether you need to adjust any of the amounts reported to you.

Interest not reported on Form 1099-INT. Even if you don't receive a Form 1099-INT, you must still report all of your interest income. For example, you may receive distributive shares of interest from partnerships or S corporations. This interest is reported to you on Schedule K-1 (Form 1065), Partner's Share of Income, Deduction, Credits, etc., or Schedule K-1 (Form 1120S), Shareholder's Share of Income, Deductions, Credits, etc.

Nominees. Generally, if someone receives interest as a nominee for you, that person must give you a Form 1099-INT showing the interest received on your behalf.

If you receive a Form 1099-INT that includes amounts belonging to another person, see the discussion on nominee distributions under *How To Report Interest Income* in chapter 1 of Pub.

550, or the Schedule B (Form 1040) instructions.

Incorrect amount. If you receive a Form 1099-INT that shows an incorrect amount or other incorrect information, you should ask the issuer for a corrected form. The new Form 1099-INT you receive will have the "CORRECTED" box checked.

Form 1099-OID. Reportable interest income also may be shown on Form 1099-OID, Original Issue Discount. For more information about amounts shown on this form, see *Original Issue Discount (OID),* later in this chapter.

Exempt-interest dividends. Exempt-interest dividends you receive from a mutual fund or other regulated investment company, including those received from a qualified fund of funds in any tax year beginning after December 22, 2010, aren't included in your taxable income. (However, see *Information-reporting requirement* next.) Exempt-interest dividends should be shown in box 11 of Form 1099-DIV. You don't reduce your basis for distributions that are exempt-interest dividends.

Information-reporting requirement. Although exempt-interest dividends aren't taxable, you must show them on your tax return if you have to file. This is an information-reporting requirement and doesn't change the exempt-interest dividends into taxable income.

Note. Exempt-interest dividends paid from specified private activity bonds may be subject to the alternative minimum tax. See *Alternative Minimum Tax (AMT)* in chapter 29 for more information. Chapter 1 of Pub. 550 contains a discussion on private activity bonds under *State or Local Government Obligations.*

Interest on VA dividends. Interest on insurance dividends left on deposit with the Department of Veterans Affairs (VA) isn't taxable. This includes interest paid on dividends on converted United States Government Life Insurance and on National Service Life Insurance policies.

Individual retirement arrangements (IRAs). Interest on a Roth IRA generally isn't taxable. Interest on a traditional IRA is tax deferred. You generally don't include interest earned in an IRA in your income until you make withdrawals from the IRA. See chapter 17.

Taxable Interest

Taxable interest includes interest you receive from bank accounts, loans you make to others, and other sources. The following are some sources of taxable interest.

Dividends that are actually interest. Certain distributions commonly called dividends are actually interest. You must report as interest so-called "dividends" on deposits or on share accounts in:

- Cooperative banks,

- Credit unions,

- Domestic building and loan associations,

- Domestic savings and loan associations,

- Federal savings and loan associations, and

- Mutual savings banks.

The "dividends" will be shown as interest income on Form 1099-INT.

Money market funds. Money market funds pay dividends and are offered by nonbank financial institutions, such as mutual funds and stock brokerage houses. Generally, amounts you receive from money market funds should be reported as dividends, not as interest.

Certificates of deposit and other deferred interest accounts. If you open any of these accounts, interest may be paid at fixed intervals of 1 year or less during the term of the account. You generally must include this interest in your income when you actually receive it or are entitled to receive it without paying a substantial penalty. The same is true for accounts that mature in 1 year or less and pay interest in a single payment at maturity. If interest is deferred for more than 1 year, see *Original Issue Discount (OID)*, later.

Interest subject to penalty for early withdrawal. If you withdraw funds from a deferred interest account before maturity, you may have to pay a penalty. You must report the total amount of interest paid or credited to your account during the year, without subtracting the penalty. See *Penalty on early withdrawal of savings* in chapter 1 of Pub. 550 for more information on how to report the interest and deduct the penalty.

Money borrowed to invest in certificate of deposit. The interest expense you pay on money borrowed from a bank or savings institution to meet the minimum deposit required for a certificate of deposit from the institution and the interest you earn on the certificate are two separate items. You must report the total interest income you earn on the certificate in your income. If you itemize deductions, you can deduct the interest you pay as investment interest, up to the amount of your net investment income. See *Interest Expenses* in chapter 3 of Pub. 550.

Example. You deposited $5,000 with a bank and borrowed $5,000 from the bank to make up the $10,000 minimum deposit required to buy a 6-month certificate of deposit. The certificate earned $575 at maturity in 2018, but you received only $265, which represented the $575 you earned minus $310 interest charged on your $5,000 loan. The bank gives you a Form 1099-INT for 2018 showing the $575 interest you earned. The bank also gives you a statement showing that you paid $310 of interest for 2018. You must include the $575 in your income. If you itemize your deductions on Schedule A (Form 1040), you can deduct $310, subject to the net investment income limit.

Gift for opening account. If you receive non-cash gifts or services for making deposits or for opening an account in a savings institution, you may have to report the value as interest.

For deposits of less than $5,000, gifts or services valued at more than $10 must be reported as interest. For deposits of $5,000 or more, gifts or services valued at more than $20 must be reported as interest. The value is determined by the cost to the financial institution.

Example. You open a savings account at your local bank and deposit $800. The account earns $20 interest. You also receive a $15 calculator. If no other interest is credited to your account during the year, the Form 1099-INT you receive will show $35 interest for the year. You must report $35 interest income on your tax return.

Interest on insurance dividends. Interest on insurance dividends left on deposit with an insurance company that can be withdrawn annually is taxable to you in the year it is credited to your account. However, if you can withdraw it only on the anniversary date of the policy (or other specified date), the interest is taxable in the year that date occurs.

Prepaid insurance premiums. Any increase in the value of prepaid insurance premiums, advance premiums, or premium deposit funds is interest if it is applied to the payment of premiums due on insurance policies or made available for you to withdraw.

U.S. obligations. Interest on U.S. obligations, such as U.S. Treasury bills, notes, and bonds, issued by any agency or instrumentality of the United States is taxable for federal income tax purposes.

Interest on tax refunds. Interest you receive on tax refunds is taxable income.

Interest on condemnation award. If the condemning authority pays you interest to compensate you for a delay in payment of an award, the interest is taxable.

Installment sale payments. If a contract for the sale or exchange of property provides for deferred payments, it also usually provides for interest payable with the deferred payments. Generally, that interest is taxable when you receive it. If little or no interest is provided for in a deferred payment contract, part of each payment may be treated as interest. See *Unstated Interest and Original Issue Discount* in Pub. 537, Installment Sales.

Interest on annuity contract. Accumulated interest on an annuity contract you sell before its maturity date is taxable.

Usurious interest. Usurious interest is interest charged at an illegal rate. This is taxable as interest unless state law automatically changes it to a payment on the principal.

Interest income on frozen deposits. Exclude from your gross income interest on frozen deposits. A deposit is frozen if, at the end of the year, you can't withdraw any part of the deposit because:

- The financial institution is bankrupt or insolvent, or

- The state where the institution is located has placed limits on withdrawals because other financial institutions in the state are bankrupt or insolvent.

The amount of interest you must exclude is the interest that was credited on the frozen deposits minus the sum of:

- The net amount you withdrew from these deposits during the year, and

- The amount you could have withdrawn as of the end of the year (not reduced by any penalty for premature withdrawals of a time deposit).

If you receive a Form 1099-INT for interest income on deposits that were frozen at the end of 2018, see *Frozen deposits* under *How To Report Interest Income* in chapter 1 of Pub. 550 for information about reporting this interest income exclusion on your tax return.

The interest you exclude is treated as credited to your account in the following year. You must include it in income in the year you can withdraw it.

Example. $100 of interest was credited on your frozen deposit during the year. You withdrew $80 but couldn't withdraw any more as of the end of the year. You must include $80 in your income and exclude $20 from your income for the year. You must include the $20 in your income for the year you can withdraw it.

Bonds traded flat. If you buy a bond at a discount when interest has been defaulted or when the interest has accrued but hasn't been paid, the transaction is described as trading a bond flat. The defaulted or unpaid interest isn't income and isn't taxable as interest if paid later. When you receive a payment of that interest, it is a return of capital that reduces the remaining cost basis of your bond. Interest that accrues after the date of purchase, however, is taxable interest income for the year it is received or accrued. See *Bonds Sold Between Interest Dates*, later, for more information.

Below-market loans. In general, a below-market loan is a loan on which no interest is charged or on which interest is charged at a rate below the applicable federal rate. See *Below-Market Loans* in chapter 1 of Pub. 550 for more information.

U.S. Savings Bonds

This section provides tax information on U.S. savings bonds. It explains how to report the interest income on these bonds and how to treat transfers of these bonds.

 For other information on U.S. savings bonds, write to:

For series HH/H:
Series HH and Series H
Treasury Retail Securities Site
P.O. Box 2186
Minneapolis, MN 55480-2186

For series EE and I paper savings bonds:
Series EE and Series I
Treasury Retail Securities Site
P.O. Box 214
Minneapolis, MN 55480-0214

For series EE and I electronic bonds:
Series EE and Series I
Treasury Retail Securities Site
P.O. Box 7015
Minneapolis, MN 55480-7015

Or, on the Internet, visit *www.treasurydirect.gov/indiv/ indiv.htm*.

Accrual method taxpayers. If you use an accrual method of accounting, you must report interest on U.S. savings bonds each year as it accrues. You can't postpone reporting interest until you receive it or until the bonds mature. Accrual methods of accounting are explained in chapter 1 under *Accounting Methods*.

Cash method taxpayers. If you use the cash method of accounting, as most individual taxpayers do, you generally report the interest on U.S. savings bonds when you receive it. The cash method of accounting is explained in chapter 1 under *Accounting Methods*. But see *Reporting options for cash method taxpayers*, later.

Series HH bonds. These bonds were issued at face value. Interest is paid twice a year by direct deposit to your bank account. If you are a cash method taxpayer, you must report interest on these bonds as income in the year you receive it.

Series HH bonds were first offered in 1980 and last offered in August 2004. Before 1980, series H bonds were issued. Series H bonds are treated the same as series HH bonds. If you are a cash method taxpayer, you must report the interest when you receive it.

Series H bonds have a maturity period of 30 years. Series HH bonds mature in 20 years. The last series H bonds matured in 2009.

Series EE and series I bonds. Interest on these bonds is payable when you redeem the bonds. The difference between the purchase price and the redemption value is taxable interest.

Series EE bonds. Series EE bonds were first offered in January 1980 and have a maturity period of 30 years.

Before July 1980, series E bonds were issued. The original 10-year maturity period of series E bonds has been extended to 40 years for bonds issued before December 1965 and 30 years for bonds issued after November 1965. Paper series EE and series E bonds are issued at a discount. The face value is payable to you at maturity. Electronic series EE bonds are issued at their face value. The face value plus accrued interest is payable to you at maturity. As of January 1, 2012, paper savings bonds were no longer sold at financial institutions.

Owners of paper series EE bonds can convert them to electronic bonds. These converted bonds don't retain the denomination listed on the paper certificate but are posted at their purchase price (with accrued interest).

Series I bonds. Series I bonds were first offered in 1998. These are inflation-indexed bonds issued at their face amount with a maturity period of 30 years. The face value plus all accrued interest is payable to you at maturity.

Reporting options for cash method taxpayers. If you use the cash method of reporting income, you can report the interest on series EE, series E, and series I bonds in either of the following ways.

1. **Method 1.** Postpone reporting the interest until the earlier of the year you cash or dispose of the bonds or the year they mature. (However, see *Savings bonds traded*, later.)

2. **Method 2.** Choose to report the increase in redemption value as interest each year.

You must use the same method for all series EE, series E, and series I bonds you own. If you don't choose method 2 by reporting the increase in redemption value as interest each year, you must use method 1.

 If you plan to cash your bonds in the same year you will pay for higher education expenses, you may want to use method 1 because you may be able to exclude the interest from your income. To learn how, see Education Savings Bond Program, *later.*

Change from method 1. If you want to change your method of reporting the interest from method 1 to method 2, you can do so without permission from the IRS. In the year of change, you must report all interest accrued to date and not previously reported for all your bonds.

Once you choose to report the interest each year, you must continue to do so for all series EE, series E, and series I bonds you own and for any you get later, unless you request permission to change, as explained next.

Change from method 2. To change from method 2 to method 1, you must request permission from the IRS. Permission for the change is automatically granted if you send the IRS a statement that meets all the following requirements.

1. You have typed or printed the following number at the top: "131."

2. It includes your name and social security number under "131."

3. It includes the year of change (both the beginning and ending dates).

4. It identifies the savings bonds for which you are requesting this change.

5. It includes your agreement to:

   a. Report all interest on any bonds acquired during or after the year of change when the interest is realized upon disposition, redemption, or final maturity, whichever is earliest; and

   b. Report all interest on the bonds acquired before the year of change when the interest is realized upon disposition, redemption, or final maturity, whichever is earliest, with the exception of the interest reported in prior tax years.

You must attach this statement to your tax return for the year of change, which you must file by the due date (including extensions).

You can have an automatic extension of 6 months from the due date of your return for the year of change (excluding extensions) to file the statement with an amended return. To get this extension, you must have filed your original return for the year of the change by the due date (including extensions).

Instead of filing this statement, you can request permission to change from method 2 to method 1 by filing Form 3115, Application for Change in Accounting Method. In that case, follow the form instructions for an automatic change. No user fee is required.

Co-owners. If a U.S. savings bond is issued in the names of co-owners, such as you and your child or you and your spouse, interest on the bond is generally taxable to the co-owner who bought the bond.

One co-owner's funds used. If you used your funds to buy the bond, you must pay the tax on the interest. This is true even if you let the other co-owner redeem the bond and keep all the proceeds. Under these circumstances, the co-owner who redeemed the bond will receive a Form 1099-INT at the time of redemption and must provide you with another Form 1099-INT showing the amount of interest from the bond taxable to you. The co-owner who redeemed the bond is a "nominee." See *Nominee distributions* under *How To Report Interest Income* in chapter 1 of Pub. 550 for more information about how a person who is a nominee reports interest income belonging to another person.

Both co-owners' funds used. If you and the other co-owner each contribute part of the bond's purchase price, the interest is generally taxable to each of you, in proportion to the amount each of you paid.

Community property. If you and your spouse live in a community property state and hold bonds as community property, one-half of the interest is considered received by each of you. If you file separate returns, each of you generally must report one-half of the bond interest. For more information about community property, see Pub. 555.

Table 7-1. These rules are also shown in Table 7-1.

Ownership transferred. If you bought series E, series EE, or series I bonds entirely with your own funds and had them reissued in your co-owner's name or beneficiary's name alone, you must include in your gross income for the year of reissue all interest that you earned on these bonds and have not previously reported. But, if the bonds were reissued in your name alone, you don't have to report the interest accrued at that time.

This same rule applies when bonds (other than bonds held as community property) are transferred between spouses or incident to divorce.

Purchased jointly. If you and a co-owner each contributed funds to buy series E, series EE, or series I bonds jointly and later have the bonds reissued in the co-owner's name alone, you must include in your gross income for the year of reissue your share of all the interest earned on the bonds that you have not previously reported. The former co-owner doesn't have to include in gross income at the time of reissue his or her share of the interest earned that was not reported before the transfer. This interest, however, as well as all interest earned after the reissue, is income to the former co-owner.

Table 7-1. Who Pays the Tax on U.S. Savings Bond Interest

IF...	THEN the interest must be reported by...
you buy a bond in your name and the name of another person as co-owners, using only your own funds	you.
you buy a bond in the name of another person, who is the sole owner of the bond	the person for whom you bought the bond.
you and another person buy a bond as co-owners, each contributing part of the purchase price	both you and the other co-owner, in proportion to the amount each paid for the bond.
you and your spouse, who live in a community property state, buy a bond that is community property	you and your spouse. If you file separate returns, both you and your spouse generally report one-half of the interest.

This income-reporting rule also applies when the bonds are reissued in the name of your former co-owner and a new co-owner. But the new co-owner will report only his or her share of the interest earned after the transfer.

If bonds that you and a co-owner bought jointly are reissued to each of you separately in the same proportion as your contribution to the purchase price, neither you nor your co-owner has to report at that time the interest earned before the bonds were reissued.

Example 1. You and your spouse each spent an equal amount to buy a $1,000 series EE savings bond. The bond was issued to you and your spouse as co-owners. You both postpone reporting interest on the bond. You later have the bond reissued as two $500 bonds, one in your name and one in your spouse's name. At that time, neither you nor your spouse has to report the interest earned to the date of reissue.

Example 2. You bought a $1,000 series EE savings bond entirely with your own funds. The bond was issued to you and your spouse as co-owners. You both postpone reporting interest on the bond. You later have the bond reissued as two $500 bonds, one in your name and one in your spouse's name. You must report half the interest earned to the date of reissue.

Transfer to a trust. If you own series E, series EE, or series I bonds and transfer them to a trust, giving up all rights of ownership, you must include in your income for that year the interest earned to the date of transfer if you have not already reported it. However, if you are considered the owner of the trust and if the increase in value both before and after the transfer continues to be taxable to you, you can continue to defer reporting the interest earned each year. You must include the total interest in your income in the year you cash or dispose of the bonds or the year the bonds finally mature, whichever is earlier.

The same rules apply to previously unreported interest on series EE or series E bonds if the transfer to a trust consisted of series HH or series H bonds you acquired in a trade for the series EE or series E bonds. See *Savings bonds traded*, later.

Decedents. The manner of reporting interest income on series E, series EE, or series I bonds, after the death of the owner (decedent), depends on the accounting and income-reporting methods previously used by the decedent. This is explained in chapter 1 of Pub. 550.

Savings bonds traded. If you postponed reporting the interest on your series EE or series E bonds, you didn't recognize taxable income when you traded the bonds for series HH or series H bonds, unless you received cash in the trade. (You can't trade series I bonds for series HH bonds. After August 31, 2004, you can't trade any other series of bonds for series HH bonds.) Any cash you received is income up to the amount of the interest earned on the bonds traded. When your series HH or series H bonds mature, or if you dispose of them before maturity, you report as interest the difference between their redemption value and your cost. Your cost is the sum of the amount you paid for the traded series EE or series E bonds plus any amount you had to pay at the time of the trade.

Example. You traded series EE bonds (on which you postponed reporting the interest) for $2,500 in series HH bonds and $223 in cash. You reported the $223 as taxable income on your tax return. At the time of the trade, the series EE bonds had accrued interest of $523 and a redemption value of $2,723. You hold the series HH bonds until maturity, when you receive $2,500. You must report $300 as interest income in the year of maturity. This is the difference between their redemption value, $2,500, and your cost, $2,200 (the amount you paid for the series EE bonds). It is also the difference between the accrued interest of $523 on the series EE bonds and the $223 cash received on the trade.

Choice to report interest in year of trade. You could have chosen to treat all of the previously unreported accrued interest on the series EE or series E bonds traded for series HH bonds as income in the year of the trade. If you made this choice, it is treated as a change from method 1. See *Change from method 1*, earlier.

Form 1099-INT for U.S. savings bonds interest. When you cash a bond, the bank or other payer that redeems it must give you a Form 1099-INT if the interest part of the payment you receive is $10 or more. Box 3 of your Form 1099-INT should show the interest as the difference between the amount you received and the amount paid for the bond. However, your Form 1099-INT may show more interest than you have to include on your income tax return. For example, this may happen if any of the following are true.

- You chose to report the increase in the redemption value of the bond each year. The interest shown on your Form 1099-INT won't be reduced by amounts previously included in income.

- You received the bond from a decedent. The interest shown on your Form 1099-INT won't be reduced by any interest reported by the decedent before death, or on the decedent's final return, or by the estate on the estate's income tax return.

- Ownership of the bond was transferred. The interest shown on your Form 1099-INT won't be reduced by interest that accrued before the transfer.

- You were named as a co-owner, and the other co-owner contributed funds to buy the bond. The interest shown on your Form 1099-INT won't be reduced by the amount you received as nominee for the other co-owner. (See *Co-owners*, earlier in this chapter, for more information about the reporting requirements.)

- You received the bond in a taxable distribution from a retirement or profit-sharing plan. The interest shown on your Form 1099-INT won't be reduced by the interest portion of the amount taxable as a distribution from the plan and not taxable as interest. (This amount is generally shown on Form 1099-R, Distributions From Pensions, Annuities, Retirement or Profit-Sharing Plans, IRAs, Insurance Contracts, etc., for the year of distribution.)

For more information on including the correct amount of interest on your return, see *How To Report Interest Income*, later. Pub. 550 includes examples showing how to report these amounts.

 Interest on U.S. savings bonds is exempt from state and local taxes. The Form 1099-INT you receive will indicate the amount that is for U.S. savings bond interest in box 3.

Education Savings Bond Program

You may be able to exclude from income all or part of the interest you receive on the redemption of qualified U.S. savings bonds during the year if you pay qualified higher educational expenses during the same year. This exclusion is known as the Education Savings Bond Program.

You don't qualify for this exclusion if your filing status is married filing separately.

Form 8815. Use Form 8815 to figure your exclusion. Attach the form to your Form 1040.

Qualified U.S. savings bonds. A qualified U.S. savings bond is a series EE bond issued after 1989 or a series I bond. The bond must be issued either in your name (sole owner) or in your and your spouse's names (co-owners). You must be at least 24 years old before the bond's issue date. For example, a bond bought by a parent and issued in the name of his or her child under age 24 doesn't qualify for the exclusion by the parent or child.

 The issue date of a bond may be earlier than the date the bond is purchased because the issue date assigned to a bond is the first day of the month in which it is purchased.

Beneficiary. You can designate any individual (including a child) as a beneficiary of the bond.

Verification by IRS. If you claim the exclusion, the IRS will check it by using bond redemption information from the Department of the Treasury.

Qualified expenses. Qualified higher education expenses are tuition and fees required for you, your spouse, or your dependent (for whom you claim an exemption) to attend an eligible educational institution.

Qualified expenses include any contribution you make to a qualified tuition program or to a Coverdell education savings account.

Qualified expenses don't include expenses for room and board or for courses involving sports, games, or hobbies that aren't part of a degree or certificate granting program.

Eligible educational institutions. These institutions include most public, private, and nonprofit universities, colleges, and vocational schools that are accredited and eligible to participate in student aid programs run by the U.S. Department of Education.

Reduction for certain benefits. You must reduce your qualified higher education expenses by all of the following tax-free benefits.

1. Tax-free part of scholarships and fellowships (see *Scholarships and fellowships* in chapter 12).

2. Expenses used to figure the tax-free portion of distributions from a Coverdell ESA.

3. Expenses used to figure the tax-free portion of distributions from a qualified tuition program.

4. Any tax-free payments (other than gifts or inheritances) received for educational expenses, such as:

    a. Veterans' educational assistance benefits,

    b. Qualified tuition reductions, or

    c. Employer-provided educational assistance.

5. Any expense used in figuring the American opportunity and lifetime learning credits.

Amount excludable. If the total proceeds (interest and principal) from the qualified U.S. savings bonds you redeem during the year aren't more than your adjusted qualified higher education expenses for the year, you may be able to exclude all of the interest. If the proceeds are more than the expenses, you may be able to exclude only part of the interest.

To determine the excludable amount, multiply the interest part of the proceeds by a fraction. The numerator of the fraction is the qualified higher education expenses you paid during the year. The denominator of the fraction is the total proceeds you received during the year.

Example. In February 2018, Mark and Joan, a married couple, cashed qualified series EE U.S. savings bonds with a total denomination of $10,000 that they bought in April 2002 for $5,000. They received proceeds of $7,244, representing principal of $5,000 and interest of $2,244. In 2018, they paid $4,000 of their daughter's college tuition. They aren't claiming an education credit for that amount, and their daughter doesn't have any tax-free educational assistance. They can exclude $1,239 ($2,244 x ($4,000 ÷ $7,244)) of interest in 2018. They must include the remaining $1,005 ($2,244 – $1,239) interest in gross income.

Modified adjusted gross income limit. The interest exclusion is limited if your modified adjusted gross income (modified AGI) is:

- $79,550 to $94,550 for taxpayers filing single or head of household, and

- $119,300 to $149,300 for married taxpayers filing jointly or for a qualifying widow(er) with dependent child.

You don't qualify for the interest exclusion if your modified AGI is equal to or more than the upper limit for your filing status.

Modified AGI, for purposes of this exclusion, is adjusted gross income (Form 1040, line 7) figured before the interest exclusion, and modified by adding back any:

1. Foreign earned income exclusion,

2. Foreign housing exclusion and deduction,

3. Exclusion of income for bona fide residents of American Samoa,

4. Exclusion for income from Puerto Rico,

5. Exclusion for adoption benefits received under an employer's adoption assistance program,

6. Deduction for student loan interest, and

7. Deduction for domestic production activities.

 At the time this publication was prepared for printing, Congress was considering legislation that would extend the tuition and fees deduction, which expired at the end of 2017. If extended, your tuition and fees may be deductible for 2018. To see if the legislation was enacted, go to Recent Developments at IRS.gov/Pub17.

Use the Line 9 Worksheet in the Form 8815 instructions to figure your modified AGI.

If you have investment interest expense incurred to earn royalties and other investment income, see *Education Savings Bond Program* in chapter 1 of Pub. 550.

 Recordkeeping. If you claim the interest exclusion, you must keep a written record of the qualified U.S. savings bonds you redeem. Your record must include the serial number, issue date, face value, and total redemption proceeds (principal and interest) of each bond. You can use Form 8818 to record this information. You should also keep bills, receipts, canceled checks, or other documentation that shows you paid qualified higher education expenses during the year.

U.S. Treasury Bills, Notes, and Bonds

Treasury bills, notes, and bonds are direct debts (obligations) of the U.S. Government.

Taxation of interest. Interest income from Treasury bills, notes, and bonds is subject to federal income tax but is exempt from all state and local income taxes. You should receive a Form 1099-INT showing the interest paid to you for the year in box 3.

Payments of principal and interest generally will be credited to your designated checking or savings account by direct deposit through the TreasuryDirect® system.

Treasury bills. These bills generally have a 4-week, 13-week, 26-week, or 52-week maturity period. They are generally issued at a discount in the amount of $100 and multiples of $100. The difference between the discounted price you pay for the bills and the face value you receive at maturity is interest income. Generally, you report this interest income when the bill is paid at maturity. If you paid a premium for a bill (more than the face value), you generally report the premium as a section 171 deduction when the bill is paid at maturity.

Treasury notes and bonds. Treasury notes have maturity periods of more than 1 year, ranging up to 10 years. Maturity periods for Treasury bonds are longer than 10 years. Both generally are issued in denominations of $100 to $1 million and generally pay interest every 6 months. Generally, you report this interest for the year paid. For more information, see *U.S. Treasury Bills, Notes, and Bonds* in chapter 1 of Pub. 550.

 For other information on Treasury notes or bonds, write to:

Treasury Retail Securities Site
P.O. Box 7015
Minneapolis, MN 55480-7015

 Or, click on the link to the Treasury website at: *www.treasurydirect.gov/ indiv/indiv.htm.*

For information on series EE, series I, and series HH savings bonds, see *U.S. Savings Bonds,* earlier.

Treasury inflation-protected securities (TIPS). These securities pay interest twice a year at a fixed rate, based on a principal amount adjusted to take into account inflation and deflation. For the tax treatment of these securities, see *Inflation-Indexed Debt Instruments* under *Original Issue Discount (OID)* in Pub. 550.

Bonds Sold Between Interest Dates

If you sell a bond between interest payment dates, part of the sales price represents interest accrued to the date of sale. You must report that part of the sales price as interest income for the year of sale.

If you buy a bond between interest payment dates, part of the purchase price represents interest accrued before the date of purchase. When that interest is paid to you, treat it as a nontaxable return of your capital investment, rather than as interest income. See *Accrued interest on bonds* under *How To Report Interest Income* in chapter 1 of Pub. 550 for information on reporting the payment.

Insurance

Life insurance proceeds paid to you as beneficiary of the insured person are usually not taxable. But if you receive the proceeds in installments, you must usually report a part of each installment payment as interest income.

For more information about insurance proceeds received in installments, see Pub. 525, Taxable and Nontaxable Income.

Annuity. If you buy an annuity with life insurance proceeds, the annuity payments you receive are taxed as pension and annuity income from a nonqualified plan, not as interest income. See chapter 10 for information on pension and annuity income from nonqualified plans.

State or Local Government Obligations

Interest on a bond used to finance government operations generally isn't taxable if the bond is issued by a state, the District of Columbia, a possession of the United States, or any of their political subdivisions.

Bonds issued after 1982 (including tribal economic development bonds issued after February 17, 2009) by an Indian tribal government are treated as issued by a state. Interest on these bonds is generally tax exempt if the bonds are part of an issue of which substantially all proceeds are to be used in the exercise of any essential government function.

For information on federally guaranteed bonds, mortgage revenue bonds, arbitrage bonds, private activity bonds, qualified tax credit bonds, and Build America bonds, see State or Local Government Obligations in chapter 1 of Pub. 550.

Information-reporting requirement. If you file a tax return, you are required to show any tax-exempt interest you received on your return. This is an information-reporting requirement only. It doesn't change tax-exempt interest to taxable interest.

Original Issue Discount (OID)

Original issue discount (OID) is a form of interest. You generally include OID in your income as it accrues over the term of the debt instrument, whether or not you receive any payments from the issuer.

A debt instrument generally has OID when the instrument is issued for a price that is less than its stated redemption price at maturity. OID is the difference between the stated redemption price at maturity and the issue price.

All debt instruments that pay no interest before maturity are presumed to be issued at a discount. Zero coupon bonds are one example of these instruments.

The OID accrual rules generally don't apply to short-term obligations (those with a fixed maturity date of 1 year or less from date of issue). See Discount on Short-Term Obligations in chapter 1 of Pub. 550.

De minimis OID. You can treat the discount as zero if it is less than one-fourth of 1% (0.0025) of the stated redemption price at maturity multiplied by the number of full years from the date of original issue to maturity. This small discount is known as "de minimis" OID.

Example 1. You bought a 10-year bond with a stated redemption price at maturity of $1,000, issued at $980 with OID of $20. One-fourth of 1% of $1,000 (stated redemption price) times 10 (the number of full years from the date of original issue to maturity) equals $25. Because the $20 discount is less than $25, the OID is treated as zero. (If you hold the bond at maturity, you will recognize $20 ($1,000 − $980) of capital gain.)

Example 2. The facts are the same as in *Example 1*, except that the bond was issued at $950. The OID is $50. Because the $50 discount is more than the $25 figured in *Example 1*, you must include the OID in income as it accrues over the term of the bond.

Debt instrument bought after original issue. If you buy a debt instrument with de minimis OID at a premium, the discount isn't includible in income. If you buy a debt instrument with de minimis OID at a discount, the discount is reported under the market discount rules. See Market Discount Bonds in chapter 1 of Pub. 550.

Exceptions to reporting OID as current income. The OID rules discussed in this chapter don't apply to the following debt instruments.

1. Tax-exempt obligations. (However, see Stripped tax-exempt obligations under Stripped Bonds and Coupons in chapter 1 of Pub. 550).

2. U.S. savings bonds.

3. Short-term debt instruments (those with a fixed maturity date of not more than 1 year from the date of issue).

4. Obligations issued by an individual before March 2, 1984.

5. Loans between individuals if all the following are true.

   a. The lender isn't in the business of lending money.

   b. The amount of the loan, plus the amount of any outstanding prior loans between the same individuals, is $10,000 or less.

   c. Avoiding any federal tax isn't one of the principal purposes of the loan.

Form 1099-OID. The issuer of the debt instrument (or your broker if you held the instrument through a broker) should give you Form 1099-OID, or a similar statement, if the total OID for the calendar year is $10 or more. Form 1099-OID will show, in box 1, the amount of OID for the part of the year that you held the bond. It also will show, in box 2, the stated interest you must include in your income. Box 8 shows OID on a U.S. Treasury obligation for the part of the year you owned it and isn't included in box 1. A copy of Form 1099-OID will be sent to the IRS. Don't file your copy with your return. Keep it for your records.

In most cases, you must report the entire amount in boxes 1, 2, and 8 of Form 1099-OID as interest income. But see Refiguring OID shown on Form 1099-OID, later in this discussion, for more information.

Form 1099-OID not received. If you had OID for the year but didn't receive a Form 1099-OID, you may have to figure the correct amount of OID to report on your return. See Pub. 1212 for details on how to figure the correct OID.

Nominee. If someone else is the holder of record (the registered owner) of an OID instrument belonging to you and receives a Form 1099-OID on your behalf, that person must give you a Form 1099-OID.

Refiguring OID shown on Form 1099-OID. You may need to refigure the OID shown in box 1 or box 8 of Form 1099-OID if either of the following apply.

- You bought the debt instrument after its original issue and paid a premium or an acquisition premium.

- The debt instrument is a stripped bond or a stripped coupon (including certain zero coupon instruments).

For information about figuring the correct amount of OID to include in your income, see Figuring OID on Long-Term Debt Instruments in Pub. 1212 and the instructions for Form 1099-OID.

Refiguring periodic interest shown on Form 1099-OID. If you disposed of a debt instrument or acquired it from another holder during the year, see Bonds Sold Between Interest Dates, earlier, for information about the treatment of periodic interest that may be shown in box 2 of Form 1099-OID for that instrument.

Certificates of deposit (CDs). If you buy a CD with a maturity of more than 1 year, you must include in income each year a part of the total interest due and report it in the same manner as other OID.

This also applies to similar deposit arrangements with banks, building and loan associations, etc., including:

- Time deposits,

- Bonus plans,

- Savings certificates,

- Deferred income certificates,

- Bonus savings certificates, and

- Growth savings certificates.

Bearer CDs. CDs issued after 1982 generally must be in registered form. Bearer CDs are CDs not in registered form. They aren't issued in the depositor's name and are transferable from one individual to another.

Banks must provide the IRS and the person redeeming a bearer CD with a Form 1099-INT.

More information. See chapter 1 of Pub. 550 for more information about OID and related topics, such as market discount bonds.

When To Report Interest Income

When to report your interest income depends on whether you use the cash method or an accrual method to report income.

Cash method. Most individual taxpayers use the cash method. If you use this method, you generally report your interest income in the year in which you actually or constructively receive it. However, there are special rules for reporting the discount on certain debt instruments. See *U.S. Savings Bonds* and *Original Issue Discount (OID)*, earlier.

Example. On September 1, 2016, you loaned another individual $2,000 at 12%, compounded annually. You aren't in the business of lending money. The note stated that principal and interest would be due on August 31, 2018. In 2018, you received $2,508.80 ($2,000 principal and $508.80 interest). If you use the cash method, you must include in income on your 2018 return the $508.80 interest you received in that year.

Constructive receipt. You constructively receive income when it is credited to your account or made available to you. You don't need to have physical possession of it. For example, you are considered to receive interest, dividends, or other earnings on any deposit or account in a bank, savings and loan, or similar financial institution, or interest on life insurance policy dividends left to accumulate, when they are credited to your account and subject to your withdrawal. This is true even if they aren't yet entered in your passbook.

You constructively receive income on the deposit or account even if you must:

- Make withdrawals in multiples of even amounts,
- Give a notice to withdraw before making the withdrawal,
- Withdraw all or part of the account to withdraw the earnings, or
- Pay a penalty on early withdrawals, unless the interest you are to receive on an early withdrawal or redemption is substantially less than the interest payable at maturity.

Accrual method. If you use an accrual method, you report your interest income when you earn it, whether or not you have received it. Interest is earned over the term of the debt instrument.

Example. If, in the previous example, you use an accrual method, you must include the interest in your income as you earn it. You would report the interest as follows: 2016, $80; 2017, $249.60; and 2018, $179.20.

Coupon bonds. Interest on bearer bonds with detachable coupons is generally taxable in the year the coupon becomes due and payable. It doesn't matter when you mail the coupon for payment.

How To Report Interest Income

Generally, you report all your taxable interest income on Form 1040, line 2b.

Form 1040. You must use Form 1040 if:

1. You forfeited interest income because of the early withdrawal of a time deposit;

2. You acquired taxable bonds after 1987, you choose to reduce interest income from the bonds by any amortizable bond premium, and you are deducting the excess of bond premium amortization for the accrual period over the qualified stated interest for the period (see *Bond Premium Amortization* in chapter 3 of Pub. 550); or

3. You received tax-exempt interest from private activity bonds issued after August 7, 1986.

Schedule B (Form 1040). You must also complete Schedule B (Form 1040), Part I, if you file Form 1040 and any of the following apply.

1. Your taxable interest income is more than $1,500.

2. You are claiming the interest exclusion under the Education Savings Bond Program (discussed earlier).

3. You received interest from a seller-financed mortgage, and the buyer used the property as a home.

4. You received a Form 1099-INT for U.S. savings bond interest that includes amounts you reported in a previous tax year.

5. You received, as a nominee, interest that actually belongs to someone else.

6. You received a Form 1099-INT for interest on frozen deposits.

7. You received a Form 1099-INT for interest on a bond you bought between interest payment dates.

8. You are reporting OID in an amount less than the amount shown on Form 1099-OID.

9. Statement (2) in the preceding list under Form 1040 is true.

In Part I, line 1, list each payer's name and the amount received from each. If you received a Form 1099-INT or Form 1099-OID from a brokerage firm, list the brokerage firm as the payer.

Reporting tax-exempt interest. Total your tax-exempt interest (such as interest or accrued OID on certain state and municipal bonds, including zero coupon municipal bonds) reported on Form 1099-INT, box 8, and exempt-interest dividends from a mutual fund or other regulated investment company reported on Form 1099-DIV, box 11. Add these amounts to any other tax-exempt interest you received. Report the total on line 2a of Form 1040.

Form 1099-INT, box 9, and Form 1099-DIV, box 12, show the tax-exempt interest subject to the alternative minimum tax on Form 6251. These amounts are already included in the amounts on Form 1099-INT, box 8, and Form 1099-DIV, box 11. Don't add the amounts in Form 1099-INT, box 9, and Form 1099-DIV, box 12, to, or subtract them from, the amounts on Form 1099-INT, box 8, and Form 1099-DIV, box 11.

 Don't report interest from an individual retirement account (IRA) as tax-exempt interest.

Form 1099-INT. Your taxable interest income, except for interest from U.S. savings bonds and Treasury obligations, is shown in box 1 of Form 1099-INT. Add this amount to any other taxable interest income you received. See the instructions for Form 1099-INT if you have interest from a security acquired at a premium. You must report all of your taxable interest income even if you don't receive a Form 1099-INT. Contact your financial institution if you don't receive a Form 1099-INT by February 15. Your identifying number may be truncated on any paper Form 1099-INT you receive.

If you forfeited interest income because of the early withdrawal of a time deposit, the deductible amount will be shown on Form 1099-INT in box 2. See *Penalty on early withdrawal of savings* in chapter 1 of Pub. 550.

Box 3 of Form 1099-INT shows the interest income you received from U.S. savings bonds, Treasury bills, Treasury notes, and Treasury bonds. Generally, add the amount shown in box 3 to any other taxable interest income you received. If part of the amount shown in box 3 was previously included in your interest income, see *U.S. savings bond interest previously reported*, later. If you acquired the security at a premium, see the instructions for Form 1099-INT.

Box 4 of Form 1099-INT will contain an amount if you were subject to backup withholding. Include the amount from box 4 on Form 1040, line 16 (federal income tax withheld).

Box 5 of Form 1099-INT shows investment expenses you may be able to deduct as an itemized deduction. See chapter 27 for more information about investment expenses.

If there are entries in boxes 6 and 7 of Form 1099-INT, you must file Form 1040. You may be able to take a credit for the amount shown in box 6 unless you deduct this amount on line 6 of Schedule A (Form 1040). To take the credit, you may have to file Form 1116, Foreign Tax Credit. For more information, see Pub. 514, Foreign Tax Credit for Individuals.

U.S. savings bond interest previously reported. If you received a Form 1099-INT for U.S. savings bond interest, the form may show interest you don't have to report. See *Form 1099-INT for U.S. savings bonds interest*, earlier.

On Schedule B (Form 1040), Part I, line 1, report all the interest shown on your Form 1099-INT. Then follow these steps.

1. Several lines above line 2, enter a subtotal of all interest listed on line 1.

2. Below the subtotal, enter "U.S. Savings Bond Interest Previously Reported" and enter amounts previously reported or interest accrued before you received the bond.

3. Subtract these amounts from the subtotal and enter the result on line 2.

More information. For more information about how to report interest income, see chapter 1 of Pub. 550 or the instructions for the form you must file.

8.

Dividends and Other Distributions

What's New

 At the time this publication went to print, Congress was considering legislation that would do the following.

1. Provide additional tax relief for those affected by certain 2018 disasters.

2. Extend certain tax benefits that expired at the end of 2017 and that currently can't be claimed on your 2018 tax return.

3. Change certain other tax provisions.

To learn whether this legislation was enacted, resulting in changes that affect your 2018 tax return, go to Recent Developments at IRS.gov/ Pub17.

Reminder

Foreign-source income. If you are a U.S. citizen with dividend income from sources outside the United States (foreign-source income), you must report that income on your tax return unless it is exempt by U.S. law. This is true whether you reside inside or outside the United States and whether or not you receive a Form 1099 from the foreign payer.

Automatic 6-month extension. If you receive your Form 1099 reporting dividends or other distributions late and you need more time to file your tax return, you can request a 6-month extension of time to file. See *Automatic Extension* in chapter 1.

Introduction

This chapter discusses the tax treatment of:

● Ordinary dividends,

● Capital gain distributions,

● Nondividend distributions, and

● Other distributions you may receive from a corporation or a mutual fund.

This chapter also explains how to report dividend income on your tax return.

Dividends are distributions of money, stock, or other property paid to you by a corporation or by a mutual fund. You also may receive dividends through a partnership, an estate, a trust, or an association that is taxed as a corporation. However, some amounts you receive that are called dividends are actually interest income. (See *Dividends that are actually interest* in chapter 7.)

Most distributions are paid in cash (or check). However, distributions can consist of more stock, stock rights, other property, or services.

Useful Items

You may want to see:

Publication

❑ **514** Foreign Tax Credit for Individuals

❑ **550** Investment Income and Expenses

Form (and Instructions)

❑ **Schedule B (Form 1040)** Interest and Ordinary Dividends

For these and other useful items, go to *IRS.gov/ Forms*.

General Information

This section discusses general rules for dividend income.

Tax for certain dependent children. The tax for certain dependent children under age 18 (and certain older children) with $2,100 of unearned income is no longer taxed at the parent's tax rate. This change in figuring the tax for certain dependent children is in effect for tax years 2018 through 2025 as a result of the Tax Cuts and Jobs Act. See the Instructions for Form 8615 for more information.

For more information, see chapter 30.

Beneficiary of an estate or trust. Dividends and other distributions you receive as a beneficiary of an estate or trust are generally taxable income. You should receive a Schedule K-1 (Form 1041), Beneficiary's Share of Income, Deductions, Credits, etc., from the fiduciary. Your copy of Schedule K-1 (Form 1041) and its instructions will tell you where to report the income on your Form 1040.

Social security number (SSN) or individual taxpayer identification number (ITIN). You must give your SSN or ITIN to any person required by federal tax law to make a return, statement, or other document that relates to you. This includes payers of dividends. If you don't give your SSN or ITIN to the payer of dividends, you may have to pay a penalty.

For more information on SSNs and ITINs, see *Social Security Number (SSN)* in chapter 1.

Backup withholding. Your dividend income is generally not subject to regular withholding. However, it may be subject to backup withholding to ensure that income tax is collected on the income. Under backup withholding, the payer of dividends must withhold income tax on the

amount you are paid, by applying the appropriate withholding rate.

Backup withholding may also be required if the IRS has determined that you underreported your interest or dividend income. For more information, see *Backup Withholding* in chapter 4.

Stock certificate in two or more names. If two or more persons hold stock as joint tenants, tenants by the entirety, or tenants in common, each person's share of any dividends from the stock is determined by local law.

Form 1099-DIV. Most corporations and mutual funds use Form 1099-DIV, Dividends and Distributions, to report the distributions you received from them during the year. Keep this form with your records. You don't have to attach it to your tax return.

Dividends not reported on Form 1099-DIV. Even if you don't receive a Form 1099-DIV, you must still report all your taxable dividend income. For example, you may receive distributive shares of dividends from partnerships or S corporations. These dividends are reported to you on Schedule K-1 (Form 1065), Partner's Share of Income, Deductions, Credits, etc., and Schedule K-1 (Form 1120S), Shareholder's Share of Income, Deductions, Credits, etc.

Reporting tax withheld. If tax is withheld from your dividend income, the payer must give you a Form 1099-DIV that indicates the amount withheld.

Nominees. If someone receives distributions as a nominee for you that person should give you a Form 1099-DIV, which will show distributions received on your behalf.

Form 1099-MISC. Certain substitute payments in lieu of dividends or tax-exempt interest received by a broker on your behalf must be reported to you on Form 1099-MISC, Miscellaneous Income, or a similar statement. See *Reporting Substitute Payments* under *Short Sales* in chapter 4 of Pub. 550 for more information about reporting these payments.

Incorrect amount shown on a Form 1099. If you receive a Form 1099 that shows an incorrect amount or other incorrect information, you should ask the issuer for a corrected form. The new Form 1099 you receive will have the "CORRECTED" box checked.

Dividends on stock sold. If stock is sold, exchanged, or otherwise disposed of after a dividend is declared but before it is paid, the owner of record (usually the payee shown on the dividend check) must include the dividend in income.

Dividends received in January. If a mutual fund (or other regulated investment company) or real estate investment trust (REIT) declares a dividend (including any exempt-interest dividend or capital gain distribution) in October, November, or December payable to shareholders of record on a date in one of those months but actually pays the dividend during January of the next calendar year, you are considered to have received the dividend on December 31. You report the dividend in the year it was declared.

Ordinary Dividends

Ordinary dividends are the most common type of distribution from a corporation or a mutual fund and are taxable. They are paid out of earnings and profits and are ordinary income to you. This means they aren't capital gains. You can assume that any dividend you receive on common or preferred stock is an ordinary dividend unless the paying corporation or mutual fund tells you otherwise. Ordinary dividends will be shown in box 1a of the Form 1099-DIV you receive.

Qualified Dividends

Qualified dividends are the ordinary dividends subject to the same 0%, 15%, or 20% maximum tax rate that applies to net capital gain. They should be shown in box 1b of the Form 1099-DIV you receive.

The maximum rate of tax on qualified dividends is the following.

- 0% on any amount that otherwise would be taxed at a 10% or 15% rate.

- 15% on any amount that otherwise would be taxed at rates greater than 15% but less than 37%.

- 20% on any amount that otherwise would be taxed at a 37% rate.

To qualify for the maximum rate, all of the following requirements must be met.

- The dividends must have been paid by a U.S. corporation or a qualified foreign corporation. (See *Qualified foreign corporation*, later.)

- The dividends aren't of the type listed later under *Dividends that aren't qualified dividends*, later.

- You meet the holding period (discussed next).

Holding period. You must have held the stock for more than 60 days during the 121-day period that begins 60 days before the ex-dividend date. The ex-dividend date is the first date following the declaration of a dividend on which the buyer of a stock isn't entitled to receive the next dividend payment. Instead, the seller will get the dividend.

When counting the number of days you held the stock, include the day you disposed of the stock, but not the day you acquired it. See the examples later.

Exception for preferred stock. In the case of preferred stock, you must have held the stock more than 90 days during the 181-day period that begins 90 days before the ex-dividend date if the dividends are due to periods totaling more than 366 days. If the preferred dividends are due to periods totaling less than 367 days, the holding period in the previous paragraph applies.

Example 1. You bought 5,000 shares of XYZ Corp. common stock on July 9, 2018. XYZ Corp. paid a cash dividend of 10 cents per share. The ex-dividend date was July 16, 2018. Your Form 1099-DIV from XYZ Corp. shows $500 in box 1a (ordinary dividends) and in box 1b (qualified dividends). However, you sold the 5,000 shares on August 12, 2018. You held your shares of XYZ Corp. for only 34 days of the 121-day period (from July 10, 2018, through August 12, 2018). The 121-day period began on May 17, 2018 (60 days before the ex-dividend date), and ended on September 14, 2018. You have no qualified dividends from XYZ Corp. because you held the XYZ stock for less than 61 days.

Example 2. Assume the same facts as in *Example 1*, except that you bought the stock on July 15, 2018 (the day before the ex-dividend date), and you sold the stock on September 16, 2018. You held the stock for 63 days (from July 16, 2018, through September 16, 2018). The $500 of qualified dividends shown in box 1b of your Form 1099-DIV are all qualified dividends because you held the stock for 61 days of the 121-day period (from July 16, 2018, through September 14, 2018).

Example 3. You bought 10,000 shares of ABC Mutual Fund common stock on July 9, 2018. ABC Mutual Fund paid a cash dividend of 10 cents a share. The ex-dividend date was July 16, 2018. The ABC Mutual Fund advises you that the portion of the dividend eligible to be treated as qualified dividends equals 2 cents per share. Your Form 1099-DIV from ABC Mutual Fund shows total ordinary dividends of $1,000 and qualified dividends of $200. However, you sold the 10,000 shares on August 12, 2018. You have no qualified dividends from ABC Mutual Fund because you held the ABC Mutual Fund stock for less than 61 days.

Holding period reduced where risk of loss is diminished. When determining whether you met the minimum holding period discussed earlier, you cannot count any day during which you meet any of the following conditions.

1. You had an option to sell, were under a contractual obligation to sell, or had made (and not closed) a short sale of substantially identical stock or securities.

2. You were the grantor (writer) of an option to buy substantially identical stock or securities.

3. Your risk of loss is diminished by holding one or more other positions in substantially similar or related property.

For information about how to apply condition (3), see Regulations section 1.246-5.

Qualified foreign corporation. A foreign corporation is a qualified foreign corporation if it meets any of the following conditions.

1. The corporation is incorporated in a U.S. possession.

2. The corporation is eligible for the benefits of a comprehensive income tax treaty with the United States that the Department of the Treasury determines is satisfactory for this purpose and that includes an exchange of information program. For a list of those treaties, see Table 8-1.

3. The corporation doesn't meet (1) or (2) above, but the stock for which the dividend is paid is readily tradable on an established securities market in the United States. See *Readily tradable stock*, later.

Exception. A corporation isn't a qualified foreign corporation if it is a passive foreign investment company during its tax year in which the dividends are paid or during its previous tax year.

Readily tradable stock. Any stock (such as common, ordinary, or preferred) or an American depositary receipt in respect of that stock is considered to satisfy requirement 3 under *Qualified foreign corporation*, earlier, if it is listed on a national securities exchange that is registered under section 6 of the Securities Exchange Act of 1934 or on the Nasdaq Stock Market. For a list of the exchanges that meet these requirements, see *www.sec.gov/divisions/marketreg/mrexchanges.shtml.*

Dividends that aren't qualified dividends. The following dividends aren't qualified dividends. They aren't qualified dividends even if they are shown in box 1b of Form 1099-DIV.

- Capital gain distributions.

- Dividends paid on deposits with mutual savings banks, cooperative banks, credit unions, U.S. building and loan associations, U.S. savings and loan associations, federal savings and loan associations, and similar financial institutions. (Report these amounts as interest income.)

- Dividends from a corporation that is a tax-exempt organization or farmer's cooperative during the corporation's tax year in which the dividends were paid or during the corporation's previous tax year.

- Dividends paid by a corporation on employer securities held on the date of record by an employee stock ownership plan (ESOP) maintained by that corporation.

- Dividends on any share of stock to the extent you are obligated (whether under a short sale or otherwise) to make related payments for positions in substantially similar or related property.

- Payments in lieu of dividends, but only if you know or have reason to know the payments aren't qualified dividends.

- Payments shown in Form 1099-DIV, box 1b, from a foreign corporation to the extent you know or have reason to know the payments aren't qualified dividends.

Table 8-1. **Income Tax Treaties**

Income tax treaties the United States has with the following countries satisfy requirement 2 under *Qualified foreign corporation*, earlier.

Armenia	Ireland	Slovenia
Australia	Israel	South Africa
Austria	Italy	Spain
Azerbaijan	Jamaica	Sri Lanka
Bangladesh	Japan	Sweden
Barbados	Kazakhstan	Switzerland
Belarus	Korea	Tajikistan
Belgium	Kyrgyzstan	Thailand
Bulgaria	Latvia	Trinidad and
Canada	Lithuania	Tobago
China	Luxembourg	Tunisia
Cyprus	Malta	Turkey
Czech	Mexico	Turkmenistan
Republic	Moldova	Ukraine
Denmark	Morocco	Union of
Egypt	Netherlands	Soviet
Estonia	New Zealand	Socialist
Finland	Norway	Republics
France	Pakistan	(USSR)
Georgia	Philippines	United
Germany	Poland	Kingdom
Greece	Portugal	United States
Hungary	Romania	Model
Iceland	Russia	Uzbekistan
India	Slovak	Venezuela
Indonesia	Republic	

Dividends Used To Buy More Stock

The corporation in which you own stock may have a dividend reinvestment plan. This plan lets you choose to use your dividends to buy (through an agent) more shares of stock in the corporation instead of receiving the dividends in cash. Most mutual funds also permit shareholders to automatically reinvest distributions in more shares in the fund, instead of receiving cash. If you use your dividends to buy more stock at a price equal to its fair market value, you still must report the dividends as income.

If you are a member of a dividend reinvestment plan that lets you buy more stock at a price less than its fair market value, you must report as dividend income the fair market value of the additional stock on the dividend payment date.

You also must report as dividend income any service charge subtracted from your cash dividends before the dividends are used to buy the additional stock. But you may be able to deduct the service charge. See chapter 27 for more information about deducting expenses of producing income.

In some dividend reinvestment plans, you can invest more cash to buy shares of stock at a price less than fair market value. If you choose to do this, you must report as dividend income the difference between the cash you invest and the fair market value of the stock you

buy. When figuring this amount, use the fair market value of the stock on the dividend payment date.

Money Market Funds

Report amounts you receive from money market funds as dividend income. Money market funds are a type of mutual fund and shouldn't be confused with bank money market accounts that pay interest.

Capital Gain Distributions

Capital gain distributions (also called capital gain dividends) are paid to you or credited to your account by mutual funds (or other regulated investment companies) and real estate investment trusts (REITs). They will be shown in box 2a of the Form 1099-DIV you receive from the mutual fund or REIT.

Report capital gain distributions as long-term capital gains, regardless of how long you owned your shares in the mutual fund or REIT.

Qualified Opportunity Fund. Effective December 22, 2017, IRC 1400Z-2 provides a temporary deferral of inclusion in gross income for capital gains invested in Qualified Opportunity Funds, and permanent exclusion of capital gains from the sale or exchange of an investment in the Qualified Opportunity Fund if the investment is held for at least 10 years. See Form 8949 instructions on how to report your election to defer eligible gains invested in a Qualified Opportunity Fund. For additional information, please see Opportunity Zones Frequently Asked Questions available at *www.irs.gov/ newsroom/opportunity-zones-frequently-asked-questions*.

Undistributed capital gains of mutual funds and REITs. Some mutual funds and REITs keep their long-term capital gains and pay tax on them. You must treat your share of these gains as distributions, even though you didn't actually receive them. However, they aren't included on Form 1099-DIV. Instead, they are reported to you in box 1a of Form 2439.

Report undistributed capital gains (box 1a of Form 2439) as long-term capital gains on Schedule D (Form 1040), line 11, column (h).

The tax paid on these gains by the mutual fund or REIT is shown in box 2 of Form 2439. You take credit for this tax by including it on Schedule 5 (Form 1040), line 74a, and following the instructions there.

Basis adjustment. Increase your basis in your mutual fund, or your interest in a REIT, by the difference between the gain you report and the credit you claim for the tax paid.

Additional information. For more information on the treatment of distributions from mutual funds, see Pub. 550.

Nondividend Distributions

A nondividend distribution is a distribution that isn't paid out of the earnings and profits of a corporation or a mutual fund. You should receive a Form 1099-DIV or other statement showing the nondividend distribution. On Form 1099-DIV, a nondividend distribution will be shown in box 3. If you don't receive such a statement, you report the distribution as an ordinary dividend.

Basis adjustment. A nondividend distribution reduces the basis of your stock. It isn't taxed until your basis in the stock is fully recovered. This nontaxable portion is also called a return of capital; it is a return of your investment in the stock of the company. If you buy stock in a corporation in different lots at different times, and you cannot definitely identify the shares subject to the nondividend distribution, reduce the basis of your earliest purchases first.

When the basis of your stock has been reduced to zero, report any additional nondividend distribution you receive as a capital gain. Whether you report it as a long-term or short-term capital gain depends on how long you have held the stock. See *Holding Period* in chapter 14.

Example. You bought stock in 2005 for $100. In 2008, you received a nondividend distribution of $80. You didn't include this amount in your income, but you reduced the basis of your stock to $20. You received a nondividend distribution of $30 in 2018. The first $20 of this amount reduced your basis to zero. You report the other $10 as a long-term capital gain for 2018. You must report as a long-term capital gain any nondividend distribution you receive on this stock in later years.

Liquidating Distributions

Liquidating distributions, sometimes called liquidating dividends, are distributions you receive during a partial or complete liquidation of a corporation. These distributions are, at least in part, one form of a return of capital. They may be paid in one or more installments. You will receive Form 1099-DIV from the corporation showing you the amount of the liquidating distribution in box 9 or 10.

For more information on liquidating distributions, see chapter 1 of Pub. 550.

Distributions of Stock and Stock Rights

Distributions by a corporation of its own stock are commonly known as stock dividends. Stock rights (also known as stock options) are distributions by a corporation of rights to acquire the corporation's stock. Generally, stock dividends and stock rights aren't taxable to you, and you don't report them on your return.

Taxable stock dividends and stock rights. Distributions of stock dividends and stock rights are taxable to you if any of the following apply.

1. You or any other shareholder have the choice to receive cash or other property instead of stock or stock rights.

2. The distribution gives cash or other property to some shareholders and an increase in the percentage interest in the corporation's assets or earnings and profits to other shareholders.

3. The distribution is in convertible preferred stock and has the same result as in (2).

4. The distribution gives preferred stock to some common stock shareholders and common stock to other common stock shareholders.

5. The distribution is on preferred stock. (The distribution, however, isn't taxable if it is an increase in the conversion ratio of convertible preferred stock made solely to take into account a stock dividend, stock split, or similar event that would otherwise result in reducing the conversion right.)

The term "stock" includes rights to acquire stock, and the term "shareholder" includes a holder of rights or of convertible securities.

If you receive taxable stock dividends or stock rights, include their fair market value at the time of distribution in your income.

Preferred stock redeemable at a premium. If you receive preferred stock having a redemption price higher than its issue price, the difference (the redemption premium) generally is taxable as a constructive distribution of additional stock on the preferred stock. For more information, see chapter 1 of Pub. 550.

Basis. Your basis in stock or stock rights received in a taxable distribution is their fair market value when distributed. If you receive stock or stock rights that aren't taxable to you, see *Stocks and Bonds* under *Basis of Investment Property* in chapter 4 of Pub. 550 for information on how to figure their basis.

Fractional shares. You may not own enough stock in a corporation to receive a full share of stock if the corporation declares a stock dividend. However, with the approval of the shareholders, the corporation may set up a plan in which fractional shares aren't issued but instead are sold, and the cash proceeds are given to the shareholders. Any cash you receive for fractional shares under such a plan is treated as an amount realized on the sale of the fractional shares. Report this transaction on Form 8949, Sales and Other Dispositions of Capital Assets. Enter your gain or loss (the difference between the cash you receive and the basis of the fractional shares sold) in column (h) of Schedule D (Form 1040) in Part I or Part II, whichever is appropriate.

 Report these transactions on Form 8949. Also, check the correct box to show how the transaction was reported on Form 1099-B.

For more information on Form 8949 and Schedule D (Form 1040), see chapter 4 of Pub. 550. Also see the Instructions for Form 8949 and the Instructions for Schedule D (Form 1040).

Example. You own one share of common stock that you bought on January 3, 2009, for $100. The corporation declared a common stock dividend of 5% on June 30, 2018. The fair market value of the stock at the time the stock dividend was declared was $200. You were paid $10 for the fractional-share stock dividend under a plan described in the discussion above. You figure your gain or loss as follows:

Fair market value of old stock	$200.00
Fair market value of stock dividend (cash received)	+10.00
Fair market value of old stock and stock dividend	$210.00
Basis (cost) of old stock after the stock dividend (($200 ÷ $210) × $100)	$95.24
Basis (cost) of stock dividend (($10 ÷ $210) × $100)	+4.76
Total	$100.00
Cash received	$10.00
Basis (cost) of stock dividend	– 4.76
Gain	$5.24

Because you had held the share of stock for more than 1 year at the time the stock dividend was declared, your gain on the stock dividend is a long-term capital gain.

Scrip dividends. A corporation that declares a stock dividend may issue you a scrip certificate that entitles you to a fractional share. The certificate is generally nontaxable when you receive it. If you choose to have the corporation sell the certificate for you and give you the proceeds, your gain or loss is the difference between the proceeds and the portion of your basis in the corporation's stock allocated to the certificate.

However, if you receive a scrip certificate that you can choose to redeem for cash instead of stock, the certificate is taxable when you receive it. You must include its fair market value in income on the date you receive it.

Other Distributions

You may receive any of the following distributions during the year.

Exempt-interest dividends. Exempt-interest dividends you receive from a mutual fund or other regulated investment company, including those received from a qualified fund of funds in any tax year beginning after December 22, 2010, aren't included in your taxable income. Exempt-interest dividends should be shown in box 11 of Form 1099-DIV.

Information-reporting requirement. Although exempt-interest dividends aren't taxable, you must show them on your tax return if you have to file a return. This is an information-reporting requirement and doesn't change the exempt-interest dividends to taxable income.

Alternative minimum tax treatment. Exempt-interest dividends paid from specified private activity bonds may be subject to the alternative minimum tax. See *Alternative Minimum Tax (AMT)* in chapter 29 for more information.

Dividends on insurance policies. Insurance policy dividends the insurer keeps and uses to pay your premiums aren't taxable. However, you must report as taxable interest income the interest that is paid or credited on dividends left with the insurance company.

If dividends on an insurance contract (other than a modified endowment contract) are distributed to you, they are a partial return of the premiums you paid. Don't include them in your gross income until they are more than the total of all net premiums you paid for the contract. Report any taxable distributions on insurance policies on Schedule 1 (Form 1040), line 21.

Dividends on veterans' insurance. Dividends you receive on veterans' insurance policies aren't taxable. In addition, interest on dividends left with the Department of Veterans Affairs isn't taxable.

Patronage dividends. Generally, patronage dividends you receive in money from a cooperative organization are included in your income.

Don't include in your income patronage dividends you receive on:

- Property bought for your personal use, or

- Capital assets or depreciable property bought for use in your business. But you must reduce the basis (cost) of the items bought. If the dividend is more than the adjusted basis of the assets, you must report the excess as income.

These rules are the same whether the cooperative paying the dividend is a taxable or tax-exempt cooperative.

Alaska Permanent Fund dividends. Don't report these amounts as dividends. Instead, include these amounts on Schedule 1 (Form 1040), line 21.

How To Report Dividend Income

Generally, you must use Form 1040 to report your dividend income. Report the total of your ordinary dividends on line 3b of Form 1040. Report qualified dividends on line 3a of Form 1040.

If you receive capital gain distributions, you must use Form 1040. See *Exceptions to filing Form 8949 and Schedule D (Form 1040)* in chapter 16. If you receive nondividend distributions required to be reported as capital gains, you must use Form 1040.

Form 1099-DIV. If you owned stock on which you received $10 or more in dividends and other distributions, you should receive a Form 1099-DIV. Even if you don't receive Form 1099-DIV, you must report all your dividend income.

See Form 1099-DIV for more information on how to report dividend income.

Form 1040. You must complete Schedule B (Form 1040), Part II, and attach it to your Form 1040 if:

- Your ordinary dividends, which are reported on Form 1099-DIV, box 1a, are more than $1,500; or

- You received, as a nominee, dividends that actually belong to someone else.

If your ordinary dividends are more than $1,500, you also must complete Schedule B (Form 1040), Part III.

List on Schedule B (Form 1040), Part II, line 5, each payer's name and the ordinary dividends you received. If your securities are held by a brokerage firm (in "street name"), list the name of the brokerage firm shown on Form 1099-DIV as the payer. If your stock is held by a nominee who is the owner of record, and the nominee credited or paid you dividends on the stock, show the name of the nominee and the dividends you received or for which you were credited.

Enter on line 6 the total of the amounts listed on line 5. Also enter this total on line 3b of Form 1040.

Qualified dividends. Report qualified dividends (Form 1099-DIV, box 1b) on line 3a of Form 1040. The amount in box 1b is already included in box 1a. Don't add the amount in box 1b to, or subtract it from, the amount in box 1a.

Don't include any of the following on line 3a.

- Qualified dividends you received as a nominee. See *Nominees* under *How To Report Dividend Income* in chapter 1 of Pub. 550.

- Dividends on stock for which you didn't meet the holding period. See *Holding period*, earlier, under *Qualified Dividends*.

- Dividends on any share of stock to the extent you are obligated (whether under a short sale or otherwise) to make related payments for positions in substantially similar or related property.

- Payments in lieu of dividends, but only if you know or have reason to know the payments aren't qualified dividends.

- Payments shown in Form 1099-DIV, box 1b, from a foreign corporation to the extent you know or have reason to know the payments aren't qualified dividends.

If you have qualified dividends, you must figure your tax by completing the Qualified Dividends and Capital Gain Tax Worksheet in the Form 1040 instructions or the Schedule D Tax Worksheet in the Schedule D (Form 1040) instructions, whichever applies. Enter qualified dividends on line 2 of the worksheet.

Investment interest deducted. If you claim a deduction for investment interest, you may have to reduce the amount of your qualified dividends that are eligible for the 0%, 15%, or 20% tax rate. Reduce it by the qualified dividends you choose to include in investment income when figuring the limit on your investment interest deduction. This is done on the Qualified Dividends and Capital Gain Tax Worksheet or the Schedule D Tax Worksheet. For more information about the limit on investment interest, see *Investment expenses* in chapter 24.

Expenses related to dividend income. You may be able to deduct expenses related to dividend income if you itemize your deductions on Schedule A (Form 1040). See chapter 27 for general information about deducting expenses of producing income.

More information. For more information about how to report dividend income, see chapter 1 of Pub. 550 or the instructions for the form you must file.

9.

Rental Income and Expenses

What's New

 At the time this publication went to print, Congress was considering legislation that would do the following.

1. *Provide additional tax relief for those affected by certain 2018 disasters.*

2. *Extend certain tax benefits that expired at the end of 2017 and that currently can't be claimed on your 2018 tax return.*

3. *Change certain other tax provisions.*

To learn whether this legislation was enacted resulting in changes that affect your 2018 tax return, go to Recent Developments at *IRS.gov/ Pub17.*

Introduction

This chapter discusses rental income and expenses. It also covers the following topics.

- Personal use of dwelling unit (including vacation home).

- Depreciation.

- Limits on rental losses.

- How to report your rental income and expenses.

If you sell or otherwise dispose of your rental property, see Pub. 544, Sales and Other Dispositions of Assets.

If you have a loss from damage to, or theft of, rental property, see Pub. 547, Casualties, Disasters, and Thefts.

If you rent a condominium or a cooperative apartment, some special rules apply to you even though you receive the same tax treatment as other owners of rental property. See Pub. 527, Residential Rental Property, for more information.

Useful Items

You may want to see:

Publication

❑ **527** Residential Rental Property

❑ **534** Depreciating Property Placed in Service Before 1987

❑ **535** Business Expenses

❑ **925** Passive Activity and At-Risk Rules

❑ **946** How To Depreciate Property

Form (and Instructions)

❑ **4562** Depreciation and Amortization

❑ **6251** Alternative Minimum Tax—Individuals

❑ **8582** Passive Activity Loss Limitations

❑ **Schedule E (Form 1040)** Supplemental Income and Loss

For these and other useful items, go to *IRS.gov/ Forms.*

Rental Income

In most cases, you must include in your gross income all amounts you receive as rent. Rental income is any payment you receive for the use or occupation of property. It isn't limited to amounts you receive as normal rental payments.

When to report. If you are a cash-basis taxpayer, you report rental income on your return for the year you actually or constructively receive it. You are a cash-basis taxpayer if you report income in the year you receive it, regardless of when it was earned. You constructively receive income when it is made available to you, for example, by being credited to your bank account.

For more information about when you constructively receive income, see *Accounting Methods* in chapter 1.

Advance rent. Advance rent is any amount you receive before the period that it covers. Include advance rent in your rental income in the year you receive it regardless of the period covered or the method of accounting you use.

Example. You sign a 10-year lease to rent your property. In the first year, you receive $5,000 for the first year's rent and $5,000 as rent for the last year of the lease. You must include $10,000 in your income in the first year.

Canceling a lease. If your tenant pays you to cancel a lease, the amount you receive is rent. Include the payment in your income in the year you receive it regardless of your method of accounting.

Expenses paid by tenant. If your tenant pays any of your expenses, those payments are rental income. Because you must include this amount in income, you also can deduct the expenses if they are deductible rental expenses. See *Rental Expenses*, later, for more information.

Property or services. If you receive property or services, instead of money, as rent, include the fair market value of the property or services in your rental income.

If the services are provided at an agreed upon or specified price, that price is the fair market value unless there is evidence to the contrary.

Security deposits. Don't include a security deposit in your income when you receive it if you plan to return it to your tenant at the end of the lease. But if you keep part or all of the security deposit during any year because your tenant doesn't live up to the terms of the lease, include the amount you keep in your income in that year.

If an amount called a security deposit is to be used as a final payment of rent, it is advance rent. Include it in your income when you receive it.

Part interest. If you own a part interest in rental property, you must report your part of the rental income from the property.

Rental of property also used as your home. If you rent property that you also use as your home and you rent it less than 15 days during the tax year, don't include the rent you receive in your income and don't deduct rental expenses. However, you can deduct on Schedule A (Form 1040) the interest, taxes, and casualty and theft losses that are allowed for nonrental property. See *Personal Use of Dwelling Unit (Including Vacation Home)*, later.

Rental Expenses

This part discusses expenses of renting property that you ordinarily can deduct from your rental income. It includes information on the expenses you can deduct if you rent part of your property, or if you change your property to rental use. Depreciation, which you can also deduct from your rental income, is discussed later under *Depreciation of Rental Property*.

Personal use of rental property. If you sometimes use your rental property for personal purposes, you must divide your expenses between rental and personal use. Also, your rental expense deductions may be limited. See *Personal Use of Dwelling Unit (Including Vacation Home)*, later.

Part interest. If you own a part interest in rental property, you can deduct expenses that you paid according to your percentage of ownership.

When to deduct. If you are a cash-basis taxpayer, you generally deduct your rental expenses in the year you pay them.

Depreciation. You can begin to depreciate rental property when it is ready and available for rent. See *Placed in Service* under *When Does Depreciation Begin and End* in chapter 2 of Pub. 527.

Pre-rental expenses. You can deduct your ordinary and necessary expenses for managing, conserving, or maintaining rental property from the time you make it available for rent.

Uncollected rent. If you are a cash-basis taxpayer, don't deduct uncollected rent. Because you haven't included it in your income, it isn't deductible.

Vacant rental property. If you hold property for rental purposes, you may be able to deduct your ordinary and necessary expenses (including depreciation) for managing, conserving, or maintaining the property while the property is vacant. However, you can't deduct any loss of rental income for the period the property is vacant.

Vacant while listed for sale. If you sell property you held for rental purposes, you can deduct the ordinary and necessary expenses for managing, conserving, or maintaining the property until it is sold. If the property isn't held out and available for rent while listed for sale, the expenses aren't deductible rental expenses.

Repairs and Improvements

Generally, an expense for repairing or maintaining your rental property may be deducted if you aren't required to capitalize the expense.

Improvements. You must capitalize any expense you pay to improve your rental property. An expense is for an improvement if it results in a betterment to your property, restores your property, or adapts your property to a new or different use.

Betterments. Expenses that may result in a betterment to your property include expenses for fixing a pre-existing defect or condition, enlarging or expanding your property, or increasing the capacity, strength, or quality of your property.

Restoration. Expenses that may be for restoration include expenses for replacing a substantial structural part of your property, repairing damage to your property after you properly adjusted the basis of your property as a result of a casualty loss, or rebuilding your property to a like-new condition.

Adaptation. Expenses that may be for adaptation include expenses for altering your property to a use that isn't consistent with the intended ordinary use of your property when you began renting the property.

Safe harbor for routine maintenance. If you determine that your cost was for an improvement to a building or equipment, you still may be able to deduct your cost under the routine maintenance safe harbor. See Pub. 535 for more information.

 Separate the costs of repairs and improvements, and keep accurate records. You will need to know the cost of improvements when you sell or depreciate your property. The expenses you capitalize for improving your property generally can be depreciated as if the improvement were separate property.

Other Expenses

Other expenses you can deduct from your rental income include advertising, cleaning and maintenance, utilities, fire and liability insurance, taxes, interest, commissions for the collection of rent, ordinary and necessary travel and transportation, and other expenses, discussed next.

Insurance premiums paid in advance. If you pay an insurance premium for more than 1 year in advance, you can't deduct the total premium in the year you pay it. For each year of coverage, you deduct only the part of the premium payment that applies to that year.

Legal and other professional fees. You can deduct, as a rental expense, legal and other professional expenses, such as tax return preparation fees you paid to prepare Schedule E (Form 1040), Part I. For example, on your 2018 Schedule E, you also can deduct fees paid in 2018 to prepare your 2017 Schedule E, Part I. You can also deduct, as a rental expense, any expense (other than federal taxes and penalties) you paid to resolve a tax underpayment related to your rental activities.

Local benefits taxes. In most cases, you can't deduct charges for local benefits that increase the value of your property, such as charges for putting in streets, sidewalks, or water and sewer systems. These charges are nondepreciable capital expenditures, and must be added to the basis of your property. However, you can deduct local benefit taxes that are for maintaining, repairing, or paying interest charges for the benefits.

Local transportation expenses. You may be able to deduct your ordinary and necessary local transportation expenses if you incur them to collect rental income or to manage, conserve, or maintain your rental property. However, transportation expenses incurred to travel between your home and a rental property generally constitute nondeductible commuting costs unless you use your home as your principal place of business. See Pub. 587, Business Use of Your Home, for information on determining if your home office qualifies as a principal place of business.

Generally, if you use your personal car, pickup truck, or light van for rental activities, you can deduct the expenses using one of two methods: actual expenses or the standard mileage rate. For 2018, the standard mileage rate for business use is 54.5 cents per mile. For more information, see *Transportation Expenses* in chapter 20.

 To deduct car expenses under either method, you must keep records that follow the rules in *Recordkeeping* in chapter 20. In addition, you must complete Form 4562, Part V, and attach it to your tax return.

Rental of equipment. You can deduct the rent you pay for equipment that you use for rental purposes. However, in some cases, lease contracts are actually purchase contracts. If so, you can't deduct these payments. You can recover the cost of purchased equipment through depreciation.

Rental of property. You can deduct the rent you pay for property that you use for rental purposes. If you buy a leasehold for rental purposes, you can deduct an equal part of the cost each year over the term of the lease.

Travel expenses. You can deduct the ordinary and necessary expenses of traveling away from home if the primary purpose of the trip is to collect rental income or to manage, conserve, or maintain your rental property. You must properly allocate your expenses between rental and nonrental activities. You can't deduct the cost of traveling away from home if the primary purpose of the trip was to improve your property. You recover the cost of improvements by taking depreciation. For information on travel expenses, see *Travel Expenses* in chapter 20.

 To deduct *Travel Expenses*, you must keep records that follow the rules in chapter 20.

See *Rental Expenses* in Pub. 527 for more information.

Property Changed to Rental Use

If you change your home or other property (or a part of it) to rental use at any time other than the beginning of your tax year, you must divide yearly expenses, such as taxes and insurance, between rental use and personal use.

You can deduct as rental expenses only the part of the expense that is for the part of the year the property was used or held for rental purposes.

You can't deduct depreciation or insurance for the part of the year the property was held for personal use. However, you can include the home mortgage interest and real estate tax expenses for the part of the year the property was held for personal use when figuring the amount you can deduct on Schedule A.

Example. Your tax year is the calendar year. You moved from your home in May and started renting it out on June 1. You can deduct as rental expenses seven-twelfths of your yearly expenses, such as taxes and insurance.

Starting with June, you can deduct as rental expenses the amounts you pay for items generally billed monthly, such as utilities.

Renting Part of Property

If you rent part of your property, you must divide certain expenses between the part of the property used for rental purposes and the part of the property used for personal purposes, as though you actually had two separate pieces of property.

You can deduct the expenses related to the part of the property used for rental purposes, such as home mortgage interest and real estate taxes, as rental expenses on Schedule E (Form 1040). You also can deduct as rental expenses a portion of other expenses that normally are nondeductible personal expenses, such as expenses for electricity or painting the outside of your house.

There is no change in the types of expenses deductible for the personal-use part of your property. Generally, these expenses may be deducted only if you itemize your deductions on Schedule A (Form 1040).

You can't deduct any part of the cost of the first phone line even if your tenants have unlimited use of it.

You don't have to divide the expenses that belong only to the rental part of your property. For example, if you paint a room that you rent, or if you pay premiums for liability insurance in connection with renting a room in your home, your entire cost is a rental expense. If you install a second phone line strictly for your tenants' use, all of the cost of the second line is deductible as a rental expense. You can deduct depreciation, discussed later, on the part of the house used for rental purposes as well as on the furniture and equipment you use for rental purposes.

How to divide expenses. If an expense is for both rental use and personal use, such as mortgage interest or heat for the entire house, you must divide the expense between the rental use and the personal use. You can use any reasonable method for dividing the expense. It may be reasonable to divide the cost of some items (for example, water) based on the number of people using them. The two most common methods for dividing an expense are based on (1) the number of rooms in your home, and (2) the square footage of your home.

Not Rented for Profit

If you don't rent your property to make a profit, you can deduct your rental expenses only up to the amount of your rental income. You can't deduct a loss or carry forward to the next year any rental expenses that are more than your rental income for the year. For more information about the rules for an activity not engaged in for profit, see *Not-for-Profit Activities* in chapter 1 of Pub. 535.

Where to report. Report your not-for-profit rental income on Schedule 1 (Form 1040), line 21, or Form 1040NR, line 21. If you itemize your deductions, include your mortgage interest (if you use the property as your main home or second home), real estate taxes, and casualty losses from your not-for-profit rental activity when figuring the amount you can deduct on Schedule A.

Personal Use of Dwelling Unit (Including Vacation Home)

If you have any personal use of a dwelling unit (including a vacation home) that you rent, you must divide your expenses between rental use and personal use. In general, your rental expenses will be no more than your total expenses multiplied by a fraction, the denominator of which is the total number of days the dwelling unit is used and the numerator of which is the total number of days actually rented at a fair rental price. Only your rental expenses may be deducted on Schedule E (Form 1040). Some of your personal expenses may be deductible if you itemize your deductions on Schedule A (Form 1040).

You also must determine if the dwelling unit is considered a home. The amount of rental expenses that you can deduct may be limited if the dwelling unit is considered a home. Whether a dwelling unit is considered a home depends on how many days during the year are considered to be days of personal use. There is a special rule if you used the dwelling unit as a home and you rented it for less than 15 days during the year.

Dwelling unit. A dwelling unit includes a house, apartment, condominium, mobile home, boat, vacation home, or similar property. It also includes all structures or other property belonging to the dwelling unit. A dwelling unit has basic living accommodations, such as sleeping space, a toilet, and cooking facilities.

A dwelling unit doesn't include property (or part of the property) used solely as a hotel, motel, inn, or similar establishment. Property is used solely as a hotel, motel, inn, or similar establishment if it is regularly available for occupancy by paying customers and isn't used by an owner as a home during the year.

Example. You rent a room in your home that is always available for short-term occupancy by paying customers. You don't use the room yourself, and you allow only paying customers to use the room. The room is used solely as a hotel, motel, inn, or similar establishment and isn't a dwelling unit.

Dividing Expenses

If you use a dwelling unit for both rental and personal purposes, divide your expenses between the rental use and the personal use based on the number of days used for each purpose.

When dividing your expenses, follow these rules.

- Any day that the unit is rented at a fair rental price is a day of rental use even if you used the unit for personal purposes that day. (This rule doesn't apply when determining whether you used the unit as a home.)

- Any day that the unit is available for rent but not actually rented isn't a day of rental use.

Example. Your beach cottage was available for rent from June 1 through August 31 (92 days). During that time, except for the first week in August (7 days) when you were unable to find a renter, you rented the cottage at a fair rental price. The person who rented the cottage for July allowed you to use it over the weekend (2 days) without any reduction in or refund of rent. Your family also used the cottage during the last 2 weeks of May (14 days). The cottage wasn't used at all before May 17 or after August 31.

You figure the part of the cottage expenses to treat as rental expenses as follows.

- The cottage was used for rental purposes for a total of 85 days (92 − 7). The days it was available for rent but not rented (7 days) aren't days of rental use. The July weekend (2 days) you used it is rental use because you received a fair rental price for the weekend.

- You used the cottage for personal purposes for 14 days (the last 2 weeks in May).

- The total use of the cottage was 99 days (14 days personal use + 85 days rental use).

- Your rental expenses are 85/99 (86%) of the cottage expenses.

Note. When determining whether you used the cottage as a home, the July weekend (2 days) you used it is considered personal use even though you received a fair rental price for the weekend. Therefore, you had 16 days of personal use and 83 days of rental use for this purpose. Because you used the cottage for personal purposes more than 14 days and more than 10% of the days of rental use (8 days), you used it as a home. If you have a net loss, you may not be able to deduct all of the rental expenses. See *Dwelling Unit Used as a Home* next.

Dwelling Unit Used as a Home

If you use a dwelling unit for both rental and personal purposes, the tax treatment of the rental expenses you figured earlier under *Dividing Expenses* and rental income depends on whether you are considered to be using the dwelling unit as a home.

You use a dwelling unit as a home during the tax year if you use it for personal purposes more than the greater of:

1. 14 days, or
2. 10% of the total days it is rented to others at a fair rental price.

See *What is a day of personal use*, later.

Fair rental price. A fair rental price for your property generally is the amount of rent that a person who isn't related to you would be willing to pay. The rent you charge isn't a fair rental price if it is substantially less than the rents charged for other properties that are similar to your property in your area.

If a dwelling unit is used for personal purposes on a day it is rented at a fair rental price, don't count that day as a day of rental use in applying (2) just described. Instead, count it as a day of personal use in applying both (1) and (2) just described.

What is a day of personal use? A day of personal use of a dwelling unit is any day that the unit is used by any of the following persons.

1. You or any other person who owns an interest in the unit, unless you rent it to another owner as his or her main home under a shared equity financing agreement (defined later). However, see *Days used as a main home before or after renting*, later.
2. A member of your family or a member of the family of any other person who owns an interest in the unit, unless the family member uses the dwelling unit as his or her main home and pays a fair rental price. Family includes only your spouse, brothers and sisters, half-brothers and half-sisters, ancestors (parents, grandparents, etc.), and lineal descendants (children, grandchildren, etc.).
3. Anyone under an arrangement that lets you use some other dwelling unit.
4. Anyone at less than a fair rental price.

Main home. If the other person or member of the family in (1) or (2) just described has

more than one home, his or her main home is ordinarily the one he or she lived in most of the time.

Shared equity financing agreement. This is an agreement under which two or more persons acquire undivided interests for more than 50 years in an entire dwelling unit, including the land, and one or more of the co-owners is entitled to occupy the unit as his or her main home upon payment of rent to the other co-owner or owners.

Donation of use of property. You use a dwelling unit for personal purposes if:

- You donate the use of the unit to a charitable organization,
- The organization sells the use of the unit at a fundraising event, and
- The "purchaser" uses the unit.

Examples. The following examples show how to determine days of personal use.

Example 1. You and your neighbor are co-owners of a condominium at the beach. Last year, you rented the unit to vacationers whenever possible. The unit wasn't used as a main home by anyone. Your neighbor used the unit for 2 weeks last year; you didn't use it at all.

Because your neighbor has an interest in the unit, both of you are considered to have used the unit for personal purposes during those 2 weeks.

Example 2. You and your neighbors are co-owners of a house under a shared equity financing agreement. Your neighbors live in the house and pay you a fair rental price.

Even though your neighbors have an interest in the house, the days your neighbors live there aren't counted as days of personal use by you. This is because your neighbors rent the house as their main home under a shared equity financing agreement.

Example 3. You own a rental property that you rent to your son. Your son doesn't own any interest in this property. He uses it as his main home and pays you a fair rental price.

Your son's use of the property isn't personal use by you because your son is using it as his main home, he owns no interest in the property, and he is paying you a fair rental price.

Example 4. You rent your beach house to Joshua. Joshua rents his cabin in the mountains to you. You each pay a fair rental price.

You are using your beach house for personal purposes on the days that Joshua uses it because your house is used by Joshua under an arrangement that allows you to use his cabin.

Days used for repairs and maintenance. Any day that you spend working substantially full time repairing and maintaining (not improving) your property isn't counted as a day of personal use. Don't count such a day as a day of personal use even if family members use the property for recreational purposes on the same day.

Days used as a main home before or after renting. For purposes of determining

whether a dwelling unit was used as a home, you may not have to count days you used the property as your main home before or after renting it or offering it for rent as days of personal use. Don't count them as days of personal use if:

- You rented or tried to rent the property for 12 or more consecutive months.
- You rented or tried to rent the property for a period of less than 12 consecutive months and the period ended because you sold or exchanged the property.

However, this special rule doesn't apply when dividing expenses between rental and personal use.

Examples. The following examples show how to determine whether you used your rental property as a home.

Example 1. You converted the basement of your home into an apartment with a bedroom, a bathroom, and a small kitchen. You rented the basement apartment at a fair rental price to college students during the regular school year. You rented to them on a 9-month lease (273 days). You figured 10% of the total days rented to others at a fair rental price is 27 days.

During June (30 days), your brothers stayed with you and lived in the basement apartment rent free.

Your basement apartment was used as a home because you used it for personal purposes for 30 days. Rent-free use by your brothers is considered personal use. Your personal use (30 days) is more than the greater of 14 days or 10% of the total days it was rented (27 days).

Example 2. You rented the guest bedroom in your home at a fair rental price during the local college's homecoming, commencement, and football weekends (a total of 27 days). Your sister-in-law stayed in the room, rent free, for the last 3 weeks (21 days) in July. You figured 10% of the total days rented to others at a fair rental price is 3 days.

The room was used as a home because you used it for personal purposes for 21 days. That is more than the greater of 14 days or 10% of the 27 days it was rented (3 days).

Example 3. You own a condominium apartment in a resort area. You rented it at a fair rental price for a total of 170 days during the year. For 12 of those days, the tenant wasn't able to use the apartment and allowed you to use it even though you didn't refund any of the rent. Your family actually used the apartment for 10 of those days. Therefore, the apartment is treated as having been rented for 160 (170 – 10) days. You figured 10% of the total days rented to others at a fair rental price is 16 days. Your family also used the apartment for 7 other days during the year.

You used the apartment as a home because you used it for personal purposes for 17 days. That is more than the greater of 14 days or 10% of the 160 days it was rented (16 days).

Minimal rental use. If you use the dwelling unit as a home and you rent it less than 15 days during the year, that period isn't treated as rental activity. See *Used as a home but rented less than 15 days*, later, for more information.

Limit on deductions. Renting a dwelling unit that is considered a home isn't a passive activity. Instead, if your rental expenses are more than your rental income, some or all of the excess expenses can't be used to offset income from other sources. The excess expenses that can't be used to offset income from other sources are carried forward to the next year and treated as rental expenses for the same property. Any expenses carried forward to the next year will be subject to any limits that apply for that year. This limitation will apply to expenses carried forward to another year even if you don't use the property as your home for that subsequent year.

To figure your deductible rental expenses for this year and any carryover to next year, use Worksheet 9-1.

Reporting Income and Deductions

Property not used for personal purposes. If you don't use a dwelling unit for personal purposes, see *How To Report Rental Income and Expenses*, later, for how to report your rental income and expenses.

Property used for personal purposes. If you do use a dwelling unit for personal purposes, then how you report your rental income and expenses depends on whether you used the dwelling unit as a home.

Not used as a home. If you use a dwelling unit for personal purposes, but not as a home, report all the rental income in your income. Because you used the dwelling unit for personal purposes, you must divide your expenses between the rental use and the personal use, as described earlier in *Dividing Expenses*. The expenses for personal use aren't deductible as rental expenses.

Your deductible rental expenses can be more than your gross rental income; however, see *Limits on Rental Losses*, later.

Used as a home but rented less than 15 days. If you use a dwelling unit as a home and you rent it less than 15 days during the year, its primary function isn't considered to be rental and it shouldn't be reported on Schedule E (Form 1040). You aren't required to report the rental income and rental expenses from this activity. The expenses, including mortgage interest, property taxes, and any qualified casualty loss, will be reported as normally allowed on Schedule A (Form 1040). See the Instructions for Schedule A (Form 1040) for more information on deducting these expenses.

Used as a home and rented 15 days or more. If you use a dwelling unit as a home and rent it 15 days or more during the year, include all your rental income in your income. Since you used the dwelling unit for personal purposes, you must divide your expenses between the rental use and the personal use, as described earlier in *Dividing Expenses*. The expenses for personal use aren't deductible as rental expenses.

If you had a net profit from renting the dwelling unit for the year (that is, if your rental income is more than the total of your rental expenses, including depreciation), deduct all of your rental

expenses. You don't need to use Worksheet 9-1.

However, if you had a net loss from renting the dwelling unit for the year, your deduction for certain rental expenses is limited. To figure your deductible rental expenses and any carryover to next year, use Worksheet 9-1.

Depreciation of Rental Property

You recover the cost of income-producing property through yearly tax deductions. You do this by depreciating the property; that is, by deducting some of the cost each year on your tax return.

Three factors determine how much depreciation you can deduct each year: (1) your basis in the property, (2) the recovery period for the property, and (3) the depreciation method used. You can't simply deduct your mortgage or principal payments, or the cost of furniture, fixtures, and equipment, as an expense.

You can deduct depreciation only on the part of your property used for rental purposes. Depreciation reduces your basis for figuring gain or loss on a later sale or exchange.

You may have to use Form 4562 to figure and report your depreciation. See *How To Report Rental Income and Expenses*, later.

Alternative minimum tax (AMT). If you use accelerated depreciation, you may be subject to the AMT. Accelerated depreciation allows you to deduct more depreciation earlier in the recovery period than you could deduct using a straight line method (same deduction each year).

Claiming the correct amount of depreciation. You should claim the correct amount of depreciation each tax year. If you didn't claim all the depreciation you were entitled to deduct, you must still reduce your basis in the property by the full amount of depreciation that you could have deducted.

If you deducted an incorrect amount of depreciation for property in any year, you may be able to make a correction by filing Form 1040X, Amended U.S. Individual Income Tax Return. If you aren't allowed to make the correction on an amended return, you can change your accounting method to claim the correct amount of depreciation. See *Claiming the Correct Amount of Depreciation* in chapter 2 of Pub. 527 for more information.

Changing your accounting method to deduct unclaimed depreciation. To change your accounting method, you generally must file Form 3115 to get the consent of the IRS. In some instances, that consent is automatic. For more information, see chapter 1 of Pub. 946.

Land. You can't depreciate the cost of land because land generally doesn't wear out, become obsolete, or get used up. The costs of clearing, grading, planting, and landscaping are usually all part of the cost of land and can't be depreciated.

More information. See Pub. 527 for more information about depreciating rental property

and see Pub. 946 for more information about depreciation.

Limits on Rental Losses

If you have a loss from your rental real estate activity, two sets of rules may limit the amount of loss you can report on Schedule E. You must consider these rules in the order shown below.

1. At-risk rules. These rules are applied first if there is investment in your rental real estate activity for which you aren't at risk. This applies only if the real property was placed in service after 1986.

2. Passive activity limits. Generally, rental real estate activities are considered passive activities and losses aren't deductible unless you have income from other passive activities to offset them. However, there are exceptions.

In addition to at-risk rules and passive activity limits, excess business loss rules apply to losses from all noncorporate trades or businesses. This loss limitation is figured using Form 461 after you complete your Schedule E. Any limitation to your loss resulting from these rules will not be reflected on your Schedule E. Instead, it will be added to your income on Form 1040 and treated as a net operating loss that must be carried forward and deducted in a subsequent year.

At-Risk Rules

You may be subject to the at-risk rules if you have:

- A loss from an activity carried on as a trade or business or for the production of income, and

- Amounts invested in the activity for which you aren't fully at risk.

Losses from holding real property (other than mineral property) placed in service before 1987 aren't subject to the at-risk rules.

In most cases, any loss from an activity subject to the at-risk rules is allowed only to the extent of the total amount you have at risk in the activity at the end of the tax year. You are considered at risk in an activity to the extent of cash and the adjusted basis of other property you contributed to the activity and certain amounts borrowed for use in the activity. See Pub. 925 for more information.

Passive Activity Limits

In most cases, all rental real estate activities (except those of certain real estate professionals, discussed later) are passive activities. For this purpose, a rental activity is an activity from which you receive income mainly for the use of tangible property, rather than for services.

Limits on passive activity deductions and credits. Deductions or losses from passive activities are limited. You generally can't offset income, other than passive income, with losses from passive activities. Nor can you offset taxes on income, other than passive income, with credits resulting from passive activities. Any excess loss or credit is carried forward to the next tax year.

For a detailed discussion of these rules, see Pub. 925.

You may have to complete Form 8582 to figure the amount of any passive activity loss for the current tax year for all activities and the amount of the passive activity loss allowed on your tax return.

Real estate professionals. Rental activities in which you materially participated during the year aren't passive activities if, for that year, you were a real estate professional. For a detailed discussion of the requirements, see Pub. 527. For a detailed discussion of material participation, see Pub. 925.

Exception for Personal Use of Dwelling Unit

If you used the rental property as a home during the year, any income, deductions, gain, or loss allocable to such use is not taken into account for purposes of the passive activity loss limitation. Instead, follow the rules explained in *Personal Use of Dwelling Unit (Including Vacation Home)*, earlier.

Exception for Rental Real Estate Activities With Active Participation

If you or your spouse actively participated in a passive rental real estate activity, you may be able to deduct up to $25,000 of loss from the activity from your nonpassive income. This special allowance is an exception to the general rule disallowing losses in excess of income from passive activities. Similarly, you may be able to offset credits from the activity against the tax on up to $25,000 of nonpassive income after taking into account any losses allowed under this exception.

Active participation. You actively participated in a rental real estate activity if you (and your spouse) owned at least 10% of the rental property and you made management decisions or arranged for others to provide services (such as repairs) in a significant and bona fide sense. Management decisions that may count as active participation include approving new tenants, deciding on rental terms, approving expenditures, and similar decisions.

Maximum special allowance. The maximum special allowance is:

- $25,000 for single individuals and married individuals filing a joint return for the tax year,
- $12,500 for married individuals who file separate returns for the tax year and lived apart from their spouses at all times during the tax year, and
- $25,000 for a qualifying estate reduced by the special allowance for which the surviving spouse qualified.

If your modified adjusted gross income (MAGI) is $100,000 or less ($50,000 or less if married filing separately), you can deduct your loss up to the amount specified above. If your MAGI is more than $100,000 (more than $50,000 if married filing separately), your special allowance is limited to 50% of the difference between $150,000 ($75,000 if married filing separately) and your MAGI.

Generally, if your MAGI is $150,000 or more ($75,000 or more if you are married filing separately), there is no special allowance.

More information. See Pub. 925 for more information on the passive loss limits, including information on the treatment of unused disallowed passive losses and credits and the treatment of gains and losses realized on the disposition of a passive activity.

How To Report Rental Income and Expenses

The basic form for reporting residential rental income and expenses is Schedule E (Form 1040). However, don't use that schedule to report a not-for-profit activity. See *Not Rented for Profit*, earlier.

Providing substantial services. If you provide substantial services that are primarily for your tenant's convenience, such as regular cleaning, changing linen, or maid service, report your rental income and expenses on Schedule C (Form 1040), Profit or Loss From Business, or Schedule C-EZ (Form 1040), Net Profit From Business (Sole Proprietorship). Substantial services don't include the furnishing of heat and light, cleaning of public areas, trash collec-

tion, etc. For information, see Pub. 334, Tax Guide for Small Business. You also may have to pay self-employment tax on your rental income using Schedule SE (Form 1040), Self-Employment Tax.

Use Form 1065, U.S. Return of Partnership Income, if your rental activity is a partnership (including a partnership with your spouse unless it is a qualified joint venture).

Qualified joint venture. If you and your spouse each materially participate as the only members of a jointly owned and operated real estate business, and you file a joint return for the tax year, you can make a joint election to be treated as a qualified joint venture instead of a partnership. This election, in most cases, won't increase the total tax owed on the joint return, but it does give each of you credit for social security earnings on which retirement benefits are based and for Medicare coverage if your rental income is subject to self-employment tax. For more information, see Pub. 527.

Form 1098, Mortgage Interest Statement. If you paid $600 or more of mortgage interest on your rental property to any one person, you should receive a Form 1098, or a similar statement showing the interest you paid for the year. If you and at least one other person (other than your spouse if you file a joint return) were liable for and paid interest on the mortgage, and the other person received the Form 1098, report your share of the interest on Schedule E (Form 1040), line 13. Attach a statement to your return showing the name and address of the other person. See the Instructions for Schedule E (Form 1040) for more information.

Schedule E (Form 1040)

If you rent buildings, rooms, or apartments, and provide basic services such as heat and light, trash collection, etc., you normally report your rental income and expenses on Schedule E (Form 1040), Part I.

Page 2 of Schedule E is used to report income or loss from partnerships, S corporations, estates, trusts, and real estate mortgage investment conduits. If you need to use page 2 of Schedule E, be sure to use page 2 of the same Schedule E you used to enter your rental activity on page 1. See the Instructions for Schedule E (Form 1040).

Worksheet 9-1. Worksheet for Figuring Rental Deductions for a Dwelling Unit Used as a Home

Keep for Your Records

Use this worksheet only if you answer "Yes" to all of the following questions.
- Did you use the dwelling unit as a home this year? (See *Dwelling Unit Used as a Home*, earlier.)
- Did you rent the dwelling unit at a fair rental price 15 days or more this year?
- Is the total of your rental expenses and depreciation more than your rental income?

PART I. Rental Use Percentage

A. Total days available for rent at fair rental price .... A. _____

B. Total days available for rent (line A) but not rented .... B. _____

C. **Total days of rental use.** Subtract line B from line A .... C. _____

D. **Total days of personal use** (including days rented at less than fair rental price) .... D. _____

E. **Total days of rental and personal use.** Add lines C and D .... E. _____

F. **Percentage of expenses allowed for rental.** Divide line C by line E .... F. _____

PART II. Allowable Rental Expenses

1. Enter rents received .... 1. _____

2a. Enter the rental portion of deductible home mortgage interest. See instructions .... 2a. _____

b. Enter the rental portion of deductible real estate taxes. See instructions .... b. _____

c. Enter the rental portion of deductible casualty and theft losses. See instructions .... c. _____

d. Enter direct rental expenses. See instructions .... d. _____

e. **Fully deductible rental expenses.** Add lines 2a–2d. Enter here and on the appropriate lines on Schedule E. See instructions .... 2e. _____

3. Subtract line 2e from line 1. If zero or less, enter -0- .... 3. _____

4a. Enter the rental portion of expenses directly related to operating or maintaining the dwelling unit (such as repairs, insurance, and utilities) .... 4a. _____

b. Enter the rental portion of excess mortgage interest. See instructions .... b. _____

c. Enter the rental portion of excess real estate taxes. See instructions .... c. _____

d. Carryover of operating expenses from 2017 worksheet .... d. _____

e. Add lines 4a–4d .... e. _____

f. **Allowable expenses.** Enter the **smaller** of line 3 or line 4e. See instructions .... 4f. _____

5. Subtract line 4f from line 3. If zero or less, enter -0- .... 5. _____

6a. Enter the rental portion of excess casualty and theft losses. See instructions .... 6a. _____

b. Enter the rental portion of depreciation of the dwelling unit .... b. _____

c. Carryover of excess casualty and theft losses and depreciation from 2017 worksheet ..... c. _____

d. Add lines 6a–6c .... d. _____

e. **Allowable excess casualty and theft losses and depreciation.** Enter the **smaller** of line 5 or line 6d. See instructions .... 6e. _____

PART III. Carryover of Unallowed Expenses to Next Year

7a. **Operating expenses to be carried over to next year.** Subtract line 4f from line 4e .... 7a. _____

b. **Excess casualty and theft losses and depreciation to be carried over to next year.** Subtract line 6e from line 6d .... b. _____

Caution. Use the percentage determined in Part I, line F, to figure the rental portions to enter on lines 2a–2c, 4a–4c, and 6a–6b of Part II.

Line 2a. Figure the mortgage interest on the dwelling unit that you could deduct on Schedule A as if you had not rented the unit. Don't include interest on a loan that didn't benefit the dwelling unit. For example, don't include interest on a home equity loan used to pay off credit cards or other personal loans, buy a car, or pay college tuition. Include interest on a loan used to buy, build, or improve the dwelling unit, or to refinance such a loan. Enter the rental portion of this interest in the total on line 2a of the worksheet.

Note. If you itemize your deductions on Schedule A, be sure to claim only the personal portion of your deductible mortgage interest on Schedule A. The personal portion of mortgage interest on the dwelling unit doesn't include the rental portion you reported on line 2a of this Worksheet 9-1 or any portion that you deducted on other forms, such as Schedule C or F.

Line 2b. Figure the real estate taxes on the dwelling unit that you could deduct on Schedule A as if you had not rented the unit. If your combined state and local estate taxes, income taxes, and personal property taxes exceed the Schedule A limit for deducting state and local taxes, you will need to separate the Schedule A limit between your real estate taxes and other state and local taxes. When figuring the rental portion of real estate taxes, be sure to use only the portion of the Schedule A limit that is attributable to real estate taxes. Enter the rental portion of these real estate taxes on line 2b of this Worksheet 9-1.

Note. If you itemize your deductions on Schedule A, be sure to report only the personal portion of your real estate taxes on line 5b of Schedule A. The personal portion of real estate taxes on the dwelling unit doesn't include the rental portion you reported on line 2b of this Worksheet 9-1 or any portion that you deducted on other forms, such as Schedule C or F.

Line 2c. Figure the casualty and theft losses related to the dwelling unit resulting from a federally declared disaster that you could deduct on Schedule A as if you had not rented the unit. To do this, complete Section A of Form 4684 as a worksheet. When completing line 17 of the worksheet version of Form 4684, enter 10% of your adjusted gross income figured without your rental income and expenses from the dwelling unit. Enter the rental portion of the amount on lines 15 and 18 of your worksheet version of Form 4684 on line 2c of this Worksheet 9-1. Don't file the worksheet version of Form 4684. Instead, keep it for your records. You will complete a separate Form 4684 to attach to your return.

Note. To figure the casualty and theft losses that you can include in your itemized deductions on Schedule A or the qualified disaster losses by which you may be able to increase your standard deduction, complete Section A on the separate Form 4684 using the personal portion of your casualty losses. You will report casualty and theft losses attributable to your rental activity in Section B of that separate Form 4684.

Line 2d. Enter the total of your rental expenses that are directly related only to the rental activity. These include interest on loans used for rental activities other than to buy, build, or improve the dwelling unit. Also include rental agency fees, advertising, office supplies, and depreciation on office equipment used in your rental activity.

Line 2e. You can deduct the amounts on lines 2a, 2b, 2c, and 2d as rental expenses on Schedule E even if your rental expenses are more than your rental income. Enter the amounts on lines 2a, 2b, 2c, and 2d on the appropriate lines of Schedule E.

Line 4b. On line 2a, you entered the rental portion of the mortgage interest you could deduct on Schedule A if you had not rented the dwelling unit. If you had additional mortgage interest that wouldn't be deductible on Schedule A because of limits imposed on them, enter on line 4b of this worksheet the rental portion of those excess amounts. Don't include interest on a loan that didn't benefit the dwelling unit (as explained in the line 2a instructions).

Line 4c. On line 2b, you entered the rental portion of the real estate taxes you could deduct on Schedule A if you had not rented the dwelling unit. If you had additional real estate taxes that wouldn't be deductible on Schedule A because of the limit imposed on state and local taxes, enter on line 4c of this Worksheet 9-1 the rental portion of those excess real estate taxes.

Line 4f. You can deduct the amounts on lines 4a, 4b, 4c, and 4d, as rental expenses on Schedule E only to the extent they aren't more than the amount on line 4f.*

Line 6a. To find the rental portion of excess casualty and theft losses resulting from a federally declared disaster, use the worksheet version of Form 4684 (Section A) from the line 2c instructions for line A.

If you have casualty and theft losses related to the dwelling unit that aren't the result of a federally declared disaster, treat them as trade or business expenses and complete Section B of Form 4684 as a worksheet. Don't file the worksheet version of Form 4684. Instead, keep it for your records. You'll report just the portion of casualty and theft losses attributable to your rental activity in Section B of a separate Form 4684 according to the Instructions for Form 4684 (Section B) for line E.

> A. Enter the amount from the worksheet version of Form 4684, line 10 . . . . _____
> B. Enter the rental portion of line A . . . . _____
> C. Enter the amount from line 2c of this worksheet . . . . _____
> D. Subtract line C from line B . . . . _____
> E. Enter the amount from the worksheet version of Form 4684, line 28 . . . . _____
> F. Enter the rental portion of line E . . . . _____
> G. Add lines D and F. Enter the result here and on line 6a of this worksheet . . . . _____

Line 6e. You can deduct the amounts on lines 6a, 6b, and 6c as rental expenses on Schedule E only to the extent they aren't more than the amount on line 6e.*

* **Allocating the limited deduction.** If you can't deduct all of the amount on line 4e or line 6d this year, you can allocate the allowable deduction in any way you wish among the expenses included on line 4e or line 6d. Enter the amount you allocate to each expense on the appropriate line of Schedule E, Part I.

10.

Retirement Plans, Pensions, and Annuities

What's New

At the time this publication went to print, Congress was considering legislation that would do the following.

1. Provide additional tax relief for those affected by certain 2018 disasters.

2. Extend certain tax benefits that expired at the end of 2017 and that currently can't be claimed on your 2018 tax return.

3. Change certain other tax provisions.

To learn whether this legislation was enacted resulting in changes that affect your 2018 tax return, go to Recent Developments at *IRS.gov/Pub17*.

Reminders

Net Investment Income Tax (NIIT). For purposes of the NIIT, net investment income doesn't include distributions from a qualified retirement plan (for example, 401(a), 403(a), 403(b), 408, 408A, or 457(b) plans). However, these distributions are taken into account when determining the modified adjusted gross income threshold. Distributions from a nonqualified retirement plan are included in net investment income. See Form 8960, Net Investment Income Tax—Individuals, Estates, and Trusts, and its instructions for more information.

Introduction

This chapter discusses the tax treatment of distributions you receive from:

- An employee pension or annuity from a qualified plan,

- A disability retirement, and

- A purchased commercial annuity.

What isn't covered in this chapter. The following topics are not discussed in this chapter.

The General Rule. This is the method generally used to determine the tax treatment of pension and annuity income from nonqualified plans (including commercial annuities). For a qualified plan, you generally can't use the General Rule unless your annuity starting date is before November 19, 1996. For more

information about the General Rule, see Pub. 939, General Rule for Pensions and Annuities.

Individual retirement arrangements (IRAs). Information on the tax treatment of amounts you receive from an IRA is in chapter 17.

Civil service retirement benefits. If you are retired from the federal government (regular, phased, or disability retirement), see Pub. 721, Tax Guide to U.S. Civil Service Retirement Benefits. Pub. 721 also covers the information that you need if you are the survivor or beneficiary of a federal employee or retiree who died.

Useful Items

You may want to see:

Publication

- ❑ **560** Retirement Plans for Small Business

- ❑ **575** Pension and Annuity Income

- ❑ **721** Tax Guide to U.S. Civil Service Retirement Benefits

- ❑ **939** General Rule for Pensions and Annuities

Form (and Instructions)

- ❑ **W-4P** Withholding Certificate for Pension or Annuity Payments

- ❑ **1099-R** Distributions From Pensions, Annuities, Retirement or Profit-Sharing Plans, IRAs, Insurance Contracts, etc.

- ❑ **4972** Tax on Lump-Sum Distributions

- ❑ **5329** Additional Taxes on Qualified Plans (Including IRAs) and Other Tax-Favored Accounts

For these and other useful items, go to *IRS.gov/Forms*.

General Information

Designated Roth accounts. A designated Roth account is a separate account created under a qualified Roth contribution program to which participants may elect to have part or all of their elective deferrals to a 401(k), 403(b), or 457(b) plan designated as Roth contributions. Elective deferrals that are designated as Roth contributions are included in your income. However, qualified distributions aren't included in your income. See Pub. 575 for more information.

In-plan rollovers to designated Roth accounts. If you are a participant in a 401(k), 403(b), or 457(b) plan, your plan may permit you to roll over amounts in those plans to a designated Roth account within the same plan. The rollover of any untaxed amounts must be included in income in the year you receive the distribution. See Pub. 575 for more information.

More than one program. If you receive benefits from more than one program under a single trust or plan of your employer, such as a pension plan and a profit-sharing plan, you may have to figure the taxable part of each pension or annuity contract separately. Your former employer or the plan administrator should be able

to tell you if you have more than one pension or annuity contract.

Section 457 deferred compensation plans. If you work for a state or local government or for a tax-exempt organization, you may be able to participate in a section 457 deferred compensation plan. If your plan is an eligible plan, you aren't taxed currently on pay that is deferred under the plan or on any earnings from the plan's investment of the deferred pay. You generally are taxed on amounts deferred in an eligible state or local government plan only when they are distributed from the plan. You are taxed on amounts deferred in an eligible tax-exempt organization plan when they are distributed or otherwise made available to you.

Your 457(b) plan may have a designated Roth account option. If so, you may be able to roll over amounts to the designated Roth account or make contributions. Elective deferrals to a designated Roth account are included in your income. Qualified distributions from a designated Roth account aren't subject to tax.

This chapter covers the tax treatment of benefits under eligible section 457 plans, but it doesn't cover the treatment of deferrals. For information on deferrals under section 457 plans, see *Retirement Plan Contributions* under *Employee Compensation* in Pub. 525.

For general information on these deferred compensation plans, see *Section 457 Deferred Compensation Plans* in Pub. 575.

Disability pensions. If you retired on disability, you generally must include in income any disability pension you receive under a plan that is paid for by your employer. You must report your taxable disability payments as wages on line 1 of Form 1040 until you reach minimum retirement age. Minimum retirement age generally is the age at which you can first receive a pension or annuity if you aren't disabled.

 You may be entitled to a tax credit if you were permanently and totally disabled when you retired. For information on the credit for the elderly or the disabled, see chapter 32.

Beginning on the day after you reach minimum retirement age, payments you receive are taxable as a pension or annuity. Report the payments on Form 1040, lines 4a and 4b.

 Disability payments for injuries incurred as a direct result of a terrorist attack directed against the United States (or its allies) aren't included in income. For more information about payments to survivors of terrorist attacks, see Pub. 3920.

For more information on how to report disability pensions, including military and certain government disability pensions, see chapter 5.

Retired public safety officers. An eligible retired public safety officer can elect to exclude from income distributions of up to $3,000 made directly from a government retirement plan to the provider of accident, health, or long-term disability insurance. See *Insurance Premiums for Retired Public Safety Officers* in Pub. 575 for more information.

Railroad retirement benefits. Part of any railroad retirement benefits you receive is treated for tax purposes as social security benefits, and part is treated as an employee pension. For information about railroad retirement benefits treated as social security benefits, see Pub. 915. For information about railroad retirement benefits treated as an employee pension, see *Railroad Retirement Benefits* in Pub. 575.

Withholding and estimated tax. The payer of your pension, profit-sharing, stock bonus, annuity, or deferred compensation plan will withhold income tax on the taxable parts of amounts paid to you. You can tell the payer how much to withhold, or not to withhold, by filing Form W-4P. If you choose not to have tax withheld, or you don't have enough tax withheld, you may have to pay estimated tax.

If you receive an eligible rollover distribution, you can't choose not to have tax withheld. Generally, 20% will be withheld, but no tax will be withheld on a direct rollover of an eligible rollover distribution. See *Direct rollover option* under *Rollovers*, later.

For more information, see *Pensions and Annuities* under *Tax Withholding for 2019* in chapter 4.

Qualified plans for self-employed individuals. Qualified plans set up by self-employed individuals are sometimes called Keogh or H.R. 10 plans. Qualified plans can be set up by sole proprietors, partnerships (but not a partner), and corporations. They can cover self-employed persons, such as the sole proprietor or partners, as well as regular (common-law) employees.

Distributions from a qualified plan usually are fully taxable because most recipients have no cost basis. If you have an investment (cost) in the plan, however, your pension or annuity payments from a qualified plan are taxed under the Simplified Method. For more information about qualified plans, see Pub. 560.

Purchased annuities. If you receive pension or annuity payments from a privately purchased annuity contract from a commercial organization, such as an insurance company, you generally must use the General Rule to figure the tax-free part of each annuity payment. For more information about the General Rule, see Pub. 939. Also, see *Variable Annuities* in Pub. 575 for the special provisions that apply to these annuity contracts.

Loans. If you borrow money from your retirement plan, you must treat the loan as a nonperiodic distribution from the plan unless certain exceptions apply. This treatment also applies to any loan under a contract purchased under your retirement plan, and to the value of any part of your interest in the plan or contract that you pledge or assign. This means that you must include in income all or part of the amount borrowed. Even if you don't have to treat the loan as a nonperiodic distribution, you may not be able to deduct the interest on the loan in some situations. For details, see *Loans Treated as Distributions* in Pub. 575. For information on the deductibility of interest, see chapter 24.

Tax-free exchange. No gain or loss is recognized on an exchange of an annuity contract for another annuity contract if the insured or annuitant remains the same. However, if an annuity contract is exchanged for a life insurance or en-

dowment contract, any gain due to interest accumulated on the contract is ordinary income. See *Transfers of Annuity Contracts* in Pub. 575 for more information about exchanges of annuity contracts.

How To Report

If you file Form 1040, report your total annuity on line 4a, and the taxable part on line 4b. If your pension or annuity is fully taxable, enter it on line 4b; don't make an entry on line 4a.

More than one annuity. If you receive more than one annuity and at least one of them isn't fully taxable, enter the total amount received from all annuities on Form 1040, line 4a, and enter the taxable part on Form 1040, line 4b. If all the annuities you receive are fully taxable, enter the total of all of them on Form 1040, line 4b.

Joint return. If you file a joint return and you and your spouse each receive one or more pensions or annuities, report the total of the pensions and annuities on Form 1040, line 4a, and report the taxable part on Form 1040, line 4b.

Cost (Investment in the Contract)

Before you can figure how much, if any, of a distribution from your pension or annuity plan is taxable, you must determine your cost (your investment in the contract) in the pension or annuity. Your total cost in the plan includes the total premiums, contributions, or other amounts you paid. This includes the amounts your employer contributed that were taxable to you when paid. Cost doesn't include any amounts you deducted or were excluded from your income.

From this total cost, subtract any refunds of premiums, rebates, dividends, unrepaid loans that weren't included in your income, or other tax-free amounts that you received by the later of the annuity starting date or the date on which you received your first payment.

Your annuity starting date is the later of the first day of the first period for which you received a payment or the date the plan's obligations became fixed.

Designated Roth accounts. Your cost in these accounts is your designated Roth contributions that were included in your income as wages subject to applicable withholding requirements. Your cost also will include any in-plan Roth rollovers you included in income.

Foreign employment contributions. If you worked in a foreign country and contributions were made to your retirement plan, special rules apply in determining your cost. See *Foreign employment contributions* under *Cost (Investment in the Contract)* in Pub. 575.

Taxation of Periodic Payments

Fully taxable payments. Generally, if you didn't pay any part of the cost of your employee pension or annuity and your employer didn't

withhold part of the cost from your pay while you worked, the amounts you receive each year are fully taxable. You must report them on your income tax return.

Partly taxable payments. If you paid part of the cost of your pension or annuity, you aren't taxed on the part of the pension or annuity you receive that represents a return of your cost. The rest of the amount you receive generally is taxable. You figure the tax-free part of the payment using either the Simplified Method or the General Rule. Your annuity starting date and whether or not your plan is qualified determine which method you must or may use.

If your annuity starting date is after November 18, 1996, and your payments are from a qualified plan, you must use the Simplified Method. Generally, you must use the General Rule if your annuity is paid under a nonqualified plan, and you can't use this method if your annuity is paid under a qualified plan.

If you had more than one partly taxable pension or annuity, figure the tax-free part and the taxable part of each separately.

If your annuity is paid under a qualified plan and your annuity starting date is after July 1, 1986, and before November 19, 1996, you could have chosen to use either the General Rule or the Simplified Method.

Exclusion limit. Your annuity starting date determines the total amount of annuity payments that you can exclude from your taxable income over the years. Once your annuity starting date is determined, it doesn't change. If you calculate the taxable portion of your annuity payments using the Simplified Method Worksheet, the annuity starting date determines the recovery period for your cost. That recovery period begins on your annuity starting date and isn't affected by the date you first complete the worksheet.

Exclusion limited to cost. If your annuity starting date is after 1986, the total amount of annuity income that you can exclude over the years as a recovery of the cost can't exceed your total cost.

Exclusion not limited to cost. If your annuity starting date is before 1987, you can continue to take your monthly exclusion for as long as you receive your annuity. If you chose a joint and survivor annuity, your survivor can continue to take the survivor's exclusion figured as of the annuity starting date. The total exclusion may be more than your cost.

Simplified Method

Under the Simplified Method, you figure the tax-free part of each annuity payment by dividing your cost by the total number of anticipated monthly payments. For an annuity that is payable for the lives of the annuitants, this number is based on the annuitants' ages on the annuity starting date and is determined from a table. For any other annuity, this number is the number of monthly annuity payments under the contract.

Who must use the Simplified Method. You must use the Simplified Method if your annuity starting date is after November 18, 1996, and you both:

1. Receive pension or annuity payments from a qualified employee plan, qualified employee annuity, or a tax-sheltered annuity (403(b)) plan; and

2. On your annuity starting date, you were either under age 75, or entitled to less than 5 years of guaranteed payments.

Guaranteed payments. Your annuity contract provides guaranteed payments if a minimum number of payments or a minimum amount (for example, the amount of your investment) is payable even if you and any survivor annuitant don't live to receive the minimum. If the minimum amount is less than the total amount of the payments you are to receive, barring death, during the first 5 years after payments begin (figured by ignoring any payment increases), you are entitled to less than 5 years of guaranteed payments.

How to use the Simplified Method. Complete the Simplified Method Worksheet in Pub. 575 to figure your taxable annuity for 2018.

Single-life annuity. If your annuity is payable for your life alone, use Table 1 at the bottom of the worksheet to determine the total number of expected monthly payments. Enter on line 3 the number shown for your age at the annuity starting date.

Multiple-lives annuity. If your annuity is payable for the lives of more than one annuitant, use Table 2 at the bottom of the worksheet to determine the total number of expected monthly payments. Enter on line 3 the number shown for the combined ages of you and the youngest survivor annuitant at the annuity starting date.

However, if your annuity starting date is before 1998, don't use Table 2 and don't combine the annuitants' ages. Instead, you must use Table 1 and enter on line 3 the number shown for the primary annuitant's age on the annuity starting date.

 Be sure to keep a copy of the completed worksheet; it will help you figure your taxable annuity next year.

Example. Bill Smith, age 65, began receiving retirement benefits in 2018, under a joint and survivor annuity. Bill's annuity starting date is January 1, 2018. The benefits are to be paid for the joint lives of Bill and his wife Kathy, age 65. Bill had contributed $31,000 to a qualified plan and had received no distributions before the annuity starting date. Bill is to receive a retirement benefit of $1,200 a month, and Kathy is to receive a monthly survivor benefit of $600 upon Bill's death.

Bill must use the Simplified Method to figure his taxable annuity because his payments are from a qualified plan and he is under age 75. Because his annuity is payable over the lives of more than one annuitant, he uses his and Kathy's combined ages and Table 2 at the bottom of the worksheet in completing line 3 of the worksheet. His completed worksheet is shown in Worksheet 10-A.

Bill's tax-free monthly amount is $100 ($31,000 ÷ 310) as shown on line 4 of the worksheet. Upon Bill's death, if Bill hasn't recovered the full $31,000 investment, Kathy also will exclude $100 from her $600 monthly payment. The full amount of any annuity payments received after 310 payments are paid must be included in gross income.

1. Enter the total pension or annuity payments received this year. Also, add this amount to the total for Form 1040, line 4a .... **1.** _14,400_

2. Enter your cost in the plan (contract) at the annuity starting date plus any death benefit exclusion.* See *Cost (Investment in the Contract)*, earlier .... **2.** _31,000_
   Note. If your annuity starting date was **before this year** and you completed this worksheet last year, skip line 3 and enter the amount from line 4 of last year's worksheet on line 4 below (even if the amount of your pension or annuity has changed). Otherwise, go to line 3.

3. Enter the appropriate number from Table 1 below. **But** if your annuity starting date was **after 1997 and** the payments are for your life and that of your beneficiary, enter the appropriate number from Table 2 below ..... **3.** _310_

4. Divide line 2 by the number on line 3 .... **4.** _100_

5. Multiply line 4 by the number of months for which this year's payments were made. If your annuity starting date was *before* 1987, enter this amount on line 8 below and skip lines 6, 7, 10, and 11. Otherwise, go to line 6 .... **5.** _1,200_

6. Enter any amounts previously recovered tax free in years after 1986. This is the amount shown on line 10 of your worksheet for last year .... **6.** _-0-_

7. Subtract line 6 from line 2 .... **7.** _31,000_

8. Enter the **smaller** of line 5 or line 7 .... **8.** _1,200_

9. **Taxable amount for year.** Subtract line 8 from line 1. Enter the result, but not less than zero. Also, add this amount to the total for Form 1040, line 4b .... **9.** _13,200_
   Note. If your Form 1099-R shows a larger taxable amount, use the amount figured on this line instead. If you are a retired public safety officer, see *Insurance Premiums for Retired Public Safety Officers* in Pub. 575 before entering an amount on your tax return.

10. Was your annuity starting date before 1987?
    ☐ Yes. **STOP.** Don't complete the rest of this worksheet.
    ☑ No. Add lines 6 and 8. This is the amount you have recovered tax free through 2018. You will need this number if you need to fill out this worksheet next year .... **10.** _1,200_

11. **Balance of cost to be recovered.** Subtract line 10 from line 2. If zero, you won't have to complete this worksheet next year. The payments you receive next year will generally be fully taxable .... **11.** _29,800_

* A death benefit exclusion (up to $5,000) applied to certain benefits received by employees who died before August 21, 1996.

Table 1 for Line 3 Above		
	AND your annuity starting date was—	
IF the age at annuity starting date was...	BEFORE November 19, 1996, enter on line 3...	AFTER November 18, 1996, enter on line 3...
55 or under	300	360
56–60	260	310
61–65	240	260
66–70	170	210
71 or older	120	160

Table 2 for Line 3 Above	
IF the combined ages at annuity starting date were...	THEN enter on line 3...
110 or under	410
111–120	360
121–130	310
131–140	260
141 or older	210

Who must use the General Rule. You must use the General Rule if you receive pension or annuity payments from:

- A nonqualified plan (such as a private annuity, a purchased commercial annuity, or a nonqualified employee plan), or

- A qualified plan if you are age 75 or older on your annuity starting date and your annuity payments are guaranteed for at least 5 years.

Annuity starting before November 19, 1996. If your annuity starting date is after July 1, 1986, and before November 19, 1996, you had to use the General Rule for either circumstance just described. You also had to use it for any fixed-period annuity. If you didn't have to use the General Rule, you could have chosen to use it. If your annuity starting date is before July 2, 1986, you had to use the General Rule unless you could use the Three-Year Rule.

If you had to use the General Rule (or chose to use it), you must continue to use it each year that you recover your cost.

Who can't use the General Rule. You can't use the General Rule if you receive your pension or annuity from a qualified plan and none of the circumstances described in the preceding discussions apply to you. See *Who must use the Simplified Method*, earlier.

More information. For complete information on using the General Rule, including the actuarial tables you need, see Pub. 939.

Taxation of Nonperiodic Payments

Nonperiodic distributions also are known as amounts not received as an annuity. They include all payments other than periodic payments and corrective distributions. Examples of nonperiodic payments are cash withdrawals, distributions of current earnings, certain loans, and the value of annuity contracts transferred without full and adequate consideration.

Corrective distributions of excess plan contributions. Generally, if the contributions made for you during the year to certain retirement plans exceed certain limits, the excess is taxable to you. To correct an excess, your plan may distribute it to you (along with any income earned on the excess). For information on plan contribution limits and how to report corrective distributions of excess contributions, see *Retirement Plan Contributions* under *Employee Compensation* in Pub. 525.

Figuring the taxable amount of nonperiodic payments. How you figure the taxable amount of a nonperiodic distribution depends on whether it is made before the annuity starting date, or on or after the annuity starting date. If it is made before the annuity starting date, its tax treatment also depends on whether it is made under a qualified or nonqualified plan. If it is made under a nonqualified plan, its tax treatment depends on whether it fully discharges the contract, is received under certain life insurance or endowment contracts, or is allocable to an investment you made before August 14, 1982.

Annuity starting date. The annuity starting date is either the first day of the first period for which you receive an annuity payment under the contract or the date on which the obligation under the contract becomes fixed, whichever is later.

Distribution on or after annuity starting date. If you receive a nonperiodic payment from your annuity contract on or after the annuity starting date, you generally must include all of the payment in gross income.

Distribution before annuity starting date. If you receive a nonperiodic distribution before the annuity starting date from a qualified retirement plan, you generally can allocate only part of it to the cost of the contract. You exclude from your gross income the part that you allocate to the cost. You include the remainder in your gross income.

Distribution before annuity starting date from a nonqualified plan. If you receive a nonperiodic distribution before the annuity starting date from a plan other than a qualified retirement plan (nonqualified plan), it is allocated first to earnings (the taxable part) and then to the cost of the contract (the tax-free part). This allocation rule applies, for example, to a commercial annuity contract you bought directly from the issuer.

 Distributions from nonqualified plans are subject to the NIIT. See the Instructions for Form 8960.

For more information, see *Figuring the Taxable Amount* under *Taxation of Nonperiodic Payments* in Pub. 575.

Lump-Sum Distributions

 This section on lump-sum distributions only applies if the plan participant was born before January 2, 1936. If the plan participant was born after January 1, 1936, the taxable amount of this nonperiodic payment is reported as discussed earlier.

A lump-sum distribution is the distribution or payment in 1 tax year of a plan participant's entire balance from all of the employer's qualified plans of one kind (for example, pension, profit-sharing, or stock bonus plans). A distribution from a nonqualified plan (such as a privately purchased commercial annuity or a section 457 deferred compensation plan of a state or local government or tax-exempt organization) can't qualify as a lump-sum distribution.

The participant's entire balance from a plan doesn't include certain forfeited amounts. It also doesn't include any deductible voluntary employee contributions allowed by the plan after 1981 and before 1987. For more information about distributions that don't qualify as lump-sum distributions, see *Distributions that don't qualify* under *Lump-Sum Distributions* in Pub. 575.

If you receive a lump-sum distribution from a qualified employee plan or qualified employee annuity and the plan participant was born before January 2, 1936, you may be able to elect optional methods of figuring the tax on the distribution. The part from active participation in the plan before 1974 may qualify as capital gain subject to a 20% tax rate. The part from participation after 1973 (and any part from participation before 1974 that you don't report as capital gain) is ordinary income. You may be able to use the 10-year tax option, discussed later, to figure tax on the ordinary income part.

Use Form 4972 to figure the separate tax on a lump-sum distribution using the optional methods. The tax figured on Form 4972 is added to the regular tax figured on your other income. This may result in a smaller tax than you would pay by including the taxable amount of the distribution as ordinary income in figuring your regular tax.

How to treat the distribution. If you receive a lump-sum distribution, you may have the following options for how you treat the taxable part.

- Report the part of the distribution from participation before 1974 as a capital gain (if you qualify) and the part from participation after 1973 as ordinary income.

- Report the part of the distribution from participation before 1974 as a capital gain (if you qualify) and use the 10-year tax option to figure the tax on the part from participation after 1973 (if you qualify).

- Use the 10-year tax option to figure the tax on the total taxable amount (if you qualify).

- Roll over all or part of the distribution. See *Rollovers*, later. No tax is currently due on the part rolled over. Report any part not rolled over as ordinary income.

- Report the entire taxable part of the distribution as ordinary income on your tax return.

The first three options are explained in the following discussions.

Electing optional lump-sum treatment. You can choose to use the 10-year tax option or capital gain treatment only once after 1986 for any plan participant. If you make this choice, you can't use either of these optional treatments for any future distributions for the participant.

Taxable and tax-free parts of the distribution. The taxable part of a lump-sum distribution is the employer's contributions and income earned on your account. You may recover your cost in the lump sum and any net unrealized appreciation (NUA) in employer securities tax free.

Cost. In general, your cost is the total of:

- The plan participant's nondeductible contributions to the plan,

- The plan participant's taxable costs of any life insurance contract distributed,

- Any employer contributions that were taxable to the plan participant, and

- Repayments of any loans that were taxable to the plan participant.

You must reduce this cost by amounts previously distributed tax free.

Net unrealized appreciation (NUA). The NUA in employer securities (box 6 of Form 1099-R) received as part of a lump-sum distribution generally is tax free until you sell or exchange the securities. For more information, see *Distributions of employer securities* under *Taxation of Nonperiodic Payments* in Pub. 575.

Capital Gain Treatment

Capital gain treatment applies only to the taxable part of a lump-sum distribution resulting from participation in the plan before 1974. The amount treated as capital gain is taxed at a 20% rate. You can elect this treatment only once for any plan participant, and only if the plan participant was born before January 2, 1936.

Complete Part II of Form 4972 to choose the 20% capital gain election. For more information, see *Capital Gain Treatment* under *Lump-Sum Distributions* in Pub. 575.

10-Year Tax Option

The 10-year tax option is a special formula used to figure a separate tax on the ordinary income part of a lump-sum distribution. You pay the tax only once, for the year in which you receive the distribution, not over the next 10 years. You can elect this treatment only once for any plan participant, and only if the plan participant was born before January 2, 1936.

The ordinary income part of the distribution is the amount shown in box 2a of the Form 1099-R given to you by the payer, minus the amount, if any, shown in box 3. You also can treat the capital gain part of the distribution (box 3 of Form 1099-R) as ordinary income for the 10-year tax option if you don't choose capital gain treatment for that part.

Complete Part III of Form 4972 to choose the 10-year tax option. You must use the special Tax Rate Schedule shown in the instructions for Part III to figure the tax. Pub. 575

illustrates how to complete Form 4972 to figure the separate tax.

Rollovers

If you withdraw cash or other assets from a qualified retirement plan in an eligible rollover distribution, you generally can defer tax on the distribution by rolling it over into another qualified retirement plan, a traditional IRA, or, after 2 years of participation in a SIMPLE IRA plan sponsored by your employer, a SIMPLE IRA under that plan.

For this purpose, the following plans are qualified retirement plans.

- A qualified employee plan.
- A qualified employee annuity.
- A tax-sheltered annuity plan (403(b) plan).
- An eligible state or local government section 457 deferred compensation plan.

Rollovers to SIMPLE retirement accounts. You can roll over amounts from a qualified retirement plan (as described next) or an IRA into a SIMPLE retirement account as follows.

1. During the first 2 years of participation in a SIMPLE retirement account, you may roll over amounts from one SIMPLE retirement account into another SIMPLE retirement account.

2. After 2 years of participation in a SIMPLE retirement account, you may roll over amounts from a SIMPLE retirement, a qualified retirement plan, or an IRA into a SIMPLE retirement account.

Eligible rollover distributions. Generally, an eligible rollover distribution is any distribution of all or any part of the balance to your credit in a qualified retirement plan. For information about exceptions to eligible rollover distributions, see Pub. 575.

Rollover of nontaxable amounts. You may be able to roll over the nontaxable part of a distribution (such as your after-tax contributions) made to another qualified retirement plan that is a qualified employee plan or a 403(b) plan, or to a traditional or Roth IRA. The transfer must be made either through a direct rollover to a qualified plan or 403(b) plan that separately accounts for the taxable and nontaxable parts of the rollover or through a rollover to a traditional or Roth IRA.

If you roll over only part of a distribution that includes both taxable and nontaxable amounts, the amount you roll over is treated as coming first from the taxable part of the distribution.

Any after-tax contributions that you roll over into your traditional IRA become part of your basis (cost) in your IRAs. To recover your basis when you take distributions from your IRA, you must complete Form 8606 for the year of the distribution. For more information, see the Form 8606 instructions.

Direct rollover option. You can choose to have any part or all of an eligible rollover distribution paid directly to another qualified retirement plan that accepts rollover distributions or to a traditional or Roth IRA. If you choose the direct rollover option, or have an automatic roll-

over, no tax will be withheld from any part of the distribution that is directly paid to the trustee of the other plan.

Payment to you option. If an eligible rollover distribution is paid to you, 20% generally will be withheld for income tax. However, the full amount is treated as distributed to you even though you actually receive only 80%. You generally must include in income any part (including the part withheld) that you don't roll over within 60 days to another qualified retirement plan or to a traditional or Roth IRA. (See *Pensions and Annuities* under *Tax Withholding for 2019* in chapter 4.)

 Rolling over more than amount received. If you decide to roll over an amount equal to the distribution before withholding, your contribution to the new plan or IRA must include other money (for example, from savings or amounts borrowed) to replace the amount withheld.

Time for making rollover. You generally must complete the rollover of an eligible rollover distribution paid to you by the 60th day following the day on which you receive the distribution from your employer's plan. (If an amount distributed to you becomes a frozen deposit in a financial institution during the 60-day period after you receive it, the rollover period is extended for the period during which the distribution is in a frozen deposit in a financial institution.)

The IRS may waive the 60-day requirement where the failure to do so would be against equity or good conscience, such as in the event of a casualty, disaster, or other event beyond your reasonable control.

The administrator of a qualified plan must give you a written explanation of your distribution options within a reasonable period of time before making an eligible rollover distribution.

Qualified domestic relations order (QDRO). You may be able to roll over tax free all or part of a distribution from a qualified retirement plan that you receive under a QDRO. If you receive the distribution as an employee's spouse or former spouse (not as a nonspousal beneficiary), the rollover rules apply to you as if you were the employee. You can roll over the distribution from the plan into a traditional IRA or to another eligible retirement plan. See *Rollovers* in Pub. 575 for more information on benefits received under a QDRO.

Rollover by surviving spouse. You may be able to roll over tax free all or part of a distribution from a qualified retirement plan you receive as the surviving spouse of a deceased employee. The rollover rules apply to you as if you were the employee. You can roll over a distribution into a qualified retirement plan or a traditional or Roth IRA. For a rollover to a Roth IRA, see *Rollovers to Roth IRAs*, later.

A distribution paid to a beneficiary other than the employee's surviving spouse generally is not an eligible rollover distribution. However, see *Rollovers by nonspouse beneficiary* next.

Rollovers by nonspouse beneficiary. If you are a designated beneficiary (other than a surviving spouse) of a deceased employee, you may be able to roll over tax free all or a portion of a distribution you receive from an eligible re-

tirement plan of the employee. The distribution must be a direct trustee-to-trustee transfer to your traditional or Roth IRA that was set up to receive the distribution. The transfer will be treated as an eligible rollover distribution and the receiving plan will be treated as an inherited IRA. For information on inherited IRAs, see *What if You Inherit an IRA?* in chapter 1 of Pub. 590-B.

Retirement bonds. If you redeem retirement bonds purchased under a qualified bond purchase plan, you can roll over the proceeds that exceed your basis tax free into an IRA (as discussed in Pub. 590-A) or a qualified employer plan.

Designated Roth accounts. You can roll over an eligible rollover distribution from a designated Roth account into another designated Roth account or a Roth IRA. If you want to roll over the part of the distribution that isn't included in income, you must make a direct rollover of the entire distribution or you can roll over the entire amount (or any portion) to a Roth IRA. For more information on rollovers from designated Roth accounts, see *Rollovers* in Pub. 575.

In-plan rollovers to designated Roth accounts. If you are a plan participant in a 401(k), 403(b), or 457(b) plan, your plan may permit you to roll over amounts in those plans to a designated Roth account within the same plan. The rollover of any untaxed amounts must be included in income. See *Designated Roth accounts* under *Rollovers* in Pub. 575 for more information.

Rollovers to Roth IRAs. You can roll over distributions directly from a qualified retirement plan (other than a designated Roth account) to a Roth IRA.

You must include in your gross income distributions from a qualified retirement plan (other than a designated Roth account) that you would have had to include in income if you hadn't rolled them over into a Roth IRA. You don't include in gross income any part of a distribution from a qualified retirement plan that is a return of contributions to the plan that were taxable to you when paid. In addition, the 10% tax on early distributions doesn't apply.

More information. For more information on the rules for rolling over distributions, see *Rollovers* in Pub. 575.

Special Additional Taxes

To discourage the use of pension funds for purposes other than normal retirement, the law imposes additional taxes on early distributions of those funds and on failures to withdraw the funds timely. Ordinarily, you won't be subject to these taxes if you roll over all early distributions you receive, as explained earlier, and begin drawing out the funds at a normal retirement age, in reasonable amounts over your life expectancy. These special additional taxes are the taxes on:

- Early distributions, and
- Excess accumulation (not receiving minimum distributions).

These taxes are discussed in the following sections.

If you must pay either of these taxes, report them on Form 5329. However, you don't have to file Form 5329 if you owe only the tax on early distributions and all your Forms 1099-R correctly show a "1" in box 7. Instead, enter 10% of the taxable part of the distribution on Schedule 4, Form 1040, line 59, and write "No" under the heading "Other Taxes" to the left of line 59.

Even if you don't owe any of these taxes, you may have to complete Form 5329 and attach it to your Form 1040. This applies if you meet an exception to the tax on early distributions but box 7 of your Form 1099-R doesn't indicate an exception.

Tax on Early Distributions

Most distributions (both periodic and nonperiodic) from qualified retirement plans and nonqualified annuity contracts made to you before you reach age 59½ are subject to an additional tax of 10%. This tax applies to the part of the distribution that you must include in gross income.

For this purpose, a qualified retirement plan is:

- A qualified employee plan,
- A qualified employee annuity plan,
- A tax-sheltered annuity plan, or
- An eligible state or local government section 457 deferred compensation plan (to the extent that any distribution is attributable to amounts the plan received in a direct transfer or rollover from one of the other plans listed here or an IRA).

5% rate on certain early distributions from deferred annuity contracts. If an early withdrawal from a deferred annuity is otherwise subject to the 10% additional tax, a 5% rate may apply instead. A 5% rate applies to distributions under a written election providing a specific schedule for the distribution of your interest in the contract if, as of March 1, 1986, you had begun receiving payments under the election. On line 4 of Form 5329, multiply the line 3 amount by 5% (0.05) instead of 10% (0.10). Attach an explanation to your return.

Distributions from Roth IRAs allocable to a rollover from an eligible retirement plan within the 5-year period. If, within the 5-year period starting with the first day of your tax year in which you rolled over an amount from an eligible retirement plan to a Roth IRA, you take a distribution from the Roth IRA, you may have to pay the additional 10% tax on early distributions. You generally must pay the 10% additional tax on any amount attributable to the part of the rollover that you had to include in income. The additional tax is figured on Form 5329. For more information, see Form 5329 and its instructions. For information on qualified distributions from Roth IRAs, see *Additional Tax on Early Distributions* in chapter 2 of Pub. 590-B.

Distributions from designated Roth accounts allocable to in-plan Roth rollovers within the 5-year period. If, within the 5-year

period starting with the first day of your tax year in which you rolled over an amount from a 401(k), 403(b), or 457(b) plan to a designated Roth account, you take a distribution from the designated Roth account, you may have to pay the additional 10% tax on early distributions. You generally must pay the 10% additional tax on any amount attributable to the part of the in-plan rollover that you had to include in income. The additional tax is figured on Form 5329. For more information, see Form 5329 and its instructions. For information on qualified distributions from designated Roth accounts, see *Designated Roth accounts* under *Taxation of Periodic Payments* in Pub. 575.

Exceptions to tax. Certain early distributions are excepted from the early distribution tax. If the payer knows that an exception applies to your early distribution, distribution code "2," "3," or "4" should be shown in box 7 of your Form 1099-R and you don't have to report the distribution on Form 5329. If an exception applies but distribution code "1" (early distribution, no known exception) is shown in box 7, you must file Form 5329. Enter the taxable amount of the distribution shown in box 2a of your Form 1099-R on line 1 of Form 5329. On line 2, enter the amount that can be excluded and the exception number shown in the Form 5329 instructions.

 If distribution code "1" is incorrectly shown on your Form 1099-R for a distribution received when you were age 59½ or older, include that distribution on Form 5329. Enter exception number "12" on line 2.

General exceptions. The tax doesn't apply to distributions that are:

- Made as part of a series of substantially equal periodic payments (made at least annually) for your life (or life expectancy) or the joint lives (or joint life expectancies) of you and your designated beneficiary (if from a qualified retirement plan, the payments must begin after your separation from service),

- Made because you are totally and permanently disabled (see *Exceptions to Tax* under *Tax on Early Distributions* in Pub. 575), or

- Made on or after the death of the plan participant or contract holder.

Additional exceptions for qualified retirement plans. The tax doesn't apply to distributions that are:

- From a qualified retirement plan (other than an IRA) after your separation from service in or after the year you reached age 55 (age 50 for qualified public safety employees);

- From a qualified retirement plan (other than an IRA) to an alternate payee under a qualified domestic relations order;

- From a qualified retirement plan to the extent you have deductible medical expenses that exceed 7.5% of your adjusted gross income, whether or not you itemize your deductions for the year;

- From an employer plan under a written election that provides a specific schedule

for distribution of your entire interest if, as of March 1, 1986, you had separated from service and had begun receiving payments under the election;

- From an employee stock ownership plan for dividends on employer securities held by the plan;

- From a qualified retirement plan due to an IRS levy of the plan;

- From elective deferral accounts under 401(k) or 403(b) plans or similar arrangements that are qualified reservist distributions; or

- Phased retirement annuity payments made to federal employees. See Pub. 721 for more information on the phased retirement program.

Qualified public safety employees. If you are a qualified public safety employee, distributions made from a governmental defined benefit pension plan aren't subject to the additional tax on early distributions. You are a qualified public safety employee if you provide police protection, firefighting services, or emergency medical services for a state or municipality, and you separated from service in or after the year you attained age 50.

Note. For tax years after December 31, 2015, the definition of qualified public safety employees is expanded to include the following.

- Federal law enforcement officers.
- Federal customs and border protection officers.
- Federal firefighters.
- Air traffic controllers.
- Nuclear materials couriers.
- Members of the United States Capitol Police.
- Members of the Supreme Court Police.
- Diplomatic security special agents of the United States Department of State.

Qualified reservist distributions. A qualified reservist distribution isn't subject to the additional tax on early distributions. A qualified reservist distribution is a distribution (a) from elective deferrals under a section 401(k) or 403(b) plan, or a similar arrangement; (b) to an individual ordered or called to active duty (because he or she is a member of a reserve component) for a period of more than 179 days or for an indefinite period; and (c) made during the period beginning on the date of the order or call and ending at the close of the active duty period. You must have been ordered or called to active duty after September 11, 2001. For more information, see *Qualified reservist distributions* under *Special Additional Taxes* in Pub. 575.

Additional exceptions for nonqualified annuity contracts. The tax doesn't apply to distributions from:

- A deferred annuity contract to the extent allocable to investment in the contract before August 14, 1982;

- A deferred annuity contract under a qualified personal injury settlement;

- A deferred annuity contract purchased by your employer upon termination of a qualified employee plan or qualified employee annuity plan and held by your employer until your separation from service; or

- An immediate annuity contract (a single premium contract providing substantially equal annuity payments that start within 1 year from the date of purchase and are paid at least annually).

Tax on Excess Accumulation

To make sure that most of your retirement benefits are paid to you during your lifetime, rather than to your beneficiaries after your death, the payments that you receive from qualified retirement plans must begin no later than your required beginning date (defined later). The payments each year can't be less than the required minimum distribution.

Required distributions not made. If the actual distributions to you in any year are less than the minimum required distribution for that year, you are subject to an additional tax. The tax equals 50% of the part of the required minimum distribution that wasn't distributed.

For this purpose, a qualified retirement plan includes:

- A qualified employee plan,

- A qualified employee annuity plan,

- An eligible section 457 deferred compensation plan, or

- A tax-sheltered annuity plan (403(b) plan) (for benefits accruing after 1986).

Waiver. The tax may be waived if you establish that the shortfall in distributions was due to reasonable error and that reasonable steps are being taken to remedy the shortfall. See the Instructions for Form 5329 for the procedure to follow if you believe you qualify for a waiver of this tax.

State insurer delinquency proceedings. You might not receive the minimum distribution because assets are invested in a contract issued by an insurance company in state insurer delinquency proceedings. If your payments are reduced below the minimum due to these proceedings, you should contact your plan administrator. Under certain conditions, you won't have to pay the 50% excise tax.

Required beginning date. Unless the rule for 5% owners applies, you generally must begin to receive distributions from your qualified retirement plan by April 1 of the year that follows the later of:

- The calendar year in which you reach age 70½, or

- The calendar year in which you retire from employment with the employer maintaining the plan.

However, your plan may require you to begin to receive distributions by April 1 of the year that follows the year in which you reach age 70½, even if you haven't retired.

If you reached age 70½ in 2018, you may be required to receive your first distribution by April 1, 2019. Your required distribution then must be made for 2018 by December 31, 2019.

5% owners. If you are a 5% owner, you must begin to receive distributions by April 1 of the year that follows the calendar year in which you reach age 70½.

You are a 5% owner if, for the plan year ending in the calendar year in which you reach age 70½, you own (or are considered to own under section 318 of the Internal Revenue Code) more than 5% of the outstanding stock (or more than 5% of the total voting power of all stock) of the employer, or more than 5% of the capital or profits interest in the employer.

Age 70½. You reach age 70½ on the date that is 6 calendar months after the date of your 70th birthday.

For example, if you are retired and your 70th birthday was on June 30, 2018, you were age 70½ on December 30, 2018. If your 70th birthday was on July 1, 2018, you reached age 70½ on January 1, 2019.

Required distributions. By the required beginning date, as explained earlier, you must either:

- Receive your entire interest in the plan (for a tax-sheltered annuity, your entire benefit accruing after 1986), or

- Begin receiving periodic distributions in annual amounts calculated to distribute your entire interest (for a tax-sheltered annuity, your entire benefit accruing after 1986) over your life or life expectancy or over the joint lives or joint life expectancies of you and a designated beneficiary (or over a shorter period).

Additional information. For more information on this rule, see *Tax on Excess Accumulation* in Pub. 575.

Form 5329. You must file Form 5329 if you owe tax because you didn't receive a minimum required distribution from your qualified retirement plan.

Survivors and Beneficiaries

Generally, a survivor or beneficiary reports pension or annuity income in the same way the plan participant would have. However, some special rules apply. See Pub. 575 for more information.

Survivors of employees. If you are entitled to receive a survivor annuity on the death of an employee who died, you can exclude part of each annuity payment as a tax-free recovery of the employee's investment in the contract. You must figure the taxable and tax-free parts of your annuity payments using the method that applies as if you were the employee.

Survivors of retirees. If you receive benefits as a survivor under a joint and survivor annuity, include those benefits in income in the same way the retiree would have included them in income. If you receive a survivor annuity because of the death of a retiree who had reported the annuity under the Three-Year Rule and recovered all of the cost tax free, your survivor payments are fully taxable.

If the retiree was reporting the annuity payments under the General Rule, you must apply the same exclusion percentage to your initial survivor annuity payment called for in the contract. The resulting tax-free amount will then remain fixed. Any increases in the survivor annuity are fully taxable.

If the retiree was reporting the annuity payments under the Simplified Method, the part of each payment that is tax free is the same as the tax-free amount figured by the retiree at the annuity starting date. This amount remains fixed even if the annuity payments are increased or decreased. See *Simplified Method*, earlier.

In any case, if the annuity starting date is after 1986, the total exclusion over the years can't be more than the cost.

Estate tax deduction. If your annuity was a joint and survivor annuity that was included in the decedent's estate, an estate tax may have been paid on it. You can deduct the part of the total estate tax that was based on the annuity. The deceased annuitant must have died after the annuity starting date. (For details, see section 1.691(d)-1 of the regulations.) Deduct it in equal amounts over your remaining life expectancy.

If the decedent died before the annuity starting date of a deferred annuity contract and you receive a death benefit under that contract, the amount you receive (either in a lump sum or as periodic payments) in excess of the decedent's cost is included in your gross income as income in respect of a decedent for which you may be able to claim an estate tax deduction.

You can take the estate tax deduction as an itemized deduction on Schedule A, Form 1040. See Pub. 559 for more information on the estate tax deduction.

11.

Social Security and Equivalent Railroad Retirement Benefits

What's New

 At the time this publication went to print, Congress was considering legislation that would do the following.

1. *Provide additional tax relief for those affected by certain 2018 disasters.*

2. Extend certain tax benefits that expired at the end of 2017 and that currently can't be claimed on your 2018 tax return.

3. Change certain other tax provisions.

To learn whether this legislation was enacted resulting in changes that affect your 2018 tax return, go to Recent Developments at IRS.gov/Pub17.

Introduction

This chapter explains the federal income tax rules for social security benefits and equivalent tier 1 railroad retirement benefits. It explains the following topics.

- How to figure whether your benefits are taxable.

- How to report your taxable benefits.

- How to use the social security benefits worksheet (with examples).

- Deductions related to your benefits and how to treat repayments that are more than the benefits you received during the year.

Social security benefits include monthly retirement, survivor, and disability benefits. They don't include Supplemental Security Income (SSI) payments, which aren't taxable.

Equivalent tier 1 railroad retirement benefits are the part of tier 1 benefits that a railroad employee or beneficiary would have been entitled to receive under the social security system. They are commonly called the social security equivalent benefit (SSEB) portion of tier 1 benefits.

If you received these benefits during 2018, you should have received a Form SSA-1099, Social Security Benefit Statement; or Form RRB-1099, Payments by the Railroad Retirement Board. These forms show the amounts received and repaid, and taxes withheld for the year. You may receive more than one of these forms for the same year. You should add the amounts shown on all the Forms SSA-1099 and Forms RRB-1099 you receive for the year to determine the total amounts received and repaid, and taxes withheld for that year. See the *Appendix* at the end of Pub. 915 for more information.

Note. When the term "benefits" is used in this chapter, it applies to both social security benefits and the SSEB portion of tier 1 railroad retirement benefits.

my Social Security account. Social Security beneficiaries may quickly and easily obtain various information from the SSA's website with a *my Social Security* account to:

- Keep track of your earnings and verify them every year,

- Get an estimate of your future benefits if you are still working,

- Get a letter with proof of your benefits if you currently receive them,

- Change your address,

- Start or change your direct deposit,

- Get a replacement Medicare card, and

- Get a replacement Form SSA-1099 for the tax season.

For more information and to set up an account, go to SSA.gov/myaccount.

What isn't covered in this chapter. This chapter doesn't cover the tax rules for the following railroad retirement benefits.

- Non-social security equivalent benefit (NSSEB) portion of tier 1 benefits.

- Tier 2 benefits.

- Vested dual benefits.

- Supplemental annuity benefits.

For information on these benefits, see Pub. 575, Pension and Annuity Income.

This chapter doesn't cover the tax rules for social security benefits reported on Form SSA-1042S, Social Security Benefit Statement; or Form RRB-1042S, Statement for Nonresident Alien Recipients of: Payments by the Railroad Retirement Board. For information about these benefits, see Pub. 519, U.S. Tax Guide for Aliens; and Pub. 915, Social Security and Equivalent Railroad Retirement Benefits.

This chapter also doesn't cover the tax rules for foreign social security benefits. These benefits are taxable as annuities, unless they are exempt from U.S. tax or treated as a U.S. social security benefit under a tax treaty.

Useful Items

You may want to see:

Publication

- ❏ **505** Tax Withholding and Estimated Tax

- ❏ **575** Pension and Annuity Income

- ❏ **590-A** Contributions to Individual Retirement Arrangements (IRAs)

- ❏ **915** Social Security and Equivalent Railroad Retirement Benefits

Forms (and Instructions)

- ❏ **1040-ES** Estimated Tax for Individuals

- ❏ **SSA-1099** Social Security Benefit Statement

- ❏ **RRB-1099** Payments by the Railroad Retirement Board

- ❏ **W-4V** Voluntary Withholding Request

For these and other useful items, go to IRS.gov/Forms.

Are Any of Your Benefits Taxable?

To find out whether any of your benefits may be taxable, compare the base amount for your filing status with the total of:

1. One-half of your benefits; plus

2. All your other income, including tax-exempt interest.

Exclusions. When making this comparison, don't reduce your other income by any exclusions for:

- Interest from qualified U.S. savings bonds,

- Employer-provided adoption benefits,

- Foreign earned income or foreign housing, or

- Income earned by bona fide residents of American Samoa or Puerto Rico.

Children's benefits. The rules in this chapter apply to benefits received by children. See *Who is taxed*, later.

Figuring total income. To figure the total of one-half of your benefits plus your other income, use Worksheet 11-1 later in this discussion. If the total is more than your base amount, part of your benefits may be taxable.

If you are married and file a joint return for 2018, you and your spouse must combine your incomes and your benefits to figure whether any of your combined benefits are taxable. Even if your spouse didn't receive any benefits, you must add your spouse's income to yours to figure whether any of your benefits are taxable.

TIP *If the only income you received during 2018 was your social security or the SSEB portion of tier 1 railroad retirement benefits, your benefits generally aren't taxable and you probably don't have to file a return. If you have income in addition to your benefits, you may have to file a return even if none of your benefits are taxable. See* Do I Have To File a Return? *in chapter 1, earlier; Pub. 501, Dependents, Standard Deduction, and Filing Information; or your tax return instructions to find out if you have to file a return.*

Base amount. Your base amount is:

- $25,000 if you are single, head of household, or qualifying widow(er);

- $25,000 if you are married filing separately and lived apart from your spouse for all of 2018;

- $32,000 if you are married filing jointly; or

- $0 if you are married filing separately and lived with your spouse at any time during 2018.

Worksheet 11-1. You can use Worksheet 11-1 to figure the amount of income to compare with your base amount. This is a quick way to check whether some of your benefits may be taxable.

Worksheet 11-1. **A Quick Way To Check if Your Benefits May Be Taxable**

Note. If you plan to file a joint income tax return, include your spouse's amounts, if any, on lines A, C, and D.

A. Enter the amount from *box 5* of all your Forms SSA-1099 and RRB-1099. Include the full amount of any lump-sum benefit payments received in 2018, for 2018 and earlier years. (If you received more than one form, combine the amounts from box 5 and enter the total.) . . . . A. _____

Note. If the amount on line A is zero or less, stop here; none of your benefits are taxable this year.

B. Enter one-half of line A . . . B. _____

C. Enter your total income that is taxable (excluding line A), such as pensions, wages, interest, ordinary dividends, and capital gain distributions. Don't reduce your income by any deductions, exclusions (listed earlier), or exemptions . . . . C. _____

D. Enter any tax-exempt interest income such as interest on municipal bonds . . . . D. _____

E. Add lines B, C, and D . . . E. _____

Note. Compare the amount on line E to your **base amount** for your filing status. If the amount on line E equals or is less than the **base amount** for your filing status, none of your benefits are taxable this year. If the amount on line E is more than your **base amount,** some of your benefits may be taxable. You need to complete Worksheet 1 in Pub. 915 (or the Social Security Benefits Worksheet in your tax form instructions). If none of your benefits are taxable, but you otherwise must file a tax return, see *Benefits not taxable,* later, under *How To Report Your Benefits.*

Example. You and your spouse (both over 65) are filing a joint return for 2018 and you both received social security benefits during the year. In January 2019, you received a Form SSA-1099 showing net benefits of $6,500 in box 5. Your spouse received a Form SSA-1099 showing net benefits of $3,500 in box 5. You also received a taxable pension of $26,200 and interest income of $700. You didn't have any tax-exempt interest income. Your benefits aren't taxable for 2018 because your income, as figured in Worksheet 11-1, isn't more than your base amount ($32,000) for married filing jointly.

Even though none of your benefits are taxable, you must file a return for 2018 because your taxable gross income ($26,900) exceeds the minimum filing requirement amount for your filing status.

Filled-in Worksheet 11-1. **A Quick Way To Check if Your Benefits May Be Taxable**

Note. If you plan to file a joint income tax return, include your spouse's amounts, if any, on lines A, C, and D.

A. Enter the amount from *box 5* of all your Forms SSA-1099 and RRB-1099. Include the full amount of any lump-sum benefit payments received in 2018, for 2018 and earlier years. (If you received more than one form, combine the amounts from box 5 and enter the total.) . . . . A. $10,000

Note. If the amount on line A is zero or less, stop here; none of your benefits are taxable this year.

B. Enter one-half of line A . . . B. 5,000

C. Enter your total income that is taxable (excluding line A), such as pensions, wages, interest, ordinary dividends, and capital gain distributions. Don't reduce your income by any deductions, exclusions (listed earlier), or exemptions . . . . C. 26,900

D. Enter any tax-exempt interest income such as interest on municipal bonds . . . . D. -0-

E. Add lines B, C, and D . . . E. $31,900

Note. Compare the amount on line E to your **base amount** for your filing status. If the amount on line E equals or is less than the **base amount** for your filing status, none of your benefits are taxable this year. If the amount on line E is more than your **base amount,** some of your benefits may be taxable. You need to complete Worksheet 1 in Pub. 915 (or the Social Security Benefits Worksheet in your tax form instructions). If none of your benefits are taxable, but you otherwise must file a tax return, see *Benefits not taxable,* later, under *How To Report Your Benefits.*

Who is taxed. Benefits are included in the taxable income (to the extent they are taxable) of the person who has the legal right to receive the benefits. For example, if you and your child receive benefits, but the check for your child is made out in your name, you must use only your part of the benefits to see whether any benefits are taxable to you. One-half of the part that belongs to your child must be added to your child's other income to see whether any of those benefits are taxable to your child.

Repayment of benefits. Any repayment of benefits you made during 2018 must be subtracted from the gross benefits you received in 2018. It doesn't matter whether the repayment was for a benefit you received in 2018 or in an earlier year. If you repaid more than the gross benefits you received in 2018, see *Repayments More Than Gross Benefits,* later.

Your gross benefits are shown in box 3 of Form SSA-1099 or RRB-1099. Your repayments are shown in box 4. The amount in box 5 shows your net benefits for 2018 (box 3 minus box 4). Use the amount in box 5 to figure whether any of your benefits are taxable.

Tax withholding and estimated tax. You can choose to have federal income tax withheld from your social security benefits and/or the SSEB portion of your tier 1 railroad retirement benefits. If you choose to do this, you must complete a Form W-4V.

If you don't choose to have income tax withheld, you may have to request additional withholding from other income or pay estimated tax during the year. For details, see chapter 4, earlier; Pub. 505; or the instructions for Form 1040-ES.

How To Report Your Benefits

If part of your benefits are taxable, you must use Form 1040.

Reporting on Form 1040. Report your net benefits (the total amount from box 5 of all your Forms SSA-1099 and Forms RRB-1099) on line 5a and the taxable part on line 5b. If you are married filing separately and you lived apart from your spouse for all of 2018, also enter "D" to the right of the word "benefits" on line 5a.

Benefits not taxable. Report your net benefits (the total amount from box 5 of all your Forms SSA-1099 and Forms RRB-1099) on Form 1040, line 5a. Enter -0- on Form 1040, line 5b. If you are married filing separately and you lived apart from your spouse for all of 2018, also enter "D" to the right of the word "benefits" on Form 1040, line 5a.

How Much Is Taxable?

If part of your benefits are taxable, how much is taxable depends on the total amount of your benefits and other income. Generally, the higher that total amount, the greater the taxable part of your benefits.

Maximum taxable part. Generally, up to 50% of your benefits will be taxable. However, up to 85% of your benefits can be taxable if either of the following situations applies to you.

- The total of one-half of your benefits and all your other income is more than $34,000 ($44,000 if you are married filing jointly).

- You are married filing separately and lived with your spouse at any time during 2018.

Which worksheet to use. A worksheet you can use to figure your taxable benefits is in the instructions for your Form 1040. You can use either that worksheet or Worksheet 1 in Pub. 915, unless any of the following situations applies to you.

1. You contributed to a traditional individual retirement arrangement (IRA) and you or your spouse is covered by a retirement plan at work. In this situation, you must use the special worksheets in *Appendix B*

of Pub. 590-A to figure both your IRA deduction and your taxable benefits.

2. Situation 1 doesn't apply and you take an exclusion for interest from qualified U.S. savings bonds (Form 8815), for adoption benefits (Form 8839), for foreign earned income or housing (Form 2555 or Form 2555-EZ), or for income earned in American Samoa (Form 4563) or Puerto Rico by bona fide residents. In this situation, you must use Worksheet 1 in Pub. 915 to figure your taxable benefits.

3. You received a lump-sum payment for an earlier year. In this situation, also complete Worksheet 2 or 3 and Worksheet 4 in Pub. 915. See *Lump-sum election* next.

Lump-sum election. You must include the taxable part of a lump-sum (retroactive) payment of benefits received in 2018 in your 2018 income, even if the payment includes benefits for an earlier year.

 This type of lump-sum benefit payment shouldn't be confused with the lump-sum death benefit that both the SSA and RRB pay to many of their beneficiaries. No part of the lump-sum death benefit is subject to tax.

Generally, you use your 2018 income to figure the taxable part of the total benefits received in 2018. However, you may be able to figure the taxable part of a lump-sum payment for an earlier year separately, using your income for the earlier year. You can elect this method if it lowers your taxable benefits.

Making the election. If you received a lump-sum benefit payment in 2018 that includes benefits for one or more earlier years, follow the instructions in Pub. 915 under *Lump-Sum Election* to see whether making the election will lower your taxable benefits. That discussion also explains how to make the election.

 Because the earlier year's taxable benefits are included in your 2018 income, no adjustment is made to the earlier year's return. Don't file an amended return for the earlier year.

Examples

The following are a few examples you can use as a guide to figure the taxable part of your benefits.

Example 1. George White is single and files Form 1040 for 2018. He received the following income in 2018.

Fully taxable pension	$18,600
Wages from part-time job	9,400
Taxable interest income	990
Total	$28,990

George also received social security benefits during 2018. The Form SSA-1099 he received in January 2019 shows $5,980 in box 5. To figure his taxable benefits, George completes the worksheet shown here.

Filled-in Worksheet 1.
Figuring Your Taxable Benefits

1. Enter the total amount from box 5 of ALL your Forms SSA-1099 and RRB-1099. Also enter this amount on Form 1040, line 5a **$5,980**

2. Enter one-half of line 1 . . . . **2,990**

3. Combine the amounts from Form 1040, lines 1, 2b, 3b, 4b, and Schedule 1 (Form 1040), line 22 . . . **28,990**

4. Enter the amount, if any, from Form 1040, line 2a . . . . **-0-**

5. Enter the total of any exclusions/adjustments for:
   - Adoption benefits (Form 8839, line 28),
   - Foreign earned income or housing (Form 2555, lines 45 and 50; or Form 2555-EZ, line 18), and
   - Certain income of bona fide residents of American Samoa (Form 4563, line 15) or Puerto Rico . . . . **-0-**

6. Combine lines 2, 3, 4, and 5 . . . . . . **31,980**

7. Enter the amounts from Schedule 1 (Form 1040), lines 23 through 32, and any write-in adjustments you entered on the dotted line next to line Schedule 1, (Form 1040), line 36 . . . . **-0-**

8. Is the amount on line 7 less than the amount on line 6?

   No. None of your social security benefits are taxable. Enter -0- on Form 1040, line 5b.

   Yes. Subtract line 7 from line 6 . . . . . **31,980**

9. If you are:
   - Married filing jointly, enter $32,000
   - Single, head of household, qualifying widow(er), or married filing separately and you **lived apart** from your spouse for all of 2018, enter $25,000 . . . . **25,000**

Note. If you are married filing separately and you lived with your spouse at any time in 2018, skip lines 9 through 16; multiply line 8 by 85% (0.85) and enter the result on line 17. Then go to line 18.

10. Is the amount on line 9 less than the amount on line 8?

    No. None of your benefits are taxable. Enter -0- on Form 1040, line 5b. If you are married filing separately and you **lived apart** from your spouse for all of 2018, be sure you entered "D" to the right of the word "benefits" on Form 1040, line 5a.

    Yes. Subtract line 9 from line 8 . . . . **6,980**

11. Enter $12,000 if married filing jointly; $9,000 if single, head of household, qualifying widow(er), or married filing separately and you **lived apart** from your spouse for all of 2018 . . . . **9,000**

12. Subtract line 11 from line 10. If zero or less, enter -0- . . . . **-0-**

13. Enter the **smaller** of line 10 or line 11 . . . . **6,980**

14. Enter one-half of line 13 . . . . **3,490**

15. Enter the **smaller** of line 2 or line 14 . . **2,990**

16. Multiply line 12 by 85% (0.85). If line 12 is zero, enter -0- . . . . **-0-**

17. Add lines 15 and 16 . . . . **2,990**

18. Multiply line 1 by 85% (0.85) **5,083**

19. **Taxable benefits.** Enter the **smaller** of line 17 or line 18. Also enter this amount on Form 1040, line 5b **$2,990**

The amount on line 19 of George's worksheet shows that $2,990 of his social security benefits is taxable. On line 5a of his Form 1040, George enters his net benefits of $5,980. On line 5b, he enters his taxable benefits of $2,990.

Example 2. Ray and Alice Hopkins file a joint return on Form 1040 for 2018. Ray is retired and received a fully taxable pension of $15,500. He also received social security benefits, and his Form SSA-1099 for 2018 shows net benefits of $5,600 in box 5. Alice worked during the year and had wages of $14,000. She made a deductible payment to her IRA account of $1,000 and isn't covered by a retirement plan at work. Ray and Alice have two savings accounts with a total of $250 in taxable interest income. They complete Worksheet 1, entering $29,750 ($15,500 + $14,000 + $250) on line 3. They find none of Ray's social security benefits are taxable. On Form 1040, they enter $5,600 on line 5a and -0- on line 5b.

Filled-in Worksheet 1.
Figuring Your Taxable Benefits

1. Enter the total amount from box 5 of ALL your Forms SSA-1099 and RRB-1099. Also enter this amount on Form 1040, line 5a $5,600
2. Enter one-half of line 1 . . . . . . **2,800**
3. Combine the amounts from Form 1040, lines 1, 2b, 3b, 4b, and Schedule 1 (Form 1040), line 22 . . . . **29,750**
4. Enter the amount, if any, from Form 1040, line 2a . . . . **-0-**
5. Enter the total of any exclusions/ adjustments for:
   • Adoption benefits (Form 8839, line 28),
   • Foreign earned income or housing (Form 2555, lines 45 and 50; or Form 2555-EZ, line 18), and
   • Certain income of bona fide residents of American Samoa (Form 4563, line 15) or Puerto Rico . . . . **-0-**
6. Combine lines 2, 3, 4, and 5 . . . **32,550**
7. Enter the amounts from Schedule 1 (Form 1040), lines 23 through 32, and any write-in adjustments you entered on the dotted line next to line Schedule 1, (Form 1040), line 36 . . . . . . **1,000**
8. Is the amount on line 7 less than the amount on line 6?

   No. (STOP) None of your social security benefits are taxable. Enter -0- on Form 1040, line 5b.
   Yes. Subtract line 7 from line 6 . . . . **31,550**
9. If you are:
   • Married filing jointly, enter $32,000
   • Single, head of household, qualifying widow(er), or married filing separately and you **lived apart** from your spouse for all of 2018, enter $25,000 . . . . . **32,000**

   Note. If you are married filing separately and you lived with your spouse at any time in 2018, skip lines 9 through 16; multiply line 8 by 85% (0.85) and enter the result on line 17. Then go to line 18.
10. Is the amount on line 9 less than the amount on line 8?

    No. (STOP) None of your benefits are taxable. Enter -0- on Form 1040, line 5b. If you are married filing separately and you **lived apart** from your spouse for all of 2018, be sure you entered "D" to the right of the word "benefits" on Form 1040, line 5a.
    Yes. Subtract line 9 from line 8 . . . .

11. Enter $12,000 if married filing jointly; $9,000 if single, head of household, qualifying widow(er), or married filing separately and you **lived apart** from your spouse for all of 2018 . . . . ____
12. Subtract line 11 from line 10. If zero or less, enter -0- . . . . ____
13. Enter the **smaller** of line 10 or line 11 . . . . ____
14. Enter one-half of line 13 . . . . ____
15. Enter the **smaller** of line 2 or line 14 . . ____
16. Multiply line 12 by 85% (0.85). If line 12 is zero, enter -0- . . . . ____
17. Add lines 15 and 16 . . . . ____
18. Multiply line 1 by 85% (0.85) . . . . . . ____
19. **Taxable benefits.** Enter the **smaller** of line 17 or line 18. Also enter this amount on Form 1040, line 5b . . . . ════

Example 3. Joe and Betty Johnson file a joint return on Form 1040 for 2018. Joe is a retired railroad worker and in 2018 received the SSEB portion of tier 1 railroad retirement benefits. Joe's Form RRB-1099 shows $10,000 in box 5. Betty is a retired government worker and received a fully taxable pension of $38,000. They had $2,300 in taxable interest income plus interest of $200 on a qualified U.S. savings bond. The savings bond interest qualified for the exclusion. They figure their taxable benefits by completing Worksheet 1. Because they have qualified U.S. savings bond interest, they follow the note at the beginning of the worksheet and use the amount from line 2 of their Schedule B (Form 1040) on line 3 of the worksheet instead of the amount from line 2b of their Form 1040. On line 3 of the worksheet, they enter $40,500 ($38,000 + $2,500).

Filled-in Worksheet 1.
Figuring Your Taxable Benefits

Before you begin:
• If you are married filing separately and you lived apart from your spouse for all of 2018, enter "D" to the right of the word "benefits" on Form 1040, line 5a.
• Don't use this worksheet if you repaid benefits in 2018 and your total repayments (box 4 of Forms SSA-1099 and RRB-1099) were more than your gross benefits for 2018 (box 3 of Forms SSA-1099 and RRB-1099). None of your benefits are taxable for 2018. For more information, see *Repayments More Than Gross Benefits*, later.
• If you are filing Form 8815, Exclusion of Interest From Series EE and I U.S. Savings Bonds Issued After 1989, don't include the amount from line 2b of Form 1040 on line 3 of this worksheet. Instead, include the amount from Schedule B (Form 1040), line 2.

1. Enter the total amount from box 5 of ALL your Forms SSA-1099 and RRB-1099. Also enter this amount on Form 1040, line 5a $10,000
2. Enter one-half of line 1 . . . . **5,000**
3. Combine the amounts from Form 1040, lines 1, 2b, 3b, 4b, and Schedule 1 (Form 1040), line 22 . . . **40,500**
4. Enter the amount, if any, from Form 1040, line 2a . . . . **-0-**
5. Enter the total of any exclusions/ adjustments for:
   • Adoption benefits (Form 8839, line 28),
   • Foreign earned income or housing (Form 2555, lines 45 and 50; or Form 2555-EZ, line 18), and
   • Certain income of bona fide residents of American Samoa (Form 4563, line 15) or Puerto Rico . . . . **-0-**
6. Combine lines 2, 3, 4, and 5 . . . . **45,500**
7. Enter the amounts from Schedule 1 (Form 1040), lines 23 through 32, and any write-in adjustments you entered on the dotted line next to Schedule 1 (Form 1040), line 36 . . . . **-0-**
8. Is the amount on line 7 less than the amount on line 6?

   No. (STOP) None of your social security benefits are taxable. Enter -0- on Form 1040, line 5b.
   Yes. Subtract line 7 from line 6 . . . . . **45,500**
9. If you are:
   • Married filing jointly, enter $32,000
   • Single, head of household, qualifying widow(er), or married filing separately and you **lived apart** from your spouse for all of 2018, enter $25,000 . . . . **32,000**

Note. If you are married filing separately and you lived with your spouse at any time in 2018, skip lines 9 through 16; multiply line 8 by 85% (0.85) and enter the result on line 17. Then go to line 18.

10. Is the amount on line 9 less than the amount on line 8?

   No. None of your benefits are taxable. Enter -0- on Form 1040, line 5b. If you are married filing separately and you **lived apart** from your spouse for all of 2018, be sure you entered "D" to the right of the word "benefits" on Form 1040, line 5a.

   Yes. Subtract line 9 from line 8 13,500

11. Enter $12,000 if married filing jointly; $9,000 if single, head of household, qualifying widow(er), or married filing separately and you **lived apart** from your spouse for all of 2018 12,000

12. Subtract line 11 from line 10. If zero or less, enter -0- 1,500

13. Enter the **smaller** of line 10 or line 11 12,000

14. Enter one-half of line 13 6,000

15. Enter the **smaller** of line 2 or line 14 . . 5,000

16. Multiply line 12 by 85% (0.85). If line 12 is zero, enter -0- 1,275

17. Add lines 15 and 16 6,275

18. Multiply line 1 by 85% (0.85) 8,500

19. **Taxable benefits.** Enter the **smaller** of line 17 or line 18. Also enter this amount on Form 1040, line 5b $6,275

More than 50% of Joe's net benefits are taxable because the income on line 8 of the worksheet ($45,500) is more than $44,000. Joe and Betty enter $10,000 on Form 1040, line 5a; and $6,275 on Form 1040, line 5b.

Deductions Related to Your Benefits

You may be entitled to deduct certain amounts related to the benefits you receive.

Disability payments. You may have received disability payments from your employer or an insurance company that you included as income on your tax return in an earlier year. If you received a lump-sum payment from the SSA or RRB, and you had to repay the employer or insurance company for the disability payments, you can take an itemized deduction for the part of the payments you included in gross income in the earlier year. If the amount you repay is more than $3,000, you may be able to claim a tax credit instead. Claim the deduction or credit in the same way explained under *Repayments More Than Gross Benefits* next.

Repayments More Than Gross Benefits

In some situations, your Form SSA-1099 or Form RRB-1099 will show that the total benefits you repaid (box 4) are more than the gross benefits (box 3) you received. If this occurred, your net benefits in box 5 will be a negative figure (a figure in parentheses) and none of your benefits will be taxable. Don't use a worksheet in this case. If you receive more than one form, a

negative figure in box 5 of one form is used to offset a positive figure in box 5 of another form for that same year.

If you have any questions about this negative figure, contact your local *SSA office* or your local *RRB field office*.

Joint return. If you and your spouse file a joint return, and your Form SSA-1099 or RRB-1099 has a negative figure in box 5, but your spouse's doesn't, subtract the amount in box 5 of your form from the amount in box 5 of your spouse's form. You do this to get your net benefits when figuring if your combined benefits are taxable.

Example. John and Mary file a joint return for 2018. John received Form SSA-1099 showing $3,000 in box 5. Mary also received Form SSA-1099 and the amount in box 5 was ($500). John and Mary will use $2,500 ($3,000 minus $500) as the amount of their net benefits when figuring if any of their combined benefits are taxable.

Repayment of benefits received in an earlier year. If the total amount shown in box 5 of all of your Forms SSA-1099 and RRB-1099 is a negative figure, you can take an itemized deduction for the part of this negative figure that represents benefits you included in gross income in an earlier year. If the figure is more than $3,000, you should figure your tax two ways.

Deduction more than $3,000.

1. Figure your tax for 2018 with the itemized deduction included on Schedule A (Form 1040), line 16.

2. Figure your tax for 2018 in the following steps.

   a. Figure the tax without the itemized deduction included on Schedule A (Form 1040), line 16.

   b. For each year after 1983 for which part of the negative figure represents a repayment of benefits, refigure your taxable benefits as if your total benefits for the year were reduced by that part of the negative figure. Then refigure the tax for that year.

   c. Subtract the total of the refigured tax amounts in (b) from the total of your actual tax amounts.

   d. Subtract the result in (c) from the result in (a).

Compare the tax figured in methods 1 and 2. Your tax for 2018 is the smaller of the two amounts. If method 1 results in less tax, take the itemized deduction on Schedule A (Form 1040), line 16. If method 2 results in less tax, claim a credit for the amount from step 2c above on Schedule 5 (Form 1040), line 74. Check box d and enter "I.R.C. 1341" in the space next to that box. If both methods produce the same tax, deduct the repayment on Schedule A (Form 1040), line 16.

12.

Other Income

What's New

 At the time this publication went to print, Congress was considering legislation that would do the following.

1. Provide additional tax relief for those affected by certain 2018 disasters.

2. Extend certain tax benefits that expired at the end of 2017 and that currently can't be claimed on your 2018 tax return.

3. Change certain other tax provisions.

To learn whether this legislation was enacted, resulting in changes that affect your 2018 tax return, go to Recent Developments at *IRS.gov/ Pub17*.

Repeal of deduction for alimony payments. You can't deduct alimony or separate maintenance payments made under a divorce or separation agreement (1) executed after 2018, or (2) executed before 2019 but later modified if the modification expressly states the repeal of the deduction for alimony payments applies to the modification. Alimony and separate maintenance payments you receive under such an agreement are not included in your gross income.

Reminder

Automatic 6-month extension. If you receive your Form 1099 and/or Schedule K-1, reporting your other income, late and you need more time to file your tax return, you can request a 6-month extension of time to file. See *Automatic Extension* in chapter 1.

Introduction

You must include on your return all items of income you receive in the form of money, property, and services unless the tax law states that you don't include them. Some items, however, are only partly excluded from income. This chapter discusses many kinds of income and explains whether they're taxable or nontaxable.

- Income that's taxable must be reported on your tax return and is subject to tax.

- Income that's nontaxable may have to be shown on your tax return but isn't taxable.

This chapter begins with discussions of the following income items.

- Bartering.

- Canceled debts.

- Sales parties at which you're the host or hostess.

- Life insurance proceeds.

- Partnership income.
- S corporation income.
- Recoveries (including state income tax refunds).
- Rents from personal property.
- Repayments.
- Royalties.
- Unemployment benefits.
- Welfare and other public assistance benefits.

These discussions are followed by brief discussions of other income items.

Useful Items

You may want to see:

Publication

❏ **525** Taxable and Nontaxable Income

❏ **544** Sales and Other Dispositions of Assets

❏ **4681** Canceled Debts, Foreclosures, Repossessions, and Abandonments

For these and other useful items, go to *IRS.gov/ Forms*.

Bartering

Bartering is an exchange of property or services. You must include in your income, at the time received, the fair market value of property or services you receive in bartering. If you exchange services with another person and you both have agreed ahead of time on the value of the services, that value will be accepted as fair market value unless the value can be shown to be otherwise.

Generally, you report this income on Schedule C (Form 1040), Profit or Loss From Business, or Schedule C-EZ (Form 1040), Net Profit From Business. However, if the barter involves an exchange of something other than services, such as in *Example 3* below, you may have to use another form or schedule instead.

Example 1. You're a self-employed attorney who performs legal services for a client, a small corporation. The corporation gives you shares of its stock as payment for your services. You must include the fair market value of the shares in your income on Schedule C (Form 1040) or Schedule C-EZ (Form 1040) in the year you receive them.

Example 2. You're self-employed and a member of a barter club. The club uses "credit units" as a means of exchange. It adds credit units to your account for goods or services you provide to members, which you can use to purchase goods or services offered by other members of the barter club. The club subtracts credit units from your account when you receive goods or services from other members. You must include in your income the value of the credit units that are added to your account, even though you may not actually receive goods or services from other members until a later tax year.

Example 3. You own a small apartment building. In return for 6 months rent-free use of an apartment, an artist gives you a work of art she created. You must report as rental income on Schedule E (Form 1040), Supplemental Income and Loss, the fair market value of the artwork, and the artist must report as income on Schedule C (Form 1040) or Schedule C-EZ (Form 1040) the fair rental value of the apartment.

Form 1099-B from barter exchange. If you exchanged property or services through a barter exchange, Form 1099-B, Proceeds From Broker and Barter Exchange Transactions, or a similar statement from the barter exchange should be sent to you by February 15, 2019. It should show the value of cash, property, services, credits, or scrip you received from exchanges during 2018. The IRS also will receive a copy of Form 1099-B.

Canceled Debts

In most cases, if a debt you owe is canceled or forgiven, other than as a gift or bequest, you must include the canceled amount in your income. You have no income from the canceled debt if it's intended as a gift to you. A debt includes any indebtedness for which you're liable or which attaches to property you hold.

If the debt is a nonbusiness debt, report the canceled amount on Schedule 1 (Form 1040), line 21. If it's a business debt, report the amount on Schedule C (Form 1040) or Schedule C-EZ (Form 1040) (or on Schedule F (Form 1040), Profit or Loss From Farming, if the debt is farm debt and you're a farmer).

Form 1099-C. If a federal government agency, financial institution, or credit union cancels or forgives a debt you owe of $600 or more, you will receive a Form 1099-C, Cancellation of Debt. The amount of the canceled debt is shown in box 2.

Interest included in canceled debt. If any interest is forgiven and included in the amount of canceled debt in box 2, the amount of interest also will be shown in box 3. Whether or not you must include the interest portion of the canceled debt in your income depends on whether the interest would be deductible when you paid it. See *Deductible debt* under *Exceptions*, later.

If the interest wouldn't be deductible (such as interest on a personal loan), include in your income the amount from Form 1099-C, box 2. If the interest would be deductible (such as on a business loan), include in your income the net amount of the canceled debt (the amount shown in box 2 less the interest amount shown in box 3).

Discounted mortgage loan. If your financial institution offers a discount for the early payment of your mortgage loan, the amount of the discount is canceled debt. You must include the canceled amount in your income.

Mortgage relief upon sale or other disposition. If you're personally liable for a mortgage (recourse debt), and you're relieved of the mortgage when you dispose of the property, you may realize gain or loss up to the fair market value of the property. Also, to the extent the mortgage discharge exceeds the fair market value of the property, it's income from discharge of indebtedness unless it qualifies for exclusion under *Excluded debt*, later. Report any income from discharge of indebtedness on nonbusiness debt that doesn't qualify for exclusion as other income on Schedule 1 (Form 1040), line 21.

If you aren't personally liable for a mortgage (nonrecourse debt), and you're relieved of the mortgage when you dispose of the property (such as through foreclosure), that relief is included in the amount you realize. You may have a taxable gain if the amount you realize exceeds your adjusted basis in the property. Report any gain on nonbusiness property as a capital gain.

See Pub. 4681 for more information.

Stockholder debt. If you're a stockholder in a corporation and the corporation cancels or forgives your debt to it, the canceled debt is a constructive distribution that's generally dividend income to you. For more information, see Pub. 542, Corporations.

If you're a stockholder in a corporation and you cancel a debt owed to you by the corporation, you generally don't realize income. This is because the canceled debt is considered as a contribution to the capital of the corporation equal to the amount of debt principal that you canceled.

Repayment of canceled debt. If you included a canceled amount in your income and later pay the debt, you may be able to file a claim for refund for the year the amount was included in income. You can file a claim on Form 1040X if the statute of limitations for filing a claim is still open. The statute of limitations generally doesn't end until 3 years after the due date of your original return.

Exceptions

There are several exceptions to the inclusion of canceled debt in income. These are explained next.

Student loans. Certain student loans contain a provision that all or part of the debt incurred to attend the qualified educational institution will be canceled if you work for a certain period of time in certain professions for any of a broad class of employers.

You don't have income if your student loan is canceled after you agreed to this provision and then performed the services required. To qualify, the loan must have been made by:

1. The federal government, a state or local government, or an instrumentality, agency, or subdivision thereof;

2. A tax-exempt public benefit corporation that has assumed control of a state, county, or municipal hospital, and whose employees are considered public employees under state law; or

3. An educational institution:

    a. Under an agreement with an entity described in (1) or (2) that provided the funds to the institution to make the loan, or

b. As part of a program of the institution designed to encourage its students to serve in occupations with unmet needs or in areas with unmet needs and under which the services provided by the students (or former students) are for or under the direction of a governmental unit or a tax-exempt organization described in section 501(c)(3).

A loan to refinance a qualified student loan also will qualify if it was made by an educational institution or a qualified tax-exempt organization under its program designed as described in item 3b above.

Education loan repayment assistance. Education loan repayments made to you by the National Health Service Corps Loan Repayment Program (NHSC Loan Repayment Program), a state education loan repayment program eligible for funds under the Public Health Service Act, or any other state loan repayment or loan forgiveness program that's intended to provide for the increased availability of health services in underserved or health professional shortage areas aren't taxable.

Deductible debt. You don't have income from the cancellation of a debt if your payment of the debt would be deductible. This exception applies only if you use the cash method of accounting. For more information, see chapter 5 of Pub. 334, Tax Guide for Small Business.

Price reduced after purchase. In most cases, if the seller reduces the amount of debt you owe for property you purchased, you don't have income from the reduction. The reduction of the debt is treated as a purchase price adjustment and reduces your basis in the property.

Excluded debt. Don't include a canceled debt in your gross income in the following situations.

- The debt is canceled in a bankruptcy case under title 11 of the U.S. Code. See Pub. 908, Bankruptcy Tax Guide.

- The debt is canceled when you're insolvent. However, you can't exclude any amount of canceled debt that's more than the amount by which you're insolvent. See Pub. 908.

- The debt is qualified farm debt and is canceled by a qualified person. See chapter 3 of Pub. 225, Farmer's Tax Guide.

- The debt is qualified real property business debt. See chapter 5 of Pub. 334.

- The cancellation is intended as a gift.

 At the time this publication was prepared for printing, Congress was considering legislation to extend the exclusion of qualified principal residence indebtedness from income that had expired at the end of 2017. If extended, you may be able to exclude your qualified principal residence indebtedness from your income for 2018. To see if the legislation was enacted, go to Recent Developments at IRS.gov/Pub17.

Host or Hostess

If you host a party or event at which sales are made, any gift or gratuity you receive for giving the event is a payment for helping a direct seller make sales. You must report this item as income at its fair market value.

Your out-of-pocket party expenses are subject to the 50% limit for meal expenses. For tax years 2018 through 2025, no deduction is allowed for any expenses related to activities generally considered entertainment, amusement, or recreation. Taxpayers may continue to deduct 50% of the cost of business meals if the taxpayer (or an employee of the taxpayer) is present and the food or beverages are not considered lavish or extravagant. The meals may be provided to a current or potential business customer, client, consultant, or similar business contact. Food and beverages that are provided during entertainment events will not be considered entertainment if purchased separately from the event.

For more information about the 50% limit for meal expenses, see Pub. 463.

Life Insurance Proceeds

Life insurance proceeds paid to you because of the death of the insured person aren't taxable unless the policy was turned over to you for a price. This is true even if the proceeds were paid under an accident or health insurance policy or an endowment contract. However, interest income received as a result of life insurance proceeds may be taxable.

Proceeds not received in installments. If death benefits are paid to you in a lump sum or other than at regular intervals, include in your income only the benefits that are more than the amount payable to you at the time of the insured person's death. If the benefit payable at death isn't specified, you include in your income the benefit payments that are more than the present value of the payments at the time of death.

Proceeds received in installments. If you receive life insurance proceeds in installments, you can exclude part of each installment from your income.

To determine the excluded part, divide the amount held by the insurance company (generally, the total lump sum payable at the death of the insured person) by the number of installments to be paid. Include anything over this excluded part in your income as interest.

Surviving spouse. If your spouse died before October 23, 1986, and insurance proceeds paid to you because of the death of your spouse are received in installments, you can exclude up to $1,000 a year of the interest included in the installments. If you remarry, you can continue to take the exclusion.

Surrender of policy for cash. If you surrender a life insurance policy for cash, you must include in income any proceeds that are more than the cost of the life insurance policy. In most cases, your cost (or investment in the contract)

is the total of premiums that you paid for the life insurance policy, less any refunded premiums, rebates, dividends, or unrepaid loans that weren't included in your income.

You should receive a Form 1099-R showing the total proceeds and the taxable part. Report these amounts on lines 4a and 4b of Form 1040.

More information. For more information, see *Life Insurance Proceeds* in Pub. 525.

Endowment Contract Proceeds

An endowment contract is a policy under which you're paid a specified amount of money on a certain date unless you die before that date, in which case the money is paid to your designated beneficiary. Endowment proceeds paid in a lump sum to you at maturity are taxable only if the proceeds are more than the cost of the policy. To determine your cost, subtract any amount that you previously received under the contract and excluded from your income from the total premiums (or other consideration) paid for the contract. Include in your income the part of the lump-sum payment that's more than your cost.

Accelerated Death Benefits

Certain amounts paid as accelerated death benefits under a life insurance contract or viatical settlement before the insured's death are excluded from income if the insured is terminally or chronically ill.

Viatical settlement. This is the sale or assignment of any part of the death benefit under a life insurance contract to a viatical settlement provider. A viatical settlement provider is a person who regularly engages in the business of buying or taking assignment of life insurance contracts on the lives of insured individuals who are terminally or chronically ill and who meets the requirements of section 101(g)(2)(B) of the Internal Revenue Code.

Exclusion for terminal illness. Accelerated death benefits are fully excludable if the insured is a terminally ill individual. This is a person who has been certified by a physician as having an illness or physical condition that can reasonably be expected to result in death within 24 months from the date of the certification.

Exclusion for chronic illness. If the insured is a chronically ill individual who's not terminally ill, accelerated death benefits paid on the basis of costs incurred for qualified long-term care services are fully excludable. Accelerated death benefits paid on a per diem or other periodic basis are excludable up to a limit. For 2018, this limit is $360. It applies to the total of the accelerated death benefits and any periodic payments received from long-term care insurance contracts. For information on the limit and the definitions of chronically ill individual, qualified long-term care services, and long-term care insurance contracts, see *Long-Term Care Insurance Contracts* under *Sickness and Injury Benefits* in Pub. 525.

Exception. The exclusion doesn't apply to any amount paid to a person (other than the insured) who has an insurable interest in the life of the insured because the insured:

- Is a director, officer, or employee of the person; or
- Has a financial interest in the person's business.

Form 8853. To claim an exclusion for accelerated death benefits made on a per diem or other periodic basis, you must file Form 8853, Archer MSAs and Long-Term Care Insurance Contracts, with your return. You don't have to file Form 8853 to exclude accelerated death benefits paid on the basis of actual expenses incurred.

Public Safety Officer Killed or Injured in the Line of Duty

A spouse, former spouse, and child of a public safety officer killed in the line of duty can exclude from gross income survivor benefits received from a governmental section 401(a) plan attributable to the officer's service. See section 101(h).

A public safety officer who's permanently and totally disabled or killed in the line of duty and a surviving spouse or child can exclude from income death or disability benefits received from the federal Bureau of Justice Assistance or death benefits paid by a state program. See section 104(a)(6).

For this purpose, the term "public safety officer" includes law enforcement officers, firefighters, chaplains, and rescue squad and ambulance crew members. For more information, see Pub. 559, Survivors, Executors, and Administrators.

Partnership Income

A partnership generally isn't a taxable entity. The income, gains, losses, deductions, and credits of a partnership are passed through to the partners based on each partner's distributive share of these items.

Schedule K-1 (Form 1065). Although a partnership generally pays no tax, it must file an information return on Form 1065, U.S. Return of Partnership Income, and send Schedule K-1 (Form 1065) to each partner. In addition, the partnership will send each partner a copy of the Partner's Instructions for Schedule K-1 (Form 1065) to help each partner report his or her share of the partnership's income, deductions, credits, and tax preference items.

 Keep Schedule K-1 (Form 1065) for your records. Don't attach it to your Form 1040, unless you're specifically required to do so.

For more information on partnerships, see Pub. 541, Partnerships.

Qualified joint venture. If you and your spouse each materially participate as the only members of a jointly owned and operated business, and you file a joint return for the tax year,

you can make a joint election to be treated as a qualified joint venture instead of a partnership. To make this election, you must divide all items of income, gain, loss, deduction, and credit attributable to the business between you and your spouse in accordance with your respective interests in the venture. For further information on how to make the election and which schedule(s) to file, see the instructions for your individual tax return.

S Corporation Income

In most cases, an S corporation doesn't pay tax on its income. Instead, the income, losses, deductions, and credits of the corporation are passed through to the shareholders based on each shareholder's pro rata share.

Schedule K-1 (Form 1120S). An S corporation must file a return on Form 1120S, U.S. Income Tax Return for an S Corporation, and send Schedule K-1 (Form 1120S) to each shareholder. In addition, the S corporation will send each shareholder a copy of the Shareholder's Instructions for Schedule K-1 (Form 1120S) to help each shareholder report his or her share of the S corporation's income, losses, credits, and deductions.

 Keep Schedule K-1 (Form 1120S) for your records. Don't attach it to your Form 1040, unless you're specifically required to do so.

For more information on S corporations and their shareholders, see the Instructions for Form 1120S.

Recoveries

A recovery is a return of an amount you deducted or took a credit for in an earlier year. The most common recoveries are refunds, reimbursements, and rebates of deductions itemized on Schedule A (Form 1040). You also may have recoveries of nonitemized deductions (such as payments on previously deducted bad debts) and recoveries of items for which you previously claimed a tax credit.

Tax benefit rule. You must include a recovery in your income in the year you receive it up to the amount by which the deduction or credit you took for the recovered amount reduced your tax in the earlier year. For this purpose, any increase to an amount carried over to the current year that resulted from the deduction or credit is considered to have reduced your tax in the earlier year. For more information, see Pub. 525.

Federal income tax refund. Refunds of federal income taxes aren't included in your income because they're never allowed as a deduction from income.

State tax refund. If you received a state or local income tax refund (or credit or offset) in 2018, you generally must include it in income if you deducted the tax in an earlier year. The payer should send Form 1099-G, Certain Government Payments, to you by January 31, 2019. The IRS also will receive a copy of the Form 1099-G. If you file Form 1040, use the State and Local Income Tax Refund Worksheet in the 2018 Instructions for Schedule 1 (Form 1040) to

figure the amount (if any) to include in your income. See Pub. 525 for when you must use another worksheet.

If you could choose to deduct for a tax year either:

- State and local income taxes, or
- State and local general sales taxes, then

the maximum refund that you may have to include in income is limited to the excess of the tax you chose to deduct for that year over the tax you didn't choose to deduct for that year. For examples, see Pub. 525.

Mortgage interest refund. If you received a refund or credit in 2018 of mortgage interest paid in an earlier year, the amount should be shown in box 4 of your Form 1098, Mortgage Interest Statement. Don't subtract the refund amount from the interest you paid in 2018. You may have to include it in your income under the rules explained in the following discussions.

Interest on recovery. Interest on any of the amounts you recover must be reported as interest income in the year received. For example, report any interest you received on state or local income tax refunds on Form 1040, line 2b.

Recovery and expense in same year. If the refund or other recovery and the expense occur in the same year, the recovery reduces the deduction or credit and isn't reported as income.

Recovery for 2 or more years. If you receive a refund or other recovery that's for amounts you paid in 2 or more separate years, you must allocate, on a pro rata basis, the recovered amount between the years in which you paid it. This allocation is necessary to determine the amount of recovery from any earlier years and to determine the amount, if any, of your allowable deduction for this item for the current year. For information on how to figure the allocation, see Recoveries in Pub. 525.

Itemized Deduction Recoveries

If you recover any amount that you deducted in an earlier year on Schedule A (Form 1040), you generally must include the full amount of the recovery in your income in the year you receive it.

Where to report. Enter your state or local income tax refund on Schedule 1 (Form 1040), line 10, and the total of all other recoveries as other income on Schedule 1 (Form 1040), line 21.

Standard deduction limit. You generally are allowed to claim the standard deduction if you don't itemize your deductions. Only your itemized deductions that are more than your standard deduction are subject to the recovery rule (unless you're required to itemize your deductions). If your total deductions on the earlier year return weren't more than your income for that year, include in your income this year the lesser of:

- Your recoveries, or
- The amount by which your itemized deductions exceeded the standard deduction.

Example. For 2017, you filed a joint return. Your taxable income was $60,000 and you weren't entitled to any tax credits. Your standard deduction was $12,700, and you had itemized deductions of $14,000. In 2018, you received the following recoveries for amounts deducted on your 2017 return.

Medical expenses	$200
State and local income tax refund	400
Refund of mortgage interest	325
Total recoveries	$925

None of the recoveries were more than the deductions taken for 2017. The difference between the state and local income tax you deducted and your local general sales tax was more than $400.

Your total recoveries are less than the amount by which your itemized deductions exceeded the standard deduction ($14,000 − 12,700 = $1,300), so you must include your total recoveries in your income for 2018. Report the state and local income tax refund of $400 on Schedule 1 (Form 1040), line 10, and the balance of your recoveries, $525, on Schedule 1 (Form 1040), line 21.

Standard deduction for earlier years. To determine if amounts recovered in the current year must be included in your income, you must know the standard deduction for your filing status for the year the deduction was claimed. Look in the instructions for your tax return from prior years to locate the standard deduction for the filing status for that prior year.

Example. You filed a joint return on Form 1040 for 2017 with taxable income of $45,000. Your itemized deductions were $12,850. The standard deduction that you could have claimed was $12,700. In 2018, you recovered $2,100 of your 2017 itemized deductions. None of the recoveries were more than the actual deductions for 2017. Include $150 of the recoveries in your 2018 income. This is the smaller of your recoveries ($2,100) or the amount by which your itemized deductions were more than the standard deduction ($12,850 − $12,700 = $150).

Recovery limited to deduction. You don't include in your income any amount of your recovery that's more than the amount you deducted in the earlier year. The amount you include in your income is limited to the smaller of:

- The amount deducted on Schedule A (Form 1040), or
- The amount recovered.

Example. During 2017, you paid $1,700 for medical expenses. Of this amount, you deducted $200 on your 2017 Schedule A (Form 1040). In 2018, you received a $500 reimbursement from your medical insurance for your 2017 expenses. The only amount of the $500 reimbursement that must be included in your income for 2018 is $200—the amount actually deducted.

Other recoveries. See *Recoveries* in Pub. 525 if:

- You have recoveries of items other than itemized deductions, or

- You received a recovery for an item for which you claimed a tax credit (other than investment credit or foreign tax credit) in a prior year.

Rents From Personal Property

If you rent out personal property, such as equipment or vehicles, how you report your income and expenses is in most cases determined by:

- Whether or not the rental activity is a business, and
- Whether or not the rental activity is conducted for profit.

In most cases, if your primary purpose is income or profit and you're involved in the rental activity with continuity and regularity, your rental activity is a business. See Pub. 535, Business Expenses, for details on deducting expenses for both business and not-for-profit activities.

Reporting business income and expenses. If you're in the business of renting personal property, report your income and expenses on Schedule C (Form 1040) or Schedule C-EZ (Form 1040). The form instructions have information on how to complete them.

Reporting nonbusiness income. If you aren't in the business of renting personal property, report your rental income on Schedule 1 (Form 1040), line 21. List the type and amount of the income on the dotted line next to line 21.

Reporting nonbusiness expenses. If you rent personal property for profit, include your rental expenses in the total amount you enter on Schedule 1 (Form 1040), line 36, and see the instructions there.

If you don't rent personal property for profit, your deductions are limited and you can't report a loss to offset other income. See *Activity not for profit* under *Other Income*, later.

Repayments

If you had to repay an amount that you included in your income in an earlier year, you may be able to deduct the amount repaid from your income for the year in which you repaid it. Or, if the amount you repaid is more than $3,000, you may be able to take a credit against your tax for the year in which you repaid it. Generally, you can claim a deduction or credit only if the repayment qualifies as an expense or loss incurred in your trade or business or in a for-profit transaction.

Type of deduction. The type of deduction you're allowed in the year of repayment depends on the type of income you included in the earlier year. You generally deduct the repayment on the same form or schedule on which you previously reported it as income. For example, if you reported it as self-employment income, deduct it as a business expense on Schedule C (Form 1040) or Schedule C-EZ (Form 1040) or Schedule F (Form 1040). If you reported it as a capital gain, deduct it as a capital loss as explained in the Instructions for Schedule D (Form 1040). If you reported it as wages, unemployment compensation, or other

nonbusiness income, you may be able to deduct it as an other itemized deduction if the amount repaid is over $3,000.

 Beginning in 2018, you can no longer claim any miscellaneous itemized deductions, so if the amount repaid was $3,000 or less, you are not able to deduct it from your income in the year you repaid it.

Repaid social security benefits. If you repaid social security benefits or equivalent railroad retirement benefits, see *Repayment of benefits* in chapter 11.

Repayment of $3,000 or less. If the amount you repaid was $3,000 or less, deduct it from your income in the year you repaid it.

Repayment over $3,000. If the amount you repaid was more than $3,000, you can deduct the repayment as an other itemized deduction on Schedule A (Form 1040), line 16, if you included the income under a claim of right. This means that at the time you included the income, it appeared that you had an unrestricted right to it. However, you can choose to take a credit for the year of repayment. Figure your tax under both methods and compare the results. Use the method (deduction or credit) that results in less tax.

 When determining whether the amount you repaid was more or less than $3,000, consider the total amount being repaid on the return. Each instance of repayment isn't considered separately.

Method 1. Figure your tax for 2018 claiming a deduction for the repaid amount. If you deduct it as an other itemized deduction, enter it on Schedule A (Form 1040), line 16.

Method 2. Figure your tax for 2018 claiming a credit for the repaid amount. Follow these steps.

1. Figure your tax for 2018 without deducting the repaid amount.

2. Refigure your tax from the earlier year without including in income the amount you repaid in 2018.

3. Subtract the tax in (2) from the tax shown on your return for the earlier year. This is the credit.

4. Subtract the answer in (3) from the tax for 2018 figured without the deduction (step 1).

If method 1 results in less tax, deduct the amount repaid. If method 2 results in less tax, claim the credit figured in (3) above on Schedule 5 (Form 1040), line 74, by adding the amount of the credit to any other credits on this line, and see the instructions there.

An example of this computation can be found in Pub. 525.

Repaid wages subject to social security and Medicare taxes. If you had to repay an amount that you included in your wages or compensation in an earlier year on which social security, Medicare, or tier 1 RRTA taxes were paid, ask your employer to refund the excess amount to you. If the employer refuses to refund the taxes, ask for a statement indicating the amount of the overcollection to support your claim. File a claim for refund using Form 843, Claim for Refund and Request for Abatement.

Repaid wages subject to Additional Medicare Tax. Employers can't make an adjustment or file a claim for refund for Additional Medicare Tax withholding when there is a repayment of wages received by an employee in a prior year because the employee determines liability for Additional Medicare Tax on the employee's income tax return for the prior year. If you had to repay an amount that you included in your wages or compensation in an earlier year, and on which Additional Medicare Tax was paid, you may be able to recover the Additional Medicare Tax paid on the amount. To recover Additional Medicare Tax on the repaid wages or compensation, you must file Form 1040X, Amended U.S. Individual Income Tax Return, for the prior year in which the wages or compensation was originally received. See the Instructions for Form 1040X.

Royalties

Royalties from copyrights, patents, and oil, gas, and mineral properties are taxable as ordinary income.

In most cases, you report royalties in Part I of Schedule E (Form 1040). However, if you hold an operating oil, gas, or mineral interest or are in business as a self-employed writer, inventor, artist, etc., report your income and expenses on Schedule C (Form 1040) or Schedule C-EZ (Form 1040).

Copyrights and patents. Royalties from copyrights on literary, musical, or artistic works, and similar property, or from patents on inventions, are amounts paid to you for the right to use your work over a specified period of time. Royalties generally are based on the number of units sold, such as the number of books, tickets to a performance, or machines sold.

Oil, gas, and minerals. Royalty income from oil, gas, and mineral properties is the amount you receive when natural resources are extracted from your property. The royalties are based on units, such as barrels, tons, etc., and are paid to you by a person or company that leases the property from you.

Depletion. If you're the owner of an economic interest in mineral deposits or oil and gas wells, you can recover your investment through the depletion allowance. For information on this subject, see chapter 9 of Pub. 535.

Coal and iron ore. Under certain circumstances, you can treat amounts you receive from the disposal of coal and iron ore as payments from the sale of a capital asset, rather than as royalty income. For information about gain or loss from the sale of coal and iron ore, see chapter 2 of Pub. 544.

Sale of property interest. If you sell your complete interest in oil, gas, or mineral rights, the amount you receive is considered payment for the sale of property used in a trade or business under section 1231, not royalty income. Under certain circumstances, the sale is subject to capital gain or loss treatment as explained in the Instructions for Schedule D (Form 1040).

For more information on selling section 1231 property, see chapter 3 of Pub. 544.

If you retain a royalty, an overriding royalty, or a net profit interest in a mineral property for the life of the property, you have made a lease or a sublease, and any cash you receive for the assignment of other interests in the property is ordinary income subject to a depletion allowance.

Part of future production sold. If you own mineral property but sell part of the future production, in most cases you treat the money you receive from the buyer at the time of the sale as a loan from the buyer. Don't include it in your income or take depletion based on it.

When production begins, you include all the proceeds in your income, deduct all the production expenses, and deduct depletion from that amount to arrive at your taxable income from the property.

Unemployment Benefits

The tax treatment of unemployment benefits you receive depends on the type of program paying the benefits.

Unemployment compensation. You must include in income all unemployment compensation you receive. You should receive a Form 1099-G showing in box 1 the total unemployment compensation paid to you. In most cases, you enter unemployment compensation on Schedule 1 (Form 1040), line 19.

Types of unemployment compensation. Unemployment compensation generally includes any amount received under an unemployment compensation law of the United States or of a state. It includes the following benefits.

- Benefits paid by a state or the District of Columbia from the Federal Unemployment Trust Fund.

- State unemployment insurance benefits.

- Railroad unemployment compensation benefits.

- Disability payments from a government program paid as a substitute for unemployment compensation. (Amounts received as workers' compensation for injuries or illness aren't unemployment compensation. See chapter 5 for more information.)

- Trade readjustment allowances under the Trade Act of 1974.

- Unemployment assistance under the Disaster Relief and Emergency Assistance Act.

- Unemployment assistance under the Airline Deregulation Act of 1978 Program.

Governmental program. If you contribute to a governmental unemployment compensation program and your contributions aren't deductible, amounts you receive under the program aren't included as unemployment compensation until you recover your contributions. If you deducted all of your contributions to

the program, the entire amount you receive under the program is included in your income.

Repayment of unemployment compensation. If you repaid in 2018 unemployment compensation you received in 2018, subtract the amount you repaid from the total amount you received and enter the difference on Schedule 1 (Form 1040), line 19. On the dotted line next to your entry, enter "Repaid" and the amount you repaid. If you repaid unemployment compensation in 2018 that you included in income in an earlier year, you can deduct the amount repaid on Schedule A (Form 1040), line 16, if you itemize deductions and the amount is more than $3,000. See *Repayments*, earlier.

Tax withholding. You can choose to have federal income tax withheld from your unemployment compensation. To make this choice, complete Form W-4V, Voluntary Withholding Request, and give it to the paying office. Tax will be withheld at 10% of your payment.

 If you don't choose to have tax withheld from your unemployment compensation, you may be liable for estimated tax. If you don't pay enough tax, either through withholding or estimated tax, or a combination of both, you may have to pay a penalty. For more information on estimated tax, see chapter 4.

Supplemental unemployment benefits. Benefits received from an employer-financed fund (to which the employees didn't contribute) aren't unemployment compensation. They are taxable as wages. For more information, see *Supplemental Unemployment Benefits* in section 5 of Pub. 15-A, Employer's Supplemental Tax Guide. Report these payments on line 1 of Form 1040.

Repayment of benefits. You may have to repay some of your supplemental unemployment benefits to qualify for trade readjustment allowances under the Trade Act of 1974. If you repay supplemental unemployment benefits in the same year you receive them, reduce the total benefits by the amount you repay. If you repay the benefits in a later year, you must include the full amount of the benefits received in your income for the year you received them.

Deduct the repayment in the later year as an adjustment to gross income on Form 1040. Include the repayment on Schedule 1 (Form 1040), line 36, and see the instructions there. If the amount you repay in a later year is more than $3,000, you may be able to take a credit against your tax for the later year instead of deducting the amount repaid. For more information on this, see *Repayments*, earlier.

Private unemployment fund. Unemployment benefit payments from a private (nonunion) fund to which you voluntarily contribute are taxable only if the amounts you receive are more than your total payments into the fund. Report the taxable amount on Schedule 1 (Form 1040), line 21.

Payments by a union. Benefits paid to you as an unemployed member of a union from regular union dues are included in your income on Schedule 1 (Form 1040), line 21. However, if you contribute to a special union fund and your payments to the fund aren't deductible, the unemployment benefits you receive from the fund are includible in your income only to the extent they're more than your contributions.

Guaranteed annual wage. Payments you receive from your employer during periods of unemployment, under a union agreement that guarantees you full pay during the year, are taxable as wages. Include them on line 1 of Form 1040.

State employees. Payments similar to a state's unemployment compensation may be made by the state to its employees who aren't covered by the state's unemployment compensation law. Although the payments are fully taxable, don't report them as unemployment compensation. Report these payments on Schedule 1 (Form 1040), line 21.

Welfare and Other Public Assistance Benefits

Don't include in your income governmental benefit payments from a public welfare fund based upon need, such as payments to blind individuals under a state public assistance law. Payments from a state fund for the victims of crime shouldn't be included in the victims' incomes if they're in the nature of welfare payments. Don't deduct medical expenses that are reimbursed by such a fund. You must include in your income any welfare payments that are compensation for services or that are obtained fraudulently.

Reemployment Trade Adjustment Assistance (RTAA) payments. RTAA payments received from a state must be included in your income. The state must send you Form 1099-G to advise you of the amount you should include in income. The amount should be reported on Schedule 1 (Form 1040), line 21.

Persons with disabilities. If you have a disability, you must include in income compensation you receive for services you perform unless the compensation is otherwise excluded. However, you don't include in income the value of goods, services, and cash that you receive, not in return for your services, but for your training and rehabilitation because you have a disability. Excludable amounts include payments for transportation and attendant care, such as interpreter services for the deaf, reader services for the blind, and services to help individuals with an intellectual disability do their work.

Disaster relief grants. Don't include post-disaster grants received under the Robert T. Stafford Disaster Relief and Emergency Assistance Act in your income if the grant payments are made to help you meet necessary expenses or serious needs for medical, dental, housing, personal property, transportation, child care, or funeral expenses. Don't deduct casualty losses or medical expenses that are specifically reimbursed by these disaster relief grants. If you have deducted a casualty loss for the loss of your personal residence and you later receive a disaster relief grant for the loss of the same residence, you may have to include part or all of the grant in your taxable income. See *Recoveries*, earlier. Unemployment assistance pay-

ments under the Act are taxable unemployment compensation. See *Unemployment compensation* under *Unemployment Benefits*, earlier.

Disaster relief payments. You can exclude from income any amount you receive that's a qualified disaster relief payment. A qualified disaster relief payment is an amount paid to you:

1. To reimburse or pay reasonable and necessary personal, family, living, or funeral expenses that result from a qualified disaster;
2. To reimburse or pay reasonable and necessary expenses incurred for the repair or rehabilitation of your home or repair or replacement of its contents to the extent it's due to a qualified disaster;
3. By a person engaged in the furnishing or sale of transportation as a common carrier because of the death or personal physical injuries incurred as a result of a qualified disaster; or
4. By a federal, state, or local government, agency, or instrumentality in connection with a qualified disaster in order to promote the general welfare.

You can exclude this amount only to the extent any expense it pays for isn't paid for by insurance or otherwise. The exclusion doesn't apply if you were a participant or conspirator in a terrorist action or a representative of one.

A qualified disaster is:

- A disaster which results from a terrorist or military action;
- A federally declared disaster; or
- A disaster which results from an accident involving a common carrier, or from any other event, which is determined to be catastrophic by the Secretary of the Treasury or his or her delegate.

For amounts paid under item (4), a disaster is qualified if it's determined by an applicable federal, state, or local authority to warrant assistance from the federal, state, or local government, agency, or instrumentality.

Disaster mitigation payments. You can exclude from income any amount you receive that's a qualified disaster mitigation payment. Qualified disaster mitigation payments are most commonly paid to you in the period immediately following damage to property as a result of a natural disaster. However, disaster mitigation payments are used to mitigate (reduce the severity of) potential damage from future natural disasters. They're paid to you through state and local governments based on the provisions of the Robert T. Stafford Disaster Relief and Emergency Assistance Act or the National Flood Insurance Act.

You can't increase the basis or adjusted basis of your property for improvements made with nontaxable disaster mitigation payments.

Home Affordable Modification Program (HAMP). If you benefit from Pay-for-Performance Success Payments under HAMP, the payments aren't taxable.

Mortgage assistance payments under section 235 of the National Housing Act. Payments made under section 235 of the National

Housing Act for mortgage assistance aren't included in the homeowner's income. Interest paid for the homeowner under the mortgage assistance program can't be deducted.

Medicare. Medicare benefits received under title XVIII of the Social Security Act aren't includible in the gross income of the individuals for whom they're paid. This includes basic (Part A (Hospital Insurance Benefits for the Aged)) and supplementary (Part B (Supplementary Medical Insurance Benefits for the Aged)).

Social security benefits (including lump-sum payments attributable to prior years), Supplemental Security Income (SSI) benefits, and lump-sum death benefits. The Social Security Administration (SSA) provides benefits such as old-age benefits, benefits to disabled workers, and benefits to spouses and dependents. These benefits may be subject to federal income tax depending on your filing status and other income. See chapter 11 in this publication and Pub. 915, Social Security and Equivalent Railroad Retirement Benefits, for more information. An individual originally denied benefits, but later approved, may receive a lump-sum payment for the period when benefits were denied (which may be prior years). See Pub. 915 for information on how to make a lump-sum election, which may reduce your tax liability. There are also other types of benefits paid by the SSA. However, SSI benefits and lump-sum death benefits (one-time payment to spouse and children of deceased) aren't subject to federal income tax. For more information on these benefits, go to *SSA.gov*.

Nutrition Program for the Elderly. Food benefits you receive under the Nutrition Program for the Elderly aren't taxable. If you prepare and serve free meals for the program, include in your income as wages the cash pay you receive, even if you're also eligible for food benefits.

Payments to reduce cost of winter energy. Payments made by a state to qualified people to reduce their cost of winter energy use aren't taxable.

Other Income

The following brief discussions are arranged in alphabetical order. Other income items briefly discussed below are referenced to publications which provide more topical information.

Activity not for profit. You must include on your return income from an activity from which you don't expect to make a profit. An example of this type of activity is a hobby or a farm you operate mostly for recreation and pleasure. Enter this income on Schedule 1 (Form 1040), line 21. Deductions for expenses related to the activity are limited. They can't total more than the income you report and can be taken only if you itemize deductions on Schedule A (Form 1040). See *Not-for-Profit Activities* in chapter 1 of Pub. 535 for information on whether an activity is considered carried on for a profit.

Alaska Permanent Fund dividend. If you received a payment from Alaska's mineral income fund (Alaska Permanent Fund dividend), report it as income on Schedule 1 (Form 1040), line 21. The state of Alaska sends each recipient a document that shows the amount of the payment with the check. The amount is also reported to the IRS.

Alimony. Include in your income on Schedule 1 (Form 1040), line 11, any alimony payments you receive. Amounts you receive for child support aren't income to you. Alimony and child support payments are discussed in chapter 18.

 Don't include alimony payments you receive under a divorce or separation agreement (1) executed after 2018, or (2) executed before 2019 but later modified if the modification expressly states the repeal of the deduction for alimony payments applies to the modification.

Bribes. If you receive a bribe, include it in your income.

Campaign contributions. These contributions aren't income to a candidate unless they're diverted to his or her personal use. To be nontaxable, the contributions must be spent for campaign purposes or kept in a fund for use in future campaigns. However, interest earned on bank deposits, dividends received on contributed securities, and net gains realized on sales of contributed securities are taxable and must be reported on Form 1120-POL, U.S. Income Tax Return for Certain Political Organizations. Excess campaign funds transferred to an office account must be included in the officeholder's income on Schedule 1 (Form 1040), line 21, in the year transferred.

Car pools. Don't include in your income amounts you receive from the passengers for driving a car in a car pool to and from work. These amounts are considered reimbursement for your expenses. However, this rule doesn't apply if you have developed car pool arrangements into a profit-making business of transporting workers for hire.

Cash rebates. A cash rebate you receive from a dealer or manufacturer of an item you buy isn't income, but you must reduce your basis by the amount of the rebate.

Example. You buy a new car for $24,000 cash and receive a $2,000 rebate check from the manufacturer. The $2,000 isn't income to you. Your basis in the car is $22,000. This is the basis on which you figure gain or loss if you sell the car and depreciation if you use it for business.

Casualty insurance and other reimbursements. You generally shouldn't report these reimbursements on your return unless you're figuring gain or loss from the casualty or theft. See chapter 26 for more information.

Child support payments. You shouldn't report these payments on your return. See chapter 18 for more information.

Court awards and damages. To determine if settlement amounts you receive by compromise or judgment must be included in your income, you must consider the item that the settlement replaces. The character of the income as ordinary income or capital gain depends on the nature of the underlying claim. Include the following as ordinary income.

1. Interest on any award.

2. Compensation for lost wages or lost profits in most cases.

3. Punitive damages, in most cases. It doesn't matter if they relate to a physical injury or physical sickness.

4. Amounts received in settlement of pension rights (if you didn't contribute to the plan).

5. Damages for:

    a. Patent or copyright infringement,

    b. Breach of contract, or

    c. Interference with business operations.

6. Back pay and damages for emotional distress received to satisfy a claim under title VII of the Civil Rights Act of 1964.

7. Attorney fees and costs (including contingent fees) where the underlying recovery is included in gross income.

8. Attorney fees and costs relating to whistleblower awards where the underlying recovery is included in gross income.

Don't include in your income compensatory damages for personal physical injury or physical sickness (whether received in a lump sum or installments).

Emotional distress. Emotional distress itself isn't a physical injury or physical sickness, but damages you receive for emotional distress due to a physical injury or sickness are treated as received for the physical injury or sickness. Don't include them in your income.

If the emotional distress is due to a personal injury that isn't due to a physical injury or sickness (for example, employment discrimination or injury to reputation), you must include the damages in your income, except for any damages that aren't more than amounts paid for medical care due to that emotional distress. Emotional distress includes physical symptoms that result from emotional distress, such as headaches, insomnia, and stomach disorders.

Credit card insurance. In most cases, if you receive benefits under a credit card disability or unemployment insurance plan, the benefits are taxable to you. These plans make the minimum monthly payment on your credit card account if you can't make the payment due to injury, illness, disability, or unemployment. Report on Schedule 1 (Form 1040), line 21, the amount of benefits you received during the year that's more than the amount of the premiums you paid during the year.

Down payment assistance. If you purchase a home and receive assistance from a nonprofit corporation to make the down payment, that assistance isn't included in your income. If the corporation qualifies as a tax-exempt charitable organization, the assistance is treated as a gift and is included in your basis of the house. If the corporation doesn't qualify, the assistance is treated as a rebate or reduction of the purchase price and isn't included in your basis.

Employment agency fees. If you get a job through an employment agency, and the fee is paid by your employer, the fee isn't includible in your income if you aren't liable for it. However, if

you pay it and your employer reimburses you for it, it's includible in your income.

Energy conservation subsidies. You can exclude from gross income any subsidy provided, either directly or indirectly, by public utilities for the purchase or installation of an energy conservation measure for a dwelling unit.

Energy conservation measure. This includes installations or modifications that are primarily designed to reduce consumption of electricity or natural gas, or improve the management of energy demand.

Dwelling unit. This includes a house, apartment, condominium, mobile home, boat, or similar property. If a building or structure contains both dwelling and other units, any subsidy must be properly allocated.

Estate and trust income. An estate or trust, unlike a partnership, may have to pay federal income tax. If you're a beneficiary of an estate or trust, you may be taxed on your share of its income distributed or required to be distributed to you. However, there is never a double tax. Estates and trusts file their returns on Form 1041, U.S. Income Tax Return for Estates and Trusts, and your share of the income is reported to you on Schedule K-1 (Form 1041).

Current income required to be distributed. If you're the beneficiary of an estate or trust that must distribute all of its current income, you must report your share of the distributable net income, whether or not you actually received it.

Current income not required to be distributed. If you're the beneficiary of an estate or trust and the fiduciary has the choice of whether to distribute all or part of the current income, you must report:

- All income that's required to be distributed to you, whether or not it's actually distributed, plus

- All other amounts actually paid or credited to you,

up to the amount of your share of distributable net income.

How to report. Treat each item of income the same way that the estate or trust would treat it. For example, if a trust's dividend income is distributed to you, you report the distribution as dividend income on your return. The same rule applies to distributions of tax-exempt interest and capital gains.

The fiduciary of the estate or trust must tell you the type of items making up your share of the estate or trust income and any credits you're allowed on your individual income tax return.

Losses. Losses of estates and trusts generally aren't deductible by the beneficiaries.

Grantor trust. Income earned by a grantor trust is taxable to the grantor, not the beneficiary, if the grantor keeps certain control over the trust. (The grantor is the one who transferred property to the trust.) This rule applies if the property (or income from the property) put into the trust will or may revert (be returned) to the grantor or the grantor's spouse.

Generally, a trust is a grantor trust if the grantor has a reversionary interest valued (at the date of transfer) at more than 5% of the value of the transferred property.

Expenses paid by another. If your personal expenses are paid for by another person, such as a corporation, the payment may be taxable to you depending upon your relationship with that person and the nature of the payment. But if the payment makes up for a loss caused by that person, and only restores you to the position you were in before the loss, the payment isn't includible in your income.

Fees for services. Include all fees for your services in your income. Examples of these fees are amounts you receive for services you perform as:

- A corporate director;
- An executor, administrator, or personal representative of an estate;
- A manager of a trade or business you operated before declaring Chapter 11 bankruptcy;
- A notary public; or
- An election precinct official.

Nonemployee compensation. If you aren't an employee and the fees for your services from a single payer in the course of the payer's trade or business total $600 or more for the year, the payer should send you a Form 1099-MISC. You may need to report your fees as self-employment income. See *Self-Employed Persons* in chapter 1 for a discussion of when you're considered self-employed.

Corporate director. Corporate director fees are self-employment income. Report these payments on Schedule C (Form 1040) or Schedule C-EZ (Form 1040).

Personal representatives. All personal representatives must include in their gross income fees paid to them from an estate. If you aren't in the trade or business of being an executor (for instance, you're the executor of a friend's or relative's estate), report these fees on Schedule 1 (Form 1040), line 21. If you're in the trade or business of being an executor, report these fees as self-employment income on Schedule C (Form 1040) or Schedule C-EZ (Form 1040). The fee isn't includible in income if it's waived.

Manager of trade or business for bankruptcy estate. Include in your income all payments received from your bankruptcy estate for managing or operating a trade or business that you operated before you filed for bankruptcy. Report this income on Schedule 1 (Form 1040), line 21.

Notary public. Report payments for these services on Schedule C (Form 1040) or Schedule C-EZ (Form 1040). These payments aren't subject to self-employment tax. See the separate Instructions for Schedule SE (Form 1040) for details.

Election precinct official. You should receive a Form W-2 showing payments for services performed as an election official or election worker. Report these payments on line 1 of Form 1040.

Foster care providers. Generally, payment you receive from a state, political subdivision, or a qualified foster care placement agency for caring for a qualified foster individual in your home is excluded from your income. However, you must include in your income payment to the extent it's received for the care of more than five qualified foster individuals age 19 years or older.

A qualified foster individual is a person who:

1. Is living in a foster family home; and
2. Was placed there by:
    a. An agency of a state or one of its political subdivisions, or
    b. A qualified foster care placement agency.

Difficulty-of-care payments. These are payments that are designated by the payer as compensation for providing the additional care that's required for physically, mentally, or emotionally handicapped qualified foster individuals. A state must determine that this compensation is needed, and the care for which the payments are made must be provided in the foster care provider's home in which the qualified foster individual was placed.

Certain Medicaid waiver payments are treated as difficulty-of-care payments when received by an individual care provider for caring for an eligible individual (whether related or unrelated) living in the provider's home. See Notice 2014-7, available at *IRS.gov/irb/2014-4 IRB/ar06.html*, and related questions and answers, available at *IRS.gov/Individuals/Certain-Medicaid-Waiver-Payments-May-Be-Excludable-From-Income*, for more information.

You must include in your income difficulty-of-care payments to the extent they're received for more than:

- 10 qualified foster individuals under age 19, or
- Five qualified foster individuals age 19 or older.

Maintaining space in home. If you're paid to maintain space in your home for emergency foster care, you must include the payment in your income.

Reporting taxable payments. If you receive payments that you must include in your income and you're in business as a foster care provider, report the payments on Schedule C (Form 1040) or Schedule C-EZ (Form 1040). See Pub. 587, Business Use of Your Home, to help you determine the amount you can deduct for the use of your home.

Found property. If you find and keep property that doesn't belong to you that has been lost or abandoned (treasure trove), it's taxable to you at its fair market value in the first year it's your undisputed possession.

Free tour. If you received a free tour from a travel agency for organizing a group of tourists, you must include its value in your income. Report the fair market value of the tour on Schedule 1 (Form 1040), line 21, if you aren't in the trade or business of organizing tours. You can't deduct your expenses in serving as the voluntary leader of the group at the group's request. If

you organize tours as a trade or business, report the tour's value on Schedule C (Form 1040) or Schedule C-EZ (Form 1040).

Gambling winnings. You must include your gambling winnings in income on Schedule 1 (Form 1040), line 21. If you itemize your deductions on Schedule A (Form 1040), you can deduct gambling losses you had during the year, but only up to the amount of your winnings. If you're in the trade or business of gambling, use Schedule C (Form 1040).

Lotteries and raffles. Winnings from lotteries and raffles are gambling winnings. In addition to cash winnings, you must include in your income the fair market value of bonds, cars, houses, and other noncash prizes.

 If you win a state lottery prize payable in installments, see Pub. 525 for more information.

Form W-2G. You may have received a Form W-2G, Certain Gambling Winnings, showing the amount of your gambling winnings and any tax taken out of them. Include the amount from box 1 on Schedule 1 (Form 1040), line 21. Include the amount shown in box 4 on Form 1040, line 16, as federal income tax withheld.

Reporting winnings and recordkeeping. For more information on reporting gambling winnings and recordkeeping, see *Gambling Losses up to the Amount of Gambling Winnings* in chapter 27.

Gifts and inheritances. In most cases, property you receive as a gift, bequest, or inheritance isn't included in your income. However, if property you receive this way later produces income such as interest, dividends, or rents, that income is taxable to you. If property is given to a trust and the income from it is paid, credited, or distributed to you, that income is also taxable to you. If the gift, bequest, or inheritance is the income from the property, that income is taxable to you.

Inherited pension or individual retirement arrangement (IRA). If you inherited a pension or an IRA, you may have to include part of the inherited amount in your income. See *Survivors and Beneficiaries* in Pub. 575 if you inherited a pension. See *What if You Inherit an IRA?* in Pubs. 590-A and 590-B if you inherited an IRA.

Hobby losses. Losses from a hobby aren't deductible from other income. A hobby is an activity from which you don't expect to make a profit. See *Activity not for profit*, earlier.

 If you collect stamps, coins, or other items as a hobby for recreation and pleasure, and you sell any of the items, your gain is taxable as a capital gain. (See chapter 16.) However, if you sell items from your collection at a loss, you can't deduct the loss.

Illegal activities. Income from illegal activities, such as money from dealing illegal drugs, must be included in your income on Schedule 1 (Form 1040), line 21, or on Schedule C (Form 1040) or Schedule C-EZ (Form 1040) if from your self-employment activity.

Indian fishing rights. If you're a member of a qualified Indian tribe that has fishing rights secured by treaty, executive order, or an Act of Congress as of March 17, 1988, don't include in your income amounts you receive from activities related to those fishing rights. The income isn't subject to income tax, self-employment tax, or employment taxes.

Interest on frozen deposits. In general, you exclude from your income the amount of interest earned on a frozen deposit. See *Interest income on frozen deposits* in chapter 7.

Interest on qualified savings bonds. You may be able to exclude from income the interest from qualified U.S. savings bonds you redeem if you pay qualified higher education expenses in the same year. For more information on this exclusion, see *Education Savings Bond Program* under *U.S. Savings Bonds* in chapter 7.

Job interview expenses. If a prospective employer asks you to appear for an interview and either pays you an allowance or reimburses you for your transportation and other travel expenses, the amount you receive is generally not taxable. You include in income only the amount you receive that's more than your actual expenses.

Jury duty. Jury duty pay you receive must be included in your income on Schedule 1 (Form 1040), line 21. If you gave any of your jury duty pay to your employer because your employer continued to pay you while you served jury duty, include the amount you gave your employer as an income adjustment on Schedule 1 (Form 1040), line 36, and see the instructions there.

Kickbacks. You must include kickbacks, side commissions, push money, or similar payments you receive in your income on Schedule 1 (Form 1040), line 21, or on Schedule C (Form 1040) or Schedule C-EZ (Form 1040) if from your self-employment activity.

Example. You sell cars and help arrange car insurance for buyers. Insurance brokers pay back part of their commissions to you for referring customers to them. You must include the kickbacks in your income.

Medical savings accounts (Archer MSAs and Medicare Advantage MSAs). In most cases, you don't include in income amounts you withdraw from your Archer MSA or Medicare Advantage MSA if you use the money to pay for qualified medical expenses. Generally, qualified medical expenses are those you can deduct on Schedule A (Form 1040). For more information about qualified medical expenses, see chapter 22. For more information about Archer MSAs or Medicare Advantage MSAs, see Pub. 969, Health Savings Accounts and Other Tax-Favored Health Plans.

Prizes and awards. If you win a prize in a lucky number drawing, television or radio quiz program, beauty contest, or other event, you must include it in your income. For example, if you win a $50 prize in a photography contest, you must report this income on Schedule 1 (Form 1040), line 21. If you refuse to accept a prize, don't include its value in your income.

Prizes and awards in goods or services must be included in your income at their fair market value.

Employee awards or bonuses. Cash awards or bonuses given to you by your employer for good work or suggestions generally must be included in your income as wages. However, certain noncash employee achievement awards can be excluded from income. See *Bonuses and awards* in chapter 5.

Pulitzer, Nobel, and similar prizes. If you were awarded a prize in recognition of accomplishments in religious, charitable, scientific, artistic, educational, literary, or civic fields, you generally must include the value of the prize in your income. However, you don't include this prize in your income if you meet all of the following requirements.

- You were selected without any action on your part to enter the contest or proceeding.

- You aren't required to perform substantial future services as a condition to receiving the prize or award.

- The prize or award is transferred by the payer directly to a governmental unit or tax-exempt charitable organization as designated by you.

See Pub. 525 for more information about the conditions that apply to the transfer.

Qualified Opportunity Fund (QOF). Effective December 22, 2017, Code section 1400Z-2 provides a temporary deferral on inclusion in gross income for capital gains invested in QOFs, and permanent exclusion of capital gains from the sale or exchange of an investment in the QOF if the investment is held for at least 10 years. See the Instructions for Form 8949 on how to report your election to defer eligible gains invested in a QOF. For additional information, see Opportunity Zones Frequently Asked Questions at *IRS.gov/Newsroom/ Opportunity-Zones-Frequently-Asked-Questions*.

Qualified tuition programs (QTPs). A QTP (also known as a 529 program) is a program set up to allow you to either prepay or contribute to an account established for paying a student's qualified higher education expenses at an eligible educational institution. A program can be established and maintained by a state, an agency or instrumentality of a state, or an eligible educational institution.

The part of a distribution representing the amount paid or contributed to a QTP isn't included in income. This is a return of the investment in the program.

In most cases, the beneficiary doesn't include in income any earnings distributed from a QTP if the total distribution is less than or equal to adjusted qualified higher education expenses. See Pub. 970 for more information.

Railroad retirement annuities. The following types of payments are treated as pension or annuity income and are taxable under the rules explained in Pub. 575, Pension and Annuity Income.

- Tier 1 railroad retirement benefits that are more than the social security equivalent benefit.

- Tier 2 benefits.

- Vested dual benefits.

Rewards. If you receive a reward for providing information, include it in your income.

Sale of home. You may be able to exclude from income all or part of any gain from the sale or exchange of your main home. See chapter 15.

Sale of personal items. If you sold an item you owned for personal use, such as a car, refrigerator, furniture, stereo, jewelry, or silverware, your gain is taxable as a capital gain. Report it as explained in the Instructions for Schedule D (Form 1040). You can't deduct a loss.

However, if you sold an item you held for investment, such as gold or silver bullion, coins, or gems, any gain is taxable as a capital gain and any loss is deductible as a capital loss.

Example. You sold a painting on an online auction website for $100. You bought the painting for $20 at a garage sale years ago. Report your gain as a capital gain as explained in the Instructions for Schedule D (Form 1040).

Scholarships and fellowships. A candidate for a degree can exclude amounts received as a qualified scholarship or fellowship. A qualified scholarship or fellowship is any amount you receive that's for:

- Tuition and fees to enroll at or attend an educational institution; or

- Fees, books, supplies, and equipment required for courses at the educational institution.

Amounts used for room and board don't qualify for the exclusion. See Pub. 970 for more information on qualified scholarships and fellowship grants.

Payment for services. In most cases, you must include in income the part of any scholarship or fellowship that represents payment for past, present, or future teaching, research, or other services. This applies even if all candidates for a degree must perform the services to receive the degree.

For information about the rules that apply to a tax-free qualified tuition reduction provided to employees and their families by an educational institution, see Pub. 970.

Department of Veterans Affairs (VA) payments. Allowances paid by the VA aren't included in your income. These allowances aren't considered scholarship or fellowship grants.

Prizes. Scholarship prizes won in a contest aren't scholarships or fellowships if you don't have to use the prizes for educational purposes. You must include these amounts in your income on Schedule 1 (Form 1040), line 21, whether or not you use the amounts for educational purposes.

Stolen property. If you steal property, you must report its fair market value in your income in the year you steal it unless you return it to its rightful owner in the same year.

Transporting school children. Don't include in your income a school board mileage allowance for taking children to and from school if you aren't in the business of taking children to school. You can't deduct expenses for providing this transportation.

Union benefits and dues. Amounts deducted from your pay for union dues, assessments, contributions, or other payments to a union can't be excluded from your income.

Strike and lockout benefits. Benefits paid to you by a union as strike or lockout benefits, including both cash and the fair market value of other property, are usually included in your income as compensation. You can exclude these benefits from your income only when the facts clearly show that the union intended them as gifts to you.

Utility rebates. If you're a customer of an electric utility company and you participate in the utility's energy conservation program, you may receive on your monthly electric bill either:

- A reduction in the purchase price of electricity furnished to you (rate reduction), or
- A nonrefundable credit against the purchase price of the electricity.

The amount of the rate reduction or nonrefundable credit isn't included in your income.

Part Three.

Gains and Losses

The four chapters in this part discuss investment gains and losses, including how to figure your basis in property. They will help you to determine if a gain from selling or trading stocks, bonds, or other investment property is taxable and if a loss is or isn't deductible. These chapters also discuss gains from selling property you personally use — including the special rules for selling your home. Nonbusiness casualty and theft losses are discussed in chapter 26 in Part Five.

The new Form 1040 schedule that is discussed in these chapters is:

* *Schedule 1, Additional Income and Adjustments to Income.*

13.

Basis of Property

What's New

At the time this publication went to print, Congress was considering legislation that would do the following.

1. *Provide additional tax relief for those affected by certain 2018 disasters.*

2. *Extend certain tax benefits that expired at the end of 2017 and that currently can't be claimed on your 2018 tax return.*

3. *Change certain other tax provisions.*

To learn whether this legislation was enacted resulting in changes that affect your 2018 tax return, go to Recent Developments at IRS.gov/ Pub17.

Special rules for capital gains invested in Qualified Opportunity Funds. Effective December 22, 2017, code section 1400Z-2 provides a temporary deferral of inclusion in gross income for certain capital gains invested in Qualified Opportunity Funds (QOFs), and a potential permanent exclusion of gains from the sale or exchange of an investment in a QOF if the investment is held for at least 10 years. For more information, see the Instructions for Form 8949. For additional information, please see the *Frequently Asked Questions* for Opportunity Zones.

Exchanges limited to real property. Beginning after 2017, section 1031 like-kind exchange treatment applies only to exchanges of real property held for use in a trade or business

or for investment, other than real property held primarily for sale.

Introduction

This chapter discusses how to figure your basis in property. It is divided into the following sections.

* Cost basis.
* Adjusted basis.
* Basis other than cost.

Your basis is the amount of your investment in property for tax purposes. Use the basis to figure the gain or loss on the sale, exchange, or other disposition of property. Also use it to figure deductions for depreciation, amortization, depletion, and casualty losses.

If you use property for both business or for production of income purposes, and for personal purposes, you must allocate the basis based on the use. Only the basis allocated to the business or the production of income part of the property can be depreciated.

Your original basis in property is adjusted (increased or decreased) by certain events. For example, if you make improvements to the property, increase your basis. If you take deductions for depreciation or casualty losses, or claim certain credits, reduce your basis.

Keep accurate records of all items that affect the basis of your property. For more information on keeping records, see chapter 1.

Useful Items

You may want to see:

Publication

❏ **15-B** Employer's Tax Guide to Fringe Benefits

❏ **525** Taxable and Nontaxable Income

❏ **535** Business Expenses

❏ **537** Installment Sales

❏ **544** Sales and Other Dispositions of Assets

❏ **550** Investment Income and Expenses

❏ **551** Basis of Assets

❏ **946** How To Depreciate Property

For these and other useful items, go to IRS.gov/ forms.

Cost Basis

The basis of property you buy is usually its cost. The cost is the amount you pay in cash, debt obligations, other property, or services. Your cost also includes amounts you pay for the following items.

* Sales tax.
* Freight.
* Installation and testing.
* Excise taxes.
* Legal and accounting fees (when they must be capitalized).
* Revenue stamps.
* Recording fees.
* Real estate taxes (if you assume liability for the seller).

In addition, the basis of real estate and business assets may include other items.

Loans with low or no interest. If you buy property on a time-payment plan that charges little or no interest, the basis of your property is your stated purchase price minus any amount considered to be unstated interest. You generally have unstated interest if your interest rate is less than the applicable federal rate.

For more information, see *Unstated Interest and Original Issue Discount (OID)* in Pub. 537.

Real Property

Real property, also called real estate, is land and generally anything built on, growing on, or attached to land.

If you buy real property, certain fees and other expenses you pay are part of your cost basis in the property.

Lump-sum purchase. If you buy buildings and the land on which they stand for a lump sum, allocate the cost basis between the land and the buildings. Allocate the cost basis according to the respective fair market values (FMVs) of the land and buildings at the time of purchase. Figure the basis of each asset by multiplying the lump sum by a fraction. The numerator is the FMV of that asset and the denominator is the FMV of the whole property at the time of purchase.

 If you are not certain of the FMVs of the land and buildings, you can allocate the basis according to their assessed values for real estate tax purposes.

Fair market value (FMV). FMV is the price at which the property would change hands between a willing buyer and a willing seller, neither having to buy or sell, and both having reasonable knowledge of all the necessary facts. Sales of similar property on or about the same date may be helpful in figuring the FMV of the property.

Assumption of mortgage. If you buy property and assume (or buy the property subject to) an existing mortgage on the property, your basis includes the amount you pay for the property plus the amount to be paid on the mortgage.

Settlement costs. Your basis includes the settlement fees and closing costs you paid for buying the property. (A fee for buying property is a cost that must be paid even if you buy the property for cash.) Do not include fees and costs for getting a loan on the property in your basis.

The following are some of the settlement fees or closing costs you can include in the basis of your property.

- Abstract fees (abstract of title fees).
- Charges for installing utility services.
- Legal fees (including fees for the title search and preparation of the sales contract and deed).
- Recording fees.
- Survey fees.
- Transfer taxes.
- Owner's title insurance.
- Any amounts the seller owes that you agree to pay, such as back taxes or interest, recording or mortgage fees, charges for improvements or repairs, and sales commissions.

Settlement costs do not include amounts placed in escrow for the future payment of items such as taxes and insurance.

The following are some of the settlement fees and closing costs you cannot include in the basis of property.

- Casualty insurance premiums.
- Rent for occupancy of the property before closing.
- Charges for utilities or other services related to occupancy of the property before closing.
- Charges connected with getting a loan, such as points (discount points, loan origination fees), mortgage insurance premiums, loan assumption fees, cost of a credit report, and fees for an appraisal required by a lender.
- Fees for refinancing a mortgage.

Real estate taxes. If you pay real estate taxes the seller owed on real property you bought,

and the seller did not reimburse you, treat those taxes as part of your basis. You cannot deduct the taxes as an expense.

If you reimburse the seller for taxes the seller paid for you, you can usually deduct that amount as an expense in the year of purchase. Do not include the amount of real estate taxes you deducted as an expense in the basis of your property. If you did not reimburse the seller, you must reduce your basis by the amount of those taxes.

Points. If you pay points to get a loan (including a mortgage, second mortgage, line of credit, or a home equity loan), do not add the points to the basis of the related property. Generally, you deduct the points over the term of the loan. For more information on how to deduct points, see chapter 24.

Points on home mortgage. Special rules may apply to points you and the seller pay when you get a mortgage to buy your main home. If certain requirements are met, you can deduct the points in full for the year in which they are paid. Reduce the basis of your home by any seller-paid points.

Adjusted Basis

Before figuring gain or loss on a sale, exchange, or other disposition of property or figuring allowable depreciation, depletion, or amortization, you must usually make certain adjustments (increases and decreases) to the cost basis or basis other than cost (discussed later) of the property. The result is the adjusted basis.

Increases to Basis

Increase the basis of any property by all items properly added to a capital account. Examples of items that increase basis are shown in Table 13-1. These include the items discussed below.

Improvements. Add to your basis in property the cost of improvements having a useful life of more than 1 year that increase the value of the property, lengthen its life, or adapt it to a different use. For example, improvements include putting a recreation room in your unfinished basement, adding another bathroom or bedroom, putting up a fence, putting in new plumbing or wiring, installing a new roof, or paving your driveway.

Assessments for local improvements. Add to the basis of property assessments for improvements such as streets and sidewalks if they increase the value of the property assessed. Do not deduct them as taxes. However, you can deduct as taxes assessments for maintenance or repairs, or for meeting interest charges related to the improvements.

Example. Your city changes the street in front of your store into an enclosed pedestrian mall and assesses you and other affected property owners for the cost of the conversion. Add the assessment to your property's basis. In this example, the assessment is a depreciable asset.

Decreases to Basis

Decrease the basis of any property by all items that represent a return of capital for the period during which you held the property. Examples of items that decrease basis are shown in Table 13-1. These include the items discussed below.

Casualty and theft losses. If you have a casualty or theft loss, decrease the basis in your property by any insurance proceeds or other reimbursement and by any deductible loss not covered by insurance.

You must increase your basis in the property by the amount you spend on repairs that restore the property to its pre-casualty condition.

For more information on casualty and theft losses, see chapter 26.

Depreciation and section 179 deduction. Decrease the basis of your qualifying business property by any section 179 deduction you take and the depreciation you deducted, or could have deducted (including any special depreciation allowance), on your tax returns under the method of depreciation you selected.

For more information about depreciation and the section 179 deduction, see Pub. 946 and the Instructions for Form 4562.

Example. You owned a duplex used as rental property that cost you $40,000, of which $35,000 was allocated to the building and $5,000 to the land. You added an improvement to the duplex that cost $10,000. In February last year, the duplex was damaged by fire. Up to that time, you had been allowed depreciation of $23,000. You sold some salvaged material for $1,300 and collected $19,700 from your insurance company. You deducted a casualty loss of $1,000 on your income tax return for last year. You spent $19,000 of the insurance proceeds for restoration of the duplex, which was completed this year. You must use the duplex's adjusted basis after the restoration to determine depreciation for the rest of the property's recovery period. Figure the adjusted basis of the duplex as follows:

Original cost of duplex		$35,000
Addition to duplex		10,000
Total cost of duplex		$45,000
Minus: Depreciation		23,000
Adjusted basis before casualty		$22,000
Minus: Insurance proceeds	$19,700	
Deducted casualty loss	1,000	
Salvage proceeds	1,300	22,000
Adjusted basis after casualty		$-0-
Add: Cost of restoring duplex		19,000
Adjusted basis after restoration		**$19,000**

Note. Your basis in the land is its original cost of $5,000.

Easements. The amount you receive for granting an easement generally is considered to be proceeds from the sale of an interest in real property. It reduces the basis of the affected part of the property. If the amount received is more than the basis of the part of the property affected by the easement, reduce your basis in that part to zero and treat the excess as a recognized gain.

If the gain is on a capital asset, see chapter 16 for information about how to report it. If the gain is on property used in a trade or business, see Pub. 544 for information about how to report it.

Exclusion of subsidies for energy conservation measures. You can exclude from gross income any subsidy you received from a public utility company for the purchase or installation of an energy conservation measure for a dwelling unit. Reduce the basis of the property for which you received the subsidy by the excluded amount. For more information about this subsidy, see chapter 12.

Postponed gain from sale of home. If you postponed gain from the sale of your main home under rules in effect before May 7, 1997, you must reduce the basis of the home you acquired as a replacement by the amount of the postponed gain. For more information on the rules for the sale of a home, see chapter 15.

Basis Other Than Cost

There are many times when you cannot use cost as basis. In these cases, the fair market value or the adjusted basis of the property can be used. Fair market value (FMV) and adjusted basis were discussed earlier.

Property Received for Services

If you receive property for your services, include the FMV of the property in income. The amount you include in income becomes your basis. If the services were performed for a price agreed on beforehand, it will be accepted as the FMV of the property if there is no evidence to the contrary.

Restricted property. If you receive property for your services and the property is subject to certain restrictions, your basis in the property is its FMV when it becomes substantially vested. However, this rule doesn't apply if you make an election to include in income the FMV of the property at the time it is transferred to you, less any amount you paid for it. Property is substantially vested when it is transferable or when it is not subject to a substantial risk of forfeiture (you do not have a good chance of losing it). For more information, see *Restricted Property* in Pub. 525.

Bargain purchases. A bargain purchase is a purchase of an item for less than its FMV. If, as compensation for services, you buy goods or other property at less than FMV, include the difference between the purchase price and the property's FMV in your income. Your basis in the property is its FMV (your purchase price plus the amount you include in income).

If the difference between your purchase price and the FMV is a qualified employee discount, do not include the difference in income. However, your basis in the property is still its FMV. See *Employee Discounts* in Pub. 15-B.

Table 13-1. **Examples of Adjustments to Basis**

Increases to Basis	Decreases to Basis

• Capital improvements:
  Putting an addition on your home
  Replacing an entire roof
  Paving your driveway
  Installing central air conditioning
  Rewiring your home
	• Exclusion from income of subsidies for energy conservation measures

• Assessments for local improvements:
  Water connections
  Extending utility service lines to the property
  Sidewalks
  Roads
	• Casualty or theft loss deductions and insurance reimbursements
	
	• Postponed gain from the sale of a home
	
	• Alternative fuel vehicle refueling property credit (Form 8911)
	
	• Residential energy credit (Form 5695)

• Casualty losses: Restoring damaged property	• Depreciation and section 179 deduction

• Legal fees:
  Cost of defending and perfecting a title
  Fees for getting a reduction of an assessment
	• Nontaxable corporate distributions
	
	• Certain canceled debt excluded from income

• Zoning costs	• Easements • Adoption tax benefits

Taxable Exchanges

A taxable exchange is one in which the gain is taxable or the loss is deductible. A taxable gain or deductible loss also is known as a recognized gain or loss. If you receive property in exchange for other property in a taxable exchange, the basis of the property you receive is usually its FMV at the time of the exchange.

Nontaxable Exchanges

A nontaxable exchange is an exchange in which you are not taxed on any gain and you cannot deduct any loss. If you receive property in a nontaxable exchange, its basis generally is the same as the basis of the property you transferred. See *Nontaxable Trades* in chapter 14.

Involuntary Conversions

If you receive replacement property as a result of an involuntary conversion, such as a casualty, theft, or condemnation, figure the basis of the replacement property using the basis of the converted property.

Similar or related property. If you receive replacement property similar or related in service or use to the converted property, the replacement property's basis is the same as the converted property's basis on the date of the conversion, with the following adjustments.

1. Decrease the basis by the following.

    a. Any loss you recognize on the involuntary conversion.

    b. Any money you receive that you do not spend on similar property.

2. Increase the basis by the following.

    a. Any gain you recognize on the involuntary conversion.

    b. Any cost of acquiring the replacement property.

Money or property not similar or related. If you receive money or property not similar or related in service or use to the converted property, and you buy replacement property similar or related in service or use to the converted property, the basis of the replacement property is its cost decreased by the gain not recognized on the conversion.

Example. The state condemned your property. The adjusted basis of the property was $26,000 and the state paid you $31,000 for it. You realized a gain of $5,000 ($31,000 − $26,000). You bought replacement property similar in use to the converted property for $29,000. You recognize a gain of $2,000 ($31,000 − $29,000), the unspent part of the payment from the state. Your unrecognized gain is $3,000, the difference between the $5,000 realized gain and the $2,000 recognized gain. The basis of the replacement property is figured as follows:

Cost of replacement property	$29,000
Minus: Gain not recognized	3,000
Basis of replacement property	**$26,000**

Allocating the basis. If you buy more than one piece of replacement property, allocate your basis among the properties based on their respective costs.

Basis for depreciation. Special rules apply in determining and depreciating the basis of Modified Accelerated Cost Recovery System (MACRS) property acquired in an involuntary conversion. For information, see *What Is the Basis of Your Depreciable Property?* in chapter 1 of Pub. 946.

Like-Kind Exchanges

Beginning after 2017, section 1031 like-kind exchange treatment applies only to exchanges of real property held for use in a trade or business or for investment, other than real property held primarily for sale.

The exchange of property for the same kind of property is the most common type of nontaxable exchange. To qualify as a like-kind exchange, you must hold for business or investment purposes both the property you transfer and the property you receive. There also must be an exchange of like-kind property. For more information, see *Like-Kind Exchanges* in chapter 1 of Pub. 544.

The basis of the property you receive generally is the same as the adjusted basis of the property you gave up. If you trade property in a like-kind exchange and also pay money, the basis of the property received is the adjusted basis of the property you gave up increased by the money you paid.

Qualifying property. In a like-kind exchange, you must hold for investment or for productive use in your trade or business both the property you give up and the property you receive.

Like-kind property. There must be an exchange of like-kind property. Like-kind properties are properties of the same nature or character, even if they differ in grade or quality. The exchange of real estate for real estate and personal property for similar personal property are exchanges of like-kind property.

Example. You trade in an old truck used in your business with an adjusted basis of $1,700 for a new one costing $6,800. The dealer allows you $2,000 on the old truck, and you pay $4,800. This is a like-kind exchange. The basis of the new truck is $6,500 (the adjusted basis of the old one, $1,700, plus the amount you paid, $4,800).

If you sell your old truck to a third party for $2,000 instead of trading it in and then buy a new one from the dealer, you have a taxable gain of $300 on the sale (the $2,000 sale price minus the $1,700 adjusted basis). The basis of the new truck is the price you pay the dealer.

Partially nontaxable exchanges. A partially nontaxable exchange is an exchange in which you receive unlike property or money in addition to like-kind property. The basis of the property you receive is the same as the adjusted basis of the property you gave up, with the following adjustments.

1. Decrease the basis by the following amounts.

    a. Any money you receive.

    b. Any loss you recognize on the exchange.

2. Increase the basis by the following amounts.

    a. Any additional costs you incur.

    b. Any gain you recognize on the exchange.

If the other party to the exchange assumes your liabilities, treat the debt assumption as money you received in the exchange.

Allocation of basis. If you receive like-kind and unlike properties in the exchange, allocate the basis first to the unlike property, other than money, up to its FMV on the date of the exchange. The rest is the basis of the like-kind property.

Basis for depreciation. Special rules apply in determining and depreciating the basis of MACRS property acquired in a like-kind exchange. For information, see *What Is the Basis of Your Depreciable Property?* in chapter 1 of Pub. 946.

Property Transferred From a Spouse

The basis of property transferred to you or transferred in trust for your benefit by your spouse is the same as your spouse's adjusted basis. The same rule applies to a transfer by your former spouse that is incident to divorce. However, for property transferred in trust, adjust your basis for any gain recognized by your spouse or former spouse if the liabilities assumed, plus the liabilities to which the property is subject, are more than the adjusted basis of the property transferred.

If the property transferred to you is a series E, series EE, or series I U.S. savings bond, the transferor must include in income the interest accrued to the date of transfer. Your basis in the bond immediately after the transfer is equal to the transferor's basis increased by the interest income includible in the transferor's income. For more information on these bonds, see chapter 7.

At the time of the transfer, the transferor must give you the records needed to determine the adjusted basis and holding period of the property as of the date of the transfer.

For more information about the transfer of property from a spouse, see chapter 14.

Property Received as a Gift

To figure the basis of property you receive as a gift, you must know its adjusted basis to the donor just before it was given to you, its FMV at the time it was given to you, and any gift tax paid on it.

FMV less than donor's adjusted basis. If the FMV of the property at the time of the gift is less than the donor's adjusted basis, your basis depends on whether you have a gain or a loss when you dispose of the property. Your basis for figuring gain is the same as the donor's adjusted basis plus or minus any required adjustments to basis while you held the property. Your basis for figuring loss is its FMV when you received the gift plus or minus any required adjustments to basis while you held the property. See *Adjusted Basis*, earlier.

Example. You received an acre of land as a gift. At the time of the gift, the land had an FMV of $8,000. The donor's adjusted basis was $10,000. After you received the property, no events occurred to increase or decrease your basis. If you later sell the property for $12,000, you will have a $2,000 gain because you must use the donor's adjusted basis at the time of the gift ($10,000) as your basis to figure gain. If you sell the property for $7,000, you will have a $1,000 loss because you must use the FMV at the time of the gift ($8,000) as your basis to figure loss.

If the sales price is between $8,000 and $10,000, you have neither gain nor loss.

Business property. If you hold the gift as business property, your basis for figuring any depreciation, depletion, or amortization deductions is the same as the donor's adjusted basis plus or minus any required adjustments to basis while you hold the property.

FMV equal to or greater than donor's adjusted basis. If the FMV of the property is equal to or greater than the donor's adjusted basis, your basis is the donor's adjusted basis at the time you received the gift. Increase your basis by all or part of any gift tax paid, depending on the date of the gift, explained later.

Also, for figuring gain or loss from a sale or other disposition or for figuring depreciation, depletion, or amortization deductions on business property, you must increase or decrease your basis (the donor's adjusted basis) by any required adjustments to basis while you held the property. See *Adjusted Basis*, earlier.

If you received a gift during the tax year, increase your basis in the gift (the donor's adjusted basis) by the part of the gift tax paid on it due to the net increase in value of the gift. Figure the increase by multiplying the gift tax paid by a fraction. The numerator of the fraction is the net increase in value of the gift, and the denominator is the amount of the gift.

The net increase in value of the gift is the FMV of the gift minus the donor's adjusted basis. The amount of the gift is its value for gift tax purposes after reduction by any annual exclusion and marital or charitable deduction that applies to the gift.

Example. In 2018, you received a gift of property from your mother that had an FMV of $50,000. Her adjusted basis was $20,000. The amount of the gift for gift tax purposes was $35,000 ($50,000 minus the $15,000 annual exclusion). She paid a gift tax of $7,100 on the property. Your basis is $26,106, figured as follows:

Fair market value	$50,000
Minus: Adjusted basis	−20,000
Net increase in value	$30,000
Gift tax paid	$7,100
Multiplied by ($30,000 ÷ $35,000)	× 0.86
Gift tax due to net increase in value	$6,106
Adjusted basis of property to your mother	+20,000
Your basis in the property	**$26,106**

Inherited Property

Your basis in property you inherited from a decedent generally is one of the following.

- The FMV of the property at the date of the decedent's death.

- The FMV on the alternate valuation date if the personal representative for the estate elects to use alternate valuation.

- The value under the special-use valuation method for real property used in farming or a closely held business if elected for estate tax purposes.

- The decedent's adjusted basis in land to the extent of the value excluded from the decedent's taxable estate as a qualified conservation easement.

If a federal estate tax return doesn't have to be filed, your basis in the inherited property is its appraised value at the date of death for state inheritance or transmission taxes.

For more information, see the Instructions for Form 706, United States Estate (and Generation-Skipping Transfer) Tax Return.

Information for beneficiaries receiving Schedule A (Form 8971). Form 8971, Information Regarding Beneficiaries Acquiring Property From a Decedent, and its Schedule A, are used to comply with the reporting requirements regarding consistency of basis for assets acquired from an estate. In certain circumstances, an executor of an estate (or other person) required to file an estate tax return after July 31, 2015, will be required to provide a Schedule A (Form 8971) to a beneficiary who receives or is to receive property from an estate. For more information about when Form 8971 and Schedule A must be completed, see the Instructions for Form 8971 and Schedule A.

The beneficiary uses the final estate tax value reported on Schedule A to determine his or her basis in the property. When figuring a basis consistent with the final estate tax value, start with the reported value and then make any allowed adjustments.

Community property. In community property states (Arizona, California, Idaho, Louisiana, Nevada, New Mexico, Texas, Washington, and Wisconsin), married individuals are each usually considered to own half the community property. When either spouse dies, the total value of the community property, even the part belonging to the surviving spouse, generally becomes the basis of the entire property. For this rule to apply, at least half the value of the community property interest must be includible in the decedent's gross estate, whether or not the estate must file a return.

Example. You and your spouse owned community property that had a basis of $80,000. When your spouse died, half the FMV of the community interest was includible in your spouse's estate. The FMV of the community interest was $100,000. The basis of your half of the property after the death of your spouse is $50,000 (half of the $100,000 FMV). The basis of the other half to your spouse's heirs is also $50,000.

For more information about community property, see Pub. 555, Community Property.

Property Changed From Personal to Business or Rental Use

If you hold property for personal use and then change it to business use or use it to produce rent, you can begin to depreciate the property at the time of the change. To do so, you must figure its basis for depreciation at the time of the change. An example of changing property held for personal use to business or rental use would be renting out your former personal residence.

Basis for depreciation. The basis for depreciation is the lesser of the following amounts.

- The FMV of the property on the date of the change.

- Your adjusted basis on the date of the change.

Example. Several years ago, you paid $160,000 to have your house built on a lot that cost $25,000. You paid $20,000 for permanent improvements to the house and claimed a $2,000 casualty loss deduction for damage to the house before changing the property to rental use last year. Because land is not depreciable, you include only the cost of the house when figuring the basis for depreciation.

Your adjusted basis in the house when you changed its use to rental property was $178,000 ($160,000 + $20,000 − $2,000). On the same date, your property had an FMV of $180,000, of which $15,000 was for the land and $165,000 was for the house. The basis for figuring depreciation on the house is its FMV on the date of the change ($165,000) because it is less than your adjusted basis ($178,000).

Sale of property. If you later sell or dispose of property changed to business or rental use, the basis you use will depend on whether you are figuring gain or loss.

Gain. The basis for figuring a gain is your adjusted basis in the property when you sell the property.

Example. Assume the same facts as in the previous example, except that you sell the property at a gain after being allowed depreciation deductions of $37,500. Your adjusted basis for figuring gain is $165,500 ($178,000 + $25,000 (land) − $37,500).

Loss. Figure the basis for a loss starting with the smaller of your adjusted basis or the FMV of the property at the time of the change to business or rental use. Then make adjustments (increases and decreases) for the period after the change in the property's use, as discussed earlier under *Adjusted Basis*.

Example. Assume the same facts as in the previous example, except that you sell the property at a loss after being allowed depreciation deductions of $37,500. In this case, you would start with the FMV on the date of the change to rental use ($180,000) because it is less than the adjusted basis of $203,000 ($178,000 + $25,000 (land)) on that date. Reduce that amount ($180,000) by the depreciation deductions ($37,500). The basis for loss is $142,500 ($180,000 − $37,500).

Stocks and Bonds

The basis of stocks or bonds you buy generally is the purchase price plus any costs of purchase, such as commissions and recording or transfer fees. If you get stocks or bonds other than by purchase, your basis is usually determined by the FMV or the previous owner's adjusted basis, as discussed earlier.

You must adjust the basis of stocks for certain events that occur after purchase. For example, if you receive additional stock from nontaxable stock dividends or stock splits, reduce your basis for each share of stock by dividing the adjusted basis of the old stock by the number of shares of old and new stock. This rule applies only when the additional stock received is identical to the stock held. Also reduce your basis when you receive nontaxable distributions. The nontaxable distributions are a return of capital.

Example. In 2016, you bought 100 shares of XYZ stock for $1,000 or $10 a share. In 2017, you bought 100 shares of XYZ stock for $1,600 or $16 a share. In 2018, XYZ declared a 2-for-1 stock split. You now have 200 shares of stock with a basis of $5 a share and 200 shares with a basis of $8 a share.

Other basis. There are other ways to figure the basis of stocks or bonds depending on how you acquired them. For detailed information, see *Stocks and Bonds* under *Basis of Investment Property* in chapter 4 of Pub. 550.

Identifying stocks or bonds sold. If you can adequately identify the shares of stock or the bonds you sold, their basis is the cost or other basis of the particular shares of stocks or bonds. If you buy and sell securities at various times in varying quantities and you cannot adequately identify the shares you sell, the basis of the securities you sell is the basis of the securities you acquired first. For more information about identifying securities you sell, see *Stocks and Bonds* under *Basis of Investment Property* in chapter 4 of Pub. 550.

Mutual fund shares. If you sell mutual fund shares you acquired at various times and prices and left on deposit in an account kept by a custodian or agent, you can elect to use an average basis. For more information, see Pub. 550.

Bond premium. If you buy a taxable bond at a premium and elect to amortize the premium, reduce the basis of the bond by the amortized premium you deduct each year. See *Bond Premium Amortization* in chapter 3 of Pub. 550 for more information. Although you cannot deduct the premium on a tax-exempt bond, you must amortize the premium each year and reduce your basis in the bond by the amortized amount.

Original issue discount (OID) on debt instruments. You must increase your basis in an OID debt instrument by the OID you include in income for that instrument. See *Original Issue Discount (OID)* in chapter 7, and Pub. 1212, Guide To Original Issue Discount (OID) Instruments.

Tax-exempt obligations. OID on tax-exempt obligations generally is not taxable. However, when you dispose of a tax-exempt obligation issued after September 3, 1982, and acquired after March 1, 1984, you must accrue OID on the obligation to determine its adjusted basis. The accrued OID is added to the basis of the obligation to determine your gain or loss. See chapter 4 of Pub. 550.

14.

Sale of Property

What's New

At the time this publication went to print, Congress was considering legislation that would do the following.

1. *Provide additional tax relief for those affected by certain 2018 disasters.*

2. *Extend certain tax benefits that expired at the end of 2017 and that currently can't be claimed on your 2018 tax return.*

3. *Change certain other tax provisions.*

To learn whether this legislation was enacted resulting in changes that affect your 2018 tax return, go to Recent Developments at IRS.gov/Pub17.

Capital gains from publicly traded securities. After 2017, you cannot roll over capital gains from publicly traded securities to a specialized small business investment company as previously permitted under section 1044.

Self-created capital assets. Beginning January 1, 2018, certain self-created properties like patents, inventions, models/designs, and a secret formula or process are not considered capital assets.

Capital gains reinvested in opportunity funds. P.L. 115-97, section 13823, provides for the temporary deferral of capital gains reinvested in a qualified opportunity fund and permanent exclusion of capital gains from the sale or an exchange of an investment in a qualified opportunity fund. For further information, go to the IRS.gov Opportunity Zone Frequently Asked Questions page at *IRS.gov/Newsroom/*

Opportunity-Zones-Frequently-Asked-Questions.

Reminder

Foreign income. If you are a U.S. citizen who sells property located outside the United States, you must report all gains and losses from the sale of that property on your tax return unless it is exempt by U.S. law. This is true whether you reside inside or outside the United States and whether or not you receive a Form 1099 from the payer.

Introduction

This chapter discusses the tax consequences of selling or trading investment property. It explains the following.

- What a sale or trade is.
- Figuring gain or loss.
- Nontaxable trades.
- Related party transactions.
- Capital gains or losses.
- Capital assets and noncapital assets.
- Holding period.

Other property transactions. Certain transfers of property aren't discussed here. They are discussed in other IRS publications. These include the following.

- Sales of a main home, covered in *Selling Your Home* in chapter 15.
- Installment sales, covered in Pub. 537.
- Transactions involving business property, covered in Pub. 544.
- Dispositions of an interest in a passive activity, covered in Pub. 925.

Pub. 550 provides a more detailed discussion about sales and trades of investment property. Pub. 550 includes information about the rules covering nonbusiness bad debts, straddles, section 1256 contracts, puts and calls, commodity futures, short sales, and wash sales. It also discusses investment-related expenses.

Useful Items
You may want to see:

Publication
☐ **550** Investment Income and Expenses

Form (and Instructions)
☐ **Schedule D (Form 1040)** Capital Gains and Losses
☐ **8949** Sales and Other Dispositions of Capital Assets
☐ **8824** Like-Kind Exchanges

For these and other useful items, go to *IRS.gov/Forms.*

Sales and Trades

If you sold property such as stocks, bonds, or certain commodities through a broker during the

year, you should receive from the broker a Form 1099-B. You should receive a Form 1099-B for 2018 by February 15, 2019. It will show the gross proceeds from the sale. It may also show your basis. The IRS will also get a copy of Form 1099-B from the broker.

Use the Form 1099-B received from your broker to complete Form 8949 and/or Schedule D (Form 1040).

What Is a Sale or Trade?

This section explains what is a sale or trade. It also explains certain transactions and events that are treated as sales or trades.

A sale is generally a transfer of property for money or a mortgage, note, or other promise to pay money.

A trade is a transfer of property for other property or services and may be taxed in the same way as a sale.

Sale and purchase. Ordinarily, a transaction isn't a trade when you voluntarily sell property for cash and immediately buy similar property to replace it. The sale and purchase are two separate transactions. But see *Like-kind exchanges* under *Nontaxable Trades,* later.

Redemption of stock. A redemption of stock is treated as a sale or trade and is subject to the capital gain or loss provisions unless the redemption is a dividend or other distribution on stock.

Dividend versus sale or trade. Whether a redemption is treated as a sale, trade, dividend, or other distribution depends on the circumstances in each case. Both direct and indirect ownership of stock will be considered. The redemption is treated as a sale or trade of stock if:

- The redemption isn't essentially equivalent to a dividend (see *Dividends and Other Distributions* in chapter 8),
- There is a substantially disproportionate redemption of stock,
- There is a complete redemption of all the stock of the corporation owned by the shareholder, or
- The redemption is a distribution in partial liquidation of a corporation.

Redemption or retirement of bonds. A redemption or retirement of bonds or notes at their maturity is generally treated as a sale or trade.

In addition, a significant modification of a bond is treated as a trade of the original bond for a new bond. For details, see Regulations section 1.1001-3.

Surrender of stock. A surrender of stock by a dominant shareholder who retains ownership of more than half of the corporation's voting shares is treated as a contribution to capital rather than as an immediate loss deductible from taxable income. The surrendering shareholder must reallocate his or her basis in the surrendered shares to the shares he or she retains.

Worthless securities. Stocks, stock rights, and bonds (other than those held for sale by a securities dealer) that became completely worthless during the tax year are treated as though they were sold on the last day of the tax year. This affects whether your capital loss is long term or short term. See *Holding Period*, later.

Worthless securities also include securities that you abandon after March 12, 2008. To abandon a security, you must permanently surrender and relinquish all rights in the security and receive no consideration in exchange for it. All the facts and circumstances determine whether the transaction is properly characterized as an abandonment or other type of transaction, such as an actual sale or exchange, contribution to capital, dividend, or gift.

If you are a cash basis taxpayer and make payments on a negotiable promissory note that you issued for stock that became worthless, you can deduct these payments as losses in the years you actually make the payments. Don't deduct them in the year the stock became worthless.

How to report loss. Report worthless securities on Form 8949, Part I or Part II, whichever applies.

 Report your worthless securities transactions on Form 8949 with the correct box checked for these transactions. See Form 8949 and the Instructions for Form 8949.

 For more information on Form 8949 and Schedule D (Form 1040), see Reporting Capital Gains and Losses in chapter 16. See also Schedule D (Form 1040), Form 8949, and their separate instructions.

Filing a claim for refund. If you don't claim a loss for a worthless security on your original return for the year it becomes worthless, you can file a claim for a credit or refund due to the loss. You must use Form 1040X to amend your return for the year the security became worthless. You must file it within 7 years from the date your original return for that year had to be filed, or 2 years from the date you paid the tax, whichever is later. For more information about filing a claim, see *Amended Returns and Claims for Refund* in chapter 1.

How To Figure Gain or Loss

You figure gain or loss on a sale or trade of property by subtracting the adjusted basis of the property from the amount you realize on the sale or trade.

Gain. If the amount you realize from a sale or trade is more than the adjusted basis of the property you transfer, the difference is a gain.

Loss. If the adjusted basis of the property you transfer is more than the amount you realize, the difference is a loss.

Adjusted basis. The adjusted basis of property is your original cost or other original basis properly adjusted (increased or decreased) for certain items. See *Adjusted Basis* in chapter 13 for more information.

Amount realized. The amount you realize from a sale or trade of property is everything

you receive for the property minus your expenses related to the sale (such as redemption fees, sales commissions, sales charges, or exit fees). Amount realized includes the money you receive plus the fair market value of any property or services you receive. If you received a note or other debt instrument for the property, see *How To Figure Gain or Loss* in chapter 4 of Pub. 550 to figure the amount realized.

If you finance the buyer's purchase of your property and the debt instrument doesn't provide for adequate stated interest, the unstated interest that you must report as ordinary income will reduce the amount realized from the sale. For more information, see Pub. 537.

Fair market value. Fair market value is the price at which the property would change hands between a buyer and a seller, neither being forced to buy or sell and both having reasonable knowledge of all the relevant facts.

Example. You trade A Company stock with an adjusted basis of $7,000 for B Company stock with a fair market value of $10,000, which is your amount realized. Your gain is $3,000 ($10,000 – $7,000).

Debt paid off. A debt against the property, or against you, that is paid off as a part of the transaction, or that is assumed by the buyer, must be included in the amount realized. This is true even if neither you nor the buyer is personally liable for the debt. For example, if you sell or trade property that is subject to a nonrecourse loan, the amount you realize generally includes the full amount of the note assumed by the buyer even if the amount of the note is more than the fair market value of the property.

Example. You sell stock that you had pledged as security for a bank loan of $8,000. Your basis in the stock is $6,000. The buyer pays off your bank loan and pays you $20,000 in cash. The amount realized is $28,000 ($20,000 + $8,000). Your gain is $22,000 ($28,000 – $6,000).

Payment of cash. If you trade property and cash for other property, the amount you realize is the fair market value of the property you receive. Determine your gain or loss by subtracting the cash you pay plus the adjusted basis of the property you trade in from the amount you realize. If the result is a positive number, it is a gain. If the result is a negative number, it is a loss.

No gain or loss. You may have to use a basis for figuring gain that is different from the basis used for figuring loss. In this case, you may have neither a gain nor a loss. See *Basis Other Than Cost* in chapter 13.

Nontaxable Trades

This section discusses trades that generally don't result in a taxable gain or deductible loss. For more information on nontaxable trades, see chapter 1 of Pub. 544, Sales and Other Dispositions of Assets.

Like-kind exchanges. If you trade business or investment property for other business or investment property of a like kind, you don't pay tax on any gain or deduct any loss until you sell

or dispose of the property you receive. To be nontaxable, a trade must meet all six of the following conditions.

1. The property must be business or investment property. You must hold both the property you trade and the property you receive for productive use in your trade or business or for investment. Neither property may be property used for personal purposes, such as your home or family car.

2. The property must not be held primarily for sale. The property you trade and the property you receive must not be property you sell to customers, such as merchandise.

3. The property must not be stocks, bonds, notes, choses in action, certificates of trust or beneficial interest, or other securities or evidences of indebtedness or interest, including partnership interests. However, see *Special rules for mutual ditch, reservoir, or irrigation company stock* in chapter 4 of Pub. 550 for an exception. Also, you can have a nontaxable trade of corporate stocks under a different rule, as discussed later.

4. There must be a trade of like property. The trade of real estate for real estate, or personal property for similar personal property, is a trade of like property. The trade of an apartment house for a store building, or a panel truck for a pickup truck, is a trade of like property. The trade of a piece of machinery for a store building isn't a trade of like property. Real property located in the United States and real property located outside the United States aren't like property. Also, personal property used predominantly within the United States and personal property used predominantly outside the United States aren't like property.

5. The property to be received must be identified in writing within 45 days after the date you transfer the property given up in the trade.

6. The property to be received must be received by the earlier of:
   a. The 180th day after the date on which you transfer the property given up in the trade; or
   b. The due date, including extensions, for your tax return for the year in which the transfer of the property given up occurs.

If you trade property with a related party in a like-kind exchange, a special rule may apply. See *Related Party Transactions*, later in this chapter. Also, see chapter 1 of Pub. 544 for more information on exchanges of business property and special rules for exchanges using qualified intermediaries or involving multiple properties.

Partly nontaxable exchange. If you receive money or property that is not like-kind in addition to like-kind property, and the above six conditions are met, you have a partly nontaxable trade. You are taxed on any gain you realize, but only up to the amount of the money and the fair market value of the property that is not like-kind that you receive. You can't deduct a loss.

Like property and unlike property transferred. If you give up unlike property in addition to the like property, you must recognize gain or loss on the unlike property you give up. The gain or loss is the difference between the adjusted basis of the unlike property and its fair market value.

Like property and money transferred. If all of the above conditions (1)–(6) are met, you have a nontaxable trade even if you pay money in addition to the like property.

Basis of property received. To figure the basis of the property received, see *Nontaxable Exchanges* in chapter 13.

How to report. You must report the trade of like-kind property on Form 8824. If you figure a recognized gain or loss on Form 8824, report it on Schedule D (Form 1040), or on Form 4797, Sales of Business Property, whichever applies. See the instructions for line 22 in the Instructions for Form 8824.

For information on using Form 4797, see chapter 4 of Pub. 544.

Corporate stocks. The following trades of corporate stocks generally don't result in a taxable gain or a deductible loss.

Corporate reorganizations. In some instances, a company will give you common stock for preferred stock, preferred stock for common stock, or stock in one corporation for stock in another corporation. If this is a result of a merger, recapitalization, transfer to a controlled corporation, bankruptcy, corporate division, corporate acquisition, or other corporate reorganization, you don't recognize gain or loss.

Stock for stock of the same corporation. You can exchange common stock for common stock or preferred stock for preferred stock in the same corporation without having a recognized gain or loss. This is true for a trade between two stockholders as well as a trade between a stockholder and the corporation.

Convertible stocks and bonds. You generally will not have a recognized gain or loss if you convert bonds into stock or preferred stock into common stock of the same corporation according to a conversion privilege in the terms of the bond or the preferred stock certificate.

Property for stock of a controlled corporation. If you transfer property to a corporation solely in exchange for stock in that corporation, and immediately after the trade you are in control of the corporation, you ordinarily will not recognize a gain or loss. This rule applies both to individuals and to groups who transfer property to a corporation. It doesn't apply if the corporation is an investment company.

For this purpose, to be in control of a corporation, you or your group of transferors must own, immediately after the exchange, at least 80% of the total combined voting power of all classes of stock entitled to vote and at least 80% of the outstanding shares of each class of nonvoting stock of the corporation.

If this provision applies to you, you may have to attach to your return a complete statement of all facts pertinent to the exchange. For details, see Regulations section 1.351-3.

Additional information. For more information on trades of stock, see *Nontaxable Trades* in chapter 4 of Pub. 550.

Insurance policies and annuities. You will not have a recognized gain or loss if the insured or annuitant is the same under both contracts and you trade:

- A life insurance contract for another life insurance contract or for an endowment or annuity contract or for a qualified long-term care insurance contract,

- An endowment contract for another endowment contract that provides for regular payments beginning at a date no later than the beginning date under the old contract or for an annuity contract or for a qualified long-term insurance contract,

- An annuity contract for another annuity contract or for a qualified long-term care insurance contract, or

- A qualified long-term care insurance contract for a qualified long-term care insurance contract.

You also may not have to recognize gain or loss on an exchange of a portion of an annuity contract for another annuity contract. See Revenue Ruling 2003-76 and Revenue Procedure 2011-38.

For tax years beginning after 2010, amounts received as an annuity for a period of 10 years or more, or for the lives of one or more individuals, under any portion of an annuity, endowment, or life insurance contract, are treated as a separate contract and are considered partial annuities. A portion of an annuity, endowment, or life insurance contract may be annuitized, provided that the annuitization period is for 10 years or more or for the lives of one or more individuals. The investment in the contract is allocated between the part of the contract from which amounts are received as an annuity and the part of the contract from which amounts aren't received as an annuity.

Exchanges of contracts not included in this list, such as an annuity contract for an endowment contract, or an annuity or endowment contract for a life insurance contract, are taxable.

Demutualization of life insurance companies. If you received stock in exchange for your equity interest as a policyholder or an annuitant, you generally will not have a recognized gain or loss. See *Demutualization of Life Insurance Companies* in Pub. 550.

U.S. Treasury notes or bonds. You can trade certain issues of U.S. Treasury obligations for other issues designated by the Secretary of the Treasury, with no gain or loss recognized on the trade. See *Savings bonds traded* in chapter 1 of Pub. 550 for more information.

Transfers Between Spouses

Generally, no gain or loss is recognized on a transfer of property from an individual to (or in trust for the benefit of) a spouse, or if incident to a divorce, a former spouse. This nonrecognition rule doesn't apply in the following situations.

- The recipient spouse or former spouse is a nonresident alien.

- Property is transferred in trust and liability exceeds basis. Gain must be recognized to the extent the amount of the liabilities assumed by the trust, plus any liabilities on the property, exceed the adjusted basis of the property.

For other situations, see *Transfers Between Spouses* in chapter 4 of Pub. 550.

Any transfer of property to a spouse or former spouse on which gain or loss isn't recognized is treated by the recipient as a gift and isn't considered a sale or exchange. The recipient's basis in the property will be the same as the adjusted basis of the giver immediately before the transfer. This carryover basis rule applies whether the adjusted basis of the transferred property is less than, equal to, or greater than either its fair market value at the time of transfer or any consideration paid by the recipient. This rule applies for purposes of determining loss as well as gain. Any gain recognized on a transfer in trust increases the basis.

A transfer of property is incident to a divorce if the transfer occurs within 1 year after the date on which the marriage ends, or if the transfer is related to the ending of the marriage.

Related Party Transactions

Special rules apply to the sale or trade of property between related parties.

Gain on sale or trade of depreciable property. Your gain from the sale or trade of property to a related party may be ordinary income, rather than capital gain, if the property can be depreciated by the party receiving it. See chapter 3 of Pub. 544 for more information.

Like-kind exchanges. Generally, if you trade business or investment property for other business or investment property of a like kind, no gain or loss is recognized. See *Like-kind exchanges*, earlier, under *Nontaxable Trades*.

This rule also applies to trades of property between related parties, defined next under *Losses on sales or trades of property*. However, if either you or the related party disposes of the like property within 2 years after the trade, you both must report any gain or loss not recognized on the original trade on your return filed for the year in which the later disposition occurs. See *Related Party Transactions* in chapter 4 of Pub. 550 for exceptions.

Losses on sales or trades of property. You can't deduct a loss on the sale or trade of property, other than a distribution in complete liquidation of a corporation, if the transaction is directly or indirectly between you and the following related parties.

- Members of your family. This includes only your brothers and sisters, half-brothers and half-sisters, spouse, ancestors (parents, grandparents, etc.), and lineal descendants (children, grandchildren, etc.).

- A partnership in which you directly or indirectly own more than 50% of the capital interest or the profits interest.
- A corporation in which you directly or indirectly own more than 50% in value of the outstanding stock. (See *Constructive ownership of stock*, later.)
- A tax-exempt charitable or educational organization directly or indirectly controlled, in any manner or by any method, by you or by a member of your family, whether or not this control is legally enforceable.

In addition, a loss on the sale or trade of property isn't deductible if the transaction is directly or indirectly between the following related parties.

- A grantor and fiduciary, or the fiduciary and beneficiary, of any trust.
- Fiduciaries of two different trusts, or the fiduciary and beneficiary of two different trusts, if the same person is the grantor of both trusts.
- A trust fiduciary and a corporation of which more than 50% in value of the outstanding stock is directly or indirectly owned by or for the trust, or by or for the grantor of the trust.
- A corporation and a partnership if the same persons own more than 50% in value of the outstanding stock of the corporation and more than 50% of the capital interest, or the profits interest, in the partnership.
- Two S corporations if the same persons own more than 50% in value of the outstanding stock of each corporation.
- Two corporations, one of which is an S corporation, if the same persons own more than 50% in value of the outstanding stock of each corporation.
- An executor and a beneficiary of an estate (except in the case of a sale or trade to satisfy a pecuniary bequest).
- Two corporations that are members of the same controlled group. (Under certain conditions, however, these losses aren't disallowed but must be deferred.)
- Two partnerships if the same persons own, directly or indirectly, more than 50% of the capital interests or the profit interests in both partnerships.

Multiple property sales or trades. If you sell or trade to a related party a number of blocks of stock or pieces of property in a lump sum, you must figure the gain or loss separately for each block of stock or piece of property. The gain on each item may be taxable. However, you can't deduct the loss on any item. Also, you can't reduce gains from the sales of any of these items by losses on the sales of any of the other items.

Indirect transactions. You can't deduct your loss on the sale of stock through your broker if, under a prearranged plan, a related party buys the same stock you had owned. This doesn't apply to a trade between related parties through an exchange that is purely coincidental and isn't prearranged.

Constructive ownership of stock. In determining whether a person directly or indirectly owns any of the outstanding stock of a corporation, the following rules apply.

Rule 1. Stock directly or indirectly owned by or for a corporation, partnership, estate, or trust is considered owned proportionately by or for its shareholders, partners, or beneficiaries.

Rule 2. An individual is considered to own the stock directly or indirectly owned by or for his or her family. Family includes only brothers and sisters, half-brothers and half-sisters, spouse, ancestors, and lineal descendants.

Rule 3. An individual owning, other than by applying rule 2, any stock in a corporation is considered to own the stock directly or indirectly owned by or for his or her partner.

Rule 4. When applying rule 1, 2, or 3, stock constructively owned by a person under rule 1 is treated as actually owned by that person. But stock constructively owned by an individual under rule 2 or rule 3 isn't treated as owned by that individual for again applying either rule 2 or rule 3 to make another person the constructive owner of the stock.

Property received from a related party. If you sell or trade at a gain property you acquired from a related party, you recognize the gain only to the extent it is more than the loss previously disallowed to the related party. This rule applies only if you are the original transferee and you acquired the property by purchase or exchange. This rule doesn't apply if the related party's loss was disallowed because of the wash sale rules described in chapter 4 of Pub. 550 under *Wash Sales*. See *Example 1* below.

If you sell or trade at a loss property you acquired from a related party, you can't recognize the loss that wasn't allowed to the related party. See *Example 2* below.

Example 1. Your brother sells you stock for $7,600. His cost basis is $10,000. Your brother can't deduct the loss of $2,400. Later, you sell the same stock to an unrelated party for $10,500, realizing a gain of $2,900. Your reportable gain is $500 (the $2,900 gain minus the $2,400 loss not allowed to your brother).

Example 2. If, in *Example 1*, you sold the stock for $6,900 instead of $10,500, your recognized loss is only $700 (your $7,600 basis minus $6,900). You can't deduct the loss that wasn't allowed to your brother.

Capital Gains and Losses

This section discusses the tax treatment of gains and losses from different types of investment transactions.

Character of gain or loss. You need to classify your gains and losses as either ordinary or capital gains or losses. You then need to classify your capital gains and losses as either short term or long term. If you have long-term gains and losses, you must identify your 28% rate gains and losses. If you have a net capital gain, you must also identify any unrecaptured section 1250 gain.

The correct classification and identification helps you figure the limit on capital losses and the correct tax on capital gains. See *Reporting Gains and Losses* in chapter 16.

Capital or Ordinary Gain or Loss

If you have a taxable gain or a deductible loss from a transaction, it may be either a capital gain or loss or an ordinary gain or loss, depending on the circumstances. Generally, a sale or trade of a capital asset (defined next) results in a capital gain or loss. A sale or trade of a noncapital asset generally results in an ordinary gain or loss. Depending on the circumstances, a gain or loss on a sale or trade of property used in a trade or business may be treated as either capital or ordinary, as explained in Pub. 544. In some situations, part of your gain or loss may be a capital gain or loss and part may be an ordinary gain or loss.

Capital Assets and Noncapital Assets

For the most part, everything you own and use for personal purposes, pleasure, or investment is a capital asset. Some examples are:

- Stocks or bonds held in your personal account;
- A house owned and used by you and your family;
- Household furnishings;
- A car used for pleasure or commuting;
- Coin or stamp collections;
- Gems and jewelry; and
- Gold, silver, or any other metal.

Any property you own is a capital asset, except the following noncapital assets.

1. Property held mainly for sale to customers or property that will physically become a part of the merchandise for sale to customers. For an exception, see *Capital Asset Treatment for Self-Created Musical Works*, later.

2. Depreciable property used in your trade or business, even if fully depreciated.

3. Real property used in your trade or business.

4. A certain patent; an invention, model, or design (whether or not patented); or a secret formula or process.

5. A copyright; a literary, musical, or artistic composition; a letter or memorandum; or similar property that is:

   a. Created by your personal efforts,

   b. Prepared or produced for you (in the case of a letter, memorandum, or similar property), or

   c. Acquired under circumstances (for example, by gift) entitling you to the basis of the person who created the property or for whom it was prepared or produced.

For an exception to this rule, see *Capital Asset Treatment for Self-Created Musical Works*, later.

6. Accounts or notes receivable acquired in the ordinary course of a trade or business for services rendered or from the sale of property described in (1).

7. U.S. Government publications that you received from the government free or for less than the normal sales price, or that you acquired under circumstances entitling you to the basis of someone who received the publications free or for less than the normal sales price.

8. Certain commodities derivative financial instruments held by commodities derivatives dealers.

9. Hedging transactions, but only if the transaction is clearly identified as a hedging transaction before the close of the day on which it was acquired, originated, or entered into.

10. Supplies of a type you regularly use or consume in the ordinary course of your trade or business.

Investment Property

Investment property is a capital asset. Any gain or loss from its sale or trade is generally a capital gain or loss.

Gold, silver, stamps, coins, gems, etc. These are capital assets except when they are held for sale by a dealer. Any gain or loss you have from their sale or trade generally is a capital gain or loss.

Stocks, stock rights, and bonds. All of these (including stock received as a dividend) are capital assets except when held for sale by a securities dealer. However, if you own small business stock, see *Losses on Section 1244 (Small Business) Stock*, later, and *Losses on Small Business Investment Company Stock* in chapter 4 of Pub. 550.

Personal Use Property

Property held for personal use only, rather than for investment, is a capital asset, and you must report a gain from its sale as a capital gain. However, you can't deduct a loss from selling personal use property.

Capital Asset Treatment for Self-Created Musical Works

You can elect to treat musical compositions and copyrights in musical works as capital assets when you sell or exchange them if:

- Your personal efforts created the property, or

- You acquired the property under circumstances (for example, by gift) entitling you to the basis of the person who created the property or for whom it was prepared or produced.

You must make a separate election for each musical composition (or copyright in a musical work) sold or exchanged during the tax year.

Make the election by the due date (including extensions) of the income tax return for the tax year of the sale or exchange. Make the election on Form 8949 and your Schedule D (Form 1040) by treating the sale or exchange as the sale or exchange of a capital asset, according to Form 8949, Schedule D (Form 1040), and their separate instructions.

You can revoke the election if you have IRS approval. To get IRS approval, you must submit a request for a letter ruling under the appropriate IRS revenue procedure. See, for example, Revenue Procedure 2017-1, available at *IRS.gov/irb/2017-01_IRB#RP-2017-1*. Alternatively, you are granted an automatic 6-month extension from the due date of your income tax return (excluding extensions) to revoke the election, provided you timely file your income tax return, and within this 6-month extension period, you file Form 1040X that treats the sale or exchange as the sale or exchange of property that isn't a capital asset.

Discounted Debt Instruments

Treat your gain or loss on the sale, redemption, or retirement of a bond or other debt instrument originally issued at a discount or bought at a discount as capital gain or loss, except as explained in the following discussions.

Short-term government obligations. Treat gains on short-term federal, state, or local government obligations (other than tax-exempt obligations) as ordinary income up to your ratable share of the acquisition discount. This treatment applies to obligations with a fixed maturity date not more than 1 year from the date of issue. Acquisition discount is the stated redemption price at maturity minus your basis in the obligation.

However, don't treat these gains as income to the extent you previously included the discount in income. See *Discount on Short-Term Obligations* in chapter 1 of Pub. 550.

Short-term nongovernment obligations. Treat gains on short-term nongovernment obligations as ordinary income up to your ratable share of original issue discount (OID). This treatment applies to obligations with a fixed maturity date of not more than 1 year from the date of issue.

However, to the extent you previously included the discount in income, you don't have to include it in income again. See *Discount on Short-Term Obligations* in chapter 1 of Pub. 550.

Tax-exempt state and local government bonds. If these bonds were originally issued at a discount before September 4, 1982, or you acquired them before March 2, 1984, treat your part of OID as tax-exempt interest. To figure your gain or loss on the sale or trade of these bonds, reduce the amount realized by your part of OID.

If the bonds were issued after September 3, 1982, and acquired after March 1, 1984, increase the adjusted basis by your part of OID to figure gain or loss. For more information on the basis of these bonds, see *Discounted Debt Instruments* in chapter 4 of Pub. 550.

Any gain from market discount is usually taxable on disposition or redemption of tax-exempt bonds. If you bought the bonds before

May 1, 1993, the gain from market discount is capital gain. If you bought the bonds after April 30, 1993, the gain is ordinary income.

You figure the market discount by subtracting the price you paid for the bond from the sum of the original issue price of the bond and the amount of accumulated OID from the date of issue that represented interest to any earlier holders. For more information, see *Market Discount Bonds* in chapter 1 of Pub. 550.

A loss on the sale or other disposition of a tax-exempt state or local government bond is deductible as a capital loss.

Redeemed before maturity. If a state or local bond issued before June 9, 1980, is redeemed before it matures, the OID isn't taxable to you.

If a state or local bond issued after June 8, 1980, is redeemed before it matures, the part of OID earned while you hold the bond isn't taxable to you. However, you must report the unearned part of OID as a capital gain.

Example. On July 5, 2007, the date of issue, you bought a 20-year, 6% municipal bond for $800. The face amount of the bond was $1,000. The $200 discount was OID. At the time the bond was issued, the issuer had no intention of redeeming it before it matured. The bond was callable at its face amount beginning 10 years after the issue date.

The issuer redeemed the bond at the end of 11 years (July 5, 2018) for its face amount of $1,000 plus accrued annual interest of $60. The OID earned during the time you held the bond, $73, isn't taxable. The $60 accrued annual interest also isn't taxable. However, you must report the unearned part of OID, $127 ($200 − $73 = $127) as a capital gain.

Long-term debt instruments issued after 1954 and before May 28, 1969 (or before July 2, 1982, if a government instrument). If you sell, trade, or redeem for a gain one of these debt instruments, the part of your gain that isn't more than your ratable share of the OID at the time of the sale or redemption is ordinary income. The rest of the gain is capital gain. If, however, there was an intention to call the debt instrument before maturity, all of your gain that isn't more than the entire OID is treated as ordinary income at the time of the sale. This treatment of taxable gain also applies to corporate instruments issued after May 27, 1969, under a written commitment that was binding on May 27, 1969, and at all times thereafter.

Long-term debt instruments issued after May 27, 1969 (or after July 1, 1982, if a government instrument). If you hold one of these debt instruments, you must include a part of OID in your gross income each year you own the instrument. Your basis in that debt instrument is increased by the amount of OID that you have included in your gross income. See *Original Issue Discount (OID)* in chapter 7 for information about OID that you must report on your tax return.

If you sell or trade the debt instrument before maturity, your gain is a capital gain. However, if at the time the instrument was originally issued there was an intention to call it before its maturity, your gain generally is ordinary income to the extent of the entire OID reduced by any amounts of OID previously includible in your income. In this case, the rest of the gain is capital gain.

Market discount bonds. If the debt instrument has market discount and you chose to include the discount in income as it accrued, increase your basis in the debt instrument by the accrued discount to figure capital gain or loss on its disposition. If you didn't choose to include the discount in income as it accrued, you must report gain as ordinary interest income up to the instrument's accrued market discount. The rest of the gain is capital gain. See *Market Discount Bonds* in chapter 1 of Pub. 550.

A different rule applies to market discount bonds issued before July 19, 1984, and purchased by you before May 1, 1993. See *Market discount bonds* under *Discounted Debt Instruments* in chapter 4 of Pub. 550.

Retirement of debt instrument. Any amount you receive on the retirement of a debt instrument is treated in the same way as if you had sold or traded that instrument.

Notes of individuals. If you hold an obligation of an individual issued with OID after March 1, 1984, you generally must include the OID in your income currently, and your gain or loss on its sale or retirement is generally capital gain or loss. An exception to this treatment applies if the obligation is a loan between individuals and all the following requirements are met.

- The lender isn't in the business of lending money.
- The amount of the loan, plus the amount of any outstanding prior loans, is $10,000 or less.
- Avoiding federal tax isn't one of the principal purposes of the loan.

If the exception applies, or the obligation was issued before March 2, 1984, you don't include the OID in your income currently. When you sell or redeem the obligation, the part of your gain that isn't more than your accrued share of OID at that time is ordinary income. The rest of the gain, if any, is capital gain. Any loss on the sale or redemption is capital loss.

Deposit in Insolvent or Bankrupt Financial Institution

If you lose money you have on deposit in a bank, credit union, or other financial institution that becomes insolvent or bankrupt, you may be able to deduct your loss in one of three ways.

- Ordinary loss.
- Casualty loss.
- Nonbusiness bad debt (short-term capital loss).

For more information, see *Deposit in Insolvent or Bankrupt Financial Institution* in chapter 4 of Pub. 550.

Sale of Annuity

The part of any gain on the sale of an annuity contract before its maturity date that is based on interest accumulated on the contract is ordinary income.

Losses on Section 1244 (Small Business) Stock

You can deduct as an ordinary loss, rather than as a capital loss, your loss on the sale, trade, or worthlessness of section 1244 stock. Report an ordinary loss from the sale, exchange, or worthlessness of section 1244 stock on Form 4797. However, if the total loss is more than the maximum amount that can be treated as an ordinary loss, also report the transaction on Form 8949. See the instructions for Forms 4797 and 8949.

Any gain on section 1244 stock is a capital gain if the stock is a capital asset in your hands. Report the gain on Form 8949. See *Losses on Section 1244 (Small Business) Stock* in chapter 4 of Pub. 550.

 For more information on Form 8949 and Schedule D (Form 1040), see Reporting Capital Gains and Losses *in chapter 16. See also Schedule D (Form 1040), Form 8949, and their separate instructions.*

Holding Period

If you sold or traded investment property, you must determine your holding period for the property. Your holding period determines whether any capital gain or loss was a short-term or long-term capital gain or loss.

Long-term or short-term. If you hold investment property more than 1 year, any capital gain or loss is a long-term capital gain or loss. If you hold the property 1 year or less, any capital gain or loss is a short-term capital gain or loss.

To determine how long you held the investment property, begin counting on the date after the day you acquired the property. The day you disposed of the property is part of your holding period.

Example. If you bought investment property on February 3, 2017, and sold it on February 3, 2018, your holding period isn't more than 1 year and you have a short-term capital gain or loss. If you sold it on February 6, 2018, your holding period is more than 1 year and you will have a long-term capital gain or loss.

Securities traded on established market. For securities traded on an established securities market, your holding period begins the day after the trade date you bought the securities, and ends on the trade date you sold them.

 Don't confuse the trade date with the settlement date, which is the date by which the stock must be delivered and payment must be made.

Example. You are a cash method, calendar year taxpayer. You sold stock on December 30, 2018. According to the rules of the stock exchange, the sale was closed by delivery of the stock and payment of the sale price in January 2019. Report your gain or loss on your 2018 return, even though you received the payment in 2019. The gain or loss is long term or short term depending on whether you held the stock more than 1 year. Your holding period ended on December 30.

U.S. Treasury notes and bonds. The holding period of U.S. Treasury notes and bonds sold at auction on the basis of yield starts the day after the Secretary of the Treasury, through news releases, gives notification of acceptance to successful bidders. The holding period of U.S. Treasury notes and bonds sold through an offering on a subscription basis at a specified yield starts the day after the subscription is submitted.

Automatic investment service. In determining your holding period for shares bought by the bank or other agent, full shares are considered bought first and any fractional shares are considered bought last. Your holding period starts on the day after the bank's purchase date. If a share was bought over more than one purchase date, your holding period for that share is a split holding period. A part of the share is considered to have been bought on each date that stock was bought by the bank with the proceeds of available funds.

Nontaxable trades. If you acquire investment property in a trade for other investment property and your basis for the new property is determined, in whole or in part, by your basis in the old property, your holding period for the new property begins on the day following the date you acquired the old property.

Property received as a gift. If you receive a gift of property and your basis is determined by the donor's adjusted basis, your holding period is considered to have started on the same day the donor's holding period started.

If your basis is determined by the fair market value of the property, your holding period starts on the day after the date of the gift.

Inherited property. Generally, if you inherited investment property, your capital gain or loss on any later disposition of that property is long-term capital gain or loss. This is true regardless of how long you actually held the property.

Real property bought. To figure how long you have held real property bought under an unconditional contract, begin counting on the day after you received title to it or on the day after you took possession of it and assumed the burdens and privileges of ownership, whichever happened first. However, taking delivery or possession of real property under an option agreement isn't enough to start the holding period. The holding period can't start until there is an actual contract of sale. The holding period of the seller can't end before that time.

Real property repossessed. If you sell real property but keep a security interest in it, and then later repossess the property under the terms of the sales contract, your holding period for a later sale includes the period you held the property before the original sale and the period after the repossession. Your holding period doesn't include the time between the original sale and the repossession; that is, it doesn't include the period during which the first buyer held the property. However, the holding period for any improvements made by the first buyer begins at the time of repossession.

Stock dividends. The holding period for stock you received as a taxable stock dividend begins on the date of distribution.

The holding period for new stock you received as a nontaxable stock dividend begins on the same day as the holding period of the old stock. This rule also applies to stock acquired in a "spin-off," which is a distribution of stock or securities in a controlled corporation.

Nontaxable stock rights. Your holding period for nontaxable stock rights begins on the same day as the holding period of the underlying stock. The holding period for stock acquired through the exercise of stock rights begins on the date the right was exercised.

Nonbusiness Bad Debts

If someone owes you money that you can't collect, you have a bad debt. You may be able to deduct the amount owed to you when you figure your tax for the year the debt becomes worthless.

Generally, nonbusiness bad debts are bad debts that didn't come from operating your trade or business, and are deductible as short-term capital losses. To be deductible, nonbusiness bad debts must be totally worthless. You can't deduct a partly worthless nonbusiness debt.

Genuine debt required. A debt must be genuine for you to deduct a loss. A debt is genuine if it arises from a debtor-creditor relationship based on a valid and enforceable obligation to repay a fixed or determinable sum of money.

Basis in bad debt required. To deduct a bad debt, you must have a basis in it—that is, you must have already included the amount in your income or loaned out your cash. For example, you can't claim a bad debt deduction for court-ordered child support not paid to you by your former spouse. If you are a cash method taxpayer (as most individuals are), you generally can't take a bad debt deduction for unpaid salaries, wages, rents, fees, interest, dividends, and similar items.

When deductible. You can take a bad debt deduction only in the year the debt becomes worthless. You don't have to wait until a debt is due to determine whether it is worthless. A debt becomes worthless when there is no longer any chance that the amount owed will be paid.

It isn't necessary to go to court if you can show that a judgment from the court would be uncollectible. You must only show that you have taken reasonable steps to collect the debt. Bankruptcy of your debtor is generally good evidence of the worthlessness of at least a part of an unsecured and unpreferred debt.

How to report bad debts. Deduct nonbusiness bad debts as short-term capital losses on Form 8949.

 Make sure you report your bad debt(s) (and any other short-term transactions for which you didn't receive a Form 1099-B) on Form 8949, Part I, with box C checked.

 For more information on Form 8949 and Schedule D (Form 1040), see Reporting Capital Gains and Losses in chapter 16. See also Schedule D (Form 1040), Form 8949, and their separate instructions.

For each bad debt, attach a statement to your return that contains:

- A description of the debt, including the amount, and the date it became due;

- The name of the debtor, and any business or family relationship between you and the debtor;

- The efforts you made to collect the debt; and

- Why you decided the debt was worthless. For example, you could show that the borrower has declared bankruptcy, or that legal action to collect would probably not result in payment of any part of the debt.

Filing a claim for refund. If you don't deduct a bad debt on your original return for the year it becomes worthless, you can file a claim for a credit or refund due to the bad debt. To do this, use Form 1040X to amend your return for the year the debt became worthless. You must file it within 7 years from the date your original return for that year had to be filed, or 2 years from the date you paid the tax, whichever is later. For more information about filing a claim, see Amended Returns and Claims for Refund in chapter 1.

Additional information. For more information, see Nonbusiness Bad Debts in Pub. 550. For information on business bad debts, see chapter 10 of Pub. 535.

Wash Sales

You can't deduct losses from sales or trades of stock or securities in a wash sale.

A wash sale occurs when you sell or trade stock or securities at a loss and within 30 days before or after the sale you:

1. Buy substantially identical stock or securities,

2. Acquire substantially identical stock or securities in a fully taxable trade,

3. Acquire a contract or option to buy substantially identical stock or securities, or

4. Acquire substantially identical stock for your individual retirement account (IRA) or Roth IRA.

If your loss was disallowed because of the wash sale rules, add the disallowed loss to the cost of the new stock or securities (except in (4) above). The result is your basis in the new stock or securities. This adjustment postpones the loss deduction until the disposition of the new stock or securities. Your holding period for the new stock or securities includes the holding period of the stock or securities sold.

For more information, see Wash Sales in chapter 4 of Pub. 550.

15

Selling Your Home

What's New

 At the time this publication went to print, Congress was considering legislation that would do the following.

1. Provide additional tax relief for those affected by certain 2018 disasters.

2. Extend certain tax benefits that expired at the end of 2017 and that currently can't be claimed on your 2018 tax return.

3. Change certain other tax provisions.

To learn whether this legislation was enacted resulting in changes that affect your 2018 tax return, go to Recent Developments at IRS.gov/Pub17.

The Tax Cuts and Jobs Act provides for the temporary deferral of gain on the sale of your home. See Deferral of Gain, later.

Reminder

Home sold with undeducted points. If you haven't deducted all the points you paid to secure a mortgage on your old home, you may be able to deduct the remaining points in the year of the sale. See Mortgage ending early under Points in chapter 24.

Introduction

This chapter explains the tax rules that apply when you sell your main home. In most cases, your main home is the one in which you live most of the time.

If you sold your main home in 2018, you may be able to exclude from income any gain up to a limit of $250,000 ($500,000 on a joint return in most cases). See Excluding the Gain, later. Generally, if you can exclude all the gain, you don't need to report the sale on your tax return.

In addition, you may be able to temporarily defer capital gains invested in a Qualified Opportunity Fund (QOF). You also may be able to permanently exclude capital gains from the sale or exchange of an investment in a QOF if the investment is held for at least 10 years.

If you have gain that is more than the exclusion amount or that otherwise can't be excluded, then you have taxable gain. Report it on Form 8949, Sales and Other Dispositions of Capital Assets, and Schedule D (Form 1040). You also may have to complete Form 4797, Sales of Business Property. See Reporting the Sale, later.

If you have a loss on the sale, you generally can't deduct it on your return. However, you may need to report it. See *Reporting the Sale*, later.

The following are main topics in this chapter.

- Figuring gain or loss.
- Basis.
- Excluding the gain.
- Ownership and use tests.
- Reporting the sale.

Other topics include the following.

- Business use or rental of home.
- Recapturing a federal mortgage subsidy.

Useful Items

You may want to see:

Publication

- ❏ **504** Divorced or Separated Individuals
- ❏ **505** Tax Withholding and Estimated Tax
- ❏ **519** U.S. Tax Guide for Aliens
- ❏ **523** Selling Your Home
- ❏ **530** Tax Information for Homeowners
- ❏ **537** Installment Sales
- ❏ **544** Sales and Other Dispositions of Assets
- ❏ **547** Casualties, Disasters, and Thefts
- ❏ **4492** Information for Taxpayers Affected by Hurricanes Katrina, Rita, and Wilma
- ❏ **4492-B** Information for Affected Taxpayers in the Midwestern Disaster Areas
- ❏ **4681** Canceled Debts, Foreclosures, Repossessions, and Abandonments
- ❏ **4895** Tax Treatment of Property Acquired From a Decedent Dying in 2010

Form (and Instructions)

- ❏ **Schedule D (Form 1040)** Capital Gains and Losses
- ❏ **982** Reduction of Tax Attributes Due to Discharge of Indebtedness
- ❏ **8828** Recapture of Federal Mortgage Subsidy
- ❏ **8949** Sales and Other Dispositions of Capital Assets

For these and other useful items, go to *IRS.gov/Forms*.

Main Home

This section explains the term "main home." Usually, the home you live in most of the time is your main home and can be a:

- House,
- Houseboat,
- Mobile home,
- Cooperative apartment, or
- Condominium.

To exclude gain under the rules of this chapter, in most cases, you must have owned and lived in the property as your main home for at least 2 years during the 5-year period ending on the date of sale.

Land. If you sell the land on which your main home is located, but not the house itself, you can't exclude any gain you have from the sale of the land. However, if you sell vacant land that is used as part of your main home and that is adjacent to the land on which your home sits, you may be able to exclude the gain from the sale under certain circumstances. See Pub. 523 for more information.

Example. You buy a piece of land and move your main home to it. Then you sell the land on which your main home was located. This sale isn't considered a sale of your main home, and you can't exclude any gain on the sale of the land.

More than one home. If you have more than one home, you can exclude gain only from the sale of your main home. You must include in income gain from the sale of any other home. If you have two homes and live in both of them, your main home is ordinarily the one you live in most of the time during the year.

Example 1. You own two homes, one in New York and one in Florida. From 2014 through 2018, you live in the New York home for 7 months and in the Florida residence for 5 months of each year. In the absence of facts and circumstances indicating otherwise, the New York home is your main home. You would be eligible to exclude the gain from the sale of the New York home but you wouldn't be eligible to exclude the gain on the Florida home in 2018.

Example 2. You own a house, but you live in another house that you rent. The rented house is your main home.

Example 3. You own two homes, one in Virginia and one in New Hampshire. In 2014 and 2015, you lived in the Virginia home. In 2016 and 2017, you lived in the New Hampshire home. In 2018, you lived again in the Virginia home. Your main home in 2014, 2015, and 2018 is the Virginia home. Your main home in 2016 and 2017 is the New Hampshire home. You would be eligible to exclude gain from the sale of either home (but not both) in 2018.

Property used partly as your main home. If you use only part of the property as your main home, the rules discussed in this publication apply only to the gain or loss on the sale of that part of the property. For details, see *Business Use or Rental of Home*, later.

Figuring Gain or Loss

To figure the gain or loss on the sale of your main home, you must know the selling price, the amount realized, and the adjusted basis. Subtract the adjusted basis from the amount realized to get your gain or loss.

```
  Selling price
- Selling expenses
  ───────────────
  Amount realized


  Amount realized
- Adjusted basis
  ───────────────
  Gain or loss
```

Selling Price

The selling price is the total amount you receive for your home. It includes money and the fair market value of any other property or any other services you receive and all notes, mortgages, or other debts assumed by the buyer as part of the sale.

Payment by employer. You may have to sell your home because of a job transfer. If your employer pays you for a loss on the sale or for your selling expenses, don't include the payment as part of the selling price. Your employer will include it as wages in box 1 of your Form W-2, and you will include it in your income on Form 1040, line 1.

Option to buy. If you grant an option to buy your home and the option is exercised, add the amount you receive for the option to the selling price of your home. If the option isn't exercised, you must report the amount as ordinary income in the year the option expires. Report this amount on Schedule 1 (Form 1040), line 21.

Form 1099-S. If you received Form 1099-S, Proceeds From Real Estate Transactions, box 2 (Gross proceeds) should show the total amount you received for your home.

However, box 2 won't include the fair market value of any services or property other than cash or notes you received or will receive. Instead, box 4 will be checked to indicate your receipt or expected receipt of these items.

Amount Realized

The amount realized is the selling price minus selling expenses.

Selling expenses. Selling expenses include:

- Commissions;
- Advertising fees;
- Legal fees; and
- Loan charges paid by the seller, such as loan placement fees or "points."

Adjusted Basis

While you owned your home, you may have made adjustments (increases or decreases) to the basis. This adjusted basis must be determined before you can figure gain or loss on the sale of your home. For information on how to figure your home's adjusted basis, see *Determining Basis*, later.

Amount of Gain or Loss

To figure the amount of gain or loss, compare the amount realized to the adjusted basis.

Gain on sale. If the amount realized is more than the adjusted basis, the difference is a gain and, except for any part you can exclude, in most cases is taxable.

Loss on sale. If the amount realized is less than the adjusted basis, the difference is a loss. A loss on the sale of your main home can't be deducted.

Jointly owned home. If you and your spouse sell your jointly owned home and file a joint return, you figure your gain or loss as one taxpayer.

Separate returns. If you file separate returns, each of you must figure your own gain or loss according to your ownership interest in the home. Your ownership interest generally is determined by state law.

Joint owners not married. If you and a joint owner other than your spouse sell your jointly owned home, each of you must figure your own gain or loss according to your ownership interest in the home. Each of you applies the rules discussed in this chapter on an individual basis.

Dispositions Other Than Sales

Some special rules apply to other dispositions of your main home.

Foreclosure or repossession. If your home was foreclosed on or repossessed, you have a disposition. See Pub. 4681 to determine if you have ordinary income, gain, or loss.

Abandonment. If you abandon your home, see Pub. 4681 to determine if you have ordinary income, gain, or loss.

Trading (exchanging) homes. If you trade your old home for another home, treat the trade as a sale and a purchase.

Example. You owned and lived in a home with an adjusted basis of $41,000. A real estate dealer accepted your old home as a trade-in and allowed you $50,000 toward a new home priced at $80,000. This is treated as a sale of your old home for $50,000 with a gain of $9,000 ($50,000 – $41,000).

If the dealer had allowed you $27,000 and assumed your unpaid mortgage of $23,000 on your old home, your sales price would still be $50,000 (the $27,000 trade-in allowed plus the $23,000 mortgage assumed).

Transfer to spouse. If you transfer your home to your spouse or you transfer it to your former spouse incident to your divorce, in most cases, you have no gain or loss. This is true even if you receive cash or other consideration for the home. As a result, the rules in this chapter don't apply.

More information. If you need more information, see Pub. 523 and *Property Settlements* in Pub. 504.

Involuntary conversion. You have a disposition when your home is destroyed or condemned and you receive other property or money in payment, such as insurance or a condemnation award. This is treated as a sale and

you may be able to exclude all or part of any gain from the destruction or condemnation of your home, as explained later under *Special Situations*.

Determining Basis

You need to know your basis in your home to figure any gain or loss when you sell it. Your basis in your home is determined by how you got the home. Generally, your basis is its cost if you bought it or built it. If you got it in some other way (inheritance, gift, etc.), your basis generally is either its fair market value when you received it or the adjusted basis of the previous owner.

While you owned your home, you may have made adjustments (increases or decreases) to your home's basis. The result of these adjustments is your home's adjusted basis, which is used to figure gain or loss on the sale of your home. See *Adjusted Basis*, later.

You can find more information on basis and adjusted basis in chapter 13 of this publication and in Pub. 523.

Cost as Basis

The cost of property is the amount you paid for it in cash, debt obligations, other property, or services.

Purchase. If you bought your home, your basis is its cost to you. This includes the purchase price and certain settlement or closing costs. In most cases, your purchase price includes your down payment and any debt, such as a first or second mortgage or notes you gave the seller in payment for the home. If you build, or contract to build, a new home, your purchase price can include costs of construction, as discussed in Pub. 523.

Settlement fees or closing costs. When you bought your home, you may have paid settlement fees or closing costs in addition to the contract price of the property. You can include in your basis some of the settlement fees and closing costs you paid for buying the home, but not the fees and costs for getting a mortgage loan. A fee paid for buying the home is any fee you would have had to pay even if you paid cash for the home (that is, without the need for financing).

Chapter 13 lists some of the settlement fees and closing costs that you can include in the basis of property, including your home. It also lists some settlement costs that can't be included in basis.

Also see Pub. 523 for additional items and a discussion of basis other than cost.

Adjusted Basis

Adjusted basis is your cost or other basis increased or decreased by certain amounts. To figure your adjusted basis, see Pub. 523.

 If you are selling a home in which you acquired an interest from a decedent who died in 2010, see Pub. 4895 to determine your basis.

Increases to basis. These include the following.

- Additions and other improvements that have a useful life of more than 1 year.
- Special assessments for local improvements.
- Amounts you spent after a casualty to restore damaged property.

Improvements. These add to the value of your home, prolong its useful life, or adapt it to new uses. You add the cost of additions and other improvements to the basis of your property.

For example, putting a recreation room or another bathroom in your unfinished basement, putting up a new fence, putting in new plumbing or wiring, putting on a new roof, or paving your unpaved driveway is an improvement. An addition to your house, such as a new deck, a sun room, or a new garage, also is an improvement.

Repairs. These maintain your home in good condition but don't add to its value or prolong its life. You don't add their cost to the basis of your property.

Examples of repairs include repainting your house inside or outside, fixing your gutters or floors, repairing leaks or plastering, and replacing broken window panes.

Decreases to basis. These include the following.

- Discharge of qualified principal residence indebtedness which was discharged before January 1, 2018, or was subject to an arrangement that was entered into and evidenced in writing before January 1, 2018.
- Some or all of the cancellation of debt income that was excluded due to your bankruptcy or insolvency. For details, see Pub. 4681.
- Gain you postponed from the sale of a previous home before May 7, 1997.
- Deductible casualty losses.
- Insurance payments you received or expect to receive for casualty losses.
- Payments you received for granting an easement or right-of-way.
- Depreciation allowed or allowable if you used your home for business or rental purposes.
- Adoption credit you claimed for improvements added to the basis of your home.
- Nontaxable payments from your employer's adoption assistance program that you used for improvements you added to the basis of your home.
- Energy conservation subsidy excluded from your gross income because you received it (directly or indirectly) from a public utility after 1992 to buy or install any energy conservation measure. An energy conservation measure is an installation or modification primarily designed either to reduce consumption of electricity or natural gas or to improve the management of energy demand for a home.

- General sales taxes (beginning in 2004) claimed as an itemized deduction on Schedule A (Form 1040) that were imposed on the purchase of personal property, such as a houseboat used as your home or a mobile home.

 Recordkeeping. You should keep records to prove your home's adjusted basis. Ordinarily, you must keep records for 3 years after the due date for filing your return for the tax year in which you sold your home. But if you sold a home before May 7, 1997, and postponed tax on any gain, the basis of that home affects the basis of the new home you bought. Keep records proving the basis of both homes as long as they are needed for tax purposes.

The records you should keep include:

- Proof of the home's purchase price and purchase expenses;

- Receipts and other records for all improvements, additions, and other items that affect the home's adjusted basis;

- Any worksheets or other computations you used to figure the adjusted basis of the home you sold, the gain or loss on the sale, the exclusion, and the taxable gain;

- Any Form 982 you filed to report any discharge of qualified principal residence indebtedness;

- Any Form 2119, Sale of Your Home, you filed to postpone gain from the sale of a previous home before May 7, 1997; and

- Any worksheets you used to prepare Form 2119, such as the Adjusted Basis of Home Sold Worksheet or the Capital Improvements Worksheet from the Form 2119 instructions, or other source of computations.

Excluding the Gain

You may qualify to exclude from your income all or part of any gain from the sale of your main home. This means that, if you qualify, you won't have to pay tax on the gain up to the limit described under *Maximum Exclusion*, next. To qualify, you must meet the ownership and use tests described later.

You can choose not to take the exclusion by including the gain from the sale in your gross income on your tax return for the year of the sale.

See Pub. 523 to figure the amount of your exclusion and your taxable gain, if any.

 If you have any taxable gain from the sale of your home, you may have to increase your withholding or make estimated tax payments. See Pub. 505 for more information.

Maximum Exclusion

You can exclude up to $250,000 of the gain (other than gain allocated to periods of nonqualified use) on the sale of your main home if all of the following are true.

- You meet the ownership test.

- You meet the use test.

- During the 2-year period ending on the date of the sale, you didn't exclude gain from the sale of another home.

For details on gain allocated to periods of nonqualified use, see *Periods of nonqualified use*, later.

You may be able to exclude up to $500,000 of the gain (other than gain allocated to periods of nonqualified use) on the sale of your main home if you are married, file a joint return, and meet the requirements listed in the discussion of the special rules for joint returns, later, under *Married Persons*.

Ownership and Use Tests

To claim the exclusion, you must meet the ownership and use tests. This means that during the 5-year period ending on the date of the sale, you must have:

- Owned the home for at least 2 years (the ownership test), and

- Lived in the home as your main home for at least 2 years (the use test).

Exception. If you owned and lived in the property as your main home for less than 2 years, you can still claim an exclusion in some cases. However, the maximum amount you may be able to exclude will be reduced. See *Reduced Maximum Exclusion*, later.

Example 1—Home owned and occupied for at least 2 years. Mya bought and moved into her main home in September 2016. She sold the home at a gain in October 2018. During the 5-year period ending on the date of sale in October 2018, she owned and lived in the home for more than 2 years. She meets the ownership and use tests.

Example 2—Ownership test met but use test not met. Ayden bought a home, lived in it for 6 months, moved out, and never occupied the home again. He later sold the home for a gain. He owned the home during the entire 5-year period ending on the date of sale. He meets the ownership test but not the use test. He can't exclude any part of his gain on the sale unless he qualified for a reduced maximum exclusion (explained later).

Period of Ownership and Use

The required 2 years of ownership and use during the 5-year period ending on the date of the sale don't have to be continuous nor do they both have to occur at the same time.

You meet the tests if you can show that you owned and lived in the property as your main home for either 24 full months or 730 days (365 × 2) during the 5-year period ending on the date of sale.

Temporary absence. Short temporary absences for vacations or other seasonal absences, even if you rent out the property during the absences, are counted as periods of use. The following examples assume that the reduced maximum exclusion (discussed later) doesn't apply to the sales.

Example 1. David Johnson, who is single, bought and moved into his home on February 1, 2016. Each year during 2016 and 2017, David left his home for a 2-month summer vacation. David sold the house on March 1, 2018. Although the total time David used his home is less than 2 years (21 months), he meets the requirement and may exclude gain. The 2-month vacations are short temporary absences and are counted as periods of use in determining whether David used the home for the required 2 years.

Example 2. Professor Paul Beard, who is single, bought and moved into a house on August 19, 2015. He lived in it as his main home continuously until January 5, 2017, when he went abroad for a 1-year sabbatical leave. On February 5, 2018, 1 month after returning from the leave, Paul sold the house at a gain. Because his leave wasn't a short temporary absence, he can't include the period of leave to meet the 2-year use test. He can't exclude any part of his gain, because he didn't use the residence for the required 2 years.

Ownership and use tests met at different times. You can meet the ownership and use tests during different 2-year periods. However, you must meet both tests during the 5-year period ending on the date of the sale.

Example. Beginning in 2007, Helen Jones lived in a rented apartment. The apartment building was later converted to condominiums, and she bought her same apartment on December 2, 2015. In 2016, Helen became ill and on April 14 of that year she moved to her daughter's home. On July 7, 2018, while still living in her daughter's home, she sold her condominium.

Helen can exclude gain on the sale of her condominium because she met the ownership and use tests during the 5-year period from July 8, 2013, to July 7, 2018, the date she sold the condominium. She owned her condominium from December 2, 2015, to July 7, 2018 (more than 2 years). She lived in the property from July 8, 2013 (the beginning of the 5-year period), to April 14, 2016 (more than 2 years).

The time Helen lived in her daughter's home during the 5-year period can be counted toward her period of ownership, and the time she lived in her rented apartment during the 5-year period can be counted toward her period of use.

Cooperative apartment. If you sold stock as a tenant-stockholder in a cooperative housing corporation, the ownership and use tests are met if, during the 5-year period ending on the date of sale, you:

- Owned the stock for at least 2 years, and

- Lived in the house or apartment that the stock entitles you to occupy as your main home for at least 2 years.

Exceptions to Ownership and Use Tests

The following sections contain exceptions to the ownership and use tests for certain taxpayers.

Exception for individuals with a disability. There is an exception to the use test if:

- You become physically or mentally unable to care for yourself, and
- You owned and lived in your home as your main home for a total of at least 1 year during the 5-year period before the sale of your home.

Under this exception, you are considered to live in your home during any time within the 5-year period that you own the home and live in a facility (including a nursing home) licensed by a state or political subdivision to care for persons in your condition.

If you meet this exception to the use test, you still have to meet the 2-out-of-5-year ownership test to claim the exclusion.

Previous home destroyed or condemned. For the ownership and use tests, you add the time you owned and lived in a previous home that was destroyed or condemned to the time you owned and lived in the replacement home on whose sale you wish to exclude gain. This rule applies if any part of the basis of the home you sold depended on the basis of the destroyed or condemned home. Otherwise, you must have owned and lived in the same home for 2 of the 5 years before the sale to qualify for the exclusion.

Members of the uniformed services or Foreign Service, employees of the intelligence community, or employees or volunteers of the Peace Corps. You can choose to have the 5-year test period for ownership and use suspended during any period you or your spouse serve on "qualified official extended duty" as a member of the uniformed services or Foreign Service of the United States, or as an employee of the intelligence community. You can choose to have the 5-year test period for ownership and use suspended during any period you or your spouse serve outside the United States either as an employee of the Peace Corps on "qualified official extended duty" or as an enrolled volunteer or volunteer leader of the Peace Corps. This means that you may be able to meet the 2-year use test even if, because of your service, you didn't actually live in your home for at least the required 2 years during the 5-year period ending on the date of sale.

If this helps you qualify to exclude gain, you can choose to have the 5-year test period suspended by filing a return for the year of sale that doesn't include the gain.

For more information about the suspension of the 5-year test period, see *Service, Intelligence, and Peace Corps Personnel* in Pub. 523.

Married Persons

If you and your spouse file a joint return for the year of sale and one spouse meets the ownership and use tests, you can exclude up to $250,000 of the gain. (But see *Special rules for joint returns* next.)

Special rules for joint returns. You can exclude up to $500,000 of the gain on the sale of your main home if all of the following are true.

- You are married and file a joint return for the year.
- Either you or your spouse meets the ownership test.
- Both you and your spouse meet the use test.
- During the 2-year period ending on the date of the sale, neither you nor your spouse excluded gain from the sale of another home.

If either spouse doesn't satisfy all these requirements, the maximum exclusion that can be claimed by the couple is the total of the maximum exclusions that each spouse would qualify for if not married and the amounts were figured separately. For this purpose, each spouse is treated as owning the property during the period that either spouse owned the property.

Example 1—One spouse sells a home. Emily sells her home in June 2018 for a gain of $300,000. She marries Jamie later in the year. She meets the ownership and use tests, but Jamie doesn't. Emily can exclude up to $250,000 of gain on a separate or joint return for 2018. The $500,000 maximum exclusion for certain joint returns doesn't apply because Jamie doesn't meet the use test.

Example 2—Each spouse sells a home. The facts are the same as in *Example 1*, except that Jamie also sells a home in 2018 for a gain of $200,000 before he marries Emily. He meets the ownership and use tests on his home, but Emily doesn't. Emily can exclude $250,000 of gain and Jamie can exclude $200,000 of gain on the respective sales of their individual homes. However, Emily can't use Jamie's unused exclusion to exclude more than $250,000 of gain. Therefore, Emily and Jamie must recognize $50,000 of gain on the sale of Emily's home. The $500,000 maximum exclusion for certain joint returns doesn't apply because Emily and Jamie don't both meet the use test for the same home.

Sale of main home by surviving spouse. If your spouse died and you didn't remarry before the date of sale, you are considered to have owned and lived in the property as your main home during any period of time when your spouse owned and lived in it as a main home.

If you meet all of the following requirements, you may qualify to exclude up to $500,000 of any gain from the sale or exchange of your main home.

- The sale or exchange took place after 2007.
- The sale or exchange took place no more than 2 years after the date of death of your spouse.
- You haven't remarried.
- You and your spouse met the use test at the time of your spouse's death.
- You or your spouse met the ownership test at the time of your spouse's death.

- Neither you nor your spouse excluded gain from the sale of another home during the last 2 years.

Example. Harry owned and used a house as his main home since 2014. Harry and Wilma married on July 1, 2018, and from that date they use Harry's house as their main home. Harry died on August 15, 2018, and Wilma inherited the property. Wilma sold the property on September 2, 2018, at which time she hadn't remarried. Although Wilma owned and used the house for less than 2 years, Wilma is considered to have satisfied the ownership and use tests because her period of ownership and use includes the period that Harry owned and used the property before death.

Home transferred from spouse. If your home was transferred to you by your spouse (or former spouse if the transfer was incident to divorce), you are considered to have owned it during any period of time when your spouse owned it.

Use of home after divorce. You are considered to have used property as your main home during any period when:

- You owned it, and
- Your spouse or former spouse is allowed to live in it under a divorce or separation instrument and uses it as his or her main home.

Reduced Maximum Exclusion

If you fail to meet the requirements to qualify for the $250,000 or $500,000 exclusion, you may still qualify for a reduced exclusion. This applies to those who:

- Fail to meet the ownership and use tests, or
- Have used the exclusion within 2 years of selling their current home.

In both cases, to qualify for a reduced exclusion, the sale of your main home must be due to one of the following reasons.

- A change in place of employment.
- Health.
- Unforeseen circumstances.

Unforeseen circumstances. The sale of your main home is because of an unforeseen circumstance if your primary reason for the sale is the occurrence of an event that you couldn't reasonably have anticipated before buying and occupying your main home.

See Pub. 523 for more information.

Deferral of Gain

The Tax Cuts and Jobs Act provides for the temporary deferral of capital gains reinvested in a qualified opportunity fund and permanent exclusion of capital gains from the sale or an exchange of an investment in a qualified opportunity fund. See *Rev. Proc. 2018-16* and *Rev. Proc. 2018-48* for further information. Also see

Worksheet. Taxable Gain on Sale of Home—Completed Example 1 for Amy

Part 1. Gain or (Loss) on Sale

1.	Selling price of home	1.
2.	Selling expenses (including commissions, advertising and legal fees, and seller-paid loan charges)	2.
3.	Subtract line 2 from line 1. This is the amount realized	3.
4.	Adjusted basis of home sold. See Pub. 523	4.
5.	**Gain or (loss) on the sale.** Subtract line 4 from line 3. If this is a loss, stop here	5. 200,000

Part 2. Exclusion and Taxable Gain

6.	Enter any depreciation allowed or allowable on the property for periods after May 6, 1997. If none, enter -0-	6. 10,000
7.	Subtract line 6 from line 5. If the result is less than zero, enter -0-	7. 190,000
8.	Aggregate number of days of nonqualified use after 2008. If none, enter -0-. If line 8 is equal to zero, skip to line 12 and enter the amount from line 7 on line 12	8. 670
9.	Number of days taxpayer owned the property	9. 2,076
10.	Divide the amount on line 8 by the amount on line 9. Enter the result as a decimal (rounded to at least 3 places). **Don't** enter an amount greater than 1.000	10. 0.323
11.	Gain allocated to nonqualified use (line 7 multiplied by line 10)	11. 61,370
12.	Gain eligible for exclusion. Subtract line 11 from line 7	12. 128,630
13.	If you qualify to exclude gain on the sale, enter your maximum exclusion. If you qualify for a reduced maximum exclusion, enter your reduced maximum exclusion. If you don't qualify to exclude gain, enter -0-. See Pub. 523	13. 250,000
14.	**Exclusion.** Enter the smaller of line 12 or line 13	14. 128,630
15.	**Taxable gain.** Subtract line 14 from line 5. **If the amount on line 6 is more than zero, complete line 16**	15. 71,370
16.	Enter the **smaller** of line 6 or line 15. Enter this amount on line 12 of the Unrecaptured Section 1250 Gain Worksheet in the Instructions for Schedule D (Form 1040)	16. 10,000

the Opportunity Zone Frequently Asked Questions page at *IRS.gov/Newsroom/Opportunity-Zones-Frequently-Asked-Questions*.

Business Use or Rental of Home

You may be able to exclude gain from the sale of a home you have used for business or to produce rental income. But you must meet the ownership and use tests.

Periods of nonqualified use. In most cases, gain from the sale or exchange of your main home won't qualify for the exclusion to the extent that the gains are allocated to periods of nonqualified use. Nonqualified use is any period after 2008 during which neither you nor your spouse (or your former spouse) used the property as a main home with the following exceptions.

Exceptions. A period of nonqualified use doesn't include:

1. Any portion of the 5-year period ending on the date of the sale or exchange after the last date you (or your spouse) use the property as a main home;

2. Any period (not to exceed an aggregate period of 10 years) during which you (or your spouse) are serving on qualified official extended duty:

    a. As a member of the uniformed services,

    b. As a member of the Foreign Service of the United States, or

    c. As an employee of the intelligence community; and

3. Any other period of temporary absence (not to exceed an aggregate period of 2 years) due to change of employment, health conditions, or such other unforeseen circumstances as may be specified by the IRS.

The gain resulting from the sale of the property is allocated between qualified and nonqualified use periods based on the amount of time the property was held for qualified and nonqualified use. Gain from the sale or exchange of a main home allocable to periods of qualified use will continue to qualify for the exclusion for the sale of your main home. Gain from the sale or exchange of property allocable to nonqualified use won't qualify for the exclusion.

Calculation. To figure the portion of the gain allocated to the period of nonqualified use, multiply the gain by the following fraction.

$$\frac{\text{Total nonqualified use during the period of ownership after 2008}}{\text{Total period of ownership}}$$

Example 1. On May 24, 2012, Amy, who is single for all years in this example, bought a house. She moved in on that date and lived in it until May 31, 2014, when she moved out of the house and put it up for rent. The house was rented from June 1, 2014, to March 31, 2016. Amy claimed depreciation deductions in 2014 through 2016 totaling $10,000. Amy moved back into the house on April 1, 2016, and lived there until she sold it on January 28, 2018, for a gain of $200,000. During the 5-year period ending on the date of the sale (January 29, 2013–January 28, 2018), Amy owned and lived in the house for more than 2 years as shown in the following table.

Five-Year Period	Used as Home	Used as Rental
1/29/13 – 5/31/14	16 months	
6/1/14 – 3/31/16		22 months
4/1/16 – 1/28/18	21 months	
	37 months	22 months

Next, Amy must figure how much of her gain is allocated to nonqualified use and how much is allocated to qualified use. During the period Amy owned the house (2,076 days), her period of nonqualified use was 670 days. Amy divides 670 by 2,076 and obtains a decimal (rounded to at least three decimal places) of 0.323. To figure her gain attributable to the period of nonqualified use, she multiplies $190,000 (the gain not attributable to the $10,000 depreciation deduction) by 0.323. Because the gain attributable to periods of nonqualified use is $61,370, Amy can exclude $128,630 of her gain.

See the worksheet for *Taxable Gain on Sale of Home—Completed Example 1 for Amy*, for how to figure Amy's taxable gain and exclusion.

Example 2. William owned and used a house as his main home from 2012 through 2015. On January 1, 2016, he moved to another state. He rented his house from that date until April 29, 2018, when he sold it. During the 5-year period ending on the date of sale (April 30, 2013–April 29, 2018), William owned and lived in the house for more than 2 years. He must report the sale on Form 4797 because it was rental property at the time of sale. Because the period of nonqualified use doesn't include any part of the 5-year period after the last date William lived in the house, he has no period of nonqualified use. Because he met the ownership and use tests, he can exclude gain up to $250,000. However, he can't exclude the part of the gain equal to the depreciation he claimed or could have claimed for renting the house, as explained next.

Depreciation after May 6, 1997. If you were entitled to take depreciation deductions because you used your home for business purposes or as rental property, you can't exclude the part of your gain equal to any depreciation allowed or allowable as a deduction for periods after May 6, 1997. If you can show by adequate records or other evidence that the depreciation allowed was less than the amount allowable, then you may limit the amount of gain recognized to the depreciation allowed. See Pub. 544 for more information.

Property used partly for business or rental. If you used property partly as a home and partly for business or to produce rental income, see Pub. 523.

Reporting the Sale

Don't report the 2018 sale of your main home on your tax return unless:

- You have a gain and don't qualify to exclude all of it,
- You have a gain and choose not to exclude it, or
- You received Form 1099-S.

If any of these conditions apply, report the entire gain or loss. For details on how to report the gain or loss, see the Instructions for Schedule D (Form 1040) and the Instructions for Form 8949.

If you used the home for business or to produce rental income, you may have to use Form 4797 to report the sale of the business or rental part (or the sale of the entire property if used entirely for business or rental). See Pub. 523 and the Instructions for Form 4797 for additional information.

Installment sale. Some sales are made under arrangements that provide for part or all of the selling price to be paid in a later year. These sales are called "installment sales." If you finance the buyer's purchase of your home yourself instead of having the buyer get a loan or mortgage from a bank, you probably have an installment sale. You may be able to report the part of the gain you can't exclude on the installment basis.

Use Form 6252, Installment Sale Income, to report the sale. Enter your exclusion on line 15 of Form 6252.

Seller-financed mortgage. If you sell your home and hold a note, mortgage, or other financial agreement, the payments you receive in most cases consist of both interest and principal. You must separately report as interest income the interest you receive as part of each payment. If the buyer of your home uses the property as a main or second home, you also

must report the name, address, and social security number (SSN) of the buyer on line 1 of Schedule B (Form 1040). The buyer must give you his or her SSN, and you must give the buyer your SSN. Failure to meet these requirements may result in a $50 penalty for each failure. If either you or the buyer doesn't have and isn't eligible to get an SSN, see *Social Security Number (SSN)* in chapter 1.

More information. For more information on installment sales, see Pub. 537.

Special Situations

The situations that follow may affect your exclusion.

Sale of home acquired in a like-kind exchange. You can't claim the exclusion if:

1. (a) You acquired your home in a like-kind exchange (also known as a section 1031 exchange), or (b) your basis in your home is determined by reference to a previous owner's basis, and that previous owner acquired the property in a like-kind exchange (for example, the owner acquired the home and then gave it to you as a gift); and

2. You sold the home within 5 years of the date your home was acquired in the like-kind exchange.

Gain from a like-kind exchange isn't taxable at the time of the exchange. This means that gain won't be taxed until you sell or otherwise dispose of the property you receive. To defer gain from a like-kind exchange, you must have exchanged business or investment property for business or investment property of a like kind. For more information about like-kind exchanges, see Pub. 544.

Home relinquished in a like-kind exchange. If you use your main home partly for business or rental purposes and then exchange the home for another property, see Pub. 523.

Expatriates. You can't claim the exclusion if the expatriation tax applies to you. The expatriation tax applies to certain U.S. citizens who have renounced their citizenship (and to certain long-term residents who have ended their residency). For more information about the expatriation tax, see *Expatriation Tax* in chapter 4 of Pub. 519.

Home destroyed or condemned. If your home was destroyed or condemned, any gain (for example, because of insurance proceeds you received) qualifies for the exclusion.

Any part of the gain that can't be excluded (because it's more than the maximum exclusion) can be postponed under the rules explained in:

- Pub. 547, in the case of a home that was destroyed; or
- Pub. 544, chapter 1, in the case of a home that was condemned.

Sale of remainder interest. Subject to the other rules in this chapter, you can choose to exclude gain from the sale of a remainder interest in your home. If you make this choice, you can't choose to exclude gain from your sale of

any other interest in the home that you sell separately.

Exception for sales to related persons. You can't exclude gain from the sale of a remainder interest in your home to a related person. Related persons include your brothers, sisters, half-brothers, half-sisters, spouse, ancestors (parents, grandparents, etc.), and lineal descendants (children, grandchildren, etc.). Related persons also include certain corporations, partnerships, trusts, and exempt organizations.

Recapturing (Paying Back) a Federal Mortgage Subsidy

If you financed your home under a federally subsidized program (loans from tax-exempt qualified mortgage bonds or loans with mortgage credit certificates), you may have to recapture all or part of the benefit you received from that program when you sell or otherwise dispose of your home. You recapture the benefit by increasing your federal income tax for the year of the sale. You may have to pay this recapture tax even if you can exclude your gain from income under the rules discussed earlier; that exclusion doesn't affect the recapture tax.

Loans subject to recapture rules. The recapture applies to loans that:

1. Came from the proceeds of qualified mortgage bonds, or

2. Were based on mortgage credit certificates.

The recapture also applies to assumptions of these loans.

When recapture applies. Recapture of the federal mortgage subsidy applies only if you meet both of the following conditions.

- You sell or otherwise dispose of your home at a gain within the first 9 years after the date you close your mortgage loan.

- Your income for the year of disposition is more than that year's adjusted qualifying income for your family size for that year (related to the income requirements a person must meet to qualify for the federally subsidized program).

When recapture doesn't apply. Recapture doesn't apply in any of the following situations.

- Your mortgage loan was a qualified home improvement loan (QHIL) of not more than $15,000 used for alterations, repairs, and improvements that protect or improve the basic livability or energy efficiency of your home.

- Your mortgage loan was a QHIL of not more than $150,000 in the case of a QHIL used to repair damage from Hurricane Katrina to homes in the hurricane disaster area; a QHIL funded by a qualified mortgage bond that is a qualified Gulf Opportunity Zone Bond; or a QHIL for an owner-occupied home in the Gulf Opportunity Zone (GO Zone), Rita GO Zone, or

Wilma GO Zone. For more information, see Pub. 4492 and Pub. 4492-B.

- The home is disposed of as a result of your death.

- You dispose of the home more than 9 years after the date you closed your mortgage loan.

- You transfer the home to your spouse, or to your former spouse incident to a divorce, where no gain is included in your income.

- You dispose of the home at a loss.

- Your home is destroyed by a casualty, and you replace it on its original site within 2 years after the end of the tax year when the destruction happened. The replacement period is extended for main homes destroyed in a federally declared disaster area, a Midwestern disaster area, the Kansas disaster area, and the Hurricane Katrina disaster area. For more information, see *Replacement Period* in Pub. 547.

- You refinance your mortgage loan (unless you later meet the conditions listed previously under *When recapture applies*, earlier).

Notice of amounts. At or near the time of settlement of your mortgage loan, you should receive a notice that provides the federally subsidized amount and other information you will need to figure your recapture tax.

How to figure and report the recapture. The recapture tax is figured on Form 8828. If you sell your home and your mortgage is subject to recapture rules, you must file Form 8828 even if you don't owe a recapture tax. Attach Form 8828 to your Form 1040. For more information, see Form 8828 and its instructions.

16.

Reporting Gains and Losses

What's New

 At the time this publication went to print, Congress was considering legislation that would do the following.

1. Provide additional tax relief for those affected by certain 2018 disasters.

2. Extend certain tax benefits that expired at the end of 2017 and that currently can't be claimed on your 2018 tax return.

3. Change certain other tax provisions.

To learn whether this legislation was enacted resulting in changes that affect your 2018 tax

return, go to Recent Developments at *IRS.gov/Pub17*.

Special rules for capital gains invested in Qualified Opportunity Funds. Effective December 22, 2017, IRC 1400Z-2 provides a temporary deferral of inclusion in gross income for certain capital gains invested in Qualified Opportunity Funds (QOF), and a potential permanent exclusion of gains from the sale or exchange of an investment in a QOF if the investment is held for at least 10 years. For more information, see the Instructions for Form 8949. For additional information, please see *IRS.gov/OpportunityZoneFrequentlyAskedQuestions*.

Introduction

This chapter discusses how to report capital gains and losses from sales, exchanges, and other dispositions of investment property on Form 8949 and Schedule D (Form 1040). The discussion includes the following topics.

- How to report short-term gains and losses.

- How to report long-term gains and losses.

- How to figure capital loss carryovers.

- How to figure your tax on a net capital gain.

If you sell or otherwise dispose of property used in a trade or business or for the production of income, see Pub. 544, Sales and Other Dispositions of Assets, before completing Schedule D (Form 1040).

Useful Items

You may want to see:

Publication

- ❏ **537** Installment Sales

- ❏ **544** Sales and Other Dispositions of Assets

- ❏ **550** Investment Income and Expenses

Form (and Instructions)

- ❏ **Schedule D (Form 1040)** Capital Gains and Losses

- ❏ **4797** Sales of Business Property

- ❏ **6252** Installment Sale Income

- ❏ **8582** Passive Activity Loss Limitations

- ❏ **8949** Sales and Other Dispositions of Capital Assets

For these and other useful items, go to *IRS.gov/Forms*.

Reporting Capital Gains and Losses

Generally, report capital gains and losses on Form 8949. Complete Form 8949 before you complete line 1b, 2, 3, 8b, 9, or 10 of Schedule D (Form 1040).

Use Form 8949 to report:

- The sale or exchange of a capital asset not reported on another form or schedule,

- Gains from involuntary conversions (other than from casualty or theft) of capital assets not held for business or profit,

- Nonbusiness bad debts, and

- Securities that become worthless.

Use Schedule D (Form 1040) to report:

- Overall gain or loss from transactions reported on Form 8949;

- Certain transactions you do not have to report on Form 8949;

- Gain from Form 2439 or 6252 or Part I of Form 4797;

- Gain or loss from Form 4684, 6781, or 8824;

- Gain or loss from a partnership, S corporation, estate, or trust;

- Capital gain distributions not reported directly on your Form 1040; and

- Capital loss carryover from the previous year to the current year.

On Form 8949, enter all sales and exchanges of capital assets, including stocks, bonds, etc., and real estate (if not reported on Form 4684, 4797, 6252, 6781, or 8824, or line 1a or 8a of Schedule D (Form 1040)). Include these transactions even if you did not receive a Form 1099-B or 1099-S for the transaction. Report short-term gains or losses in Part I. Report long-term gains or losses in Part II. Use as many Forms 8949 as you need.

Exceptions to filing Form 8949 and Schedule D (Form 1040). There are certain situations where you may not have to file Form 8949 and/or Schedule D (Form 1040).

Exception 1. You do not have to file Form 8949 or Schedule D (Form 1040) if you have no capital losses and your only capital gains are capital gain distributions from Form(s) 1099-DIV, box 2a. If any Form(s) 1099-DIV you receive have an amount in box 2b (unrecaptured section 1250 gain), box 2c (section 1202 gain), or box 2d (collectibles (28%) gain), you do not qualify for this exception.

If you qualify for this exception, report your capital gain distributions directly on Schedule 1 (Form 1040), line 13, and check the box on that line. Also, use the Qualified Dividends and Capital Gain Tax Worksheet in the Form 1040 instructions to figure your tax.

Exception 2. You must file Schedule D (Form 1040), but generally do not have to file Form 8949, if *Exception 1* above does not apply and your only capital gains and losses are:

- Capital gain distributions;

- A capital loss carryover;

- A gain from Form 2439 or 6252 or Part I of Form 4797;

- A gain or loss from Form 4684, 6781, or 8824;

- A gain or loss from a partnership, S corporation, estate, or trust; or

- Gains and losses from transactions for which you received a Form 1099-B that shows the basis was reported to the IRS and for which you do not need to make any adjustments in column (g) of Form 8949 or enter any codes in column (f) of Form 8949.

Installment sales. You can't use the installment method to report a gain from the sale of stock or securities traded on an established securities market. You must report the entire gain in the year of sale (the year in which the trade date occurs).

Passive activity gains and losses. If you have gains or losses from a passive activity, you may also have to report them on Form 8582. In some cases, the loss may be limited under the passive activity rules. Refer to Form 8582 and its instructions for more information about reporting capital gains and losses from a passive activity.

Form 1099-B transactions. If you sold property, such as stocks, bonds, or certain commodities, through a broker, you should receive a Form 1099-B from the broker. Use the Form 1099-B to complete Form 8949 and/or Schedule D (Form 1040).

If you received a Form 1099-B for a transaction, you usually report the transaction on Form 8949. Report the proceeds shown in box 1d of Form 1099-B in column (d) of either Part I or Part II of Form 8949, whichever applies. Include in column (g) any selling expenses or option premiums not reflected in Form 1099-B, box 1d or box 1e. If you include a selling expense in column (g), enter "E" in column (f). Enter the basis shown in box 1e in column (e). If the basis shown on Form 1099-B is not correct, see *How To Complete Form 8949, Columns (f) and (g)* in the Instructions for Form 8949 for the adjustment you must make. If no basis is shown on Form 1099-B, enter the correct basis of the property in column (e). See the instructions for Form 1099-B, Form 8949, and Schedule D (Form 1040) for more information.

Form 1099-CAP transactions. If a corporation in which you own stock has had a change in control or a substantial change in capital structure, you should receive Form 1099-CAP from the corporation. Use the Form 1099-CAP to fill in Form 8949. If your computations show that you would have a loss because of the change, do not enter any amounts on Form 8949 or Schedule D (Form 1040). You cannot claim a loss on Schedule D (Form 1040) as a result of this transaction.

Report the aggregate amount received shown in box 2 of Form 1099-CAP as the sales price in column (d) of either Part I or Part II of Form 8949, whichever applies.

Form 1099-S transactions. If you sold or traded land (including air rights), a building or similar structure, a condominium unit, or co-op stock, you may receive a Form 1099-S, Proceeds From Real Estate Transactions, showing your proceeds and other important information.

See the Instructions for Form 8949 and the Instructions for Schedule D (Form 1040) for how to report these transactions and include them in Part I or Part II of Form 8949 as appropriate. However, report like-kind exchanges on Form 8824 instead.

See Form 1099-S and the Instructions for Form 1099-S for more information.

Nominees. If you receive gross proceeds as a nominee (that is, the gross proceeds are in your name but actually belong to someone else), see the Instructions for Form 8949 for how to report these amounts on Form 8949.

File Form 1099-B or Form 1099-S with the IRS. If you received gross proceeds as a nominee in 2018, you must file a Form 1099-B or Form 1099-S for those proceeds with the IRS. Send the Form 1099-B or Form 1099-S with a Form 1096, Annual Summary and Transmittal of U.S. Information Returns, to your Internal Revenue Service Center by February 28, 2019 (April 1, 2019, if you file Form 1099-B or Form 1099-S electronically). Give the actual owner of the proceeds Copy B of the Form 1099-B or Form 1099-S by February 15, 2019. On Form 1099-B, you should be listed as the "Payer." The actual owner should be listed as the "Recipient." On Form 1099-S, you should be listed as the "Filer." The actual owner should be listed as the "Transferor." You do not have to file a Form 1099-B or Form 1099-S to show proceeds for your spouse. For more information about the reporting requirements and the penalties for failure to file (or furnish) certain information returns, see the General Instructions for Certain Information Returns. If you are filing electronically, see Pub. 1220.

Sale of property bought at various times. If you sell a block of stock or other property that you bought at various times, report the short-term gain or loss from the sale on one row in Part I of Form 8949, and the long-term gain or loss on one row in Part II of Form 8949. Write "Various" in column (b) for the "Date acquired."

Sale expenses. On Form 8949, include in column (g) any expense of sale, such as broker's fees, commissions, state and local transfer taxes, and option premiums, unless you reported the net sales price in column (d). If you include an expense of sale in column (g), enter "E" in column (f).

For information about adjustments to basis, see chapter 13.

Short-term gains and losses. Capital gain or loss on the sale or trade of investment property held 1 year or less is a short-term capital gain or loss. You report it in Part I of Form 8949.

You combine your share of short-term capital gain or loss from partnerships, S corporations, estates, and trusts, and any short-term capital loss carryover, with your other short-term capital gains and losses to figure your net short-term capital gain or loss on line 7 of Schedule D (Form 1040).

Long-term gains and losses. A capital gain or loss on the sale or trade of investment property held more than 1 year is a long-term capital gain or loss. You report it in Part II of Form 8949.

You report the following in Part II of Schedule D (Form 1040).

- Undistributed long-term capital gains from a mutual fund (or other regulated investment company) or real estate investment trust (REIT).

- Your share of long-term capital gains or losses from partnerships, S corporations, estates, and trusts.

- All capital gain distributions from mutual funds and REITs not reported directly on Schedule 1 (Form 1040), line 13.

- Long-term capital loss carryovers.

The result after combining these items with your other long-term capital gains and losses is your net long-term capital gain or loss (Schedule D (Form 1040), line 15).

Total net gain or loss. To figure your total net gain or loss, combine your net short-term capital gain or loss (Schedule D (Form 1040), line 7) with your net long-term capital gain or loss (Schedule D (Form 1040), line 15). Enter the result on Schedule D (Form 1040), Part III, line 16. If your losses are more than your gains, see *Capital Losses* next. If both lines 15 and 16 of your Schedule D (Form 1040) are gains and your taxable income on your Form 1040 is more than zero, see *Capital Gain Tax Rates*, later.

Capital Losses

If your capital losses are more than your capital gains, you can claim a capital loss deduction. Report the amount of the deduction on Schedule 1 (Form 1040), line 13, in parentheses.

Limit on deduction. Your allowable capital loss deduction, figured on Schedule D (Form 1040), is the lesser of:

- $3,000 ($1,500 if you are married and file a separate return), or

- Your total net loss as shown on line 16 of Schedule D (Form 1040).

You can use your total net loss to reduce your income dollar for dollar, up to the $3,000 limit.

Capital loss carryover. If you have a total net loss on line 16 of Schedule D (Form 1040) that is more than the yearly limit on capital loss deductions, you can carry over the unused part to the next year and treat it as if you had incurred it in that next year. If part of the loss is still unused, you can carry it over to later years until it is completely used up.

When you figure the amount of any capital loss carryover to the next year, you must take the current year's allowable deduction into account, whether or not you claimed it and whether or not you filed a return for the current year.

When you carry over a loss, it remains long term or short term. A long-term capital loss you carry over to the next tax year will reduce that year's long-term capital gains before it reduces that year's short-term capital gains.

Figuring your carryover. The amount of your capital loss carryover is the amount of your total net loss that is more than the lesser of:

1. Your allowable capital loss deduction for the year, or

2. Your taxable income increased by your allowable capital loss deduction for the year and your deduction for personal exemptions.

If your deductions are more than your gross income for the tax year, use your negative taxable income in figuring the amount in item (2) above.

Table 16-1. What Is Your Maximum Capital Gain Rate?

IF your net capital gain is from ...	THEN your maximum capital gain rate is ...
collectibles gain	28%
eligible gain on qualified small business stock minus the section 1202 exclusion	28%
unrecaptured section 1250 gain	25%
other gain[1] and the regular tax rate that would apply is 37%	20%
other gain[1] and the regular tax rate that would apply is 22%, 24%, 32%, or 35%	15%
other gain[1] and the regular tax rate that would apply is 10% or 12%	0%

[1]"Other gain" means any gain that is not collectibles gain, gain on small business stock, or unrecaptured section 1250 gain.

Complete the Capital Loss Carryover Worksheet in the Instructions for Schedule D or Pub. 550 to determine the part of your capital loss that you can carry over.

Example. Brian and Jackie sold securities in 2018. The sales resulted in a capital loss of $7,000. They had no other capital transactions. Their taxable income was $26,000. On their joint 2018 return, they can deduct $3,000. The unused part of the loss, $4,000 ($7,000 − $3,000), can be carried over to 2019.

If their capital loss had been $2,000, their capital loss deduction would have been $2,000. They would have no carryover.

Use short-term losses first. When you figure your capital loss carryover, use your short-term capital losses first, even if you incurred them after a long-term capital loss. If you have not reached the limit on the capital loss deduction after using the short-term capital losses, use the long-term capital losses until you reach the limit.

Decedent's capital loss. A capital loss sustained by a decedent during his or her last tax year (or carried over to that year from an earlier year) can be deducted only on the final income tax return filed for the decedent. The capital loss limits discussed earlier still apply in this situation. The decedent's estate cannot deduct any of the loss or carry it over to following years.

Joint and separate returns. If you and your spouse once filed separate returns and are now filing a joint return, combine your separate capital loss carryovers. However, if you and your spouse once filed a joint return and are now filing separate returns, any capital loss carryover from the joint return can be deducted only on the return of the spouse who actually had the loss.

Capital Gain Tax Rates

The tax rates that apply to a net capital gain are generally lower than the tax rates that apply to other income. These lower rates are called the maximum capital gain rates.

The term "net capital gain" means the amount by which your net long-term capital gain for the year is more than your net short-term capital loss.

For 2018, the maximum capital gain rates are 0%, 15%, 20%, 25%, and 28%. See Table 16-1 for details.

 If you figure your tax using the maximum capital gain rate and the regular tax computation results in a lower tax, the regular tax computation applies.

Example. All of your net capital gain is from selling collectibles, so the capital gain rate would be 28%. If you are otherwise subject to a rate lower than 28%, the 28% rate does not apply.

Investment interest deducted. If you claim a deduction for investment interest, you may have to reduce the amount of your net capital gain that is eligible for the capital gain tax rates. Reduce it by the amount of the net capital gain you choose to include in investment income when figuring the limit on your investment interest deduction. This is done on the Schedule D Tax Worksheet or the Qualified Dividends and Capital Gain Tax Worksheet. For more information about the limit on investment interest, see *Interest Expenses* in chapter 3 of Pub. 550.

Collectibles gain or loss. This is gain or loss from the sale or trade of a work of art, rug, antique, metal (such as gold, silver, and platinum bullion), gem, stamp, coin, or alcoholic beverage held more than 1 year.

Collectibles gain includes gain from sale of an interest in a partnership, S corporation, or trust due to unrealized appreciation of collectibles.

Gain on qualified small business stock. If you realized a gain from qualified small business stock that you held more than 5 years, you generally can exclude some or all of your gain under section 1202. The eligible gain minus your section 1202 exclusion is a 28% rate gain. See *Gains on Qualified Small Business Stock* in chapter 4 of Pub. 550.

Unrecaptured section 1250 gain. Generally, this is any part of your capital gain from selling section 1250 property (real property) that is due to depreciation (but not more than your net section 1231 gain), reduced by any net loss in the 28% group. Use the Unrecaptured Section 1250 Gain Worksheet in the Schedule D (Form 1040) instructions to figure your unrecaptured section 1250 gain. For more information about section 1250 property and section 1231 gain, see chapter 3 of Pub. 544.

Tax computation using maximum capital gain rates. Use the Qualified Dividends and Capital Gain Tax Worksheet or the Schedule D Tax Worksheet (whichever applies) to figure your tax if you have qualified dividends or net capital gain. You have net capital gain if Schedule D (Form 1040), lines 15 and 16, are both gains.

Schedule D Tax Worksheet. Use the Schedule D Tax Worksheet in the Schedule D (Form 1040) instructions to figure your tax if:

- You have to file Schedule D (Form 1040); and

- Schedule D (Form 1040), line 18 (28% rate gain) or line 19 (unrecaptured section 1250 gain), is more than zero.

Qualified Dividends and Capital Gain Tax Worksheet. If you do not have to use the Schedule D Tax Worksheet (as explained above) and any of the following apply, use the Qualified Dividends and Capital Gain Tax Worksheet in the instructions for Form 1040 to figure your tax.

- You received qualified dividends. (See *Qualified Dividends* in chapter 8.)

- You do not have to file Schedule D (Form 1040) and you received capital gain distributions. (See *Exceptions to filing Form 8949 and Schedule D (Form 1040)*, earlier.)

- Schedule D (Form 1040), lines 15 and 16, are both more than zero.

Alternative minimum tax. These capital gain rates are also used in figuring alternative minimum tax.

Part Four.

Adjustments to Income

The four chapters in this part discuss some of the adjustments to income that you can make in figuring your adjusted gross income. These chapters cover:

- Contributions you make to traditional and Roth individual retirement arrangements (IRAs) — chapter 17;
- Alimony you pay — chapter 18;
- Student loan interest you pay — chapter 19; and
- Business expenses you pay as an Armed Forces reservist, a performing artist, or a fee-basis government official — chapter 20.

Other adjustments to income are discussed elsewhere. See Table V.

The new Form 1040 schedules that are discussed in these chapters are:

- Schedule 1, Additional Income and Adjustments to Income.
- Schedule 4, Other Taxes.

Table V. **Other Adjustments to Income**

Use this table to find information about other adjustments to income not covered in this part of the publication.

IF you are looking for more information about the deduction for...	THEN see...
contributions to a health savings account	Pub. 969, Health Savings Accounts and Other Tax-Favored Health Plans.
moving expenses	Pub. 521, Moving Expenses.
part of your self-employment tax	chapter 23.
self-employed health insurance	chapter 22.
payments to self-employed SEP, SIMPLE, and qualified plans	Pub. 560, Retirement Plans for Small Business.
penalty on the early withdrawal of savings	chapter 7.
contributions to an Archer MSA	Pub. 969.
reforestation amortization or expense	chapters 7 and 8 of Pub. 535, Business Expenses.
contributions to Internal Revenue Code section 501(c)(18)(D) pension plans	Pub. 525, Taxable and Nontaxable Income.
expenses from the rental of personal property	chapter 12.
certain required repayments of supplemental unemployment benefits (sub-pay)	chapter 12.
foreign housing costs	chapter 4 of Pub. 54, Tax Guide for U.S. Citizens and Resident Aliens Abroad.
jury duty pay given to your employer	chapter 12.
contributions by certain ministers or chaplains to Internal Revenue Code section 403(b) plans	Pub. 517, Social Security and Other Information for Members of the Clergy and Religious Workers.
attorney fees and certain costs for actions involving IRS awards to whistleblowers	Pub. 525.
domestic production activities deduction for patrons of specified agricultural or horticultural cooperatives (specified cooperatives)	Instructions for Form 8903, Domestic Production Activities Deduction.

17.

Individual Retirement Arrangements (IRAs)

What's New

 At the time this publication went to print, Congress was considering legislation that would do the following.

1. Provide additional tax relief for those affected by certain 2018 disasters.

2. Extend certain tax benefits that expired at the end of 2017 and that currently can't be claimed on your 2018 tax return.

3. Change certain other tax provisions.

To learn whether this legislation was enacted resulting in changes that affect your 2018 tax return, go to Recent Developments at IRS.gov/ Pub17.

Extended rollover period for qualified plan loan off-sets in 2018 or later. For distributions made in tax years beginning after December 31, 2017, you have until the due date (including extensions) for your tax return for the tax year in which the offset occurs to roll over a qualified plan loan offset amount. For more information, see Pub. 590-A.

No recharacterizations of conversions made in 2018 or later. A conversion of a traditional IRA to a Roth IRA, and a rollover from any other eligible retirement plan to a Roth IRA, made after December 31, 2017, can't be recharacterized as having been made to a traditional IRA. For more information, see Pub. 590-A.

Reminders

Modified AGI limit for traditional IRA contributions. For 2018, if you are covered by a retirement plan at work, your deduction for contributions to a traditional IRA is reduced (phased out) if your modified AGI is:

- More than $101,000 but less than $121,000 for a married couple filing a joint return or a qualifying widow(er),

- More than $63,000 but less than $73,000 for a single individual or head of household, or

- Less than $10,000 for a married individual filing a separate return.

If you either live with your spouse or file a joint return, and your spouse is covered by a

retirement plan at work but you aren't, your deduction is phased out if your modified AGI is more than $189,000 but less than $199,000. If your modified AGI is $199,000 or more, you can't take a deduction for contributions to a traditional IRA. See How Much Can You Deduct, later.

Modified AGI limit for Roth IRA contributions. For 2018, your Roth IRA contribution limit is reduced (phased out) in the following situations.

- Your filing status is married filing jointly or qualifying widow(er) and your modified AGI is at least $189,000. You can't make a Roth IRA contribution if your modified AGI is $199,000 or more.

- Your filing status is single, head of household, or married filing separately and you didn't live with your spouse at any time in 2018 and your modified AGI is at least $120,000. You can't make a Roth IRA contribution if your modified AGI is $135,000 or more.

- Your filing status is married filing separately, you lived with your spouse at any time during the year, and your modified AGI is more than zero. You can't make a Roth IRA contribution if your modified AGI is $10,000 or more.

See Can You Contribute to a Roth IRA, later.

2019 limits. You can find information about the 2019 contribution and AGI limits in Pub. 590-A.

Contributions to both traditional and Roth IRAs. For information on your combined contribution limit if you contribute to both traditional and Roth IRAs, see Roth IRAs and traditional IRAs, later.

Statement of required minimum distribution. If a minimum distribution from your IRA is required, the trustee, custodian, or issuer that held the IRA at the end of the preceding year must either report the amount of the required minimum distribution to you, or offer to figure it for you. The report or offer must include the date by which the amount must be distributed. The report is due January 31 of the year in which the minimum distribution is required. It can be provided with the year-end fair market value statement that you normally get each year. No report is required for IRAs of owners who have died.

IRA interest. Although interest earned from your IRA is generally not taxed in the year earned, it isn't tax-exempt interest. Tax on your traditional IRA is generally deferred until you take a distribution. Don't report this interest on your tax return as tax-exempt interest.

Net Investment Income Tax. For purposes of the Net Investment Income Tax (NIIT), net investment income doesn't include distributions from a qualified retirement plan including IRAs (for example, 401(a), 403(a), 403(b), 408, 408A, or 457(b) plans). However, these distributions are taken into account when determining the modified AGI threshold. Distributions from a nonqualified retirement plan are included in net investment income. See Form 8960, Net Investment Income Tax—Individuals, Estates, and Trusts, and its instructions for more information.

Form 8606. To designate contributions as nondeductible, you must file Form 8606, Nondeductible IRAs.

 The term "50 or older" is used several times in this chapter. It refers to an IRA owner who is age 50 or older by the end of the tax year.

Introduction

An IRA is a personal savings plan that gives you tax advantages for setting aside money for your retirement.

This chapter discusses the following topics.

- The rules for a traditional IRA (any IRA that isn't a Roth or SIMPLE IRA).

- The Roth IRA, which features nondeductible contributions and tax-free distributions.

Simplified Employee Pensions (SEPs) and Savings Incentive Match Plans for Employees (SIMPLEs) aren't discussed in this chapter. For more information on these plans and employees' SEP IRAs and SIMPLE IRAs that are part of these plans, see Pub. 560, Retirement Plans for Small Business.

For information about contributions, deductions, withdrawals, transfers, rollovers, and other transactions, see Pub. 590-A and Pub. 590-B.

Useful Items

You may want to see:

Publication

❏ **560** Retirement Plans for Small Business

❏ **590-A** Contributions to Individual Retirement Arrangements (IRAs)

❏ **590-B** Distributions from Individual Retirement Arrangements (IRAs)

Form (and Instructions)

❏ **5329** Additional Taxes on Qualified Plans (Including IRAs) and Other Tax-Favored Accounts

❏ **8606** Nondeductible IRAs

For these and other useful items, go to IRS.gov/ Forms.

Traditional IRAs

In this chapter, the original IRA (sometimes called an ordinary or regular IRA) is referred to as a "traditional IRA." A traditional IRA is any IRA that isn't a Roth IRA or a SIMPLE IRA. Two advantages of a traditional IRA are:

- You may be able to deduct some or all of your contributions to it, depending on your circumstances; and

- Generally, amounts in your IRA, including earnings and gains, aren't taxed until they are distributed.

Who Can Open a Traditional IRA?

You can open and make contributions to a traditional IRA if:

- You (or, if you file a joint return, your spouse) received taxable compensation during the year, and

- You weren't age 70½ by the end of the year.

What is compensation? Generally, compensation is what you earn from working. Compensation includes wages, salaries, tips, professional fees, bonuses, and other amounts you receive for providing personal services. The IRS treats as compensation any amount properly shown in box 1 (Wages, tips, other compensation) of Form W-2, Wage and Tax Statement, provided that this amount is reduced by any amount properly shown in box 11 (Nonqualified plans).

Scholarship and fellowship payments are compensation for this purpose only if shown in box 1 of Form W-2.

Compensation also includes commissions and taxable alimony and separate maintenance payments.

Self-employment income. If you are self-employed (a sole proprietor or a partner), compensation is the net earnings from your trade or business (provided your personal services are a material income-producing factor) reduced by the total of:

- The deduction for contributions made on your behalf to retirement plans, and

- The deductible part of your self-employment tax.

Compensation includes earnings from self-employment even if they aren't subject to self-employment tax because of your religious beliefs.

Nontaxable combat pay. For IRA purposes, if you were a member of the U.S. Armed Forces, your compensation includes any nontaxable combat pay you receive.

What isn't compensation? Compensation doesn't include any of the following items.

- Earnings and profits from property, such as rental income, interest income, and dividend income.

- Pension or annuity income.

- Deferred compensation received (compensation payments postponed from a past year).

- Income from a partnership for which you don't provide services that are a material income-producing factor.

- Conservation Reserve Program (CRP) payments reported on Schedule SE (Form 1040), line 1b.

- Any amounts (other than combat pay) you exclude from income, such as foreign earned income and housing costs.

When and How Can a Traditional IRA Be Opened?

You can open a traditional IRA at any time. However, the time for making contributions for any year is limited. See *When Can Contributions Be Made*, later.

You can open different kinds of IRAs with a variety of organizations. You can open an IRA at a bank or other financial institution or with a mutual fund or life insurance company. You can also open an IRA through your stockbroker. Any IRA must meet Internal Revenue Code requirements.

Kinds of traditional IRAs. Your traditional IRA can be an individual retirement account or annuity. It can be part of either a SEP or an employer or employee association trust account.

How Much Can Be Contributed?

There are limits and other rules that affect the amount that can be contributed to a traditional IRA. These limits and other rules are explained below.

Community property laws. Except as discussed later under *Kay Bailey Hutchison Spousal IRA limit*, each spouse figures his or her limit separately, using his or her own compensation. This is the rule even in states with community property laws.

Brokers' commissions. Brokers' commissions paid in connection with your traditional IRA are subject to the contribution limit.

Trustees' fees. Trustees' administrative fees aren't subject to the contribution limit.

Qualified reservist repayments. If you are (or were) a member of a reserve component and you were ordered or called to active duty after September 11, 2001, you may be able to contribute (repay) to an IRA amounts equal to any qualified reservist distributions you received. You can make these repayment contributions even if they would cause your total contributions to the IRA to be more than the general limit on contributions. To be eligible to make these repayment contributions, you must have received a qualified reservist distribution from an IRA or from a section 401(k) or 403(b) plan or similar arrangement.

For more information, see *Qualified reservist repayments* under *How Much Can Be Contributed?* in chapter 1 of Pub. 590-A.

 Contributions on your behalf to a traditional IRA reduce your limit for contributions to a Roth IRA. (See Roth IRAs, later.)

General limit. For 2018, the most that can be contributed to your traditional IRA generally is the smaller of the following amounts.

- $5,500 ($6,500 if you are 50 or older).

- Your taxable compensation (defined earlier) for the year.

This is the most that can be contributed regardless of whether the contributions are to one or more traditional IRAs or whether all or part of the contributions are nondeductible. (See *Nondeductible Contributions*, later.) Qualified reservist repayments don't affect this limit.

Example 1. Betty, who is 34 years old and single, earned $24,000 in 2018. Her IRA contributions for 2018 are limited to $5,500.

Example 2. John, an unmarried college student working part time, earned $3,500 in 2018. His IRA contributions for 2018 are limited to $3,500, the amount of his compensation.

Kay Bailey Hutchison Spousal IRA limit. For 2018, if you file a joint return and your taxable compensation is less than that of your spouse, the most that can be contributed for the year to your IRA is the smaller of the following amounts.

1. $5,500 ($6,500 if you are 50 or older).

2. The total compensation includible in the gross income of both you and your spouse for the year, reduced by the following two amounts.

    a. Your spouse's IRA contribution for the year to a traditional IRA.

    b. Any contribution for the year to a Roth IRA on behalf of your spouse.

This means that the total combined contributions that can be made for the year to your IRA and your spouse's IRA can be as much as $11,000 ($12,000 if only one of you is 50 or older, or $13,000 if both of you are 50 or older).

When Can Contributions Be Made?

As soon as you open your traditional IRA, contributions can be made to it through your chosen sponsor (trustee or other administrator). Contributions must be in the form of money (cash, check, or money order). Property can't be contributed.

Contributions must be made by due date. Contributions can be made to your traditional IRA for a year at any time during the year or by the due date for filing your return for that year, not including extensions.

Age 70½ rule. Contributions can't be made to your traditional IRA for the year in which you reach age 70½ or for any later year.

You attain age 70½ on the date that is 6 calendar months after the 70th anniversary of your birth. If you were born on or before June 30, 1947, you can't contribute for 2018 or any later year.

Designating year for which contribution is made. If an amount is contributed to your traditional IRA between January 1 and April 15, you should tell the sponsor which year (the current year or the previous year) the contribution is for. If you don't tell the sponsor which year it is for, the sponsor can assume, and report to the IRS, that the contribution is for the current year (the year the sponsor received it).

Filing before a contribution is made. You can file your return claiming a traditional IRA contribution before the contribution is actually made. Generally, the contribution must be made by the due date of your return, not including extensions.

Contributions not required. You don't have to contribute to your traditional IRA for every tax year, even if you can.

How Much Can You Deduct?

Generally, you can deduct the lesser of:

- The contributions to your traditional IRA for the year, or

- The general limit (or the Kay Bailey Hutchison Spousal IRA limit, if it applies).

However, if you or your spouse was covered by an employer retirement plan, you may not be able to deduct this amount. See *Limit if Covered by Employer Plan*, later.

 You may be able to claim a credit for contributions to your traditional IRA. For more information, see chapter 37.

Trustees' fees. Trustees' administrative fees that are billed separately and paid in connection with your traditional IRA aren't deductible as IRA contributions. You are also not able to deduct these fees as an itemized deduction.

Brokers' commissions. Brokers' commissions are part of your IRA contribution and, as such, are deductible subject to the limits.

Full deduction. If neither you nor your spouse was covered for any part of the year by an employer retirement plan, you can take a deduction for total contributions to one or more traditional IRAs of up to the lesser of:

- $5,500 ($6,500 if you are age 50 or older in 2018), or

- 100% of your compensation.

This limit is reduced by any contributions made to a 501(c)(18) plan on your behalf.

Kay Bailey Hutchison Spousal IRA. In the case of a married couple with unequal compensation who file a joint return, the deduction for contributions to the traditional IRA of the spouse with less compensation is limited to the lesser of the following amounts.

1. $5,500 ($6,500 if the spouse with the lower compensation is age 50 or older in 2018).

2. The total compensation includible in the gross income of both spouses for the year reduced by the following three amounts.

   a. The IRA deduction for the year of the spouse with the greater compensation.

   b. Any designated nondeductible contribution for the year made on behalf of the spouse with the greater compensation.

   c. Any contributions for the year to a Roth IRA on behalf of the spouse with the greater compensation.

This limit is reduced by any contributions to a 501(c)(18) plan on behalf of the spouse with the lesser compensation.

Note. If you were divorced or legally separated (and didn't remarry) before the end of the year, you can't deduct any contributions to your spouse's IRA. After a divorce or legal separation, you can deduct only contributions to your own IRA. Your deductions are subject to the rules for single individuals.

Covered by an employer retirement plan. If you or your spouse was covered by an employer retirement plan at any time during the year for which contributions were made, your deduction may be further limited. This is discussed later under *Limit if Covered by Employer Plan*. Limits on the amount you can deduct don't affect the amount that can be contributed. See *Nondeductible Contributions*, later.

Are You Covered by an Employer Plan?

The Form W-2 you receive from your employer has a box used to indicate whether you were covered for the year. The "Retirement plan" box should be checked if you were covered.

Reservists and volunteer firefighters should also see *Situations in Which You Aren't Covered by an Employer Plan*, later.

If you aren't certain whether you were covered by your employer's retirement plan, you should ask your employer.

Federal judges. For purposes of the IRA deduction, federal judges are covered by an employer retirement plan.

For Which Year(s) Are You Covered?

Special rules apply to determine the tax years for which you are covered by an employer plan. These rules differ depending on whether the plan is a defined contribution plan or a defined benefit plan.

Tax year. Your tax year is the annual accounting period you use to keep records and report income and expenses on your income tax return. For almost all people, the tax year is the calendar year.

Defined contribution plan. Generally, you are covered by a defined contribution plan for a tax year if amounts are contributed or allocated to your account for the plan year that ends with or within that tax year.

A defined contribution plan is a plan that provides for a separate account for each person covered by the plan. Types of defined contribution plans include profit-sharing plans, stock bonus plans, and money purchase pension plans. For additional information, see Pub. 590-A.

Defined benefit plan. If you are eligible to participate in your employer's defined benefit plan for the plan year that ends within your tax year, you are covered by the plan. This rule applies even if you:

- Declined to participate in the plan,

- Didn't make a required contribution, or

- Didn't perform the minimum service required to accrue a benefit for the year.

A defined benefit plan is any plan that isn't a defined contribution plan. In a defined benefit plan, the level of benefits to be provided to each participant is spelled out in the plan. The plan administrator figures the amount needed to provide those benefits and those amounts are contributed to the plan. Defined benefit plans include pension plans and annuity plans.

No vested interest. If you accrue a benefit for a plan year, you are covered by that plan even if you have no vested interest in (legal right to) the accrual.

Situations in Which You Aren't Covered

Unless you are covered under another employer plan, you aren't covered by an employer plan if you are in one of the situations described below.

Social security or railroad retirement. Coverage under social security or railroad retirement isn't coverage under an employer retirement plan.

Benefits from a previous employer's plan. If you receive retirement benefits from a previous employer's plan, you aren't covered by that plan.

Reservists. If the only reason you participate in a plan is because you are a member of a reserve unit of the U.S. Armed Forces, you may not be covered by the plan. You aren't covered by the plan if both of the following conditions are met.

1. The plan you participate in is established for its employees by:

   a. The United States,

   b. A state or political subdivision of a state, or

   c. An instrumentality of either (a) or (b) above.

2. You didn't serve more than 90 days on active duty during the year (not counting duty for training).

Volunteer firefighters. If the only reason you participate in a plan is because you are a volunteer firefighter, you may not be covered by the plan. You aren't covered by the plan if both of the following conditions are met.

1. The plan you participate in is established for its employees by:

   a. The United States,

   b. A state or political subdivision of a state, or

   c. An instrumentality of either (a) or (b) above.

2. Your accrued retirement benefits at the beginning of the year won't provide more than $1,800 per year at retirement.

Limit if Covered by Employer Plan

If either you or your spouse was covered by an employer retirement plan, you may be entitled

Table 17-1. Effect of Modified AGI[1] on Deduction if You Are Covered by Retirement Plan at Work

If you are covered by a retirement plan at work, use this table to determine if your modified AGI affects the amount of your deduction.

IF your filing status is...	AND your modified AGI is...	THEN you can take...
Single	$63,000 or less	a full deduction.
or	more than $63,000 but less than $73,000	a partial deduction.
Head of household	$73,000 or more	no deduction.
Married filing jointly	$101,000 or less	a full deduction.
or	more than $101,000 but less than $121,000	a partial deduction.
Qualifying widow(er)	$121,000 or more	no deduction.
Married filing separately[2]	less than $10,000	a partial deduction.
	$10,000 or more	no deduction.

[1] Modified AGI (adjusted gross income). See *Modified adjusted gross income (AGI)*, later.

[2] If you didn't live with your spouse at any time during the year, your filing status is considered Single for this purpose (therefore, your IRA deduction is determined under the "Single" column).

Table 17-2. Effect of Modified AGI[1] on Deduction if You Are NOT Covered by Retirement Plan at Work

If you aren't covered by a retirement plan at work, use this table to determine if your modified AGI affects the amount of your deduction.

IF your filing status is...	AND your modified AGI is...	THEN you can take...
Single, **Head of household,** or **Qualifying widow(er)**	any amount	a full deduction.
Married filing jointly or **separately** with a spouse who **isn't** covered by a plan at work	any amount	a full deduction.
Married filing jointly with a spouse who **is** covered by a plan at work	$189,000 or less	a full deduction.
	more than $189,000 but less than $199,000	a partial deduction.
	$199,000 or more	no deduction.
Married filing separately with a spouse who **is** covered by a plan at work[2]	less than $10,000	a partial deduction.
	$10,000 or more	no deduction.

[1] Modified AGI (adjusted gross income). See *Modified adjusted gross income (AGI)*, later.

[2] You are entitled to the full deduction if you didn't live with your spouse at any time during the year.

to only a partial (reduced) deduction or no deduction at all, depending on your income and your filing status.

Your deduction begins to decrease (phase out) when your income rises above a certain amount and is eliminated altogether when it reaches a higher amount. These amounts vary depending on your filing status.

To determine if your deduction is subject to phaseout, you must determine your modified AGI and your filing status. See *Filing status* and *Modified adjusted gross income (AGI)*, later. Then use Table 17-1 or Table 17-2 to determine if the phaseout applies.

Social security recipients. Instead of using Table 17-1 or Table 17-2, use the worksheets in Appendix B of Pub. 590-A if, for the year, all of the following apply.

- You received social security benefits.
- You received taxable compensation.

- Contributions were made to your traditional IRA.
- You or your spouse was covered by an employer retirement plan.

Use those worksheets to figure your IRA deduction, your nondeductible contribution, and the taxable portion, if any, of your social security benefits.

Deduction phaseout. If you are covered by an employer retirement plan and you didn't receive any social security retirement benefits, your IRA deduction may be reduced or eliminated depending on your filing status and modified AGI as shown in Table 17-1.

If your spouse is covered. If you aren't covered by an employer retirement plan, but your spouse is, and you didn't receive any social security benefits, your IRA deduction may be reduced or eliminated entirely depending on your filing status and modified AGI as shown in Table 17-2.

Filing status. Your filing status depends primarily on your marital status. For this purpose, you need to know if your filing status is single or head of household, married filing jointly or qualifying widow(er), or married filing separately. If you need more information on filing status, see chapter 2.

Lived apart from spouse. If you didn't live with your spouse at any time during the year and you file a separate return, your filing status, for this purpose, is single.

Modified adjusted gross income (AGI). You may be able to use Worksheet 17-1 to figure your modified AGI. However, if you made contributions to your IRA for 2018 and received a distribution from your IRA in 2018, see Pub. 590-A.

 Don't assume that your modified AGI is the same as your compensation. Your modified AGI may include income in addition to your compensation (discussed earlier), such as interest, dividends, and income from IRA distributions.

When filing Form 1040, refigure the AGI amount on line 7 without taking into account any of the following amounts.

- IRA deduction.
- Student loan interest deduction.
- Domestic production activities deduction.
- Foreign earned income exclusion.
- Foreign housing exclusion or deduction.
- Exclusion of qualified savings bond interest shown on Form 8815, Exclusion of Interest From Series EE and I U.S. Savings Bonds Issued After 1989.
- Exclusion of employer-provided adoption benefits shown on Form 8839, Qualified Adoption Expenses.

This is your modified AGI.

Worksheet 17-1. Figuring Your Modified AGI

Use this worksheet to figure your modified adjusted gross income for traditional IRA purposes.

1.	Enter your adjusted gross income (AGI) from Form 1040, line 7, figured without taking into account the amount from Schedule 1 (Form 1040), line 32	1. _____
2.	Enter any student loan interest deduction from Schedule 1 (Form 1040), line 33	2. _____
3.	Enter any domestic production activities deduction from Schedule 1 (Form 1040), line 36	3. _____
4.	Enter any foreign earned income and/or housing exclusion from Form 2555, line 45, or Form 2555-EZ, line 18	4. _____
5.	Enter any foreign housing deduction from Form 2555, line 50	5. _____
6.	Enter any excludable savings bond interest from Form 8815, line 14	6. _____
7.	Enter any excluded employer-provided adoption benefits from Form 8839, line 28	7. _____
8.	Add lines 1 through 7. This is your **modified AGI** for traditional IRA purposes	8. _____

Both contributions for 2018 and distributions in 2018. If all three of the following apply, any IRA distributions you received in 2018 may be partly tax free and partly taxable.

- You received distributions in 2018 from one or more traditional IRAs.

- You made contributions to a traditional IRA for 2018.

- Some of those contributions may be nondeductible contributions.

If this is your situation, you must figure the taxable part of the traditional IRA distribution before you can figure your modified AGI. To do this, you can use Worksheet 1-1, Figuring the Taxable Part of Your IRA Distribution, in Pub. 590-B.

If at least one of the above doesn't apply, figure your modified AGI using Worksheet 17-1.

How to figure your reduced IRA deduction. You can figure your reduced IRA deduction for Form 1040 by using the worksheets in chapter 1 of Pub. 590-A. Also, the Instructions for Form 1040 include similar worksheets that you may be able to use instead.

Reporting Deductible Contributions

When filing Form 1040, enter your IRA deduction on Schedule 1 (Form 1040), line 32.

Nondeductible Contributions

Although your deduction for IRA contributions may be reduced or eliminated, contributions can be made to your IRA up to the *general limit* or, if it applies, the *Kay Bailey Hutchison Spousal IRA limit*. The difference between your total permitted contributions and your IRA deduction, if any, is your nondeductible contribution.

Example. Mike is 30 years old and single. In 2018, he was covered by a retirement plan at work. His salary was $67,000. His modified AGI was $80,000. Mike made a $5,500 IRA contribution for 2018. Because he was covered by a retirement plan and his modified AGI was over $73,000, he can't deduct his $5,500 IRA contribution. He must designate this contribution as a

nondeductible contribution by reporting it on Form 8606, as explained next.

Form 8606. To designate contributions as nondeductible, you must file Form 8606.

You don't have to designate a contribution as nondeductible until you file your tax return. When you file, you can even designate otherwise deductible contributions as nondeductible.

You must file Form 8606 to report nondeductible contributions even if you don't have to file a tax return for the year.

 A Form 8606 isn't used for the year that you make a rollover from a qualified retirement plan to a traditional IRA and the rollover includes nontaxable amounts. In those situations, a Form 8606 is completed for the year you take a distribution from that IRA. See Form 8606 *under Distributions Fully or Partly Taxable, later.*

Failure to report nondeductible contributions. If you don't report nondeductible contributions, all of the contributions to your traditional IRA will be treated as deductible contributions when withdrawn. All distributions from your IRA will be taxed unless you can show, with satisfactory evidence, that nondeductible contributions were made.

Penalty for overstatement. If you overstate the amount of nondeductible contributions on your Form 8606 for any tax year, you must pay a penalty of $100 for each overstatement, unless it was due to reasonable cause.

Penalty for failure to file Form 8606. You will have to pay a $50 penalty if you don't file a required Form 8606, unless you can prove that the failure was due to reasonable cause.

Tax on earnings on nondeductible contributions. As long as contributions are within the contribution limits, none of the earnings or gains on contributions (deductible or nondeductible) will be taxed until they are distributed. See *When Can You Withdraw or Use IRA Assets,* later.

Cost basis. You will have a cost basis in your traditional IRA if you made any nondeductible contributions. Your cost basis is the sum of the nondeductible contributions to your IRA minus any withdrawals or distributions of nondeductible contributions.

Inherited IRAs

If you inherit a traditional IRA, you are called a beneficiary. A beneficiary can be any person or entity the owner chooses to receive the benefits of the IRA after he or she dies. Beneficiaries of a traditional IRA must include in their gross income any taxable distributions they receive.

Inherited from spouse. If you inherit a traditional IRA from your spouse, you generally have the following three choices. You can do one of the following:

1. Treat it as your own IRA by designating yourself as the account owner.

2. Treat it as your own by rolling it over into your IRA, or to the extent it is taxable, into a:

   a. Qualified employer plan,

   b. Qualified employee annuity plan (section 403(a) plan),

   c. Tax-sheltered annuity plan (section 403(b) plan), or

   d. Deferred compensation plan of a state or local government (section 457 plan).

3. Treat yourself as the beneficiary rather than treating the IRA as your own.

Treating it as your own. You will be considered to have chosen to treat the IRA as your own if:

- Contributions (including rollover contributions) are made to the inherited IRA, or

- You don't take the required minimum distribution for a year as a beneficiary of the IRA.

You will only be considered to have chosen to treat the IRA as your own if:

- You are the sole beneficiary of the IRA, and

- You have an unlimited right to withdraw amounts from it.

However, if you receive a distribution from your deceased spouse's IRA, you can roll that distribution over into your own IRA within the 60-day time limit, as long as the distribution isn't a required distribution, even if you aren't the sole beneficiary of your deceased spouse's IRA.

Inherited from someone other than spouse. If you inherit a traditional IRA from anyone other than your deceased spouse, you can't treat the inherited IRA as your own. This means that you can't make any contributions to the IRA. It also means you can't roll over any amounts into or out of the inherited IRA. However, you can make a trustee-to-trustee transfer as long as the IRA into which amounts are being moved is set up and maintained in the name of the deceased IRA owner for the benefit of you as beneficiary.

For more information, see the discussion of Inherited IRAs under *Rollover From One IRA Into Another*, later.

Can You Move Retirement Plan Assets?

You can transfer, tax free, assets (money or property) from other retirement plans (including traditional IRAs) to a traditional IRA. You can make the following kinds of transfers.

- Transfers from one trustee to another.
- Rollovers.
- Transfers incident to a divorce.

Transfers to Roth IRAs. Under certain conditions, you can move assets from a traditional IRA or from a designated Roth account to a Roth IRA. You can also move assets from a qualified retirement plan to a Roth IRA. See *Can You Move Amounts Into a Roth IRA?* under *Roth IRAs*, later.

Trustee-to-Trustee Transfer

A transfer of funds in your traditional IRA from one trustee directly to another, either at your request or at the trustee's request, isn't a rollover. This includes the situation where the current trustee issues a check to the new trustee, but gives it to you to deposit. Because there is no distribution to you, the transfer is tax free. Because it isn't a rollover, it isn't affected by the 1-year waiting period required between rollovers, discussed later under *Rollover From One IRA Into Another*. For information about direct transfers to IRAs from retirement plans other than IRAs, see *Can You Move Retirement Plan Assets?* in chapter 1 and *Can You Move Amounts Into a Roth IRA?* in chapter 2 of Pub. 590-A.

Rollovers

Generally, a rollover is a tax-free distribution to you of cash or other assets from one retirement plan that you contribute (roll over) to another retirement plan. The contribution to the second retirement plan is called a "rollover contribution."

Note. An amount rolled over tax free from one retirement plan to another is generally includible in income when it is distributed from the second plan.

Kinds of rollovers to a traditional IRA. You can roll over amounts from the following plans into a traditional IRA.

- A traditional IRA.

- An employer's qualified retirement plan for its employees.
- A deferred compensation plan of a state or local government (section 457 plan).
- A tax-sheltered annuity plan (section 403(b) plan).

Treatment of rollovers. You can't deduct a rollover contribution, but you must report the rollover distribution on your tax return as discussed later under *Reporting rollovers from IRAs* and under *Reporting rollovers from employer plans*.

Rollover notice. A written explanation of rollover treatment must be given to you by the plan (other than an IRA) making the distribution. See Written explanation to recipients, in Pub. 590-A.

Kinds of rollovers from a traditional IRA. You may be able to roll over, tax free, a distribution from your traditional IRA into a qualified plan. These plans include the federal Thrift Savings Fund (for federal employees), deferred compensation plans of state or local governments (section 457 plans), and tax-sheltered annuity plans (section 403(b) plans). The part of the distribution that you can roll over is the part that would otherwise be taxable (includible in your income). Qualified plans may, but aren't required to, accept such rollovers.

Time limit for making a rollover contribution. You generally must make the rollover contribution by the 60th day after the day you receive the distribution from your traditional IRA or your employer's plan.

The IRS may waive the 60-day requirement where the failure to do so would be against equity or good conscience, such as in the event of a casualty, disaster, or other event beyond your reasonable control. For more information, see *Can You Move Retirement Plan Assets?* in chapter 1 of Pub. 590-A.

Extension of rollover period. If an amount distributed to you from a traditional IRA or a qualified employer retirement plan is a frozen deposit at any time during the 60-day period allowed for a rollover, special rules extend the rollover period. For more information, see *Can You Move Retirement Plan Assets?* in chapter 1 of Pub. 590-A.

Rollover From One IRA Into Another

You can withdraw, tax free, all or part of the assets from one traditional IRA if you reinvest them within 60 days in the same or another traditional IRA. Because this is a rollover, you can't deduct the amount that you reinvest in an IRA.

Waiting period between rollovers. Generally, if you make a tax-free rollover of any part of a distribution from a traditional IRA, you can't, within a 1-year period, make a tax-free rollover of any later distribution from that same IRA. You also can't make a tax-free rollover of any amount distributed, within the same 1-year period, from the IRA into which you made the tax-free rollover.

The 1-year period begins on the date you receive the IRA distribution, not on the date you roll it over into an IRA. Rules apply to the number of rollovers you can have with your traditional IRAs. See *Application of one-rollover limitation*, next.

Application of one-rollover limitation. You can make only one rollover from an IRA to another (or the same) IRA in any 1-year period, regardless of the number of IRAs you own. The limit applies by aggregating all of an individual's IRAs, including SEP and SIMPLE IRAs, as well as traditional and Roth IRAs, effectively treating them as one IRA for purposes of the limit. However, trustee-to-trustee transfers between IRAs aren't limited and rollovers from traditional IRAs to Roth IRAs (conversions) aren't limited.

Example. John has three traditional IRAs: IRA-1, IRA-2, and IRA-3. John didn't take any distributions from his IRAs in 2018. On January 1, 2019, John took a distribution from IRA-1 and rolled it over into IRA-2 on the same day. For 2019, John can't roll over any other 2019 IRA distribution, including a rollover distribution involving IRA-3. This wouldn't apply to a trustee-to-trustee transfer or a Roth IRA conversion.

Partial rollovers. If you withdraw assets from a traditional IRA, you can roll over part of the withdrawal tax free and keep the rest of it. The amount you keep will generally be taxable (except for the part that is a return of nondeductible contributions). The amount you keep may be subject to the 10% additional tax on early distributions, discussed later under *What Acts Result in Penalties or Additional Taxes*.

Required distributions. Amounts that must be distributed during a particular year under the required minimum distribution rules (discussed later) aren't eligible for rollover treatment.

Inherited IRAs. If you inherit a traditional IRA from your spouse, you generally can roll it over, or you can choose to make the inherited IRA your own. See *Treating it as your own*, earlier.

Not inherited from spouse. If you inherit a traditional IRA from someone other than your spouse, you can't roll it over or allow it to receive a rollover contribution. You must withdraw the IRA assets within a certain period. For more information, see *When Must You Withdraw Assets? (Required Minimum Distributions)* in chapter 1 of Pub. 590-B.

Reporting rollovers from IRAs. Report any rollover from one traditional IRA to the same or another traditional IRA on Form 1040 as follows.

Enter the total amount of the distribution on Form 1040, line 4a. If the total amount on Form 1040, line 4a, was rolled over, enter zero on Form 1040, line 4b. If the total distribution wasn't rolled over, enter the taxable portion of the part that wasn't rolled over on Form 1040, line 4b. Put "Rollover" next to Form 1040, line 4b. For more information, see the Form 1040 instructions.

If you rolled over the distribution into a qualified plan (other than an IRA) or you make the rollover in 2019, attach a statement explaining what you did.

Rollover From Employer's Plan Into an IRA

You can roll over into a traditional IRA all or part of an eligible rollover distribution you receive from your (or your deceased spouse's):

- Employer's qualified pension, profit-sharing, or stock bonus plan;
- Annuity plan;
- Tax-sheltered annuity plan (section 403(b) plan); or
- Governmental deferred compensation plan (section 457 plan).

A qualified plan is one that meets the requirements of the Internal Revenue Code.

Eligible rollover distribution. Generally, an eligible rollover distribution is any distribution of all or part of the balance to your credit in a qualified retirement plan except the following.

1. A required minimum distribution (explained later under *When Must You Withdraw IRA Assets? (Required Minimum Distributions)*).
2. A hardship distribution.
3. Any of a series of substantially equal periodic distributions paid at least once a year over:
   a. Your lifetime or life expectancy,
   b. The lifetimes or life expectancies of you and your beneficiary, or
   c. A period of 10 years or more.
4. Corrective distributions of excess contributions or excess deferrals, and any income allocable to the excess, or of excess annual additions and any allocable gains.
5. A loan treated as a distribution because it doesn't satisfy certain requirements either when made or later (such as upon default), unless the participant's accrued benefits are reduced (offset) to repay the loan. For more information, see the discussion for Plan loan offsets, under *Time Limit for Making a Rollover Contribution*, in Pub. 590-A.
6. Dividends on employer securities.
7. The cost of life insurance coverage.

Your rollover into a traditional IRA may include both amounts that would be taxable and amounts that wouldn't be taxable if they were distributed to you, but not rolled over. To the extent the distribution is rolled over into a traditional IRA, it isn't includible in your income.

 Any nontaxable amounts that you roll over into your traditional IRA become part of your basis (cost) in your IRAs. To recover your basis when you take distributions from your IRA, you must complete Form 8606 for the year of the distribution. See Form 8606 under Distributions Fully or Partly Taxable, *later.*

Rollover by nonspouse beneficiary. A direct transfer from a deceased employee's qualified pension, profit-sharing, or stock bonus plan; annuity plan; tax-sheltered annuity (section 403(b)) plan; or governmental deferred com-

pensation (section 457) plan to an IRA set up to receive the distribution on your behalf can be treated as an eligible rollover distribution if you are the designated beneficiary of the plan and not the employee's spouse. The IRA is treated as an inherited IRA. For more information about inherited IRAs, see *Inherited IRAs*, earlier.

Reporting rollovers from employer plans. Enter the total distribution (before income tax or other deductions were withheld) on Form 1040, line 4a. This amount should be shown in box 1 of Form 1099-R. From this amount, subtract any contributions (usually shown in box 5 of Form 1099-R) that were taxable to you when made. From that result, subtract the amount that was rolled over either directly or within 60 days of receiving the distribution. Enter the remaining amount, even if zero, on Form 1040, line 4b. Also, enter "Rollover" next to Form 1040, line 4b.

Transfers Incident to Divorce

If an interest in a traditional IRA is transferred from your spouse or former spouse to you by a divorce or separate maintenance decree or a written document related to such a decree, the interest in the IRA, starting from the date of the transfer, is treated as your IRA. The transfer is tax free. For detailed information, see *Distributions under divorce or similar proceedings (alternate payees)* under *Rollover From Employer's Plan Into an IRA* in Pub. 590-A.

Converting From Any Traditional IRA to a Roth IRA

Allowable conversions. You can withdraw all or part of the assets from a traditional IRA and reinvest them (within 60 days) in a Roth IRA. The amount that you withdraw and timely contribute (convert) to the Roth IRA is called a conversion contribution. If properly (and timely) rolled over, the 10% additional tax on early distributions won't apply. However, a part or all of the conversion from your traditional IRA is included in your gross income.

Required distributions. You can't convert amounts that must be distributed from your traditional IRA for a particular year (including the calendar year in which you reach age 70½) under the required minimum distribution rules (discussed later).

Income. You must include in your gross income distributions from a traditional IRA that you would have had to include in income if you hadn't converted them into a Roth IRA. These amounts are normally included in income on your return for the year that you converted them from a traditional IRA to a Roth IRA.

You don't include in gross income any part of a distribution from a traditional IRA that is a return of your basis, as discussed later.

You must file Form 8606 to report 2018 conversions from traditional, SEP, or SIMPLE IRAs to a Roth IRA in 2018 (unless you recharacterized the entire amount) and to figure the amount to include in income.

If you must include any amount in your gross income, you may have to increase your withholding or make estimated tax payments. See chapter 4.

Recharacterizations

You may be able to treat a contribution made to one type of IRA as having been made to a different type of IRA. This is called recharacterizing the contribution. See *Can You Move Retirement Plan Assets?* in chapter 1 of Pub. 590-A for more detailed information.

How to recharacterize a contribution. To recharacterize a contribution, you generally must have the contribution transferred from the first IRA (the one to which it was made) to the second IRA in a trustee-to-trustee transfer. If the transfer is made by the due date (including extensions) for your tax return for the year during which the contribution was made, you can elect to treat the contribution as having been originally made to the second IRA instead of to the first IRA. If you recharacterize your contribution, you must do all three of the following.

- Include in the transfer any net income allocable to the contribution. If there was a loss, the net income you must transfer may be a negative amount.
- Report the recharacterization on your tax return for the year during which the contribution was made.
- Treat the contribution as having been made to the second IRA on the date that it was actually made to the first IRA.

No recharacterizations of conversions made in 2018 or later. A conversion of a traditional IRA to a Roth IRA, and a rollover from any other eligible retirement plan to a Roth IRA, made in tax years beginning after December 31, 2017, can't be recharacterized as having been made to a traditional IRA. If you made a conversion in the 2017 tax year, you have until the due date (with extensions) for filing the return for that tax year to recharacterize it.

No deduction allowed. You can't deduct the contribution to the first IRA. Any net income you transfer with the recharacterized contribution is treated as earned in the second IRA.

How do you recharacterize a contribution? To recharacterize a contribution, you must notify both the trustee of the first IRA (the one to which the contribution was actually made) and the trustee of the second IRA (the one to which the contribution is being moved) that you have elected to treat the contribution as having been made to the second IRA rather than the first. You must make the notifications by the date of the transfer. Only one notification is required if both IRAs are maintained by the same trustee. The notification(s) must include all of the following information.

- The type and amount of the contribution to the first IRA that is to be recharacterized.
- The date on which the contribution was made to the first IRA and the year for which it was made.
- A direction to the trustee of the first IRA to transfer in a trustee-to-trustee transfer the amount of the contribution and any net income (or loss) allocable to the contribution to the trustee of the second IRA.
- The name of the trustee of the first IRA and the name of the trustee of the second IRA.

- Any additional information needed to make the transfer.

Reporting a recharacterization. If you elect to recharacterize a contribution to one IRA as a contribution to another IRA, you must report the recharacterization on your tax return as directed by Form 8606 and its instructions. You must treat the contribution as having been made to the second IRA.

When Can You Withdraw or Use IRA Assets?

There are rules limiting use of your IRA assets and distributions from it. Violation of the rules generally results in additional taxes in the year of violation. See *What Acts Result in Penalties or Additional Taxes*, later.

Contributions returned before the due date of return. If you made IRA contributions in 2018, you can withdraw them tax free by the due date of your return. If you have an extension of time to file your return, you can withdraw them tax free by the extended due date. You can do this if, for each contribution you withdraw, both of the following conditions apply.

- You didn't take a deduction for the contribution.

- You withdraw any interest or other income earned on the contribution. You can take into account any loss on the contribution while it was in the IRA when figuring the amount that must be withdrawn. If there was a loss, the net income earned on the contribution may be a negative amount.

Note. To figure the amount you must withdraw, see Worksheet 1-4 under *When Can You Withdraw or Use Assets?* in chapter 1 of Pub. 590-A.

Earnings includible in income. You must include in income any earnings on the contributions you withdraw. Include the earnings in income for the year in which you made the contributions, not in the year in which you withdraw them.

 Generally, except for any part of a withdrawal that is a return of nondeductible contributions (basis), any withdrawal of your contributions after the due date (or extended due date) of your return will be treated as a taxable distribution. Excess contributions can also be recovered tax free as discussed under What Acts Result in Penalties or Additional Taxes, *later.*

Early distributions tax. The 10% additional tax on distributions made before you reach age 59½ doesn't apply to these tax-free withdrawals of your contributions. However, the distribution of interest or other income must be reported on Form 5329 and, unless the distribution qualifies as an exception to the age 59½ rule, it will be subject to this tax. See *Early Distributions* under *What Acts Result in Penalties or Additional Taxes*, in Pub. 590-B.

When Must You Withdraw IRA Assets? (Required Minimum Distributions)

You can't keep funds in a traditional IRA indefinitely. Eventually, they must be distributed. If there are no distributions, or if the distributions aren't large enough, you may have to pay a 50% excise tax on the amount not distributed as required. See *Excess Accumulations (Insufficient Distributions)*, later. The requirements for distributing IRA funds differ depending on whether you are the IRA owner or the beneficiary of a decedent's IRA.

Required minimum distribution. The amount that must be distributed each year is referred to as the required minimum distribution.

Distributions not eligible for rollover. Amounts that must be distributed (required minimum distributions) during a particular year aren't eligible for rollover treatment.

IRA owners. If you are the owner of a traditional IRA, you generally must start receiving distributions from your IRA by April 1 of the year following the year in which you reach age 70½. April 1 of the year following the year in which you reach age 70½ is referred to as the required beginning date.

Distributions by the required beginning date. You must receive at least a minimum amount for each year starting with the year you reach age 70½ (your 70½ year). If you don't (or didn't) receive that minimum amount in your 70½ year, then you must receive distributions for your 70½ year by April 1 of the next year.

If an IRA owner dies after reaching age 70½, but before April 1 of the next year, no minimum distribution is required because death occurred before the required beginning date.

 Even if you begin receiving distributions before you attain age 70½, you must begin figuring and receiving required minimum distributions by your required beginning date.

Distributions after the required beginning date. The required minimum distribution for any year after the year you turn age 70½ must be made by December 31 of that later year.

Beneficiaries. If you are the beneficiary of a decedent's traditional IRA, the requirements for distributions from that IRA generally depend on whether the IRA owner died before or after the required beginning date for distributions.

More information. For more information, including how to figure your minimum required distribution each year and how to figure your required distribution if you are a beneficiary of a decedent's IRA, see *When Must You Withdraw Assets? (Required Minimum Distributions)* in chapter 1 of Pub. 590-B.

Are Distributions Taxable?

In general, distributions from a traditional IRA are taxable in the year you receive them.

Exceptions. Exceptions to distributions from traditional IRAs being taxable in the year you receive them are:

- Rollovers;
- Qualified charitable distributions (QCDs), discussed later;
- Tax-free withdrawals of contributions; discussed earlier, and
- The return of nondeductible contributions, discussed later under *Distributions Fully or Partly Taxable*.

 Although a conversion of a traditional IRA is considered a rollover for Roth IRA purposes, it isn't an exception to the rule that distributions from a traditional IRA are taxable in the year you receive them. Conversion distributions are includible in your gross income subject to this rule and the special rules for conversions explained in Converting From Any Traditional IRA Into a Roth IRA *under* Can You Move Retirement Plan Assets? *in chapter 1 of Pub. 590-A.*

Qualified charitable distributions (QCDs). A QCD is generally a nontaxable distribution made directly by the trustee of your IRA to an organization eligible to receive tax deductible contributions. See *Qualified Charitable Distributions* in Pub. 590-B for more information.

Ordinary income. Distributions from traditional IRAs that you include in income are taxed as ordinary income.

No special treatment. In figuring your tax, you can't use the 10-year tax option or capital gain treatment that applies to lump-sum distributions from qualified retirement plans.

Distributions Fully or Partly Taxable

Distributions from your traditional IRA may be fully or partly taxable, depending on whether your IRA includes any nondeductible contributions.

Fully taxable. If only deductible contributions were made to your traditional IRA (or IRAs, if you have more than one), you have no basis in your IRA. Because you have no basis in your IRA, any distributions are fully taxable when received. See *Reporting taxable distributions on your return*, later.

Partly taxable. If you made nondeductible contributions or rolled over any after-tax amounts to any of your traditional IRAs, you have a cost basis (investment in the contract) equal to the amount of those contributions. These nondeductible contributions aren't taxed when they are distributed to you. They are a return of your investment in your IRA.

Only the part of the distribution that represents nondeductible contributions and rolled over after-tax amounts (your cost basis) is tax free. If nondeductible contributions have been made or after-tax amounts have been rolled over to your IRA, distributions consist partly of nondeductible contributions (basis) and partly of deductible contributions, earnings, and gains (if there are any). Until all of your basis has been distributed, each distribution is partly nontaxable and partly taxable.

Form 8606. You must complete Form 8606 and attach it to your return if you receive a distribution from a traditional IRA and have ever made nondeductible contributions or rolled over after-tax amounts to any of your traditional IRAs. Using the form, you will figure the nontaxable distributions for 2018 and your total IRA basis for 2018 and earlier years.

Note. If you are required to file Form 8606, but you aren't required to file an income tax return, you still must file Form 8606. Send it to the IRS at the time and place you would otherwise file an income tax return.

Distributions reported on Form 1099-R. If you receive a distribution from your traditional IRA, you will receive Form 1099-R, Distributions From Pensions, Annuities, Retirement or Profit-Sharing Plans, IRAs, Insurance Contracts, etc., or a similar statement. IRA distributions are shown in boxes 1 and 2a of Form 1099-R. The number or letter codes in box 7 tell you what type of distribution you received from your IRA.

Withholding. Federal income tax is withheld from distributions from traditional IRAs unless you choose not to have tax withheld. See chapter 4.

IRA distributions delivered outside the United States. In general, if you are a U.S. citizen or resident alien and your home address is outside the United States or its possessions, you can't choose exemption from withholding on distributions from your traditional IRA.

Reporting taxable distributions on your return. Report fully taxable distributions, including early distributions, on Form 1040, line 4b (no entry is required on Form 1040, line 4a). If only part of the distribution is taxable, enter the total amount on Form 1040, line 4a, and the taxable part on Form 1040, line 4b.

What Acts Result in Penalties or Additional Taxes?

The tax advantages of using traditional IRAs for retirement savings can be offset by additional taxes and penalties if you don't follow the rules.

There are additions to the regular tax for using your IRA funds in prohibited transactions. There are also additional taxes for the following activities.

- Investing in collectibles.
- Having unrelated business income, see Pub. 590-B.
- Making excess contributions.
- Taking early distributions.
- Allowing excess amounts to accumulate (failing to take required distributions).

There are penalties for overstating the amount of nondeductible contributions and for failure to file a Form 8606, if required.

Prohibited Transactions

Generally, a prohibited transaction is any improper use of your traditional IRA by you, your beneficiary, or any disqualified person.

Disqualified persons include your fiduciary and members of your family (spouse, ancestor, lineal descendent, and any spouse of a lineal descendent).

The following are examples of prohibited transactions with a traditional IRA.

- Borrowing money from it, see Pub. 590-B.
- Selling property to it.
- Using it as security for a loan.
- Buying property for personal use (present or future) with IRA funds.

Effect on an IRA account. Generally, if you or your beneficiary engages in a prohibited transaction in connection with your traditional IRA account at any time during the year, the account stops being an IRA as of the first day of that year.

Effect on you or your beneficiary. If your account stops being an IRA because you or your beneficiary engaged in a prohibited transaction, the account is treated as distributing all its assets to you at their fair market values on the first day of the year. If the total of those values is more than your basis in the IRA, you will have a taxable gain that is includible in your income. For information on figuring your gain and reporting it in income, see *Are Distributions Taxable*, earlier. The distribution may be subject to additional taxes or penalties.

Taxes on prohibited transactions. If someone other than the owner or beneficiary of a traditional IRA engages in a prohibited transaction, that person may be liable for certain taxes. In general, there is a 15% tax on the amount of the prohibited transaction and a 100% additional tax if the transaction isn't corrected.

More information. For more information on prohibited transactions, see *What Acts Result in Penalties or Additional Taxes?* in chapter 1 of Pub. 590-A.

Investment in Collectibles

If your traditional IRA invests in collectibles, the amount invested is considered distributed to you in the year invested. You may have to pay the 10% additional tax on early distributions, discussed later.

Collectibles. These include:

- Artworks,
- Rugs,
- Antiques,
- Metals,
- Gems,
- Stamps,
- Coins,
- Alcoholic beverages, and
- Certain other tangible personal property.

Exception. Your IRA can invest in one-, one-half-, one-quarter-, or one-tenth-ounce

U.S. gold coins, or one-ounce silver coins minted by the Treasury Department. It can also invest in certain platinum coins and certain gold, silver, palladium, and platinum bullion.

Excess Contributions

Generally, an excess contribution is the amount contributed to your traditional IRA(s) for the year that is more than the smaller of:

- The maximum deductible amount for the year (for 2018, this is $5,500 ($6,500 if you are 50 or older)); or
- Your taxable compensation for the year.

Contributions for the year you reach age 70½ and any later year are also excess contributions.

An excess contribution could be the result of your contribution, your spouse's contribution, your employer's contribution, or an improper rollover contribution. If your employer makes contributions on your behalf to a SEP IRA, see chapter 2 of Pub. 560.

Tax on excess contributions. In general, if the excess contributions for a year aren't withdrawn by the date your return for the year is due (including extensions), you are subject to a 6% tax. You must pay the 6% tax each year on excess amounts that remain in your traditional IRA at the end of your tax year. The tax can't be more than 6% of the combined value of all your IRAs as of the end of your tax year. The additional tax is figured on Form 5329.

Excess contributions withdrawn by due date of return. You won't have to pay the 6% tax if you withdraw an excess contribution made during a tax year and you also withdraw interest or other income earned on the excess contribution. You must complete your withdrawal by the date your tax return for that year is due, including extensions.

How to treat withdrawn contributions. Don't include in your gross income an excess contribution that you withdraw from your traditional IRA before your tax return is due if both the following conditions are met.

- No deduction was allowed for the excess contribution.
- You withdraw the interest or other income earned on the excess contribution.

You can take into account any loss on the contribution while it was in the IRA when figuring the amount that must be withdrawn. If there was a loss, the net income you must withdraw may be a negative amount.

How to treat withdrawn interest or other income. You must include in your gross income the interest or other income that was earned on the excess contribution. Report it on your return for the year in which the excess contribution was made. Your withdrawal of interest or other income may be subject to an additional 10% tax on early distributions, discussed later.

Excess contributions withdrawn after due date of return. In general, you must include all distributions (withdrawals) from your traditional IRA in your gross income. However, if the following conditions are met, you can withdraw excess contributions from your IRA and not include the amount withdrawn in your gross income.

- Total contributions (other than rollover contributions) for 2018 to your IRA weren't more than $5,500 ($6,500 if you are 50 or older).
- You didn't take a deduction for the excess contribution being withdrawn.

The withdrawal can take place at any time, even after the due date, including extensions, for filing your tax return for the year.

Excess contribution deducted in an earlier year. If you deducted an excess contribution in an earlier year for which the total contributions weren't more than the maximum deductible amount for that year (see the following table), you can still remove the excess from your traditional IRA and not include it in your gross income. To do this, file Form 1040X for that year and don't deduct the excess contribution on the amended return. Generally, you can file an amended return within 3 years after you filed your return, or 2 years from the time the tax was paid, whichever is later.

Year(s)	Contribution limit	Contribution limit if age 50 or older at the end of the year
2013 through 2018	$5,500	$6,500
2008 through 2012	$5,000	$6,000
2006 or 2007	$4,000	$5,000
2005	$4,000	$4,500
2002 through 2004	$3,000	$3,500
1997 through 2001	$2,000	—
before 1997	$2,250	—

Excess due to incorrect rollover information. If an excess contribution in your traditional IRA is the result of a rollover and the excess occurred because the information the plan was required to give you was incorrect, you can withdraw the excess contribution. The limits mentioned above are increased by the amount of the excess that is due to the incorrect information. You will have to amend your return for the year in which the excess occurred to correct the reporting of the rollover amounts in that year. Don't include in your gross income the part of the excess contribution caused by the incorrect information. For additional information on Excess Contributions, see Pub. 590-A.

Early Distributions

You must include early distributions of taxable amounts from your traditional IRA in your gross income. Early distributions are also subject to an additional 10% tax. See the discussion of Form 5329 under *Reporting Additional Taxes*, later, to figure and report the tax.

Early distributions defined. Early distributions generally are amounts distributed from your traditional IRA account or annuity before you are age 59 1/2.

Age 59 1/2 rule. Generally, if you are under age 59 1/2, you must pay a 10% additional tax on the distribution of any assets (money or other property) from your traditional IRA. Distributions before you are age 59 1/2 are called early distributions.

The 10% additional tax applies to the part of the distribution that you have to include in gross income. It is in addition to any regular income tax on that amount.

After age 59 1/2 and before age 70 1/2. After you reach age 59 1/2, you can receive distributions without having to pay the 10% additional tax. Even though you can receive distributions after you reach age 59 1/2, distributions aren't required until you reach age 70 1/2. See *When Must You Withdraw IRA Assets? (Required Minimum Distributions)*, earlier.

Exceptions. There are several exceptions to the age 59 1/2 rule. Even if you receive a distribution before you are age 59 1/2, you may not have to pay the 10% additional tax if you are in one of the following situations.

- You have unreimbursed medical expenses that are more than 7.5% of your adjusted gross income.
- The distributions aren't more than the cost of your medical insurance due to a period of unemployment.
- You are totally and permanently disabled.
- You are the beneficiary of a deceased IRA owner.
- You are receiving distributions in the form of an annuity.
- The distributions aren't more than your qualified higher education expenses.
- You use the distributions to buy, build, or rebuild a first home.
- The distribution is due to an IRS levy of the qualified plan.
- The distribution is a qualified reservist distribution.

Most of these exceptions are explained under *Early Distributions* in *What Acts Result in Penalties or Additional Taxes?* in chapter 1 of Pub. 590-B.

Note. Distributions that are timely and properly rolled over, as discussed earlier, aren't subject to either regular income tax or the 10% additional tax. Certain withdrawals of excess contributions after the due date of your return are also tax free and therefore not subject to the 10% additional tax. (See *Excess contributions withdrawn after due date of return*, earlier.) This also applies to transfers incident to divorce, as discussed earlier.

Receivership distributions. Early distributions (with or without your consent) from savings institutions placed in receivership are subject to this tax unless one of the exceptions listed earlier applies. This is true even if the distribution is from a receiver that is a state agency.

Additional 10% tax. The additional tax on early distributions is 10% of the amount of the early distribution that you must include in your gross income. This tax is in addition to any regular income tax resulting from including the distribution in income.

Nondeductible contributions. The tax on early distributions doesn't apply to the part of a distribution that represents a return of your nondeductible contributions (basis).

More information. For more information on early distributions, see *What Acts Result in Penalties or Additional Taxes?* in chapter 1 of Pub. 590-B.

Excess Accumulations (Insufficient Distributions)

You can't keep amounts in your traditional IRA indefinitely. Generally, you must begin receiving distributions by April 1 of the year following the year in which you reach age 70 1/2. The required minimum distribution for any year after the year in which you reach age 70 1/2 must be made by December 31 of that later year.

Tax on excess. If distributions are less than the required minimum distribution for the year, you may have to pay a 50% excise tax for that year on the amount not distributed as required.

Request to waive the tax. If the excess accumulation is due to reasonable error, and you have taken, or are taking, steps to remedy the insufficient distribution, you can request that the tax be waived. If you believe you qualify for this relief, attach a statement of explanation and complete Form 5329 as instructed under *Waiver of tax* in the Instructions for Form 5329.

Exemption from tax. If you are unable to take required distributions because you have a traditional IRA invested in a contract issued by an insurance company that is in state insurer delinquency proceedings, the 50% excise tax doesn't apply if the conditions and requirements of Revenue Procedure 92-10 are satisfied.

More information. For more information on excess accumulations, see *What Acts Result in Penalties or Additional Taxes?* in chapter 1 of Pub. 590-B.

Reporting Additional Taxes

Generally, you must use Form 5329 to report the tax on excess contributions, early distributions, and excess accumulations.

Filing a tax return. If you must file an individual income tax return, complete Form 5329 and attach it to your Form 1040. Enter the total additional taxes due on Schedule 4 (Form 1040), line 59.

Not filing a tax return. If you don't have to file a tax return but do have to pay one of the additional taxes mentioned earlier, file the completed Form 5329 with the IRS at the time and place you would have filed your Form 1040. Be sure to include your address on page 1 and your signature and date on page 2. Enclose, but don't attach, a check or money order payable to "United States Treasury" for the tax you owe, as shown on Form 5329. Enter your social security number and "2018 Form 5329" on your check or money order.

Form 5329 not required. You don't have to use Form 5329 if either of the following situations exists.

- Distribution code 1 (early distribution) is correctly shown in box 7 of all your Forms 1099-R. If you don't owe any other additional tax on a distribution, multiply the taxable part of the early distribution by 10% and enter the result on Schedule 4 (Form 1040), line 59. Put "No" to the left of the line to indicate that you don't have to file Form 5329. However, if you owe this tax and also owe any other additional tax on a distribution, don't enter this 10% additional tax directly on your Form 1040. You must file Form 5329 to report your additional taxes.

- If you rolled over part or all of a distribution from a qualified retirement plan, the part rolled over isn't subject to the tax on early distributions.

- If you have a qualified 2017 disaster distribution.

Roth IRAs

Regardless of your age, you may be able to establish and make nondeductible contributions to a retirement plan called a Roth IRA.

Contributions not reported. You don't report Roth IRA contributions on your return.

What Is a Roth IRA?

A Roth IRA is an individual retirement plan that, except as explained in this chapter, is subject to the rules that apply to a traditional IRA (defined earlier). It can be either an account or an annuity. Individual retirement accounts and annuities are described under *How Can a Traditional IRA Be Opened?* in chapter 1 of Pub. 590-A.

To be a Roth IRA, the account or annuity must be designated as a Roth IRA when it is opened. A deemed IRA can be a Roth IRA, but neither a SEP IRA nor a SIMPLE IRA can be designated as a Roth IRA.

Unlike a traditional IRA, you can't deduct contributions to a Roth IRA. But, if you satisfy the requirements, qualified distributions (discussed later) are tax free. Contributions can be made to your Roth IRA after you reach age 70½ and you can leave amounts in your Roth IRA as long as you live.

When Can a Roth IRA Be Opened?

You can open a Roth IRA at any time. However, the time for making contributions for any year is limited. See *When Can You Make Contributions*, later, under *Can You Contribute to a Roth IRA*.

Can You Contribute to a Roth IRA?

Generally, you can contribute to a Roth IRA if you have taxable compensation (defined later) and your modified AGI (defined later) is less than:

- $199,000 for married filing jointly or qualifying widow(er);

- $135,000 for single, head of household, or married filing separately and you didn't live with your spouse at any time during the year; or

- $10,000 for married filing separately and you lived with your spouse at any time during the year.

 You may be eligible to claim a credit for contributions to your Roth IRA. For more information, see chapter 37.

Is there an age limit for contributions? Contributions can be made to your Roth IRA regardless of your age.

Can you contribute to a Roth IRA for your spouse? You can contribute to a Roth IRA for your spouse provided the contributions satisfy the Kay Bailey Hutchison Spousal IRA limit (discussed in *How Much Can Be Contributed*, earlier, under *Traditional IRAs*), you file jointly, and your modified AGI is less than $199,000.

Compensation. Compensation includes wages, salaries, tips, professional fees, bonuses, and other amounts received for providing personal services. It also includes commissions, self-employment income, nontaxable combat pay, military differential pay, and taxable alimony and separate maintenance payments.

Modified AGI. Your modified AGI for Roth IRA purposes is your adjusted gross income (AGI) as shown on your return with some adjustments. Use Worksheet 17-2 below to determine your modified AGI.

Use this worksheet to figure your modified adjusted gross income for Roth IRA purposes.

1.	Enter your adjusted gross income from Form 1040, line 7	1. _____
2.	Enter any income resulting from the conversion of an IRA (other than a Roth IRA) to a Roth IRA (included on Form 1040, line 4b) and a rollover from a qualified retirement plan to a Roth IRA (included on Form 1040, line 4b)	2. _____
3.	Subtract line 2 from line 1	3. _____
4.	Enter any traditional IRA deduction from Schedule 1 (Form 1040), line 32	4. _____
5.	Enter any student loan interest deduction from Schedule 1 (Form 1040), line 33	5. _____
6.	Enter any domestic production activities deduction from Schedule 1 (Form 1040), line 36	6. _____
7.	Enter any foreign earned income and/or housing exclusion from Form 2555, line 45, or Form 2555-EZ, line 18	7. _____
8.	Enter any foreign housing deduction from Form 2555, line 50	8. _____
9.	Enter any excludable savings bond interest from Form 8815, line 14	9. _____
10.	Enter any excluded employer-provided adoption benefits from Form 8839, line 28	10. _____
11.	Add the amounts on lines 3 through 10	11. _____
12.	Enter: • $199,000 if married filing jointly or qualifying widow(er), • $10,000 if married filing separately and you lived with your spouse at any time during the year, or • $135,000 for all others.	12. _____

Is the amount on line 11 more than the amount on line 12?
If yes, then see the *Note* below.
If no, then the amount on line 11 is your **modified AGI** for Roth IRA purposes.

Note. If the amount on line 11 is more than the amount on line 12 and you have other income or loss items, such as social security income or passive activity losses, that are subject to AGI-based phaseouts, you can refigure your AGI solely for the purpose of figuring your modified AGI for Roth IRA purposes. (If you receive social security benefits, use Worksheet 1 in *Appendix B* of Pub. 590-A to refigure your AGI.) Then go to line 3 above in this Worksheet 17-2 to refigure your modified AGI. If you don't have other income or loss items subject to AGI-based phaseouts, your modified AGI for Roth IRA purposes is the amount on line 11.

How Much Can Be Contributed?

The contribution limit for Roth IRAs generally depends on whether contributions are made only to Roth IRAs or to both traditional IRAs and Roth IRAs.

Roth IRAs only. If contributions are made only to Roth IRAs, your contribution limit generally is the lesser of the following amounts.

- $5,500 ($6,500 if you are 50 or older in 2018).
- Your taxable compensation.

However, if your modified AGI is above a certain amount, your contribution limit may be reduced, as explained later under *Contribution limit reduced*.

Roth IRAs and traditional IRAs. If contributions are made to both Roth IRAs and traditional IRAs established for your benefit, your contribution limit for Roth IRAs generally is the same as your limit would be if contributions were made only to Roth IRAs, but then reduced by all contributions for the year to all IRAs other than Roth IRAs. Employer contributions under a SEP or SIMPLE IRA plan don't affect this limit.

This means that your contribution limit is generally the lesser of the following amounts.

- $5,500 ($6,500 if you are 50 or older in 2018) minus all contributions (other than employer contributions under a SEP or SIMPLE IRA plan) for the year to all IRAs other than Roth IRAs.

- Your taxable compensation minus all contributions (other than employer contributions under a SEP or SIMPLE IRA plan) for the year to all IRAs other than Roth IRAs.

However, if your modified AGI is above a certain amount, your contribution limit may be reduced, as explained next under *Contribution limit reduced*.

Contribution limit reduced. If your modified AGI is above a certain amount, your contribution limit is gradually reduced. Use Table 17-3 to determine if this reduction applies to you.

Table 17-3. Effect of Modified AGI on Roth IRA Contribution

This table shows whether your contribution to a Roth IRA is affected by the amount of your modified adjusted gross income (modified AGI).

IF you have taxable compensation and your filing status is...	AND your modified AGI is...	THEN...
Married filing jointly, or **Qualifying widow(er)**	less than $189,000	you can contribute up to $5,500 ($6,500 if you are 50 or older in 2018).
	at least $189,000 but less than $199,000	the amount you can contribute is reduced as explained under *Contribution limit reduced* in chapter 2 of Pub. 590-A.
	$199,000 or more	you can't contribute to a Roth IRA.
Married filing separately and you lived with your spouse at any time during the year	zero (-0-)	you can contribute up to $5,500 ($6,500 if you are 50 or older in 2018).
	more than zero (-0-) but less than $10,000	the amount you can contribute is reduced as explained under *Contribution limit reduced* in chapter 2 of Pub. 590-A.
	$10,000 or more	you can't contribute to a Roth IRA.
Single, **Head of household,** or **Married filing separately** and you didn't live with your spouse at any time during the year	less than $120,000	you can contribute up to $5,500 ($6,500 if you are 50 or older in 2018).
	at least $120,000 but less than $135,000	the amount you can contribute is reduced as explained under *Contribution limit reduced* in chapter 2 of Pub. 590-A.
	$135,000 or more	you can't contribute to a Roth IRA.

Figuring the reduction. If the amount you can contribute to your Roth IRA is reduced, see Worksheet 2-2 under *Can You Contribute to a Roth IRA?* in chapter 2 of Pub. 590-A for how to figure the reduction.

When Can You Make Contributions?

You can make contributions to a Roth IRA for a year at any time during the year or by the due date of your return for that year (not including extensions).

 You can make contributions for 2018 by the due date (not including extensions) for filing your 2018 tax return.

What if You Contribute Too Much?

A 6% excise tax applies to any excess contribution to a Roth IRA.

Excess contributions. These are the contributions to your Roth IRAs for a year that equal the total of:

1. Amounts contributed for the tax year to your Roth IRAs (other than amounts properly and timely rolled over from a Roth IRA or properly converted from a traditional IRA or rolled over from a qualified retirement plan, as described later) that are more than your contribution limit for the year; plus

2. Any excess contributions for the preceding year, reduced by the total of:

   a. Any distributions out of your Roth IRAs for the year, plus

   b. Your contribution limit for the year minus your contributions to all your IRAs for the year.

Withdrawal of excess contributions. For purposes of determining excess contributions, any contribution that is withdrawn on or before the due date (including extensions) for filing your tax return for the year is treated as an amount not contributed. This treatment applies only if any earnings on the contributions are also withdrawn. The earnings are considered to have been earned and received in the year the excess contribution was made.

Applying excess contributions. If contributions to your Roth IRA for a year were more than the limit, you can apply the excess contribution in one year to a later year if the contributions for that later year are less than the maximum allowed for that year.

Can You Move Amounts Into a Roth IRA?

You may be able to convert amounts from either a traditional, SEP, or SIMPLE IRA into a Roth IRA. You may be able to roll amounts over from a qualified retirement plan to a Roth IRA. You may be able to recharacterize contributions made to one IRA as having been made directly to a different IRA. You can roll amounts over from a designated Roth account or from one Roth IRA to another Roth IRA.

Conversions

You can convert a traditional IRA to a Roth IRA. The conversion is treated as a rollover, regardless of the conversion method used. Most of the rules for rollovers, described earlier under *Rollover From One IRA Into Another* under *Traditional IRAs,* apply to these rollovers. However, the 1-year waiting period doesn't apply.

Conversion methods. You can convert amounts from a traditional IRA to a Roth IRA in any of the following ways.

- *Rollover.* You can receive a distribution from a traditional IRA and roll it over (contribute it) to a Roth IRA within 60 days after the distribution.

- *Trustee-to-trustee transfer.* You can direct the trustee of the traditional IRA to transfer an amount from the traditional IRA to the trustee of the Roth IRA.

- *Same trustee transfer.* If the trustee of the traditional IRA also maintains the Roth IRA, you can direct the trustee to transfer an amount from the traditional IRA to the Roth IRA.

Same trustee. Conversions made with the same trustee can be made by redesignating the traditional IRA as a Roth IRA, rather than opening a new account or issuing a new contract.

Rollover from a qualified retirement plan into a Roth IRA. You can roll over into a Roth IRA all or part of an eligible rollover distribution you receive from your (or your deceased spouse's):

- Employer's qualified pension, profit-sharing, or stock bonus plan;

- Annuity plan;

- Tax-sheltered annuity plan (section 403(b) plan); or

- Governmental deferred compensation plan (section 457 plan).

Any amount rolled over is subject to the same rules as those for converting a traditional IRA into a Roth IRA. Also, the rollover contribution must meet the rollover requirements that apply to the specific type of retirement plan.

Income. You must include in your gross income distributions from a qualified retirement plan that you would have had to include in income if you hadn't rolled them over into a Roth IRA. You don't include in gross income any part of a distribution from a qualified retirement plan that is a return of basis (after-tax contributions) to the plan that were taxable to you when paid. These amounts are normally included in income on your return for the year of the rollover from the qualified employer plan to a Roth IRA.

 If you must include any amount in your gross income, you may have to increase your withholding or make estimated tax payments. See Pub. 505, Tax Withholding and Estimated Tax.

For more information, see *Rollover From Employer's Plan Into a Roth IRA* in chapter 2 of Pub. 590-A.

Converting from a SIMPLE IRA. Generally, you can convert an amount in your SIMPLE IRA to a Roth IRA under the same rules explained earlier under *Converting From Any Traditional IRA to a Roth IRA* under *Traditional IRAs.*

However, you can't convert any amount distributed from the SIMPLE IRA during the 2-year period beginning on the date you first participated in any SIMPLE IRA plan maintained by your employer.

More information. For more detailed information on conversions, see *Can You Move Amounts Into a Roth IRA?* in chapter 2 in Pub. 590-A.

Rollover From a Roth IRA

You can withdraw, tax free, all or part of the assets from one Roth IRA if you contribute them within 60 days to another Roth IRA. Most of the rules for rollovers, explained earlier under *Rollover From One IRA Into Another* under *Traditional IRAs,* apply to these rollovers.

Rollover from designated Roth account. A rollover from a designated Roth account can only be made to another designated Roth account or to a Roth IRA. For more information about designated Roth accounts, see *chapter 10.*

Are Distributions Taxable?

You don't include in your gross income qualified distributions or distributions that are a return of your regular contributions from your Roth IRA(s). You also don't include distributions from your Roth IRA that you roll over tax free into another Roth IRA. You may have to include part of other distributions in your income. See *Ordering rules for distributions,* later.

What are qualified distributions? A qualified distribution is any payment or distribution from your Roth IRA that meets the following requirements.

1. It is made after the 5-year period beginning with the first tax year for which a contribution was made to a Roth IRA set up for your benefit.

2. The payment or distribution is:

a. Made on or after the date you reach age 59½,

b. Made because you are disabled,

c. Made to a beneficiary or to your estate after your death, or

d. To pay up to $10,000 (lifetime limit) of certain qualified first-time homebuyer amounts. See *First home* under *What Acts Result in Penalties or Additional Taxes?* in chapter 1 of Pub. 590-B for more information.

Additional tax on distributions of conversion and certain rollover contributions within 5-year period. If, within the 5-year period starting with the first day of your tax year in which you convert an amount from a traditional IRA or roll over an amount from a qualified retirement plan to a Roth IRA, you take a distribution from a Roth IRA, you may have to pay the 10% additional tax on early distributions. You generally must pay the 10% additional tax on any amount attributable to the part of the amount converted or rolled over (the conversion or rollover contribution) that you had to include in income. A separate 5-year period applies to each conversion and rollover. See *Ordering rules for distributions,* later, to determine the amount, if any, of the distribution that is attributable to the part of the conversion or rollover contribution that you had to include in income.

Additional tax on other early distributions. Unless an exception applies, you must pay the 10% additional tax on the taxable part of any distributions that aren't qualified distributions. See Pub. 590-B for more information.

Ordering rules for distributions. If you receive a distribution from your Roth IRA that isn't a qualified distribution, part of it may be taxable. There is a set order in which contributions (including conversion contributions and rollover contributions from qualified retirement plans) and earnings are considered to be distributed from your Roth IRA. Regular contributions are distributed first. See *Ordering Rules for Distributions* under *Are Distributions Taxable?* in chapter 2 of Pub. 590-B for more information.

Must you withdraw or use Roth IRA assets? You aren't required to take distributions from your Roth IRA at any age. The minimum distribution rules that apply to traditional IRAs don't apply to Roth IRAs while the owner is alive. However, after the death of a Roth IRA owner, certain minimum distribution rules that apply to traditional IRAs also apply to Roth IRAs.

More information. For more detailed information on Roth IRAs, see chapter 2 of Pub. 590-A and Pub. 590-B.

18.

Alimony

What's New

 At the time this publication went to print, Congress was considering legislation that would do the following.

1. *Provide additional tax relief for those affected by certain 2018 disasters.*

2. *Extend certain tax benefits that expired at the end of 2017 and that currently can't be claimed on your 2018 tax return.*

3. *Change certain other tax provisions.*

To learn whether this legislation was enacted resulting in changes that affect your 2018 tax return, go to Recent Developments at IRS.gov/ Pub17.

Nondeductibility of alimony. Generally, for divorce or separation agreements executed after December 31, 2018, you may no longer deduct an amount equal to the alimony or separate maintenance payments paid during the tax year, nor will the alimony or separate maintenance payments be included in the gross income of the recipient spouse.

Introduction

This chapter discusses the rules that apply if you pay or receive alimony. It covers the following topics.

- What payments are alimony.

- What payments are not alimony, such as child support.

- How to deduct alimony you paid.

- How to report alimony you received as income.

- Whether you must recapture the tax benefits of alimony. Recapture means adding back in your income all or part of a deduction you took in a prior year.

Alimony is a payment to or for a spouse or former spouse under a divorce or separation instrument. It doesn't include voluntary payments that aren't made under a divorce or separation instrument.

For divorce or separation agreements executed before January 1, 2019, alimony is deductible by the payer, and the recipient must include it in income. Although this chapter is generally written for the payer of the alimony, the recipient can also use the information to determine whether an amount received is alimony.

To be alimony, a payment must meet certain requirements. There are some differences between the requirements that apply to payments under instruments executed after 1984 and to payments under instruments executed before 1985. The general requirements that apply to payments regardless of when the divorce or separation agreement was executed and the specific requirements that apply to post-1984 instruments (and, in certain cases, some pre-1985 instruments) are discussed in this chapter. If you are looking for information on the specific requirements that apply to pre-1985 instruments, get and keep a copy of the 2004 version of Pub. 504. That was the last year the information on pre-1985 instruments was included in Pub. 504.

Use Table 18-1 in this chapter as a guide to determine whether certain payments are considered alimony.

Definitions. The following definitions apply throughout this chapter.

Spouse or former spouse. Unless otherwise stated, the term "spouse" includes former spouse.

Divorce or separation instrument. The term "divorce or separation instrument" means:

- A decree of divorce or separate maintenance or a written instrument incident to that decree;

- A written separation agreement; or

- A decree or any type of court order requiring a spouse to make payments for the support or maintenance of the other spouse. This includes a temporary decree, an interlocutory (not final) decree, and a decree of alimony pendente lite (while awaiting action on the final decree or agreement).

Useful Items

You may want to see:

Publication

❏ **504** Divorced or Separated Individuals

For this and other useful items, go to *IRS.gov/Forms*.

General Rules

For divorce or separation agreements executed after December 31, 2018, you may no longer deduct an amount equal to the alimony or separate maintenance payments paid during the tax year, nor will the alimony or separate maintenance payments be included in the gross income of the recipient spouse. For divorce or separation agreements executed before January 1, 2019, the following rules apply to alimony.

Payments not alimony. Not all payments under a divorce or separation instrument are alimony. Alimony doesn't include:

- Child support;

- Noncash property settlements;

- Payments that are your spouse's part of community income, as explained under *Community Property* in Pub. 504;

- Payments to keep up the payer's property; or

- Use of the payer's property.

Payments to a third party. Cash payments, checks, or money orders to a third party on behalf of your spouse under the terms of your divorce or separation instrument can be alimony, if they otherwise qualify. These include payments for your spouse's medical expenses, housing costs (rent, utilities, etc.), taxes, tuition, etc. The payments are treated as received by your spouse and then paid to the third party.

Life insurance premiums. Alimony includes premiums you must pay under your divorce or separation instrument for insurance on your life to the extent your spouse owns the policy.

Payments for jointly owned home. If your divorce or separation instrument states that you must pay expenses for a home owned by you and your spouse, some of your payments may be alimony.

Mortgage payments. If you must pay all the mortgage payments (principal and interest) on a jointly owned home, and they otherwise qualify as alimony, you can deduct half of the total payments as alimony. If you itemize deductions and the home is a qualified home, you can claim half of the interest in figuring your deductible interest. Your spouse must report half of the payments as alimony received. If your spouse itemizes deductions and the home is a qualified home, he or she can claim half of the interest on the mortgage in figuring deductible interest.

Taxes and insurance. If you must pay all the real estate taxes or insurance on a home held as tenants in common, you can deduct half of these payments as alimony. Your spouse must report half of these payments as alimony received. If you and your spouse itemize deductions, you can each claim half of the real estate taxes and none of the home insurance.

If your home is held as tenants by the entirety or joint tenants, none of your payments for taxes or insurance are alimony. But if you itemize deductions, you can claim all of the real estate taxes and none of the home insurance.

Other payments to a third party. If you made other third-party payments, see Pub. 504 to see whether any part of the payments qualifies as alimony.

Instruments Executed After 1984 and Before 2019

The following rules for alimony apply to payments under divorce or separation instruments executed after 1984 and before 2019.

Exception for instruments executed before 1985. There are two situations where the rules for instruments executed after 1984 apply to instruments executed before 1985.

1. A divorce or separation instrument executed before 1985 and then modified after 1984 to specify that the after-1984 rules will apply.

2. A temporary divorce or separation instrument executed before 1985 and incorporated into, or adopted by, a final decree executed after 1984 that:

   a. Changes the amount or period of payment, or

   b. Adds or deletes any contingency or condition.

For the rules for alimony payments under pre-1985 instruments not meeting these exceptions, get the 2004 version of Pub. 504 at *IRS.gov/Pub504*.

Example 1. In November 1984, you and your former spouse executed a written separation agreement. In February 1985, a decree of divorce was substituted for the written separation agreement. The decree of divorce didn't change the terms for the alimony you pay your former spouse. The decree of divorce is treated as executed before 1985. Alimony payments under this decree aren't subject to the rules for payments under instruments executed after 1984.

Example 2. Assume the same facts as in *Example 1*, except that the decree of divorce changed the amount of the alimony. In this example, the decree of divorce isn't treated as executed before 1985. The alimony payments are subject to the rules for payments under instruments executed after 1984.

Alimony requirements. A payment to or for a spouse under a divorce or separation instrument is alimony if the spouses don't file a joint return with each other and all the following requirements are met.

- The payment is in cash.

- The instrument doesn't designate the payment as not alimony.

- The spouses aren't members of the same household at the time the payments are made. This requirement applies only if the spouses are legally separated under a decree of divorce or separate maintenance.

- There is no liability to make any payment (in cash or property) after the death of the recipient spouse.

- The payment isn't treated as child support.

Each of these requirements is discussed next.

Cash payment requirement. Only cash payments, including checks and money orders, qualify as alimony. The following don't qualify as alimony.

- Transfers of services or property (including a debt instrument of a third party or an annuity contract).

- Execution of a debt instrument by the payer.

- The use of the payer's property.

Payments to a third party. Cash payments to a third party under the terms of your divorce or separation instrument can qualify as cash payments to your spouse. See *Payments to a third party* under *General Rules*, earlier.

Also, cash payments made to a third party at the written request of your spouse may qualify as alimony if all the following requirements are met.

- The payments are in lieu of payments of alimony directly to your spouse.

- The written request states that both spouses intend the payments to be treated as alimony.

Table 18-1. Alimony Requirements (Instruments Executed After 1984 and Before 2019)

Payments ARE alimony if all of the following are true:	Payments are NOT alimony if any of the following are true:
Payments are required by a divorce or separation instrument.	Payments aren't required by a divorce or separation instrument.
Payer and recipient spouse don't file a joint return with each other.	Payer and recipient spouse file a joint return with each other.
Payment is in cash (including checks or money orders).	Payment is: • Not in cash, • A noncash property settlement, • Spouse's part of community income, or • To keep up the payer's property.
Payment isn't designated in the instrument as not alimony.	Payment is designated in the instrument as not alimony.
Spouses legally separated under a decree of divorce or separate maintenance aren't members of the same household.	Spouses legally separated under a decree of divorce or separate maintenance are members of the same household.
Payments aren't required after death of the recipient spouse.	Payments are required after death of the recipient spouse.
Payment isn't treated as child support.	Payment is treated as child support.
These payments are deductible by the payer and includible in income by the recipient.	*These payments are neither deductible by the payer nor includible in income by the recipient.*

• You receive the written request from your spouse before you file your return for the year you made the payments.

Payments designated as not alimony. You and your spouse can designate that otherwise qualifying payments aren't alimony. You do this by including a provision in your divorce or separation instrument that states the payments aren't deductible as alimony by you and are excludable from your spouse's income. For this purpose, any instrument (written statement) signed by both of you that makes this designation and that refers to a previous written separation agreement is treated as a written separation agreement (and therefore a divorce or separation instrument). If you are subject to temporary support orders, the designation must be made in the original or a later temporary support order.

Your spouse can exclude the payments from income only if he or she attaches a copy of the instrument designating them as not alimony to his or her return. The copy must be attached each year the designation applies.

Spouses can't be members of the same household. Payments to your spouse while you are members of the same household aren't alimony if you are legally separated under a decree of divorce or separate maintenance. A home you formerly shared is considered one household, even if you physically separate yourselves in the home.

You aren't treated as members of the same household if one of you is preparing to leave the household and does leave no later than 1 month after the date of the payment.

Exception. If you aren't legally separated under a decree of divorce or separate

maintenance, a payment under a written separation agreement, support decree, or other court order may qualify as alimony even if you are members of the same household when the payment is made.

Liability for payments after death of recipient spouse. If any part of payments you make must continue to be made for any period after your spouse's death, that part of your payments isn't alimony, whether made before or after the death. If all of the payments would continue, then none of the payments made before or after the death are alimony.

The divorce or separation instrument doesn't have to expressly state that the payments cease upon the death of your spouse if, for example, the liability for continued payments would end under state law.

Example. You must pay your former spouse $10,000 in cash each year for 10 years. Your divorce decree states that the payments will end upon your former spouse's death. You must also pay your former spouse or your former spouse's estate $20,000 in cash each year for 10 years. The death of your spouse wouldn't end these payments under state law.

The $10,000 annual payments may qualify as alimony. The $20,000 annual payments that don't end upon your former spouse's death aren't alimony.

Substitute payments. If you must make any payments in cash or property after your spouse's death as a substitute for continuing otherwise qualifying payments before the death, the otherwise qualifying payments aren't alimony. To the extent that your payments begin, accelerate, or increase because of the death of your spouse, otherwise qualifying

payments you made may be treated as payments that weren't alimony. Whether or not such payments will be treated as not alimony depends on all the facts and circumstances.

Example 1. Under your divorce decree, you must pay your former spouse $30,000 annually. The payments will stop at the end of 6 years or upon your former spouse's death, if earlier.

Your former spouse has custody of your minor children. The decree provides that if any child is still a minor at your spouse's death, you must pay $10,000 annually to a trust until the youngest child reaches the age of majority. The trust income and corpus (principal) are to be used for your children's benefit.

These facts indicate that the payments to be made after your former spouse's death are a substitute for $10,000 of the $30,000 annual payments. Of each of the $30,000 annual payments, $10,000 isn't alimony.

Example 2. Under your divorce decree, you must pay your former spouse $30,000 annually. The payments will stop at the end of 15 years or upon your former spouse's death, if earlier. The decree provides that if your former spouse dies before the end of the 15-year period, you must pay the estate the difference between $450,000 ($30,000 × 15) and the total amount paid up to that time. For example, if your spouse dies at the end of the 10th year, you must pay the estate $150,000 ($450,000 − $300,000).

These facts indicate that the lump-sum payment to be made after your former spouse's death is a substitute for the full amount of the $30,000 annual payments. None of the annual payments are alimony. The result would be the same if the payment required at death were to be discounted by an appropriate interest factor to account for the prepayment.

Child support. A payment that is specifically designated as child support or treated as specifically designated as child support under your divorce or separation instrument isn't alimony. The amount of child support may vary over time. Child support payments aren't deductible by the payer and aren't taxable to the recipient.

Specifically designated as child support. A payment will be treated as specifically designated as child support to the extent that the payment is reduced either:

• On the happening of a contingency relating to your child, or

• At a time that can be clearly associated with the contingency.

A payment may be treated as specifically designated as child support even if other separate payments are specifically designated as child support.

Contingency relating to your child. A contingency relates to your child if it depends on any event relating to that child. It doesn't matter whether the event is certain or likely to occur. Events relating to your child include the child's:

• Becoming employed,

• Dying,

- Leaving the household,
- Leaving school,
- Marrying, or
- Reaching a specified age or income level.

Clearly associated with a contingency. Payments that would otherwise qualify as alimony are presumed to be reduced at a time clearly associated with the happening of a contingency relating to your child only in the following situations.

- The payments are to be reduced not more than 6 months before or after the date the child will reach 18, 21, or local age of majority.
- The payments are to be reduced on two or more occasions that occur not more than 1 year before or after a different one of your children reaches a certain age from 18 to 24. This certain age must be the same for each child, but needn't be a whole number of years.

In all other situations, reductions in payments are not treated as clearly associated with the happening of a contingency relating to your child.

Either you or the IRS can overcome the presumption in the two situations above. This is done by showing that the time at which the payments are to be reduced was determined independently of any contingencies relating to your children. For example, if you can show that the period of alimony payments is customary in the local jurisdiction, such as a period equal to half of the duration of the marriage, you can overcome the presumption and may be able to treat the amount as alimony.

How To Deduct Alimony Paid Before 2019

You can deduct alimony you paid before January 1, 2019, whether or not you itemize deductions on your return. You must file Form 1040. You can't use Form 1040NR.

Enter the amount of alimony you paid on Schedule 1 (Form 1040), line 31a. In the space provided on Schedule 1 (Form 1040), line 31b, enter the recipient's social security number (SSN) or individual taxpayer identification number (ITIN).

If you paid alimony to more than one person, enter the SSN or ITIN of one of the recipients. Show the SSN or ITIN and amount paid to each additional recipient on an attached statement. Enter your total payments on Schedule 1 (Form 1040), line 31a.

 If you don't provide your spouse's SSN or ITIN, you may have to pay a $50 penalty and your deduction may be disallowed. For more information on SSNs and ITINs, see Social Security Number (SSN) *in chapter 1.*

How To Report Alimony Received Before 2019

Report alimony you received before January 1, 2019, as income on Schedule 1 (Form 1040), line 11, or on Schedule NEC (Form 1040NR), line 12.

 You must give the person who paid the alimony your SSN or ITIN. If you don't, you may have to pay a $50 penalty.

Recapture Rule

If your alimony payments decrease or end during the first 3 calendar years, you may be subject to the recapture rule. If you are subject to this rule, you have to include in income in the third year part of the alimony payments you previously deducted. Your spouse can deduct in the third year part of the alimony payments he or she previously included in income.

The 3-year period starts with the first calendar year you make a payment qualifying as alimony under a decree of divorce or separate maintenance or a written separation agreement. Don't include any time in which payments were being made under temporary support orders. The second and third years are the next 2 calendar years, whether or not payments are made during those years.

The reasons for a reduction or end of alimony payments that can require a recapture include:

- A change in your divorce or separation instrument,
- A failure to make timely payments,
- A reduction in your ability to provide support, or
- A reduction in your spouse's support needs.

When to apply the recapture rule. You are subject to the recapture rule in the third year if the alimony you pay in the third year decreases by more than $15,000 from the second year or the alimony you pay in the second and third years decreases significantly from the alimony you pay in the first year.

When you figure a decrease in alimony, don't include the following amounts.

- Payments made under a temporary support order.
- Payments required over a period of at least 3 calendar years that vary because they are a fixed part of your income from a business or property, or from compensation for employment or self-employment.
- Payments that decrease because of the death of either spouse or the remarriage of the spouse receiving the payments before the end of the third year.

Figuring the recapture. You can use Worksheet 1 in Pub. 504 to figure recaptured alimony.

Including the recapture in income. If you must include a recaptured amount in income, show it on Schedule 1 (Form 1040), line 11 ("Alimony received"). Cross out "received" and enter "recapture." On the dotted line next to the amount, enter your spouse's last name and SSN or ITIN.

Deducting the recapture. If you can deduct a recaptured amount, show it on Schedule 1 (Form 1040), line 31a ("Alimony paid"). Cross out "paid" and enter "recapture." In the space provided, enter your spouse's SSN or ITIN.

19.

Education-Related Adjustments

Introduction

This chapter discusses the education-related adjustments you can deduct in figuring your adjusted gross income.

This chapter covers the student loan interest deduction, tuition and fees deduction, and the deduction for educator expenses.

Useful Items
You may want to see:

Publication

❑ **970** Tax Benefits for Education

For these and other useful items, go to *IRS.gov/ Forms.*

What's New

 At the time this publication went to print, Congress was considering legislation that would do the following.

1. *Provide additional tax relief for those affected by certain 2018 disasters.*

2. *Extend certain tax benefits that expired at the end of 2017 and that currently can't be claimed on your 2018 tax return.*

3. *Change certain other tax provisions.*

To learn whether this legislation was enacted resulting in changes that affect your 2018 tax return, go to Recent Developments *at IRS.gov/ Pub17.*

Student loan interest deduction. For 2018, the amount of your student loan interest deduction is gradually reduced (phased out) if your MAGI is between $65,000 and $80,000 ($135,000 and $165,000 if you file a joint return). You can't claim the deduction if your

MAGI is $80,000 or more ($165,000 or more if you file a joint return).

Tuition and fees deduction. The tuition and fees deduction has expired and you can no longer take this deduction. If extended (see Caution above), information about this deduction will be available in the Recent Developments at *IRS.gov/Pub17*.

Student Loan Interest Deduction

Generally, personal interest you pay, other than certain mortgage interest, isn't deductible on your tax return. However, if your modified adjusted gross income (MAGI) is less than $80,000 ($165,000 if filing a joint return), you may be allowed a special deduction for paying interest on a student loan (also known as an education loan) used for higher education. For most taxpayers, MAGI is the adjusted gross income as figured on their federal income tax return before subtracting any deduction for student loan interest. This deduction can reduce the amount of your income subject to tax by up to $2,500. Table 19-1 summarizes the features of the student loan interest deduction.

Table 19-1. Student Loan Interest Deduction at a Glance
Don't rely on this table alone.
Refer to the text for more details.

Feature	Description
Maximum benefit	You can reduce your income subject to tax by up to $2,500.
Loan qualifications	Your student loan: • Must have been taken out solely to pay qualified education expenses, and • Can't be from a related person or made under a qualified employer plan.
Student qualifications	The student must be: • You, your spouse, or your dependent (as defined later for this purpose); and • Enrolled at least half-time in a program leading to a degree, certificate, or other recognized educational credential at an eligible educational institution.
Limit on modified adjusted gross income (MAGI)	$165,000 if married filing a joint return; $80,000 if single, head of household, or qualifying widow(er).

Student Loan Interest Defined

Student loan interest is interest you paid during the year on a qualified student loan. It includes both required and voluntary interest payments.

Qualified Student Loan

This is a loan you took out solely to pay qualified education expenses (defined later) that were:

• For you, your spouse, or a person who was your dependent (as defined later for this purpose) when you took out the loan;

• Paid or incurred within a reasonable period of time before or after you took out the loan; and

• For education provided during an academic period for an eligible student.

Loans from the following sources aren't qualified student loans.

• A related person.

• A qualified employer plan.

Your dependent. Generally, your dependent is someone who is either a:

• Qualifying child, or

• Qualifying relative.

You can find more information about dependents in chapter 3.

For this purpose, the term "dependent" also includes any person you could have claimed as a dependent on your return except that:

• You, or your spouse if filing jointly, could be claimed as a dependent of another taxpayer (such as your parent's tax return);

• The person filed a joint return; or

• The person had gross income for the year that was equal to or more than $4,150 for 2018.

Reasonable period of time. Qualified education expenses are treated as paid or incurred within a reasonable period of time before or after you take out the loan if they are paid with the proceeds of student loans that are part of a federal postsecondary education loan program.

Even if not paid with the proceeds of that type of loan, the expenses are treated as paid or incurred within a reasonable period of time if both of the following requirements are met.

• The expenses relate to a specific academic period.

• The loan proceeds are disbursed within a period that begins 90 days before the start of that academic period and ends 90 days after the end of that academic period.

If neither of the above situations applies, the reasonable period of time usually is determined based on all the relevant facts and circumstances.

Academic period. An academic period includes a semester, trimester, quarter, or other period of study (such as a summer school session) as reasonably determined by an educational institution. If an educational institution uses credit hours or clock hours and doesn't have academic terms, each payment period can be treated as an academic period.

Eligible student. An eligible student is a student who was enrolled at least half-time in a program leading to a degree, certificate, or other recognized educational credential.

Enrolled at least half-time. A student was enrolled at least half-time if the student was taking at least half the normal full-time workload for his or her course of study.

The standard for what is half of the normal full-time workload is determined by each eligible educational institution. However, the standard may not be lower than any of those established by the U.S. Department of Education under the Higher Education Act of 1965.

Related person. You can't deduct interest on a loan you get from a related person. Related persons include:

• Your spouse;

• Your brothers and sisters;

• Your half brothers and half sisters;

• Your ancestors (parents, grandparents, etc.);

• Your lineal descendants (children, grandchildren, etc.); and

• Certain corporations, partnerships, trusts, and exempt organizations.

Qualified employer plan. You can't deduct interest on a loan made under a qualified employer plan or under a contract purchased under such a plan.

Qualified Education Expenses

For purposes of the student loan interest deduction, these expenses are the total costs of attending an eligible educational institution. They include amounts paid for the following items.

• Tuition and fees.

• Room and board.

• Books, supplies, and equipment.

• Other necessary expenses (such as transportation).

The cost of room and board qualifies only to the extent it isn't more than:

• The allowance for room and board, as determined by the eligible educational institution, that was included in the cost of attendance (for federal financial aid purposes) for a particular academic period and living arrangement of the student; or

• If greater, the actual amount charged if the student is residing in housing owned or operated by the eligible educational institution.

Eligible educational institution. An eligible educational institution is generally any accredited public, nonprofit, or proprietary (privately owned profit-making) college, university, vocational school, or other postsecondary educational institution. Also, the institution must be eligible to participate in a student aid program administered by the U.S. Department of Education. Virtually all accredited postsecondary institutions meet this definition.

An eligible educational institution also includes certain educational institutions located outside the United States that are eligible to participate in the U.S. Department of Education's Federal Student Aid (FSA) programs.

For purposes of the student loan interest deduction, an eligible educational institution also includes an institution conducting an internship or residency program leading to a degree or certificate from an institution of higher education, a hospital, or a health care facility that offers postgraduate training.

An educational institution must meet the above criteria only during the academic period(s) for which the student loan was incurred. The deductibility of interest on the loan isn't affected by the institution's subsequent loss of eligibility.

 The educational institution should be able to tell you if it is an eligible educational institution.

Adjustments to qualified education expenses. You must reduce your qualified education expenses by certain tax-free items (such as the tax-free part of scholarships and fellowship grants). See chapter 4 of Pub. 970 for details.

Include as Interest

In addition to simple interest on the loan, if all other requirements are met, the items discussed below can be student loan interest.

Loan origination fee. In general, this is a one-time fee charged by the lender when a loan is made. To be deductible as interest, a loan origination fee must be for the use of money rather than for property or services (such as commitment fees or processing costs) provided by the lender. A loan origination fee treated as interest accrues over the life of the loan.

Capitalized interest. This is unpaid interest on a student loan that is added by the lender to the outstanding principal balance of the loan.

Interest on revolving lines of credit. This interest, which includes interest on credit card debt, is student loan interest if the borrower uses the line of credit (credit card) only to pay qualified education expenses. See *Qualified Education Expenses*, earlier.

Interest on refinanced and consolidated student loans. This includes interest on a loan used solely to refinance a qualified student loan of the same borrower. It also includes a single consolidation loan used solely to refinance two or more qualified student loans of the same borrower.

 If you refinance a qualified student loan for more than your original loan and you use the additional amount for any purpose other than qualified education expenses, you can't deduct any interest paid on the refinanced loan.

Don't Include as Interest

You can't claim a student loan interest deduction for any of the following items.

- Interest you paid on a loan if, under the terms of the loan, you aren't legally obligated to make interest payments.
- Loan origination fees that are payments for property or services provided by the

lender, such as commitment fees or processing costs.

- Interest you paid on a loan to the extent payments were made through your participation in the National Health Service Corps Loan Repayment Program (the "NHSC Loan Repayment Program") or certain other loan repayment assistance programs. For more information, see *Student Loan Repayment Assistance* in chapter 5 of Pub. 970.

Can You Claim the Deduction?

Generally, you can claim the deduction if all of the following requirements are met.

- Your filing status is any filing status except married filing separately.
- No one else is claiming you as a dependent on his or her tax return.
- You are legally obligated to pay interest on a qualified student loan.
- You paid interest on a qualified student loan.

Interest paid by others. If you are the person legally obligated to make interest payments and someone else makes a payment of interest on your behalf, you are treated as receiving the payments from the other person and, in turn, paying the interest. See chapter 4 of Pub. 970 for more information.

No Double Benefit Allowed

You can't deduct as interest on a student loan any amount that is an allowable deduction under any other provision of the tax law (for example, home mortgage interest).

How Much Can You Deduct?

Your student loan interest deduction is generally the smaller of:

- $2,500, or
- The interest you paid during the tax year.

However, the amount determined above is phased out (gradually reduced) if your MAGI is between $65,000 and $80,000 ($135,000 and $165,000 if you file a joint return). You can't take a student loan interest deduction if your MAGI is $80,000 or more ($165,000 or more if you file a joint return). For details on figuring your MAGI, see chapter 4 of Pub. 970.

How Do You Figure the Deduction?

Generally, you figure the deduction using the Student Loan Interest Deduction Worksheet in the Instructions for Form 1040. However, if you are filing Form 2555, 2555-EZ, or 4563, or you are excluding income from sources within Puerto Rico, you must complete Worksheet 4-1 in chapter 4 of Pub. 970.

Form 1098-E. To help you figure your student loan interest deduction, you should receive Form 1098-E, Student Loan Interest Statement. Generally, an institution (such as a bank or governmental agency) that received interest payments of $600 or more during 2018 on one or more qualified student loans must send Form 1098-E (or an acceptable substitute) to each borrower by January 31, 2019.

For qualified student loans taken out before September 1, 2004, the institution is required to include on Form 1098-E only payments of stated interest. Other interest payments, such as certain loan origination fees and capitalized interest, may not appear on the form you receive. However, if you pay qualifying interest that isn't included on Form 1098-E, you can also deduct those amounts. For information on allocating payments between interest and principal, see chapter 4 of Pub. 970.

To claim the deduction, enter the allowable amount on Schedule 1 (Form 1040), line 33.

Educator Expenses

If you were an eligible educator in 2018, you can deduct up to $250 of qualified expenses you paid in 2018 as an adjustment to gross income on Schedule 1 (Form 1040), line 23. If you and your spouse are filing jointly and both of you were eligible educators, the maximum deduction is $500. However, neither spouse can deduct more than $250 of his or her qualified expenses.

Eligible educator. An eligible educator is a kindergarten through grade 12 teacher, instructor, counselor, principal, or aide in school for at least 900 hours during a school year.

Qualified expenses. Qualified expenses include ordinary and necessary expenses paid in connection with books, supplies, equipment (including computer equipment, software, and services), and other materials used in the classroom. An ordinary expense is one that is common and accepted in your educational field. A necessary expense is one that is helpful and appropriate for your profession as an educator. An expense doesn't have to be required to be considered necessary.

Qualified expenses also include those expenses you incur while participating in professional development courses related to the curriculum in which you provide instruction. It also includes those expenses related to those students for whom you provide that instruction.

Qualified expenses don't include expenses for home schooling or for nonathletic supplies for courses in health or physical education. You must reduce your qualified expenses by the following amounts.

- Excludable U.S. series EE and I savings bond interest from Form 8815.
- Nontaxable qualified state tuition program earnings.
- Nontaxable earnings from Coverdell education savings accounts.
- Any reimbursements you received for those expenses that weren't reported to you in box 1 of your Form W-2.

If you were an educator in 2018 and you had qualified expenses that you couldn't take as an adjustment to gross income, you can no longer deduct the rest as a miscellaneous itemized deduction.

20.

Other Adjustments to Income

What's New

 At the time this publication went to print, Congress was considering legislation that would do the following.

1. *Provide additional tax relief for those affected by certain 2018 disasters.*

2. *Extend certain tax benefits that expired at the end of 2017 and that currently can't be claimed on your 2018 tax return.*

3. *Change certain other tax provisions.*

To learn whether this legislation was enacted resulting in changes that affect your 2018 tax return, go to Recent Developments at *IRS.gov/ Pub17.*

Deduction for miscellaneous itemized deductions suspended. For tax years beginning after 2017, the deduction for job-related or other miscellaneous itemized deductions subject to the 2%-of-adjusted-gross-income floor is suspended. Armed Forces reservists, qualified performing artists, and fee-based state or local government officials can continue to claim eligible business expenses as adjustments in determining adjusted gross income. Employees with impairment-related work expenses can continue to claim eligible impairment-related work expenses as itemized deductions.

Deduction for moving expenses suspended. For tax years beginning after 2017, the deduction for moving expenses is suspended unless you are a member of the Armed Forces who moves pursuant to a military order and incident to a permanent change of station.

Standard mileage rate. For 2018, the standard mileage rate for the cost of operating your car for business use is 54.5 cents (0.545) per mile.

Car expenses and use of the standard mileage rate are explained under *Transportation Expenses,* later.

Depreciation limits on cars, trucks, and vans. For 2018, the first-year limit on depreciation, the special depreciation allowance, and the section 179 deduction for vehicles acquired before September 28, 2017, and placed in service during 2018 is $16,400. The first-year limit on depreciation, the special depreciation allowance, and the section 179 deduction for vehicles acquired after September 27, 2017, and placed in service during 2018 is $18,000. If you elect not to claim a special depreciation allowance for a vehicle placed in service in 2018, the first-year limit is $10,000.

Special depreciation allowance. For 2018, the first-year special ("bonus") depreciation allowance on qualified property (including cars, trucks, and vans) is 100% for qualified property acquired and placed in service after September 27, 2017, and before January 1, 2023. The special depreciation allowance is explained in chapter 4 of Pub. 463.

Meals and entertainment. Beginning in 2018, entertainment expenses generally are no longer deductible. Only non-entertainment-related meals are deductible, and the 50% limitation on the deduction of meals has not changed.

Introduction

You may be able to deduct the ordinary and necessary business-related expenses you have for:

- Travel,
- Non-entertainment-related meals,
- Gifts, or
- Transportation.

An ordinary expense is one that is common and accepted in your trade or business. A necessary expense is one that is helpful and appropriate for your business. An expense doesn't have to be required to be considered necessary.

This chapter explains the following.

- What expenses are deductible.
- How to report your expenses on your return.
- What records you need to prove your expenses.
- How to treat any expense reimbursements you may receive.

Who doesn't need to use this chapter. If you are an employee, you won't need to read this chapter if all of the following are true.

- You fully accounted to your employer for your work-related expenses.
- You received full reimbursement for your expenses.
- Your employer required you to return any excess reimbursement and you did so.
- There is no amount shown with a code L in box 12 of your Form W-2, Wage and Tax Statement.

If you meet all of these conditions, there is no need to show the expenses or the reimbursements on your return. See *Reimbursements,* later, if you would like more information on reimbursements and accounting to your employer.

 If you meet these conditions and your employer included reimbursements on your Form W-2 in error, ask your employer for a corrected Form W-2.

Useful Items

You may want to see:

Publication

❑ **463** Travel, Gift, and Car Expenses

❑ **535** Business Expenses

Form (and Instructions)

❑ **Schedule A (Form 1040)** Itemized Deductions

❑ **Schedule C (Form 1040)** Profit or Loss From Business

❑ **Schedule C-EZ (Form 1040)** Net Profit From Business

❑ **Schedule F (Form 1040)** Profit or Loss From Farming

❑ **Form 2106** Employee Business Expenses

For these and other useful items, go to *IRS.gov/ Forms.*

Travel Expenses

If you temporarily travel away from your tax home, you can use this section to determine if you have deductible travel expenses. This section discusses:

- Traveling away from home,
- Tax home,
- Temporary assignment or job, and
- What travel expenses are deductible.

It also discusses the standard meal allowance, rules for travel inside and outside the United States, and deductible convention expenses.

Travel expenses defined. For tax purposes, travel expenses are the ordinary and necessary expenses (defined earlier) of traveling away from home for your business, profession, or job.

You will find examples of deductible travel expenses in Table 20-1.

Traveling Away From Home

You are traveling away from home if:

- Your duties require you to be away from the general area of your tax home (defined later) substantially longer than an ordinary day's work, and
- You need to sleep or rest to meet the demands of your work while away from home.

This rest requirement isn't satisfied by merely napping in your car. You don't have to be away from your tax home for a whole day or from dusk to dawn as long as your relief from duty is long enough to get necessary sleep or rest.

Example 1. You are a railroad conductor. You leave your home terminal on a regularly scheduled round-trip run between two cities and return home 16 hours later. During the run, you have 6 hours off at your turnaround point where you eat two meals and rent a hotel room to get necessary sleep before starting the return trip. You are considered to be away from home.

Example 2. You are a truck driver. You leave your terminal and return to it later the same day. You get an hour off at your turn-around point to eat. Because you aren't off to get necessary sleep and the brief time off isn't an adequate rest period, you aren't traveling away from home.

Members of the Armed Forces. If you are a member of the U.S. Armed Forces on a permanent duty assignment overseas, you aren't traveling away from home. You can't deduct your expenses for meals and lodging. You can't deduct these expenses even if you have to maintain a home in the United States for your family members who aren't allowed to accompany you overseas. If you are transferred from one permanent duty station to another, you may have deductible moving expenses, which are explained in Pub. 521, Moving Expenses.

A naval officer assigned to permanent duty aboard a ship that has regular eating and living facilities has a tax home aboard ship for travel expense purposes.

Tax Home

To determine whether you are traveling away from home, you must first determine the location of your tax home.

Generally, your tax home is your regular place of business or post of duty, regardless of where you maintain your family home. It includes the entire city or general area in which your business or work is located.

If you have more than one regular place of business, your tax home is your main place of business. See *Main place of business or work*, later.

If you don't have a regular or a main place of business because of the nature of your work, then your tax home may be the place where you regularly live. See *No main place of business or work*, later.

If you don't have a regular or a main place of business or post of duty and there is no place where you regularly live, you are considered an itinerant (a transient) and your tax home is wherever you work. As an itinerant, you can't claim a travel expense deduction because you are never considered to be traveling away from home.

Main place of business or work. If you have more than one place of business or work, consider the following when determining which one is your main place of business or work.

- The total time you ordinarily spend in each place.
- The level of your business activity in each place.
- Whether your income from each place is significant or insignificant.

Example. You live in Cincinnati where you have a seasonal job for 8 months each year and

earn $40,000. You work the other 4 months in Miami, also at a seasonal job, and earn $15,000. Cincinnati is your main place of work because you spend most of your time there and earn most of your income there.

No main place of business or work. You may have a tax home even if you don't have a regular or main place of business or work. Your tax home may be the home where you regularly live.

Factors used to determine tax home. If you don't have a regular or main place of business or work, use the following three factors to determine where your tax home is.

1. You perform part of your business in the area of your main home and use that home for lodging while doing business in the area.

2. You have living expenses at your main home that you duplicate because your business requires you to be away from that home.

3. You haven't abandoned the area in which both your historical place of lodging and your claimed main home are located; you have a member or members of your family living at your main home; or you often use that home for lodging.

If you satisfy all three factors, your tax home is the home where you regularly live. If you satisfy only two factors, you may have a tax home depending on all the facts and circumstances. If you satisfy only one factor, you are an itinerant; your tax home is wherever you work and you can't deduct travel expenses.

Example. You are single and live in Boston in an apartment you rent. You have worked for your employer in Boston for a number of years. Your employer enrolls you in a 12-month executive training program. You don't expect to return to work in Boston after you complete your training.

During your training, you don't do any work in Boston. Instead, you receive classroom and on-the-job training throughout the United States. You keep your apartment in Boston and return to it frequently. You use your apartment to conduct your personal business. You also keep up your community contacts in Boston. When you complete your training, you are transferred to Los Angeles.

You don't satisfy factor (1) because you didn't work in Boston. You satisfy factor (2) because you had duplicate living expenses. You also satisfy factor (3) because you didn't abandon your apartment in Boston as your main home, you kept your community contacts, and you frequently returned to live in your apartment. Therefore, you have a tax home in Boston.

Tax home different from family home. If you (and your family) don't live at your tax home (defined earlier), you can't deduct the cost of traveling between your tax home and your family home. You also can't deduct the cost of meals and lodging while at your tax home. See *Example 1* below.

If you are working temporarily in the same city where you and your family live, you may be

considered as traveling away from home. See *Example 2* below.

Example 1. You are a truck driver and you and your family live in Tucson. You are employed by a trucking firm that has its terminal in Phoenix. At the end of your long runs, you return to your home terminal in Phoenix and spend one night there before returning home. You can't deduct any expenses you have for meals and lodging in Phoenix or the cost of traveling from Phoenix to Tucson. This is because Phoenix is your tax home.

Example 2. Your family home is in Pittsburgh, where you work 12 weeks a year. The rest of the year you work for the same employer in Baltimore. In Baltimore, you eat in restaurants and sleep in a rooming house. Your salary is the same whether you are in Pittsburgh or Baltimore.

Because you spend most of your working time and earn most of your salary in Baltimore, that city is your tax home. You can't deduct any expenses you have for meals and lodging there. However, when you return to work in Pittsburgh, you are away from your tax home even though you stay at your family home. You can deduct the cost of your round trip between Baltimore and Pittsburgh. You can also deduct your part of your family's living expenses for non-entertainment-related meals and lodging while you are living and working in Pittsburgh.

Temporary Assignment or Job

You may regularly work at your tax home and also work at another location. It may not be practical to return to your tax home from this other location at the end of each work day.

Temporary assignment vs. indefinite assignment. If your assignment or job away from your main place of work is temporary, your tax home doesn't change. You are considered to be away from home for the whole period you are away from your main place of work. You can deduct your travel expenses if they otherwise qualify for deduction. Generally, a temporary assignment in a single location is one that is realistically expected to last (and does in fact last) for 1 year or less.

However, if your assignment or job is indefinite, the location of the assignment or job becomes your new tax home and you can't deduct your travel expenses while there. An assignment or job in a single location is considered indefinite if it is realistically expected to last for more than 1 year, whether or not it actually lasts for more than 1 year.

If your assignment is indefinite, you must include in your income any amounts you receive from your employer for living expenses, even if they are called travel allowances and you account to your employer for them.

Exception for federal crime investigations or prosecutions. If you are a federal employee participating in a federal crime investigation or prosecution, you aren't subject to the 1-year rule. This means you may be able to deduct travel expenses even if you are away from your tax home for more than 1 year, provided you meet the other requirements for deductibility.

For you to qualify, the Attorney General (or his or her designee) must certify that you are traveling:

- For the federal government;

- In a temporary duty status; and

- To investigate or prosecute, or provide support services for the investigation or prosecution of, a federal crime.

Determining temporary or indefinite. You must determine whether your assignment is temporary or indefinite when you start work. If you expect an assignment or job to last for 1 year or less, it is temporary unless there are facts and circumstances that indicate otherwise. An assignment or job that is initially temporary may become indefinite due to changed circumstances. A series of assignments to the same location, all for short periods but that together cover a long period, may be considered an indefinite assignment.

Going home on days off. If you go back to your tax home from a temporary assignment on your days off, you aren't considered away from home while you are in your hometown. You can't deduct the cost of your meals and lodging there. However, you can deduct your travel expenses, including meals and lodging, while traveling between your temporary place of work and your tax home. You can claim these expenses up to the amount it would have cost you to stay at your temporary place of work.

If you keep your hotel room during your visit home, you can deduct the cost of your hotel room. In addition, you can deduct your expenses of returning home up to the amount you would have spent for meals had you stayed at your temporary place of work.

Probationary work period. If you take a job that requires you to move, with the understanding that you will keep the job if your work is satisfactory during a probationary period, the job is indefinite. You can't deduct any of your expenses for meals and lodging during the probationary period.

What Travel Expenses Are Deductible?

Once you have determined that you are traveling away from your tax home, you can determine what travel expenses are deductible.

You can deduct ordinary and necessary expenses you have when you travel away from home on business. The type of expense you can deduct depends on the facts and your circumstances.

Table 20-1 summarizes travel expenses you may be able to deduct. You may have other deductible travel expenses that aren't covered there, depending on the facts and your circumstances.

 When you travel away from home on business, you should keep records of all the expenses you have and any advances you receive from your employer. You can use a log, diary, notebook, or any other written record to keep track of your expenses.

The types of expenses you need to record, along with supporting documentation, are described in Table 20-2.

Separating costs. If you have one expense that includes the costs of non-entertainment-related meals and other services (such as lodging or transportation), you must allocate that expense between the cost of non-entertainment-related meals and the cost of other services. You must have a reasonable basis for making this allocation. For example, you must allocate your expenses if a hotel includes one or more meals in its room charge.

Travel expenses for another individual. If a spouse, dependent, or other individual goes with you (or your employee) on a business trip or to a business convention, you generally can't deduct his or her travel expenses.

Employee. You can deduct the travel expenses of someone who goes with you if that person:

1. Is your employee,

2. Has a bona fide business purpose for the travel, and

3. Would otherwise be allowed to deduct the travel expenses.

Business associate. If a business associate travels with you and meets the conditions in (2) and (3) above, you can deduct the travel expenses you have for that person. A business associate is someone with whom you could reasonably expect to engage or deal in the active conduct of your business. A business associate can be a current or prospective (likely to become) customer, client, supplier, employee, agent, partner, or professional advisor.

Bona fide business purpose. A bona fide business purpose exists if you can prove a real business purpose for the individual's presence. Incidental services, such as typing notes or assisting in entertaining customers, aren't enough to make the expenses deductible.

Example. Jerry drives to Chicago on business and takes his wife, Linda, with him. Linda isn't Jerry's employee. Linda occasionally types notes, performs similar services, and accompanies Jerry to luncheons and dinners. The performance of these services doesn't establish that her presence on the trip is necessary to the conduct of Jerry's business. Her expenses aren't deductible.

Jerry pays $199 a day for a double room. A single room costs $149 a day. He can deduct the total cost of driving his car to and from Chicago, but only $149 a day for his hotel room. If both Jerry and Linda use public transportation, Jerry can deduct only his fare.

Meals and Incidental Expenses

You can deduct the cost of non-entertainment-related meals if it is necessary for you to stop for substantial sleep or rest to properly perform your duties while traveling away from home on business.

The elimination of the deduction for entertainment expenses is discussed under *Meals and Entertainment Expenses*, later. The

following discussion deals with meals (and incidental expenses).

50% limit on meals. You can figure your meal expenses using either of the following methods.

- Actual cost.

- The standard meal allowance.

Both of these methods are explained below. But, regardless of the method you use, you generally can deduct only 50% of the unreimbursed cost of your non-entertainment-related meals.

If you are reimbursed for the cost of your meals, how you apply the 50% limit depends on whether your employer's reimbursement plan was accountable or nonaccountable. If you aren't reimbursed, the 50% limit applies even if the unreimbursed meal expense is for business travel. The 50% limit is explained later under *Meals and Entertainment Expenses*. Accountable and nonaccountable plans are discussed later under *Reimbursements*.

Actual cost. You can use the actual cost of your meals to figure the amount of your expense before reimbursement and application of the 50% deduction limit. If you use this method, you must keep records of your actual cost.

Standard meal allowance. Generally, you can use the "standard meal allowance" method as an alternative to the actual cost method. It allows you to use a set amount for your daily meals and incidental expenses (M&IE), instead of keeping records of your actual costs. The set amount varies depending on where and when you travel. In this chapter, "standard meal allowance" refers to the federal rate for M&IE, discussed later under *Amount of standard meal allowance*. If you use the standard meal allowance, you still must keep records to prove the time, place, and business purpose of your travel. See *Recordkeeping*, later.

Incidental expenses. The term "incidental expenses" means fees and tips given to porters, baggage carriers, hotel staff, and staff on ships. Incidental expenses don't include expenses for laundry, cleaning and pressing of clothing, lodging taxes, costs of telegrams or telephone calls, transportation between places of lodging or business and places where meals are taken, or the mailing cost of filing travel vouchers and paying employer-sponsored charge card billings.

Incidental expenses only method. You can use an optional method (instead of actual cost) for deducting incidental expenses only. The amount of the deduction is $5 a day. You can use this method only if you didn't pay or incur any meal expenses. You can't use this method on any day that you use the standard meal allowance.

 Federal employees should refer to the Federal Travel Regulations at GSA.gov. Find "Policy and Regulations" and click on "Regulations" for links to Federal Travel Regulation (FTR) for changes affecting claims for reimbursement.

50% limit may apply. If you use the standard meal allowance method for non-entertainment-related meal expenses and you aren't

Table 20-1. **Travel Expenses You Can Deduct**
This chart summarizes expenses you can deduct when you travel away from home for business purposes.

IF you have expenses for...	THEN you can deduct the cost of...
transportation	travel by airplane, train, bus, or car between your home and your business destination. If you were provided with a ticket or you are riding free as a result of a frequent traveler or similar program, your cost is zero. If you travel by ship, see *Luxury Water Travel* and *Cruise Ships* (under *Conventions*) in Pub. 463 for additional rules and limits.
taxi, commuter bus, and airport limousine	fares for these and other types of transportation that take you between: • The airport or station and your hotel; and • The hotel and the work location of your customers or clients, your business meeting place, or your temporary work location.
baggage and shipping	sending baggage and sample or display material between your regular and temporary work locations.
car	operating and maintaining your car when traveling away from home on business. You can deduct actual expenses or the standard mileage rate as well as business-related tolls and parking. If you rent a car while away from home on business, you can deduct only the business-use portion of the expenses.
lodging and meals	your lodging and non-entertainment-related meals if your business trip is overnight or long enough that you need to stop for sleep or rest to properly perform your duties. Meals include amounts spent for food, beverages, taxes, and related tips. See *Meals and Incidental Expenses*, earlier, for additional rules and limits.
cleaning	dry cleaning and laundry.
telephone	business calls while on your business trip. This includes business communication by fax machine or other communication devices.
tips	tips you pay for any expenses in this chart.
other	other similar ordinary and necessary expenses related to your business travel. These expenses might include transportation to or from a business meal, public stenographer's fees, computer rental fees, and operating and maintaining a house trailer.

reimbursed or you are reimbursed under a non-accountable plan, you can generally deduct only 50% of the standard meal allowance. If you are reimbursed under an accountable plan and you are deducting amounts that are more than your reimbursements, you can deduct only 50% of the excess amount. The 50% limit is explained later under *Meals and Entertainment Expenses*. Accountable and nonaccountable plans are discussed later under *Reimbursements*.

 There is no optional standard lodging amount similar to the standard meal allowance. Your allowable lodging expense deduction is your actual cost.

Who can use the standard meal allowance. You can use the standard meal allowance whether you are an employee or self-employed, and whether or not you are reimbursed for your traveling expenses.

Use of the standard meal allowance for other travel. You can use the standard meal allowance to figure your meal expenses when you travel in connection with investment and other income-producing property. You can also use it to figure your meal expenses when you travel for qualifying educational purposes. You can't use the standard meal allowance to figure the cost of your meals when you travel for medical or charitable purposes.

Amount of standard meal allowance. The standard meal allowance is the federal M&IE rate. For travel between January 1 and September 30, 2018, the rate for most small localities in the United States is $51 a day. For travel between October 1 and December 31, 2018, the rate for most small localities in the United States is $60 a day.

Most major cities and many other localities in the United States are designated as high-cost areas, qualifying for higher standard meal allowances. You can find this information (organized by year and location) on the Internet at *GSA.gov/perdiem*.

If you travel to more than one location in one day, use the rate in effect for the area where you stop for sleep or rest. If you work in the transportation industry, however, see *Special rate for transportation workers*, later.

Standard meal allowance for areas outside the continental United States. The standard meal allowance rates above don't apply to travel in Alaska, Hawaii, or any other location outside the continental United States. The Department of Defense establishes per diem rates for Alaska, Hawaii, Puerto Rico, American Samoa, Guam, Midway, the Northern Mariana Islands, the U.S. Virgin Islands, Wake Island, and other non-foreign areas outside the continental United States. The Department of State establishes per diem rates for all other foreign areas.

 You can access per diem rates for non-foreign areas outside the continental United States at *www.Defensetravel.dod.mil/site/perdiemCalc.cfm*. You can access all other foreign per diem rates at *State.gov/travel/*. Click on "Travel Per Diem Allowances for Foreign Areas" under "Foreign Per Diem Rates" to obtain the latest foreign per diem rates.

Special rate for transportation workers. You can use a special standard meal allowance if you work in the transportation industry. You are in the transportation industry if your work:

• Directly involves moving people or goods by airplane, barge, bus, ship, train, or truck; and

• Regularly requires you to travel away from home and, during any single trip, usually involves travel to areas eligible for different standard meal allowance rates.

If this applies to you, you can claim a standard daily meal allowance of $63 a day ($68 for travel outside the continental United States) for travel between January 1 and September 30, 2018. You can claim a standard meal allowance of $66 a day ($71 for travel outside the continental United States) for travel between October 1 and December 31, 2018. To determine which rate you should use, see *Transition Rules* in Pub. 463.

Using the special rate for transportation workers eliminates the need for you to determine the standard meal allowance for every area where you stop for sleep or rest. If you choose to use the special rate for any trip, you must use the special rate (and not use the regular standard meal allowance rates) for all trips you take that year.

Travel for days you depart and return. For both the day you depart for and the day you return from a business trip, you must prorate the standard meal allowance (figure a reduced amount for each day). You can do so by one of two methods.

- Method 1: You can claim 3/4 of the standard meal allowance.

- Method 2: You can prorate using any method that you consistently apply and that is in accordance with reasonable business practice.

Example. Jen is employed in New Orleans as a convention planner. In March, her employer sent her on a 3-day trip to Washington, DC, to attend a planning seminar. She left her home in New Orleans at 10 a.m. on Wednesday and arrived in Washington, DC, at 5:30 p.m. After spending two nights there, she flew back to New Orleans on Friday and arrived back home at 8 p.m. Jen's employer gave her a flat amount to cover her expenses and included it with her wages.

Under Method 1, Jen can claim 2½ days of the standard meal allowance for Washington, DC: 3/4 of the daily rate for Wednesday and Friday (the days she departed and returned), and the full daily rate for Thursday.

Under Method 2, Jen could also use any method that she applies consistently and that is in accordance with reasonable business practice. For example, she could claim 3 days of the standard meal allowance even though a federal employee would have to use Method 1 and be limited to only 2½ days.

Travel in the United States

The following discussion applies to travel in the United States. For this purpose, the United States includes only the 50 states and the District of Columbia. The treatment of your travel expenses depends on how much of your trip was business related and on how much of your trip occurred within the United States. See *Part of Trip Outside the United States*, later.

Trip Primarily for Business

You can deduct all your travel expenses if your trip was entirely business related. If your trip was primarily for business and, while at your business destination, made a personal side trip, or had other personal activities, you can deduct your business-related travel expenses. These expenses include the travel costs of getting to and from your business destination and any business-related expenses at your business destination.

Example. You work in Atlanta and take a business trip to New Orleans in May. Your business travel totals 900 miles round trip. On your way home, you stop in Mobile to visit your parents. You spend $2,165 for the 9 days you are away from home for travel, non-entertainment-related meals, lodging, and other travel expenses. If you hadn't stopped in Mobile, you would've been gone only 6 days, and your total cost would have been $1,633.50. You can deduct $1,633.50 for your trip, including the cost of round-trip transportation to and from New Orleans. The deduction for your non-entertainment-related meals is subject to the 50% limit on meals mentioned earlier.

Trip Primarily for Personal Reasons

If your trip was primarily for personal reasons, such as a vacation, the entire cost of the trip is a nondeductible personal expense. However, you can deduct any expenses you have while at your destination that are directly related to your business.

A trip to a resort or on a cruise ship may be a vacation even if the promoter advertises that it is primarily for business. The scheduling of incidental business activities during a trip, such as viewing videotapes or attending lectures dealing with general subjects, won't change what is really a vacation into a business trip.

Part of Trip Outside the United States

If part of your trip is outside the United States, use the rules described later under *Travel Outside the United States* for that part of the trip. For the part of your trip that is inside the United States, use the rules for travel in the United States. Travel outside the United States doesn't include travel from one point in the United States to another point in the United States. The following discussion can help you determine whether your trip was entirely within the United States.

Public transportation. If you travel by public transportation, any place in the United States where that vehicle makes a scheduled stop is a point in the United States. Once the vehicle leaves the last scheduled stop in the United States on its way to a point outside the United States, you apply the rules under *Travel Outside the United States*, later.

Example. You fly from New York to Puerto Rico with a scheduled stop in Miami. You return to New York nonstop. The flight from New York to Miami is in the United States, so only the flight from Miami to Puerto Rico is outside the United States. Because there are no scheduled stops between Puerto Rico and New York, all of the return trip is outside the United States.

Private car. Travel by private car in the United States is travel between points in the United States, even when you are on your way to a destination outside the United States.

Example. You travel by car from Denver to Mexico City and return. Your travel from Denver to the border and from the border back to Denver is travel in the United States, and the rules in this section apply. The rules below under *Travel Outside the United States* apply to your trip from the border to Mexico City and back to the border.

Travel Outside the United States

If any part of your business travel is outside the United States, some of your deductions for the cost of getting to and from your destination may be limited. For this purpose, the United States includes only the 50 states and the District of Columbia.

How much of your travel expenses you can deduct depends in part upon how much of your trip outside the United States was business related.

See chapter 1 of Pub. 463 for information on luxury water travel.

Travel Entirely for Business or Considered Entirely for Business

You can deduct all your travel expenses of getting to and from your business destination if your trip is entirely for business or considered entirely for business.

Travel entirely for business. If you travel outside the United States and you spend the entire time on business activities, you can deduct all of your travel expenses.

Travel considered entirely for business. Even if you didn't spend your entire time on business activities, your trip is considered entirely for business if you meet at least one of the following four exceptions.

Exception 1—No substantial control. Your trip is considered entirely for business if you didn't have substantial control over arranging the trip. The fact that you control the timing of your trip doesn't, by itself, mean that you have substantial control over arranging your trip.

You don't have substantial control over your trip if you:

- Are an employee who was reimbursed or paid a travel expense allowance,

- Aren't related to your employer, or

- Aren't a managing executive.

"Related to your employer" is defined later in this chapter under *Per Diem and Car Allowances*.

A "managing executive" is an employee who has the authority and responsibility, without being subject to the veto of another, to decide on the need for the business travel.

A self-employed person generally has substantial control over arranging business trips.

Exception 2—Outside United States no more than a week. Your trip is considered entirely for business if you were outside the United States for a week or less, combining business and nonbusiness activities. One week means 7 consecutive days. In counting the days, don't count the day you leave the United States, but do count the day you return to the United States.

Exception 3—Less than 25% of time on personal activities. Your trip is considered entirely for business if:

- You were outside the United States for more than a week, and

- You spent less than 25% of the total time you were outside the United States on nonbusiness activities.

For this purpose, count both the day your trip began and the day it ended.

Exception 4—Vacation not a major consideration. Your trip is considered entirely for business if you can establish that a personal vacation wasn't a major consideration, even if you have substantial control over arranging the trip.

Travel Primarily for Business

If you travel outside the United States primarily for business but spend some of your time on nonbusiness activities, you generally can't deduct all of your travel expenses. You only can deduct the business portion of your cost of getting to and from your destination. You must allocate the costs between your business and nonbusiness activities to determine your deductible amount. These travel allocation rules are discussed in chapter 1 of Pub. 463.

 You don't have to allocate your travel expense deduction if you meet one of the four exceptions listed earlier under Travel considered entirely for business. *In those cases, you can deduct the total cost of getting to and from your destination.*

Travel Primarily for Personal Reasons

If you travel outside the United States primarily for vacation or for investment purposes, the entire cost of the trip is a nondeductible personal expense. If you spend some time attending brief professional seminars or a continuing education program, you can deduct your registration fees and other expenses you have that are directly related to your business.

Conventions

You can deduct your travel expenses when you attend a convention if you can show that your attendance benefits your trade or business. You can't deduct the travel expenses for your family.

If the convention is for investment, political, social, or other purposes unrelated to your trade or business, you can't deduct the expenses.

 Your appointment or election as a delegate doesn't, in itself, determine whether you can deduct travel expenses. You can deduct your travel expenses only if your attendance is connected to your own trade or business.

Convention agenda. The convention agenda or program generally shows the purpose of the convention. You can show your attendance at the convention benefits your trade or business by comparing the agenda with the official duties and responsibilities of your position. The agenda doesn't have to deal specifically with your official duties and responsibilities; it will be enough if the agenda is so related to your position that it shows your attendance was for business purposes.

Conventions held outside the North American area. See chapter 1 of Pub. 463 for information on conventions held outside the North American area.

Meals and Entertainment Expenses

For expenses paid or incurred after 2017, generally no deduction is available for entertainment expenses, including entertainment-related meals. Entertainment includes any activity generally considered to provide entertainment, amusement, or recreation, and includes meals provided to a customer or client. Generally, entertainment expenses paid after 2017 (including entertainment-related meals) are not deductible. If you have one expense that includes the costs of entertainment and other services (such as lodging or transportation), you must allocate that expense between the cost of entertainment and the cost of other services. You must have a reasonable basis for making the allocation. For example, you must allocate your expenses if a hotel includes entertainment in its lounge on the same bill with your room charge. In certain limited cases, you may be able to deduct entertainment expenses, such as when you treat the expense as compensation to an employee and as wages to the employee for tax purposes. For more information, see chapter 2 of Pub. 463.

 If food or beverages are provided during or at an entertainment event, and the food and beverages were purchased separately from the entertainment or the cost of the food and beverages was stated separately from the cost of the entertainment on one or more bills, invoices, or receipts, you may be able to deduct the separately stated costs as a meal expense. See Notice 2018-76 for examples and more information. Notice 2018-76 is available at IRS.gov/irb/ 2018-42 IRB#NOT-2018-76.

50% Limit on Meals

In general, you can deduct only 50% of your non-entertainment business-related meal, unless an exception applies. (If you are subject to the Department of Transportation's "hours of service" limits, you can deduct 80% of your business-related meal and entertainment expenses. See *Individuals subject to "hours of service" limits,* later.)

The 50% limit applies to employees or their employers, and to self-employed persons (including independent contractors) or their clients, depending on whether the expenses are reimbursed.

Figure 20-A summarizes the general rules explained in this section.

Examples of non-entertainment-related meals might include:

- Meals while traveling away from home (whether eating alone or with others) on business, and

- Meals at a business convention or business league meeting.

Included expenses. Expenses subject to the 50% limit include:

- Taxes and tips relating to a business meal, and

- Rent paid for a room in which you hold a dinner or cocktail party.

However, the cost of transportation to and from a business meal isn't subject to the 50% limit.

Application of 50% limit. The 50% limit on non-entertainment-related meal expenses applies if the expense is otherwise deductible and isn't covered by one of the exceptions discussed later in this section.

The 50% limit also applies to certain meal expenses that aren't business related. It applies to meal expenses you have for the production of income, including rental or royalty income. It also applies to the cost of meals included in deductible educational expenses.

When to apply the 50% limit. You apply the 50% limit after determining the amount that would otherwise qualify for a deduction. You first have to determine the amount of non-entertainment-related meal expenses that would be deductible under the other rules discussed in this chapter.

Example 1. You spend $200 (including tax and tip) for a non-entertainment-related business meal. If $110 of that amount isn't allowable because it is lavish and extravagant, the remaining $90 is subject to the 50% limit. Your deduction can't be more than $45 (50% (0.50) × $90).

Example 2. You purchase two tickets to a concert for you and your client. Your deduction is zero because no deduction is allowed for entertainment expenses.

Exceptions to the 50% Limit

Generally, non-entertainment-related business meal expenses are subject to the 50% limit. Figure 20-A can help you determine if the 50% limit applies to you.

Your meal expense isn't subject to the 50% limit and an expense for entertainment may be deductible if the expense meets one of the following exceptions.

Expenses treated as compensation. In general, expenses for goods, services, and facilities aren't subject to the 50% limit to the extent the expenses are treated by the taxpayer with respect to entertainment, amusement, or recreation, as compensation to an employee and as wages to the employee for tax purposes.

Employee's reimbursed expenses. If you are an employee, you aren't subject to the 50% limit on expenses for which your employer reimburses you under an accountable plan. Accountable plans are discussed later under *Reimbursements.*

Individuals subject to "hours of service" limits. You can deduct a higher percentage of your meal expenses while traveling away from your tax home if the meals take place during or incident to any period subject to the Department of Transportation's "hours of service" limits. The percentage is 80%.

Individuals subject to the Department of Transportation's "hours of service" limits include the following persons.

- Certain air transportation workers (such as pilots, crew, dispatchers, mechanics, and control tower operators) who are under Federal Aviation Administration regulations.

- Interstate truck operators and bus drivers who are under Department of Transportation regulations.

- Certain railroad employees (such as engineers, conductors, train crews, dispatchers, and control operations personnel) who are under Federal Railroad Administration regulations.

- Certain merchant mariners who are under Coast Guard regulations.

Other exceptions. There are also exceptions for the self-employed; expenses for recreational, social, or similar activities (such as a holiday party); meals furnished as advertising expenses; and selling meals. These are discussed in Pub. 463.

What Meal Expenses Are Deductible?

This section explains the rules for deducting non-entertainment-related meal expenses. Beginning in 2018, you may not deduct any entertainment expenses.

Entertainment. Entertainment includes any activity generally considered to provide entertainment, amusement, or recreation. Examples include entertaining guests at nightclubs; at social, athletic, and sporting clubs; at theaters; at sporting events; or on hunting, fishing, vacation, and similar trips.

A meal as a form of entertainment. Entertainment includes the cost of a meal you provide to a customer or client, whether the meal is a part of other entertainment or by itself. A meal expense includes the cost of food, beverages, taxes, and tips for the meal.

Separating costs. If you have one expense that includes the costs of entertainment and other services (such as lodging or transportation), you must allocate that expense between the cost of entertainment and the cost of other services. You must have a reasonable basis for making this allocation. For example, you must allocate your expenses if a hotel includes entertainment in its lounge on the same bill with your room charge. You can deduct the lodging costs but not the entertainment costs.

Taking turns paying for meals. If a group of business acquaintances take turns picking up each others' non-entertainment-related meal checks without regard to whether any business purposes are served, no member of the group can deduct any part of the expense.

Trade association meetings. You can deduct expenses that are directly related to, and necessary for, attending business meetings or conventions of certain exempt organizations if the expenses of your attendance are related to your active trade or business. These organizations

Figure 20-A. **Does the 50% Limit Apply to Your Expenses?**

There are exceptions to these rules. See *Exceptions to the 50% Limit.*

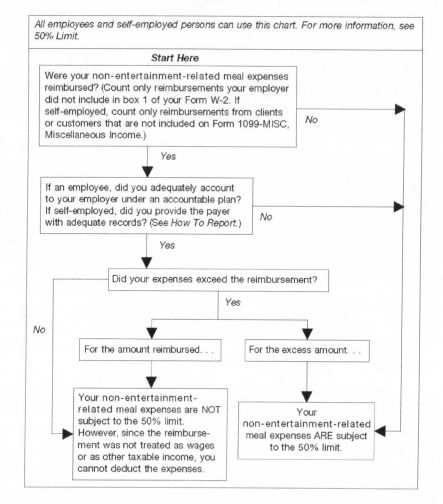

include business leagues, chambers of commerce, real estate boards, trade associations, and professional associations.

Gift Expenses

If you give gifts in the course of your trade or business, you can deduct all or part of the cost. This section explains the limits and rules for deducting the costs of gifts.

$25 limit. You can deduct no more than $25 for business gifts you give directly or indirectly to each person during your tax year. A gift to a company that is intended for the eventual personal use or benefit of a particular person or a limited class of people will be considered an indirect gift to that particular person or to the individuals within that class of people who receive the gift.

If you give a gift to a member of a customer's family, the gift is generally considered to be an indirect gift to the customer. This rule doesn't apply if you have a bona fide independent business connection with that family member and the gift isn't intended for the customer's eventual use or benefit.

If you and your spouse both give gifts, both of you are treated as one taxpayer. It doesn't matter whether you have separate businesses, are separately employed, or whether each of you has an independent connection with the recipient. If a partnership gives gifts, the partnership and the partners are treated as one taxpayer.

Incidental costs. Incidental costs, such as engraving on jewelry, or packaging, insuring, and mailing, are generally not included in determining the cost of a gift for purposes of the $25 limit.

A cost is incidental only if it doesn't add substantial value to the gift. For example, the cost of customary gift wrapping is an incidental cost. However, the purchase of an ornamental basket for packaging fruit isn't an incidental cost if the value of the basket is substantial compared to the value of the fruit.

Exceptions. The following items aren't considered gifts for purposes of the $25 limit.

1. An item that costs $4 or less and:

    a. Has your name clearly and permanently imprinted on the gift, and

b. Is one of a number of identical items you widely distribute. Examples include pens, desk sets, and plastic bags and cases.

2. Signs, display racks, or other promotional material to be used on the business premises of the recipient.

Gift or entertainment. Any item that might be considered either a gift or entertainment generally will be considered entertainment. You can't deduct entertainment expenses. However, if you give a customer packaged food or beverages you intend the customer to use at a later date, treat it as a gift.

If you give a customer tickets to a theater performance or sporting event and you don't go with the customer to the performance or event, you have a choice. You can treat the cost of the tickets as either a gift expense or an entertainment expense. However, you can only deduct the cost if you treat it as a gift expense.

If you go with the customer to the event, you must treat the cost of the tickets as a non-deductible entertainment expense. You can't choose, in this case, to treat the cost of the tickets as a gift expense.

Transportation Expenses

This section discusses expenses you can deduct for business transportation when you aren't traveling away from home as defined earlier under *Travel Expenses*. These expenses include the cost of transportation by air, rail, bus, taxi, etc., and the cost of driving and maintaining your car.

Transportation expenses include the ordinary and necessary costs of all of the following.

- Getting from one workplace to another in the course of your business or profession when you are traveling within the area of your tax home. (Tax home is defined earlier under *Travel Expenses*.)

- Visiting clients or customers.

- Going to a business meeting away from your regular workplace.

- Getting from your home to a temporary workplace when you have one or more regular places of work. These temporary workplaces can be either within the area of your tax home or outside that area.

Transportation expenses don't include expenses you have while traveling away from home overnight. Those expenses are travel expenses, discussed earlier. However, if you use your car while traveling away from home overnight, use the rules in this section to figure your car expense deduction. See *Car Expenses*, later.

Illustration of transportation expenses. Figure 20-B illustrates the rules for when you can deduct transportation expenses when you have a regular or main job away from your home. You may want to refer to it when deciding whether you can deduct your transportation expenses. Daily transportation expenses you incur while traveling from home to one or more regular places of business are generally nondeductible commuting expenses. However, there are many exceptions for deducting transportation expenses, like whether your work location is temporary (inside or outside the metropolitan area), traveling for the same trade or business, or if you have a home office.

Temporary work location. If you have one or more regular work locations away from your home and you commute to a temporary work location in the same trade or business, you can deduct the expenses of the daily round-trip transportation between your home and the temporary location, regardless of distance.

If your employment at a work location is realistically expected to last (and does in fact last) for 1 year or less, the employment is temporary unless there are facts and circumstances that would indicate otherwise.

If your employment at a work location is realistically expected to last for more than 1 year or if there is no realistic expectation that the employment will last for 1 year or less, the employment isn't temporary, regardless of whether it actually lasts for more than 1 year.

If employment at a work location initially is realistically expected to last for 1 year or less, but at some later date the employment is realistically expected to last more than 1 year, that employment will be treated as temporary (unless there are facts and circumstances that would indicate otherwise) until your expectation changes. It won't be treated as temporary after the date you determine it will last more than 1 year.

If the temporary work location is beyond the general area of your regular place of work and you stay overnight, you are traveling away from home. You may have deductible travel expenses as discussed earlier in this chapter.

No regular place of work. If you have no regular place of work but ordinarily work in the metropolitan area where you live, you can deduct daily transportation costs between home and a temporary work site outside that metropolitan area.

Generally, a metropolitan area includes the area within the city limits and the suburbs that are considered part of that metropolitan area.

You can't deduct daily transportation costs between your home and temporary work sites within your metropolitan area. These are nondeductible commuting expenses.

Two places of work. If you work at two places in one day, whether or not for the same employer, you can deduct the expense of getting from one workplace to the other. However, if for some personal reason you don't go directly from one location to the other, you can't deduct more than the amount it would have cost you to go directly from the first location to the second.

Transportation expenses you have in going between home and a part-time job on a day off from your main job are commuting expenses. You can't deduct them.

Armed Forces reservists. A meeting of an Armed Forces reserve unit is a second place of business if the meeting is held on a day on which you work at your regular job. You can deduct the expense of getting from one workplace to the other as just discussed under *Two places of work*, earlier.

You usually can't deduct the expense if the reserve meeting is held on a day on which you don't work at your regular job. In this case, your transportation generally is a nondeductible commuting expense. However, you can deduct your transportation expenses if the location of the meeting is temporary and you have one or more regular places of work.

If you ordinarily work in a particular metropolitan area but not at any specific location and the reserve meeting is held at a temporary location outside that metropolitan area, you can deduct your transportation expenses.

If you travel away from home overnight to attend a guard or reserve meeting, you can deduct your travel expenses. These expenses are discussed earlier under *Travel Expenses*.

If you travel more than 100 miles away from home in connection with your performance of services as a member of the reserves, you may be able to deduct some of your reserve-related travel costs as an adjustment to income rather than as an itemized deduction. See *Armed Forces reservists traveling more than 100 miles from home* under *Special Rules*, later.

Commuting expenses. You can't deduct the costs of taking a bus, trolley, subway, or taxi, or of driving a car between your home and your main or regular place of work. These costs are personal commuting expenses. You can't deduct commuting expenses no matter how far your home is from your regular place of work. You can't deduct commuting expenses even if you work during the commuting trip.

Example. You sometimes use your cell phone to make business calls while commuting to and from work. Sometimes business associates ride with you to and from work, and you have a business discussion in the car. These activities don't change the trip from personal to business. You can't deduct your commuting expenses.

Parking fees. Fees you pay to park your car at your place of business are nondeductible commuting expenses. You can, however, deduct business-related parking fees when visiting a customer or client.

Advertising display on car. Putting display material that advertises your business on your car doesn't change the use of your car from personal use to business use. If you use this car for commuting or other personal uses, you still can't deduct your expenses for those uses.

Car pools. You can't deduct the cost of using your car in a nonprofit car pool. Don't include payments you receive from the passengers in your income. These payments are considered reimbursements of your expenses. However, if you operate a car pool for a profit, you must include payments from passengers in your income. You can then deduct your car expenses (using the rules in this chapter).

Hauling tools or instruments. Hauling tools or instruments in your car while commuting to and from work doesn't make your car expenses deductible. However, you can deduct any additional costs you have for hauling tools or instruments (such as for renting a trailer you tow with your car).

Figure 20-B. **When Are Transportation Expenses Deductible?**

Most employees and self-employed persons can use this chart. (Don't use this chart if your home is your principal place of business. See *Office in the home*.)

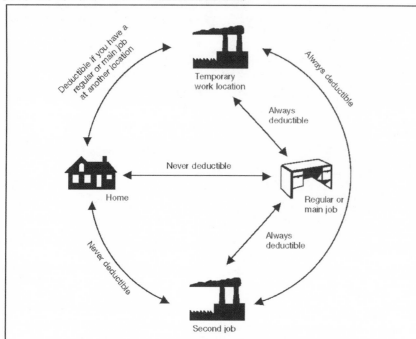

Home: The place where you reside. Transportation expenses between your home and your main or regular place of work are personal commuting expenses.

Regular or main job: Your principal place of business. If you have more than one job, you must determine which one is your regular or main job. Consider the time you spend at each, the activity you have at each, and the income you earn at each.

Temporary work location: A place where your work assignment is realistically expected to last (and does in fact last) one year or less. Unless you have a regular place of business, you can only deduct your transportation expenses to a temporary work location <u>outside</u> your metropolitan area.

Second job: If you regularly work at two or more places in one day, whether or not for the same employer, you can deduct your transportation expenses of getting from one workplace to another. If you do not go directly from your first job to your second job, you can only deduct the transportation expenses of going directly from your first job to your second job. You cannot deduct your transportation expenses between your home and a second job on a day off from your main job.

Union members' trips from a union hall. If you get your work assignments at a union hall and then go to your place of work, the costs of getting from the union hall to your place of work are nondeductible commuting expenses. Although you need the union to get your work assignments, you are employed where you work, not where the union hall is located.

Office in the home. If you have an office in your home that qualifies as a principal place of business, you can deduct your daily transportation costs between your home and another work location in the same trade or business. (See Pub. 587 for information on determining if your home office qualifies as a principal place of business.)

Examples of deductible transportation. The following examples show when you can deduct transportation expenses based on the location of your work and your home.

Example 1. You regularly work in an office in the city where you live. Your employer sends you to a 1-week training session at a different office in the same city. You travel directly from your home to the training location and return each day. You can deduct the cost of your daily round-trip transportation between your home and the training location.

Example 2. Your principal place of business is in your home. You can deduct the cost of round-trip transportation between your qualifying home office and your client's or customer's place of business.

Example 3. You have no regular office, and you don't have an office in your home. In this case, the location of your first business contact inside the metropolitan area is considered your office. Transportation expenses between your home and this first contact are nondeductible commuting expenses. Transportation expenses between your last business contact and your home are also nondeductible commuting expenses. While you can't deduct the costs of these first and last trips, you can deduct the

costs of going from one client or customer to another. With no regular or home office, the costs of travel between two or more business contacts in a metropolitan area are deductible while the costs of travel between the home to (and from) business contacts aren't deductible.

Car Expenses

If you use your car for business purposes, you may be able to deduct car expenses. You generally can use one of the following two methods to figure your deductible expenses.

- *Standard Mileage Rate*.

- *Actual Car Expenses*.

If you use actual car expenses to figure your deduction for a car you lease, there are rules that affect the amount of your lease payments you can deduct. See *Leasing a car* under *Actual Car Expenses*, later.

In this chapter, the term "car" includes a van, pickup, or panel truck.

Standard Mileage Rate

You may be able to use the standard mileage rate to figure the deductible costs of operating your car for business purposes. For 2018, the standard mileage rate for business use is 54.5 cents (0.545) per mile.

 If you use the standard mileage rate for a year, you can't deduct your actual car expenses for that year, but see Parking fees and tolls, *later.*

You generally can use the standard mileage rate whether or not you are reimbursed and whether or not any reimbursement is more or less than the amount figured using the standard mileage rate. See *Reimbursements* under *How To Report*, later.

Choosing the standard mileage rate. If you want to use the standard mileage rate for a car you own, you must choose to use it in the first year the car is available for use in your business. Then, in later years, you can choose to use either the standard mileage rate or actual expenses.

If you want to use the standard mileage rate for a car you lease, you must use it for the entire lease period.

You must make the choice to use the standard mileage rate by the due date (including extensions) of your return. You can't revoke the choice. However, in a later year, you can switch from the standard mileage rate to the actual expenses method. If you change to the actual expenses method in a later year, but before your car is fully depreciated, you have to estimate the remaining useful life of the car and use straight line depreciation.

For more information about depreciation included in the standard mileage rate, see the exception in *Methods of depreciation* under *Depreciation Deduction* in chapter 4 of Pub. 463.

Standard mileage rate not allowed. You can't use the standard mileage rate if you:

- Use five or more cars at the same time (as in fleet operations),

- Claimed a depreciation deduction for the car using any method other than straight line depreciation,
- Claimed a section 179 deduction on the car,
- Claimed the special depreciation allowance on the car, or
- Claimed actual car expenses after 1997 for a car you leased.

Five or more cars. If you own or lease five or more cars that are used for business at the same time, you can't use the standard mileage rate for the business use of any car. However, you may be able to deduct your actual expenses for operating each of the cars in your business. See *Actual Car Expenses* in chapter 4 of Pub. 463 for information on how to figure your deduction.

You aren't using five or more cars for business at the same time if you alternate using (use at different times) the cars for business.

Note. You can elect to use the standard mileage rate if you used a car for hire (such as a taxi).

Parking fees and tolls. In addition to using the standard mileage rate, you can deduct any business-related parking fees and tolls. (Parking fees you pay to park your car at your place of work are nondeductible commuting expenses.)

Actual Car Expenses

If you don't use the standard mileage rate, you may be able to deduct your actual car expenses.

 If you qualify to use both methods, you may want to figure your deduction both ways to see which gives you a larger deduction.

Actual car expenses include:

Depreciation	Lease	Registration
Licenses	payments	fees
Gas	Insurance	Repairs
Oil	Garage rent	Tires
Tolls	Parking fees	

Business and personal use. If you use your car for both business and personal purposes, you must divide your expenses between business and personal use. You can divide your expenses based on the miles driven for each purpose.

Example. You are a contractor and drive your car 20,000 miles during the year: 12,000 miles for business and 8,000 miles for personal use. You can claim only 60% (12,000 ÷ 20,000) of the cost of operating your car as a business expense.

Interest on car loans. If you are an employee, you can't deduct any interest paid on a car loan. This interest is treated as personal interest and isn't deductible. However, if you are self-employed and use your car in that business, see chapter 4 of Pub. 535.

Taxes paid on your car. If you are an employee, you can deduct personal property taxes paid on your car if you itemize deductions. Enter the amount paid on line 5c of Schedule A (Form 1040). (See chapter 23 for more information on taxes.) If you aren't an employee, see your form instructions for information on how to deduct personal property taxes paid on your car.

Sales taxes. Generally, sales taxes on your car are part of your car's basis and are recovered through depreciation, discussed later.

Fines and collateral. You can't deduct fines you pay and collateral you forfeited for traffic violations.

Depreciation and section 179 deductions. Generally, the cost of a car, plus sales tax and improvements, is a capital expense. Because the benefits last longer than 1 year, you generally can't deduct a capital expense. However, you can recover this cost through the section 179 deduction and depreciation deductions. Depreciation allows you to recover the cost over more than 1 year by deducting part of it each year. The section 179 deduction and the depreciation deductions are discussed in more detail in chapter 4 of Pub. 463.

Generally, there are limits on these deductions. Special rules apply if you use your car 50% or less in your work or business.

Leasing a car. If you lease a car, truck, or van that you use in your business, you can use the standard mileage rate or actual expenses to figure your deductible car expense.

Deductible payments. If you choose to use actual expenses, you can deduct the part of each lease payment that is for the use of the vehicle in your business. You can't deduct any part of a lease payment that is for personal use of the vehicle, such as commuting.

You must spread any advance payments over the entire lease period. You can't deduct any payments you make to buy a vehicle, even if the payments are called lease payments.

If you lease a car, truck, or van for 30 days or more, you may have to reduce your lease payment deduction by an "inclusion amount." For information on reporting lease inclusion amounts, see *Leasing a Car* in chapter 4 of Pub. 463.

Sale, Trade-in, or Other Disposition

If you sell, trade in, or otherwise dispose of your car, you may have a taxable gain or a deductible loss. This is true whether you used the standard mileage rate or actual car expenses to deduct the business use of your car. Pub. 544 has information on sales of property used in a trade or business, and details on how to report the disposition.

Recordkeeping

If you deduct travel, gift, or transportation expenses, you must be able to prove (substantiate) certain elements of the expense. This section discusses the records you need to keep to prove these expenses.

 If you keep timely and accurate records, you will have support to show the IRS if your tax return is ever examined. You will also have proof of expenses that your employer may require if you are reimbursed under an accountable plan. These plans are discussed later under *Reimbursements*.

How To Prove Expenses

Table 20-2 is a summary of records you need to prove each expense discussed in this chapter. You must be able to prove the elements listed across the top portion of the table. You prove them by having the information and receipts (where needed) for the expenses listed in the first column.

 You can't deduct amounts that you approximate or estimate.

You should keep adequate records to prove your expenses or have sufficient evidence that will support your own statement. You must generally prepare a written record for it to be considered adequate. This is because written evidence is more reliable than oral evidence alone.

 However, if you contemporaneously prepare a record on a computer, it is considered an adequate record.

What Are Adequate Records?

You should keep the proof you need in an account book, diary, statement of expense, or similar record. You should also keep documentary evidence that, together with your records, will support each element of an expense.

Documentary evidence. You generally must have documentary evidence, such as receipts, canceled checks, or bills, to support your expenses.

Exception. Documentary evidence is not needed if any of the following conditions apply.

- You have meals or lodging expenses while traveling away from home for which you account to your employer under an accountable plan and you use a per diem allowance method that includes meals and/or lodging. (Accountable plans and per diem allowances are discussed later under *Reimbursements*.)

- Your expense, other than lodging, is less than $75.

- You have a transportation expense for which a receipt is not readily available.

Adequate evidence. Documentary evidence ordinarily will be considered adequate if it shows the amount, date, place, and essential character of the expense.

For example, a hotel receipt is enough to support expenses for business travel if it has all of the following information.

- The name and location of the hotel.
- The dates you stayed there.
- Separate amounts for charges such as lodging, meals, and telephone calls.

A restaurant receipt is enough to prove an expense for a business meal if it has all of the following information.

- The name and location of the restaurant.
- The number of people served.
- The date and amount of the expense.

If a charge is made for items other than food and beverages, the receipt must show that this is the case.

Canceled check. A canceled check, together with a bill from the payee, ordinarily establishes the cost. However, a canceled check by itself doesn't prove a business expense without other evidence to show that it was for a business purpose.

Duplicate information. You don't have to record information in your account book or other record that duplicates information shown on a receipt as long as your records and receipts complement each other in an orderly manner.

You don't have to record amounts your employer pays directly for any ticket or other travel item. However, if you charge these items to your employer, through a credit card or otherwise, you must keep a record of the amounts you spend.

Timely kept records. You should record the elements of an expense or of a business use at or near the time of the expense or use and support it with sufficient documentary evidence. A timely kept record has more value than a statement prepared later when generally there is a lack of accurate recall.

You don't need to write down the elements of every expense on the day of the expense. If you maintain a log on a weekly basis which accounts for use during the week, the log is considered a timely kept record.

If you give your employer, client, or customer an expense account statement, it can also be considered a timely kept record. This is true if you copy it from your account book, diary, statement of expense, or similar record.

Proving business purpose. You must generally provide a written statement of the business purpose of an expense. However, the degree of proof varies according to the circumstances in each case. If the business purpose of an expense is clear from the surrounding circumstances, then you don't need to give a written explanation.

Confidential information. You don't need to put confidential information relating to an element of a deductible expense (such as the place, business purpose, or business relationship) in your account book, diary, or other record. However, you do have to record the information elsewhere at or near the time of the expense and have it available to fully prove that element of the expense.

What if I Have Incomplete Records?

If you don't have complete records to prove an element of an expense, then you must prove the element with:

- Your own written or oral statement, containing specific information about the element; and
- Other supporting evidence that is sufficient to establish the element.

Destroyed records. If you can't produce a receipt because of reasons beyond your control, you can prove a deduction by reconstructing your records or expenses. Reasons beyond your control include fire, flood, and other casualty.

Separating and Combining Expenses

This section explains when expenses must be kept separate and when expenses can be combined.

Separating expenses. Each separate payment is generally considered a separate expense. For example, if you travel to a business meeting and have a non-entertainment-related meal, you have two separate expenses. You must record them separately in your records.

Combining items. You can make one daily entry in your record for reasonable categories of expenses. Examples are taxi fares, telephone calls, or other incidental travel costs. Non-entertainment-related meals should be in a separate category. You can include tips for meal-related services with the costs of the meals.

Expenses of a similar nature occurring during the course of a single event are considered a single expense.

Allocating total cost. If you can prove the total cost of travel but you can't prove how much it cost for each person who participated in the event, you may have to allocate the total cost among you and your guests on a pro rata basis. An allocation would be needed, for example, if you didn't have a business relationship with all of your guests.

If your return is examined. If your return is examined, you may have to provide additional information to the IRS. This information could be needed to clarify or to establish the accuracy or reliability of information contained in your records, statements, testimony, or documentary evidence before a deduction is allowed.

How Long To Keep Records and Receipts

You must keep records as long as they may be needed for the administration of any provision of the Internal Revenue Code. Generally, this means you must keep your records that support your deduction (or an item of income) for 3 years from the date you file the income tax return on which the deduction is claimed. A return filed early is considered filed on the due date. For a more complete explanation, see Pub. 583, Starting a Business and Keeping Records.

Reimbursed for expenses. Employees who give their records and documentation to their employers and are reimbursed for their expenses generally don't have to keep copies of this information. However, you may have to prove your expenses if any of the following conditions apply.

- You claim deductions for expenses that are more than reimbursements.
- Your expenses are reimbursed under a nonaccountable plan.
- Your employer doesn't use adequate accounting procedures to verify expense accounts.
- You are related to your employer, as defined later under *Related to employer*.

See the next section, *How To Report*, for a discussion of reimbursements, adequate accounting, and nonaccountable plans.

Additional information. Chapter 5 of Pub. 463 has more information on recordkeeping, including examples.

How To Report

This section explains where and how to report the expenses discussed in this chapter. It discusses reimbursements and how to treat them under accountable and nonaccountable plans. It also explains rules for independent contractors and clients, fee-basis officials, certain performing artists, Armed Forces reservists, and certain disabled employees. This section ends with an illustration of how to report travel, gift, and car expenses on Form 2106.

Self-employed. You must report your income and expenses on Schedule C or C-EZ (Form 1040) if you are a sole proprietor, or on Schedule F (Form 1040) if you are a farmer. You don't use Form 2106. See your form instructions for information on how to complete your tax return. You can also find information in Pub. 535 if you are a sole proprietor, or in Pub. 225, Farmer's Tax Guide, if you are a farmer.

Both self-employed and an employee. If you are both self-employed and an employee, you must keep separate records for each business activity. Report your business expenses for self-employment on Schedule C, C-EZ, or F (Form 1040), as discussed earlier. Report your business expenses for your work as an employee on Form 2106, as discussed next.

 Form 2106 is only used by Armed Forces reservists, qualified performing artists, fee-based state or local government officials, and employees with impairment-related work expenses. Due to the suspension of miscellaneous itemized deductions subject to the 2% floor under section 67(a), employees who do not fit into one of the listed categories may not use Form 2106.

Employees. If you are an employee, you generally must complete Form 2106 to deduct your travel and transportation expenses.

For more information on how to report your expenses on Form 2106, see *Completing Form 2106*, later.

Table 20-2. **How To Prove Certain Business Expenses**

IF you have expenses for...	THEN you must keep records that show details of the following elements...			
	Amount	Time	Place or Description	Business Purpose and Business Relationship
Travel	Cost of each separate expense for travel, lodging, and meals. Incidental expenses may be totaled in reasonable categories such as taxis, fees and tips, etc.	Dates you left and returned for each trip and number of days spent on business.	Destination or area of your travel (name of city, town, or other designation).	Purpose: Business purpose for the expense or the business benefit gained or expected to be gained. Relationship: N/A
Gifts	Cost of the gift.	Date of the gift.	Description of the gift.	Purpose: Business purpose for the expense or the business benefit gained or expected to be gained. Relationship: Occupations or other information (such as names, titles, or other designations) about the recipients that shows their business relationship to you.
Transportation	Cost of each separate expense. For car expenses, the cost of the car and any improvements, the date you started using it for business, the mileage for each business use, and the total miles for the year.	Date of the expense. For car expenses, the date of the use of the car.	Your business destination.	Purpose: Business purpose for the expense. Relationship: N/A

Statutory employees. If you received a Form W-2 and the "Statutory employee" box in box 13 was checked, report your income and expenses related to that income on Schedule C or C-EZ (Form 1040). Don't complete Form 2106.

Statutory employees include full-time life insurance salespersons, certain agent or commission drivers, traveling salespersons, and certain homeworkers.

 If you are entitled to a reimbursement from your employer but you don't claim it, you can't claim a deduction for the expenses to which that unclaimed reimbursement applies.

Reimbursement for personal expenses. If your employer reimburses you for nondeductible personal expenses, such as for vacation trips, your employer must report the reimbursement as wage income in box 1 of your Form W-2. You can't deduct personal expenses.

Reimbursements

This section explains what to do when you receive an advance or are reimbursed for any of the employee business expenses discussed in this chapter.

If you received an advance, allowance, or reimbursement for your expenses, how you report this amount and your expenses depends on whether your employer reimbursed you under an accountable plan or a nonaccountable plan.

This section explains the two types of plans, how per diem and car allowances simplify proving the amount of your expenses, and the tax treatment of your reimbursements and expenses.

No reimbursement. You aren't reimbursed or given an allowance for your expenses if you are paid a salary or commission with the understanding that you will pay your own expenses. In this situation, you have no reimbursement or allowance arrangement, and you don't have to read this section on reimbursements. Instead, see *Completing Form 2106*, later, for information on completing your tax return.

Reimbursement, allowance, or advance. A reimbursement or other expense allowance arrangement is a system or plan that an employer uses to pay, substantiate, and recover the expenses, advances, reimbursements, and amounts charged to the employer for employee business expenses. Arrangements include per diem and car allowances.

A per diem allowance is a fixed amount of daily reimbursement your employer gives you for your lodging, meal, and incidental expenses when you are away from home on business. (The term "incidental expenses" is defined earlier under *Meals and Incidental Expenses*.) A car allowance is an amount your employer gives you for the business use of your car.

Your employer should tell you what method of reimbursement is used and what records you must provide.

Accountable Plans

To be an accountable plan, your employer's reimbursement or allowance arrangement must include all of the following rules.

1. Your expenses must have a business connection—that is, you must have paid or incurred deductible expenses while performing services as an employee of your employer.

2. You must adequately account to your employer for these expenses within a reasonable period of time.

3. You must return any excess reimbursement or allowance within a reasonable period of time.

See *Adequate Accounting* and *Returning Excess Reimbursements*, later.

An excess reimbursement or allowance is any amount you are paid that is more than the business-related expenses that you adequately accounted for to your employer.

Reasonable period of time. The definition of a reasonable period of time depends on the facts and circumstances of your situation. However, regardless of the facts and circumstances of your situation, actions that take place within the times specified in the following list will be treated as taking place within a reasonable period of time.

- You receive an advance within 30 days of the time you have an expense.

- You adequately account for your expenses within 60 days after they were paid or incurred.

- You return any excess reimbursement within 120 days after the expense was paid or incurred.

- You are given a periodic statement (at least quarterly) that asks you to either return or adequately account for outstanding advances and you comply within 120 days of the statement.

Employee meets accountable plan rules. If you meet the three rules for accountable plans, your employer shouldn't include any reimbursements in your income in box 1 of your Form W-2. If your expenses equal your reimbursement, you don't complete Form 2106. You have no deduction since your expenses and reimbursement are equal.

 If your employer included reimbursements in box 1 of your Form W-2 and you meet all the rules for accountable plans, ask your employer for a corrected Form W-2.

Accountable plan rules not met. Even though you are reimbursed under an accountable plan, some of your expenses may not meet all the rules. Those expenses that fail to meet all three rules for accountable plans are treated as having been reimbursed under a nonaccountable plan (discussed later).

Reimbursement of nondeductible expenses. You may be reimbursed under your employer's accountable plan for expenses related to that employer's business, some of which are deductible as employee business expenses and some of which aren't deductible. The reimbursements you receive for the nondeductible expenses don't meet rule (1) for accountable plans, and they are treated as paid under a nonaccountable plan.

Example. Your employer's plan reimburses you for travel expenses while away from home on business and also for meals when you work late at the office, even though you aren't away from home. The part of the arrangement that reimburses you for the nondeductible meals when you work late at the office is treated as paid under a nonaccountable plan.

 The employer makes the decision whether to reimburse employees under an accountable plan or a nonaccountable plan. If you are an employee who receives payments under a nonaccountable plan, you can't convert these amounts to payments under an accountable plan by voluntarily accounting to your employer for the expenses and voluntarily returning excess reimbursements to the employer.

Adequate Accounting

One of the rules for an accountable plan is that you must adequately account to your employer for your expenses. You adequately account by giving your employer a statement of expense, an account book, a diary, or a similar record in which you entered each expense at or near the time you had it, along with documentary

evidence (such as receipts) of your travel, mileage, and other employee business expenses. (See Table 20-2 for details you need to enter in your record and documents you need to prove certain expenses.) A per diem or car allowance satisfies the adequate accounting requirement under certain conditions. See *Per Diem and Car Allowances*, later.

You must account for all amounts you received from your employer during the year as advances, reimbursements, or allowances. This includes amounts you charged to your employer by credit card or other method. You must give your employer the same type of records and supporting information that you would have to give to the IRS if the IRS questioned a deduction on your return. You must pay back the amount of any reimbursement or other expense allowance for which you don't adequately account or that is more than the amount for which you accounted.

Per Diem and Car Allowances

If your employer reimburses you for your expenses using a per diem or car allowance, you can generally use the allowance as proof of the amount of your expenses. A per diem or car allowance satisfies the adequate accounting requirements for the amount of your expenses only if all the following conditions apply.

- Your employer reasonably limits payments of your expenses to those that are ordinary and necessary in the conduct of the trade or business.

- The allowance is similar in form to and not more than the federal rate (discussed later).

- You prove the time (dates), place, and business purpose of your expenses to your employer (as explained in Table 20-2) within a reasonable period of time.

- You aren't related to your employer (as defined next). If you are related to your employer, you must be able to prove your expenses to the IRS even if you have already adequately accounted to your employer and returned any excess reimbursement.

If the IRS finds that an employer's travel allowance practices aren't based on reasonably accurate estimates of travel costs (including recognition of cost differences in different areas for per diem amounts), you won't be considered to have accounted to your employer. In this case, you must be able to prove your expenses to the IRS.

Related to employer. You are related to your employer if:

1. Your employer is your brother or sister, half brother or half sister, spouse, ancestor, or lineal descendant;

2. Your employer is a corporation in which you own, directly or indirectly, more than 10% in value of the outstanding stock; or

3. Certain relationships (such as grantor, fiduciary, or beneficiary) exist between you, a trust, and your employer.

You may be considered to indirectly own stock, for purposes of (2), if you have an interest in a

corporation, partnership, estate, or trust that owns the stock or if a member of your family or your partner owns the stock.

The federal rate. The federal rate can be figured using any one of the following methods.

1. For per diem amounts:
   a. The regular federal per diem rate.
   b. The standard meal allowance.
   c. The high-low rate.

2. For car expenses:
   a. The standard mileage rate.
   b. A fixed and variable rate (FAVR).

 For per diem amounts, use the rate in effect for the area where you stop for sleep or rest.

Regular federal per diem rate. The regular federal per diem rate is the highest amount that the federal government will pay to its employees for lodging, meal, and incidental expenses (or meal and incidental expenses only) while they are traveling away from home in a particular area. The rates are different for different locations. Your employer should have these rates available. (They are also available at GSA.gov/Perdiem.)

The standard meal allowance. The standard meal allowance (discussed earlier) is the federal rate for meals and incidental expenses (M&IE). For travel between January 1 and September 30, 2018, the rate for most small localities in the United States is $51 a day. For travel between October 1 and December 31, 2018, the rate for most localities in the United States is $60. Most major cities and many other localities qualify for higher rates. You can find this information at GSA.gov/Perdiem.

You receive an allowance only for meals and incidental expenses when your employer does one of the following.

- Provides you with lodging (furnishes it in kind).

- Reimburses you, based on your receipts, for the actual cost of your lodging.

- Pays the hotel, motel, etc., directly for your lodging.

- Doesn't have a reasonable belief that you had (or will have) lodging expenses, such as when you stay with friends or relatives or sleep in the cab of your truck.

- Figures the allowance on a basis similar to that used in figuring your compensation, such as number of hours worked or miles traveled.

High-low rate. This is a simplified method of figuring the federal per diem rate for travel within the continental United States. It eliminates the need to keep a current list of the per diem rate for each city.

Under the high-low method, the per diem amount for travel during January through September 2018 is $284 (including $68 for M&IE) for certain high-cost locations. All other areas have a per diem amount of $191 (including $57 for M&IE). (You can find the areas eligible for the $284 per diem amount under the high-low method for all or part of this period at *GSA.gov/ Perdiem*.)

 Effective October 1, 2018 (FY2019), the per diem amount for travel under the high-low method for high-cost locations increased to $287 (including $71 for M&IE). The rate for all other locations increased to $195 (including $60 for M&IE). Employers who didn't use the high-low method during the first 9 months of 2018 can't begin to use it before 2019. For more information, see Notice 2018-77, which can be found at IRS.gov/irb/ 2018-42_IRB#NOT-2018-77, and Revenue Procedure 2011-47 at IRS.gov/irb/ 2011-42_IRB#RP-2011-47.

Prorating the standard meal allowance on partial days of travel. The standard meal allowance is for a full 24-hour day of travel. If you travel for part of a day, such as on the days you depart and return, you must prorate the full-day M&IE rate. This rule also applies if your employer uses the regular federal per diem rate or the high-low rate.

You can use either of the following methods to figure the federal M&IE for that day.

1. *Method 1:*

   a. For the day you depart, add 3/4 of the standard meal allowance amount for that day.

   b. For the day you return, add 3/4 of the standard meal allowance amount for the preceding day.

2. *Method 2:* Prorate the standard meal allowance using any method you consistently apply in accordance with reasonable business practice.

The standard mileage rate. This is a set rate per mile that you can use to figure your deductible car expenses. For 2018, the standard mileage rate for the cost of operating your car is 54.5 cents (0.545) per mile.

Fixed and variable rate (FAVR). This is an allowance your employer may use to reimburse your car expenses. Under this method, your employer pays an allowance that includes a combination of payments covering fixed and variable costs, such as a cents-per-mile rate to cover your variable operating costs (such as gas, oil, etc.) plus a flat amount to cover your fixed costs (such as depreciation (or lease payments), insurance, etc.). If your employer chooses to use this method, your employer will request the necessary records from you.

Reporting your expenses with a per diem or car allowance. If your reimbursement is in the form of an allowance received under an accountable plan, the following facts affect your reporting.

- The federal rate.
- Whether the allowance or your actual expenses were more than the federal rate.

The following discussions explain where to report your expenses depending upon how the amount of your allowance compares to the federal rate.

Allowance less than or equal to the federal rate. If your allowance is less than or equal to the federal rate, the allowance won't be included in box 1 of your Form W-2. You don't need to report the related expenses or the allowance on your return if your expenses are equal to or less than the allowance.

However, if your actual expenses are more than your allowance, you can complete Form 2106 and deduct the excess amount if you are an Armed Forces reservist, fee-based state or local government official, qualified performing artist, or disabled employee with impairment-related work expenses. If you are using actual expenses, you must be able to prove to the IRS the total amount of your expenses and reimbursements for the entire year. If you are using the standard meal allowance or the standard mileage rate, you don't have to prove that amount.

Example. Nicole drives 10,000 miles in 2018 for business. Under her employer's accountable plan, she accounts for the time (dates), place, and business purpose of each trip. Her employer pays her a mileage allowance of 40 cents (0.40) a mile.

Nicole's $5,450 expense figured under the standard mileage rate (10,000 miles x 54.5 cents (0.545)) is more than her $4,000 reimbursement (10,000 miles x 40 cents (0.40)). Nicole completes Form 2106 (showing all her expenses and reimbursements) and enters $1,450 ($5,450 – $4,000) on Schedule 1 (Form 1040), line 24.

Allowance more than the federal rate. If your allowance is more than the federal rate, your employer must include the allowance amount up to the federal rate under code L in box 12 of your Form W-2. This amount isn't taxable. However, the excess allowance will be included in box 1 of your Form W-2. You must report this part of your allowance as if it were wage income.

If your actual expenses are less than or equal to the federal rate, you don't complete Form 2106 or claim any of your expenses on your return.

However, if your actual expenses are more than the federal rate, you can complete Form 2106 and deduct those excess expenses. You must report on Form 2106 your reimbursements up to the federal rate (as shown under code L in box 12 of your Form W-2) and all your expenses. You should be able to prove these amounts to the IRS.

Example. Joe lives and works in Austin. In May, his employer sent him to San Diego for 4 days and paid the hotel directly for Joe's hotel bill. The employer reimbursed Joe $75 a day for his meals and incidental expenses. The federal rate for San Diego is $64 a day.

Joe can prove that his actual non-entertainment-related meal expenses totaled $380. His employer's accountable plan won't pay more than $75 a day for travel to San Diego, so Joe doesn't give his employer the records that prove that he actually spent $380. However, he does account for the time, place, and business purpose of the trip. This is Joe's only business trip this year.

Joe was reimbursed $300 ($75 x 4 days), which is $44 more than the federal rate of $256 ($64 x 4 days). His employer includes the $44 as income on Joe's Form W-2 in box 1. His employer also enters $256 under code L in box 12 of Joe's Form W-2.

Joe completes Form 2106 to figure his deductible expenses. He enters the total of his actual expenses for the year ($380) on Form 2106. He also enters the reimbursements that weren't included in his income ($256). His total deductible expense, before the 50% limit, is $124. After he figures the 50% limit on his unreimbursed meals, he will include the balance, $62, on Schedule 1 (Form 1040), line 24.

Returning Excess Reimbursements

Under an accountable plan, you are required to return any excess reimbursement or other expense allowances for your business expenses to the person paying the reimbursement or allowance. Excess reimbursement means any amount for which you didn't adequately account within a reasonable period of time. For example, if you received a travel advance and you didn't spend all the money on business-related expenses or you don't have proof of all your expenses, you have an excess reimbursement.

For more information, see *Adequate Accounting*, earlier.

Travel advance. You receive a travel advance if your employer provides you with an expense allowance before you actually have the expense, and the allowance is reasonably expected to be no more than your expense. Under an accountable plan, you are required to adequately account to your employer for this advance and to return any excess within a reasonable period of time.

If you don't adequately account for or don't return any excess advance within a reasonable period of time, the amount you don't account for or return will be treated as having been paid under a nonaccountable plan (discussed later).

Unproven amounts. If you don't prove that you actually traveled on each day for which you received a per diem or car allowance (proving the elements described in Table 20-2), you must return this unproven amount of the travel advance within a reasonable period of time. If you don't do this, the unproven amount will be considered paid under a nonaccountable plan (discussed later).

Per diem allowance more than federal rate. If your employer's accountable plan pays you an allowance that is higher than the federal rate, you don't have to return the difference between the two rates for the period you can prove business-related travel expenses. However, the difference will be reported as wages on your Form W-2. This excess amount is considered paid under a nonaccountable plan (discussed later).

Example. Your employer sends you on a 5-day business trip to Phoenix in March 2018 and gives you a $400 ($80 x 5 days) advance to cover your meals and incidental expenses. The federal per diem for meals and incidental expenses for Phoenix is $59. Your trip lasts only 3 days. Under your employer's accountable plan, you must return the $160 ($80 x 2 days) advance for the 2 days you didn't travel. For the 3 days you did travel, you don't have to return

Table 20-3. **Reporting Travel, Non-Entertainment-Related Meal, Gift, and Car Expenses and Reimbursements**

IF the type of reimbursement (or other expense allowance) arrangement is under...	THEN the employer reports on Form W-2...	AND the employee reports on Form 2106...
An accountable plan with:		
Actual expense reimbursement: Adequate accounting made <u>and</u> excess returned.	No amount.	No amount.
Actual expense reimbursement: Adequate accounting and return of excess both required <u>but</u> excess not returned.	The excess amount as wages in box 1.	No amount.
Per diem or mileage allowance up to the federal rate: Adequate accounting made <u>and</u> excess returned.	No amount.	All expenses and reimbursements only if excess expenses are claimed. Otherwise, form isn't filed.
Per diem or mileage allowance up to the federal rate: Adequate accounting and return of excess both required <u>but</u> excess not returned.	The excess amount as wages in box 1. The amount up to the federal rate is reported only in box 12—it is not reported in box 1.	No amount.
Per diem or mileage allowance exceeds the federal rate: Adequate accounting up to the federal rate only <u>and</u> excess not returned.	The excess amount as wages in box 1. The amount up to the federal rate is reported only in box 12—it isn't reported in box 1.	All expenses (and reimbursement reported on Form W-2, box 12) only if expenses in excess of the federal rate are claimed. Otherwise, form isn't required.
A nonaccountable plan with:		
Either adequate accounting or return of excess, or both, not required by plan.	The entire amount as wages in box 1.	All expenses.
No reimbursement plan:	The entire amount as wages in box 1.	All expenses.

the $63 difference between the allowance you received and the federal rate for Phoenix (($80 – $59) × 3 days). However, the $63 will be reported on your Form W-2 as wages.

Nonaccountable Plans

A nonaccountable plan is a reimbursement or expense allowance arrangement that doesn't meet one or more of the three rules listed earlier under *Accountable Plans*.

In addition, even if your employer has an accountable plan, the following payments will be treated as being paid under a nonaccountable plan.

- Excess reimbursements you fail to return to your employer.

- Reimbursement of nondeductible expenses related to your employer's business. See *Reimbursement of nondeductible expenses* under *Accountable Plans*, earlier.

If you aren't sure if the reimbursement or expense allowance arrangement is an accountable or nonaccountable plan, ask your employer.

Reporting your expenses under a nonaccountable plan. Your employer will combine the amount of any reimbursement or other expense allowance paid to you under a nonaccountable plan with your wages, salary, or other pay. Your employer will report the total in box 1 of your Form W-2.

You must be an Armed Forces reservist, fee-based state or local government official, qualified performing artist, or disabled employee with impairment-related work expenses and complete Form 2106 to deduct your expenses for travel, transportation, or meals. Your non-entertainment-related meal expenses will be subject to the 50% limit discussed earlier under *Meals and Entertainment Expenses*.

Example. Kim's employer gives her $1,000 a month ($12,000 for the year) for her business expenses. Kim doesn't have to provide any proof of her expenses to her employer, and Kim can keep any funds that she doesn't spend.

Kim is being reimbursed under a nonaccountable plan. Her employer will include the $12,000 on Kim's Form W-2 as if it were wages. If Kim wants to deduct her business expenses, she must complete Form 2106.

Completing Form 2106

This section briefly describes how employees complete Form 2106. Table 20-3 explains what the employer reports on Form W-2 and what the employee reports on Form 2106. The instructions for the forms have more information on completing them.

 If you are self-employed, don't file Form 2106. Report your expenses on Schedule C, C-EZ, or F (Form 1040). See the instructions for the form that you must file.

Car expenses. If you used a car to perform your job as an employee, you may be able to deduct certain car expenses. These are generally figured on Form 2106, Part II, and then claimed on Form 2106, Part I, line 1, column A.

Transportation expenses. Show your transportation expenses that didn't involve overnight travel on Form 2106, line 2, column A. Also include on this line business expenses you have for parking fees and tolls. Don't include expenses of operating your car or expenses of commuting between your home and work.

Employee business expenses other than non-entertainment-related meals. Show your other employee business expenses on Form 2106, lines 3 and 4, column A. Don't include expenses for non-entertainment-related meals on those lines. Line 4 is for expenses such as gifts, educational expenses (tuition and books), office-in-the-home expenses, and trade and professional publications.

Non-entertainment-related meal expenses. Show the full amount of your expenses for non-entertainment-related meals on Form 2106, line 5, column B. Include meals while away from your tax home overnight and other non-entertainment-related business meals. Enter 50% of the line 8, column B, meal expenses on line 9, column B.

"Hours of service" limits. If you are subject to the Department of Transportation's "hours of service" limits, use 80% instead of 50% for meals while away from your tax home.

Reimbursements. Enter on Form 2106, line 7, the amounts your employer (or third party) reimbursed you that weren't included in box 1 of your Form W-2. This includes any reimbursement reported under code L in box 12 of Form W-2.

Allocating your reimbursement. If you were reimbursed under an accountable plan and want to deduct excess expenses that weren't reimbursed, you may have to allocate your reimbursement. This is necessary if your employer pays your reimbursement in the following manner.

- Pays you a single amount that covers non-entertainment-related meals, as well as other business expenses.
- Doesn't clearly identify how much is for deductible non-entertainment-related meals.

You must allocate that single payment so that you know how much to enter on Form 2106, line 7, column A and column B.

Example. Rob's employer paid him an expense allowance of $12,000 this year under an accountable plan. The $12,000 payment consisted of $5,000 for airfare and $7,000 for non-entertainment-related meals and car expenses. Rob's employer didn't clearly show how much of the $7,000 was for the cost of deductible non-entertainment-related meals. Rob actually spent $14,000 during the year ($5,500 for airfare, $4,500 for non-entertainment-related meals, and $4,000 for car expenses).

Since the airfare allowance was clearly identified, Rob knows that $5,000 of the payment goes in column A, line 7 of Form 2106. To allocate the remaining $7,000, Rob uses the worksheet from the instructions for Form 2106. His completed worksheet follows.

Reimbursement Allocation Worksheet
(keep for your records)

1. Enter the total amount of reimbursements your employer gave you that weren't reported to you in box 1 of Form W-2	$7,000
2. Enter the total amount of your expenses for the periods covered by this reimbursement ($4,500 for non-entertainment-related meals and $4,000 for car expenses)	8,500
3. Enter the part of the amount on line 2 that was your total expense for non-entertainment-related meals	4,500
4. Divide line 3 by line 2. Enter the result as a decimal (rounded to at least three places)	0.529
5. Multiply line 1 by line 4. Enter the result here and in column B, line 7	3,703
6. Subtract line 5 from line 1. Enter the result here and in column A, line 7	$3,297

On line 7 of Form 2106, Rob enters $8,297 ($5,000 airfare and $3,297 of the $7,000) in column A and $3,703 (of the $7,000) in column B.

After you complete the form. If you are a government official paid on a fee basis, a performing artist, an Armed Forces reservist, or a disabled employee with impairment-related work expenses, see *Special Rules*, later.

Limits on employee business expenses. Your employee business expenses may be subject to either of the limits described next.

These limits are figured in the following order on the specified form.

1. Limit on meals. Certain non-entertainment-related meal expenses are subject to a 50% limit. Entertainment expenses paid or incurred after 2017 are not deductible. If you are an employee, you figure the 50% limit on line 9 of Form 2106. See *50% Limit on Meals* under *Meals and Entertainment Expenses*, earlier.

2. Suspension of limit on total itemized deductions. The limitation on itemized deductions is suspended for tax years beginning after 2017.

Special Rules

This section discusses special rules that apply to Armed Forces reservists, government officials who are paid on a fee basis, performing artists, and disabled employees with impairment-related work expenses. For tax years beginning after 2017, they are the only taxpayers that can use Form 2106.

Armed Forces reservists traveling more than 100 miles from home. If you are a member of a reserve component of the Armed Forces of the United States and you travel more than 100 miles away from home in connection with your performance of services as a member of the reserves, you can deduct your travel expenses as an adjustment to gross income. The amount of expenses you can deduct as an adjustment to gross income is limited to the regular federal per diem rate (for lodging, meals, and incidental expenses) and the standard mileage rate (for car expenses) plus any parking fees, ferry fees, and tolls. The federal rate is explained earlier under *Per Diem and Car Allowances*. Any expenses in excess of these amounts can't be deducted.

Member of a reserve component. You are a member of a reserve component of the Armed Forces of the United States if you are in the Army, Navy, Marine Corps, Air Force, or Coast Guard Reserve, the Army National Guard of the United States, the Air National Guard of the United States, or the Reserve Corps of the Public Health Service.

How to report. If you have reserve-related travel that takes you more than 100 miles from home, you should first complete Form 2106. Then include your expenses for reserve travel over 100 miles from home, up to the federal rate, from Form 2106, line 10, in the total on Schedule 1 (Form 1040), line 24.

You can't deduct expenses of travel that doesn't take you more than 100 miles from home as an adjustment to gross income.

Officials paid on a fee basis. Certain fee-basis officials can claim their employee business expenses on Form 2106.

Fee-basis officials are persons who are employed by a state or local government and who are paid in whole or in part on a fee basis. They can deduct their business expenses in performing services in that job as an adjustment to gross income.

If you are a fee-basis official, include your employee business expenses from Form 2106, line 10, on Schedule 1 (Form 1040), line 24.

Expenses of certain performing artists. If you are a performing artist, you may qualify to deduct your employee business expenses as an adjustment to gross income. To qualify, you must meet all of the following requirements.

1. During the tax year, you perform services in the performing arts as an employee for at least two employers.

2. You receive at least $200 each from any two of these employers.

3. Your related performing-arts business expenses are more than 10% of your gross income from the performance of those services.

4. Your adjusted gross income isn't more than $16,000 before deducting these business expenses.

Special rules for married persons. If you are married, you must file a joint return unless you lived apart from your spouse at all times during the tax year.

If you file a joint return, you must figure requirements (1), (2), and (3) separately for both you and your spouse. However, requirement (4) applies to your and your spouse's combined adjusted gross income.

Where to report. If you meet all of the above requirements, you should first complete Form 2106. Then you include your performing-arts-related expenses from line 10 of Form 2106 in the total on Schedule 1 (Form 1040), line 24.

If you don't meet all of the above requirements, you don't qualify to deduct your expenses as an adjustment to gross income.

Impairment-related work expenses of disabled employees. If you are an employee with a physical or mental disability, you can deduct your impairment-related work expenses. After you complete Form 2106, enter your impairment-related work expenses from Form 2106, line 10, on Schedule A (Form 1040), line 16, and identify the type and amount of this expense on the line next to line 16. You can't deduct your employee business expenses.

Impairment-related work expenses are your allowable expenses for attendant care at your workplace and other expenses you have in connection with your workplace that are necessary for you to be able to work. For more information, see chapter 22.

Part Five.

Standard Deduction, Itemized Deductions, and Other Deductions

After you have figured your adjusted gross income, you are ready to subtract the deductions used to figure taxable income. You can subtract either the standard deduction or itemized deductions, and, if you qualify, the qualified business income deduction. Itemized deductions are deductions for certain expenses that are listed on Schedule A (Form 1040). The eight chapters in this part discuss the standard deduction and each itemized deduction. See chapter 21 for the factors to consider when deciding whether to take the standard deduction or itemized deductions. See chapter 28 for information on the new qualified business income deduction.

The new Form 1040 schedules that are discussed in these chapters are:

- *Schedule 1, Additional Income and Adjustments to Income.*
- *Schedule 3, Nonrefundable Credits.*

21.

Standard Deduction

What's New

 At the time this publication went to print, Congress was considering legislation that would do the following.

1. *Provide additional tax relief for those affected by certain 2018 disasters.*
2. *Extend certain tax benefits that expired at the end of 2017 and that currently can't be claimed on your 2018 tax return.*
3. *Change certain other tax provisions.*

To learn whether this legislation was enacted resulting in changes that affect your 2018 tax return, go to Recent Developments at IRS.gov/Pub17.

Standard deduction increased. For 2018, the standard deduction for taxpayers who don't itemize their deductions has been increased for all filers. The amount depends on your filing status. You can use the 2018 Standard Deduction Tables in this chapter to figure your standard deduction.

In addition, your 2018 standard deduction may be increased by any net qualified disaster loss. See the instructions to Form 1040 and Schedule A (Form 1040) for more information on how to claim the increased standard deduction.

Personal exemption suspended. For 2018, you can't claim a personal exemption for yourself, your spouse, or your dependents.

Changes to itemized deductions. For 2018, your itemized deductions are no longer limited if

your AGI is over a certain limit. However, your deduction for state and local income, sales, real estate, and property taxes is limited to a combined total deduction of $10,000 ($5,000 if married filing separately). Also, you can no longer deduct job-related expenses or other miscellaneous itemized deductions that were subject to the 2%-of-adjusted-gross-income floor.

These changes will impact your choice of whether to take a standard deduction or to itemize deductions. There may be other changes that impact the amount of your itemized deductions. See the instructions to Schedule A (Form 1040) for more information.

Introduction

This chapter discusses the following topics.

- How to figure the amount of your standard deduction.
- The standard deduction for dependents.
- Who should itemize deductions.

Most taxpayers have a choice of either taking a standard deduction or itemizing their deductions. If you have a choice, you can use the method that gives you the lower tax.

The standard deduction is a dollar amount that reduces your taxable income. It is a benefit that eliminates the need for many taxpayers to itemize actual deductions, such as medical expenses, charitable contributions, and taxes, on Schedule A (Form 1040). The standard deduction is higher for taxpayers who:

- Are 65 or older, or
- Are blind.

 You benefit from the standard deduction if your standard deduction is more than the total of your allowable itemized deductions.

Persons not eligible for the standard deduction. Your standard deduction is zero and you should itemize any deductions you have if:

- Your filing status is married filing separately, and your spouse itemizes deductions on his or her return;
- You are filing a tax return for a short tax year because of a change in your annual accounting period; or
- You are a nonresident or dual-status alien during the year. You are considered a dual-status alien if you were both a nonresident and resident alien during the year.

If you are a nonresident alien who is married to a U.S. citizen or resident alien at the end of the year, you can choose to be treated as a U.S. resident. (See Pub. 519.) If you make this choice, you can take the standard deduction.

 If you can be claimed as a dependent on another person's return (such as your parents' return), your standard deduction may be limited. See Standard Deduction for Dependents, later.

Standard Deduction Amount

The standard deduction amount depends on your filing status, whether you are 65 or older or blind, and whether another taxpayer can claim you as a dependent. Generally, the standard deduction amounts are adjusted each year for inflation. The standard deduction amounts for most people are shown in Table 21-1.

Decedent's final return. The standard deduction for a decedent's final tax return is the same as it would have been had the decedent continued to live. However, if the decedent wasn't 65 or older at the time of death, the higher standard deduction for age can't be claimed.

Higher Standard Deduction for Age (65 or Older)

If you are age 65 or older on the last day of the year and don't itemize deductions, you are entitled to a higher standard deduction. You are considered 65 on the day before your 65th birthday. Therefore, you can take a higher standard deduction for 2018 if you were born before January 2, 1954.

Use Table 21-2 to figure the standard deduction amount.

Death of a taxpayer. If you are preparing a return for someone who died in 2018, see *Death of taxpayer* in *Pub. 501* before using Table 21-2 or Table 21-3.

Higher Standard Deduction for Blindness

If you are blind on the last day of the year and you don't itemize deductions, you are entitled to a higher standard deduction.

Not totally blind. If you aren't totally blind, you must get a certified statement from an eye doctor (ophthalmologist or optometrist) that:

- You can't see better than 20/200 in the better eye with glasses or contact lenses, or
- Your field of vision is 20 degrees or less.

If your eye condition isn't likely to improve beyond these limits, the statement should include this fact. Keep the statement in your records.

If your vision can be corrected beyond these limits only by contact lenses that you can wear only briefly because of pain, infection, or ulcers, you can take the higher standard deduction for blindness if you otherwise qualify.

Spouse 65 or Older or Blind

You can take the higher standard deduction if your spouse is age 65 or older or blind and:

- You file a joint return, or
- You file a separate return and your spouse had no gross income and can't be claimed as a dependent by another taxpayer.

Death of a spouse. If your spouse died in 2018 before reaching age 65, you can't take a higher standard deduction because of your spouse. Even if your spouse was born before January 2, 1954, he or she isn't considered 65 or older at the end of 2018 unless he or she was 65 or older at the time of death.

A person is considered to reach age 65 on the day before his or her 65th birthday.

Example. Your spouse was born on February 14, 1953, and died on February 13, 2018. Your spouse is considered age 65 at the time of death. However, if your spouse died on February 12, 2018, your spouse isn't considered age 65 at the time of death and isn't 65 or older at the end of 2018.

 You can't claim the higher standard deduction for an individual other than yourself and your spouse.

Higher Standard Deduction for Net Disaster Loss

Your standard deduction may be increased by any net qualified disaster loss.

See the instructions to Form 1040 and Schedule A (Form 1040) for more information on how to figure your increased standard deduction and how to report it on Form 1040.

 At the time this publication was prepared for printing, Congress was considering legislation to allow your standard deduction to be increased by losses resulting from certain 2018 disasters. If allowed, you may able to increase your standard deduction for 2018. To see if the legislation was enacted, go to Recent Developments *at* IRS.gov/Pub17.

Examples

The following examples illustrate how to determine your standard deduction using Tables 21-1 and 21-2.

Example 1. Larry, 46, and Donna, 33, are filing a joint return for 2018. Neither is blind, and neither can be claimed as a dependent. They decide not to itemize their deductions. They use Table 21-1. Their standard deduction is $24,000.

Example 2. The facts are the same as in *Example 1* except that Larry is blind at the end of 2018. Larry and Donna use Table 21-2. Their standard deduction is $25,300.

Example 3. Bill and Lisa are filing a joint return for 2018. Both are over age 65. Neither is blind, and neither can be claimed as a dependent. If they don't itemize deductions, they use Table 21-2. Their standard deduction is $26,600.

Standard Deduction for Dependents

The standard deduction for an individual who can be claimed as a dependent on another person's tax return is generally limited to the greater of:

- $1,050, or
- The individual's earned income for the year plus $350 (but not more than the regular standard deduction amount, generally $12,000).

However, if the individual is 65 or older or blind, the standard deduction may be higher.

If you (or your spouse, if filing jointly) can be claimed as a dependent on someone else's return, use Table 21-3 to determine your standard deduction.

Earned income defined. Earned income is salaries, wages, tips, professional fees, and other amounts received as pay for work you actually perform.

For purposes of the standard deduction, earned income also includes any part of a taxable scholarship or fellowship grant. See *Scholarships and fellowships* in chapter 12 for more information on what qualifies as a scholarship or fellowship grant.

Example 1. Michael is 16 years old and single. His parents can claim him as a dependent on their 2018 tax return. He has interest income of $780 and wages of $150. He has no itemized deductions. Michael uses Table 21-3 to find his standard deduction. He enters $150 (his earned income) on line 1, $500 ($150 + $350) on line 3, $1,050 (the larger of $500 and $1,050) on line 5, and $12,000 on line 6. His standard deduction, on line 7a, is $1,050 (the smaller of $1,050 and $12,000).

Example 2. Joe, a 22-year-old full-time college student, is his parents' dependent. Joe is married and files a separate return. His wife doesn't itemize deductions on her separate return. Joe has $1,500 in interest income and wages of $3,800. He has no itemized deductions. Joe finds his standard deduction by using Table 21-3. He enters his earned income, $3,800, on line 1. He adds lines 1 and 2 and enters $4,150 on line 3. On line 5, he enters $4,150, the larger of lines 3 and 4. Because Joe is married filing a separate return, he enters $12,000 on line 6. On line 7a, he enters $4,150 as his standard deduction because it is smaller than $12,000, the amount on line 6.

Example 3. Amy, who is single, is her parents' dependent. She is 18 years old and blind. She has interest income of $1,300 and wages of $2,900. She has no itemized deductions. Amy uses Table 21-3 to find her standard deduction. She enters her wages of $2,900 on line 1. She adds lines 1 and 2 and enters $3,250 ($2,900 + $350) on line 3. On line 5, she enters $3,250, the larger of lines 3 and 4. Because she is single, Amy enters $12,000 on line 6. She enters $3,250 on line 7a. This is the smaller of the amounts on lines 5 and 6. Because she checked the box in the top part of the worksheet, indicating she is blind, she enters $1,600 on line 7b. She then adds the amounts on lines 7a and 7b and enters her standard deduction of $4,850 on line 7c.

Example 4. Ed is 18 years old and single. His parents can claim him as a dependent on their 2018 tax return. He has wages of $7,000, interest income of $500, and a business loss of $3,000. He has no itemized deductions. Ed uses Table 21-3 to figure his standard deduction. He enters $4,000 ($7,000 − $3,000) on line 1. He adds lines 1 and 2 and enters $4,350 on line 3. On line 5, he enters $4,350, the larger of lines 3 and 4. Because he is single, Ed enters $12,000 on line 6. On line 7a, he enters $4,350 as his standard deduction because it is smaller than $12,000, the amount on line 6.

Who Should Itemize

You should itemize deductions if your total deductions are more than the standard deduction amount. Also, you should itemize if you don't qualify for the standard deduction, as discussed earlier under *Persons not eligible for the standard deduction*.

You should first figure your itemized deductions and compare that amount to your standard deduction to make sure you are using the method that gives you the greater benefit.

When to itemize. You may benefit from itemizing your deductions on Schedule A (Form 1040) if you:

- Don't qualify for the standard deduction;
- Had large uninsured medical and dental expenses during the year;
- Paid interest and taxes on your home;
- Had large uninsured casualty or theft losses;

- Made large contributions to qualified charities; or
- Have total itemized deductions that are more than the standard deduction to which you otherwise are entitled.

These deductions are explained in chapters 22–28.

If you decide to itemize your deductions, complete Schedule A and attach it to your Form 1040. Enter the amount from Schedule A, line 17, on Form 1040, line 8.

Electing to itemize for state tax or other purposes. Even if your itemized deductions are less than your standard deduction, you can elect to itemize deductions on your federal return rather than take the standard deduction. You may want to do this if, for example, the tax benefit of itemizing your deductions on your state tax return is greater than the tax benefit you lose on your federal return by not taking the standard deduction. To make this election, you must check the box on line 18 of Schedule A.

Changing your mind. If you don't itemize your deductions and later find that you should have itemized—or if you itemize your deductions and later find you shouldn't have—you can change your return by filing Form 1040X, Amended U.S. Individual Income Tax Return. See *Amended Returns and Claims for Refund* in chapter 1 for more information on amended returns.

Married persons who filed separate returns. You can change methods of taking deductions only if you and your spouse both make the same changes. Both of you must file a consent to assessment for any additional tax either one may owe as a result of the change.

You and your spouse can use the method that gives you the lower total tax, even though one of you may pay more tax than you would have paid by using the other method. You both must use the same method of claiming deductions. If one itemizes deductions, the other should itemize because he or she won't qualify for the standard deduction. See *Persons not eligible for the standard deduction,* earlier.

2018 Standard Deduction Tables

 If you are married filing a separate return and your spouse itemizes deductions, or if you are a dual-status alien, you can't take the standard deduction even if you were born before January 2, 1954, or are blind.

Table 21-1. Standard Deduction Chart for Most People*

IF your filing status is...	THEN your standard deduction is...
Single or Married filing separately	$12,000
Married filing jointly or Qualifying widow(er)	24,000
Head of household	18,000

*Don't use this chart if you were born before January 2, 1954, are blind, or if someone else can claim you (or your spouse, if filing jointly) as a dependent. Use Table 21-2 or 21-3 instead.

Table 21-2. Standard Deduction Chart for People Born Before January 2, 1954, or Who Are Blind*

Check the correct number of boxes below. Then go to the chart.
You: Born before January 2, 1954 ☐   Blind ☐
Your spouse: Born before January 2, 1954 ☐   Blind ☐

Total number of boxes checked ☐

IF your filing status is...	AND the number in the box above is...	THEN your standard deduction is...
Single	1	$13,600
	2	15,200
Married filing jointly	1	$25,300
	2	26,600
	3	27,900
	4	29,200
Qualifying widow(er)	1	$25,300
	2	26,600
Married filing separately**	1	$13,300
	2	14,600
	3	15,900
	4	17,200
Head of household	1	$19,600
	2	21,200

*If someone else can claim you (or your spouse, if filing jointly) as a dependent, use Table 21-3 instead.
**You can check the boxes for *Your Spouse* if your filing status is married filing separately and your spouse had no income, isn't filing a return, and can't be claimed as a dependent on another person's return.

Table 21-3. Standard Deduction Worksheet for Dependents

Use this worksheet only if someone else can claim you (or your spouse, if filing jointly) as a dependent.

Check the correct number of boxes below. Then go to the worksheet.
You: Born before January 2, 1954 ☐   Blind ☐
Your spouse: Born before January 2, 1954 ☐   Blind ☐

Total number of boxes checked ☐

1.	Enter your earned income (defined below). If none, enter -0-.	1.	
2.	Additional amount.	2.	$350
3.	Add lines 1 and 2.	3.	
4.	Minimum standard deduction.	4.	$1,050
5.	Enter the larger of line 3 or line 4.	5.	
6.	Enter the amount shown below for your filing status. • Single or Married filing separately— $12,000 • Married filing jointly— $24,000 • Head of household— $18,000	6.	

7.	Standard deduction.
	  a. Enter the smaller of line 5 or line 6. If born after January 1, 1954, and not blind, stop here. This is your standard deduction. Otherwise, go on to line 7b.
	  b. If born before January 2, 1954, or blind, multiply $1,600 ($1,300 if married) by the number in the box above.
	  c. Add lines 7a and 7b. This is your standard deduction for 2018.
		7a.
		7b.
		7c.	

Earned income includes wages, salaries, tips, professional fees, and other compensation received for personal services you performed. It also includes any taxable scholarship or fellowship grant.

22.

Medical and Dental Expenses

What's New

 At the time this publication went to print, Congress was considering legislation that would do the following.

1. Provide additional tax relief for those affected by certain 2018 disasters.

2. Extend certain tax benefits that expired at the end of 2017 and that currently can't be claimed on your 2018 tax return.

3. Change certain other tax provisions.

To learn whether this legislation was enacted resulting in changes that affect your 2018 tax return, go to Recent Developments at *IRS.gov/ Pub17*.

Medical and dental expenses. Beginning January 1, 2017, and ending before January 1, 2019, you can deduct only the part of your medical and dental expenses that exceeds 7.5% of your adjusted gross income (AGI).

Standard mileage rate. The standard mileage rate allowed for operating expenses for a car when you use it for medical reasons is 18 cents per mile. See *Transportation* under *What Medical Expenses Are Includible*, later.

Introduction

This chapter will help you determine the following.

- What medical expenses are.
- What expenses you can include this year.
- How much of the expenses you can deduct.
- Whose medical expenses you can include.
- What medical expenses are includible.
- How to treat reimbursements.
- How to report the deduction on your tax return.
- How to report impairment-related work expenses.
- How to report health insurance costs if you are self-employed.

Useful Items

You may want to see:

Publication

❏ **502** Medical and Dental Expenses

❏ **969** Health Savings Accounts and Other Tax-Favored Health Plans

Form (and Instructions)

❏ **1040** U.S. Individual Tax Return

❏ **Schedule A (Form 1040)** Itemized Deductions

❏ **8885** Health Coverage Tax Credit

❏ **8962** Premium Tax Credit (PTC)

For these and other useful items, go to *IRS.gov/ Forms*.

What Are Medical Expenses?

Medical expenses are the costs of diagnosis, cure, mitigation, treatment, or prevention of disease, or for the purpose of affecting any part or function of the body. These expenses include payments for legal medical services rendered by physicians, surgeons, dentists, and other medical practitioners. They include the costs of equipment, supplies, and diagnostic devices needed for these purposes.

Medical care expenses must be primarily to alleviate or prevent a physical or mental disability or illness. They don't include expenses that are merely beneficial to general health, such as vitamins or a vacation.

Medical expenses include the premiums you pay for insurance that covers the expenses of medical care, and the amounts you pay for transportation to get medical care. Medical expenses also include amounts paid for qualified long-term care services and limited amounts paid for any qualified long-term care insurance contract.

What Expenses Can You Include This Year?

You can include only the medical and dental expenses you paid this year, but generally not payments for medical or dental care you will receive in a future year. This is not the rule for determining whether an expense can be reimbursed by a flexible spending arrangement (FSA). If you pay medical expenses by check, the day you mail or deliver the check generally is the date of payment. If you use a "pay-by-phone" or "online" account to pay your medical expenses, the date reported on the statement of the financial institution showing when payment was made is the date of payment. If you use a credit card, include medical expenses you charge to your credit card in the year the charge is made, not when you actually pay the amount charged.

Separate returns. If you and your spouse live in a noncommunity property state and file separate returns, each of you can include only the medical expenses each actually paid. Any medical expenses paid out of a joint checking account in which you and your spouse have the same interest are considered to have been paid equally by each of you, unless you can show otherwise.

Community property states. If you and your spouse live in a community property state and file separate returns, or are registered domestic partners in Nevada, Washington, or California, any medical expenses paid out of community funds are divided equally. Each of you should include half the expenses. If medical expenses are paid out of the separate funds of one individual, only the individual who paid the medical expenses can include them. If you live in a community property state and aren't filing a joint return, see Pub. 555.

How Much of the Expenses Can You Deduct?

Generally, you can deduct on Schedule A (Form 1040) only the amount of your medical and dental expenses that is more than 7.5% of your adjusted gross income (AGI), found on Form 1040, line 7.

 If you contributed to a health savings account or a medical savings account in 2018, see Pub. 969 to figure your deduction.

Whose Medical Expenses Can You Include?

You generally can include medical expenses you pay for yourself, as well as those you pay for someone who was your spouse or your dependent either when the services were provided or when you paid for them. There are different rules for decedents and for individuals who are the subject of multiple support agreements. See *Support claimed under a multiple support agreement*, later.

Spouse

You can include medical expenses you paid for your spouse. To include these expenses, you must have been married either at the time your spouse received the medical services or at the time you paid the medical expenses.

Example 1. Mary received medical treatment before she married Bill. Bill paid for the treatment after they married. Bill can include these expenses in figuring his medical expense deduction even if Bill and Mary file separate returns.

If Mary had paid the expenses, Bill couldn't include Mary's expenses in his separate return. Mary would include the amounts she paid during the year in her separate return. If they filed a joint return, the medical expenses both paid during the year would be used to figure their medical expense deduction.

Example 2. This year, John paid medical expenses for his wife Louise, who died last year. John married Belle this year and they file a joint return. Because John was married to Louise when she received the medical services, he can include those expenses in figuring his medical expense deduction for this year.

Dependent

You can include medical expenses you paid for your dependent. For you to include these expenses, the person must have been your dependent either at the time the medical services were provided or at the time you paid the expenses. A person generally qualifies as your dependent for purposes of the medical expense deduction if both of the following requirements are met.

1. The person was a qualifying child (defined later) or a qualifying relative (defined later).

2. The person was a U.S. citizen or national, or a resident of the United States, Canada, or Mexico. If your qualifying child was adopted, see *Exception for adopted child* next.

You can include medical expenses you paid for an individual that would have been your dependent except that:

1. He or she received gross income of $4,150 or more in 2018;

2. He or she filed a joint return for 2018; or

3. You, or your spouse if filing jointly, could be claimed as a dependent on someone else's 2018 return.

Exception for adopted child. If you are a U.S. citizen or U.S. national and your adopted child lived with you as a member of your household for 2018, that child doesn't have to be a U.S. citizen or national or a resident of the United States, Canada, or Mexico.

Qualifying Child

A qualifying child is a child who:

1. Is your son, daughter, stepchild, foster child, brother, sister, stepbrother, stepsister, half brother, half sister, or a descendant of any of them (for example, your grandchild, niece, or nephew);

2. Was:
   a. Under age 19 at the end of 2018 and younger than you (or your spouse if filing jointly);
   b. Under age 24 at the end of 2018, a full-time student, and younger than you (or your spouse if filing jointly); or
   c. Any age and permanently and totally disabled;

3. Lived with you for more than half of 2018;

4. Didn't provide over half of his or her own support for 2018; and

5. Didn't file a joint return, or, if he or she did, it was only to claim a refund.

Adopted child. A legally adopted child is treated as your own child. This includes a child lawfully placed with you for legal adoption.

You can include medical expenses that you paid for a child before adoption if the child qualified as your dependent when the medical services were provided or when the expenses were paid.

If you pay back an adoption agency or other persons for medical expenses they paid under an agreement with you, you are treated as having paid those expenses, provided you clearly substantiate that the payment is directly attributable to the medical care of the child.

But if you pay the agency or other person for medical care that was provided and paid for before adoption negotiations began, you can't include them as medical expenses.

 You may be able to take an adoption credit for other expenses related to an adoption. See the Instructions for Form 8839, Qualified Adoption Expenses, for more information.

Child of divorced or separated parents. For purposes of the medical and dental expenses deduction, a child of divorced or separated parents can be treated as a dependent of both parents. Each parent can include the medical expenses he or she pays for the child, even if the other parent claims the child as a dependent, if:

1. The child is in the custody of one or both parents for more than half the year;

2. The child receives over half of his or her support during the year from his or her parents; and

3. The child's parents:
   a. Are divorced or legally separated under a decree of divorce or separate maintenance,
   b. Are separated under a written separation agreement, or
   c. Live apart at all times during the last 6 months of the year.

This doesn't apply if the child is being claimed as a dependent under a multiple support agreement (discussed later).

Qualifying Relative

A qualifying relative is a person:

1. Who is your:
   a. Son, daughter, stepchild, foster child, or a descendant of any of them (for example, your grandchild);
   b. Brother, sister, half brother, half sister, or a son or daughter of any of them;
   c. Father, mother, or an ancestor or sibling of either of them (for example, your grandmother, grandfather, aunt, or uncle);
   d. Stepbrother, stepsister, stepfather, stepmother, son-in-law, daughter-in-law, father-in-law, mother-in-law, brother-in-law, or sister-in-law; or
   e. Any other person (other than your spouse) who lived with you all year as a member of your household if your relationship didn't violate local law;

2. Who wasn't a qualifying child (see *Qualifying Child*, earlier) of any other person for 2018; and

3. For whom you provided over half of the support in 2018. But see *Child of divorced or separated parents*, earlier; *Support claimed under a multiple support agreement* next; and *Kidnapped child* under *Qualifying Relative* in Pub. 501, Dependents, Standard Deduction, and Filing Information.

Support claimed under a multiple support agreement. If you are considered to have provided more than half of a qualifying relative's support under a multiple support agreement, you can include medical expenses you pay for that person. A multiple support agreement is used when two or more people provide more than half of a person's support, but no one alone provides more than half.

Any medical expenses paid by others who joined you in the agreement can't be included as medical expenses by anyone. However, you can include the entire unreimbursed amount you paid for medical expenses.

Example. You and your three brothers each provide one-fourth of your mother's total support. Under a multiple support agreement, you treat your mother as your dependent. You paid all of her medical expenses. Your brothers repaid you for three-fourths of these expenses. In figuring your medical expense deduction, you can include only one-fourth of your mother's medical expenses. Your brothers can't include any part of the expenses. However, if you and your brothers share the nonmedical support items and you separately pay all of your mother's medical expenses, you can include the unreimbursed amount you paid for her medical expenses in your medical expenses.

Decedent

Medical expenses paid before death by the decedent are included in figuring any deduction for medical and dental expenses on the decedent's final income tax return. This includes expenses for the decedent's spouse and dependents as well as for the decedent.

The survivor or personal representative of a decedent can choose to treat certain expenses paid by the decedent's estate for the decedent's medical care as paid by the decedent at the time the medical services were provided. The expenses must be paid within the 1-year period beginning with the day after the date of death. If you are the survivor or personal representative making this choice, you must attach a statement to the decedent's Form 1040 (or the decedent's amended return, Form 1040X) saying that the expenses haven't been and won't be claimed on the estate tax return.

 Qualified medical expenses paid before death by the decedent aren't deductible if paid with a tax-free distribution from any Archer MSA, Medicare Advantage MSA, or health savings account.

Amended returns and claims for refund are discussed in chapter 1.

What if you pay medical expenses of a deceased spouse or dependent? If you paid medical expenses for your deceased spouse or dependent, include them as medical expenses on your Schedule A (Form 1040) in the year paid, whether they are paid before or after the decedent's death. The expenses can be included if the person was your spouse or dependent either at the time the medical services were provided or at the time you paid the expenses.

What Medical Expenses Are Includible?

Use Table 22-1 as a guide to determine which medical and dental expenses you can include on Schedule A (Form 1040).

This table doesn't include all possible medical expenses. To determine if an expense not listed can be included in figuring your medical expense deduction, see *What Are Medical Expenses*, earlier.

Insurance Premiums

You can include in medical expenses insurance premiums you pay for policies that cover medical care. Medical care policies can provide payment for treatment that includes:

- Hospitalization, surgical services, X-rays;
- Prescription drugs and insulin;
- Dental care;
- Replacement of lost or damaged contact lenses; and
- Long-term care (subject to additional limitations). See *Qualified Long-Term Care Insurance Contracts* in Pub. 502.

If you have a policy that provides payments for other than medical care, you can include the premiums for the medical care part of the policy if the charge for the medical part is reasonable. The cost of the medical part must be separately stated in the insurance contract or given to you in a separate statement.

Premium tax credit. When figuring the amount of insurance premiums you can deduct on Schedule A, don't include the amount of net premium tax credit you are claiming on Form 1040.

If advance payments of the premium tax credit were made, or you think you may be eligible to claim a premium tax credit, fill out Form 8962 before filling out Schedule A. See Pub. 502 for more information on how to figure your deduction.

Health coverage tax credit. If, during 2018, you were an eligible trade adjustment assistance (TAA) recipient, an alternative TAA (ATAA) recipient, reemployment TAA (RTAA) recipient, or Pension Benefit Guaranty Corporation (PBGC) payee, you must complete Form 8885 before completing Schedule A, line 1. When figuring the amount of insurance premiums you can deduct on Schedule A, do not include any of the following.

- Any amounts you included on Form 8885, line 4, or on Form 14095, The Health Coverage Tax Credit (HCTC) Reimbursement Request Form, to receive a reimbursement of the HCTC during the year.

- Any qualified health insurance coverage premiums you paid to "U.S. Treasury—HCTC" for eligible coverage months for which you received the benefit of the advance monthly payment program.

- Any advance monthly payments from your health plan administrator received from the IRS, as shown on Form 1099-H, Health Coverage Tax Credit (HCTC) Advance Payments.

Employer-sponsored health insurance plan. Don't include in your medical and dental expenses any insurance premiums paid by an employer-sponsored health insurance plan unless the premiums are included on your Form W-2. Also, don't include any other medical and dental expenses paid by the plan unless the amount paid is included on your Form W-2.

Example. You are a federal employee participating in the premium conversion plan of the Federal Employee Health Benefits (FEHB) program. Your share of the FEHB premium is paid by making a pre-tax reduction in your salary. Because you are an employee whose insurance premiums are paid with money that is never included in your gross income, you can't deduct the premiums paid with that money.

Long-term care services. Contributions made by your employer to provide coverage for qualified long-term care services under a flexible spending or similar arrangement must be included in your income. This amount will be reported as wages on your Form W-2.

Retired public safety officers. If you are a retired public safety officer, don't include as medical expenses any health or long-term care premiums that you elected to have paid with tax-free distributions from your retirement plan. This applies only to distributions that would otherwise be included in income.

Health reimbursement arrangement (HRA). If you have medical expenses that are reimbursed by a health reimbursement arrangement, you can't include those expenses in your medical expenses. This is because an HRA is funded solely by the employer.

Medicare A. If you are covered under social security (or if you are a government employee who paid Medicare tax), you are enrolled in Medicare A. The payroll tax paid for Medicare A isn't a medical expense.

If you aren't covered under social security (or weren't a government employee who paid Medicare tax), you can voluntarily enroll in Medicare A. In this situation, you can include the premiums you paid for Medicare A as a medical expense.

Medicare B. Medicare B is supplemental medical insurance. Premiums you pay for Medicare B are a medical expense. Check the information you received from the Social Security Administration to find out your premium.

Medicare D. Medicare D is a voluntary prescription drug insurance program for persons with Medicare A or B. You can include as a medical expense premiums you pay for Medicare D.

Prepaid insurance premiums. Premiums you pay before you are age 65 for insurance for medical care for yourself, your spouse, or your dependents after you reach age 65 are medical care expenses in the year paid if they are:

- Payable in equal yearly installments, or more often; and
- Payable for at least 10 years, or until you reach age 65 (but not for less than 5 years).

Unused sick leave used to pay premiums. You must include in gross income cash payments you receive at the time of retirement for unused sick leave. You also must include in gross income the value of unused sick leave that, at your option, your employer applies to the cost of your continuing participation in your employer's health plan after you retire. You can include this cost of continuing participation in the health plan as a medical expense.

If you participate in a health plan where your employer automatically applies the value of unused sick leave to the cost of your continuing participation in the health plan (and you don't have the option to receive cash), don't include the value of the unused sick leave in gross income. You can't include this cost of continuing participation in that health plan as a medical expense.

Meals and Lodging

You can include in medical expenses the cost of meals and lodging at a hospital or similar institution if a principal reason for being there is to get medical care. See *Nursing home*, later.

You may be able to include in medical expenses the cost of lodging not provided in a hospital or similar institution. You can include the cost of such lodging while away from home if all of the following requirements are met.

- The lodging is primarily for and essential to medical care.
- The medical care is provided by a doctor in a licensed hospital or in a medical care facility related to, or the equivalent of, a licensed hospital.
- The lodging isn't lavish or extravagant under the circumstances.
- There is no significant element of personal pleasure, recreation, or vacation in the travel away from home.

The amount you include in medical expenses for lodging can't be more than $50 for each night for each person. You can include lodging for a person traveling with the person receiving the medical care. For example, if a parent is traveling with a sick child, up to $100 per night can be included as a medical expense for lodging. Meals aren't included.

Nursing home. You can include in medical expenses the cost of medical care in a nursing home, home for the aged, or similar institution, for yourself, your spouse, or your dependents. This includes the cost of meals and lodging in the home if a principal reason for being there is to get medical care.

Table 22-1. Medical and Dental Expenses Checklist. See Pub. 502 for more information about these and other expenses.

You can include:		You can't include:	
• Bandages • Birth control pills prescribed by your doctor • Body scan • Braille books • Breast pump and supplies • Capital expenses for equipment or improvements to your home needed for medical care (see Worksheet A, Capital Expense Worksheet, in Pub. 502) • Diagnostic devices • Expenses of an organ donor • Eye surgery (to promote the correct function of the eye) • Fertility enhancement, certain procedures • Guide dogs or other animals aiding the blind, deaf, and disabled • Hospital services fees (lab work, therapy, nursing services, surgery, etc.) • Lead-based paint removal • Legal abortion • Legal operation to prevent having children such as a vasectomy or tubal ligation • Long-term care contracts, qualified • Meals and lodging provided by a hospital during medical treatment • Medical services fees (from doctors, dentists, surgeons, specialists, and other medical practitioners) • Medicare Part D premiums	• Medical and hospital insurance premiums • Nursing services • Oxygen equipment and oxygen • Part of life-care fee paid to retirement home designated for medical care • Physical examination • Pregnancy test kit • Prescription medicines (prescribed by a doctor) and insulin • Psychiatric and psychological treatment • Social security tax, Medicare tax, FUTA, and state employment tax for worker providing medical care (see Wages for nursing services below) • Special items (artificial limbs, false teeth, eyeglasses, contact lenses, hearing aids, crutches, wheelchair, etc.) • Special education for mentally or physically disabled persons • Stop-smoking programs • Transportation for needed medical care • Treatment at a drug or alcohol center (includes meals and lodging provided by the center) • Wages for nursing services • Weight loss, certain expenses for obesity	• Baby sitting and childcare • Bottled water • Contributions to Archer MSAs (see Pub. 969) • Diaper service • Expenses for your general health (even if following your doctor's advice) such as— —Health club dues —Household help (even if recommended by a doctor) —Social activities, such as dancing or swimming lessons —Trip for general health improvement • Flexible spending account reimbursements for medical expenses (if contributions were on a pre-tax basis) • Funeral, burial, or cremation expenses • Health savings account payments for medical expenses • Operation, treatment, or medicine that is illegal under federal or state law • Life insurance or income protection policies, or policies providing payment for loss of life, limb, sight, etc. • Maternity clothes	• Medical insurance included in a car insurance policy covering all persons injured in or by your car • Medicine you buy without a prescription • Nursing care for a healthy baby • Prescription drugs you brought in (or ordered shipped) from another country, in most cases • Nutritional supplements, vitamins, herbal supplements, "natural medicines," etc., unless recommended by a medical practitioner as a treatment for a specific medical condition diagnosed by a physician • Surgery for purely cosmetic reasons • Toothpaste, toiletries, cosmetics, etc. • Teeth whitening • Weight-loss expenses not for the treatment of obesity or other disease

Don't include the cost of meals and lodging if the reason for being in the home is personal. You can, however, include in medical expenses the part of the cost that is for medical or nursing care.

Transportation

Include in medical expenses amounts paid for transportation primarily for, and essential to, medical care. You can include:

- Bus, taxi, train, or plane fares, or ambulance service;

- Transportation expenses of a parent who must go with a child who needs medical care;

- Transportation expenses of a nurse or other person who can give injections, medications, or other treatment required by a patient who is traveling to get medical care and is unable to travel alone; and

- Transportation expenses for regular visits to see a mentally ill dependent, if these visits are recommended as a part of treatment.

Car expenses. You can include out-of-pocket expenses, such as the cost of gas and oil, when you use your car for medical reasons. You can't include depreciation, insurance, general repair, or maintenance expenses.

If you don't want to use your actual expenses for 2018, you can use the standard medical mileage rate of 18 cents per mile.

You also can include parking fees and tolls. You can add these fees and tolls to your medical expenses whether you use actual expenses or use the standard mileage rate.

Example. In 2018, Bill Jones drove 2,800 miles for medical reasons. He spent $400 for gas, $30 for oil, and $100 for tolls and parking. He wants to figure the amount he can include in medical expenses both ways to see which gives him the greater deduction.

He figures the actual expenses first. He adds the $400 for gas, the $30 for oil, and the $100 for tolls and parking for a total of $530.

He then figures the standard mileage amount. He multiplies 2,800 miles by 18 cents per mile for a total of $504. He then adds the $100 tolls and parking for a total of $604.

Bill includes the $604 of car expenses with his other medical expenses for the year because the $604 is more than the $530 he figured using actual expenses.

Transportation expenses you can't include. You can't include in medical expenses the cost of transportation in the following situations.

- Going to and from work, even if your condition requires an unusual means of transportation.

- Travel for purely personal reasons to another city for an operation or other medical care.

- Travel that is merely for the general improvement of one's health.

- The costs of operating a specially equipped car for other than medical reasons.

Disabled Dependent Care Expenses

Some disabled dependent care expenses may qualify as either:

- Medical expenses, or

- Work-related expenses for purposes of taking a credit for dependent care. (See chapter 31 and Pub. 503, Child and Dependent Care Expenses.)

You can choose to apply them either way as long as you don't use the same expenses to claim both a credit and a medical expense deduction.

How Do You Treat Reimbursements?

You can include in medical expenses only those amounts paid during the tax year for which you received no insurance or other reimbursement.

Figure 22-A. **Is Your Excess Medical Reimbursement Taxable?**

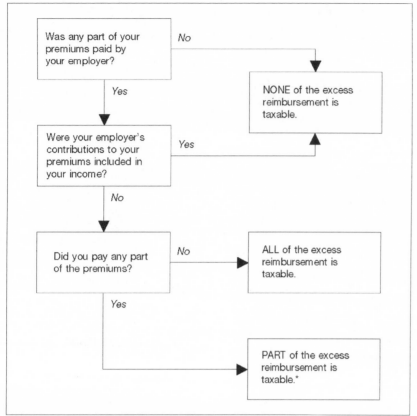

*See *Premiums paid by you and your employer* in this chapter.

Insurance Reimbursement

You must reduce your total medical expenses for the year by all reimbursements for medical expenses that you receive from insurance or other sources during the year. This includes payments from Medicare.

Even if a policy provides reimbursement for only certain specific medical expenses, you must use amounts you receive from that policy to reduce your total medical expenses, including those it doesn't reimburse.

Example. You have insurance policies that cover your hospital and doctors' bills but not your nursing bills. The insurance you receive for the hospital and doctors' bills is more than their charges. In figuring your medical deduction, you must reduce the total amount you spent for medical care by the total amount of insurance you received, even if the policies don't cover some of your medical expenses.

Health reimbursement arrangement (HRA). A health reimbursement arrangement is an employer-funded plan that reimburses employees for medical care expenses and allows unused amounts to be carried forward. An HRA is funded solely by the employer and the reimbursements for medical expenses, up to a maximum dollar amount for a coverage period, aren't included in your income.

Other reimbursements. Generally, you don't reduce medical expenses by payments you receive for:

- Permanent loss or loss of use of a member or function of the body (loss of limb, sight, hearing, etc.) or disfigurement to the extent the payment is based on the nature of the injury without regard to the amount of time lost from work; or

- Loss of earnings.

You must, however, reduce your medical expenses by any part of these payments that is designated for medical costs. See *How Do You Figure and Report the Deduction on Your Tax Return*, later.

For how to treat damages received for personal injury or sickness, see *Damages for Personal Injuries*, later.

You don't have a medical deduction if you are reimbursed for all of your medical expenses for the year.

Excess reimbursement. If you are reimbursed more than your medical expenses, you may have to include the excess in income. You may want to use Figure 21-A to help you decide if any of your reimbursement is taxable.

Premiums paid by you. If you pay either the entire premium for your medical insurance or all of the costs of a plan similar to medical insurance and your insurance payments or other reimbursements are more than your total medical expenses for the year, you have an excess reimbursement. Generally, you don't include the excess reimbursement in your gross income.

Premiums paid by you and your employer. If both you and your employer contribute to your medical insurance plan and your employer's contributions aren't included in your gross income, you must include in your gross income the part of your excess reimbursement that is from your employer's contribution.

See Pub. 502 to figure the amount of the excess reimbursement you must include in gross income.

Reimbursement in a later year. If you are reimbursed in a later year for medical expenses you deducted in an earlier year, you generally must report the reimbursement as income up to the amount you previously deducted as medical expenses.

However, don't report as income the amount of reimbursement you received up to the amount of your medical deductions that didn't reduce your tax for the earlier year. For more information about the recovery of an amount that you claimed as an itemized deduction in an earlier year, see *Itemized Deduction Recoveries* in chapter 12.

Medical expenses not deducted. If you didn't deduct a medical expense in the year you paid it because your medical expenses weren't more than 7.5% of your AGI, or because you didn't itemize deductions, don't include the reimbursement up to the amount of the expense in income. However, if the reimbursement is more than the expense, see *Excess reimbursement*, earlier.

Example. In 2018, you had $500 of medical expenses. You can't deduct the $500 because it is less than 7.5% of your AGI. If, in a later year, you are reimbursed for any of the $500 in medical expenses, you don't include the amount reimbursed in your gross income.

Damages for Personal Injuries

If you receive an amount in settlement of a personal injury suit, part of that award may be for medical expenses that you deducted in an earlier year. If it is, you must include that part in your income in the year you receive it to the extent it reduced your taxable income in the earlier year. See *Reimbursement in a later year*, discussed under *How Do You Treat Reimbursements*, earlier.

Future medical expenses. If you receive an amount in settlement of a damage suit for personal injuries, part of that award may be for future medical expenses. If it is, you must reduce any future medical expenses for these injuries until the amount you received has been completely used.

How Do You Report the Deduction on Your Tax Return?

Once you have determined which medical expenses you can include, you figure and report the deduction on your tax return.

What Tax Form Do You Use?

You report your medical expense deduction on Schedule A (Form 1040). If you need more information on itemized deductions or you aren't sure if you can itemize, see chapter 21.

Impairment-Related Work Expenses

If you are a person with a disability, you can take a business deduction for expenses that are necessary for you to be able to work. If you take a business deduction for impairment-related work expenses, they aren't subject to the 7.5% limit that applies to medical expenses.

You have a disability if you have:

- A physical or mental disability (for example, blindness or deafness) that functionally limits your being employed; or

- A physical or mental impairment (for example, a sight or hearing impairment) that substantially limits one or more of your major life activities, such as performing manual tasks, walking, speaking, breathing, learning, or working.

Impairment-related expenses defined. Impairment-related expenses are those ordinary and necessary business expenses that are:

- Necessary for you to do your work satisfactorily;

- For goods and services not required or used, other than incidentally, in your personal activities; and

- Not specifically covered under other income tax laws.

Where to report. If you are self-employed, deduct the business expenses on the appropriate form (Schedule C, C-EZ, E, or F) used to report your business income and expenses.

If you are an employee, complete Form 2106, Employee Business Expenses. Enter on Schedule A (Form 1040) that part of the amount on Form 2106 that is related to your impairment.

Example. You are blind. You must use a reader to do your work. You use the reader both during your regular working hours at your place of work and outside your regular working hours away from your place of work. The reader's services are only for your work. You can deduct your expenses for the reader as business expenses.

Health Insurance Costs for Self-Employed Persons

If you were self-employed and had a net profit for the year, you may be able to deduct, as an adjustment to income, amounts paid for medical and qualified long-term care insurance on behalf of yourself, your spouse, your dependents, and your children who were under age 27 at the end of 2018. For this purpose, you were self-employed if you were a general partner (or a limited partner receiving guaranteed payments) or you received wages from an S corporation in which you were more than a 2% shareholder. The insurance plan must be established under your trade or business and the deduction can't be more than your earned income from that trade or business.

You can't deduct payments for medical insurance for any month in which you were eligible to participate in a health plan subsidized by your employer, your spouse's employer, or an employer of your dependent or your child under age 27 at the end of 2018. You can't deduct payments for a qualified long-term care insurance contract for any month in which you were eligible to participate in a long-term care insurance plan subsidized by your employer or your spouse's employer.

If you qualify to take the deduction, use the Self-Employed Health Insurance Deduction Worksheet in the Instructions for Form 1040 to figure the amount you can deduct. But if any of the following applies, don't use that worksheet. Instead, use the worksheet in Pub. 535, Business Expenses, to figure your deduction.

- You had more than one source of income subject to self-employment tax.

- You file Form 2555, Foreign Earned Income, or Form 2555-EZ, Foreign Earned Income Exclusion.

- You are using amounts paid for qualified long-term care insurance to figure the deduction.

Use Pub. 974, Premium Tax Credit, instead of the worksheet in the Instructions for Form 1040 if you, your spouse, or a dependent enrolled in health insurance through the Health Insurance Marketplace and you are claiming the premium tax credit.

Note. If, during 2018, you are completing the Self-Employed Health Insurance Deduction Worksheet in your tax return instructions and you were an eligible trade adjustment assistance (TAA) recipient, alternative TAA (ATAA) recipient, reemployment TAA (RTAA) recipient, or Pension Benefit Guaranty Corporation (PBGC) payee, you must complete Form 8885 before completing that worksheet. When figuring the amount to enter on line 1 of the worksheet, do not include any of the following.

- Any amounts you included on Form 8885, line 4, or on Form 14095, The Health Coverage Tax Credit (HCTC) Reimbursement Request Form, to receive a reimbursement of the HCTC during the year.

- Any qualified health insurance coverage premiums you paid to "U.S. Treasury—HCTC" for eligible coverage months for which you received the benefit of the advance monthly payment program.

- Any advance monthly payments your health plan administrator received from the IRS, as shown on Form 1099-H, Health Coverage Tax Credit (HCTC) Advance Payments.

Don't include amounts paid for health insurance coverage with retirement plan distributions that were tax free because you are a retired public safety officer.

Where to report. You take this deduction on Form 1040. If you itemize your deductions and don't claim 100% of your self-employed health insurance on Form 1040, you generally can include any remaining premiums with all other medical expenses on Schedule A (Form 1040) subject to the 7.5% limit. See *Self-Employed Health Insurance Deduction* in Pub. 535 and *Medical and Dental Expenses* in the Instructions for Schedule A (Form 1040) for more information.

23.

Taxes

What's New

 At the time this publication went to print, Congress was considering legislation that would do the following.

1. Provide additional tax relief for those affected by certain 2018 disasters.

2. Extend certain tax benefits that expired at the end of 2017 and that currently can't be claimed on your 2018 tax return.

3. Change certain other tax provisions.

To learn whether this legislation was enacted resulting in changes that affect your 2018 tax return, go to Recent Developments at IRS.gov/ Pub17.

Limitation on deduction for state and local taxes. The Tax Cuts and Jobs Act provides for the temporary limitation of deductions for state and local taxes. See *Limitation on deduction for state and local taxes,* later.

No deduction for foreign taxes paid for real estate. You can no longer deduct foreign taxes you paid on real estate.

Introduction

This chapter discusses which taxes you can deduct if you itemize deductions on Schedule A (Form 1040). It also explains which taxes you can deduct on other schedules or forms and which taxes you cannot deduct.

This chapter covers the following topics.

- Income taxes (federal, state, local, and foreign).
- General sales taxes (state and local).
- Real estate taxes (state, local, and foreign).
- Personal property taxes (state and local).
- Taxes and fees you cannot deduct.

Use Table 23-1 as a guide to determine which taxes you can deduct.

The end of the chapter contains a section that explains which forms you use to deduct different types of taxes.

Business taxes. You can deduct certain taxes only if they are ordinary and necessary expenses of your trade or business or of producing income. For information on these taxes, see Pub. 535, Business Expenses.

State or local taxes. These are taxes imposed by the 50 states, U.S. possessions, or any of their political subdivisions (such as a county or city), or by the District of Columbia.

Indian tribal government. An Indian tribal government recognized by the Secretary of the Treasury as performing substantial government functions will be treated as a state for purposes of claiming a deduction for taxes. Income taxes, real estate taxes, and personal property taxes imposed by that Indian tribal government (or by any of its subdivisions that are treated as political subdivisions of a state) are deductible.

General sales taxes. These are taxes imposed at one rate on retail sales of a broad range of classes of items.

Foreign taxes. These are taxes imposed by a foreign country or any of its political subdivisions.

Useful Items

You may want to see:

Publication

- ❑ **514** Foreign Tax Credit for Individuals
- ❑ **530** Tax Information for Homeowners

Form (and Instructions)

- ❑ **Schedule A (Form 1040)** Itemized Deductions
- ❑ **Schedule E (Form 1040)** Supplemental Income and Loss
- ❑ **1116** Foreign Tax Credit

For these and other useful items, go to *IRS.gov/Forms*.

Tests To Deduct Any Tax

The following two tests must be met for you to deduct any tax.

- The tax must be imposed on you.
- You must pay the tax during your tax year.

The tax must be imposed on you. In general, you can deduct only taxes imposed on you.

Generally, you can deduct property taxes only if you are an owner of the property. If your spouse owns the property and pays the real estate taxes, the taxes are deductible on your spouse's separate return or on your joint return.

You must pay the tax during your tax year. If you are a cash basis taxpayer, you can deduct only those taxes you actually paid during your tax year. If you pay your taxes by check and the check is honored by your financial institution, the day you mail or deliver the check is the date of payment. If you use a pay-by-phone account (such as a credit card or electronic funds withdrawal), the date reported on the statement of the financial institution showing when payment was made is the date of payment. If you contest a tax liability and are a cash basis taxpayer, you can deduct the tax only in the year you actually pay it (or transfer money or other property to provide for satisfaction of the contested liability). See Pub. 538, Accounting Periods and Methods, for details.

If you use an accrual method of accounting, see Pub. 538 for more information.

Income Taxes

This section discusses the deductibility of state and local income taxes (including employee contributions to state benefit funds) and foreign income taxes.

State and Local Income Taxes

You can deduct state and local income taxes.

Exception. You can't deduct state and local income taxes you pay on income that is exempt from federal income tax, unless the exempt income is interest income. For example, you can't deduct the part of a state's income tax that is on a cost-of-living allowance exempt from federal income tax.

What To Deduct

Your deduction may be for withheld taxes, estimated tax payments, or other tax payments as follows.

Withheld taxes. You can deduct state and local income taxes withheld from your salary in the year they are withheld. Your Form(s) W-2 will show these amounts. Forms W-2G, 1099-B, 1099-DIV, 1099-G, 1099-K, 1099-MISC, 1099-OID, and 1099-R may also show state and local income taxes withheld.

Estimated tax payments. You can deduct estimated tax payments you made during the year to a state or local government. However, you must have a reasonable basis for making the estimated tax payments. Any estimated state or local tax payments that aren't made in good faith at the time of payment aren't deductible.

Example. You made an estimated state income tax payment. However, the estimate of your state tax liability shows that you will get a

refund of the full amount of your estimated payment. You had no reasonable basis to believe you had any additional liability for state income taxes and you can't deduct the estimated tax payment.

Refund applied to taxes. You can deduct any part of a refund of prior-year state or local income taxes that you chose to have credited to your 2018 estimated state or local income taxes.

Don't reduce your deduction by either of the following items.

- Any state or local income tax refund (or credit) you expect to receive for 2018.
- Any refund of (or credit for) prior-year state and local income taxes you actually received in 2018.

However, part or all of this refund (or credit) may be taxable. See *Refund (or credit) of state or local income taxes*, later.

Separate federal returns. If you and your spouse file separate state, local, and federal income tax returns, each of you can deduct on your federal return only the amount of your own state and local income tax that you paid during the tax year.

Joint state and local returns. If you and your spouse file joint state and local returns and separate federal returns, each of you can deduct on your separate federal return a part of the total state and local income taxes paid during the tax year. You can deduct only the amount of the total taxes that is proportionate to your gross income compared to the combined gross income of you and your spouse. However, you can't deduct more than the amount you actually paid during the year. You can avoid this calculation if you and your spouse are jointly and individually liable for the full amount of the state and local income taxes. If so, you and your spouse can deduct on your separate federal returns the amount you each actually paid.

Joint federal return. If you file a joint federal return, you can deduct the total of the state and local income taxes both of you paid.

Contributions to state benefit funds. As an employee, you can deduct mandatory contributions to state benefit funds withheld from your wages that provide protection against loss of wages. For example, certain states require employees to make contributions to state funds providing disability or unemployment insurance benefits. Mandatory payments made to the following state benefit funds are deductible as state income taxes on Schedule A (Form 1040), line 5.

- Alaska Unemployment Compensation Fund.
- California Nonoccupational Disability Benefit Fund.
- New Jersey Nonoccupational Disability Benefit Fund.
- New Jersey Unemployment Compensation Fund.
- New York Nonoccupational Disability Benefit Fund.

- Pennsylvania Unemployment Compensation Fund.
- Rhode Island Temporary Disability Benefit Fund.
- Washington State Supplemental Workmen's Compensation Fund.

 Employee contributions to private or voluntary disability plans aren't deductible.

Refund (or credit) of state or local income taxes. If you receive a refund of (or credit for) state or local income taxes in a year after the year in which you paid them, you may have to include the refund in income on Schedule 1 (Form 1040), line 10, in the year you receive it. This includes refunds resulting from taxes that were overwithheld, applied from a prior year return, not figured correctly, or figured again because of an amended return. If you didn't itemize your deductions in the previous year, don't include the refund in income. If you deducted the taxes in the previous year, include all or part of the refund on Schedule 1 (Form 1040), line 10, in the year you receive the refund. For a discussion of how much to include, see *Recoveries* in chapter 12.

Foreign Income Taxes

Generally, you can take either a deduction or a credit for income taxes imposed on you by a foreign country or a U.S. possession. However, you can't take a deduction or credit for foreign income taxes paid on income that is exempt from U.S. tax under the foreign earned income exclusion or the foreign housing exclusion. For information on these exclusions, see Pub. 54, Tax Guide for U.S. Citizens and Resident Aliens Abroad. For information on the foreign tax credit, see Pub. 514.

State and Local General Sales Taxes

You can elect to deduct state and local general sales taxes, instead of state and local income taxes, as an itemized deduction on Schedule A (Form 1040), line 5a. You can use either your actual expenses or the state and local sales tax tables to figure your sales tax deduction.

Actual expenses. Generally, you can deduct the actual state and local general sales taxes (including compensating use taxes) if the tax rate was the same as the general sales tax rate.

Food, clothing, and medical supplies. Sales taxes on food, clothing, and medical supplies are deductible as a general sales tax even if the tax rate was less than the general sales tax rate.

Motor vehicles. Sales taxes on motor vehicles are deductible as a general sales tax even if the tax rate was less than the general sales tax rate. However, if you paid sales tax on a motor vehicle at a rate higher than the general sales tax, you can deduct only the amount of the tax that you would have paid at the general sales tax rate on that vehicle. Include any state and local general sales taxes paid for a leased motor vehicle. For purposes of this section,

motor vehicles include cars, motorcycles, motor homes, recreational vehicles, sport utility vehicles, trucks, vans, and off-road vehicles.

 If you use the actual expenses method, you must have receipts to show the general sales taxes paid.

Trade or business items. Don't include sales taxes paid on items used in your trade or business on Schedule A (Form 1040). Instead, go to the instructions for the form you are using to report business income and expenses to see if you can deduct these taxes.

Optional sales tax tables. Instead of using your actual expenses, you can figure your state and local general sales tax deduction using the state and local sales tax tables in the Instructions for Schedule A (Form 1040). You may also be able to add the state and local general sales taxes paid on certain specified items.

Your applicable table amount is based on the state where you live, your income, and the number of exemptions claimed on your tax return. Your income is your adjusted gross income plus any nontaxable items such as the following.

- Tax-exempt interest.
- Veterans' benefits.
- Nontaxable combat pay.
- Workers' compensation.
- Nontaxable part of social security and railroad retirement benefits.
- Nontaxable part of IRA, pension, or annuity distributions, excluding rollovers.
- Public assistance payments.

If you lived in different states during the same tax year, you must prorate your applicable table amount for each state based on the days you lived in each state. See the instructions for Schedule A (Form 1040), line 5a, for details.

State and Local Real Estate Taxes

Deductible real estate taxes are any state and local taxes on real property levied for the general public welfare. You can deduct these taxes only if they are assessed uniformly against all property under the jurisdiction of the taxing authority. The proceeds must be for general community or governmental purposes and not be a payment for a special privilege granted or service rendered to you.

Deductible real estate taxes generally don't include taxes charged for local benefits and improvements that increase the value of the property. They also don't include itemized charges for services (such as trash collection) assessed against specific property or certain people, even if the charge is paid to the taxing authority. For more information about taxes and charges that aren't deductible, see *Real Estate-Related Items You Can't Deduct*, later.

Tenant-shareholders in a cooperative housing corporation. Generally, if you are a tenant-stockholder in a cooperative housing corporation, you can deduct the amount paid to the

corporation that represents your share of the real estate taxes the corporation paid or incurred for your dwelling unit. The corporation should provide you with a statement showing your share of the taxes. For more information, see *Special Rules for Cooperatives* in Pub. 530.

Division of real estate taxes between buyers and sellers. If you bought or sold real estate during the year, the real estate taxes must be divided between the buyer and the seller.

The buyer and the seller must divide the real estate taxes according to the number of days in the real property tax year (the period to which the tax is imposed relates) that each owned the property. The seller is treated as paying the taxes up to, but not including, the date of sale. The buyer is treated as paying the taxes beginning with the date of sale. This applies regardless of the lien dates under local law. Generally, this information is included on the settlement statement provided at the closing.

If you (the seller) can't deduct taxes until they are paid because you use the cash method of accounting, and the buyer of your property is personally liable for the tax, you are considered to have paid your part of the tax at the time of the sale. This lets you deduct the part of the tax to the date of sale even though you didn't actually pay it. However, you must also include the amount of that tax in the selling price of the property. The buyer must include the same amount in his or her cost of the property.

You figure your deduction for taxes on each property bought or sold during the real property tax year as follows.

Worksheet 23-1. **Figuring Your State and Local Real Estate Tax Deduction**
Keep for Your Records

1.	Enter the total state and local real estate taxes for the real property tax year . . . . _____
2.	Enter the number of days in the real property tax year that you owned the property . . . . _____
3.	Divide line 2 by 365 (for leap years, divide line 2 by 366) . . . . _____
4.	Multiply line 1 by line 3. This is your deduction. Enter it on Schedule A (Form 1040), line 5b . . . . _____

Note. Repeat steps 1 through 4 for each property you bought or sold during the real property tax year. Your total deduction is the sum of the line 4 amounts for all of the properties.

Real estate taxes for prior years. Don't divide delinquent taxes between the buyer and seller if the taxes are for any real property tax year before the one in which the property is sold. Even if the buyer agrees to pay the delinquent taxes, the buyer can't deduct them. The buyer must add them to the cost of the property. The seller can deduct these taxes paid by the buyer. However, the seller must include them in the selling price.

Examples. The following examples illustrate how real estate taxes are divided between buyer and seller.

Example 1. Dennis and Beth White's real property tax year for both their old home and their new home is the calendar year, with payment due August 1. The tax on their old home, sold on May 7, was $620. The tax on their new home, bought on May 3, was $732. Dennis and Beth are considered to have paid a proportionate share of the real estate taxes on the old home even though they didn't actually pay them to the taxing authority. On the other hand, they can claim only a proportionate share of the taxes they paid on their new property even though they paid the entire amount.

Dennis and Beth owned their old home during the real property tax year for 126 days (January 1 to May 6, the day before the sale). They figure their deduction for taxes on their old home as follows.

Worksheet 23-1. **Figuring Your State and Local Real Estate Tax Deduction — Taxes on Old Home**

1.	Enter the total state and local real estate taxes for the real property tax year	$620
2.	Enter the number of days in the real property tax year that you owned the property	126
3.	Divide line 2 by 365 (for leap years, divide line 2 by 366)	0.3452
4.	Multiply line 1 by line 3. This is your deduction. Enter it on Schedule A (Form 1040), line 5b	$214

Since the buyers of their old home paid all of the taxes, Dennis and Beth also include the $214 in the selling price of the old home. (The buyers add the $214 to their cost of the home.)

Dennis and Beth owned their new home during the real property tax year for 243 days (May 3 to December 31, including their date of purchase). They figure their deduction for taxes on their new home as follows.

Worksheet 23-1. **Figuring Your State and Local Real Estate Tax Deduction — Taxes on New Home**

1.	Enter the total state and local real estate taxes for the real property tax year	$732
2.	Enter the number of days in the real property tax year that you owned the property	243
3.	Divide line 2 by 365 (for leap years, divide line 2 by 366)	0.6658
4.	Multiply line 1 by line 3. This is your deduction. Enter it on Schedule A (Form 1040), line 5b	$487

Since Dennis and Beth paid all of the taxes on the new home, they add $245 ($732 paid less $487 deduction) to their cost of the new home. (The sellers add this $245 to their selling price and deduct the $245 as a real estate tax.)

Dennis and Beth's real estate tax deduction for their old and new homes is the sum of $214 and $487, or $701. They will enter this amount on Schedule A (Form 1040), line 5b.

Example 2. George and Helen Brown bought a new home on May 3, 2018. Their real property tax year for the new home is the calendar year. Real estate taxes for 2017 were assessed in their state on January 1, 2018. The taxes became due on May 31, 2018, and October 31, 2018.

The Browns agreed to pay all taxes due after the date of purchase. Real estate taxes for 2017 were $680. They paid $340 on May 31, 2018, and $340 on October 31, 2018. These taxes were for the 2017 real property tax year. The Browns cannot deduct them since they didn't own the property until 2018. Instead, they must add $680 to the cost of their new home.

In January 2019, the Browns receive their 2018 property tax statement for $752, which they will pay in 2019. The Browns owned their new home during the 2018 real property tax year for 243 days (May 3 to December 31). They will figure their 2019 deduction for taxes as follows.

Worksheet 23-1. **Figuring Your State and Local Real Estate Tax Deduction — Taxes on New Home**

1.	Enter the total state and local real estate taxes for the real property tax year	$752
2.	Enter the number of days in the real property tax year that you owned the property	243
3.	Divide line 2 by 365 (for leap years, divide line 2 by 366)	0.6658
4.	Multiply line 1 by line 3. This is your deduction. Claim it on Schedule A (Form 1040), line 5b	$501

The remaining $251 ($752 paid less $501 deduction) of taxes paid in 2019, along with the $680 paid in 2018, is added to the cost of their new home.

Because the taxes up to the date of sale are considered paid by the seller on the date of sale, the seller is entitled to a 2018 tax deduction of $931. This is the sum of the $680 for 2017 and the $251 for the 122 days the seller owned the home in 2018. The seller must also include the $931 in the selling price when he or she figures the gain or loss on the sale. The seller should contact the Browns in January 2019 to find out how much real estate tax is due for 2018.

Form 1099-S. For certain sales or exchanges of real estate, the person responsible for closing the sale (generally, the settlement agent) prepares Form 1099-S, Proceeds From Real Estate Transactions, to report certain information to the IRS and to the seller of the property. Box 2 of Form 1099-S is for the gross proceeds from the sale and should include the portion of the seller's real estate tax liability that the buyer will pay after the date of sale. The buyer includes these taxes in the cost basis of the property, and the seller both deducts this amount as a tax paid and includes it in the sales price of the property.

For a real estate transaction that involves a home, any real estate tax the seller paid in advance but that is the liability of the buyer appears on Form 1099-S, box 6. The buyer deducts this amount as a real estate tax, and the seller reduces his or her real estate tax deduction (or includes it in income) by the same amount. See *Refund (or rebate)*, later.

Taxes placed in escrow. If your monthly mortgage payment includes an amount placed in escrow (put in the care of a third party) for real estate taxes, you may not be able to deduct the total amount placed in escrow. You can deduct only the real estate tax that the third party actually paid to the taxing authority. If the third party doesn't notify you of the amount of real estate tax that was paid for you, contact the third party or the taxing authority to find the proper amount to show on your return.

Tenants by the entirety. If you and your spouse held property as tenants by the entirety and you file separate federal returns, each of you can deduct only the taxes each of you paid on the property.

Divorced individuals. If your divorce or separation agreement states that you must pay the real estate taxes for a home owned by you and your spouse, part of your payments may be deductible as alimony and part as real estate taxes. See *Taxes and insurance* in chapter 18 for more information.

Ministers' and military housing allowances. If you are a minister or a member of the uniformed services and receive a housing allowance that you can exclude from income, you still can deduct all of the real estate taxes you pay on your home.

Refund (or rebate). If you received a refund or rebate in 2018 of real estate taxes you paid in 2018, you must reduce your deduction by the amount refunded to you. If you received a refund or rebate in 2018 of real estate taxes you deducted in an earlier year, you generally must include the refund or rebate in income in the year you receive it. However, the amount you include in income is limited to the amount of the deduction that reduced your tax in the earlier year. For more information, see *Recoveries* in chapter 12.

Real Estate-Related Items You Can't Deduct

Payments for the following items generally aren't deductible as real estate taxes.

- Taxes for local benefits.
- Itemized charges for services (such as trash and garbage pickup fees).
- Transfer taxes (or stamp taxes).
- Rent increases due to higher real estate taxes.
- Homeowners' association charges.

Taxes for local benefits. Deductible real estate taxes generally don't include taxes charged for local benefits and improvements tending to increase the value of your property. These include assessments for streets, sidewalks, water mains, sewer lines, public parking facilities, and similar improvements. You should increase the basis of your property by the amount of the assessment.

Local benefit taxes are deductible only if they are for maintenance, repair, or interest charges related to those benefits. If only a part of the taxes is for maintenance, repair, or interest, you must be able to show the amount of that part to claim the deduction. If you can't determine what part of the tax is for maintenance, repair, or interest, none of it is deductible.

Table 23-1. Which Taxes Can You Deduct?

Type of Tax	You Can Deduct	You Can't Deduct
Fees and Charges	Fees and charges that are expenses of your trade or business or of producing income.	Fees and charges that aren't expenses of your trade or business or of producing income, such as fees for driver's licenses, car inspections, parking, or charges for water bills (see *Taxes and Fees You Can't Deduct*). Fines and penalties.
Income Taxes	State and local income taxes. Foreign income taxes. Employee contributions to state funds listed under *Contributions to state benefit funds*.	Federal income taxes. Employee contributions to private or voluntary disability plans. State and local general sales taxes if you choose to deduct state and local income taxes.
General Sales Taxes	State and local general sales taxes, including compensating use taxes.	State and local income taxes if you choose to deduct state and local general sales taxes.
Other Taxes	Taxes that are expenses of your trade or business. Taxes on property producing rent or royalty income. One-half of self-employment tax paid.	Federal excise taxes, such as tax on gasoline, that aren't expenses of your trade or business or of producing income. Per capita taxes.
Personal Property Taxes	State and local personal property taxes.	Customs duties that aren't expenses of your trade or business or of producing income.
Real Estate Taxes	State and local real estate taxes. Tenant's share of real estate taxes paid by cooperative housing corporation.	Real estate taxes that are treated as imposed on someone else (see *Division of real estate taxes between buyers and sellers*). Foreign real estate taxes. Taxes for local benefits (with exceptions). See *Real Estate-Related Items You Can't Deduct*. Trash and garbage pickup fees (with exceptions). See *Real Estate-Related Items You Can't Deduct*. Rent increase due to higher real estate taxes. Homeowners' association charges.

Taxes for local benefits may be included in your real estate tax bill. If your taxing authority (or mortgage lender) doesn't furnish you a copy of your real estate tax bill, ask for it. You should use the rules above to determine if the local benefit tax is deductible. Contact the taxing authority if you need additional information about a specific charge on your real estate tax bill.

Itemized charges for services. An itemized charge for services assessed against specific property or certain people isn't a tax, even if the charge is paid to the taxing authority. For example, you can't deduct the charge as a real estate tax if it is:

- A unit fee for the delivery of a service (such as a $5 fee charged for every 1,000 gallons of water you use),
- A periodic charge for a residential service (such as a $20 per month or $240 annual fee charged to each homeowner for trash collection), or
- A flat fee charged for a single service provided by your government (such as a $30 charge for mowing your lawn because it was allowed to grow higher than permitted under your local ordinance).

You must look at your real estate tax bill to determine if any nondeductible itemized charges, such as those listed above, are included in the bill. If your taxing authority (or mortgage lender) doesn't furnish you a copy of your real estate tax bill, ask for it.

Exception. Service charges used to maintain or improve services (such as trash collection or police and fire protection) are deductible as real estate taxes if:

- The fees or charges are imposed at a like rate against all property in the taxing jurisdiction;
- The funds collected are not earmarked; instead, they are commingled with general revenue funds; and
- Funds used to maintain or improve services are not limited to or determined by the amount of these fees or charges collected.

Transfer taxes (or stamp taxes). Transfer taxes and similar taxes and charges on the sale of a personal home aren't deductible. If they are paid by the seller, they are expenses of the sale and reduce the amount realized on the sale. If paid by the buyer, they are included in the cost basis of the property.

Rent increase due to higher real estate taxes. If your landlord increases your rent in the form of a tax surcharge because of increased real estate taxes, you can't deduct the increase as taxes.

Homeowners' association charges. These charges aren't deductible because they are imposed by the homeowners' association, rather than the state or local government.

Personal Property Taxes

Personal property tax is deductible if it is a state or local tax that is:

- Charged on personal property;
- Based only on the value of the personal property; and
- Charged on a yearly basis, even if it is collected more or less than once a year.

A tax that meets the above requirements can be considered charged on personal property even if it is for the exercise of a privilege. For example, a yearly tax based on value qualifies as a personal property tax even if it is called a registration fee and is for the privilege of registering motor vehicles or using them on the highways.

If the tax is partly based on value and partly based on other criteria, it may qualify in part.

Example. Your state charges a yearly motor vehicle registration tax of 1% of value plus 50 cents per hundredweight. You paid $32 based on the value ($1,500) and weight (3,400 lbs.) of your car. You can deduct $15 (1% × $1,500) as a personal property tax because it is based on the value. The remaining $17 ($0.50 × 34), based on the weight, isn't deductible.

Taxes and Fees You Can't Deduct

Many federal, state, and local government taxes aren't deductible because they don't fall within the categories discussed earlier. Other taxes and fees, such as federal income taxes, aren't deductible because the tax law specifically prohibits a deduction for them. See Table 23-1.

Taxes and fees that are generally not deductible include the following items.

- **Employment taxes.** This includes social security, Medicare, and railroad retirement taxes withheld from your pay. However, one-half of self-employment tax you pay is deductible. In addition, the social security and other employment taxes you pay on the wages of a household worker may be included in medical expenses that you can deduct, or child care expenses that allow you to claim the child and dependent care credit. For more information, see chapters 22 and 31.

- **Estate, inheritance, legacy, or succession taxes.** You can deduct the estate tax attributable to income in respect of a decedent if you, as a beneficiary, must include that income in your gross income. In that case, deduct the estate tax on Schedule A (Form 1040), line 16. You can no longer claim any miscellaneous itemized deductions. Miscellaneous itemized deductions are those deductions that would have been subject to the 2%-of-adjusted-gross-income limitation. For more information, see Pub. 559, Survivors, Executors, and Administrators.

- **Federal income taxes.** This includes income taxes withheld from your pay.

- **Fines and penalties.** You can't deduct fines and penalties paid to a government for violation of any law, including related amounts forfeited as collateral deposits.

- **Foreign personal or real property taxes.**

- **Gift taxes.**

- **License fees.** You can't deduct license fees for personal purposes (such as marriage, driver's, and pet license fees).

- **Per capita taxes.** You can't deduct state or local per capita taxes.

Many taxes and fees other than those listed above are also nondeductible, unless they are ordinary and necessary expenses of a business or income-producing activity. For other nondeductible items, see *Real Estate-Related Items You Can't Deduct*, earlier.

Where To Deduct

You deduct taxes on the following schedules.

State and local income taxes. These taxes are deducted on Schedule A (Form 1040), lines 5a, 5b, and 5c, even if your only source of income is from business, rents, or royalties.

Limitation on deduction for state and local taxes. The deduction for state and local taxes is limited to $10,000 ($5,000 if married filing separately). State and local taxes are the taxes that you include on Schedule A (Form 1040), lines 5a, 5b, and 5c. Include taxes imposed by a U.S. possession with your state and local taxes on Schedule A (Form 1040), lines 5a, 5b, and 5c. However, don't include any U.S. possession taxes you paid that are allocable to excluded income.

 You may want to take a credit for U.S. possession tax instead of a deduction. See the instructions for Schedule 3 (Form 1040), line 48, for details.

General sales taxes. Sales taxes are deducted on Schedule A (Form 1040), line 5a. You must check the box on line 5a. If you elect to deduct sales taxes, you can't deduct state and local income taxes on Schedule A (Form 1040), line 5a.

Foreign income taxes. Generally, income taxes you pay to a foreign country or U.S. possession can be claimed as an itemized deduction on Schedule A (Form 1040), line 6, or as a credit against your U.S. income tax on Schedule 3 (Form 1040), line 48. To claim the credit, you may have to complete and attach Form 1116. For more information, see chapter 37, the Form 1040 instructions, or Pub. 514.

Real estate taxes and personal property taxes. Real estate and personal property taxes are deducted on Schedule A (Form 1040), lines 5b and 5c, respectively, unless they are paid on property used in your business, in which case they are deducted on Schedule C, Schedule C-EZ, or Schedule F (Form 1040). Taxes on property that produces rent or royalty income are deducted on Schedule E (Form 1040).

Self-employment tax. Deduct one-half of your self-employment tax on Form 1040, line 27.

Other taxes. All other deductible taxes are deducted on Schedule A (Form 1040), line 6.

24.

Interest Expense

What's New

At the time this publication went to print, Congress was considering legislation that would do the following.

1. Provide additional tax relief for those affected by certain 2018 disasters.

2. Extend certain tax benefits that expired at the end of 2017 and that currently can't be claimed on your 2018 tax return.

3. Change certain other tax provisions.

To learn whether this legislation was enacted resulting in changes that affect your 2018 tax return, go to Recent Developments at *IRS.gov/Pub17*.

Home equity loan interest. No matter when the indebtedness was incurred, you can no longer deduct the interest from a loan secured by your home to the extent the loan proceeds weren't used to buy, build, or substantially improve your home.

Home mortgage interest. You can deduct mortgage interest on the first $750,000 ($375,000 if married filing separately) of indebtedness. However, higher limitations ($1 million ($500,000 if filing separately)) apply if you are deducting mortgage interest from indebtedness incurred before December 16, 2017.

Modification of Hardest Hit Fund safe harbor. Homeowners who may be affected by the new $10,000 limitation on deductible property taxes may allocate mortgage payments actually made first to deductible mortgage interest, and then use any reasonable method to allocate the remaining balance of payments made to real property taxes, mortgage insurance premiums, home insurance premiums, and principal.

Reminder

Mortgage insurance premiums. The itemized deduction for mortgage insurance premiums expired on December 31, 2017.

At the time this publication was prepared for printing, Congress was considering legislation that would extend the mortgage insurance premiums deduction after 2017. If extended, your mortgage insurance premiums may be deductible for 2018. To see if the legislation was enacted, go to Recent Developments at IRS.gov/Pub17.

Introduction

This chapter discusses what interest expenses you can deduct. Interest is the amount you pay for the use of borrowed money.

The following are types of interest you can deduct as itemized deductions on Schedule A (Form 1040).

- Home mortgage interest, including certain points.
- Investment interest.

This chapter explains these deductions. It also explains where to deduct other types of interest and lists some types of interest you can't deduct.

Use Table 24-1 to find out where to get more information on various types of interest, including investment interest.

Useful Items

You may want to see:

Publication

- ❑ **936** Home Mortgage Interest Deduction
- ❑ **550** Investment Income and Expenses
- ❑ **970** Tax Benefits for Education
- ❑ **535** Business Expenses
- ❑ **527** Residential Rental Property
- ❑ **225** Farmer's Tax Guide

For these and other useful items, go to IRS.gov/Forms.

Home Mortgage Interest

Generally, home mortgage interest is any interest you pay on a loan secured by your home (main home or a second home). The loan may be a mortgage to buy your home or a second mortgage.

You can deduct home mortgage interest if all the following conditions are met.

- You file Form 1040 and itemize deductions on Schedule A (Form 1040).
- The mortgage is a secured debt on a qualified home in which you have an ownership interest. (Generally, your mortgage is a secured debt if you put your home up as collateral to protect the interest of the lender. The term "qualified home" means your main home or second home. For details, see Pub. 936.)

Both you and the lender must intend that the loan be repaid.

Amount Deductible

Note. Interest on home equity loans and lines of credit are deductible only if the borrowed funds are used to buy, build, or substantially improve the taxpayer's home that secures the loan. As under prior law, the loan must be secured by the taxpayer's main home or second home (qualified residence), not exceed the cost of the home, and meet other requirements.

In most cases, you can deduct all of your home mortgage interest. How much you can deduct depends on the date of the mortgage, the amount of the mortgage, and how you use the mortgage proceeds.

Fully deductible interest. If all of your mortgages fit into one or more of the following three categories at all times during the year, you can deduct all of the interest on those mortgages. (If any one mortgage fits into more than one category, add the debt that fits in each category to your other debt in the same category.)

The three categories are as follows.

1. Mortgages you took out on or before October 13, 1987 (called grandfathered debt).

2. Mortgages you (or your spouse if married filing a joint return) took out after October 13, 1987, and prior to December 16, 2017 (but see binding contract exception below), to buy, build, or substantially improve your home (called home acquisition debt), but only if throughout 2018 these mortgages plus any grandfathered debt totaled $1 million or less ($500,000 or less if married filing separately).

   Exception. A taxpayer who enters into a written binding contract before December 15, 2017, to close on the purchase of a principal residence before January 1, 2018, and who purchases such residence before April 1, 2018, is considered to have incurred the home acquisition debt prior to December 16, 2017.

3. Mortgages you (or your spouse if married filing a joint return) took out after December 15, 2017, to buy, build, or substantially improve your home (called home acquisition debt), but only if throughout 2018 these mortgages plus any grandfathered debt totaled $750,000 or less ($375,000 or less if married filing separately).

The dollar limits for the second and third categories apply to the combined mortgages on your main home and second home.

See *Part II* of Pub. 936 for more detailed definitions of grandfathered debt and home acquisition debt.

You can use Figure 24-A to check whether your home mortgage interest is fully deductible.

Limits on deduction. You can't fully deduct interest on a mortgage that doesn't fit into any of the three categories listed earlier. If this applies to you, see *Part II* of Pub. 936 to figure the amount of interest you can deduct.

Special Situations

This section describes certain items that can be included as home mortgage interest and others

that can't. It also describes certain special situations that may affect your deduction.

Late payment charge on mortgage payment. You can deduct as home mortgage interest a late payment charge if it wasn't for a specific service performed in connection with your mortgage loan.

Mortgage prepayment penalty. If you pay off your home mortgage early, you may have to pay a penalty. You can deduct that penalty as home mortgage interest provided the penalty isn't for a specific service performed or cost incurred in connection with your mortgage loan.

Sale of home. If you sell your home, you can deduct your home mortgage interest (subject to any limits that apply) paid up to, but not including, the date of sale.

Example. John and Peggy Harris sold their home on May 7. Through April 30, they made home mortgage interest payments of $1,220. The settlement sheet for the sale of the home showed $50 interest for the 6-day period in May up to, but not including, the date of sale. Their mortgage interest deduction is $1,270 ($1,220 + $50).

Prepaid interest. If you pay interest in advance for a period that goes beyond the end of the tax year, you must spread this interest over the tax years to which it applies. You can deduct in each year only the interest that qualifies as home mortgage interest for that year. However, there is an exception that applies to points, discussed later.

Mortgage interest credit. You may be able to claim a mortgage interest credit if you were issued a mortgage credit certificate (MCC) by a state or local government. Figure the credit on Form 8396, Mortgage Interest Credit. If you take this credit, you must reduce your mortgage interest deduction by the amount of the credit.

For more information on the credit, see chapter 37.

Ministers' and military housing allowance. If you are a minister or a member of the uniformed services and receive a housing allowance that isn't taxable, you can still deduct your home mortgage interest.

Hardest Hit Fund and Emergency Homeowners' Loan Programs. You can use a special method to figure your deduction for mortgage interest and real estate taxes on your main home if you meet the following two conditions.

1. You received assistance under:

   a. A State Housing Finance Agency (State HFA) Hardest Hit Fund program in which program payments could be used to pay mortgage interest, or

   b. An Emergency Homeowners' Loan Program administered by the Department of Housing and Urban Development (HUD) or a state.

2. You meet the rules to deduct all of the mortgage interest on your loan and all of the real estate taxes on your main home.

Figure 24-A. Is My Home Mortgage Interest Fully Deductible?

*(Instructions: Include balances of **ALL** mortgages secured by your main home and second home.)*

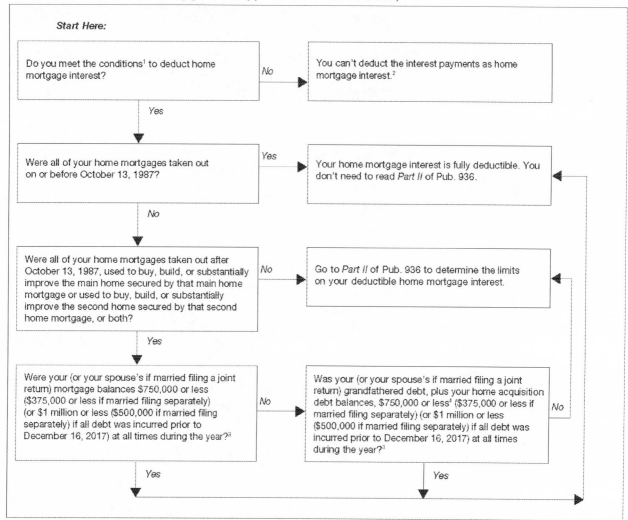

[1] You must itemize deductions on Schedule A (Form 1040). The loan must be a secured debt on a qualified home. See *Home Mortgage Interest* in *Part I* of Pub. 936.

[2] See Table 2 in *Part II* of Pub. 936 for where to deduct other types of interest payments.

[3] A taxpayer who enters into a written binding contract before December 15, 2017, to close on the purchase of a principal residence before January 1, 2018, and who purchases such residence before April 1, 2018, is considered to have incurred the home acquisition debt prior to December 16, 2017, and may use the 2017 threshold amounts of $1,000,000 ($500,000 if married filing separately).

[4] See *Part II* of Pub. 936 for more information about grandfathered debt and home acquisition debt.

If you meet these conditions, then you can deduct all of the payments you actually made during the year to your mortgage servicer, the State HFA, or HUD on the home mortgage (including the amount shown in box 3 of Form 1098-MA, Mortgage Assistance Payments), but not more than the sum of the amounts shown on Form 1098, Mortgage Interest Statement, in box 1 (mortgage interest received from payer(s)/borrower(s)) and box 10 (real property taxes).

You may first allocate amounts paid to mortgage interest up to the amount shown on Form 1098. You may then use any reasonable method to allocate the remaining balance of the payments to real property taxes, mortgage insurance premiums, and principal. Regardless of how you determine the deductible amount under this special safe harbor method, any amount allocated to state or local property taxes is subject to the limitation on the deduction for state and local taxes. However, you're not required to use this special method to figure your deduction for mortgage interest and real estate taxes on your main home.

Mortgage assistance payments under section 235 of the National Housing Act. If you qualify for mortgage assistance payments for lower-income families under section 235 of the National Housing Act, part or all of the interest on your mortgage may be paid for you. You can't deduct the interest that is paid for you.

No other effect on taxes. Don't include these mortgage assistance payments in your income. Also, don't use these payments to reduce other deductions, such as real estate taxes.

Divorced or separated individuals. If a divorce or separation agreement requires you or your spouse or former spouse to pay home mortgage interest on a home owned by both of you, the payment of interest may be alimony. See the discussion of *Payments for jointly owned home* in chapter 18.

Redeemable ground rents. If you make annual or periodic rental payments on a redeemable ground rent, you can deduct them as mortgage interest.

Payments made to end the lease and to buy the lessor's entire interest in the land aren't deductible as mortgage interest. For more information, see Pub. 936.

Nonredeemable ground rents. Payments on a nonredeemable ground rent aren't mortgage interest. You can deduct them as rent if they are a business expense or if they are for rental property.

Reverse mortgages. A reverse mortgage is a loan where the lender pays you (in a lump sum, a monthly advance, a line of credit, or a combination of all three) while you continue to live in your home. With a reverse mortgage, you retain title to your home. Depending on the plan, your reverse mortgage becomes due with interest when you move, sell your home, reach the end of a pre-selected loan period, or die. Because reverse mortgages are considered loan advances and not income, the amount you receive isn't taxable. Any interest (including original issue discount) accrued on a reverse mortgage is

considered home equity debt and isn't deductible.

Rental payments. If you live in a house before final settlement on the purchase, any payments you make for that period are rent and not interest. This is true even if the settlement papers call them interest. You can't deduct these payments as home mortgage interest.

Mortgage proceeds invested in tax-exempt securities. You can't deduct the home mortgage interest on grandfathered debt if you used the proceeds of the mortgage to buy securities or certificates that produce tax-free income. "Grandfathered debt" is defined earlier under *Amount Deductible*.

Refunds of interest. If you receive a refund of interest in the same tax year you paid it, you must reduce your interest expense by the amount refunded to you. If you receive a refund of interest you deducted in an earlier year, you generally must include the refund in income in the year you receive it. However, you need to include it only up to the amount of the deduction that reduced your tax in the earlier year. This is true whether the interest overcharge was refunded to you or was used to reduce the outstanding principal on your mortgage. If you need to include the refund in income, report it on Schedule 1 (Form 1040), line 21.

If you received a refund of interest you overpaid in an earlier year, you generally will receive a Form 1098, Mortgage Interest Statement, showing the refund in box 4. For information about Form 1098, see *Form 1098, Mortgage Interest Statement*, later.

For more information on how to treat refunds of interest deducted in earlier years, see *Recoveries* in chapter 12.

Points

The term "points" is used to describe certain charges paid, or treated as paid, by a borrower to obtain a home mortgage. Points may also be called loan origination fees, maximum loan charges, loan discount, or discount points.

A borrower is treated as paying any points that a home seller pays for the borrower's mortgage. See *Points paid by the seller*, later.

General Rule

You generally can't deduct the full amount of points in the year paid. Because they are prepaid interest, you generally deduct them ratably over the life (term) of the mortgage. See *Deduction Allowed Ratably* next. If the loan is a home equity, line of credit, or credit card loan and the proceeds from the loan are not used to buy, build, or substantially improve the home, the points are not deductible.

For exceptions to the general rule, see *Deduction Allowed in Year Paid*, later.

Deduction Allowed Ratably

If you don't meet the tests listed under *Deduction Allowed in Year Paid* next, the loan isn't a home improvement loan, or you choose not to deduct your points in full in the year paid, you can deduct the points ratably (equally) over the

life of the loan if you meet all of the following tests.

1. You use the cash method of accounting. This means you report income in the year you receive it and deduct expenses in the year you pay them. Most individuals use this method.

2. Your loan is secured by a home. (The home doesn't need to be your main home.)

3. Your loan period isn't more than 30 years.

4. If your loan period is more than 10 years, the terms of your loan are the same as other loans offered in your area for the same or longer period.

5. Either your loan amount is $250,000 or less, or the number of points isn't more than:

   a. Four, if your loan period is 15 years or less; or

   b. Six, if your loan period is more than 15 years.

Deduction Allowed in Year Paid

You can fully deduct points in the year paid if you meet all the following tests. (You can use Figure 24-B as a quick guide to see whether your points are fully deductible in the year paid.)

1. Your loan is secured by your main home. (Your main home is the one you ordinarily live in most of the time.)

2. Paying points is an established business practice in the area where the loan was made.

3. The points paid weren't more than the points generally charged in that area.

4. You use the cash method of accounting. This means you report income in the year you receive it and deduct expenses in the year you pay them. (If you want more information about this method, see *Accounting Methods* in chapter 1.)

5. The points weren't paid in place of amounts that ordinarily are stated separately on the settlement statement, such as appraisal fees, inspection fees, title fees, attorney fees, and property taxes.

6. The funds you provided at or before closing, plus any points the seller paid, were at least as much as the points charged. The funds you provided aren't required to have been applied to the points. They can include a down payment, an escrow deposit, earnest money, and other funds you paid at or before closing for any purpose. You can't have borrowed these funds from your lender or mortgage broker.

7. You use your loan to buy or build your main home.

8. The points were figured as a percentage of the principal amount of the mortgage.

9. The amount is clearly shown on the settlement statement (such as the Settlement Statement, Form HUD-1) as points charged for the mortgage. The points may

be shown as paid from either your funds or the seller's.

Note. If you meet all of these tests, you can choose to either fully deduct the points in the year paid, or deduct them over the life of the loan.

Home improvement loan. You can also fully deduct in the year paid points paid on a loan to substantially improve your main home, if tests (1) through (6) are met. See Pub. 530 for details.

 Second home. *You can't fully deduct in the year paid points you pay on loans secured by your second home. You can deduct these points only over the life of the loan.*

Refinancing. Generally, points you pay to refinance a mortgage aren't deductible in full in the year you pay them. This is true even if the new mortgage is secured by your main home.

However, if you use part of the refinanced mortgage proceeds to substantially improve your main home and you meet the first six tests listed under *Deduction Allowed in Year Paid*, earlier, you can fully deduct the part of the points related to the improvement in the year you paid them with your own funds. You can deduct the rest of the points over the life of the loan.

Example 1. In 2001, Bill Fields got a mortgage to buy a home. In 2018, Bill refinanced that mortgage with a 15-year $100,000 mortgage loan. The mortgage is secured by his home. To get the new loan, he had to pay three points ($3,000). Two points ($2,000) were for prepaid interest, and one point ($1,000) was charged for services, in place of amounts that ordinarily are stated separately on the settlement statement. Bill paid the points out of his private funds, rather than out of the proceeds of the new loan. The payment of points is an established practice in the area, and the points charged aren't more than the amount generally charged there. Bill's first payment on the new loan was due July 1. He made six payments on the loan in 2018 and is a cash-basis taxpayer.

Bill used the funds from the new mortgage to repay his existing mortgage. Although the new mortgage loan was for Bill's continued ownership of his main home, it wasn't for the purchase or substantial improvement of that home. He can't deduct all of the points in 2018. He can deduct two points ($2,000) ratably over the life of the loan. He deducts $67 [($2,000 ÷ 180 months) × 6 payments] of the points in 2018. The other point ($1,000) was a fee for services and isn't deductible.

Example 2. The facts are the same as in *Example 1,* except that Bill used $25,000 of the loan proceeds to substantially improve his home and $75,000 to repay his existing mortgage. Bill deducts 25% ($25,000 ÷ $100,000) of the points ($2,000) in 2018. His deduction is $500 ($2,000 × 25% (0.25)).

Bill also deducts the ratable part of the remaining $1,500 ($2,000 − $500) that must be spread over the life of the loan. This is $50 [($1,500 ÷ 180 months) × 6 payments] in 2018.

The total amount Bill deducts in 2018 is $550 ($500 + $50).

Special Situations

This section describes certain special situations that may affect your deduction of points.

Original issue discount (OID). If you don't qualify to either deduct the points in the year paid or deduct them ratably over the life of the loan, or if you choose not to use either of these methods, the points reduce the issue price of the loan. This reduction results in OID, which is discussed in chapter 4 of Pub. 535.

Amounts charged for services. Amounts charged by the lender for specific services connected to the loan aren't interest. Examples of these charges include the following.

- Appraisal fees.
- Notary fees.
- Preparation costs for the mortgage note or deed of trust.
- Mortgage insurance premiums.
- Department of Veterans Affairs (VA) funding fees.

You can't deduct these amounts as points either in the year paid or over the life of the mortgage.

Points paid by the seller. The term "points" includes loan placement fees that the seller pays to the lender to arrange financing for the buyer.

Treatment by seller. The seller can't deduct these fees as interest. But they are a selling expense that reduces the amount realized by the seller. See chapter 15 for information on selling your home.

Treatment by buyer. The buyer reduces the basis of the home by the amount of the seller-paid points and treats the points as if he or she had paid them. If all the tests under *Deduction Allowed in Year Paid*, earlier, are met, the buyer can deduct the points in the year paid. If any of those tests aren't met, the buyer deducts the points over the life of the loan.

For information about basis, see chapter 13.

Funds provided are less than points. If you meet all the tests in *Deduction Allowed in Year Paid*, earlier, except that the funds you provided were less than the points charged to you (test (6)), you can deduct the points in the year paid, up to the amount of funds you provided. In addition, you can deduct any points paid by the seller.

Example 1. When you took out a $100,000 mortgage loan to buy your home in December, you were charged one point ($1,000). You meet all the tests for deducting points in the year paid, except the only funds you provided were a $750 down payment. Of the $1,000 charged for points, you can deduct $750 in the year paid. You spread the remaining $250 over the life of the mortgage.

Example 2. The facts are the same as in *Example 1,* except that the person who sold you your home also paid one point ($1,000) to help

you get your mortgage. In the year paid, you can deduct $1,750 ($750 of the amount you were charged plus the $1,000 paid by the seller). You spread the remaining $250 over the life of the mortgage. You must reduce the basis of your home by the $1,000 paid by the seller.

Excess points. If you meet all the tests in *Deduction Allowed in Year Paid*, earlier, except that the points paid were more than generally paid in your area (test (3)), you deduct in the year paid only the points that are generally charged. You must spread any additional points over the life of the mortgage.

Mortgage ending early. If you spread your deduction for points over the life of the mortgage, you can deduct any remaining balance in the year the mortgage ends. However, if you refinance the mortgage with the same lender, you can't deduct any remaining balance of spread points. Instead, deduct the remaining balance over the term of the new loan.

A mortgage may end early due to a prepayment, refinancing, foreclosure, or similar event.

Example. Dan paid $3,000 in points in 2007 that he had to spread out over the 15-year life of the mortgage. He deducts $200 in points per year. Through 2018, Dan has deducted $2,200 of the points.

Dan prepaid his mortgage in full in 2018. He can deduct the remaining $800 of points in 2018.

Limits on deduction. You can't fully deduct points paid on a mortgage unless the mortgage fits into one of the categories listed earlier under *Fully deductible interest*. See Pub. 936 for details.

Form 1098, Mortgage Interest Statement

If you paid $600 or more of mortgage interest (including certain points) during the year on any one mortgage, you generally will receive a Form 1098 or a similar statement from the mortgage holder. You will receive the statement if you pay interest to a person (including a financial institution or a cooperative housing corporation) in the course of that person's trade or business. A governmental unit is a person for purposes of furnishing the statement.

The statement for each year should be sent to you by January 31 of the following year. A copy of this form will also be sent to the IRS.

The statement will show the total interest you paid during the year, and if you purchased a principal residence during the year, it also will show the points paid during the year, including seller-paid points, that are deductible as interest to the extent you do not exceed the home acquisition debt limit. See Pub. 936. However, the statement shouldn't show any interest that was paid for you by a government agency.

As a general rule, Form 1098 will include only points that you can fully deduct in the year paid. However, it may report points that you can't deduct, particularly if you are filing married filing separately or have mortgages for multiple properties. You must take care to deduct only those points legally allowable. Additionally, certain points not included on Form 1098 also may

Figure 24-B. Are My Points Fully Deductible This Year?

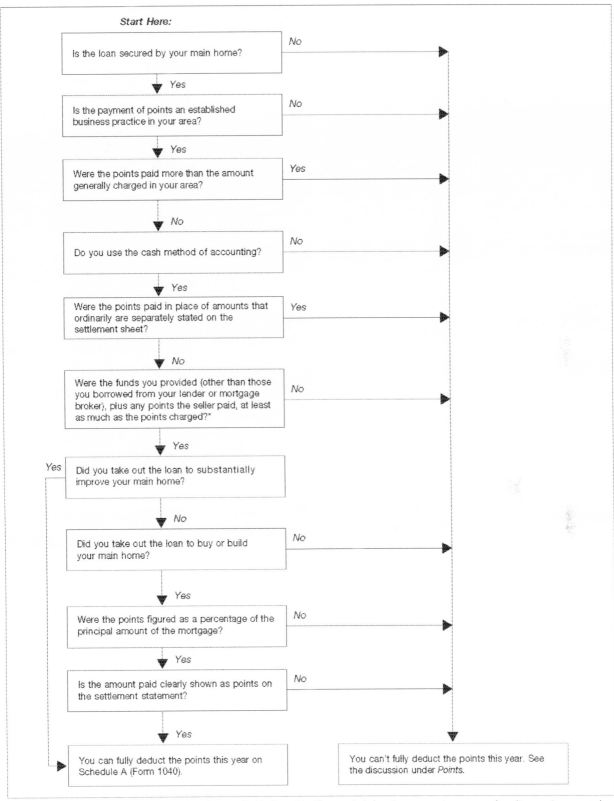

Start Here:

Is the loan secured by your main home? — **No** →

↓ **Yes**

Is the payment of points an established business practice in your area? — **No** →

↓ **Yes**

Were the points paid more than the amount generally charged in your area? — **Yes** →

↓ **No**

Do you use the cash method of accounting? — **No** →

↓ **Yes**

Were the points paid in place of amounts that ordinarily are separately stated on the settlement sheet? — **Yes** →

↓ **No**

Were the funds you provided (other than those you borrowed from your lender or mortgage broker), plus any points the seller paid, at least as much as the points charged?* — **No** →

↓ **Yes**

Did you take out the loan to substantially improve your main home? — **Yes** →

↓ **No**

Did you take out the loan to buy or build your main home? — **No** →

↓ **Yes**

Were the points figured as a percentage of the principal amount of the mortgage? — **No** →

↓ **Yes**

Is the amount paid clearly shown as points on the settlement statement? — **No** →

↓ **Yes**

You can fully deduct the points this year on Schedule A (Form 1040).

You can't fully deduct the points this year. See the discussion under *Points*.

* The funds you provided aren't required to have been applied to the points. They can include a down payment, an escrow deposit, earnest money, and other funds you paid at or before closing for any purpose.

be deductible, either in the year paid or over the life of the loan. See *Points*, earlier, to determine whether you can deduct points not shown on Form 1098.

Prepaid interest on Form 1098. If you prepaid interest in 2018 that accrued in full by January 15, 2019, this prepaid interest may be included in box 1 of Form 1098. However, you can't deduct the prepaid amount for January 2019 in 2018. (See *Prepaid interest*, earlier.) You will have to figure the interest that accrued for 2019 and subtract it from the amount in box 1. You will include the interest for January 2019 with the other interest you pay for 2019. See *How To Report*, later.

Refunded interest. If you received a refund of mortgage interest you overpaid in an earlier year, you generally will receive a Form 1098 showing the refund in box 4. See *Refunds of interest*, earlier.

Investment Interest

This section discusses interest expenses you may be able to deduct as an investor.

If you borrow money to buy property you hold for investment, the interest you pay is investment interest. You can deduct investment interest subject to the limit discussed later. However, you can't deduct interest you incurred to produce tax-exempt income. Nor can you deduct interest expenses on straddles.

Investment interest doesn't include any qualified home mortgage interest or any interest taken into account in figuring income or loss from a passive activity.

Investment Property

Property held for investment includes property that produces interest, dividends, annuities, or royalties not derived in the ordinary course of a trade or business. It also includes property that produces gain or loss (not derived in the ordinary course of a trade or business) from the sale or trade of property producing these types of income or held for investment (other than an interest in a passive activity). Investment property also includes an interest in a trade or business activity in which you didn't materially participate (other than a passive activity).

Partners, shareholders, and beneficiaries. To determine your investment interest, combine your share of investment interest from a partnership, S corporation, estate, or trust with your other investment interest.

Allocation of Interest Expense

If you borrow money for business or personal purposes as well as for investment, you must allocate the debt among those purposes. Only the interest expense on the part of the debt used for investment purposes is treated as investment interest. The allocation isn't affected by the use of property that secures the debt.

Limit on Deduction

Generally, your deduction for investment interest expense is limited to the amount of your net investment income.

You can carry over the amount of investment interest that you couldn't deduct because of this limit to the next tax year. The interest carried over is treated as investment interest paid or accrued in that next year.

You can carry over disallowed investment interest to the next tax year even if it's more than your taxable income in the year the interest was paid or accrued.

Net Investment Income

Determine the amount of your net investment income by subtracting your investment expenses (other than interest expense) from your investment income.

Investment income. This generally includes your gross income from property held for investment (such as interest, dividends, annuities, and royalties). Investment income doesn't include Alaska Permanent Fund dividends. It also doesn't include qualified dividends or net capital gain unless you choose to include them.

Choosing to include qualified dividends. Investment income generally doesn't include qualified dividends, discussed in chapter 8. However, you can choose to include all or part of your qualified dividends in investment income.

You make this choice by completing Form 4952, line 4g, according to its instructions.

If you choose to include any amount of your qualified dividends in investment income, you must reduce your qualified dividends that are eligible for the lower capital gains tax rates by the same amount.

Choosing to include net capital gain. Investment income generally doesn't include net capital gain from disposing of investment property (including capital gain distributions from mutual funds). However, you can choose to include all or part of your net capital gain in investment income.

You make this choice by completing Form 4952, line 4g, according to its instructions.

If you choose to include any amount of your net capital gain in investment income, you must reduce your net capital gain that is eligible for the lower capital gains tax rates by the same amount.

TIP *Before making either choice, consider the overall effect on your tax liability. Compare your tax if you make one or both of these choices with your tax if you don't make either choice.*

Investment income of child reported on parent's return. Investment income includes the part of your child's interest and dividend income that you choose to report on your return. If the child doesn't have qualified dividends, Alaska Permanent Fund dividends, or capital gain distributions, this is the amount on line 6 of Form 8814, Parents' Election To Report Child's Interest and Dividends.

Child's qualified dividends. If part of the amount you report is your child's qualified dividends, that part (which is reported on Form 1040, line 3a) generally doesn't count as investment income. However, you can choose to include all or part of it in investment income, as explained under *Choosing to include qualified dividends*, earlier.

Your investment income also includes the amount on Form 8814, line 12 (or, if applicable, the reduced amount figured next under *Child's Alaska Permanent Fund dividends*).

Child's Alaska Permanent Fund dividends. If part of the amount you report is your child's Alaska Permanent Fund dividends, that part doesn't count as investment income. To figure the amount of your child's income that you can consider your investment income, start with the amount on Form 8814, line 6. Multiply that amount by a percentage that is equal to the Alaska Permanent Fund dividends divided by the total amount on Form 8814, line 4. Subtract the result from the amount on Form 8814, line 12.

Child's capital gain distributions. If part of the amount you report is your child's capital gain distributions, that part (which is reported on Schedule D, line 13, or Schedule 1 (Form 1040), line 13) generally doesn't count as investment income. However, you can choose to include all or part of it in investment income, as explained in *Choosing to include net capital gain*, earlier.

Your investment income also includes the amount on Form 8814, line 12 (or, if applicable, the reduced amount figured under *Child's Alaska Permanent Fund dividends*, earlier).

Investment expenses. Investment expenses are your allowed deductions (other than interest expense) directly connected with the production of investment income.

Losses from passive activities. Income or expenses that you used in figuring income or loss from a passive activity aren't included in determining your investment income or investment expenses (including investment interest expense). See Pub. 925, Passive Activity and At-Risk Rules, for information about passive activities.

Form 4952

Use Form 4952, Investment Interest Expense Deduction, to figure your deduction for investment interest.

Exception to use of Form 4952. You don't have to complete Form 4952 or attach it to your return if you meet all of the following tests.

- Your investment interest expense isn't more than your investment income from interest and ordinary dividends minus any qualified dividends.

- You don't have any other deductible investment expenses.

- You have no carryover of investment interest expense from 2017.

If you meet all of these tests, you can deduct all of your investment interest.

More Information

For more information on investment interest, see *Interest Expenses* in chapter 3 of Pub. 550.

Items You Can't Deduct

Some interest payments aren't deductible. Certain expenses similar to interest also aren't deductible. Nondeductible expenses include the following items.

- Personal interest (discussed later).
- Service charges (however, see *Expenses You Can't Deduct* in chapter 27).
- Annual fees for credit cards.
- Loan fees.
- Credit investigation fees.
- Mortgage insurance premiums.
- VA funding fees.
- Interest to purchase or carry tax-exempt securities.

Penalties. You can't deduct fines and penalties paid to a government for violations of law, regardless of their nature.

Personal Interest

Personal interest isn't deductible. Personal interest is any interest that isn't home mortgage interest, investment interest, business interest, or other deductible interest. It includes the following items.

- Interest on car loans (unless you use the car for business).
- Interest on federal, state, or local income tax.
- Finance charges on credit cards, retail installment contracts, and revolving charge accounts incurred for personal expenses.
- Late payment charges by a public utility.

 You may be able to deduct interest you pay on a qualified student loan. For details, see Pub. 970, Tax Benefits for Education.

Allocation of Interest

If you use the proceeds of a loan for more than one purpose (for example, personal and business), you must allocate the interest on the loan to each use. However, you don't have to allocate home mortgage interest if it is fully deductible, regardless of how the funds are used.

You allocate interest (other than fully deductible home mortgage interest) on a loan in the same way as the loan itself is allocated. You do this by tracing disbursements of the debt proceeds to specific uses. For details on how to do this, see chapter 4 of Pub. 535.

How To Report

You must file Form 1040 to deduct any home mortgage interest expense on your tax return.

Table 24-1. Where To Deduct Your Interest Expense

IF you have ...	THEN deduct it on ...	AND for more information, go to ...
deductible student loan interest	Schedule 1 (Form 1040), line 33	Pub. 970.
deductible home mortgage interest and points reported on Form 1098	Schedule A (Form 1040), line 8	Pub. 936.
deductible home mortgage interest not reported on Form 1098	Schedule A (Form 1040), line 8	Pub. 936.
deductible points not reported on Form 1098	Schedule A (Form 1040), line 8	Pub. 936.
deductible investment interest (other than incurred to produce rents or royalties)	Schedule A (Form 1040), line 9	Pub. 550.
deductible business interest (non-farm)	Schedule C or C-EZ (Form 1040)	Pub. 535.
deductible farm business interest	Schedule F (Form 1040)	Pub. 225 and Pub. 535.
deductible interest incurred to produce rents or royalties	Schedule E (Form 1040)	Pub. 527 and Pub. 535.
personal interest	not deductible.	

Where you deduct your interest expense generally depends on how you use the loan proceeds. See Table 24-1 for a summary of where to deduct your interest expense.

Home mortgage interest and points. Generally, you can deduct the home mortgage interest and points reported to you on Form 1098 on Schedule A (Form 1040), line 8a. However, any interest showing in box 1 of Form 1098 from a home equity loan, or a line of credit or credit card loan secured by the property is not deductible if the proceeds were not used to buy, build, or substantially improve a qualified home. If you paid more deductible interest to the financial institution than the amount shown on Form 1098, show the portion of the deductible interest that was omitted from Form 1098 on line 8b. Attach a statement explaining the difference and print "See attached" next to line 8b.

If you paid home mortgage interest to the person from whom you bought your home, show that person's name, address, and taxpayer identification number (TIN) on the dotted lines next to line 8b. The seller must give you this number and you must give the seller your TIN. A Form W-9, Request for Taxpayer Identification Number and Certification, can be used for this purpose. Failure to meet any of these requirements may result in a $50 penalty for each failure. The TIN can be either a social security number, an individual taxpayer identification number (issued by the IRS), or an employer identification number. See *Social Security Number (SSN)* in chapter 1 for more information about TINs.

If you can take a deduction for points that weren't reported to you on Form 1098, deduct those points on Schedule A (Form 1040), line 8c.

More than one borrower. If you and at least one other person (other than your spouse if you file a joint return) were liable for and paid interest on a mortgage that was for your home, and the other person received a Form 1098 showing the interest that was paid during the year, attach a statement to your return explaining this. Show how much of the interest each of you paid, and give the name and address of the person who received the form. Deduct your share of the interest on Schedule A (Form 1040), line 8b, and print "See attached" next to the line.

Similarly, if you are the payer of record on a mortgage on which there are other borrowers entitled to a deduction for the interest shown on the Form 1098 you received, deduct only your share of the interest on Schedule A (Form 1040), line 8a. You should let each of the other borrowers know what his or her share is.

Mortgage proceeds used for business or investment. If your home mortgage interest deduction is limited, but all or part of the mortgage proceeds were used for business, investment, or other deductible activities, see Table 24-1. It shows where to deduct the part of your excess interest that is for those activities.

Investment interest. Deduct investment interest, subject to certain limits discussed in Pub. 550, on Schedule A (Form 1040), line 9.

Amortization of bond premium. There are various ways to treat the premium you pay to buy taxable bonds. See *Bond Premium Amortization* in Pub. 550.

Income-producing rental or royalty interest. Deduct interest on a loan for income-producing rental or royalty property that isn't used in your business in Part I of Schedule E (Form 1040).

Example. You rent out part of your home and borrow money to make repairs. You can deduct only the interest payment for the rented part in Part I of Schedule E (Form 1040). Deduct the rest of the interest payment on Schedule A (Form 1040) if it is deductible home mortgage interest.

25.

Contributions

What's New

 At the time this publication went to print, Congress was considering legislation that would do the following.

1. *Provide additional tax relief for those affected by certain 2018 disasters.*

2. *Extend certain tax benefits that expired at the end of 2017 and that currently can't be claimed on your 2018 tax return.*

3. *Change certain other tax provisions.*

To learn whether this legislation was enacted resulting in changes that affect your 2018 tax return, go to Recent Developments at IRS.gov/Pub17.

Overall limitation on itemized deductions no longer applies. There is no longer an overall limitation on itemized deductions based on your adjusted gross income. However, your contributions still may be subject to limitations. See *Limits on Deductions*, later.

Higher limitation for certain charitable contributions. For most cash contributions the total amount of such contributions that can be deducted is now limited to 60% of your adjusted gross income.

No deduction for athletic events seating rights. No deduction is allowed for amounts paid in exchange for college or university athletic event seating rights.

Introduction

This chapter explains how to claim a deduction for your charitable contributions. It discusses the following topics.

- The types of organizations to which you can make deductible charitable contributions.

- The types of contributions you can deduct.

- How much you can deduct.

- What records you must keep.

- How to report your charitable contributions.

A charitable contribution is a donation or gift to, or for the use of, a qualified organization. It is voluntary and is made without getting, or expecting to get, anything of equal value.

Form 1040 required. To deduct a charitable contribution, you must file Form 1040 and itemize deductions on Schedule A. The amount of your deduction may be limited if certain rules and limits explained in this chapter apply to you. The limits are explained in detail in Pub. 526.

Useful Items

You may want to see:

Publication

- ❑ **526** Charitable Contributions
- ❑ **561** Determining the Value of Donated Property
- ❑ **976** Disaster Relief

Form (and Instructions)

- ❑ **Schedule A (Form 1040)** Itemized Deductions
- ❑ **8283** Noncash Charitable Contributions

For these and other useful items, go to *IRS.gov/Forms*.

Organizations That Qualify To Receive Deductible Contributions

You can deduct your contributions only if you make them to a qualified organization. Most organizations other than churches and governments must apply to the IRS to become a qualified organization.

How to check whether an organization can receive deductible charitable contributions. You can ask any organization whether it is a qualified organization, and most will be able to tell you. Or, use the Exempt Organizations Select Check tool at *IRS.gov/EOSelectCheck*. This online tool will enable you to search for qualified organizations.

Types of Qualified Organizations

Generally, only the following types of organizations can be qualified organizations.

1. A community chest, corporation, trust, fund, or foundation organized or created in or under the laws of the United States, any state, the District of Columbia, or any possession of the United States (including Puerto Rico). It must, however, be organized and operated only for charitable, religious, scientific, literary, or educational purposes, or for the prevention of cruelty to children or animals. Certain organizations that foster national or international amateur sports competition also qualify.

2. War veterans' organizations, including posts, auxiliaries, trusts, or foundations, organized in the United States or any of its possessions (including Puerto Rico).

3. Domestic fraternal societies, orders, and associations operating under the lodge system. (Your contribution to this type of organization is deductible only if it is to be used solely for charitable, religious, scientific, literary, or educational purposes, or for the prevention of cruelty to children or animals.)

4. Certain nonprofit cemetery companies or corporations. (Your contribution to this

type of organization isn't deductible if it can be used for the care of a specific lot or mausoleum crypt.)

5. The United States or any state, the District of Columbia, a U.S. possession (including Puerto Rico), a political subdivision of a state or U.S. possession, or an Indian tribal government or any of its subdivisions that perform substantial government functions. (Your contribution to this type of organization is only deductible if it is to be used solely for public purposes.)

Examples. The following list gives some examples of qualified organizations.

- Churches, a convention or association of churches, temples, synagogues, mosques, and other religious organizations.

- Most nonprofit charitable organizations, such as the American Red Cross and the United Way.

- Most nonprofit educational organizations, including the Boy Scouts of America, Girl Scouts of America, colleges, and museums. This also includes nonprofit daycare centers that provide childcare to the general public if substantially all the childcare is provided to enable parents and guardians to be gainfully employed. However, if your contribution is a substitute for tuition or other enrollment fee, it isn't deductible as a charitable contribution, as explained later under *Contributions You Can't Deduct*.

- Nonprofit hospitals and medical research organizations.

- Utility company emergency energy programs, if the utility company is an agent for a charitable organization that assists individuals with emergency energy needs.

- Nonprofit volunteer fire companies.

- Nonprofit organizations that develop and maintain public parks and recreation facilities.

- Civil defense organizations.

Certain foreign charitable organizations. Under income tax treaties with Canada, Israel, and Mexico, you may be able to deduct contributions to certain Canadian, Israeli, or Mexican charitable organizations. Generally, you must have income from sources in that country. For additional information on the deduction of contributions to Canadian charities, see Pub. 597, Information on the United States - Canada Income Tax Treaty. If you need more information on how to figure your contribution to Mexican and Israeli charities, see Pub. 526.

Contributions You Can Deduct

Generally, you can deduct contributions of money or property you make to, or for the use of, a qualified organization. A contribution is "for the use of" a qualified organization when it is held in a legally enforceable trust for the qualified organization or in a similar legal arrangement. The contributions must be made to a qualified organization and not set aside for use by a specific person.

If you give property to a qualified organization, you generally can deduct the fair market value of the property at the time of the contribution. See *Contributions of Property*, later, in this chapter.

Your deduction for charitable contributions generally can't be more than 60% of your adjusted gross income (AGI), but in some cases 20%, 30%, or 50% limits may apply. See *Limits on Deductions*, later.

Table 25-1 gives examples of contributions you can and can't deduct.

Contributions From Which You Benefit

If you receive a benefit as a result of making a contribution to a qualified organization, you can deduct only the amount of your contribution that is more than the value of the benefit you receive. Also see *Contributions From Which You Benefit* under *Contributions You Can't Deduct*, later.

If you pay more than fair market value to a qualified organization for goods or services, the excess may be a charitable contribution. For the excess amount to qualify, you must pay it with the intent to make a charitable contribution.

Example 1. You pay $65 for a ticket to a dinner dance at a church. Your entire $65 payment goes to the church. The ticket to the dinner dance has a fair market value of $25. When you buy your ticket, you know that its value is less than your payment. To figure the amount of your charitable contribution, subtract the value of the benefit you receive ($25) from your total payment ($65). You can deduct $40 as a contribution to the church.

Example 2. At a fundraising auction conducted by a charity, you pay $600 for a week's stay at a beach house. The amount you pay is no more than the fair rental value. You haven't made a deductible charitable contribution.

Athletic events. No deduction is allowed, if you make any payment to, or for the benefit of, a college or university in exchange for tickets (or the right to buy tickets) to an athletic event in an athletic stadium of the college or university.

Charity benefit events. If you pay a qualified organization more than fair market value for the right to attend a charity ball, banquet, show, sporting event, or other benefit event, you can deduct only the amount that is more than the value of the privileges or other benefits you receive.

If there is an established charge for the event, that charge is the value of your benefit. If there is no established charge, the reasonable value of the right to attend the event is the value of your benefit. Whether you use the tickets or other privileges has no effect on the amount you can deduct. However, if you return the ticket to the qualified organization for resale, you can deduct the entire amount you paid for the ticket.

Table 25-1. **Examples of Charitable Contributions—A Quick Check**

Use the following lists for a quick check of whether you can deduct a contribution. See the rest of this chapter for more information and additional rules and limits that may apply.	
Deductible As Charitable Contributions	**Not Deductible As Charitable Contributions**
Money or property you give to: • Churches, synagogues, temples, mosques, and other religious organizations • Federal, state, and local governments, if your contribution is solely for public purposes (for example, a gift to reduce the public debt or maintain a public park) • Nonprofit schools and hospitals • The Salvation Army, American Red Cross, CARE, Goodwill Industries, United Way, Boy Scouts of America, Girl Scouts of America, Boys and Girls Clubs of America, etc. • War veterans' groups	Money or property you give to: • Civic leagues, social and sports clubs, labor unions, and chambers of commerce • Foreign organizations (except certain Canadian, Israeli, and Mexican charities) • Groups that are run for personal profit • Groups whose purpose is to lobby for law changes • Homeowners' associations • Individuals • Political groups or candidates for public office
Expenses paid for a student living with you, sponsored by a qualified organization	Cost of raffle, bingo, or lottery tickets
Out-of-pocket expenses when you serve a qualified organization as a volunteer	Dues, fees, or bills paid to country clubs, lodges, fraternal orders, or similar groups
	Tuition
	Value of your time or services
	Value of blood given to a blood bank

 Even if the ticket or other evidence of payment indicates that the payment is a "contribution," this doesn't mean you can deduct the entire amount. If the ticket shows the price of admission and the amount of the contribution, you can deduct the contribution amount.

Example. You pay $40 to see a special showing of a movie for the benefit of a qualified organization. Printed on the ticket is "Contribution—$40." If the regular price for the movie is $8, your contribution is $32 ($40 payment – $8 regular price).

State or local tax credit. If you receive or expect to receive a state or local tax credit or a state or local tax deduction for a charitable contribution, then the amount treated as a charitable deduction may be reduced. For more information, see Pub. 526.

Membership fees or dues. You may be able to deduct membership fees or dues you pay to a qualified organization. However, you can deduct only the amount that is more than the value of the benefits you receive.

You can't deduct dues, fees, or assessments paid to country clubs and other social organizations. They aren't qualified organizations.

Certain membership benefits can be disregarded. Both you and the organization can disregard the following membership benefits if you receive them in return for an annual payment of $75 or less.

1. Any rights or privileges that you can use frequently while you are a member, such as:

   a. Free or discounted admission to the organization's facilities or events,

   b. Free or discounted parking,

   c. Preferred access to goods or services, and

   d. Discounts on the purchase of goods and services.

2. Admission, while you are a member, to events open only to members of the organization, if the organization reasonably projects that the cost per person (excluding any allocated overhead) isn't more than $10.80.

Token items. You don't have to reduce your contribution by the value of any benefit you receive if both of the following are true.

1. You receive only a small item or other benefit of token value.

2. The qualified organization correctly determines that the value of the item or benefit you received isn't substantial and informs you that you can deduct your payment in full.

Written statement. A qualified organization must give you a written statement if you make a payment of more than $75 that is partly a contribution and partly for goods or services. The statement must say that you can deduct only the amount of your payment that is more than the value of the goods or services you received.

Table 25-2. **Volunteers' Questions and Answers**

If you volunteer for a qualified organization, the following questions and answers may apply to you. All of the rules explained in this chapter also apply. See, in particular, *Out-of-Pocket Expenses in Giving Services*.

Question	Answer
I volunteer 6 hours a week in the office of a qualified organization. The receptionist is paid $10 an hour for the same work. Can I deduct $60 a week for my time?	No, you can't deduct the value of your time or services.
The office is 30 miles from my home. Can I deduct any of my car expenses for these trips?	Yes, you can deduct the costs of gas and oil that are directly related to getting to and from the place where you volunteer. If you don't want to figure your actual costs, you can deduct 14 cents for each mile.
I volunteer as a Red Cross nurse's aide at a hospital. Can I deduct the cost of the uniforms I must wear?	Yes, you can deduct the cost of buying and cleaning your uniforms if the hospital is a qualified organization, the uniforms aren't suitable for everyday use, and you must wear them when volunteering.
I pay a babysitter to watch my children while I volunteer for a qualified organization. Can I deduct these costs?	No, you can't deduct payments for childcare expenses as a charitable contribution, even if you would be unable to volunteer without childcare. (If you have childcare expenses so you can work for pay, see chapter 31.)

It must also give you a good faith estimate of the value of those goods or services.

The organization can give you the statement either when it solicits or when it receives the payment from you.

Exception. An organization won't have to give you this statement if one of the following is true.

1. The organization is:

   a. A governmental organization described in (5) under *Types of Qualified Organizations*, earlier; or

   b. An organization formed only for religious purposes, and the only benefit you receive is an intangible religious benefit (such as admission to a religious ceremony) that generally isn't sold in commercial transactions outside the donative context.

2. You receive only items whose value isn't substantial as described under *Token items*, earlier.

3. You receive only membership benefits that can be disregarded, as described under *Membership fees or dues*, earlier.

Expenses Paid for Student Living With You

You may be able to deduct some expenses of having a student live with you. You can deduct qualifying expenses for a foreign or American student who:

1. Lives in your home under a written agreement between you and a qualified organization as part of a program of the organization to provide educational opportunities for the student,

2. Isn't your relative or dependent, and

3. Is a full-time student in the twelfth or any lower grade at a school in the United States.

 You can deduct up to $50 a month for each full calendar month the student lives with you. Any month when conditions (1) through (3) are met for 15 days or more counts as a full month.

For additional information, see *Expenses Paid for Student Living With You* in Pub. 526.

Mutual exchange program. You can't deduct the costs of a foreign student living in your home under a mutual exchange program through which your child will live with a family in a foreign country.

Out-of-Pocket Expenses in Giving Services

Although you can't deduct the value of your services given to a qualified organization, you may be able to deduct some amounts you pay in giving services to a qualified organization. The amounts must be:

- Unreimbursed;

- Directly connected with the services;

- Expenses you had only because of the services you gave; and

- Not personal, living, or family expenses.

Table 25-2 contains questions and answers that apply to some individuals who volunteer their services.

Conventions. If a qualified organization selects you to attend a convention as its representative, you can deduct unreimbursed expenses for travel, including reasonable amounts for meals and lodging, while away from home overnight in connection with the convention. However, see *Travel*, later.

You can't deduct personal expenses for sightseeing, fishing parties, theater tickets, or nightclubs. You also can't deduct travel, meals and lodging, and other expenses for your spouse or children.

You can't deduct your travel expenses in attending a church convention if you go only as a member of your church rather than as a chosen representative. You can, however, deduct unreimbursed expenses that are directly connected with giving services for your church during the convention.

Uniforms. You can deduct the cost and upkeep of uniforms that aren't suitable for everyday use and that you must wear while performing donated services for a charitable organization.

Foster parents. You may be able to deduct as a charitable contribution some of the costs of being a foster parent (foster care provider) if you have no profit motive in providing the foster care and aren't, in fact, making a profit. A qualified organization must select the individuals you take into your home for foster care.

You can deduct expenses that meet both of the following requirements.

1. They are unreimbursed out-of-pocket expenses to feed, clothe, and care for the foster child.

2. They are incurred primarily to benefit the qualified organization.

Unreimbursed expenses that you can't deduct as charitable contributions may be considered support provided by you in determining whether you can claim the foster child as a dependent. For details, see chapter 3.

Example. You cared for a foster child because you wanted to adopt her, not to benefit the agency that placed her in your home. Your unreimbursed expenses aren't deductible as charitable contributions.

Car expenses. You can deduct as a charitable contribution any unreimbursed out-of-pocket expenses, such as the cost of gas and oil, that are directly related to the use of your car in giving services to a charitable organization. You can't deduct general repair and maintenance expenses, depreciation, registration fees, or the costs of tires or insurance.

If you don't want to deduct your actual expenses, you can use a standard mileage rate of 14 cents a mile to figure your contribution.

You can deduct parking fees and tolls whether you use your actual expenses or the standard mileage rate.

You must keep reliable written records of your car expenses. For more information, see *Car expenses* under *Records To Keep*, later.

Travel. Generally, you can claim a charitable contribution deduction for travel expenses necessarily incurred while you are away from home performing services for a charitable organization only if there is no significant element of personal pleasure, recreation, or vacation in the travel. This applies whether you pay the expenses directly or indirectly. You are paying the expenses indirectly if you make a payment to the charitable organization and the organization pays for your travel expenses.

The deduction for travel expenses won't be denied simply because you enjoy providing services to the charitable organization. Even if you enjoy the trip, you can take a charitable contribution deduction for your travel expenses if you are on duty in a genuine and substantial sense throughout the trip. However, if you have only nominal duties, or if for significant parts of the trip you don't have any duties, you can't deduct your travel expenses.

Example 1. You are a troop leader for a tax-exempt youth group and you take the group on a camping trip. You are responsible for overseeing the setup of the camp and for providing adult supervision for other activities during the entire trip. You participate in the activities of the group and enjoy your time with them. You oversee the breaking of camp and you transport the group home. You can deduct your travel expenses.

Example 2. You sail from one island to another and spend 8 hours a day counting whales and other forms of marine life. The project is sponsored by a charitable organization. In most circumstances, you can't deduct your expenses.

Example 3. You work for several hours each morning on an archaeological dig sponsored by a charitable organization. The rest of the day is free for recreation and sightseeing. You can't take a charitable contribution deduction even though you work very hard during those few hours.

Example 4. You spend the entire day attending a charitable organization's regional meeting as a chosen representative. In the evening you go to the theater. You can claim your travel expenses as charitable contributions, but you can't claim the cost of your evening at the theater.

Daily allowance (per diem). If you provide services for a charitable organization and receive a daily allowance to cover reasonable travel expenses, including meals and lodging while away from home overnight, you must include in income any part of the allowance that is more than your deductible travel expenses. You may be able to deduct any necessary travel expenses that are more than the allowance.

Deductible travel expenses. These include:

- Air, rail, and bus transportation;
- Out-of-pocket expenses for your car;
- Taxi fares or other costs of transportation between the airport or station and your hotel;
- Lodging costs; and
- The cost of meals.

Because these travel expenses aren't business related, they aren't subject to the same limits as business-related expenses. For information on business travel expenses, see *Travel Expenses* in chapter 20.

Contributions You Can't Deduct

There are some contributions you can't deduct, such as those made to specific individuals and those made to nonqualified organizations. (See *Contributions to Individuals* and *Contributions to Nonqualified Organizations* next.) There are others you can deduct only part of, as discussed later under *Contributions From Which You Benefit*.

Contributions to Individuals

You can't deduct contributions to specific individuals, including the following.

- Contributions to fraternal societies made for the purpose of paying medical or burial expenses of deceased members.
- Contributions to individuals who are needy or worthy. You can't deduct these contributions even if you make them to a qualified organization for the benefit of a specific person. But you can deduct a contribution to a qualified organization that helps needy or worthy individuals if you don't indicate that your contribution is for a specific person.

  Example. You can deduct contributions to a qualified organization for flood relief, hurricane relief, or other disaster relief. However, you can't deduct contributions earmarked for relief of a particular individual or family. See *Temporary Suspension of 60% Limit*, later.
- Payments to a member of the clergy that can be spent as he or she wishes, such as for personal expenses.
- Expenses you paid for another person who provided services to a qualified organization.

  Example. Your son does missionary work. You pay his expenses. You can't claim a deduction for your son's unreimbursed expenses related to his contribution of services.
- Payments to a hospital that are for a specific patient's care or for services for a specific patient. You can't deduct these payments even if the hospital is operated by a city, a state, or other qualified organization.

Contributions to Nonqualified Organizations

You can't deduct contributions to organizations that aren't qualified to receive tax-deductible contributions, including the following.

1. Certain state bar associations if:
   a. The bar isn't a political subdivision of a state;
   b. The bar has private, as well as public, purposes, such as promoting the professional interests of members; and
   c. Your contribution is unrestricted and can be used for private purposes.
2. Chambers of commerce and other business leagues or organizations.
3. Civic leagues and associations.
4. Country clubs and other social clubs.
5. Most foreign organizations (other than certain Canadian, Israeli, or Mexican charitable organizations). For details, see Pub. 526.
6. Homeowners' associations.
7. Labor unions.
8. Political organizations and candidates.

Contributions From Which You Benefit

If you receive or expect to receive a financial or economic benefit as a result of making a contribution to a qualified organization, you can't deduct the part of the contribution that represents the value of the benefit you receive. See *Contributions From Which You Benefit* under *Contributions You Can Deduct*, earlier. These contributions include the following.

- Contributions for lobbying. This includes amounts that you earmark for use in, or in connection with, influencing specific legislation.
- Contributions to a retirement home for room, board, maintenance, or admittance. Also, if the amount of your contribution depends on the type or size of apartment you will occupy, it isn't a charitable contribution.
- Costs of raffles, bingo, lottery, etc. You can't deduct as a charitable contribution amounts you pay to buy raffle or lottery tickets or to play bingo or other games of chance. For information on how to report gambling winnings and losses, see *Gambling winnings* in chapter 12 and *Gambling Losses up to the Amount of Gambling Winnings* in chapter 27.
- Dues to fraternal orders and similar groups. However, see *Membership fees or dues*, earlier, under *Contributions You Can Deduct*.
- Tuition, or amounts you pay instead of tuition. You can't deduct as a charitable contribution amounts you pay as tuition even if

you pay them for children to attend parochial schools or qualifying nonprofit day-care centers. You also can't deduct any fixed amount you must pay in addition to, or instead of, tuition to enroll in a private school, even if it is designated as a "donation."

Value of Time or Services

You can't deduct the value of your time or services, including:

- Blood donations to the American Red Cross or to blood banks, and
- The value of income lost while you work as an unpaid volunteer for a qualified organization.

Personal Expenses

You can't deduct personal, living, or family expenses, such as the following items.

- The cost of meals you eat while you perform services for a qualified organization unless it is necessary for you to be away from home overnight while performing the services.
- Adoption expenses, including fees paid to an adoption agency and the costs of keeping a child in your home before adoption is final (but see *Adoption Credit* in chapter 37, and the Instructions for Form 8839, Qualified Adoption Expenses). See *Adopted child* in chapter 3.

Appraisal Fees

You can't deduct as a charitable contribution any fees you pay to find the fair market value of donated property.

Contributions of Property

If you contribute property to a qualified organization, the amount of your charitable contribution is generally the fair market value of the property at the time of the contribution. However, if the property has increased in value, you may have to make some adjustments to the amount of your deduction. See *Giving Property That Has Increased in Value*, later.

For information about the records you must keep and the information you must furnish with your return if you donate property, see *Records To Keep* and *How To Report*, later.

Clothing and household items. You can't take a deduction for clothing or household items you donate unless the clothing or household items are in good used condition or better.

Exception. You can take a deduction for a contribution of an item of clothing or household item that isn't in good used condition or better if you deduct more than $500 for it and include a qualified appraisal of it with your return.

Household items. Household items include:

- Furniture and furnishings,
- Electronics,
- Appliances,
- Linens, and
- Other similar items.

Household items don't include:

- Food;
- Paintings, antiques, and other objects of art;
- Jewelry and gems; and
- Collections.

Cars, boats, and airplanes. The following rules apply to any donation of a qualified vehicle.

A qualified vehicle is:

- A car or any motor vehicle manufactured mainly for use on public streets, roads, and highways;
- A boat; or
- An airplane.

Deduction more than $500. If you donate a qualified vehicle with a claimed fair market value of more than $500, you can deduct the smaller of:

- The gross proceeds from the sale of the vehicle by the organization, or
- The vehicle's fair market value on the date of the contribution. If the vehicle's fair market value was more than your cost or other basis, you may have to reduce the fair market value to figure the deductible amount, as described under *Giving Property That Has Increased in Value*, later.

Form 1098-C. You must attach to your return Copy B of the Form 1098-C, Contributions of Motor Vehicles, Boats, and Airplanes, (or other statement containing the same information as Form 1098-C) you received from the organization. The Form 1098-C (or other statement) will show the gross proceeds from the sale of the vehicle.

If you *e-file* your return, you must:

- Attach Copy B of Form 1098-C to Form 8453, U.S. Individual Income Tax Transmittal for an IRS *e-file* Return, and mail the forms to the IRS; or
- Include Copy B of Form 1098-C as a PDF attachment if your software program allows it.

If you don't attach Form 1098-C (or other statement), you can't deduct your contribution.

You must get Form 1098-C (or other statement) within 30 days of the sale of the vehicle. But if exception 1 or 2 (described later) applies, you must get Form 1098-C (or other statement) within 30 days of your donation.

Filing deadline approaching and still no Form 1098-C. If the filing deadline is approaching and you still don't have a Form 1098-C, you have two choices.

- Request an automatic 6-month extension of time to file your return. You can get this extension by filing Form 4868, Application for Automatic Extension of Time To File U.S. Individual Income Tax Return. For more information, see *Automatic Extension* in chapter 1.
- File the return on time without claiming the deduction for the qualified vehicle. After receiving the Form 1098-C, file an amended return, Form 1040X, Amended U.S. Individual Income Tax Return, claiming the deduction. Attach Copy B of Form 1098-C (or other statement) to the amended return. For more information about amended returns, see *Amended Returns and Claims for Refund* in chapter 1.

Exceptions. There are two exceptions to the rules just described for deductions of more than $500.

Exception 1—vehicle used or improved by organization. If the qualified organization makes a significant intervening use of or material improvement to the vehicle before transferring it, you generally can deduct the vehicle's fair market value at the time of the contribution. But if the vehicle's fair market value was more than your cost or other basis, you may have to reduce the fair market value to get the deductible amount, as described under *Giving Property That Has Increased in Value*, later. The Form 1098-C (or other statement) will show whether this exception applies.

Exception 2—vehicle given or sold to needy individual. If the qualified organization will give the vehicle, or sell it for a price well below fair market value, to a needy individual to further the organization's charitable purpose, you generally can deduct the vehicle's fair market value at the time of the contribution. But if the vehicle's fair market value was more than your cost or other basis, you may have to reduce the fair market value to get the deductible amount, as described under *Giving Property That Has Increased in Value*, later. The Form 1098-C (or other statement) will show whether this exception applies.

This exception doesn't apply if the organization sells the vehicle at auction. In that case, you can't deduct the vehicle's fair market value.

Example. Anita donates a used car to a qualified organization. She bought it 3 years ago for $9,000. A used car guide shows the fair market value for this type of car is $6,000. However, Anita gets a Form 1098-C from the organization showing the car was sold for $2,900. Neither exception 1 nor exception 2 applies. If Anita itemizes her deductions, she can deduct $2,900 for her donation. She must attach Form 1098-C and Form 8283 to her return.

Deduction $500 or less. If the qualified organization sells the vehicle for $500 or less and exceptions 1 and 2 don't apply, you can deduct the smaller of:

- $500, or
- The vehicle's fair market value on the date of the contribution. But if the vehicle's fair market value was more than your cost or other basis, you may have to reduce the fair market value to get the deductible amount, as described under *Giving Property That Has Increased in Value*, later.

If the vehicle's fair market value is at least $250 but not more than $500, you must have a written statement from the qualified organization acknowledging your donation. The statement must contain the information and meet the tests for an acknowledgment described under *Deductions of at Least $250 But Not More Than $500* under *Records To Keep*, later.

Partial interest in property. Generally, you can't deduct a charitable contribution of less than your entire interest in property.

Right to use property. A contribution of the right to use property is a contribution of less than your entire interest in that property and isn't deductible. For exceptions and more information, see *Partial Interest in Property Not in Trust* in Pub. 561.

Future interests in tangible personal property. You can't deduct the value of a charitable contribution of a future interest in tangible personal property until all intervening interests in and rights to the actual possession or enjoyment of the property have either expired or been turned over to someone other than yourself, a related person, or a related organization.

Tangible personal property. This is any property, other than land or buildings, that can be seen or touched. It includes furniture, books, jewelry, paintings, and cars.

Future interest. This is any interest that is to begin at some future time, regardless of whether it is designated as a future interest under state law.

Determining Fair Market Value

This section discusses general guidelines for determining the fair market value of various types of donated property. Pub. 561 contains a more complete discussion.

Fair market value is the price at which property would change hands between a willing buyer and a willing seller, neither having to buy or sell, and both having reasonable knowledge of all the relevant facts.

Used clothing and household items. The fair market value of used clothing and household goods is usually far less than what you paid for them when they were new.

For used clothing, you should claim as the value the price that buyers of used items actually pay in used clothing stores, such as consignment or thrift shops. See *Household Goods* in Pub. 561 for information on the valuation of household goods, such as furniture, appliances, and linens.

Example. Dawn Greene donated a coat to a thrift store operated by her church. She paid $300 for the coat 3 years ago. Similar coats in the thrift store sell for $50. The fair market value of the coat is $50. Dawn's donation is limited to $50.

Cars, boats, and airplanes. If you contribute a car, boat, or airplane to a charitable organization, you must determine its fair market value. Certain commercial firms and trade organizations publish used car pricing guides, commonly called "blue books," containing complete dealer sale prices or dealer average prices for recent model years. The guides may be published monthly or seasonally and for different regions of the country. These guides also provide estimates for adjusting for unusual equipment, unusual mileage, and physical condition. The prices aren't "official" and these publications aren't considered an appraisal of any specific donated property. But they do provide clues for making an appraisal and suggest relative prices for comparison with current sales and offerings in your area.

You can also find used car pricing information on the Internet.

Example. You donate a used car in poor condition to a local high school for use by students studying car repair. A used car guide shows the dealer retail value for this type of car in poor condition is $1,600. However, the guide shows the price for a private party sale of the car is only $750. The fair market value of the car is considered to be $750.

Large quantities. If you contribute a large number of the same item, fair market value is the price at which comparable numbers of the item are being sold.

Giving Property That Has Decreased in Value

If you contribute property with a fair market value that is less than your basis in it, your deduction is limited to its fair market value. You can't claim a deduction for the difference between the property's basis and its fair market value.

Giving Property That Has Increased in Value

If you contribute property with a fair market value that is more than your basis in it, you may have to reduce the fair market value by the amount of appreciation (increase in value) when you figure your deduction.

Your basis in property is generally what you paid for it. See chapter 13 if you need more information about basis.

Different rules apply to figuring your deduction, depending on whether the property is:

- Ordinary income property, or
- Capital gain property.

Ordinary income property. Property is ordinary income property if you would have recognized ordinary income or short-term capital gain had you sold it at fair market value on the date it was contributed. Examples of ordinary income property are inventory, works of art created by the donor, manuscripts prepared by the donor, and capital assets (defined in chapter 14) held 1 year or less.

Amount of deduction. The amount you can deduct for a contribution of ordinary income property is its fair market value minus the amount that would be ordinary income or short-term capital gain if you sold the property for its fair market value. Generally, this rule limits the deduction to your basis in the property.

Example. You donate stock you held for 5 months to your church. The fair market value of the stock on the day you donate it is $1,000, but you paid only $800 (your basis). Because the $200 of appreciation would be short-term capital gain if you sold the stock, your deduction is limited to $800 (fair market value minus the appreciation).

Capital gain property. Property is capital gain property if you would have recognized long-term capital gain had you sold it at fair market value on the date of the contribution. It includes capital assets held more than 1 year, as well as certain real property and depreciable property used in your trade or business and, generally, held more than 1 year.

Amount of deduction—general rule. When figuring your deduction for a contribution of capital gain property, you generally can use the fair market value of the property.

Exceptions. However, in certain situations, you must reduce the fair market value by any amount that would have been long-term capital gain if you had sold the property for its fair market value. Generally, this means reducing the fair market value to the property's cost or other basis.

Bargain sales. A bargain sale of property is a sale or exchange for less than the property's fair market value. A bargain sale to a qualified organization is partly a charitable contribution and partly a sale or exchange. A bargain sale may result in a taxable gain.

More information. For more information on donating appreciated property, see *Giving Property That Has Increased in Value* in Pub. 526.

When To Deduct

You can deduct your contributions only in the year you actually make them in cash or other property (or in a later carryover year, as explained later under *Carryovers*). This applies whether you use the cash or an accrual method of accounting.

Time of making contribution. Usually, you make a contribution at the time of its unconditional delivery.

Checks. A check you mail to a charity is considered delivered on the date you mail it.

Text message. Contributions made by text message are deductible in the year you send the text message if the contribution is charged to your telephone or wireless account.

Credit card. Contributions charged on your credit card are deductible in the year you make the charge.

Pay-by-phone account. Contributions made through a pay-by-phone account are considered delivered on the date the financial institution pays the amount. This date should be shown on the statement the financial institution sends you.

Stock certificate. A properly endorsed stock certificate is considered delivered on the date of mailing or other delivery to the charity or to the charity's agent. However, if you give a stock certificate to your agent or to the issuing corporation for transfer to the name of the charity, your contribution isn't delivered until the date the stock is transferred on the books of the corporation.

Promissory note. If you issue and deliver a promissory note to a charity as a contribution, it isn't a contribution until you make the note payments.

Option. If you grant a charity an option to buy real property at a bargain price, it isn't a contribution until the organization exercises the option.

Borrowed funds. If you contribute borrowed funds, you can deduct the contribution in the year you deliver the funds to the charity, regardless of when you repay the loan.

Limits on Deductions

The amount you can deduct for charitable contributions can't be more than 60% of your AGI. Your deduction may be further limited to 50%, 30%, or 20% of your AGI, depending on the type of property you give and the type of organization you give it to. If your total contributions for the year are 20% or less of your AGI, these limits don't apply to you. The limits are discussed in detail under *Limits on Deductions* in Pub. 526.

A higher limit applies to certain qualified conservation contributions. See Pub. 526 for details.

Temporary suspension of 60% limit. The 60% limit does not apply to your "qualified contributions." A qualified contribution is a charitable contribution paid in cash after October 7, 2017, and before January 1, 2019, for relief efforts in the California wildfire disaster area. For what organizations qualify and more information, see *Temporary Suspension of 60% Limit for California Wildfire Contributions* in Pub. 526.

Your deduction for qualified contributions is limited to your adjusted gross income minus your deduction for all other charitable contributions. You can carry over any contributions you aren't able to deduct for 2018 because of this limit. In 2019, treat the carryover of your unused qualified contributions like a carryover of contributions subject to the 60% limit.

Exceptions. You can't deduct contributions earmarked for the relief of a particular individual or family. Moreover, you cannot make this election for a contribution to establish a new, or maintain an existing, segregated fund or account for which you (or any person you appoint or designate) has or expects to have advisory privileges with respect to distributions or investments because of being a donor.

Partners and shareholders. Each partner in a partnership and each shareholder in an S corporation makes this election separately. See Pub. 976, Disaster Relief, for details.

Carryovers

You can carry over any contributions you can't deduct in the current year because they exceed your adjusted-gross-income limits. Except for

qualified conservation contributions, you may be able to deduct the excess in each of the next 5 years until it is used up, but not beyond that time. For more information, see *Carryovers* in Pub. 526.

Records To Keep

You must keep records to prove the amount of the contributions you make during the year. The kind of records you must keep depends on the amount of your contributions and whether they are:

* Cash contributions,
* Noncash contributions, or
* Out-of-pocket expenses when donating your services.

Note. An organization generally must give you a written statement if it receives a payment from you that is more than $75 and is partly a contribution and partly for goods or services. (See *Contributions From Which You Benefit* under *Contributions You Can Deduct*, earlier.) Keep the statement for your records. It may satisfy all or part of the recordkeeping requirements explained in the following discussions.

Cash Contributions

Cash contributions include those paid by cash, check, electronic funds transfer, online payment service, debit card, credit card, payroll deduction, or a transfer of a gift card redeemable for cash.

You can't deduct a cash contribution, regardless of the amount, unless you keep one of the following.

1. A bank record that shows the name of the qualified organization, the date of the contribution, and the amount of the contribution. Bank records may include:

    a. A canceled check,

    b. A bank or credit union statement, or

    c. A credit card statement.

    d. An electronic fund transfer receipt.

    e. A scanned image of both sides of a canceled check obtained from a bank or credit union website.

2. A receipt (or a letter or other written communication) from the qualified organization showing the name of the organization, the date of the contribution, and the amount of the contribution.

3. The payroll deduction records described next.

Payroll deductions. If you make a contribution by payroll deduction, you must keep:

1. A pay stub, Form W-2, or other document furnished by your employer that shows the date and amount of the contribution; and

2. A pledge card or other document prepared by or for the qualified organization that shows the name of the organization.

If your employer withheld $250 or more from a single paycheck, see *Contributions of $250 or More* next.

Contributions of $250 or More

You can claim a deduction for a contribution of $250 or more only if you have a contemporaneous written acknowledgment of your contribution from the qualified organization or certain payroll deduction records.

If you made more than one contribution of $250 or more, you must have either a separate acknowledgment for each or one acknowledgment that lists each contribution and the date of each contribution and shows your total contributions.

Amount of contribution. In figuring whether your contribution is $250 or more, don't combine separate contributions. For example, if you gave your church $25 each week, your weekly payments don't have to be combined. Each payment is a separate contribution.

If contributions are made by payroll deduction, the deduction from each paycheck is treated as a separate contribution.

If you made a payment that is partly for goods and services, as described earlier under *Contributions From Which You Benefit*, your contribution is the amount of the payment that is more than the value of the goods and services.

Acknowledgment. The acknowledgment must meet these tests.

1. It must be written.

2. It must include:

    a. The amount of cash you contributed;

    b. Whether the qualified organization gave you any goods or services as a result of your contribution (other than certain token items and membership benefits);

    c. A description and good faith estimate of the value of any goods or services described in (b) (other than intangible religious benefits); and

    d. A statement that the only benefit you received was an intangible religious benefit, if that was the case. The acknowledgment doesn't need to describe or estimate the value of an intangible religious benefit. An intangible religious benefit is a benefit that generally isn't sold in commercial transactions outside a donative (gift) context. An example is admission to a religious ceremony.

3. You must get it on or before the earlier of:

    a. The date you file your return for the year you make the contribution; or

    b. The due date, including extensions, for filing the return.

If the acknowledgment doesn't show the date of the contribution, you must also have a bank record or receipt, as described earlier, that does show the date of the contribution. If the acknowledgment shows the date of the contribution and meets the other tests just described, you don't need any other records.

Payroll deductions. If you make a contribution by payroll deduction and your employer withholds $250 or more from a single paycheck, you must keep:

1. A pay stub, Form W-2, or other document furnished by your employer that shows the amount withheld as a contribution; and

2. A pledge card or other document prepared by or for the qualified organization that shows the name of the organization and states the organization doesn't provide goods or services in return for any contribution made to it by payroll deduction.

A single pledge card may be kept for all contributions made by payroll deduction regardless of amount as long as it contains all the required information.

If the pay stub, Form W-2, pledge card, or other document doesn't show the date of the contribution, you must have another document that does show the date of the contribution. If the pay stub, Form W-2, pledge card, or other document shows the date of the contribution, you don't need any other records except those just described in (1) and (2).

Noncash Contributions

For a contribution not made in cash, the records you must keep depend on whether your deduction for the contribution is:

1. Less than $250,

2. At least $250 but not more than $500,

3. Over $500 but not more than $5,000, or

4. Over $5,000.

Amount of deduction. In figuring whether your deduction is $500 or more, combine your claimed deductions for all similar items of property donated to any charitable organization during the year.

If you received goods or services in return, as described earlier in *Contributions From Which You Benefit*, reduce your contribution by the value of those goods or services. If you figure your deduction by reducing the fair market value of the donated property by its appreciation, as described earlier in *Giving Property That Has Increased in Value*, your contribution is the reduced amount.

Deductions of Less Than $250

If you make any noncash contribution, you must get and keep a receipt from the charitable organization showing:

1. The name of the charitable organization,

2. The date and location of the charitable contribution, and

3. A description of the property in sufficient detail for a person not generally familiar with the type of property to understand that the description is the contributed property.

A letter or other written communication from the charitable organization acknowledging receipt of the contribution and containing the information in (1), (2), and (3) will serve as a receipt.

You aren't required to have a receipt where it is impractical to get one (for example, if you leave property at a charity's unattended drop site).

Additional records. You also must keep reliable written records for each item of contributed property. Your written records must include the following information.

- The name and address of the organization to which you contributed.

- The date and location of the contribution.

- A description of the property in detail reasonable under the circumstances. For a security, keep the name of the issuer, the type of security, and whether it is regularly traded on a stock exchange or in an over-the-counter market, or quoted daily in a national newspaper in general circulation, in the case of a mutual fund share.

- If you claim a deduction for clothing or a household item, a description of the condition of the clothing or item.

- The fair market value of the property at the time of the contribution and how you figured the fair market value. If it was determined by appraisal, keep a signed copy of the appraisal.

- The cost or other basis of the property if you must reduce its fair market value by appreciation. Your records should also include the amount of the reduction and how you figured it.

- The amount you claim as a deduction for the tax year as a result of the contribution if you contribute less than your entire interest in the property during the tax year. Your records must include the amount you claimed as a deduction in any earlier years for contributions of other interests in this property. They must also include the name and address of each organization to which you contributed the other interests, the place where any such tangible property is located or kept, and the name of any person in possession of the property, other than the organization to which you contributed it.

- The terms of any conditions attached to the contribution of property.

Deductions of at Least $250 But Not More Than $500

If you claim a deduction of at least $250 but not more than $500 for a noncash charitable contribution, you must get and keep a contemporaneous written acknowledgment of your contribution from the qualified organization. If you made more than one contribution of $250 or more, you must have either a separate acknowledgment for each or one acknowledgment that shows your total contributions.

The acknowledgment must contain the information in items (1) through (3) under *Deductions of Less Than $250*, earlier, and your written records must include the information listed in that discussion under *Additional records*.

The acknowledgment must also meet these tests.

1. It must be written.

2. It must include:

   a. A description (but not necessarily the value) of any property you contributed,

   b. Whether the qualified organization gave you any goods or services as a result of your contribution (other than certain token items and membership benefits), and

   c. A description and good faith estimate of the value of any goods or services described in (b). If the only benefit you received was an intangible religious benefit (such as admission to a religious ceremony) that generally isn't sold in a commercial transaction outside the donative context, the acknowledgment must say so and doesn't need to describe or estimate the value of the benefit.

3. You must get it on or before the earlier of:

   a. The date you file your return for the year you make the contribution; or

   b. The due date, including extensions, for filing the return.

Deductions Over $500

You are required to give additional information if you claim a deduction over $500 for noncash charitable contributions. See *Records To Keep* in Pub. 526 for more information.

Out-of-Pocket Expenses

If you give services to a qualified organization and have unreimbursed out-of-pocket expenses related to those services, the following two rules apply.

1. You must have adequate records to prove the amount of the expenses.

2. If any of your unreimbursed out-of-pocket expenses, considered separately, are $250 or more (for example, you pay $250 or more for an airline ticket to attend a convention of a qualified organization as a chosen representative), you must get an acknowledgment from the qualified organization that contains:

   a. A description of the services you provided,

   b. A statement of whether or not the organization provided you any goods or services to reimburse you for the expenses you incurred,

   c. A description and a good faith estimate of the value of any goods or services (other than intangible religious benefits) provided to reimburse you, and

d. A statement that the only benefit you received was an intangible religious benefit, if that was the case. The acknowledgment doesn't need to describe or estimate the value of an intangible religious benefit (defined earlier under *Acknowledgment*).

You must get the acknowledgment on or before the earlier of:

1. The date you file your return for the year you make the contribution; or

2. The due date, including extensions, for filing the return.

Car expenses. If you claim expenses directly related to use of your car in giving services to a qualified organization, you must keep reliable written records of your expenses. Whether your records are considered reliable depends on all the facts and circumstances. Generally, they may be considered reliable if you made them regularly and at or near the time you had the expenses.

For example, your records might show the name of the organization you were serving and the dates you used your car for a charitable purpose. If you use the standard mileage rate of 14 cents a mile, your records must show the miles you drove your car for the charitable purpose. If you deduct your actual expenses, your records must show the costs of operating the car that are directly related to a charitable purpose.

See *Car expenses* under *Out-of-Pocket Expenses in Giving Services*, earlier, for the expenses you can deduct.

How To Report

Report your charitable contributions on Schedule A (Form 1040).

If your total deduction for all noncash contributions for the year is over $500, you must also file Form 8283. See *How To Report* in Pub. 526 for more information.

26.

Nonbusiness Casualty and Theft Losses

What's New

 At the time this publication went to print, Congress was considering legislation that would do the following.

1. Provide additional tax relief for those affected by certain 2018 disasters.

2. Extend certain tax benefits that expired at the end of 2017 and that currently can't be claimed on your 2018 tax return.

3. Change certain other tax provisions.

To learn whether this legislation was enacted resulting in changes that affect your 2018 tax return, go to Recent Developments *at* IRS.gov/ Pub17.

Limitation on personal casualty and theft losses. Personal casualty and theft losses of an individual sustained in a tax year beginning after 2017 are deductible only to the extent they're attributable to a federally declared disaster. The loss deduction is subject to the $100 limit per casualty and 10% of your adjusted gross income (AGI) limitation.

An exception to the rule above, limiting the personal casualty and theft loss deduction to losses attributable to a federally declared disaster, applies if you have personal casualty gains for the tax year. In this case, you can reduce your personal casualty gains by any casualty losses not attributable to a federally declared disaster. Any excess gain is used to reduce losses from a federally declared disaster. The 10% AGI limitation is applied to any remaining losses attributable to a federally declared disaster. For more information, see *Disaster Area Loss*, later.

No miscellaneous itemized deductions allowed. You can no longer claim any miscellaneous itemized deductions. Miscellaneous itemized deductions are those deductions that would have been subject to the 2%-of-AGI limitation. As a result, ordinary losses on nonfederally insured deposits in an insolvent or bankrupt financial institution as well as business casualty and theft losses of property used in performing services as an employee can't be deducted. References to these loss deductions have been revised accordingly in this chapter.

Special rules for capital gains invested in Qualified Opportunity Funds. In 2018, if you have a capital gain, you can invest that gain into a Qualified Opportunity Fund and elect to defer part or all of the gain that you would otherwise include in income until December 31, 2026. You also may be able to permanently exclude gain from the sale or exchange of an investment in a Qualified Opportunity Fund if the investment is held for at least 10 years. For information about how to elect to use these special rules, see the Instructions for Form 8949, Sales and Other Dispositions of Capital Assets. For additional information, see *Opportunity Zones Frequently Asked Questions* on IRS.gov.

Reminder

Special rules for qualified disaster losses. Personal casualty losses attributable to a major disaster declared by the President under section 401 of the Robert T. Stafford Disaster Relief and Emergency Assistance Act (Stafford Act) in 2016, as well as from Hurricane Harvey, Tropical Storm Harvey, Hurricanes Irma and Maria, and the California wildfires, may be claimed as a qualified disaster loss on your

Form 4684. You can deduct qualified disaster losses without itemizing other deductions on Schedule A (Form 1040). Moreover, your net casualty loss from these qualified disasters doesn't need to exceed 10% of your adjusted gross income to qualify for the deduction, but the $100 limit per casualty is increased to $500. See Pub. 547, Casualties, Disasters, and Thefts; Pub. 976, Disaster Relief; and *IRS.gov/ DisasterTaxRelief* for more information about these and other disaster tax relief provisions.

Introduction

This chapter explains the tax treatment of personal (not business or investment-related) casualty losses, theft losses, and losses on deposits.

The chapter also explains the following topics.

- How to figure the amount of your loss.
- How to treat insurance and other reimbursements you receive.
- The deduction limits.
- When and how to report a casualty or theft.

Forms to file. When you have a casualty or theft, you have to file Form 4684. You will also have to file one or more of the following forms.

- Schedule A (Form 1040), Itemized Deductions.
- Schedule D (Form 1040), Capital Gains and Losses.

Condemnations. For information on condemnations of property, see *Involuntary Conversions* in chapter 1 of Pub. 544, Sales and Other Dispositions of Assets.

Workbook for casualties and thefts. Pub. 584 is available to help you make a list of your stolen or damaged personal-use property and figure your loss. It includes schedules to help you figure the loss on your home, its contents, and your motor vehicles.

Business or investment-related losses. For information on a casualty or theft loss of business or income-producing property, see Pub. 547.

Useful Items

You may want to see:

Publication

❑ **544** Sales and Other Dispositions of Assets

❑ **547** Casualties, Disasters, and Thefts

❑ **584** Casualty, Disaster, and Theft Loss Workbook (Personal-Use Property)

❑ **976** Disaster Relief

Form (and Instructions)

❑ **Schedule A (Form 1040)** Itemized Deductions

❑ **Schedule D (Form 1040)** Capital Gains and Losses

For these and other useful items, go to *IRS.gov/ Forms*.

Casualty

A casualty is the damage, destruction, or loss of property resulting from an identifiable event that is sudden, unexpected, or unusual.

- A sudden event is one that is swift, not gradual or progressive.
- An unexpected event is one that is ordinarily unanticipated and unintended.
- An unusual event is one that isn't a day-to-day occurrence and that isn't typical of the activity in which you were engaged.

Casualty losses are deductible during the tax year that the loss is sustained. This is generally the tax year that the loss occurred. However, a casualty loss may be sustained in a year after the casualty occurred. See *When To Report Gains and Losses*, later.

Definitions. Three types of casualty losses are mentioned in this chapter.

1. *Federal casualty losses*,

2. *Disaster losses*, and

3. *Qualified disaster losses*.

All three types of losses refer to federally declared disasters, but the requirements for each loss vary. A federally declared disaster is a disaster determined by the President of the United States to warrant assistance by the federal government under the Stafford Act. A federally declared disaster includes (a) a major disaster declaration or (b) an emergency declaration under the Stafford Act.

Federal casualty loss. A federal casualty loss is an individual's casualty or theft loss of personal-use property that is attributable to a federally declared disaster. The casualty loss must occur in a state receiving a federal disaster declaration. If you suffered a federal casualty loss, you are eligible to claim a casualty loss deduction. If you suffered a casualty or theft loss of personal-use property that was not attributable to federally declared disaster, it is not a federal casualty loss, and you may not claim a casualty loss deduction unless the exception applies. See the *Caution* under *Deductible losses*, later.

Disaster loss. A disaster loss is a loss that is attributable to a federally declared disaster and that occurs in a an area eligible for assistance pursuant to the Presidential declaration. The disaster loss must occur in a county eligible for public or individual assistance (or both). Disaster losses are not limited to individual personal-use property and may be claimed for individual business or income-producing property and by corporations, S corporations, and partnerships. If you suffered a disaster loss, you are eligible to claim a casualty loss deduction and to elect to claim the loss in the preceding tax year. See *Disaster Area Loss*, later.

Qualified disaster loss. A qualified disaster loss is an individual's casualty or theft loss of personal-use property that is attributable to a major disaster declared by the President under section 401 of the Stafford Act in 2016, as well as from Hurricane Harvey, Tropical Storm Harvey, Hurricanes Irma and Maria, or the California wildfires. If you suffered a qualified disaster loss, you are eligible to claim a casualty loss deduction, to elect to claim the loss in the preceding tax year, and to deduct the loss without itemizing other deductions on Schedule A (Form 1040). See *Qualified disaster losses* under *Disaster Area Losses* in Pub. 547.

Deductible losses. For tax years 2018 through 2025, if you are an individual, casualty losses of personal-use property are deductible only if the loss is attributable to a federally declared disaster (federal casualty loss). If the event causing you to suffer a personal casualty loss occurred before January 1, 2018, but the casualty loss was not sustained until January 1, 2018, or later, the casualty loss is not deductible. See *When To Report Gains and Losses*, later, for more information on when a casualty loss is sustained.

Example. As a result of a storm, a tree fell on your house in April 2017, and you suffered $5,000 in damage. The President did not declare the storm a federally declared disaster. You filed a claim with your insurance company and reasonably expected the entire amount of the claim to be covered by your insurance company. In March 2018, your insurance company paid you $3,000 and determined it did not owe you the remaining $2,000 from your claim. The $2,000 personal casualty loss is sustained in 2018 even though the storm occurred in 2017. Thus, the $2,000 is not a federal casualty loss and is not deductible as a casualty loss under the new limitations.

 An exception to the rule limiting the deduction for personal casualty and theft losses to federal casualty losses applies where you have personal casualty gains. In this case, you may deduct personal casualty losses that are not attributable to a federally declared disaster to the extent they don't exceed your personal casualty gains.

Casualty losses can result from a number of different causes, including the following.

- Car accidents (but see *Nondeductible losses* next for exceptions).
- Earthquakes.
- Fires (but see *Nondeductible losses* next for exceptions).
- Floods.
- Government-ordered demolition or relocation of a home that is unsafe to use because of a disaster as discussed under *Disaster Area Losses* in Pub. 547.
- Mine cave-ins.
- Shipwrecks.
- Sonic booms.
- Storms, including hurricanes and tornadoes.
- Terrorist attacks.
- Vandalism.
- Volcanic eruptions.

Nondeductible losses. A casualty loss isn't deductible, even to the extent the loss doesn't exceed your personal casualty gains, if the damage or destruction is caused by the following.

- Accidentally breaking articles, such as glassware or china under normal conditions.
- A family pet (explained below).
- A fire if you willfully set it or pay someone else to set it.
- A car accident if your willful negligence or willful act caused it. The same is true if the willful act or willful negligence of someone acting for you caused the accident.
- Progressive deterioration (explained later).

Family pet. Loss of property due to damage by a family pet isn't deductible as a casualty loss unless the requirements discussed earlier under *Casualty* are met.

Example. Your antique oriental rug was damaged by your new puppy before it was housebroken. Because the damage wasn't unexpected and unusual, the loss isn't deductible as a casualty loss.

Progressive deterioration. Loss of property due to progressive deterioration isn't deductible as a casualty loss. This is because the damage results from a steadily operating cause or a normal process, rather than from a sudden event. The following are examples of damage due to progressive deterioration.

- The steady weakening of a building due to normal wind and weather conditions.
- The deterioration and damage to a water heater that bursts. However, the rust and water damage to rugs and drapes caused by the bursting of a water heater does qualify as a casualty.
- Most losses of property caused by droughts. To be deductible, a drought-related loss generally must be incurred in a trade or business or in a transaction entered into for profit.
- Termite or moth damage.
- The damage or destruction of trees, shrubs, or other plants by a fungus, disease, insects, worms, or similar pests. However, a sudden destruction due to an unexpected or unusual infestation of beetles or other insects may result in a casualty loss.

Damage from corrosive drywall. If you suffered property losses due to the effects of certain imported drywall installed in homes between 2001 and 2009, under a special procedure, you may be able to claim a casualty loss deduction for amounts you paid to repair damage to your home and household appliances that resulted from corrosive drywall. However, because the personal casualty losses claimed under this special procedure are not attributable to a federally declared disaster, they are only deductible to the extent such losses don't exceed your personal casualty gains and are subject to the $100 rule and the 10% rule, discussed later. For details, see Pub. 547.

Damage from deteriorating concrete foundation. Under a special safe harbor procedure, you can deduct the amounts you paid to repair damage to your home caused by a deteriorating concrete foundation containing the mineral pyrrhotite. Under this procedure, you treat the amounts paid as a casualty loss in the year of payment for amounts paid prior to 2018. For more details and for amounts paid after 2017, see Pub. 547.

Theft

A theft is the taking and removing of money or property with the intent to deprive the owner of it. The taking of property must be illegal under the laws of the state where it occurred and it must have been done with criminal intent. You don't need to show a conviction for theft.

Theft includes the taking of money or property by the following means.

- Blackmail.
- Burglary.
- Embezzlement.
- Extortion.
- Kidnapping for ransom.
- Larceny.
- Robbery.

The taking of money or property through fraud or misrepresentation is theft if it is illegal under state or local law.

Theft loss deduction limited. For tax years 2018 through 2025, if you are an individual, casualty and theft losses of personal-use property are deductible only if the losses are attributable to a federally declared disaster (federal casualty loss).

 An exception to the rule limiting the deduction for personal casualty and theft losses to federal casualty losses applies where you have personal casualty gains. In this case, you may deduct personal casualty losses that are not attributable to a federally declared disaster to the extent they don't exceed your personal casualty gains.

Example. Martin and Grace experienced multiple personal casualties in 2018. Grace's diamond necklace was stolen, resulting in a $15,500 casualty loss. Martin and Grace also lost their camper as a result of a lightning strike. They have replacement-value insurance on the camper, so they have a $13,000 gain. Finally, they lost their car in a flood determined to be a federally declared disaster, resulting in a casualty loss of $25,000. Because Martin and Grace experienced a $13,000 personal casualty gain as a result of the replacement-value insurance, they can offset that gain with a portion of their loss attributable to the stolen necklace.

Decline in market value of stock. You can't deduct as a theft loss the decline in market value of stock acquired on the open market for investment if the decline is caused by disclosure of accounting fraud or other illegal misconduct by the officers or directors of the corporation that issued the stock. However, you may be able to deduct it as a capital loss on Schedule D

(Form 1040) if the stock is sold or exchanged or becomes completely worthless. For more information about stock sales, worthless stock, and capital losses, see chapter 4 of Pub. 550.

Mislaid or lost property. The simple disappearance of money or property isn't a theft. However, an accidental loss or disappearance of property can qualify as a casualty if it results from an identifiable event that is sudden, unexpected, or unusual. Sudden, unexpected, and unusual events are defined earlier.

Example. A car door is accidentally slammed on your hand, breaking the setting of your diamond ring. The diamond falls from the ring and is never found. The loss of the diamond is a casualty.

Losses from Ponzi-type investment schemes. If you had a loss from a Ponzi-type investment scheme, see the following.

- Revenue Ruling 2009-9, 2009-14 I.R.B. 735 (available at *IRS.gov/irb/ 2009-14_IRB#RR-2009-9*).
- Revenue Procedure 2009-20, 2009-14 I.R.B. 749 (available at *IRS.gov/irb/ 2009-14_IRB#RP-2009-20*).
- Revenue Procedure 2011-58, 2011-50 I.R.B. 849 (available at *IRS.gov/irb/ 2011-50_IRB#RP-2011-58*).

If you qualify to use Revenue Procedure 2009-20, as modified by Revenue Procedure 2011-58, and you choose to follow the procedures in the guidance, first fill out Section C of Form 4684 to determine the amount to enter on Section B, line 28. Skip lines 19 through 27. Section C of Form 4684 replaces Appendix A in Revenue Procedure 2009-20. You don't need to complete Appendix A. For more information, see the above revenue ruling and revenue procedures, and the Instructions for Form 4684.

If you choose not to use the procedures in Revenue Procedure 2009-20, you may claim your theft loss by filling out Section B, lines 19 through 39, as appropriate.

Loss on Deposits

A loss on deposits can occur when a bank, credit union, or other financial institution becomes insolvent or bankrupt. If you incurred this type of loss, you can choose one of the following ways to deduct the loss.

- As a casualty loss (to the extent the loss doesn't exceed your personal casualty gains).
- As a nonbusiness bad debt.

 You can no longer claim any miscellaneous itemized deductions, including the deduction for an ordinary loss on deposits in insolvent or bankrupt financial institutions.

Casualty loss. You can choose to deduct a loss on deposits as a casualty loss for any year in which you can reasonably estimate how much of your deposits you have lost in an insolvent or bankrupt financial institution. The choice is generally made on the return you file for that year and applies to all your losses on deposits for the year in that particular financial institution.

If you treat the loss as a casualty loss, you can't treat the same amount of the loss as a nonbusiness bad debt when it actually becomes worthless. However, you can take a nonbusiness bad debt deduction for any amount of loss that is more than the estimated amount you deducted as a casualty or ordinary loss. Once you make this choice, you can't change it without permission from the IRS.

Casualty loss limitation. If you are an individual, casualty losses of personal-use property are deductible only if the loss is attributable to a federally declared disaster. An exception to the rule limiting the deduction for personal casualty and theft losses to federal casualty losses applies where you have personal casualty gains. Because a loss on deposits is not attributable to a federally declared disaster, you may deduct losses on deposits as personal casualty losses only to the extent they don't exceed your personal casualty gains.

Nonbusiness bad debt. If you don't choose to claim the loss as a casualty loss for purposes of offsetting gains, you must wait until the year the actual loss is determined and deduct the loss as a nonbusiness bad debt in that year.

How to report. The kind of deduction you choose for your loss on deposits determines how you report your loss.

- Casualty loss—report it on Form 4684.
- Nonbusiness bad debt—report it on Form 8949 first and then on Schedule D (Form 1040).

More information. For more information, see *Deposit in Insolvent or Bankrupt Financial Institution* in Pub. 550.

Proof of Loss

To deduct a casualty or theft loss, you must be able to prove that you had a casualty or theft. You also must be able to support the amount you take as a deduction.

Casualty loss proof. For a casualty loss, your records should show all the following.

- That you were the owner of the property or, if you leased the property from someone else, that you were contractually liable to the owner for the damage.
- The type of casualty (car accident, fire, storm, etc.) and when it occurred.
- That the loss was a direct result of the casualty.
- Whether a claim for reimbursement exists for which there is a reasonable expectation of recovery.

Theft loss proof. For a theft loss, your records should show all the following.

- That you were the owner of the property.
- That your property was stolen.
- When you discovered that your property was missing.
- Whether a claim for reimbursement exists for which there is a reasonable expectation of recovery.

It is important that you have records that will prove your deduction. If you don't have the actual records to support your deduction, you can use other satisfactory evidence to support it.

Figuring a Loss

Figure the amount of your loss using the following steps.

1. Determine your adjusted basis in the property before the casualty or theft.

2. Determine the decrease in fair market value (FMV) of the property as a result of the casualty or theft.

3. From the smaller of the amounts you determined in (1) and (2), subtract any insurance or other reimbursement you received or expect to receive.

For personal-use property, apply the deduction limits, discussed later, to determine the amount of your deductible loss.

Gain from reimbursement. If your reimbursement is more than your adjusted basis in the property, you have a gain. This is true even if the decrease in the FMV of the property is smaller than your adjusted basis. If you have a gain, you may have to pay tax on it, or you may be able to postpone reporting the gain. See Pub. 547 for more information on how to treat a gain from a reimbursement for a casualty or theft.

Leased property. If you are liable for casualty damage to property you lease, your loss is the amount you must pay to repair the property minus any insurance or other reimbursement you receive or expect to receive.

Decrease in FMV

FMV is the price for which you could sell your property to a willing buyer when neither of you has to sell or buy and both of you know all the relevant facts.

The decrease in FMV used to figure the amount of a casualty or theft loss is the difference between the property's FMV immediately before and immediately after the casualty or theft.

FMV of stolen property. The FMV of property immediately after a theft is considered to be zero because you no longer have the property.

Example. Several years ago, you purchased silver dollars at face value for $150. This is your adjusted basis in the property. Your silver dollars were stolen this year. The FMV of the coins was $1,000 just before they were stolen, and insurance didn't cover them. Your theft loss is $150.

Recovered stolen property. Recovered stolen property is your property that was stolen and later returned to you. If you recovered property after you had already taken a theft loss deduction, you must refigure your loss using the smaller of the property's adjusted basis (explained later) or the decrease in FMV from the

time just before it was stolen until the time it was recovered. Use this amount to refigure your total loss for the year in which the loss was deducted.

If your refigured loss is less than the loss you deducted, you generally have to report the difference as income in the recovery year. But report the difference only up to the amount of the loss that reduced your tax. For more information on the amount to report, see *Recoveries* in chapter 12.

Figuring Decrease in FMV— Items To Consider

To figure the decrease in FMV because of a casualty or theft, you generally need a competent appraisal. However, other measures can also be used to establish certain decreases.

Appraisal. An appraisal to determine the difference between the FMV of the property immediately before a casualty or theft and immediately afterward should be made by a competent appraiser. The appraiser must recognize the effects of any general market decline that may occur along with the casualty. This information is needed to limit any deduction to the actual loss resulting from damage to the property.

Several factors are important in evaluating the accuracy of an appraisal, including the following.

- The appraiser's familiarity with your property before and after the casualty or theft.

- The appraiser's knowledge of sales of comparable property in the area.

- The appraiser's knowledge of conditions in the area of the casualty.

- The appraiser's method of appraisal.

 You may be able to use an appraisal that you used to get a federal loan (or a federal loan guarantee) as the result of a federally declared disaster to establish the amount of your disaster loss. For more information on disasters, see Disaster Area Losses *in Pub. 547.*

Cost of cleaning up or making repairs. The cost of repairing damaged property isn't part of a casualty loss. Neither is the cost of cleaning up after a casualty. But you can use the cost of cleaning up or making repairs after a casualty as a measure of the decrease in FMV if you meet all the following conditions.

- The repairs are actually made.

- The repairs are necessary to bring the property back to its condition before the casualty.

- The amount spent for repairs isn't excessive.

- The repairs take care of the damage only.

- The value of the property after the repairs isn't, due to the repairs, more than the value of the property before the casualty.

Landscaping. The cost of restoring landscaping to its original condition after a casualty may indicate the decrease in FMV. You may be

able to measure your loss by what you spend on the following.

- Removing destroyed or damaged trees and shrubs minus any salvage you receive.

- Pruning and other measures taken to preserve damaged trees and shrubs.

- Replanting necessary to restore the property to its approximate value before the casualty.

Car value. Books issued by various automobile organizations that list the manufacturer and the model of your car may be useful in figuring the value of your car. You can use the retail value for your car listed in the book and modify it by such factors as mileage and the condition of your car to determine its value. The prices aren't official, but they may be useful in determining value and suggesting relative prices for comparison with current sales and offerings in your area. If your car isn't listed in the books, determine its value from other sources. A dealer's offer for your car as a trade-in on a new car isn't usually a measure of its true value.

Safe harbor procedures to determine casualty and theft loss deduction. Safe harbor procedures allow filers to determine their casualty and theft loss deductions for personal-use residential real property and personal belongings resulting from a federally declared disaster without an appraisal. See Pub. 547 for more information about the safe harbor provisions.

Figuring Decrease in FMV— Items Not To Consider

You generally shouldn't consider the following items when attempting to establish the decrease in FMV of your property.

Cost of protection. The cost of protecting your property against a casualty or theft isn't part of a casualty or theft loss. The amount you spend on insurance or to board up your house against a storm isn't part of your loss.

If you make permanent improvements to your property to protect it against a casualty or theft, add the cost of these improvements to your basis in the property. An example would be the cost of a dike to prevent flooding.

Exception. You can't increase your basis in the property by, or deduct as a business expense, any expenditures you made with respect to qualified disaster mitigation payments. See *Disaster Area Losses* in Pub. 547.

Incidental expenses. Any incidental expenses you have due to a casualty or theft, such as expenses for the treatment of personal injuries, for temporary housing, or for a rental car, aren't part of your casualty or theft loss.

Replacement cost. The cost of replacing stolen or destroyed property isn't part of a casualty or theft loss.

Sentimental value. Don't consider sentimental value when determining your loss. If a family portrait, heirloom, or keepsake is damaged, destroyed, or stolen, you must base your loss on its FMV, as limited by your adjusted basis in the property.

Decline in market value of property in or near casualty area. A decrease in the value of your property because it is in or near an area that suffered a casualty, or that might again suffer a casualty, isn't to be taken into consideration. You have a loss only for actual casualty damage to your property. However, if your home is in a federally declared disaster area, see *Disaster Area Losses* in Pub. 547.

Costs of photographs and appraisals. Photographs taken after a casualty will be helpful in establishing the condition and value of the property after it was damaged. Photographs showing the condition of the property after it was repaired, restored, or replaced may also be helpful.

Appraisals are used to figure the decrease in FMV because of a casualty or theft. See *Appraisal*, earlier, under *Figuring Decrease in FMV—Items To Consider* for information about appraisals.

The costs of photographs and appraisals used as evidence of the value and condition of property damaged as a result of a casualty aren't a part of the loss. They are expenses in determining your tax liability. For tax years 2018 through 2025, they can no longer be deducted as miscellaneous itemized deductions.

Adjusted Basis

Adjusted basis is your basis in the property (usually cost) increased or decreased by various events, such as improvements and casualty losses. For more information, see chapter 13.

Insurance and Other Reimbursements

If you receive an insurance payment or other type of reimbursement, you must subtract the reimbursement when you figure your loss. You don't have a casualty or theft loss to the extent you are reimbursed.

If in the year of the casualty there is a claim for reimbursement with a reasonable prospect of recovery, the loss is not sustained until you know with reasonable certainty whether such reimbursement will be received. If you expect to be reimbursed for part or all of your loss, you must subtract the expected reimbursement when you figure your loss. You must reduce your loss even if you don't receive payment until a later tax year. See *Reimbursement Received After Deducting Loss*, later.

Failure to file a claim for reimbursement. If your property is covered by insurance, you must file a timely insurance claim for reimbursement of your loss. Otherwise, you can't deduct this loss as a casualty or theft loss. However, this rule doesn't apply to the portion of the loss not covered by insurance (for example, a deductible).

Example. Your car insurance policy includes comprehensive coverage with a $1,000 deductible. Because your insurance doesn't cover the first $1,000 of damages resulting from a storm, the $1,000 is deductible (subject to the deduction limits discussed later). This is true

even if you don't file an insurance claim, because your insurance policy won't reimburse you for the deductible.

Types of Reimbursements

The most common type of reimbursement is an insurance payment for your stolen or damaged property. Other types of reimbursements are discussed next. Also see the Instructions for Form 4684.

Employer's emergency disaster fund. If you receive money from your employer's emergency disaster fund and you must use that money to rehabilitate or replace property on which you are claiming a casualty loss deduction, you must take that money into consideration in figuring the casualty loss deduction. Take into consideration only the amount you used to replace your destroyed or damaged property.

Example. Your home was extensively damaged by a tornado. Your loss after reimbursement from your insurance company was $10,000. Your employer set up a disaster relief fund for its employees. Employees receiving money from the fund had to use it to rehabilitate or replace their damaged or destroyed property. You received $4,000 from the fund and spent the entire amount on repairs to your home. In figuring your casualty loss, you must reduce your unreimbursed loss ($10,000) by the $4,000 you received from your employer's fund. Your casualty loss before applying the deduction limits discussed later is $6,000.

Cash gifts. If you receive excludable cash gifts as a disaster victim and there are no limits on how you can use the money, you don't reduce your casualty loss by these excludable cash gifts. This applies even if you use the money to pay for repairs to property damaged in the disaster.

Example. Your home was damaged by a hurricane. Relatives and neighbors made cash gifts to you that were excludable from your income. You used part of the cash gifts to pay for repairs to your home. There were no limits or restrictions on how you could use the cash gifts. Because it was an excludable gift, the money you received and used to pay for repairs to your home doesn't reduce your casualty loss on the damaged home.

Insurance payments for living expenses. You don't reduce your casualty loss by insurance payments you receive to cover living expenses in either of the following situations.

- You lose the use of your main home because of a casualty.

- Government authorities don't allow you access to your main home because of a casualty or threat of one.

Inclusion in income. If these insurance payments are more than the temporary increase in your living expenses, you must include the excess in your income. Report this amount on Schedule 1 (Form 1040), line 21. However, if the casualty occurs in a federally declared disaster area, none of the insurance payments are taxable. See *Qualified disaster*

relief payments under *Disaster Area Losses* in Pub. 547.

A temporary increase in your living expenses is the difference between the actual living expenses you and your family incurred during the period you couldn't use your home and your normal living expenses for that period. Actual living expenses are the reasonable and necessary expenses incurred because of the loss of your main home. Generally, these expenses include the amounts you pay for the following.

- Rent for suitable housing.

- Transportation.

- Food.

- Utilities.

- Miscellaneous services.

Normal living expenses consist of these same expenses that you would have incurred but didn't because of the casualty or the threat of one.

Example. As a result of a hurricane, you vacated your apartment for a month and moved to a motel. You normally pay $525 a month for rent. None was charged for the month the apartment was vacated. Your motel rent for this month was $1,200. You normally pay $200 a month for food. Your food expenses for the month you lived in the motel were $400. You received $1,100 from your insurance company to cover your living expenses. You determine the payment you must include in income as follows.

1)	Insurance payment for living expenses	$1,100
2)	Actual expenses during the month you are unable to use your home because of the hurricane	$1,600
3)	Normal living expenses	725
4)	Temporary increase in living expenses: Subtract line 3 from line 2	875
5)	**Amount of payment includible in income: Subtract line 4 from line 1**	**$225**

Tax year of inclusion. You include the taxable part of the insurance payment in income for the year you regain the use of your main home or, if later, for the year you receive the taxable part of the insurance payment.

Example. Your main home was destroyed by a tornado in August 2016. You regained use of your home in November 2017. The insurance payments you received in 2016 and 2017 were $1,500 more than the temporary increase in your living expenses during those years. You include this amount in income on your 2017 Form 1040. If, in 2018, you received further payments to cover the living expenses you had in 2016 and 2017, you must include those payments in income on your 2018 Form 1040.

Disaster relief. Food, medical supplies, and other forms of assistance you receive don't reduce your casualty loss unless they are replacements for lost or destroyed property.

Qualified disaster relief payments you receive for expenses you incurred as a result of a federally declared disaster aren't taxable income to you. For more information, see Disaster Area Losses *in Pub. 547.*

Disaster unemployment assistance payments are unemployment benefits that are taxable.

Generally, disaster relief grants and qualified disaster mitigation payments made under the Stafford Act or the National Flood Insurance Act (as in effect on April 15, 2005) aren't includible in your income. See Pub. 547 for more information about disaster tax relief.

Reimbursement Received After Deducting Loss

If you figured your casualty or theft loss using the amount of your expected reimbursement, you may have to adjust your tax return for the tax year in which you receive your actual reimbursement. This section explains the adjustment you may have to make.

Actual reimbursement less than expected. If you later receive less reimbursement than you expected, include that difference as a loss with your other losses (if any) on your return for the year in which you can reasonably expect no more reimbursement.

Example. Your personal car had an FMV of $2,000 when it was destroyed in a collision with another car in 2017. The accident was due to the negligence of the other driver. At the end of 2017, there was a reasonable prospect that the owner of the other car would reimburse you in full. You didn't have a deductible loss in 2017.

In January 2018, the court awarded you a judgment of $2,000. However, in July it became apparent that you will be unable to collect any amount from the other driver. You can deduct the loss in 2018 (to the extent it doesn't exceed your 2018 personal casualty gains) subject to the deduction limits discussed later.

Actual reimbursement more than expected. If you later receive a larger reimbursement amount than you expected, after you claimed a deduction for the loss, you may have to include the extra reimbursement amount in your income for the year you receive it. However, if any part of the original deduction didn't reduce your tax for the earlier year, don't include that part of the reimbursement amount in your income. You don't refigure your tax for the year you claimed the deduction. For more information, see Recoveries in chapter 12.

⚠️ CAUTION *If the total of all the reimbursements you receive is more than your adjusted basis in the destroyed or stolen property, you will have a gain on the casualty or theft. If you have already taken a deduction for a loss and you receive the reimbursement in a later year, you may have to include the gain in your income for the later year. Include the gain as ordinary income up to the amount of your deduction that reduced your tax for the earlier year. See* Figuring a Gain *in Pub. 547 for more information on how to treat a gain from the reimbursement of a casualty or theft.*

Actual reimbursement same as expected. If you receive exactly the reimbursement you expected to receive, you don't have to include any of the reimbursement in your income and you can't deduct any additional loss.

Example. In December 2018, your personal car was damaged in a flood that was a federally declared disaster. Repairs to the car cost $950. You had $100 deductible comprehensive insurance. Your insurance company agreed to reimburse you for the rest of the damage. Because you expected a reimbursement from the insurance company, you didn't have a casualty loss deduction in 2018.

Due to the $100 rule (discussed later under Deduction Limits), you can't deduct the $100 you paid as the deductible. When you receive the $850 from the insurance company in 2019, don't report it as income.

Single Casualty on Multiple Properties

Personal property. Personal property is any property that isn't real property. If your personal property is stolen or is damaged or destroyed by a casualty, you must figure your loss separately for each item of property. Then combine these separate losses to figure the total loss from that casualty or theft.

Example. A flood in your home damaged an upholstered chair, an oriental rug, and an antique table. You didn't have flood insurance to cover your loss. (This was the only casualty or theft you had during the year.) You paid $750 for the chair and you established that it had an FMV of $500 just before the flood. The rug cost $3,000 and had an FMV of $2,500 just before the flood. You bought the table at an auction for $100 before discovering it was an antique. It had been appraised at $900 before the flood. You figure your loss on each of these items as follows.

		Chair	Rug	Table
1)	Basis (cost)	$750	$3,000	$100
2)	FMV before flood	$500	$2,500	$900
3)	FMV after flood	-0-	-0-	-0-
4)	Decrease in FMV	$500	$2,500	$900
5)	Loss (smaller of (1) or (4))	$500	$2,500	$100
6)	Total loss			$3,100

Real property. In figuring a casualty loss on personal-use real property, treat the entire property (including any improvements, such as buildings, trees, and shrubs) as one item. Figure the loss using the smaller of the adjusted basis or the decrease in FMV of the entire property.

Example. You bought your home a few years ago. You paid $160,000 ($20,000 for the land and $140,000 for the house). You also spent $2,000 for landscaping. This year a tornado destroyed your home. The tornado also damaged the shrubbery and trees in your yard. The tornado was your only casualty or theft loss this year. Competent appraisers valued the

property as a whole at $200,000 before the tornado, but only $30,000 after the tornado. (The loss to your household furnishings isn't shown in this example. It would be figured separately on each item, as explained earlier under Personal property.) Shortly after the tornado, the insurance company paid you $155,000 for the loss. You figure your casualty loss as follows.

1)	Adjusted basis of the entire property (land, building, and landscaping)	$162,000
2)	FMV of entire property before tornado	$200,000
3)	FMV of entire property after tornado	30,000
4)	Decrease in FMV of entire property	$170,000
5)	Loss (smaller of (1) or (4))	$162,000
6)	Subtract insurance	155,000
7)	**Amount of loss after reimbursement**	**$7,000**

Deduction Limits

After you have figured the amount of your casualty or theft loss, you must figure how much of the loss you can deduct. If the loss was to property for your personal use or your family's use, there are two limits on the amount you can deduct for your casualty or theft loss.

1. You must reduce each casualty or theft loss by $100 ($100 rule). However, qualified disaster losses must be reduced by $500 when figuring the deduction.

2. You must further reduce the total of all your casualty or theft losses by 10% of your adjusted gross income (AGI) (10% rule).

The deduction for casualty and theft losses of personal-use property is limited. For tax years beginning after 2017 and before 2026, personal casualty and theft losses of an individual are deductible only to the extent they're attributable to a federally declared disaster. The loss deduction is subject to the $100 and 10% rules, discussed later.

An exception to the rule above limiting the personal casualty and theft loss deduction to losses attributable to a federally declared disaster applies if you have personal casualty gains for the tax year. In this case, you may reduce your personal casualty gains by any casualty losses not attributable to a federally declared disaster. Any excess gain is used to reduce losses from a federally declared disaster. The 10% rule is applied to any federal disaster losses that remain.

You make these reductions on Form 4684.

These rules are explained next and Table 26-1 summarizes how to apply the $100 rule and the 10% rule in various situations. For more detailed explanations and examples, see Pub. 547.

Property used partly for business and partly for personal purposes. When property is used partly for personal purposes and partly for business or income-producing purposes, the casualty or theft loss deduction must be figured separately for the personal-use part and for the

Table 26-1. How To Apply the Deduction Limits for Personal-Use Property

	$100 Rule	10% Rule
General Application	You must reduce each casualty or theft loss by $100 when figuring your deduction. Apply this rule after you have figured the amount of your loss.*	You must reduce your total casualty or theft loss attributable to a federally declared disaster by 10% of your AGI. Apply this rule after you reduce each loss by $100 ($100 rule).**
Single Event	Apply this rule only once, even if many pieces of property are affected.	Apply this rule only once, even if many pieces of property are affected.
More Than One Event	Apply to the loss from each event.	Apply to the total of all your losses from all federally declared disasters.
More Than One Person— With Loss From the Same Event (other than a married couple filing jointly)	Apply separately to each person.	Apply separately to each person.
Married Couple— With Loss From the Same Event / Filing Jointly	Apply as if you were one person.	Apply as if you were one person.
Filing Separately	Apply separately to each spouse.	Apply separately to each spouse.
More Than One Owner (other than a married couple filing jointly)	Apply separately to each owner of jointly owned property.	Apply separately to each owner of jointly owned property.

* Qualified disaster losses must be reduced by $500 when figuring your deduction. See Pub. 976 for more information.

** The 10% rule does not apply to qualified disaster losses. See Pub. 976 for more information.

business or income-producing part. You must figure each loss separately because the $100 rule and the 10% rule apply only to the loss on the personal-use part of the property.

$100 Rule

After you have figured your casualty or theft loss on personal-use property, you must reduce that loss by $100. This reduction applies to each total casualty or theft loss, including those losses not attributable to a federally declared disaster that are applied to reduce your personal casualty gains. It doesn't matter how many pieces of property are involved in an event. Only a single $100 reduction applies.

Example. A tornado damages your home and your car. Determine the amount of loss, as discussed earlier, for each of these items. Since the losses are due to a single event, you combine the losses and reduce the combined amount by $100.

Single event. Generally, events closely related in origin cause a single casualty. It is a single casualty when the damage is from two or more closely related causes, such as wind and flood damage caused by the same storm.

 Qualified disaster losses must be reduced by $500 instead of $100. See Pub. 976 and the Instructions for Form 4684 for more information.

10% Rule

You must reduce your total federal casualty losses by 10% of your AGI. Apply this rule after you reduce each loss by $100. For more information, see the Instructions for Form 4684. If you have both gains and losses from casualties or thefts, see *Gains and losses*, later.

Example 1. In September, your house was damaged by a tropical storm that was a federally declared disaster. Your loss after insurance

reimbursement was $2,000. Your AGI for the year the loss was sustained is $29,500. You first apply the $100 rule and then the 10% rule. Figure your casualty loss deduction as follows.

1)	Loss after insurance	$2,000
2)	Subtract $100	100
3)	Loss after $100 rule	$1,900
4)	Subtract 10% × $29,500 AGI	2,950
5)	**Casualty loss deduction**	-0-

You don't have a casualty loss deduction because your loss after you apply the $100 rule ($1,900) is less than 10% of your AGI ($2,950).

Example 2. In March, your car was destroyed in a flood that was a federally declared disaster. You didn't have insurance on your car, so you didn't receive any insurance reimbursement. Your loss on the car was $1,800. In November, another flood, which also was a federally declared disaster, damaged your basement and totally destroyed the furniture, washer, dryer, and other items stored there. Your loss on the basement items after reimbursement from your insurer was $2,100. Your AGI for the year that the floods occurred is $25,000. You figure your casualty loss deduction as follows.

		Car	Basement
1)	Loss	$1,800	$2,100
2)	Subtract $100 per incident	100	100
3)	Loss after $100 rule	$1,700	$2,000
4)	Total loss		$3,700
5)	Subtract 10% × $25,000 AGI		2,500
6)	**Casualty loss deduction**		**$1,200**

 The 10% rule does not apply to qualified disaster losses. See Pub. 976 and the Instructions for Form 4684 for more information.

Gains and losses. If you had both gains and losses from casualties or thefts to your per-

sonal-use property, you must compare your total gains to your total losses. Do this after you have reduced each loss by any reimbursements and by $100, but before you have reduced the federal casualty losses by 10% of your AGI.

 Casualty or theft gains don't include gains you choose to postpone. See Pub. 547 for information on the postponement of gain.

Losses more than gains. If your losses are more than your recognized gains, subtract your gains from your losses and reduce the result by 10% of your AGI. The rest, if any, is your deductible loss from personal-use property. If you have losses not attributable to a federally declared disaster, see *Line 14* in the Instructions for Form 4684. Losses not attributable to a federally declared disaster can only be used to offset gains.

Gains more than losses. If your recognized gains are more than your losses, subtract your losses from your gains. The difference is treated as capital gain and must be reported on Schedule D (Form 1040). The 10% rule doesn't apply to your gains. If you have losses not attributable to a federally declared disaster, see *Line 14* in the Instructions for Form 4684.

When To Report Gains and Losses

Gains. If you receive an insurance or other reimbursement that is more than your adjusted basis in the destroyed or stolen property, you have a gain from the casualty or theft. You must include this gain in your income in the year you receive the reimbursement, unless you choose to postpone reporting the gain as explained in Pub. 547.

Losses. Generally, you can deduct a casualty loss that isn't reimbursable only in the tax year in which the casualty occurred. This is true even if you don't repair or replace the damaged property until a later year. (However, see *Disaster Area Loss*, later, for an exception.)

You can deduct theft losses that aren't reimbursable only in the year you discover your property was stolen.

If in the year of the casualty there is a claim for reimbursement with a reasonable prospect of recovery, the loss is not sustained until you know with reasonable certainty whether such reimbursement will be received. If you aren't sure whether part of your casualty or theft loss will be reimbursed, don't deduct that part until the tax year when you become reasonably certain that it won't be reimbursed. This later tax year is when your loss is sustained.

If you have a loss, see Table 26-2.

Loss on deposits. If your loss is a loss on deposits in an insolvent or bankrupt financial institution, see *Loss on Deposits*, earlier.

Disaster Area Loss

A disaster loss is a loss that occurred in an area determined by the President of the United States to warrant assistance by the Federal government under the Stafford Act and that is attributable to a federally declared disaster. Disaster area includes areas warranting public or individual assistance (or both). A federally declared disaster includes a major disaster or emergency declaration.

You generally must deduct a casualty loss in the year it occurred. However, if you have a casualty loss from a federally declared disaster that occurred in an area warranting public or individual assistance (or both), you can choose to deduct the loss on your tax return or amended return for either of the following years.

- The year the loss was sustained (the disaster year). For more details, see *Disaster year* under *Disaster Area Losses* in Pub. 547.

- The year immediately preceding the disaster year.

You must make the choice to take your casualty loss for the disaster in the preceding year on or before the date that is 6 months after the regular due date for filing your original return (without extensions) for the disaster year.

If you claimed a deduction for a disaster loss in the disaster year and you wish to deduct the loss in the preceding year, you must file an amended return to remove the previously deducted loss on or before you file the return or amended return for the preceding year that includes the disaster loss deduction. For more details, see Pub. 547.

Gains. Special rules apply if you choose to postpone reporting gain on property damaged or destroyed in a federally declared disaster area. For those special rules, see Pub. 547.

Postponed tax deadlines. The IRS may postpone for up to 1 year certain tax deadlines of taxpayers who are affected by a federally declared disaster. The tax deadlines the IRS may postpone include those for filing income and employment tax returns, paying income and employment taxes, and making contributions to a traditional IRA or Roth IRA.

Table 26-2. When To Deduct a Loss

IF you have a loss...*	THEN deduct it in the year...
from a casualty*	the loss occurred.
in a federally declared disaster area	the loss was sustained or the year immediately before the loss was sustained.
from a theft	the theft was discovered.
on a deposit treated as a:	
• casualty	a reasonable estimate can be made.
• bad debt	deposits are totally worthless.

* If you are an individual, casualty and theft losses of personal-use property are deductible only if the loss is attributable to a federally declared disaster. An exception applies where you have personal casualty gains.

If any tax deadline is postponed, the IRS will publicize the postponement in your area by publishing a news release, revenue ruling, revenue procedure, notice, announcement, or other guidance in the Internal Revenue Bulletin (IRB). Go to *IRS.gov/DisasterTaxRelief* to find out if a tax deadline has been postponed for your area.

Who is eligible. If the IRS postpones a tax deadline, the following taxpayers are eligible for the postponement.

- Any individual whose main home is located in a covered disaster area (defined next).

- Any business entity or sole proprietor whose principal place of business is located in a covered disaster area.

- Any individual who is a relief worker affiliated with a recognized government or philanthropic organization who is assisting in a covered disaster area.

- Any individual, business entity, or sole proprietorship whose records are needed to meet a postponed tax deadline, provided those records are maintained in a covered disaster area. The main home or principal place of business doesn't have to be located in the covered disaster area.

- Any estate or trust that has tax records necessary to meet a postponed tax deadline, provided those records are maintained in a covered disaster area.

- The spouse on a joint return with a taxpayer who is eligible for postponements.

- Any individual, business entity, or sole proprietorship not located in a covered disaster area, but whose records necessary to meet a postponed tax deadline are located in the covered disaster area.

- Any individual visiting the covered disaster area who was killed or injured as a result of the disaster.

- Any other person determined by the IRS to be affected by a federally declared disaster.

Covered disaster area. This is an area of a federally declared disaster in which the IRS has decided to postpone tax deadlines for up to 1 year.

Abatement of interest and penalties. The IRS may abate the interest and penalties on underpaid income tax for the length of any postponement of tax deadlines.

More information. For more information, see *Disaster Area Losses* in Pub. 547.

How To Report Gains and Losses

Use Form 4684 to report a gain or a deductible loss from a casualty or theft. If you have more than one casualty or theft, use a separate Form 4684 to determine your gain or loss for each event. Combine the gains and losses on one Form 4684. Follow the form instructions as to which lines to fill out. In addition, you must use the appropriate schedule to report a gain or loss. The schedule you use depends on whether you have a gain or loss.

If you have a:	Report it on:
Gain	Schedule D (Form 1040)
Loss	Schedule A (Form 1040)

Adjustments to basis. If you have a casualty or theft loss, you must decrease your basis in the property by any insurance or other reimbursement you receive, and by any deductible loss. If you make either of the basis adjustments described above, amounts you spend on repairs to restore your property to its pre-casualty condition increase your adjusted basis. See *Adjusted Basis* in chapter 13 for more information.

Net operating loss (NOL). If your casualty or theft loss deduction causes your deductions for the year to be more than your income for the year, you may have an NOL. Generally, you can use an NOL to lower your tax in a later year. You don't have to be in business to have an NOL from a casualty or theft loss. For more information, see Pub. 536.

27.

Other Itemized Deductions

What's New

 At the time this publication went to print, Congress was considering legislation that would do the following.

1. Provide additional tax relief for those affected by certain 2018 disasters.

2. Extend certain tax benefits that expired at the end of 2017 and that currently can't be claimed on your 2018 tax return.

3. Change certain other tax provisions.

To learn whether this legislation was enacted resulting in changes that affect your 2018 tax return, go to Recent Developments at *IRS.gov/ Pub17*.

No miscellaneous itemized deductions allowed. You can no longer claim any miscellaneous itemized deductions. Miscellaneous itemized deductions are those deductions that would have been subject to the 2% of adjusted gross income limitation. See *Miscellaneous Itemized Deductions*, later.

Fines and penalties. Rules regarding deducting fines and penalties have changed. See *Fines and Penalties*, later.

Standard mileage rate. The 2018 rate for business use of a vehicle is 54.5 cents a mile.

Introduction

This chapter explains that you can no longer claim any miscellaneous itemized deductions, unless you fall into one of the qualified categories of employment claiming a deduction relating to unreimbursed employee expenses. Miscellaneous itemized deductions are those deductions that would have been subject to the 2% of adjusted gross income limitation. You can still claim certain expenses as itemized deductions on Schedule A (Form 1040 or Form 1040NR) or as an adjustment to income on Form 1040. This publication covers the following topics.

- Miscellaneous itemized deductions.

- Expenses you can't deduct.

- Expenses you can deduct.

- How to report your deductions.

 You must keep records to verify your deductions. You should keep receipts, canceled checks, substitute checks, financial account statements, and other documentary evidence. For more information on recordkeeping, see *What Records Should I Keep?* in chapter 1.

Useful Items

You may want to see:

Publication

- ❑ **463** Travel, Gift, and Car Expenses
- ❑ **525** Taxable and Nontaxable Income
- ❑ **529** Miscellaneous Deductions
- ❑ **535** Business Expenses
- ❑ **587** Business Use of Your Home (Including Use by Daycare Providers)
- ❑ **946** How To Depreciate Property

Form (and Instructions)

- ❑ **Schedule A (Form 1040)** Itemized Deductions
- ❑ **2106** Employee Business Expenses

For these and other useful items, go to *IRS.gov/ Forms.*

Miscellaneous Itemized Deductions

You can no longer claim any miscellaneous itemized deductions that are subject to the 2% of adjusted gross income limitation, including unreimbursed employee expenses. However, you may be able to deduct certain unreimbursed employee business expenses if you fall into one of the following categories of employment listed under *Unreimbursed Employee Expenses*, next.

Unreimbursed Employee Expenses

You can no longer claim a deduction for unreimbursed employee expenses unless you fall into one of the following categories of employment.

- Armed Forces reservists.

- Qualified performing artists.

- Fee-basis state or local government officials.

- Employees with impairment-related work expenses.

Categories of Employment

You can deduct unreimbursed employee expenses only if you qualify as an Armed Forces reservist, qualified performing artist, fee-basis state or local government official, and employee with impairment-related work expenses.

Armed Forces reservist (member of a reserve component). You are a member of a reserve component of the Armed Forces of the United States if you are in the Army, Navy, Marine Corps, Air Force, or Coast Guard Reserve; the Army National Guard of the United States; or the Reserve Corps of the Public Health Service.

Qualified performing artist. You are a qualified performing artist if you:

1. Performed services in the performing arts as an employee for at least two employers during the tax year,

2. Received from at least two of the employers' wages of $200 or more per employer,

3. Had allowable business expenses attributable to the performing arts of more than 10% of gross income from the performing arts, and

4. Had adjusted gross income of $16,000 or less before deducting expenses as a performing artist.

Fee-basis state or local government official. You are a qualifying fee-basis official if you are employed by a state or political subdivision of a state and are compensated, in whole or in part, on a fee basis.

Employee with impairment-related work expenses. Impairment-related work expenses are the allowable expenses of an individual with physical or mental disabilities for attendant care at his or her place of employment. They also include other expenses in connection with the place of employment that enable the employee to work. See Pub. 463 for more details.

Allowable unreimbursed employee expenses. If you qualify as an employee in one of the categories mentioned above, you may be able to deduct the following items as unreimbursed employee expenses.

Unreimbursed employee expenses for individuals in these categories of employment are deducted as adjustments to gross income. Qualified employees listed in one of the categories above must complete Form 2106 to take the deduction.

You can deduct only unreimbursed employee expenses that are:

- Paid or incurred during your tax year,

- For carrying on your trade or business of being an employee, and

- Ordinary and necessary.

An expense is ordinary if it's common and accepted in your trade, business, or profession. An expense is necessary if it's appropriate and helpful to your business. An expense doesn't have to be required to be considered necessary.

Educator Expenses

If you were an eligible educator in 2018, you can deduct up to $250 of qualified expenses you paid in 2018 as an adjustment to gross income on Schedule 1 (Form 1040), line 23, rather than as a miscellaneous itemized deduction. If you and your spouse are filing jointly and both of you were eligible educators, the maximum deduction is $500. However, neither spouse can deduct more than $250 of his or her qualified expenses. For additional information, see *Educator Expenses* in Pub. 529.

Expenses You Can't Deduct

Because of the suspension of miscellaneous itemized deductions, there are two categories of expenses you can't deduct: miscellaneous itemized deductions subject to the 2% AGI limitation, and those expenses that are traditionally nondeductible under the Internal Revenue Code. Both categories of deduction are discussed next.

Miscellaneous Deductions Subject to 2% AGI

Unless you fall into one of the qualified categories of employment under *Unreimbursed Employee Expenses*, earlier, miscellaneous itemized deductions that are subject to the 2% of adjusted gross income limitation can no longer be claimed. For expenses not related to unreimbursed employee expenses, you generally can't deduct the following expenses, even if you fall into one of the qualified categories of employment listed earlier.

Appraisal Fees

Appraisal fees you pay to figure a casualty loss or the fair market value of donated property are miscellaneous itemized deductions and can no longer be deducted.

Casualty and Theft Losses

Damaged or stolen property used in performing services as an employee is a miscellaneous deduction and can no longer be deducted. For other casualty and theft losses, see chapter 26.

Clerical Help and Office Rent

Office expenses, such as rent and clerical help, you pay in connection with your investments and collecting taxable income on those investments are miscellaneous itemized deductions and are no longer deductible.

Credit or Debit Card Convenience Fees

The convenience fee charged by the card processor for paying your income tax (including estimated tax payments) by credit or debit card is a miscellaneous itemized deduction and is no longer deductible.

Depreciation on Home Computer

If you use your home computer to produce income (for example, to manage your investments that produce taxable income), the depreciation of the computer for that part of the usage of the computer is a miscellaneous itemized deduction and is no longer deductible.

Excess Deductions of an Estate

An excess deduction resulting from an estate's total deductions being greater than its gross income, in the previous tax year, is a miscellaneous itemized deduction and beneficiaries can no longer deduct it.

Fees To Collect Interest and Dividends

Fees you pay to a broker, bank, trustee, or similar agent to collect your taxable bond interest or dividends on shares of stock are miscellaneous itemized deductions and can no longer be deducted.

Hobby Expenses

A hobby isn't a business because it isn't carried on to make a profit. Hobby expenses are miscellaneous itemized deductions and can no longer be deducted. See *Not-for-Profit Activities* in chapter 1 of Pub. 535.

Indirect Deductions of Pass-Through Entities

Pass-through entities include partnerships, S corporations, and mutual funds that aren't publicly offered. Deductions of pass-through entities are passed through to the partners or shareholders. The partners or shareholders share of passed-through deductions for investment expenses are miscellaneous itemized deductions and can no longer be deducted.

Nonpublicly offered mutual funds. These funds will send you a Form 1099-DIV, Dividends and Distributions, or a substitute form, showing your share of gross income and investment expenses. The investment expenses reported on Form 1099-DIV are a miscellaneous itemized deduction and are no longer deductible.

Investment Fees and Expenses

Investment fees, custodial fees, trust administration fees, and other expenses you paid for managing your investments that produce taxable income are miscellaneous itemized deductions and are no longer deductible.

Legal Expenses

You usually can deduct legal expenses that you incur in attempting to produce or collect taxable income or that you pay in connection with the determination, collection, or refund of any tax.

Legal expenses that you incur in attempting to produce or collect taxable income, or that you pay in connection with the determination, collection, or refund of any tax are miscellaneous itemized deductions and are no longer deductible.

You can deduct expenses of resolving tax issues relating to profit or loss from business (Schedule C or C-EZ), rentals or royalties (Schedule E), or farm income and expenses (Schedule F) on the appropriate schedule. Expenses for resolving nonbusiness tax issues are miscellaneous itemized deductions and are no longer deductible.

Loss on Deposits

For information on whether, and if so, how, you may deduct a loss on your deposit in a qualified financial institution, see *Loss on Deposits* in chapter 26.

Repayments of Income

Generally, repayments of amounts that you included in income in an earlier year is a miscellaneous itemized deduction and can no longer be deducted. If you had to repay more than $3,000 that you included in your income in an earlier year, you may be able to deduct the amount. See *Repayments Under Claim of Right*, later.

Repayments of Social Security Benefits

For information on how to deduct your repayments of certain social security benefits, see *Repayments More Than Gross Benefits* in chapter 11.

Safe Deposit Box Rent

Rent you pay for a safety deposit box you use to store taxable income-producing stocks, bonds, or investment related papers is a miscellaneous itemized deduction and can no longer be deducted. You can't deduct the rent if you use the box only for jewelry, other personal items, or tax-exempt securities.

Service Charges on Dividend Reinvestment Plans

Service charges you pay as a subscriber in a dividend reinvestment plan are a miscellaneous itemized deduction and can no longer be deducted. These service charges include payments for:

- Holding shares acquired through a plan,
- Collecting and reinvesting cash dividends, and
- Keeping individual records and providing detailed statements of accounts.

Tax Preparation Fees

Tax preparation fees on the return for the year in which you pay them are a miscellaneous itemized deduction and can no longer be deducted. These fees include the cost of tax preparation software programs and tax publications. They also include any fee you paid for electronic filing of your return.

Trustee's Administrative Fees for IRA

Trustee's administrative fees that are billed separately and paid by you in connection with your IRA are a miscellaneous itemized deduction and can no longer be deducted. For more information about IRAs, see chapter 17.

Nondeductible Expenses

In addition to the miscellaneous itemized deductions discussed earlier, you can't deduct the following expenses.

List of Nondeductible Expenses

- Adoption expenses.
- Broker's commissions.
- Burial or funeral expenses, including the cost of a cemetery lot.

- Campaign expenses.
- Capital expenses.
- Check-writing fees.
- Club dues.
- Commuting expenses.
- Fees and licenses, such as car licenses, marriage licenses, and dog tags.
- Fines or penalties.
- Health spa expenses.
- Hobby losses, but see *Hobby Expenses*, earlier.
- Home repairs, insurance, and rent.
- Home security system.
- Illegal bribes and kickbacks. See *Bribes and kickbacks* in chapter 11 of Pub. 535.
- Investment-related seminars.
- Life insurance premiums paid by the insured.
- Lobbying expenses.
- Losses from the sale of your home, furniture, personal car, etc.
- Lost or misplaced cash or property.
- Lunches with co-workers.
- Meals while working late.
- Medical expenses as business expenses other than medical examinations required by your employer.
- Personal disability insurance premiums.
- Personal legal expenses.
- Personal, living, or family expenses.
- Political contributions.
- Professional accreditation fees.
- Professional reputation, expenses to improve.
- Relief fund contributions.
- Residential telephone line.
- Stockholders' meeting, expenses of attending.
- Tax-exempt income, expenses of earning or collecting.
- The value of wages never received or lost vacation time.
- Travel expenses for another individual.
- Voluntary unemployment benefit fund contributions.
- Wristwatches.

Adoption Expenses

You can't deduct the expenses of adopting a child, but you may be able to take a credit for those expenses. See chapter 37.

Campaign Expenses

You can't deduct campaign expenses of a candidate for any office, even if the candidate is running for reelection to the office. These include qualification and registration fees for primary elections.

Legal fees. You can't deduct legal fees paid to defend charges that arise from participation in a political campaign.

Check-Writing Fees on Personal Account

If you have a personal checking account, you can't deduct fees charged by the bank for the privilege of writing checks, even if the account pays interest.

Club Dues

Generally, you can't deduct the cost of membership in any club organized for business, pleasure, recreation, or other social purpose. This includes business, social, athletic, luncheon, sporting, airline, hotel, golf, and country clubs.

You can't deduct dues paid to an organization if one of its main purposes is to:

- Conduct entertainment activities for members or their guests, or
- Provide members or their guests with access to entertainment facilities.

Dues paid to airline, hotel, and luncheon clubs aren't deductible.

Commuting Expenses

You can't deduct commuting expenses (the cost of transportation between your home and your main or regular place of work). If you haul tools, instruments, or other items in your car to and from work, you can deduct only the additional cost of hauling the items such as the rent on a trailer to carry the items.

Fines and Penalties

Generally, no deduction is allowed for fines and penalties paid to a government or specified nongovernmental entity for the violation of any law except in the following situations.

- Amounts that constitute restitution.
- Amounts paid to come into compliance with the law.
- Amounts paid or incurred as the result of certain court orders in which no government or specified nongovernmental agency is a party.
- Amounts paid or incurred for taxes due.

Nondeductible amounts include an amount paid in settlement of your actual or potential liability for a fine or penalty (civil or criminal). Fines or penalties include amounts paid such as parking tickets, tax penalties, and penalties deducted from teachers' paychecks after an illegal strike.

Beginning on December 22, 2017, no deduction is allowed for the restitution amount or amount paid to come into compliance with the law unless the amounts are specifically identified in the settlement agreement or court order. Also, any amount paid or incurred as reimbursement to the government for the costs of any investigation or litigation are not eligible for the exceptions and are nondeductible.

Health Spa Expenses

You can't deduct health spa expenses, even if there is a job requirement to stay in excellent physical condition, such as might be required of a law enforcement officer.

Home Security System

You can't deduct the cost of a home security system as a miscellaneous deduction. However, you may be able to claim a deduction for a home security system as a business expense if you have a home office. See *Security system* under *Figuring the Deduction* in Pub. 587.

Investment-Related Seminars

You can't deduct any expenses for attending a convention, seminar, or similar meeting for investment purposes.

Life Insurance Premiums

You can't deduct premiums you pay on your life insurance. You may be able to deduct, as alimony, premiums you pay on life insurance policies assigned to your former spouse. See chapter 18 for information on alimony.

Lobbying Expenses

You generally can't deduct amounts paid or incurred for lobbying expenses. These include expenses to:

- Influence legislation;
- Participate or intervene in any political campaign for, or against, any candidate for public office;
- Attempt to influence the general public, or segments of the public, about elections, legislative matters, or referendums; or
- Communicate directly with covered executive branch officials in any attempt to influence the official actions or positions of those officials.

Lobbying expenses also include any amounts paid or incurred for research, preparation, planning, or coordination of any of these activities.

Dues used for lobbying. If a tax-exempt organization notifies you that part of the dues or other amounts you pay to the organization are used to pay nondeductible lobbying expenses, you can't deduct that part. See *Lobbying Expenses* in Pub. 529 for information on exceptions.

Lost or Mislaid Cash or Property

You can't deduct a loss based on the mere disappearance of money or property. However, an accidental loss or disappearance of property can qualify as a casualty if it results from an identifiable event that is sudden, unexpected, or unusual. See chapter 26.

Lunches With Co-workers

You can't deduct the expenses of lunches with co-workers, except while traveling away from home on business. See chapter 20 for information on deductible expenses while traveling away from home.

Meals While Working Late

You can't deduct the cost of meals while working late. However, you may be able to claim a deduction if the cost of meals is a deductible entertainment expense, or if you're traveling away from home. See chapter 20 for information on deductible entertainment expenses and expenses while traveling away from home.

Personal Legal Expenses

You can't deduct personal legal expenses such as those for the following.

- Custody of children.
- Breach of promise to marry suit.
- Civil or criminal charges resulting from a personal relationship.
- Damages for personal injury, except for certain unlawful discrimination and whistle-blower claims.
- Preparation of a title (or defense or perfection of a title).
- Preparation of a will.
- Property claims or property settlement in a divorce.

You can't deduct these expenses even if a result of the legal proceeding is the loss of income-producing property.

Political Contributions

You can't deduct contributions made to a political candidate, a campaign committee, or a newsletter fund. Advertisements in convention bulletins and admissions to dinners or programs that benefit a political party or political candidate aren't deductible.

Professional Accreditation Fees

You can't deduct professional accreditation fees such as the following.

- Accounting certificate fees paid for the initial right to practice accounting.
- Bar exam fees and incidental expenses in securing initial admission to the bar.
- Medical and dental license fees paid to get initial licensing.

Professional Reputation

You can't deduct expenses of radio and TV appearances to increase your personal prestige or establish your professional reputation.

Relief Fund Contributions

You can't deduct contributions paid to a private plan that pays benefits to any covered employee who can't work because of any injury or illness not related to the job.

Residential Telephone Service

You can't deduct any charge (including taxes) for basic local telephone service for the first telephone line to your residence, even if it's used in a trade or business.

Stockholders' Meetings

You can't deduct transportation and other expenses you pay to attend stockholders' meetings of companies in which you own stock but have no other interest. You can't deduct these expenses even if you're attending the meeting to get information that would be useful in making further investments.

Tax-Exempt Income Expenses

You can't deduct expenses to produce tax-exempt income. You can't deduct interest on a debt incurred or continued to buy or carry tax-exempt securities.

If you have expenses to produce both taxable and tax-exempt income, but you can't identify the expenses that produce each type of income, you must divide the expenses based on the amount of each type of income to determine the amount that you can deduct.

Travel Expenses for Another Individual

You generally can't deduct travel expenses you pay or incur for a spouse, dependent, or other individual who accompanies you (or your employee) on business or personal travel unless the spouse, dependent, or other individual is an employee of the taxpayer, the travel is for a bona fide business purpose, and such expenses would otherwise be deductible by the spouse, dependent, or other individual. See chapter 20 for more information on deductible travel expenses.

Voluntary Unemployment Benefit Fund Contributions

You can't deduct voluntary unemployment benefit fund contributions you make to a union fund or a private fund. However, you can deduct contributions as taxes if state law requires you to make them to a state unemployment fund that covers you for the loss of wages from unemployment caused by business conditions.

Wristwatches

You can't deduct the cost of a wristwatch, even if there is a job requirement that you know the correct time to properly perform your duties.

Expenses You Can Deduct

You can deduct the items listed below as itemized deductions. Report these items on Schedule A (Form 1040), line 16, or Schedule A (Form 1040NR), line 7.

List of Deductions

Each of the following items is discussed in detail after the list (except where indicated).

- Amortizable premium on taxable bonds.
- Casualty and theft losses from income-producing property.
- Federal estate tax on income in respect of a decedent.
- Gambling losses up to the amount of gambling winnings.
- Impairment-related work expenses of persons with disabilities.
- Losses from Ponzi-type investment schemes. See *Losses from Ponzi-type investment schemes* under *Theft* in chapter 26.
- Repayments of more than $3,000 under a claim of right.
- Unlawful discrimination claims.
- Unrecovered investment in an annuity.

Amortizable Premium on Taxable Bonds

In general, if the amount you pay for a bond is greater than its stated principal amount, the excess is bond premium. You can elect to amortize the premium on taxable bonds. The amortization of the premium is generally an offset to interest income on the bond rather than a separate deduction item.

Part of the premium on some bonds may be an itemized deduction on Schedule A (Form 1040). For more information, see *Amortizable Premium on Taxable Bonds* in Pub. 529, and *Bond Premium Amortization* in chapter 3 of Pub. 550, Investment Income and Expenses.

Casualty and Theft Losses of Income-Producing Property

You can deduct a casualty or theft loss as an itemized deduction on Schedule A (Form 1040), line 16, if the damaged or stolen property was income-producing property (property held for investment, such as stocks, notes, bonds, gold, silver, vacant lots, and works of art). First, report the loss in Form 4684, Section B. You may also have to include the loss on Form 4797, if you're otherwise required to file that form. To figure your deduction, add all casualty or theft losses from this type of property included on Form 4684, lines 32 and 38b, or Form 4797, line 18a. For more information on casualty and theft losses, see chapter 26.

Federal Estate Tax on Income in Respect of a Decedent

You can deduct the federal estate tax attributable to income in respect of a decedent that you as a beneficiary include in your gross income. Income in respect of the decedent is gross income that the decedent would have received had death not occurred and that wasn't properly includible in the decedent's final income tax return. See Pub. 559 for more information.

Gambling Losses up to the Amount of Gambling Winnings

You must report the full amount of your gambling winnings for the year on Schedule 1 (Form 1040), line 21. You deduct your gambling losses for the year on Schedule A (Form 1040), line 16. You can't deduct gambling losses that are more than your winnings.

 You can't reduce your gambling winnings by your gambling losses and report the difference. You must report the full amount of your winnings as income and claim your losses (up to the amount of winnings) as an itemized deduction. Therefore, your records should show your winnings separately from your losses.

 Diary of winnings and losses. You must keep an accurate diary or similar record of your losses and winnings.

Your diary should contain at least the following information.

- The date and type of your specific wager or wagering activity.
- The name and address or location of the gambling establishment.
- The names of other persons present with you at the gambling establishment.
- The amount(s) you won or lost.

See Pub. 529 for more information.

Impairment-Related Work Expenses

If you have a physical or mental disability that limits your being employed, or substantially limits one or more of your major life activities, such as performing manual tasks, walking, speaking, breathing, learning, and working, you can deduct your impairment-related work expenses.

Impairment-related work expenses are ordinary and necessary business expenses for attendant care services at your place of work and for other expenses in connection with your place of work that are necessary for you to be able to work.

Self-employed. If you're self-employed, enter your impairment-related work expenses on the appropriate form (Schedule C, C-EZ, E, or F) used to report your business income and expenses.

Repayments Under Claim of Right

If you had to repay more than $3,000 that you included in your income in an earlier year because at the time you thought you had an unrestricted right to it, you may be able to deduct the amount you repaid or take a credit against your tax. See *Repayments* in chapter 12 for more information.

Unlawful Discrimination Claims

You may be able to deduct, as an adjustment to income on Schedule 1 (Form 1040), line 36, or Form 1040NR, line 35, attorney fees and court costs for actions settled or decided after October 22, 2004, involving a claim of unlawful discrimination, a claim against the U.S. Government, or a claim made under section 1862(b)(3)(A) of the Social Security Act. However, the amount you can deduct on Schedule 1 (Form 1040), line 36, or Form 1040NR, line 35, is limited to the amount of the judgment or settlement you are including in income for the tax year. See Pub. 525 for more information.

Unrecovered Investment in Annuity

A retiree who contributed to the cost of an annuity can exclude from income a part of each payment received as a tax-free return of the retiree's investment. If the retiree dies before the entire investment is recovered tax free, any unrecovered investment can be deducted on the retiree's final income tax return. See chapter 10 for more information about the tax treatment of pensions and annuities.

1. Provide additional tax relief for those affected by certain 2018 disasters.

2. Extend certain tax benefits that expired at the end of 2017 and that currently can't be claimed on your 2018 tax return.

3. Change certain other tax provisions.

To learn whether this legislation was enacted resulting in changes that affect your 2018 tax return, go to Recent Developments at *IRS.gov/Pub17.*

For tax years beginning after 2017, individual taxpayers may be entitled to a deduction of up to 20% of their qualified business income (QBI) from a trade or business, including income from a pass-through entity, but not from a C corporation, plus 20% of qualified real estate investment trust (REIT) dividends and qualified publicly traded partnership (PTP) income. The deduction is subject to multiple limitations depending on the taxpayer's taxable income, and may include the type of trade or business, the amount of W-2 wages paid by the trade or business, and the unadjusted basis immediately after acquisition (UBIA) of qualified property held by the trade or business. The deduction can be taken in addition to the standard or itemized deductions. For more information, see the instructions for line 9 of Form 1040; and Pub. 535, Business Expenses.

 For the complete guidance regarding this deduction, see chapter 12 of Pub. 535. For more information, see section 199A, Treasury Regulations sections 1.199A-1 through 1.199A-6, Rev. Proc. 2019-11, and Notice 2019-07.

28.

Qualified Business Income Deduction

What's New

 At the time this publication went to print, Congress was considering legislation that would do the following.

Part Six.

Figuring Your Taxes, and Refundable and Nonrefundable Credits

The nine chapters in this part explain how to figure your tax and how to figure the tax of certain children who have more than $2,100 of unearned income. They also discuss tax credits that, unlike deductions, are subtracted directly from your tax and reduce your tax dollar for dollar. *Chapter 35* discusses the earned income credit. *Chapter 37* discusses a wide variety of other credits, such as the adoption credit.

The new Form 1040 schedules that are discussed in these chapters are:

- *Schedule 1, Additional Income and Adjustments to Income.*
- *Schedule 2, Tax.*
- *Schedule 3, Nonrefundable Credits.*
- *Schedule 4, Other Taxes.*
- *Schedule 5, Other Payments and Refundable Credits.*
- *Schedule 6, Foreign Address and Third Party Designee.*

29.

How To Figure Your Tax

What's New

 At the time this publication went to print, Congress was considering legislation that would do the following.

1. Provide additional tax relief for those affected by certain 2018 disasters.

2. Extend certain tax benefits that expired at the end of 2017 and that currently can't be claimed on your 2018 tax return.

3. Change certain other tax provisions.

To learn whether this legislation was enacted resulting in changes that affect your 2018 tax return, go to Recent Developments at IRS.gov/ Pub17.

Introduction

After you have figured your income and deductions as explained in *Parts One* through *Five*, your next step is to figure your tax. This chapter discusses:

- The general steps you take to figure your tax,

- An additional tax you may have to pay called the alternative minimum tax (AMT), and

- The conditions you must meet if you want the IRS to figure your tax.

Figuring Your Tax

Your income tax is based on your taxable income. After you figure your income tax and AMT, if any, subtract your tax credits and add any other taxes you may owe. The result is your total tax. Compare your total tax with your total payments to determine whether you are entitled to a refund or must make a payment.

This section provides a general outline of how to figure your tax. You can find step-by-step directions in the Instructions for Form 1040.

Tax. Most taxpayers use either the Tax Table or the Tax Computation Worksheet to figure their income tax. However, there are special methods if your income includes any of the following items.

- A net capital gain. (See chapter 16.)

- Qualified dividends taxed at the same rates as a net capital gain. (See chapters 8 and 16.)

- Lump-sum distributions. (See chapter 10.)

- Farming or fishing income. (See Schedule J (Form 1040), Income Averaging for Farmers and Fishermen.)

- Tax for certain children who have unearned income. (See chapter 30.)

- Parent's election to report child's interest and dividends. (See chapter 30.)

- Foreign earned income exclusion or the housing exclusion. (See Form 2555, Foreign Earned Income, or Form 2555-EZ, Foreign Earned Income Exclusion, and the Foreign Earned Income Tax Worksheet in the Form 1040 instructions.)

Credits. After you figure your income tax and any AMT (discussed later), determine if you are eligible for any tax credits. Eligibility information for these tax credits is discussed in chapters 31 through 37 and your form instructions. The following table lists some of the credits you may be able to subtract from your tax and shows where you can find more information on each credit.

CREDITS	
For information on:	**See chapter:**
Adoption	37
Alternative motor vehicle	37
Child and dependent care	31
Child tax	33
Credit to holders of tax credit bonds	37
Education	34
Elderly or disabled	32
Foreign tax	37
Mortgage interest	37
Plug-in electric drive motor credit	37
Premium tax credit	36
Prior year minimum tax	37
Residential energy	37
Retirement savings contributions	37

Some credits (such as the earned income credit) aren't listed because they are treated as payments. See *Payments*, later.

There are other credits that aren't discussed in this publication. These include the following credits.

- General business credit, which is made up of several separate business-related credits. These generally are reported on Form 3800, General Business Credit, and are discussed in chapter 4 of Pub. 334, Tax Guide for Small Business.

- Renewable electricity, refined coal, and Indian coal production credit for electricity and refined coal produced at facilities placed in service after October 22, 2004 (after October 2, 2008, for electricity produced from marine and hydrokinetic renewables). See the Instructions for Form 8835.

At the time this publication was prepared for printing, Congress was considering legislation that would extend the Indian coal production credit, which expired at the end of 2017. If extended, the Indian coal production credit may be claimed for 2018. To see if the legislation was enacted, go to Recent Developments at IRS.gov/Pub17.

- Work opportunity credit. See Form 5884.
- Credit for employer social security and Medicare taxes paid on certain employee tips. See Form 8846.

Other taxes. After you subtract your tax credits, determine whether there are any other taxes you must pay. This chapter doesn't explain these other taxes. You can find that information in other chapters of this publication and your form instructions. See the following table for other taxes you may need to add to your income tax.

OTHER TAXES

For information on:	See chapter:
Additional taxes on qualified retirement plans and IRAs	10, 17
Household employment taxes	31
Recapture of an education credit	34
Social security and Medicare tax on wages	5
Social security and Medicare tax on tips	6
Uncollected social security and Medicare tax on tips	6

You also may have to pay AMT or make a shared responsibility payment (both are discussed later in this chapter).

There are other taxes that aren't discussed in this publication. These include the following items.

1. *Self-employment tax.* You must figure this tax if either of the following applies to you (or your spouse if you file a joint return).

    a. Your net earnings from self-employment from other than church employee income were $400 or more. The term "net earnings from self-employment" may include certain nonemployee compensation and other amounts reported to you on Form 1099-MISC, Miscellaneous Income. If you received a Form 1099-MISC, see the *Instructions for Recipient* on the back. Also see the Instructions for Schedule SE (Form 1040), Self-Employment Tax and Pub. 334.

    b. You had church employee income of $108.28 or more.

2. *Additional Medicare Tax.* You may be subject to a 0.9% Additional Medicare Tax that applies to Medicare wages, Railroad Retirement Act compensation, and self-employment income over a threshold based on your filing status. For more information, see the instructions for Schedule 4 (Form 1040), line 62 and Form 8959.

3. *Net Investment Income Tax (NIIT).* You may be subject to NIIT. NIIT is a 3.8% tax on the lesser of net investment income or the excess of your modified adjusted gross income over a threshold amount. For more information, see the instructions for Schedule 4 (Form 1040), line 62 and Form 8960.

4. *Recapture taxes.* You may have to pay these taxes if you previously claimed an investment credit, a low-income housing credit, a new markets credit, a qualified plug-in electric drive motor vehicle credit, an alternative motor vehicle credit, a credit for employer-provided child care facilities, an Indian employment credit, or other credits listed in the instructions for Schedule 4 (Form 1040), line 62. For more information, see the instructions for Schedule 4 (Form 1040), line 62.

5. *Section 72(m)(5) excess benefits tax.* If you are (or were) a 5% owner of a business and you received a distribution that exceeds the benefits provided for you under the qualified pension or annuity plan formula, you may have to pay this additional tax. See *Tax on Excess Benefits* in chapter 4 of Pub. 560, Retirement Plans for Small Business.

6. *Uncollected social security and Medicare tax on group-term life insurance.* If your former employer provides you with more than $50,000 of group-term life insurance coverage, you must pay the employee part of social security and Medicare taxes on those premiums. The amount should be shown in box 12 of your Form W-2 with codes M and N.

7. *Tax on golden parachute payments.* This tax applies if you received an "excess parachute payment" (EPP) due to a change in a corporation's ownership or control. The amount should be shown in box 12 of your Form W-2 with code K. See the instructions for Schedule 4 (Form 1040), line 62.

8. *Tax on accumulation distribution of trusts.* This applies if you are the beneficiary of a trust that accumulated its income instead of distributing it currently. See Form 4970 and its instructions.

9. *Additional tax on HSA, MSA, or ABLE account.* If amounts contributed to, or distributed from, your health savings account, medical savings account, or ABLE account don't meet the rules for these accounts, you may have to pay additional taxes. See Pub. 969, Health Savings Accounts and Other Tax-Favored Health Plans; Form 8853, Archer MSAs and Long-Term Care Insurance Contracts; Form 8889, Health Savings Accounts (HSAs); and Form 5329, Additional Taxes on Qualified Plans (Including IRAs) and Other Tax-Favored Accounts.

10. *Additional tax on Coverdell ESAs.* This applies if amounts contributed to, or distributed from, your Coverdell ESA don't meet the rules for these accounts. See Pub. 970, Tax Benefits for Education, and Form 5329.

11. *Additional tax on qualified tuition programs.* This applies to amounts distributed from qualified tuition programs that don't meet the rules for these accounts. See Pub. 970 and Form 5329.

12. *Excise tax on insider stock compensation from an expatriated corporation.* You may owe a 15% excise tax on the value of nonstatutory stock options and certain other stock-based compensation held by you or a member of your family from an expatriated corporation or its expanded affiliated group in which you were an officer, director, or more-than-10% owner. For more information, see the instructions for Schedule 4 (Form 1040), line 62.

13. *Additional tax on income you received from a nonqualified deferred compensation plan that fails to meet certain requirements.* This income should be shown in Form W-2, box 12, with code Z, or in Form 1099-MISC, box 15b. For more information, see the instructions for Schedule 4 (Form 1040), line 62.

14. *Interest on the tax due on installment income from the sale of certain residential lots and timeshares.* For more information, see the instructions for Schedule 4 (Form 1040), line 62.

15. *Interest on the deferred tax on gain from certain installment sales with a sales price over $150,000.* For more information, see the instructions for Schedule 4 (Form 1040), line 62.

16. *Repayment of first-time homebuyer credit.* For more information, see Form 5405, Repayment of the First-Time Homebuyer Credit, and its instructions. Also see the instructions for Schedule 4 (Form 1040), line 60b.

Payments. After you determine your total tax, figure the total payments you have already made for the year. Include credits that are treated as payments. This chapter doesn't explain these payments and credits. You can find that information in other chapters of this publication and your form instructions. See the following table for amounts you can include in your total payments.

PAYMENTS

For information on:	See chapter:
American opportunity credit	34
Child tax credit (additional)	33
Earned income credit	35
Estimated tax paid	4
Excess social security and RRTA tax withheld	37
Federal income tax withheld	4
Health coverage tax credit	37
Net premium tax credit	36
Credit for tax on undistributed capital gain	37
Tax paid with extension	1

Another credit that is treated as a payment is the credit for federal excise tax paid on fuels. This credit is for persons who have a nontaxable use of certain fuels, such as diesel fuel and kerosene. It is claimed on Schedule 5 (Form 1040), line 73. See Form 4136, Credit for Federal Tax Paid on Fuels.

Refund or balance due. To determine whether you are entitled to a refund or whether you must make a payment, compare your total payments with your total tax. If you are entitled to a refund, see your form instructions for information on having it directly deposited into one or more of your accounts (including a traditional IRA, Roth IRA, or a SEP-IRA), or to purchase U.S. savings bonds instead of receiving a paper check.

Alternative Minimum Tax (AMT)

This section briefly discusses an additional tax you may have to pay.

The tax law gives special treatment to some kinds of income and allows special deductions and credits for some kinds of expenses. Taxpayers who benefit from this special treatment may have to pay at least a minimum amount of tax through an additional tax called AMT.

You may have to pay the AMT if your taxable income for regular tax purposes, combined with certain adjustments and tax preference items, is more than a certain amount. See Form 6251, Alternative Minimum Tax—Individuals.

Adjustments and tax preference items. The more common adjustments and tax preference items include:

- Addition of the standard deduction (if claimed);
- Addition of itemized deductions claimed for state and local taxes, certain interest, most miscellaneous deductions, and part of medical expenses;
- Subtraction of any refund of state and local taxes included in gross income;
- Changes to accelerated depreciation of certain property;
- Difference between gain or loss on the sale of property reported for regular tax purposes and AMT purposes;
- Addition of certain income from incentive stock options;
- Change in certain passive activity loss deductions;
- Addition of certain depletion that is more than the adjusted basis of the property;
- Addition of part of the deduction for certain intangible drilling costs; and
- Addition of tax-exempt interest on certain private activity bonds.

More information. For more information about the AMT, see the Instructions for Form 6251.

Tax Figured by IRS

If you file by the due date of your return (not counting extensions) – April 15, 2019, for most people – you can have the IRS figure your tax for you on Form 1040.

If the IRS figures your tax and you paid too much, you will receive a refund. If you didn't pay enough, you will receive a bill for the balance. To avoid interest or the penalty for late payment, you must pay the bill within 30 days of the date of the bill or by the due date for your return, whichever is later.

The IRS also can figure the credit for the elderly or the disabled and the earned income credit for you.

When the IRS cannot figure your tax. The IRS can't figure your tax for you if any of the following apply.

1. You want your refund directly deposited into your checking or savings account.

2. You want any part of your refund applied to your 2019 estimated tax.

3. You had income for the year from sources other than wages, salaries, tips, interest, dividends, taxable social security benefits, unemployment compensation, IRA distributions, pensions, and annuities.

4. Your taxable income is $100,000 or more.

5. You itemize deductions.

6. You file any of the following forms.

   a. Form 2555, Foreign Earned Income.

   b. Form 2555-EZ, Foreign Earned Income Exclusion.

   c. Form 4137, Social Security and Medicare Tax on Unreported Tip Income.

   d. Form 4970, Tax on Accumulation Distribution of Trusts.

   e. Form 4972, Tax on Lump-Sum Distributions.

   f. Form 6198, At-Risk Limitations.

   g. Form 6251, Alternative Minimum Tax—Individuals.

   h. Form 8606, Nondeductible IRAs.

   i. Form 8615, Tax for Certain Children Who Have Unearned Income.

   j. Form 8814, Parents' Election To Report Child's Interest and Dividends.

   k. Form 8839, Qualified Adoption Expenses.

   l. Form 8853, Archer MSAs and Long-Term Care Insurance Contracts.

   m. Form 8889, Health Savings Accounts (HSAs).

   n. Form 8919, Uncollected Social Security and Medicare Tax on Wages.

7. You must make a shared responsibility payment.

Shared responsibility payment. You must make a shared responsibility payment with your tax return unless you and your spouse (if filing jointly), and anyone else you do or can claim as a dependent, had minimum essential coverage or a coverage exemption for each month during 2018. Use the Shared Responsibility Payment Worksheet in the Instructions for Form 8965 to figure your shared responsibility payment.

Filing the Return

After you complete the line entries for the tax form you are filing, fill in your name and address. Enter your social security number in the space provided. If you are married, enter the social security numbers of you and your spouse even if you file separately. Sign and date your return and enter your occupation(s). If you are filing a joint return, both you and your spouse must sign it. Enter your daytime phone number in the space provided. This may help speed the processing of your return if we have a question that can be answered over the phone. If you are filing a joint return, you may enter either your or your spouse's daytime phone number.

If you want to allow a friend, family member, or any other person you choose (other than your paid preparer) to discuss your 2018 tax return with the IRS, check the box in the "Third party designee" section of Schedule 6 (Form 1040). Also enter the designee's name, phone number, and any five digits the designee chooses as his or her personal identification number (PIN). If you check the "Yes" box, you, and your spouse if filing a joint return, are authorizing the IRS to call the designee to answer any questions that may arise during the processing of your return.

 If you want your paid preparer to be your third party designee, check the "3rd Party Designee" box on page 1 of Form 1040. Do not complete Schedule 6.

Fill in and attach any schedules and forms asked for on the lines you completed to your paper return. Attach a copy of each of your Forms W-2 to your paper return. Also attach to your paper return any Form 1099-R you received that has withholding tax in box 4.

Mail your return to the Internal Revenue Service Center for the area where you live. A list of Service Center addresses is in the instructions for your tax return.

Form 1040 Line Entries

If you want the IRS to figure your tax. Read lines 1 through 10 on the Form 1040 and Schedule 1 (Form 1040), if applicable. Fill in the lines that apply to you and attach Schedule 1 (Form 1040), if applicable. Don't complete line 11 on the Form 1040.

If you are filing a joint return, use the space on the dotted line next to the words "Taxable Income" on the second page of your return to separately show your taxable income and your spouse's taxable income.

Read lines 12 through 18 on the Form 1040 and Schedules 2 through 5 (Form 1040), if applicable. Fill in the lines that apply to you and attach Schedules 2 through 5 (Form 1040), if applicable. Don't fill in lines 13, 15, 18, or 19 through 23 on the Form 1040. Don't fill in lines 45 or 47 of Schedule 2 (Form 1040). Don't fill in line 61 of Schedule 4 (Form 1040). Also, don't complete line 54, box "c," of Schedule 3 (Form 1040) if you are completing Schedule R (Form 1040), or line 17a on the Form 1040 if you want the IRS to figure the credits shown on those lines.

 The IRS can't figure your tax for you if you must include a shared responsibility payment on Schedule 4 (Form 1040), line 61. See the Instructions for Form 1040 and Form 8965.

Payments. Enter any federal income tax withheld that is shown on Form W-2, box 2, or Form 1099, box 4, on Form 1040, line 16. Enter any estimated tax payments you made on Schedule 5 (Form 1040), line 66, and attach the schedule to your return.

Credit for child and dependent care expenses. If you can take this credit, as discussed in chapter 31, complete Form 2441 and attach it to your paper return. Enter the amount of the credit on Schedule 3 (Form 1040), line 49. The IRS will not figure this credit.

Net premium tax credit. If you take this credit, as discussed in chapter 36, complete Form 8962 and attach it to your return. Enter the amount of the credit on Schedule 5 (Form 1040), line 70. The IRS will not figure this credit.

Credit for the elderly or the disabled. If you can take this credit, as discussed in chapter 32, the IRS can figure it for you. Enter "CFE" on the line next to Schedule 3 (Form 1040), line 54, box "c" and attach Schedule R (Form 1040) to your paper return. On Schedule R (Form 1040), check the box in Part I for your filing status and age. Complete Part II and Part III, lines 11 and 13, if they apply.

Earned income credit. If you can take this credit, as discussed in chapter 35, the IRS can figure it for you. Enter "EIC" on the space to the left of line 17 on Form 1040. If you elect to use your nontaxable combat pay in figuring your EIC, enter "NCP" and the amount in the space to the left of line 17, Form 1040.

If you have a qualifying child, you must fill in Schedule EIC (Form 1040), Earned Income Credit, and attach it to your paper return. If you don't provide the child's social security number on Schedule EIC, line 2, the credit will be reduced or disallowed unless the child was born and died in 2018.

If your credit for any year after 1996 was reduced or disallowed by the IRS, you also may have to file Form 8862 with your return. For details, see the Form 1040 instructions.

30.

Tax on Unearned Income of Certain Children

What's New

At the time this publication went to print, Congress was considering legislation that would do the following.

1. *Provide additional tax relief for those affected by certain 2018 disasters.*

2. *Extend certain tax benefits that expired at the end of 2017 and that currently can't be claimed on your 2018 tax return.*

3. *Change certain other tax provisions.*

To learn whether this legislation was enacted resulting in changes that affect your 2018 tax return, go to Recent Developments *at* IRS.gov/ Pub17.

Tax for certain dependent children. The tax for certain dependent children under age 18 (and certain older children) with $2,100 of unearned income is no longer taxed at the parent's tax rate. This change in figuring the tax for certain dependent children is in effect for tax years 2018 through 2025 as a result of the Tax Cuts and Jobs Act of 2017. See the Form 8615 instructions for more information.

Reminders

Social security number (SSN). Dependents who are required to file a tax return must have an SSN. To apply for an SSN, file Form SS-5 with the Social Security Administration. For more information, see chapter 1 or go to SSA.gov.

Individual taxpayer identification number (ITIN). The IRS will issue an ITIN to a nonresident or resident alien who doesn't have and isn't eligible to get an SSN. To apply for an ITIN, file Form W-7, Application for IRS Individual Taxpayer Identification Number, with the IRS. It takes 7–11 weeks to get an ITIN. The ITIN is entered wherever an SSN is requested on a tax return. If you are a nonresident alien applying for an ITIN to file a tax return, you generally must attach your original, completed return to Form W-7 to get an ITIN. See the Form W-7 instructions for more information.

An ITIN is for tax use only. It doesn't entitle you to social security benefits or change your employment or immigration status under U.S. law. If you were assigned an ITIN before January 1, 2013, or if you have an ITIN that you haven't included on a tax return in the last 3 consecutive years, you may need to renew it. For more information, see chapter 1 and the Instructions for Form W-7.

Introduction

This chapter discusses the following two rules that may affect the tax on unearned income of certain children.

1. If the child's interest and dividend income (including capital gain distributions) total less than $10,500, the child's parent may be able to choose to include that income on the parent's return rather than file a return for the child. (See *Parent's Election To Report Child's Interest and Dividends,* later.)

2. If the child's interest, dividends, and other unearned income total more than $2,100, the child's income is taxed at special tax rates. (See *Tax for Certain Children Who Have Unearned Income,* later.)

For these rules, the term "child" includes a legally adopted child and a stepchild. These rules apply whether or not the child is a dependent. These rules don't apply if neither of the child's parents were living at the end of the year.

Useful Items

You may want to see:

Publication

❏ **929** Tax Rules for Children and Dependents

Form (and Instructions)

❏ **8615** Tax for Certain Children Who Have Unearned Income

❏ **8814** Parents' Election To Report Child's Interest and Dividends

For these and other useful items, go to IRS.gov/ Forms.

Which Parent's Return To Use

If a child's parents are married to each other and file a joint return, use the joint return when electing to report the child's unearned interest and dividend income on their return. Certain information from that joint return is also needed, as explained later under *Tax for Certain Children Who Have Unearned Income.*

Parents Who Don't File a Joint Return

For parents who don't file a joint return, the following discussions explain which parent's tax return must be used to figure the tax.

Only the parent whose tax return is used can make the election described under *Parent's Election To Report Child's Interest and Dividends,* later.

Parents are married. If the child's parents file separate returns, use the return of the parent with the greater taxable income.

Parents not living together. If the child's parents are married to each other but not living together, and the parent with whom the child lives (the custodial parent) is considered unmarried, use the return of the custodial parent. If the custodial parent isn't considered unmarried, use the return of the parent with the greater taxable income.

For an explanation of when a married person living apart from his or her spouse is considered unmarried, see *Head of Household* in chapter 2.

Parents are divorced. If the child's parents are divorced or legally separated, and the parent who had custody of the child for the greater part of the year (the custodial parent) hasn't remarried, use the return of the custodial parent.

Custodial parent remarried. If the custodial parent has remarried, the stepparent (rather than the noncustodial parent) is treated as the child's other parent. Therefore, if the custodial parent and the stepparent file a joint return, use that joint return. Don't use the return of the non-custodial parent.

If the custodial parent and the stepparent are married, but file separate returns, use the return of the one with the greater taxable income. If the custodial parent and the stepparent are married but not living together, the earlier discussion under *Parents not living together* applies.

Parents never married. If a child's parents have never been married to each other, but lived together all year, use the return of the parent with the greater taxable income. If the parents didn't live together all year, the rules explained earlier under *Parents are divorced* apply.

Widowed parent remarried. If a widow or widower remarries, the new spouse is treated as the child's other parent. The rules explained earlier under *Custodial parent remarried* apply.

Parent's Election To Report Child's Interest and Dividends

You may be able to elect to include your child's interest and dividend income (including capital gain distributions) on your tax return. If you do, your child won't have to file a return.

You can make this election only if all the following conditions are met.

- Your child was under age 19 (or under age 24 if a full-time student) at the end of the year.

- Your child had income only from interest and dividends (including capital gain distributions and Alaska Permanent Fund dividends).

- The child's gross income was less than $10,500.

- The child is required to file a return unless you make this election.

- The child doesn't file a joint return for the year.

- No estimated tax payment was made for the year, and no overpayment from the previous year (or from any amended return) was applied to this year under your child's name and SSN.

- No federal income tax was taken out of your child's income under the backup withholding rules.

- You are the parent whose return must be used when applying the special tax rules for children. (See *Which Parent's Return To Use*, earlier.)

These conditions are also shown in Figure 30-A.

Certain January 1 birthdays. A child born on January 1, 2000, is considered to be age 19 at the end of 2018. You can't make this election for such a child unless the child was a full-time student.

A child born on January 1, 1995, is considered to be age 24 at the end of 2018. You can't make this election for such a child.

Full-time student. A full-time student is a child who during some part of each of any 5 calendar months of the year was enrolled as a full-time student at a school, or took a full-time on-farm training course given by a school or a state, county, or local government agency. A school includes a technical, trade, or mechanical school. It doesn't include an on-the-job training course, correspondence school, or school offering courses only through the Internet.

How to make the election. Make the election by attaching Form 8814 to your Form 1040. Attach a separate Form 8814 for each child for whom you make the election. You can make the election for one or more children and not for others.

Effect of Making the Election

The federal income tax on your child's income may be more if you make the Form 8814 election.

Rate may be higher. If your child received qualified dividends or capital gain distributions, you may pay up to $105 more tax if you make this election instead of filing a separate tax return for the child. This is because the tax rate on the child's income between $1,050 and $2,100 is 10% if you make this election. However, if you file a separate return for the child, the tax rate may be as low as 0% because of the preferential tax rates for qualified dividends and capital gain distributions.

Deductions you can't take. By making the Form 8814 election, you can't take any of the following deductions that the child would be entitled to on his or her return.

- The additional standard deduction if the child is blind.

- The deduction for a penalty on an early withdrawal of your child's savings.

- Itemized deductions (such as your child's charitable contributions).

Alternative minimum tax (AMT). If your child received tax-exempt interest (or exempt-interest dividends paid by a regulated investment company) from certain private activity bonds, you must determine if that interest is a tax preference item for AMT purposes. If it is, you must include it with your own tax preference items when figuring your AMT. See Form 6251, Alternative Minimum Tax—Individuals, and its instructions for details.

Net Investment Income Tax (NIIT). When figuring any NIIT on Form 8960, the amount on line 12 of Form 8814 (other than Alaska Permanent Fund dividends) will increase the amount of your net investment income reported on Form 8960. See the Form 8960 instructions for more information.

Reduced deductions or credits. If you use Form 8814, your increased adjusted gross income may reduce certain deductions or credits on your return including the following.

- Deduction for contributions to a traditional individual retirement arrangement (IRA).

- Deduction for student loan interest.

- Itemized deductions for medical expenses, casualty and theft losses, and certain miscellaneous expenses.

- Credit for child and dependent care expenses.

- Child tax credit.

- Education tax credits.

- Earned income credit.

Penalty for underpayment of estimated tax. If you make this election for 2018 and didn't have enough tax withheld or pay enough estimated tax to cover the tax you owe, you may be subject to a penalty. If you plan to make this election for 2019, you may need to increase your federal income tax withholding or your estimated tax payments to avoid the penalty. See chapter 4 for more information.

Tax for Certain Children Who Have Unearned Income

Special tax rates apply to certain dependent children with unearned income of $2,100 or more. If the child's income is $2,100, you may be able to file Form 8615 to figure the tax. If the parent doesn't or can't choose to include the child's income on the parent's return, use Form 8615 to figure the child's tax. Attach the completed form to the child's Form 1040.

When Form 8615 must be filed. Form 8615 must be filed for a child if all of the following statements are true.

1. The child's unearned income was more than $2,100.

2. The child is required to file a return for 2018.

3. The child either:

    a. Was under age 18 at the end of the year,

    b. Was age 18 at the end of the year and didn't have earned income that was more than half of his or her support, or

    c. Was a full-time student at least age 19 and under age 24 at the end of 2018 and didn't have earned income that was more than half of the child's support.

4. At least one of the child's parents was alive at the end of 2018.

5. The child doesn't file a joint return for 2018.

These conditions also are shown in Figure 30-B.

Earned Income. Earned income includes wages, salaries, tips, professional fees, and other compensation received for personal services you performed. It also includes any amount received as a scholarship that you must include in income.

Unearned income defined. Unearned income is generally all income other than salaries, wages, and other amounts received as pay for work actually done. It includes taxable interest, dividends (including capital gain distributions), capital gains, unemployment compensation, taxable scholarship and fellowship grants not reported on Form W-2, the taxable part of social security and pension payments, and certain distributions from trusts. Unearned income includes amounts produced by assets the child obtained with earned income (such as interest on a savings account into which the child deposited wages).

Nontaxable income. For this purpose, unearned income includes only amounts the child must include in total income. Nontaxable unearned income, such as tax-exempt interest and the nontaxable part of social security and pension payments, isn't included.

Income from property received as a gift. A child's unearned income includes all income produced by property belonging to the child. This is true even if the property was transferred to the child, regardless of when the property was transferred or purchased or who transferred it.

A child's unearned income includes income produced by property given as a gift to the child. This includes gifts to the child from grandparents or any other person and gifts made under the Uniform Gift to Minors Act.

Example. Amanda Black, age 13, received the following income.

- Dividends — $1,000

- Wages — $2,100

- Taxable interest — $1,200

- Tax-exempt interest — $100

- Capital gains — $300

- Capital losses — ($200)

The dividends were qualified dividends on stock given to her by her grandparents.

Amanda's unearned income is $2,300. This is the total of the dividends ($1,000), taxable interest ($1,200), and capital gains reduced by capital losses ($300 – $200 = $100). Her wages are earned (not unearned) income because they are received for work actually done. Her tax-exempt interest isn't included because it's nontaxable.

Trust income. If a child is the beneficiary of a trust, distributions of taxable interest, dividends, capital gains, and other unearned income from the trust are unearned income to the child.

However, for purposes of completing Form 8615, a taxable distribution from a qualified disability trust is considered earned income, not unearned income.

Support. Your child's support includes all amounts spent to provide the child with food, lodging, clothing, education, medical and dental care, recreation, transportation, and similar necessities. To figure your child's support, count support provided by you, your child, and others. However, a scholarship received by your child isn't considered support if your child is a full-time student. See chapter 3 for details about support.

Certain January 1 birthdays. Use the following chart to determine whether certain children

Figure 30-A. **Can You Include Your Child's Income On Your Tax Return?**

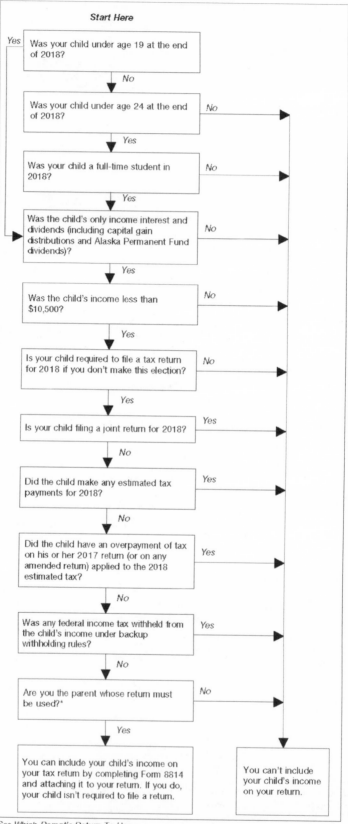

*See *Which Parent's Return To Use*

Figure 30-B. **Do You Have To Use Form 8615 To Figure Your Child's Tax?**

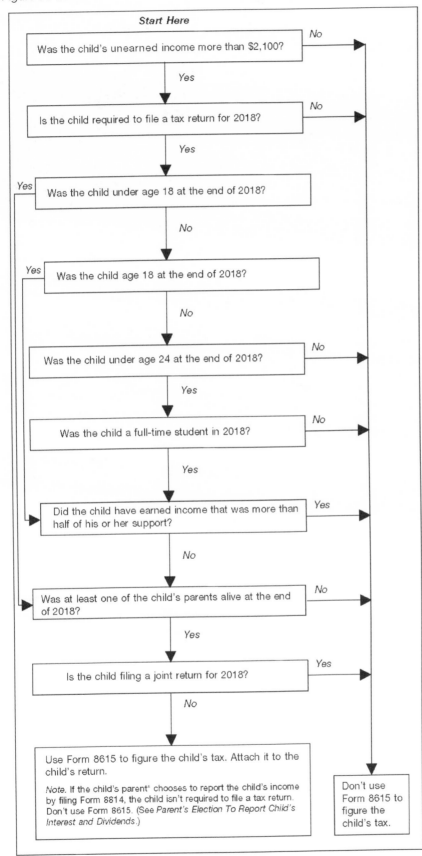

Start Here

Was the child's unearned income more than $2,100? — No →

Yes ↓

Is the child required to file a tax return for 2018? — No →

Yes ↓

Was the child under age 18 at the end of 2018? — Yes →

No ↓

Was the child age 18 at the end of 2018? — Yes →

No ↓

Was the child under age 24 at the end of 2018? — No →

Yes ↓

Was the child a full-time student in 2018? — No →

Yes ↓

Did the child have earned income that was more than half of his or her support? — Yes →

No ↓

Was at least one of the child's parents alive at the end of 2018? — No →

Yes ↓

Is the child filing a joint return for 2018? — Yes →

No ↓

Use Form 8615 to figure the child's tax. Attach it to the child's return.

Note. If the child's parent* chooses to report the child's income by filing Form 8814, the child isn't required to file a tax return. Don't use Form 8615. (See *Parent's Election To Report Child's Interest and Dividends.*)

Don't use Form 8615 to figure the child's tax.

*See *Which Parent's Return To Use*

with January 1 birthdays meet condition 3 under *When Form 8615 must be filed*, earlier.

IF a child was born on...	THEN, at the end of 2018, the child is considered to be...
January 1, 2001	18*
January 1, 2000	19**
January 1, 1995	24***

*This child isn't **under** age 18. The child meets condition 3 only if the child didn't have earned income that was more than half of the child's support.
**This child meets condition 3 only if the child was a full-time student who didn't have earned income that was more than half of the child's support.
***Don't use Form 8615 for this child.

Alternative minimum tax (AMT). A child may be subject to AMT if he or she has certain items given preferential treatment under the tax law. See *Alternative Minimum Tax (AMT)* in chapter 29.

For more information on who is liable for AMT and how to figure it, see Form 6251, Alternative Minimum Tax—Individuals. For information on special limits that apply to a child who files Form 6251, see *Certain Children Under Age 24* in the Instructions for Form 6251.

Net Investment Income Tax (NIIT). A child whose tax is figured on Form 8615 may be subject to the NIIT. NIIT is a 3.8% tax on the lesser of the net investment income or the excess of the child's modified adjusted gross income (MAGI) over the threshold amount. Use Form 8960, Net Investment Income Tax, to figure this tax. For more information on NIIT, go to *IRS.gov/NIIT*.

31.

Child and Dependent Care Credit

What's New

 At the time this publication went to print, Congress was considering legislation that would do the following.

1. *Provide additional tax relief for those affected by certain 2018 disasters.*

2. *Extend certain tax benefits that expired at the end of 2017 and that currently can't be claimed on your 2018 tax return.*

3. *Change certain other tax provisions.*

To learn whether this legislation was enacted resulting in changes that affect your 2018 tax return, go to Recent Developments at IRS.gov/ Pub17.

Personal exemption suspended. For 2018, you can't claim a personal exemption for yourself, your spouse, or your dependents.

Reminders

Future developments. For the latest information about developments related to Pub. 17 or Pub. 503, Child and Dependent Care Expenses, such as legislation enacted after it was published, go to *IRS.gov/Pub17* or *IRS.gov/ Pub503*.

Taxpayer identification number needed for each qualifying person. You must include on line 2 of Form 2441 the name and taxpayer identification number (generally, the social security number (SSN)) of each qualifying person. See *Taxpayer identification number* under *Who Is a Qualifying Person*, later.

You may have to pay employment taxes. If you pay someone to come to your home and care for your dependent or spouse, you may be a household employer who has to pay employment taxes. Usually, you aren't a household employer if the person who cares for your dependent or spouse does so at his or her home or place of business. See *Do You Have Household Employees*, later.

Introduction

This chapter discusses the credit for child and dependent care expenses and covers the following topics.

- Tests you must meet to claim the credit.
- How to figure the credit.
- How to claim the credit.
- Employment taxes you may have to pay as a household employer.

You may be able to claim the credit if you pay someone to care for your dependent who is under age 13 or for your spouse or dependent who isn't able to care for himself or herself. The credit can be up to 35% of your expenses. To qualify, you must pay these expenses so you can work or look for work.

 This credit shouldn't be confused with the child tax credit discussed in chapter 33.

Dependent care benefits. If you received any dependent care benefits from your employer during the year, you may be able to exclude all or part of them from your income. You must complete Form 2441, Part III, before you can figure the amount of your credit. See *Dependent Care Benefits* under *How To Figure the Credit*, later.

Useful Items

You may want to see:

Publication

❏ **501** Exemptions, Standard Deduction, and Filing Information

❏ **503** Child and Dependent Care Expenses

❏ **926** Household Employer's Tax Guide

Form (and Instructions)

❏ **2441** Child and Dependent Care Expenses

❏ **Schedule H (Form 1040)** Household Employment Taxes

❏ **W-7** Application for IRS Individual Taxpayer Identification Number

❏ **W-7A** Application for Taxpayer Identification Number for Pending U.S. Adoptions

❏ **W-10** Dependent Care Provider's Identification and Certification

For these and other useful items, go to *IRS.gov/ Forms.*

Can You Claim the Credit?

To be able to claim the credit for child and dependent care expenses, you must file Form 1040 or Form 1040NR, not Form 1040NR-EZ, and meet all the tests in *Tests you must meet to claim a credit for child and dependent care expenses* next.

Tests you must meet to claim a credit for child and dependent care expenses.

1. **Qualifying Person Test.** The care must be for one or more qualifying persons who are identified on Form 2441. (See *Who Is a Qualifying Person*, later.)

2. **Earned Income Test.** You (and your spouse if filing jointly) must have earned income during the year. (However, see *Rule for student-spouse or spouse not able to care for self* under *You Must Have Earned Income*, later.)

3. **Work-Related Expense Test.** You must pay child and dependent care expenses so you (and your spouse if filing jointly) can work or look for work. (See *Are These Work-Related Expenses*, later.)

4. You must make payments for child and dependent care to someone you (and your spouse) can't claim as a dependent. If you make payments to your child, he or she can't be your dependent and must be age 19 or older by the end of the year. You can't make payments to:

   a. Your spouse, or

   b. The parent of your qualifying person if your qualifying person is your child and under age 13.

   (See *Payments to Relatives or Dependents* under *Are These Work-Related Expenses?*, later.)

5. **Joint Return Test.** Your filing status may be single, head of household, or qualifying widow(er). If you're married, you must file a joint return, unless an exception applies to you. (See *What's Your Filing Status*, later.)

6. **Provider Identification Test.** You must identify the care provider on your tax return. (See *Care Provider Identification Test*, later.)

7. If you exclude or deduct dependent care benefits provided by a dependent care benefits plan, the total amount you exclude or deduct must be less than the dollar limit for qualifying expenses (generally, $3,000 if one qualifying person was cared for or $6,000 if two or more qualifying persons were cared for). (If two or more qualifying persons were cared for, the amount you exclude or deduct will always be less than the dollar limit, since the total amount you can exclude or deduct is limited to $5,000. See *Reduced Dollar Limit* under *How To Figure the Credit*, later.)

These tests are presented in Figure 31-A and are also explained in detail in this chapter.

Who Is a Qualifying Person?

Your child and dependent care expenses must be for the care of one or more qualifying persons.

A qualifying person is:

1. Your qualifying child who is your dependent and who was under age 13 when the care was provided (but see *Child of divorced or separated parents or parents living apart*, later);

2. Your spouse who wasn't physically or mentally able to care for himself or herself and lived with you for more than half the year; or

3. A person who wasn't physically or mentally able to care for himself or herself, lived with you for more than half the year, and either:

   a. Was your dependent, or

   b. Would have been your dependent except that:

      i. He or she received gross income of $4,150 or more,

      ii. He or she filed a joint return, or

      iii. You, or your spouse if filing jointly, could be claimed as a dependent on someone else's 2018 return.

Dependent defined. A dependent is a person, other than you or your spouse, whom you can claim on your tax return. To be your dependent, a person must be your qualifying child (or your qualifying relative).

Qualifying child. To be your qualifying child, a child must live with you for more than half the year and meet other requirements.

More information. For more information about who is a dependent or a qualifying child, see chapter 3.

Physically or mentally not able to care for oneself. Persons who can't dress, clean, or feed themselves because of physical or mental problems are considered not able to care for themselves. Also, persons who must have constant attention to prevent them from injuring themselves or others are considered not able to care for themselves.

Person qualifying for part of year. You determine a person's qualifying status each day. For example, if the person for whom you pay child and dependent care expenses no longer qualifies on September 16, count only those expenses through September 15. Also see *Yearly limit* under *Dollar Limit*, later.

Birth or death of otherwise qualifying person. In determining whether a person is a qualifying person, a person who was born or died in 2018 is treated as having lived with you for more than half of 2018 if your home was the person's home for more than half the time he or she was alive in 2018.

Taxpayer identification number. You must include on your return the name and taxpayer identification number (generally, the SSN) of the qualifying person(s). If the correct information isn't shown, the credit may be reduced or disallowed.

Individual taxpayer identification number (ITIN) for aliens. If your qualifying person is a nonresident or resident alien who doesn't have and can't get a SSN, use that person's ITIN. The ITIN is entered wherever an SSN is requested on a tax return. To apply for an ITIN, see Form W-7.

An ITIN is for tax use only. It doesn't entitle the holder to social security benefits or change the holder's employment or immigration status under U.S. law.

Adoption taxpayer identification number (ATIN). If your qualifying person is a child who was placed in your home for adoption and for whom you don't have an SSN, you must get an ATIN for the child. To apply for an ATIN, see Form W-7A.

Child of divorced or separated parents or parents living apart. Even if you can't claim your child as a dependent, he or she is treated as your qualifying person if:

- The child was under age 13 or wasn't physically or mentally able to care for himself or herself;

- The child received over half of his or her support during the calendar year from one or both parents who are divorced or legally separated under a decree of divorce or separate maintenance, are separated under a written separation agreement, or lived apart at all times during the last 6 months of the calendar year;

- The child was in the custody of one or both parents for more than half the year; and

- You were the child's custodial parent.

The custodial parent is the parent with whom the child lived for the greater number of nights in 2018. If the child was with each parent for an equal number of nights, the custodial parent is the parent with the higher adjusted gross income. For details and an exception for a parent who works at night, see Pub. 501.

The noncustodial parent can't treat the child as a qualifying person even if that parent is entitled to claim the child as a dependent under the special rules for a child of divorced or separated parents.

You Must Have Earned Income

To claim the credit, you (and your spouse if filing jointly) must have earned income during the year.

Earned income. Earned income includes wages, salaries, tips, other taxable employee compensation, and net earnings from self-employment. A net loss from self-employment reduces earned income. Earned income also includes strike benefits and any disability pay you report as wages.

Generally, only taxable compensation is included. However, you can elect to include nontaxable combat pay in earned income. If you're filing a joint return and both you and your spouse received nontaxable combat pay, you can each make your own election. (In other words, if one of you makes the election, the other one can also make it but doesn't have to.) You should figure your credit both ways and make the election if it gives you a greater tax benefit.

Members of certain religious faiths opposed to social security. Certain income earned by persons who are members of certain religious faiths that are opposed to participation in Social Security Act programs and have an IRS-approved form that exempts certain income from social security and Medicare taxes may not be considered earned income for this purpose. See *You Must Have Earned Income* in Pub. 503.

What isn't earned income? Earned income doesn't include:

- Pensions and annuities;

- Amounts reported on Form 1040, line 1 excluded as foreign earned income on Form 2555, line 45 or Form 2555-EZ, line 18;

- Medicaid waiver payments you exclude from income;

- Social security and railroad retirement benefits;

- Workers' compensation;

- Interest and dividends;

- Unemployment compensation;

- Scholarships or fellowship grants, except for those reported on a Form W-2 and paid to you for teaching or other services;

- Nontaxable workfare payments;

- Child support payments received;

- Income of nonresident aliens that isn't effectively connected with a U.S. trade or business; or

- Any amount received for work while an inmate in a penal institution.

Rule for student-spouse or spouse not able to care for self. Your spouse is treated as having earned income for any month that he or she is:

1. A full-time student, or

2. Physically or mentally not able to care for himself or herself. (Your spouse also must live with you for more than half the year.)

If you're filing a joint return, this rule also applies to you. You can be treated as having earned income for any month you're a full-time student or not able to care for yourself.

Figure the earned income of the nonworking spouse described under (1) or (2) above as explained under *Earned Income Limit*, later.

This rule applies to only one spouse for any 1 month. If, in the same month, both you and your spouse don't work and are either full-time students or not physically or mentally able to care for yourselves, only one of you can be treated as having earned income in that month.

Full-time student. You're a full-time student if you're enrolled at a school for the number of hours or classes that the school considers full time. You must have been a full-time student for some part of each of 5 calendar months during the year. (The months need not be consecutive.)

School. The term "school" includes high schools, colleges, universities, and technical, trade, and mechanical schools. A school doesn't include an on-the-job training course, correspondence school, or school offering courses only through the Internet.

Are These Work-Related Expenses?

Child and dependent care expenses must be work-related to qualify for the credit. Expenses are considered work-related only if both of the following are true.

- They allow you (and your spouse if filing jointly) to work or look for work.

- They are for a qualifying person's care.

Working or Looking for Work

To be work-related, your expenses must allow you to work or look for work. If you're married, generally both you and your spouse must work or look for work. One spouse is treated as working during any month he or she is a full-time student or isn't physically or mentally able to care for himself or herself.

Your work can be for others or in your own business or partnership. It can be either full time or part time.

Work also includes actively looking for work. However, if you don't find a job and have no earned income for the year, you can't take this credit. See *You Must Have Earned Income*, earlier.

An expense isn't considered work-related merely because you had it while you were working. The purpose of the expense must be to

Figure 31-A. **Can You Claim the Credit?**

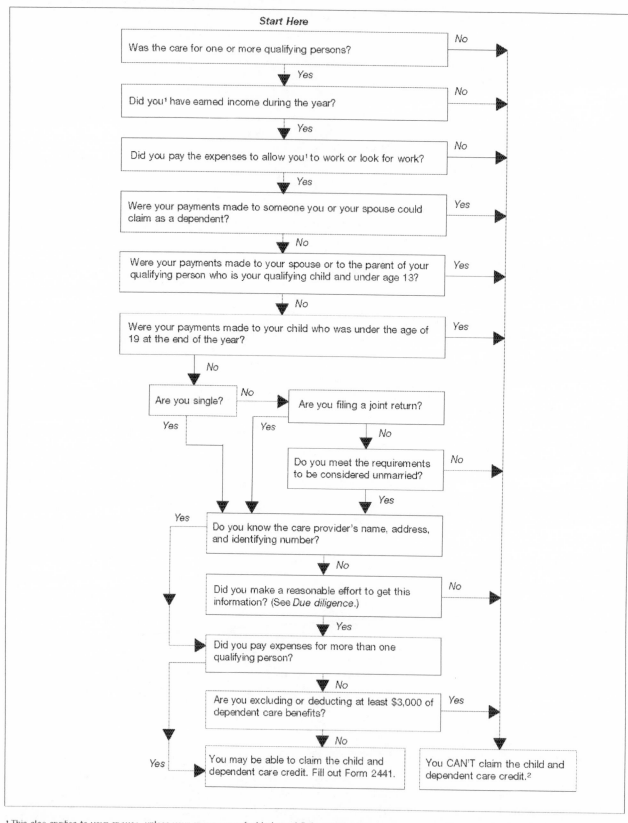

¹ This also applies to your spouse, unless your spouse was disabled or a full-time student.

² If you had expenses that met the requirements for 2017, except that you didn't pay them until 2018, you may be able to claim those expenses in 2018. See *Expenses not paid until the following year* under *How To Figure the Credit.*

Page 206   Chapter 31   **Child and Dependent Care Credit** allow you to work. Whether your expenses allow you to work or look for work depends on the facts.

Example 1. The cost of a babysitter while you and your spouse go out to eat isn't normally a work-related expense.

Example 2. You work during the day. Your spouse works at night and sleeps during the day. You pay for care of your 5-year-old child during the hours when you're working and your spouse is sleeping. Your expenses are considered work-related.

Volunteer work. For this purpose, you aren't considered to be working if you do unpaid volunteer work or volunteer work for a nominal salary.

Work for part of year. If you work or actively look for work during only part of the period covered by the expenses, then you must figure your expenses for each day. For example, if you work all year and pay care expenses of $250 a month ($3,000 for the year), all the expenses are work-related. However, if you work or look for work for only 2 months and 15 days during the year and pay work expenses of $250 a month, your work-related expenses are limited to $625 (2 1/2 months x $250).

Temporary absence from work. You don't have to figure your expenses for each day during a short, temporary absence from work, such as for vacation or a minor illness, if you have to pay for care anyway. Instead, you can figure your credit including the expenses you paid for the period of absence.

An absence of 2 weeks or less is a short, temporary absence. An absence of more than 2 weeks may be considered a short, temporary absence, depending on the circumstances.

Example. You pay a nanny to care for your 2-year-old son and 4-year-old daughter so you can work. You become ill and miss 4 months of work but receive sick pay. You continue to pay the nanny to care for the children while you're ill. Your absence isn't a short, temporary absence, and your expenses aren't considered work-related.

Part-time work. If you work part time, you generally must figure your expenses for each day. However, if you have to pay for care weekly, monthly, or in another way that includes both days worked and days not worked, you can figure your credit including the expenses you paid for days you didn't work. Any day when you work at least 1 hour is a day of work.

Example 1. You work 3 days a week. While you work, your 6-year-old child attends a dependent care center, which complies with all state and local regulations. You can pay the center $150 for any 3 days a week or $250 for 5 days a week. Your child attends the center 5 days a week. Your work-related expenses are limited to $150 a week.

Example 2. The facts are the same as in *Example 1*, except the center doesn't offer a 3-day option. The entire $250 weekly fee may be a work-related expense.

Care of a Qualifying Person

To be work-related, your expenses must be to provide care for a qualifying person.

You don't have to choose the least expensive way of providing care. The cost of a paid care provider may be an expense for the care of a qualifying person even if another care provider is available at no cost.

Expenses are for the care of a qualifying person only if their main purpose is the person's well-being and protection.

Expenses for household services qualify if part of the services is for the care of qualifying persons. See *Household Services*, later.

Expenses not for care. Expenses for care don't include amounts you pay for food, lodging, clothing, education, and entertainment. However, you can include small amounts paid for these items if they are incidental to and can't be separated from the cost of caring for the qualifying person.

Child support payments aren't for care and don't qualify for the credit.

Education. Expenses for a child in nursery school, preschool, or similar programs for children below the level of kindergarten are expenses for care. Expenses to attend kindergarten or a higher grade aren't expenses for care. Don't use these expenses to figure your credit.

However, expenses for before- or after-school care of a child in kindergarten or a higher grade may be expenses for care.

Summer school and tutoring programs aren't for care.

Example 1. You take your 3-year-old child to a nursery school that provides lunch and educational activities as a part of its preschool childcare service. The lunch and educational activities are incidental to the childcare, and their cost can't be separated from the cost of care. You can count the total cost when you figure the credit.

Example 2. You place your 10-year-old child in a boarding school so you can work full time. Only the part of the boarding school expense that's for the care of your child is a work-related expense. You can count that part of the expense in figuring your credit if it can be separated from the cost of education. You can't count any part of the amount you pay the school for your child's education.

Care outside your home. You can count the cost of care provided outside your home if the care is for your dependent under age 13 or any other qualifying person who regularly spends at least 8 hours each day in your home.

Dependent care center. You can count care provided outside your home by a dependent care center only if the center complies with all state and local regulations that apply to these centers.

A dependent care center is a place that provides care for more than six persons (other than persons who live there) and receives a fee, payment, or grant for providing services for any of those persons, even if the center isn't run for profit.

Camp. The cost of sending your child to an overnight camp isn't considered a work-related expense. The cost of sending your child to a day camp may be a work-related expense, even if the camp specializes in a particular activity, such as computers or soccer.

Transportation. If a care provider takes a qualifying person to or from a place where care is provided, that transportation is for the care of the qualifying person. This includes transportation by bus, subway, taxi, or private car. However, transportation not provided by a care provider isn't for the care of a qualifying person. Also, if you pay the transportation cost for the care provider to come to your home, that expense isn't for care of a qualifying person.

Fees and deposits. Fees you paid to an agency to get the services of a care provider, deposits you paid to an agency or preschool, application fees, and other indirect expenses are work-related expenses if you have to pay them to get care, even though they aren't directly for care. However, a forfeited deposit isn't for the care of a qualifying person if care isn't provided.

Example 1. You paid a fee to an agency to get the services of the nanny who cares for your 2-year-old daughter while you work. The fee you paid is a work-related expense.

Example 2. You placed a deposit with a preschool to reserve a place for your 3-year-old child. You later sent your child to a different preschool and forfeited the deposit. The forfeited deposit isn't for care and so isn't a work-related expense.

Household Services

Expenses you pay for household services meet the work-related expense test if they are at least partly for the well-being and protection of a qualifying person.

Definition. Household services are ordinary and usual services done in and around your home that are necessary to run your home. They include the services of a housekeeper, maid, or cook. However, they don't include the services of a chauffeur, bartender, or gardener. See *Household Services* in Pub. 503 for more information.

Housekeeper. In this publication, the term "housekeeper" refers to any household employee whose services include the care of a qualifying person.

Taxes paid on wages. The taxes you pay on wages for qualifying child and dependent care services are work-related expenses. See *Do You Have Household Employees*, later.

Payments to Relatives or Dependents

You can count work-related payments you make to relatives who aren't your dependents, even if they live in your home. However, don't count any amounts you pay to:

1. A dependent whom you (or your spouse if filing jointly) can claim on your tax return;

2. Your child who was under age 19 at the end of the year, even if he or she isn't your dependent;

3. A person who was your spouse any time during the year; or

4. The parent of your qualifying person if your qualifying person is your child and under age 13.

What's Your Filing Status?

Generally, married couples must file a joint return to take the credit. However, if you're legally separated or living apart from your spouse, you may be able to file a separate return and still take the credit.

Legally separated. You aren't considered married if you're legally separated from your spouse under a decree of divorce or separate maintenance. You may be eligible to take the credit on your return using head of household filing status.

Married and living apart. You aren't considered married and are eligible to take the credit if all the following apply.

1. You file a return apart from your spouse.

2. Your home is the home of a qualifying person for more than half the year.

3. You pay more than half the cost of keeping up your home for the year.

4. Your spouse doesn't live in your home for the last 6 months of the year.

Not legally seperated. You also may be able to claim the child and dependent care credit using the married filing separate filing status. See *Not legally separated* in Pub. 503.

Costs of keeping up a home. The costs of keeping up a home normally include property taxes, mortgage interest, rent, utility charges, home repairs, insurance on the home, and food eaten at home.

The costs of keeping up a home don't include payments for clothing, education, medical treatment, vacations, life insurance, transportation, or mortgage principal.

They also don't include the purchase, permanent improvement, or replacement of property. For example, you can't include the cost of replacing a water heater. However, you can include the cost of repairing a water heater.

Death of spouse. If your spouse died during the year and you don't remarry before the end of the year, you generally must file a joint return to take the credit. If you do remarry before the end of the year, the credit can be claimed on your deceased spouse's return.

Care Provider Identification Test

You must identify all persons or organizations that provide care for your child or dependent. Use Form 2441, Part I, to show the information.

If you don't have any care providers and you're filing Form 2441 only to report taxable income in Part III, enter "none" in line 1, column (a).

Information needed. To identify the care provider, you must give the provider's:

1. Name,

2. Address, and

3. Taxpayer identification number.

If the care provider is an individual, the taxpayer identification number is his or her SSN or ITIN. If the care provider is an organization, then it is the employer identification number (EIN).

You don't have to show the taxpayer identification number if the care provider is a tax-exempt organization (such as a church or school). In this case, enter "Tax-Exempt" in the space where Form 2441 asks for the number.

If you can't provide all of the information or if the information is incorrect, you must be able to show that you used due diligence (discussed later) in trying to furnish the necessary information.

Getting the information. You can use Form W-10 to request the required information from the care provider. If you don't use Form W-10, you can get the information from one of the other sources listed in the instructions for Form W-10 including:

1. A copy of the provider's social security card,

2. A copy of the provider's completed Form W-4 if he or she is your household employee,

3. A copy of the statement furnished by your employer if the provider is your employer's dependent care plan, or

4. A letter or invoice from the provider if it shows the information.

 You should keep this information with your tax records. Don't send Form W-10 (or other document containing this information) to the IRS.

Due diligence. If the care provider information you give is incorrect or incomplete, your credit may not be allowed. However, if you can show that you used due diligence in trying to supply the information, you can still claim the credit.

You can show due diligence by getting and keeping the provider's completed Form W-10 or one of the other sources of information just listed. Care providers can be penalized if they don't provide this information to you or if they provide incorrect information.

Provider refusal. If the provider refuses to give you their identifying information, you should report on Form 2441 whatever information you have (such as the name and address). Enter "See Attached Statement" in the columns calling for the information you don't have. Then attach a statement explaining that you requested the information from the care provider, but the provider didn't give you the information. Be sure to write your name and SSN on this statement. The statement will show that you used due diligence in trying to furnish the necessary information.

U.S. citizens and resident aliens living abroad. If you're living abroad, your care provider may not have, and may not be required to

get, a U.S. taxpayer identification number (for example, an SSN or EIN). If so, enter "LAFCP" (Living Abroad Foreign Care Provider) in the space for the care provider's taxpayer identification number.

How To Figure the Credit

Your credit is a percentage of your work-related expenses. Your expenses are subject to the earned income limit and the dollar limit. The percentage is based on your adjusted gross income.

Figuring Total Work-Related Expenses

To figure the credit for 2018 work-related expenses, count only those you paid by December 31, 2018.

Expenses prepaid in an earlier year. If you pay for services before they are provided, you can count the prepaid expenses only in the year the care is received. Claim the expenses for the later year as if they were actually paid in that later year.

Expenses not paid until the following year. Don't count 2017 expenses that you paid in 2018 as work-related expenses for 2018. You may be able to claim an additional credit for them on your 2018 return, but you must figure it separately. See *Payments for prior year's expenses* under *Amount of Credit* in Pub. 503.

 If you had expenses in 2018 that you didn't pay until 2019, you can't count them when figuring your 2018 credit. You may be able to claim a credit for them on your 2019 return.

Expenses reimbursed. If a state social services agency pays you a nontaxable amount to reimburse you for some of your child and dependent care expenses, you can't count the expenses that are reimbursed as work-related expenses.

Example. You paid work-related expenses of $3,000. You're reimbursed $2,000 by a state social services agency. You can use only $1,000 to figure your credit.

Medical expenses. Some expenses for the care of qualifying persons who aren't able to care for themselves may qualify as work-related expenses and also as medical expenses. You can use them either way, but you can't use the same expenses to claim both a credit and a medical expense deduction.

If you use these expenses to figure the credit and they are more than the earned income limit or the dollar limit, discussed later, you can add the excess to your medical expenses. However, if you use your total expenses to figure your medical expense deduction, you can't use any part of them to figure your credit.

⚠ *Amounts excluded from your income under your employer's dependent care benefits plan can't be used to claim a medical expense deduction.*

Dependent Care Benefits

If you receive dependent care benefits, your dollar limit for purposes of the credit may be reduced. See *Reduced Dollar Limit*, later. But, even if you can't take the credit, you may be able to take an exclusion or deduction for the dependent care benefits.

Dependent care benefits. Dependent care benefits include:

1. Amounts your employer paid directly to either you or your care provider for the care of your qualifying person while you work,

2. The fair market value of care in a daycare facility provided or sponsored by your employer, and

3. Pre-tax contributions you made under a dependent care flexible spending arrangement.

Your salary may have been reduced to pay for these benefits. If you received benefits as an employee, they should be shown in box 10 of your Form W-2. See *Statement for employee*, later. Benefits you received as a partner should be shown in box 13 of your Schedule K-1 (Form 1065) with code O. Enter the amount of these benefits on Form 2441, Part III, line 12.

Exclusion or deduction. If your employer provides dependent care benefits under a qualified plan, you may be able to exclude these benefits from your income. Your employer can tell you whether your benefit plan qualifies. To claim the exclusion, you must complete Part III of Form 2441.

If you're self-employed and receive benefits from a qualified dependent care benefit plan, you're treated as both employer and employee. Therefore, you wouldn't get an exclusion from wages. Instead, you would get a deduction on Form 1040, Schedule C, line 14; Schedule E, line 19 or 28; or Schedule F, line 15. To claim the deduction, you must use Form 2441.

The amount you can exclude or deduct is limited to the smallest of:

1. The total amount of dependent care benefits you received during the year,

2. The total amount of qualified expenses you incurred during the year,

3. Your earned income,

4. Your spouse's earned income, or

5. $5,000 ($2,500 if married filing separately).

The definition of earned income for the exclusion or deduction is the same as the definition used when figuring the credit except that earned income for the exclusion or deduction doesn't include any dependent care benefits you receive. See *Earned Income Limit*, later.

 You can choose to include your nontaxable combat pay in earned income when figuring your exclusion or deduction, even if you choose not to include it in earned income for the earned income credit or the credit for child and dependent care expenses.

Statement for employee. Your employer must give you a Form W-2 (or similar statement) showing in box 10 the total amount of dependent care benefits provided to you during the year under a qualified plan. Your employer will also include any dependent care benefits over $5,000 in your wages shown on your Form W-2 in box 1.

Effect of exclusion on credit. If you exclude dependent care benefits from your income, the amount of the excluded benefits:

1. Isn't included in your work-related expenses; and

2. Reduces the dollar limit, discussed later.

Earned Income Limit

The amount of work-related expenses you use to figure your credit can't be more than:

1. Your earned income for the year if you're single at the end of the year, or

2. The smaller of your or your spouse's earned income for the year if you're married at the end of the year.

Earned income is defined under *You Must Have Earned Income*, earlier.

 For purposes of item (2), use your spouse's earned income for the entire year, even if you were married for only part of the year.

Separated spouse. If you're legally separated or married and living apart from your spouse (as described under *What's Your Filing Status*, earlier), you aren't considered married for purposes of the earned income limit. Use only your income in figuring the earned income limit.

Surviving spouse. If your spouse died during the year and you file a joint return as a surviving spouse, you may, but aren't required to, take into account the earned income of your spouse who died during the year.

Community property laws. You should disregard community property laws when you figure earned income for this credit.

You or your spouse is a student or not able to care for self. Your spouse who is either a full-time student or not able to care for himself or herself is treated as having earned income. His or her earned income for each month is considered to be at least $250 if there is one qualifying person in your home, or at least $500 if there are two or more.

Spouse works. If your spouse works during that month, use the higher of $250 (or $500) or his or her actual earned income for that month.

Spouse qualifies for part of month. If your spouse is a full-time student or not able to care for himself or herself for only part of a month, the full $250 (or $500) still applies for that month.

You are a student or not able to care for yourself. These rules also apply if you're a student or not able to care for yourself and you're filing a joint return. For each month or part of a month you're a student or not able to care for yourself, your earned income is

considered to be at least $250 (or $500). If you also work during that month, use the higher of $250 (or $500) or your actual earned income for that month.

Both spouses qualify. If, in the same month, both you and your spouse are either full-time students or not able to care for yourselves, only one spouse can be considered to have this earned income of $250 (or $500) for that month.

Dollar Limit

There is a dollar limit on the amount of your work-related expenses you can use to figure the credit. This limit is $3,000 for one qualifying person, or $6,000 for two or more qualifying persons.

 If you paid work-related expenses for the care of two or more qualifying persons, the applicable dollar limit is $6,000. This $6,000 limit doesn't need to be divided equally among them. For example, if your work-related expenses for the care of one qualifying person are $3,200 and your work-related expenses for another qualifying person are $2,800, you can use the total, $6,000, when figuring the credit.

Yearly limit. The dollar limit is a yearly limit. The amount of the dollar limit remains the same no matter how long, during the year, you have a qualifying person in your household. Use the $3,000 limit if you paid work-related expenses for the care of one qualifying person at any time during the year. Use $6,000 if you paid work-related expenses for the care of more than one qualifying person at any time during the year.

Reduced Dollar Limit

If you received dependent care benefits that you exclude or deduct from your income, you must subtract that amount from the dollar limit that applies to you. Your reduced dollar limit is figured on Form 2441, Part III. See *Dependent Care Benefits*, earlier, for information on excluding or deducting these benefits.

Example 1. George is a widower with one child and earns $24,000 a year. He pays work-related expenses of $2,900 for the care of his 4-year-old child and qualifies to claim the credit for child and dependent care expenses. His employer pays an additional $1,000 under a dependent care benefit plan. This $1,000 is excluded from George's income.

Although the dollar limit for his work-related expenses is $3,000 (one qualifying person), George figures his credit on only $2,000 of the $2,900 work-related expenses he paid. This is because his dollar limit is reduced as shown next.

George's Reduced Dollar Limit

1.	Maximum allowable expenses for one qualifying person	$3,000
2.	Minus: Dependent care benefits George excludes from income	−1,000
3.	Reduced dollar limit on expenses George can use for the credit	$2,000

Example 2. Randall is married and both he and his wife are employed. Each has earned income in excess of $6,000. They have two children, Anne and Andy, ages 2 and 4, who attend a daycare facility licensed and regulated by the state. Randall's work-related expenses are $6,000 for the year.

Randall's employer has a dependent care assistance program as part of its cafeteria plan, which allows employees to make pre-tax contributions to a dependent care flexible spending arrangement. Randall has elected to take the maximum $5,000 exclusion from his salary to cover dependent care expenses through this program.

Although the dollar limit for his work-related expenses is $6,000 (two or more qualifying persons), Randall figures his credit on only $1,000 of the $6,000 work-related expenses paid. This is because his dollar limit is reduced as shown next.

Randall's Reduced Dollar Limit

1.	Maximum allowable expenses for two qualifying persons	$6,000
2.	Minus: Dependent care benefits Randall selects from employer's cafeteria plan and excludes from income	−5,000
3.	Reduced dollar limit on expenses Randall can use for the credit	$1,000

Amount of Credit

To determine the amount of your credit, multiply your work-related expenses (after applying the earned income and dollar limits) by a percentage. This percentage depends on your adjusted gross income shown on Form 1040, line 7, or Form 1040NR, line 36. The following table shows the percentage to use based on adjusted gross income.

IF your adjusted gross income is:		THEN the percentage is:
Over:	But not over:	
$ 0	$15,000	35%
15,000	17,000	34%
17,000	19,000	33%
19,000	21,000	32%
21,000	23,000	31%
23,000	25,000	30%
25,000	27,000	29%
27,000	29,000	28%
29,000	31,000	27%
31,000	33,000	26%
33,000	35,000	25%
35,000	37,000	24%
37,000	39,000	23%
39,000	41,000	22%
41,000	43,000	21%
43,000	No limit	20%

How To Claim the Credit

To claim the credit, you can file Form 1040 or Form 1040NR. You can't claim the credit on Form 1040NR-EZ.

Form 1040 or Form 1040NR. You must complete Form 2441 and attach it to your Form 1040 or Form 1040NR. Enter the credit on Schedule 3 (Form 1040), line 49, or Form 1040NR, line 47.

Limit on credit. The amount of credit you can claim is generally limited to the amount of your tax. For more information, see the Instructions for Form 2441.

Tax credit not refundable. You can't get a refund for any part of the credit that's more than this limit.

 Recordkeeping. You should keep records of your work-related expenses. Also, if your dependent or spouse isn't able to care for himself or herself, your records should show both the nature and the length of the disability. Other records you should keep to support your claim for the credit are described earlier under *Care Provider Identification Test*.

Do You Have Household Employees?

If you pay someone to come to your home and care for your dependent or spouse, you may be a household employer. If you're a household employer, you will need an EIN and you may have to pay employment taxes. If the individuals who work in your home are self-employed, you aren't liable for any of the taxes discussed in this section. Self-employed persons who are in business for themselves aren't household employees. Usually, you aren't a household employer if the person who cares for your dependent or spouse does so at his or her home or place of business.

If you use a placement agency that exercises control over what work is done and how it will be done by a babysitter or companion who works in your home, the worker isn't your employee. This control could include providing rules of conduct and appearance and requiring regular reports. In this case, you don't have to pay employment taxes. But, if an agency merely gives you a list of sitters and you hire one from that list, and pay the sitter directly, the sitter may be your employee.

If you have a household employee, you may be subject to:

1. Social security and Medicare taxes,

2. Federal unemployment tax, and

3. Federal income tax withholding.

Social security and Medicare taxes are generally withheld from the employee's pay and matched by the employer. Federal unemployment (FUTA) tax is paid by the employer only and provides for payments of unemployment compensation to workers who have lost their jobs. Federal income tax is withheld from the employee's total pay if the employee asks you to do so and you agree.

For more information on a household employer's tax responsibilities, see Pub. 926 and Schedule H (Form 1040) and its instructions.

State employment tax. You also may have to pay state unemployment tax. Contact your state unemployment tax office for information. You should also find out whether you need to pay or collect other state employment taxes or carry workers' compensation insurance. For a list of state unemployment tax agencies, visit the U.S. Department of Labor's website. A link to that website is in Pub. 926, or you can find it with an online search.

32.

Credit for the Elderly or the Disabled

What's New

 At the time this publication went to print, Congress was considering legislation that would do the following.

1. Provide additional tax relief for those affected by certain 2018 disasters.

2. Extend certain tax benefits that expired at the end of 2017 and that currently can't be claimed on your 2018 tax return.

3. Change certain other tax provisions.

To learn whether this legislation was enacted resulting in changes that affect your 2018 tax return, go to Recent Developments at *IRS.gov/ Pub17*.

Introduction

If you qualify, you may be able to reduce the tax you owe by taking the credit for the elderly or the disabled on Schedule R (Form 1040).

This chapter explains:

- Who qualifies for the credit for the elderly or the disabled, and

- How to claim the credit.

You may be able to take the credit for the elderly or the disabled if:

- You are age 65 or older at the end of 2018, or

- You retired on permanent and total disability and have taxable disability income.

Useful Items

You may want to see:

Publication

❏ **524** Credit for the Elderly or the Disabled

❏ **554** Tax Guide for Seniors

Form (and Instructions)

❏ **Schedule R (Form 1040)** Credit for the Elderly or the Disabled

For these and other useful items, go to _IRS.gov/ Forms._

Are You Eligible for the Credit?

You can take the credit for the elderly or the disabled if you meet both of the following requirements.

- You are a qualified individual.
- Your income isn't more than certain limits.

You can use Figure 32-A and Table 32-1 as guides to see if you are eligible for the credit. Use Figure 32-A first to see if you are a qualified individual. If you are, go to Table 32-1 to make sure your income isn't too high to take the credit.

Qualified Individual

You are a qualified individual for this credit if you are a U.S. citizen or resident alien, and either of the following applies.

1. You were age 65 or older at the end of 2018.

2. You were under age 65 at the end of 2018 and all three of the following statements are true.

   a. You retired on permanent and total disability (explained later).

   b. You received taxable disability income for 2018.

   c. On January 1, 2018, you had not reached mandatory retirement age (defined later under _Disability income_).

Age 65. You are considered to be age 65 on the day before your 65th birthday. Therefore, if you were born on January 1, 1954, you are considered to be age 65 at the end of 2018.

Death of a taxpayer. If you are preparing a return for someone who died in 2018, consider the taxpayer to be age 65 at the end of 2018 if he or she was age 65 or older on the day before their death. For example, if the taxpayer was born on February 14, 1953, and died on February 13, 2018, the taxpayer is considered age 65 at the time of death. However, if the taxpayer died on February 12, 2018, the taxpayer isn't considered age 65 at the time of death or at the end of 2018.

U.S. Citizen or Resident Alien

You must be a U.S. citizen or resident alien (or be treated as a resident alien) to take the credit. Generally, you can't take the credit if you were a nonresident alien at any time during the tax year.

Exceptions. You may be able to take the credit if you are a nonresident alien who is married to a U.S. citizen or resident alien at the end of the tax year and you and your spouse

choose to treat you as a U.S. resident alien. If you make that choice, both you and your spouse are taxed on your worldwide incomes.

If you were a nonresident alien at the beginning of the year and a resident alien at the end of the year, and you were married to a U.S. citizen or resident alien at the end of the year, you may be able to choose to be treated as a U.S. resident alien for the entire year. In that case, you may be allowed to take the credit.

For information on these choices, see chapter 1 of Pub. 519, U.S. Tax Guide for Aliens.

Married Persons

Generally, if you are married at the end of the tax year, you and your spouse must file a joint return to take the credit. However, if you and your spouse didn't live in the same household at any time during the tax year, you can file either a joint return or separate returns and still take the credit.

Head of household. You can file as head of household and qualify to take the credit, even if your spouse lived with you during the first 6 months of the year, if you meet certain tests. See _Head of Household_ in chapter 2 for the tests you must meet.

Under Age 65

If you are under age 65 at the end of 2018, you can qualify for the credit only if you are retired on permanent and total disability (discussed next) and have taxable disability income (discussed later under _Disability income_). You are retired on permanent and total disability if:

- You were permanently and totally disabled when you retired, and
- You retired on disability before the close of the tax year.

Even if you don't retire formally, you may be considered retired on disability when you have stopped working because of your disability.

If you retired on disability before 1977, and weren't permanently and totally disabled at the time, you can qualify for the credit if you were permanently and totally disabled on January 1, 1976, or January 1, 1977.

 You are considered to be under age 65 at the end of 2018 if you were born after January 1, 1954.

Permanent and total disability. You have a permanent and total disability if you can't engage in any substantial gainful activity because of your physical or mental condition. A qualified physician must certify that the condition has lasted or can be expected to last continuously for 12 months or more, or that the condition can be expected to result in death. See _Physician's statement_, later.

**Substantial gainful activity.** Substantial gainful activity is the performance of significant duties over a reasonable period of time while working for pay or profit, or in work generally done for pay or profit. Full-time work (or part-time work done at your employer's convenience) in a competitive work situation for at least the minimum wage conclusively shows that you are able to engage in substantial gainful activity.

Note. Information on minimum wage rates is available on the Department of Labor's Wage and Hour Division webpage at _www.dol.gov/ general/topic/wages/minimumwage._

Substantial gainful activity isn't work you do to take care of yourself or your home. It isn't unpaid work on hobbies, institutional therapy or training, school attendance, clubs, social programs, and similar activities. However, the nature of the work you perform may show that you are able to engage in substantial gainful activity.

The fact that you haven't worked or have been unemployed for some time isn't, of itself, conclusive evidence that you can't engage in substantial gainful activity. See Pub. 524 for some examples of activity that may constitute substantial gainful activity.

**Sheltered employment.** Certain work offered at qualified locations to physically or mentally impaired persons is considered sheltered employment. These qualified locations include work centers that are certified by the Department of Labor (formerly referred to as sheltered workshops), hospitals, and similar institutions; homebound programs; and Department of Veterans Affairs (VA) sponsored homes.

Compared to commercial employment, pay is lower for sheltered employment. Therefore, one usually doesn't look for sheltered employment if he or she can get other employment. The fact that one has accepted sheltered employment isn't proof of the person's ability to engage in substantial gainful activity.

Physician's statement. If you are under age 65, you must have your physician complete a statement certifying that you had a permanent and total disability on the date you retired. You can use the statement in the Instructions for Schedule R.

You don't have to file this statement with your Form 1040, but you must keep it for your records.

**Veterans.** If the Department of Veterans Affairs (VA) certifies that you have a permanent and total disability, you can substitute VA Form 21-0172, Certification of Permanent and Total Disability, for the physician's statement you are required to keep. VA Form 21-0172 must be signed by a person authorized by the VA to do so. You can get this form from your local VA regional office.

**Physician's statement obtained in earlier year.** If you got a physician's statement in an earlier year and, due to your continued disabled condition, you were unable to engage in any substantial gainful activity during 2018, you may not need to get another physician's statement for 2018. For a detailed explanation of the conditions you must meet, see the instructions for Schedule R, Part II. If you meet the required conditions, check the box on your Schedule R, Part II, line 2.

If you checked box 4, 5, or 6 in Part I of Schedule R, enter in the space above the box on line 2 in Part II the first name(s) of the spouse(s) for whom the box is checked.

Disability income. If you are under age 65, you must also have taxable disability income to qualify for the credit. Disability income must meet both of the following requirements.

Figure 32-A. **Are You a Qualified Individual?**

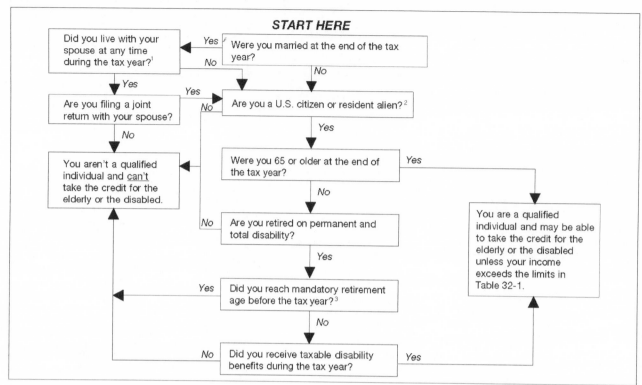

[1] However, you may be able to claim this credit even if you lived with your spouse during the first 6 months of the tax year, as long as you qualify to file as head of household. You qualify to file as head of household if you are considered unmarried and meet certain other conditions. See chapter 2 for more information.

[2] If you were a nonresident alien at any time during the tax year and were married to a U.S. citizen or resident alien at the end of the tax year, see *U.S. Citizen or Resident Alien* under *Qualified Individual*. If you and your spouse choose to treat you as a U.S. resident alien, answer "Yes" to this question.

[3] Mandatory retirement age is the age set by your employer at which you would have been required to retire, had you not become disabled.

Table 32-1. **Income Limits**

IF your filing status is...	THEN, even if you qualify (see Figure 32-A), you CAN'T take the credit if...	
	Your adjusted gross income (AGI)* is equal to or more than...	OR the total of your nontaxable social security and other nontaxable pension(s), annuities, or disability income is equal to or more than...
single, head of household, or qualifying widow(er)	$17,500	$5,000
married filing jointly **and** only one spouse qualifies in Figure 32-A	$20,000	$5,000
married filing jointly **and** both spouses qualify in Figure 32-A	$25,000	$7,500
married filing separately **and** you lived apart from your spouse for all of 2018	$12,500	$3,750

*AGI is the amount on Form 1040, line 7.

1. It must be paid under your employer's accident or health plan or pension plan.

2. It must be included in your income as wages (or payments instead of wages) for the time you are absent from work because of permanent and total disability.

Payments that aren't disability income. Any payment you receive from a plan that doesn't provide for disability retirement isn't disability income. Any lump-sum payment for accrued annual leave that you receive when you retire on disability is a salary payment and isn't disability income.

For purposes of the credit for the elderly or the disabled, disability income doesn't include amounts you receive after you reach mandatory retirement age. Mandatory retirement age is the age set by your employer at which you would have had to retire, had you not become disabled.

Income Limits

To determine if you can claim the credit, you must consider two income limits. The first limit is the amount of your adjusted gross income (AGI). The second limit is the amount of nontaxable social security and other nontaxable pensions, annuities, or disability income you received. The limits are shown in Table 32-1.

If your AGI and nontaxable pensions, annuities, or disability income are less than the income limits, you may be able to claim the credit. See *How To Claim the Credit*, later.

 If your AGI or your nontaxable pensions, annuities, or disability income are equal to or more than the income limits, you can't take the credit.

How To Claim the Credit

You can figure the credit yourself or the IRS will figure it for you. If you want to figure the credit yourself, skip to *Credit Figured by You*, later.

Credit Figured for You

If you want the IRS to figure the credit for you, read the following discussion for the form you will file Form 1040.

Form 1040. If you want the IRS to figure your credit, see *Form 1040 Line Entries* under *Tax Figured by IRS* in chapter 29.

Credit Figured by You

To figure the credit yourself, first check the box in Part I of Schedule R that applies to you. Only check one box in Part I. If you check box 2, 4, 5, 6, or 9 in Part I, also complete Part II of Schedule R.

Next, figure the amount of your credit using Part III of Schedule R. For a step-by-step discussion about filling out Part III of Schedule R, see *Figuring the Credit Yourself* in Pub. 524.

Finally, report the amount from line 22 of Schedule R on your tax return. Include the amount from line 22 of Schedule R on Schedule 3 (Form 1040), line 54; check box **c**, and enter "Sch R." on the line next to that box.

Limit on credit. The amount of the credit you can claim is generally limited to the amount of your tax. Use the Credit Limit Worksheet in the Instructions for Schedule R to determine if your credit is limited.

33.

Child Tax Credit/ Credit for Other Dependents

What's New

 At the time this publication went to print, Congress was considering legislation that would do the following.

1. *Provide additional tax relief for those affected by certain 2018 disasters.*

2. *Extend certain tax benefits that expired at the end of 2017 and that currently can't be claimed on your 2018 tax return.*

3. *Change certain other tax provisions.*

To learn whether this legislation was enacted resulting in changes that affect your 2018 tax return, go to Recent Developments at *IRS.gov/ Pub17.*

New social security number (SSN) requirement for a qualifying child. To claim the child tax credit (CTC) or additional child tax credit (ACTC), your qualifying child must have the required SSN. If you have a qualifying child who was not issued an SSN valid for employment on or before the due date of your 2018 return (including extensions), you can't use the child to claim the CTC or ACTC on either your original or amended 2018 tax return.

If your qualifying child doesn't have the required SSN but has another type of taxpayer identification number (TIN) issued on or before the due date of your 2018 return (including extensions), you may be able to claim the new credit for other dependents (ODC) for that child.

Increased child tax credit. The maximum amount of the CTC has increased to $2,000 per qualifying child.

Increased phaseout for the child tax credit. When figuring the CTC (or credit for other dependents (ODC)), the threshold amount for the limitation based on adjusted gross income has increased to $400,000 in the case of a joint return and $200,000 for all other returns.

Increased additional child tax credit. The maximum amount of the ACTC has increased to $1,400 per qualifying child.

Decreased earned income threshold. The earned income threshold for claiming the ACTC has decreased from $3,000 to $2,500.

New credit for other dependents. If you have a dependent, you may be able to claim the ODC. The ODC is a nonrefundable credit of up to $500 for each eligible dependent who can't be claimed for the child tax credit.

The ODC and CTC are both figured using the Child Tax Credit and Credit for Other Dependents Worksheet and reported on Form 1040, line 12a; or Form 1040NR, line 49. For more information, see *Credit for Other Dependents (ODC)*, later.

Reminders

Abbreviations used throughout this chapter. The following abbreviations will be used in this chapter when appropriate.

- ACTC means additional child tax credit.
- ATIN means adoption taxpayer identification number.
- CTC means child tax credit.
- ITIN means individual taxpayer identification number.
- ODC means credit for other dependents.
- SSN means social security number.
- TIN means taxpayer identification number.

Other abbreviations may be used in this chapter and will be defined as needed.

Delayed refund for returns claiming the EIC or ACTC. The IRS can't issue refunds before mid-February 2019 for returns that properly claim the earned income credit (EIC) or the ACTC. This time frame applies to the entire refund, not just the portion associated with these credits.

Introduction

The CTC is a credit that may reduce your tax by as much as $2,000 for each child who qualifies you for the CTC. See *Limits on the CTC and ODC*, later.

The ACTC is a credit you may be able to take if you're not able to claim the full amount of the CTC.

The ODC is a credit that may reduce your tax by as much as $500 for each eligible dependent.

 The CTC and the ACTC shouldn't be confused with the child and dependent care credit discussed in chapter 31.

If you have no tax. Credits, such as the CTC or the child and dependent care credit, reduce your tax. If your tax on Form 1040, line 11, is zero, you can't claim the child tax credit because there is no tax to reduce. However, you may qualify for the ACTC on line 17b (Form 1040).

Useful Items

You may want to see:

Publication

❏ **972** Child Tax Credit

Form (and Instructions)

❏ **Schedule 8812 (Form 1040)** Child Tax Credit

❏ **8862** Information To Claim Certain Credits After Disallowance

For these and other useful items, go to *IRS.gov/ Forms.*

Taxpayer Identification Number (TIN) Requirements

You must have a TIN by the due date of your return. If you, or your spouse if filing jointly, don't have an SSN or ITIN issued on or before the due date of your 2018 return (including extensions), you can't claim the CTC, ODC, or ACTC on either your original or amended 2018 tax return.

If you apply for an ITIN on or before the due date of your 2018 return (including extensions) and the IRS issues you an ITIN as a result of the application, the IRS will consider your ITIN as issued on or before the due date of your return.

Each qualifying child you use for CTC or ACTC must have the required SSN. If you have a qualifying child who doesn't have the required SSN, you can't use the child to claim the CTC or ACTC on either your original or amended 2018 tax return. The required SSN is one that is valid for employment and that is issued before the due date of your 2018 return (including extensions).

If your qualifying child doesn't have the required SSN but has another type of TIN issued on or before the due date of your 2018 return (including extensions), you may be able to claim the ODC for that child. See *Credit for Other Dependents (ODC)*, later.

Each dependent you use for the ODC must have a TIN by the due date of your return. If you have a dependent who doesn't have an SSN, ITIN, or ATIN issued on or before the due date of your 2018 return (including extensions), you can't use that dependent to claim the ODC on either your original or amended 2018 tax return.

If you apply for an ITIN or ATIN for the dependent on or before the due date of your 2018 return (including extensions) and the IRS issues the ITIN or ATIN as a result of the application, the IRS will consider the ITIN or ATIN as issued on or before the due date of your return.

Improper Claims

Two and 10-year bans for disregarding CTC or ACTC rules. If you claim the CTC, ODC, or ACTC, but you are not eligible for the credit and it is later determined that your error was due to reckless or intentional disregard of the CTC, ODC, or ACTC rules, you will not be allowed to claim any of these credits for 2 years. If it is determined that your error was due to fraud, you will not be allowed to claim any of these credits for 10 years. You also may have to pay penalties.

Form 8862 may be required. If your CTC or ACTC for a year after 2015 was denied or reduced for any reason other than a math or clerical error, you must attach Form 8862 to your tax return to claim the CTC, ACTC, or ODC, unless an exception applies. See Form 8862 and its instructions for more information, including whether an exception applies.

Child Tax Credit (CTC)

The CTC is for individuals who claim a child as a dependent if the child meets additional conditions (described later).

Note. This credit is different from and in addition to the credit for child and dependent care expenses and the earned income credit that you may also be eligible to claim.

The maximum amount you can claim for the credit is $2,000 for each child who qualifies you for the CTC. But, see *Limits on the CTC and ODC*, later.

For more information about claiming the CTC, see *Claiming the CTC and ODC*, later.

Qualifying Child for the CTC

A child qualifies you for the CTC if the child meets all of the following conditions.

1. The child is your son, daughter, stepchild, foster child, brother, sister, stepbrother, stepsister, half brother, half sister, or a descendant of any of them (for example, your grandchild, niece, or nephew).

2. The child was under age 17 at the end of 2018.

3. The child did not provide over half of his or her own support for 2018.

4. The child lived with you for more than half of 2018 (see *Exceptions to time lived with you*, later).

5. The child is claimed as a dependent on your return. See chapter 3 for more information about claiming someone as a dependent.

6. The child does not file a joint return for the year (or files it only to claim a refund of withheld income tax or estimated tax paid).

7. The child was a U.S. citizen, U.S. national, or U.S. resident alien. For more information, see Pub. 519, U.S. Tax Guide for Aliens. If the child was adopted, see *Adopted child*, later.

Example 1. Your son turned 17 on December 30, 2018. He is a citizen of the United States and you claimed him as a dependent on your return. You cannot use him to claim the CTC because he was not **under** age 17 at the end of 2018.

Example 2. Your daughter turned 8 years old in 2018. She is not a citizen of the United States, has an ITIN, and lived in Mexico all of 2018. She is not a qualifying child for the CTC because she was not a U.S. citizen or national or a resident of the United States for 2018.

 If your child is age 17 or older at the end of 2018, see Credit for Other Dependents (ODC), *later.*

Adopted child. An adopted child is always treated as your own child. An adopted child in-

cludes a child lawfully placed with you for legal adoption.

If you are a U.S. citizen or U.S. national and your adopted child lived with you all year as a member of your household in 2018, that child meets condition 7, earlier, to be a qualifying child for the child tax credit.

Exceptions to time lived with you. A child is considered to have lived with you for more than half of 2018 if the child was born or died in 2018 and your home was this child's home for more than half the time he or she was alive. Temporary absences by you or the child for special circumstances, such as school, vacation, business, medical care, military service, or detention in a juvenile facility, count as time the child lived with you.

There also are exceptions for kidnapped children and children of divorced or separated parents. For details, see *Residency Test* in chapter 3.

Qualifying child of more than one person. A special rule applies if your qualifying child is the qualifying child of more than one person. For details, see *Qualifying Child of More Than One Person* in chapter 3.

Required SSN

In addition to being a qualifying child for the CTC (defined earlier), your child must have the required SSN. The required SSN is one that is valid for employment and that is issued by the Social Security Administration before the due date of your 2018 return (including extensions). If your qualifying child does not have the required SSN, you cannot use the qualifying child to claim the CTC (or ACTC) on either your original or amended 2018 tax return.

 If your qualifying child does not have the required SSN, see Credit for Other Dependents (ODC), *later.*

If your child was a U.S. citizen when the child received the SSN, the SSN is valid for employment. If "Not Valid for Employment" is printed on your child's social security card and your child's immigration status has changed so that your child is now a U.S. citizen or permanent resident, ask the SSA for a new social security card without the legend. However, if "Valid for Work Only With DHS Authorization" is printed on your child's social security card, your child has the required SSN only as long as the Department of Homeland Security (DHS) authorization is valid.

If your child does not have the required SSN, you cannot use the child to claim the CTC (or ACTC) on either your original or amended 2018 tax return.

Credit for Other Dependents (ODC)

This credit is for individuals with a dependent who meets additional conditions (described later).

Note. This credit is different from and in addition to the credit for child and dependent care expenses that you also may be eligible to claim.

The maximum amount you can claim for this credit is $500 for each qualifying dependent. See *Limits on the CTC and ODC*, later.

For more information about claiming the ODC, see *Claiming the CTC and ODC*, later.

Qualifying Person for the ODC

A person qualifies you for the ODC if the person meets all of the following conditions.

1. The person is claimed as a dependent on your return. See chapter 3 for more information about claiming someone as a dependent.

2. The person can't be used by you to claim the CTC or ACTC. See *Child Tax Credit (CTC)*, earlier.

3. The person is a U.S. citizen, U.S. national, or U.S. resident alien. For more information, see Pub. 519. If the person is your adopted child, see *Adopted child*, earlier.

Example. Your 10-year-old nephew lives in Mexico and qualifies as your dependent. He is not a U.S. citizen, U.S. national, or U.S. resident alien. For purposes of the ODC, he is not your qualifying child or your qualifying relative.

In addition to being a qualifying person for the ODC (defined earlier), your qualifying person must have an SSN, ITIN, or ATIN issued to him or her on or before the due date of your 2018 return (including extensions). If your qualifying person has not been issued an SSN, ITIN, or ATIN by that date, you can't use the individual to claim the ODC. For more information, see *Taxpayer Identification Number (TIN) Requirements*, earlier.

You can't use the same child to claim both the CTC (or ACTC) and the ODC.

Dependent of more than one person. Special rules apply if your dependent is a qualifying child or qualifying relative of more than one person. See chapter 3 for more information.

Limits on the CTC and ODC

The maximum credit amount of your CTC or ODC may be reduced if either (1) or (2) applies.

1. The amount on Form 1040, line 11, or Form 1040NR, line 45, is less than the total of both credits. If this amount is zero, you cannot take either credit because there is no tax to reduce. But you may be able to take the ACTC if you are claiming the CTC (you can't take ACTC if you are claiming only the ODC). See *Additional Child Tax Credit (ACTC)*, later.

2. Your modified adjusted gross income (AGI) is more than the amount shown below for your filing status.

    a. Married filing jointly — $400,000.

    b. All other filing statuses — $200,000.

Modified AGI. For purposes of the CTC and ODC, your modified AGI is your AGI plus the following amounts that may apply to you.

- Any amount excluded from income because of the exclusion of income from Puerto Rico. On the dotted line next to Form 1040, line 7, enter the amount excluded and identify it as "EPRI." Also attach a copy of any Form(s) 499R-2/W-2PR to your return.

- Any amount on line 45 or line 50 of Form 2555, Foreign Earned Income.

- Any amount on line 18 of Form 2555-EZ, Foreign Earned Income Exclusion.

- Any amount on line 15 of Form 4563, Exclusion of Income for Bona Fide Residents of American Samoa.

If you do not have any of the above, your modified AGI is the same as your AGI.

AGI. Your AGI is the amount on Form 1040, line 7; or Form 1040NR, line 35.

Claiming the CTC and ODC

To claim the CTC or ODC, make sure you meet the following requirements.

- You must file Form 1040 or Form 1040NR and include the name and TIN of each dependent for whom you are claiming the CTC or ODC.

- You must file Form 8862, if applicable. See *Improper Claims*, earlier.

- You must have a timely issued TIN on your tax return for you and your spouse (if filing jointly). See *Taypayer Identification Number (TIN) Requirements*, earlier.

- For each qualifying child under 17 for whom you are claiming the CTC, you must enter the required SSN for the child in column (2) of the *Dependents* section of your tax return and check the Child tax credit box in column (4). See *Child Tax Credit (CTC)*, earlier.

- For each dependent for whom you are claiming the ODC, you must enter the timely issued TIN for the dependent in column (2) of the *Dependents* section of your tax return and check the Credit for other dependents box in column (4). See *Credit for Other Dependents (ODC)*, earlier.

Do not check both the Child tax credit box and the Credit for other dependents box for the same person.

Additional Child Tax Credit (ACTC)

This credit is for certain individuals who get less than the full amount of the CTC. The ACTC may give you a refund even if you do not owe any tax.

The ODC can't be used to figure the ACTC. Only your CTC can be used to figure your ACTC. If you are claiming the ODC but not the CTC, you can't claim the ACTC.

Foreign earned income. If you file Form 2555 or 2555-EZ (both relating to foreign earned income), you cannot claim the ACTC.

How to claim the ACTC. To claim the additional child tax credit, follow the steps below.

1. Be sure you figured the amount, if any, of your CTC and your ODC using the appropriate Child Tax Credit and Credit for Other Dependents Worksheet.

2. If you answered "Yes" on line 11 or line 12 of the Child Tax Credit and Credit for Other Dependents Worksheet in the Instructions for Form 1040, or line 16 of the Child Tax Credit and Credit for Other Dependents Worksheet in Pub. 972, and line 1 of that worksheet is more than zero, use Schedule 8812 to see if you can claim the ACTC.

3. If you have an ACTC on line 15 of Schedule 8812, carry it to Form 1040, line 17b.

4. For each qualifying child under 17 for whom you're claiming the ACTC, be sure to enter the required SSN for the child in column (2) of the *Dependents* section of your tax return and check the Child tax credit box in column (4).

If the amount on line 1 of your Child Tax Credit and Credit for Other Dependents Worksheet is zero, your ACTC also is zero. You don't need to complete Schedule 8812.

34.

Education Credits

What's New

At the time this publication went to print, Congress was considering legislation that would do the following.

1. Provide additional tax relief for those affected by certain 2018 disasters.

2. Extend certain tax benefits that expired at the end of 2017 and that currently can't be claimed on your 2018 tax return.

3. Change certain other tax provisions.

To learn whether this legislation was enacted resulting in changes that affect your 2018 tax return, go to Recent Developments at *IRS.gov/Pub17*.

Limits on modified adjusted gross income (MAGI). The lifetime learning credit MAGI limit increases to $134,000 if you are filing married filing jointly ($67,000 if you are filing single, head of household, or qualifying widow(er)). The American opportunity credit MAGI limits remain unchanged. See Table 34-1.

Reminders

Form 1098-T requirement. For tax years beginning after June 29, 2015, the law requires a taxpayer (or a dependent) to have received a Form 1098-T, Tuition Statement, from an eligible educational institution, whether domestic or foreign.

However, you may claim one of these education benefits if the student does not receive a Form 1098-T because the student's educational institution is not required to furnish a Form 1098-T to the student under existing rules (for example, if the student is a qualified nonresident alien, has qualified education expenses paid entirely with scholarships, has qualified education expenses paid under a formal billing arrangement, or is enrolled in courses for which no credit is awarded). If a student's educational institution is not required to provide a Form 1098-T to the student, you may claim one of these education benefits without a Form 1098-T if you otherwise qualify, can demonstrate that you (or a dependent) were enrolled at an eligible educational institution, and can substantiate the payment of tuition and related expense.

You also may claim this credit if the student attended an eligible educational institution required to furnish Form 1098-T but the student doesn't receive Form 1098-T before you file your tax return (for example, if the institution otherwise required to furnish the Form 1098-T doesn't furnish it or refuses to do so) and you take the following required steps. After January 31, 2019, but before the due date for your 2018 tax return, you or the student must request that the educational institution furnish a Form 1098-T. You must fully cooperate with the educational institution's efforts to gather the information needed to furnish the Form 1098-T. You also must otherwise qualify for the benefit, be able to demonstrate that you (or a dependent) were enrolled at an eligible educational institution, and substantiate the payment of qualified tuition and related expenses.

 To claim the American opportunity credit, you must provide the educational institution's employer identification number (EIN) on your Form 8863. You should be able to obtain this information from Form 1098-T or the educational institution.

Ban on claiming the American opportunity credit. If you claim the American opportunity credit even though you're not eligible, you may be banned from claiming the credit for 2 or 10 years depending on your conduct. See the Caution statement under *Introduction*, later.

Taxpayer identification number (TIN) needed by due date of return. If you haven't been issued a TIN by the due date of your 2018

return (including extensions), you can't claim the American opportunity credit on either your original or an amended 2018 return, even if you later get a TIN. Also, the American opportunity credit isn't allowed on either your original or an amended 2018 return for a student who hasn't been issued a TIN by the due date of your return (including extensions), even if that student later gets a TIN.

Form 8862 may be required. If your American opportunity credit was denied or reduced for any reason *other than a math or clerical error* for any tax year beginning after 2015, you may be required to attach a completed Form 8862, Information To Claim Certain Credits After Disallowance, to your tax return to claim the credit. See Form 8862 and its instructions for details.

Introduction

For 2018, there are two tax credits available to help you offset the costs of higher education by reducing the amount of your income tax. They are:

- The American opportunity credit, and
- The lifetime learning credit.

This chapter will present an overview of these education credits. To get the detailed information, you will need to claim either of the credits, and for examples illustrating that information, see chapters 2 and 3 of Pub. 970.

Can you claim more than one education credit this year? For each student, you can elect for any year only one of the credits. For example, if you choose to claim the American opportunity credit for a child on your 2018 tax return, you can't, for that same child, also claim the lifetime learning credit for 2018.

If you are eligible to claim the American opportunity credit and you also are eligible to claim the lifetime learning credit for the same student in the same year, you can choose to claim either credit, but not both.

If you pay qualified education expenses for more than one student in the same year, you can choose to claim the American opportunity and the lifetime learning credits on a per-student, per-year basis. This means that, for example, you can claim the American opportunity credit for one student and the lifetime learning credit for another student in the same year.

 The American opportunity credit will always be greater than or equal to the lifetime learning credit for any student who is eligible for both credits. However, if any of the conditions for the American opportunity credit, listed in *Table 34-1*, aren't met for any student, you can't take the American opportunity credit for that student. You may be able to take the lifetime learning credit for part or all of that student's qualified education expenses instead. See *chapter 19* of this publication, and Pub. 970, for information on other education benefits.

 Don't claim the American opportunity credit for 2 years after there was a final determination that your claim was due to reckless or intentional disregard of the rules, or 10 years after there was a final determination that your claim was due to fraud.

Differences between the American opportunity and lifetime learning credits. There are several differences between these two credits. These differences are summarized in Table 34-1.

Useful Items
You may want to see:

Publication
❏ **970** Tax Benefits for Education

Form (and Instructions)
❏ **8863** Education Credits (American Opportunity and Lifetime Learning Credits)

For these and other useful items, go to *IRS.gov/Forms*.

Who Can Claim an Education Credit

You may be able to claim an education credit if you, your spouse, or a dependent you claim on your tax return was a student enrolled at or attending an eligible educational institution. For 2018, the credits are based on the amount of qualified education expenses paid for the student in 2018 for academic periods beginning in 2018 and in the first 3 months of 2019.

For example, if you paid $1,500 in December 2018 for qualified tuition for the spring 2019 semester beginning in January 2019, you may be able to use that $1,500 in figuring your 2018 education credit(s).

Academic period. An academic period includes a semester, trimester, quarter, or other period of study (such as a summer school session) as reasonably determined by an educational institution. If an educational institution uses credit hours or clock hours and doesn't have academic terms, each payment period can be treated as an academic period.

Eligible educational institution. An eligible educational institution is generally any college, university, vocational school, or other postsecondary educational institution eligible to participate in a student aid program administered by the U.S. Department of Education. Virtually all accredited public, nonprofit, and proprietary (privately owned profit-making) postsecondary institutions meet this definition. The educational institution should be able to tell you if it is an eligible educational institution.

Certain educational institutions located outside the United States also participate in the U.S. Department of Education's Federal Student Aid (FSA) programs.

Who can claim a dependent's expenses. If a dependent is claimed on a tax return, all qualified education expenses of the student are treated as having been paid by the person

Table 34-1. Comparison of Education Credits for 2018

Caution. You can claim both the American opportunity credit and the lifetime learning credit on the same return—but not for the same student.

	American Opportunity Credit	Lifetime Learning Credit
Maximum credit	Up to $2,500 credit per **eligible student**	Up to $2,000 credit per **return**
Limit on modified adjusted gross income (MAGI)	$180,000 if married filing jointly; $90,000 if single, head of household, or qualifying widow(er)	$134,000 if married filing jointly; $67,000 if single, head of household, or qualifying widow(er)
Refundable or nonrefundable	40% of credit may be refundable	Nonrefundable—credit limited to the amount of tax you must pay on your taxable income
Number of years of postsecondary education	Available **ONLY** if the student had not completed the first 4 years of postsecondary education before 2018	Available for all years of postsecondary education and for courses to acquire or improve job skills
Number of tax years credit available	Available **ONLY** for 4 tax years per eligible student (including any year(s) the Hope scholarship credit was claimed)	Available for an unlimited number of tax years
Type of program required	Student must be pursuing a program leading to a degree or other recognized education credential	Student does not need to be pursuing a program leading to a degree or other recognized education credential
Number of courses	Student must be enrolled at least half-time for at least one academic period beginning during 2018 (or the first 3 months of 2019 if the qualified expenses were paid in 2018)	Available for one or more courses
Felony drug conviction	At the end of 2018, the student had not been convicted of a felony for possessing or distributing a controlled substance	Felony drug convictions do not make the student ineligible
Qualified expenses	Tuition, required enrollment fees, and course materials that the student needs for a course of study whether or not the materials are bought at the educational institution as a condition of enrollment or attendance	Tuition and required enrollment fees (including amounts required to be paid to the institution for course-related books, supplies, and equipment)
Payments for academic periods	Payments made in 2018 for academic periods beginning in 2018 or beginning in the first 3 months of 2019	
TIN needed by filing due date	Filers and students must have a TIN by the due date of their 2018 return (including extensions)	
Educational institution's EIN	You must provide the educational institution's employer identification number (EIN) on your Form 8863	

claiming the dependent. Therefore, only the person claiming the dependent on a tax return can claim an education credit for the student. If a student is not claimed as a dependent on another person's tax return, only the student can claim a credit.

Expenses paid by a third party. Qualified education expenses paid on behalf of the student by someone other than the student (such as a relative) are treated as paid by the student. However, qualified education expenses paid (or treated as paid) by a student who is claimed as a dependent on your tax return are treated as paid by you. Therefore, you are treated as having paid expenses that were paid by the third party. For more information and an example, see *Who Can Claim a Dependent's Expenses* in Pub. 970, chapter 2 or 3.

Who cannot claim a credit. You can't claim an education credit if any of the following apply.

1. Your filing status is married filing separately.

2. You are claimed as a dependent on another person's tax return, such as your parent's return.

3. You (or your spouse) were a nonresident alien for any part of 2018 and the nonresident alien did not elect to be treated as a resident alien for tax purposes.

4. You didn't have a social security number (SSN) (or individual taxpayer identification number (ITIN)) by the due date of your 2018 return (including extensions); you can't claim the American opportunity credit on either your original or an amended 2018 return, even if you later get an SSN

(or ITIN). Also, you can't claim this credit on your original or an amended 2018 return for a student who didn't have an SSN, adoption taxpayer identification number (ATIN), or ITIN by the due date of your return (including extensions), even if the student later gets one of those numbers.

5. Your MAGI is one of the following.

   a. American opportunity credit: $180,000 or more if married filing jointly; or $90,000 or more if single, head of household, or qualifying widow(er).

   b. Lifetime learning credit: $134,000 or more if married filing jointly; or $67,000 or more if single, head of household, or qualifying widow(er).

Generally, your MAGI is the amount on your Form 1040, line 7. However, if you are filing Form 2555, Form 2555-EZ, or Form 4563, or are excluding income from Puerto Rico, add to the amount on your Form 1040, line 7, the amount of income you excluded. For details, see Pub. 970.

Figure 34-A may be helpful in determining if you can claim an education credit on your tax return.

Qualified Education Expenses

Generally, qualified education expenses are amounts paid in 2018 for tuition and fees required for the student's enrollment or attendance at an eligible educational institution. It

doesn't matter whether the expenses were paid in cash, by check, by credit or debit card, or with borrowed funds.

For course-related books, supplies, and equipment, only certain expenses qualify.

- American opportunity credit: Qualified education expenses include amounts spent on books, supplies, and equipment needed for a course of study, whether or not the materials are purchased from the educational institution as a condition of enrollment or attendance.

- Lifetime learning credit: Qualified education expenses include amounts for books, supplies, and equipment **only if** required to be paid to the institution as a condition of enrollment or attendance.

Qualified education expenses include nonacademic fees, such as student activity fees, athletic fees, or other expenses unrelated to the academic course of instruction, **only if** the fee must be paid to the institution as a condition of enrollment or attendance. However, fees for personal expenses (described below) are never qualified education expenses.

Qualified education expenses for either credit **do not** include amounts paid for the following.

- Personal expenses. This means room and board, insurance, medical expenses (including student health fees), transportation, and other similar personal, living, or family expenses.

- Any course or other education involving sports, games, or hobbies, or any noncredit course, unless such course or other education is part of the student's degree program or (for the lifetime learning credit only) helps the student acquire or improve job skills.

The student may receive Form 1098-T from the institution reporting payments received in 2018 (box 1). However, the amount on your Form 1098-T may be different from the amount you paid (or are treated as having paid). In completing Form 8863, use only the amounts you actually paid (plus any amounts you are treated as having paid) in 2018, reduced as necessary, as described in *Adjustments to Qualified Education Expenses*, later. See chapters 2 and 3 of Pub. 970 for more information on Form 1098-T.

Qualified education expenses paid on behalf of the student by someone other than the student (such as a relative) are treated as paid by the student. Qualified education expenses paid (or treated as paid) by a student who is claimed as a dependent on your tax return are treated as paid by you.

If you or the student takes a deduction for higher education expenses, such as on Schedule A or C (Form 1040), you can't use those expenses in your qualified education expenses when figuring your education credits.

 Qualified education expenses for any academic period must be reduced by any tax-free educational assistance allocable to that academic period. See Adjustments to Qualified Education Expenses, *later.*

Prepaid expenses. Qualified education expenses paid in 2018 for an academic period that begins in the first 3 months of 2019 can be used in figuring an education credit for 2018 only. See *Academic period*, earlier. For example, if you pay $2,000 in December 2018 for qualified tuition for the 2019 winter quarter that begins in January 2019, you can use that $2,000 in figuring an education credit for 2018 only (if you meet all the other requirements).

 You cannot use any amount you paid in 2017 or 2019 to figure the qualified education expenses you use to figure your 2018 education credit(s).

Paid with borrowed funds. You can claim an education credit for qualified education expenses paid with the proceeds of a loan. Use the expenses to figure the credit for the year in which the expenses are paid, not the year in which the loan is repaid. Treat loan payments sent directly to the educational institution as paid on the date the institution credits the student's account.

Student withdraws from class(es). You can claim an education credit for qualified education expenses not refunded when a student withdraws.

No Double Benefit Allowed

You can't do any of the following.

- Deduct higher education expenses on your income tax return (as, for example, a business expense) and also claim an education credit based on those same expenses.

- Claim more than one education credit based on the same qualified education expenses.

- Claim an education credit based on the same expenses used to figure the tax-free portion of a distribution from a Coverdell education savings account (ESA) or qualified tuition program (QTP).

- Claim an education credit based on qualified education expenses paid with educational assistance, such as a tax-free scholarship, grant, or employer-provided educational assistance. See *Adjustments to Qualified Education Expenses* next.

Adjustments to Qualified Education Expenses

For each student, reduce the qualified education expenses paid in 2018 by or on behalf of that student under the following rules. The result is the amount of adjusted qualified education expenses for each student.

Tax-free educational assistance. For tax-free educational assistance received in 2018, reduce the qualified educational expenses for each academic period by the amount of tax-free educational assistance allocable to that academic period. See *Academic period*, earlier.

Tax-free educational assistance includes:

- The tax-free parts of scholarships and fellowship grants (including Pell grants) (see chapter 12 of this publication and chapter 1 of Pub. 970 for more information),

- The tax-free part of employer-provided educational assistance (see Pub. 970),

- Veterans' educational assistance (see chapter 1 of Pub. 970), and

- Any other nontaxable (tax-free) payments (other than gifts or inheritances) received as educational assistance.

 You may be able to increase the combined value of an education credit if the student includes some or all of a scholarship or fellowship grant in income in the year it is received. See Coordination with Pell grants and other scholarships, *later. Also, for more information, see examples in* Coordination with Pell grants and other scholarships *in chapters 2 and 3 of Pub. 970.*

Generally, any scholarship or fellowship grant is treated as tax-free educational assistance. However, a scholarship or fellowship grant isn't treated as tax-free educational assistance to the extent the **student** includes it in gross income (the **student** may or may not be required to file a tax return) for the year the scholarship or fellowship grant is received and either:

- The scholarship or fellowship grant (or any part of it) **must** be applied (by its terms) to expenses (such as room and board) other than qualified education expenses as defined in *Qualified education expenses* in Pub. 970, chapter 1; or

- The scholarship or fellowship grant (or any part of it) **may** be applied (by its terms) to expenses (such as room and board) other

than qualified education expenses as defined in *Qualified education expenses* in Pub. 970, chapter 1.

Coordination with Pell grants and other scholarships. You may be able to increase an education credit and reduce your total tax or increase your tax refund if the student (you, your spouse, or your dependent) chooses to include all or part of certain scholarships or fellowship grants in income. The scholarship or fellowship grant must be one that may qualify as a tax-free scholarship under the rules discussed in chapter 1 of Pub. 970. Also, the scholarship or fellowship grant must be one that may (by its terms) be used for expenses other than qualified education expenses (such as room and board).

The fact that the educational institution applies the scholarship or fellowship grant to qualified education expenses (such as tuition and related fees) doesn't prevent the student from choosing to apply certain scholarships or fellowship grants to other expenses (such as room and board). By choosing to do so, the student will include the part applied to other expenses (such as room and board) in gross income and may be required to file a tax return. However, this allows payments made in cash, by check, by credit or debit card, or with borrowed funds such as a student loan, to be applied to qualified education expenses. These payments, unlike certain scholarships or fellowship grants, will not reduce the qualified education expenses available to figure an education credit. The result is generally a larger education credit that reduces your total tax or increases your tax refund.

Example 1. Last year, your child graduated from high school and enrolled in college for the fall semester. You and your child meet all other requirements to claim the American opportunity credit, and you need to determine adjusted qualified education expenses to figure the credit.

Your child has $5,000 of qualified education expenses and $4,000 of room and board. Your child received a $5,000 Pell grant and took out a $2,750 student loan to pay these expenses. You paid the remaining $1,250. The Pell grant by its terms may be used for any of these expenses.

If you and your child choose to apply the Pell grant to the qualified education expenses, it will qualify as a tax-free scholarship under the rules discussed in chapter 1 of Pub. 970. Your child will not include any part of the Pell grant in gross income. After reducing qualified education expenses by the tax-free scholarship, you will have $0 ($5,000 − $5,000) of adjusted qualified education expenses available to figure your credit. Your credit will be $0.

Example 2. The facts are the same as in *Example 1*. If, unlike in *Example 1*, you and your child choose to apply only $1,000 of the Pell grant to the qualified education expenses and to apply the remaining $4,000 to room and board, only $1,000 will qualify as a tax-free scholarship.

Your child will include the $4,000 applied to room and board in gross income, and it will be treated as earned income for purposes of determining whether your child is required to file a tax return. If the $4,000 is your child's only income, your child will not be required to file a tax return.

After reducing qualified education expenses by the tax-free scholarship, you will have $4,000 ($5,000 − $1,000) of adjusted qualified education expenses available to figure your credit. Your refundable American opportunity credit will be $1,000. Your nonrefundable credit may be as much as $1,500, but this depends on your tax liability.

If you aren't otherwise required to file a tax return, you should file to get a refund of your $1,000 refundable credit, but your tax liability and nonrefundable credit will be $0.

Note. The result may be different if your child has other income or if you are the student. If you are the student and you claim the earned income credit, choosing not to apply a Pell grant to qualified education expenses may decrease your earned income credit at certain income levels by increasing your adjusted gross income. For more information, see *Coordination with Pell grants and other scholarships* in chapters 2 and 3 of Pub. 970.

Tax-free educational assistance treated as a refund. Some tax-free educational assistance received after 2018 may be treated as a refund of qualified education expenses paid in 2018. This tax-free educational assistance is any tax-free educational assistance received by you or anyone else after 2018 for qualified education expenses paid on behalf of a student in 2018 (or attributable to enrollment at an eligible educational institution during 2018).

If this tax-free educational assistance is received after 2018 but before you file your 2018 income tax return, see *Refunds received after 2018 but before your income tax return is filed*, later. If this tax-free educational assistance is received after 2018 and after you file your 2018 income tax return, see *Refunds received after 2018 and after your income tax return is filed*, later.

Refunds. A refund of qualified education expenses may reduce qualified education expenses for the tax year or may require you to repay

(recapture) the credit that you claimed in an earlier year. Some tax-free educational assistance received after 2018 may be treated as a refund. See *Tax-free educational assistance*, earlier.

Refunds received in 2018. For each student, figure the adjusted qualified education expenses for 2018 by adding all the qualified education expenses paid in 2018 and subtracting any refunds of those expenses received from the eligible educational institution during 2018.

Refunds received after 2018 but before your income tax return is filed. If anyone receives a refund after 2018 of qualified education expenses paid on behalf of a student in 2018 and the refund is received before you file your 2018 income tax return, reduce the amount of qualified education expenses for 2018 by the amount of the refund.

Refunds received after 2018 and after your income tax return is filed. If anyone receives a refund after 2018 of qualified education expenses paid on behalf of a student in 2018 and the refund is received after you file your 2018 income tax return, you may need to repay some or all of the credit that you claimed. See *Credit recapture* next.

Credit recapture. If any tax-free educational assistance for the qualified education expenses paid in 2018, or any refund of your qualified education expenses paid in 2018, is received after you file your 2018 income tax return, you must recapture (repay) any excess credit. You do this by refiguring the amount of your adjusted qualified education expenses for 2018 by reducing the expenses by the amount of the refund or tax-free educational assistance. You then refigure your education credit(s) for 2018 and figure the amount by which your 2018 tax liability would have increased if you had claimed the refigured credit(s). Include that amount as an additional tax for the year the refund or tax-free assistance was received.

Example. You paid $8,000 for tuition and fees in December 2018 for your child's spring semester beginning in January 2019. You filed your 2018 tax return on February 3, 2019, and claimed a lifetime learning credit of $1,600

($8,000 qualified education expense paid x 0.20). You claimed no other tax credits. After you filed your return, your child withdrew from two courses and you received a refund of $1,400. You must refigure your 2018 lifetime learning credit using $6,600 ($8,000 qualified education expenses − $1,400 refund). The refigured credit is $1,320 and your tax liability increased by $280. You must include the difference of $280 ($1,600 credit originally claimed − $1,320 refigured credit) as additional tax on your 2019 income tax return. See the instructions for your 2019 income tax return to determine where to include this tax.

 If you also pay qualified education expenses in both 2018 and 2019 for an academic period that begins in the first 3 months of 2019 and you receive tax-free educational assistance, or a refund, as described above, you may choose to reduce your qualified education expenses for 2019 instead of reducing your expenses for 2018.

Amounts that do not reduce qualified education expenses. Do not reduce qualified education expenses by amounts paid with funds the student receives as:

- Payment for services, such as wages;
- A loan;
- A gift;
- An inheritance; or
- A withdrawal from the student's personal savings.

Don't reduce the qualified education expenses by any scholarship or fellowship grant reported as income on the student's tax return in the following situations.

- The use of the money is restricted, by the terms of the scholarship or fellowship grant, to costs of attendance (such as room and board) other than qualified education expenses, as defined in chapter 1 of Pub. 970.
- The use of the money is not restricted.

For examples, see chapter 2 in Pub. 970.

Figure 34-A. Can You Claim an Education Credit for 2018?

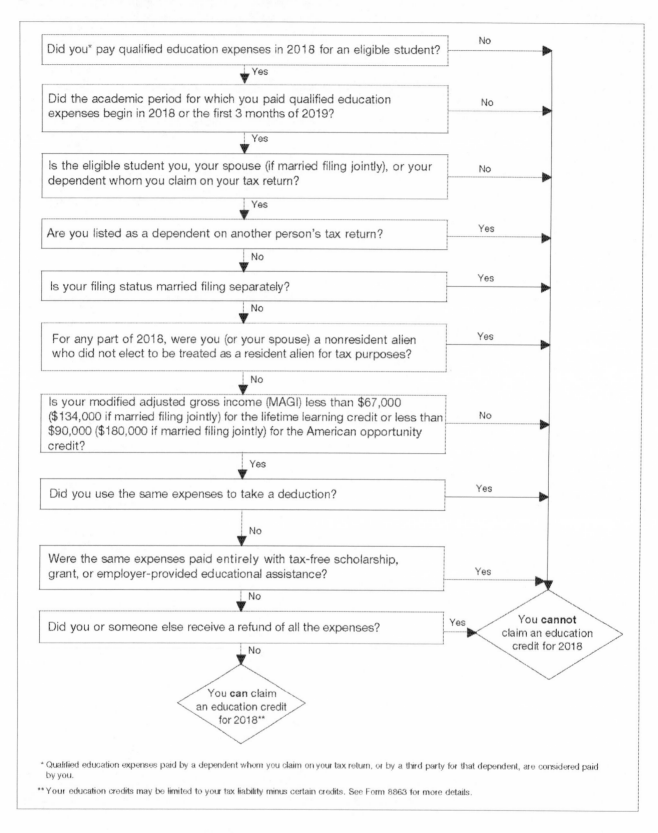

35.

Earned Income Credit (EIC)

What's New

At the time this publication went to print, Congress was considering legislation that would do the following.

1. Provide additional tax relief for those affected by certain 2018 disasters.

2. Extend certain tax benefits that expired at the end of 2017 and that currently can't be claimed on your 2018 tax return.

3. Change certain other tax provisions.

To learn whether this legislation was enacted resulting in changes that affect your 2018 tax return, go to Recent Developments at *IRS.gov/ Pub17*.

Earned income amount. The maximum amount of income you can earn and still get the credit has increased. You may be able to take the credit if:

- You have three or more qualifying children and you earned less than $49,194 ($54,884 if married filing jointly),

- You have two qualifying children and you earned less than $45,802 ($51,492 if married filing jointly),

- You have one qualifying child and you earned less than $40,320 ($46,010 if married filing jointly), or

- You don't have a qualifying child and you earned less than $15,270 ($20,950 if married filing jointly).

Your adjusted gross income also must be less than the amount in the above list that applies to you. For details, see *Rules 1* and *15*, later.

Investment income amount. The maximum amount of investment income you can have and still get the credit has increased to $3,500. See *Rule 6*, later.

Reminders

Delayed refund if claiming the EIC. Due to changes in the law, the IRS can't issue refunds before mid–February 2019, for returns that properly claim the EIC. This applies to the entire refund, not just the portion associated with the EIC.

Childless EIC. You may be able to qualify for the EIC under the rules for taxpayers without a qualifying child if you have a qualifying child for the EIC who is claimed as a qualifying child by another taxpayer.

Increased EIC on certain joint returns. A married person filing a joint return may get more EIC than someone with the same income but a different filing status. As a result, the EIC table has different columns for married persons filing jointly than for everyone else. When you look up your EIC in the EIC Table, be sure to use the correct column for your filing status and the number of children you have.

Online help. You can use the EITC Assistant at *IRS.gov/EITC* to find out if you are eligible for the credit. The EITC Assistant is available in English and Spanish.

EIC questioned by IRS. The IRS may ask you to provide documents to prove you are entitled to claim the EIC. We will tell you what documents to send us. These may include: birth certificates, school records, medical records, etc. The process of establishing your eligibility will delay your refund.

Introduction

The earned income credit (EIC) is a tax credit for certain people who work and have less than $54,884 of earned income. A tax credit usually means more money in your pocket. It reduces the amount of tax you owe. The EIC may also give you a refund.

How do you get the EIC? To claim the EIC, you must:

1. Qualify by meeting certain rules; and

2. File a tax return, even if you:

    a. Don't owe any tax,

    b. Didn't earn enough money to file a return, or

    c. Didn't have income taxes withheld from your pay.

Figure your EIC by using a worksheet in the instructions for Form 1040. Or, if you prefer, you can let the IRS figure the credit for you.

How will this chapter help you? This chapter will explain the following.

- The rules you must meet to qualify for the EIC.

- How to figure the EIC.

Useful Items

You may want to see:

Publication

❏ **596** Earned Income Credit (EIC)

Form (and Instructions)

❏ **Schedule EIC** Earned Income Credit (Qualifying Child Information)

❏ **8862** Information To Claim Certain Credits After Disallowance

For these and other useful items, go to *IRS.gov/ Forms*.

Do You Qualify for the Credit?

To qualify to claim the EIC, you must first meet all of the rules explained in *Part A. Rules for Everyone*. Then you must meet the rules in *Part B.*

Rules if You Have a Qualifying Child, or *Part C. Rules if You Don't Have a Qualifying Child*. There is one final rule you must meet in *Part D. Figuring and Claiming the EIC*. You qualify for the credit if you meet all the rules in each part that applies to you.

- If you have a qualifying child, the rules in *Parts A, B,* and *D* apply to you.

- If you don't have a qualifying child, the rules in *Parts A, C,* and *D* apply to you.

Table 35-1, Earned Income Credit in a Nutshell. Use *Table 35-1* as a guide to *Parts A, B, C,* and *D.* The table is a summary of all the rules in each part.

Do you have a qualifying child? You have a qualifying child only if you have a child who meets the four tests described in *Rule 8*, later, and illustrated in *Figure 35-1*.

If Improper Claim Made in Prior Year

If your EIC for any year after 1996 was denied or reduced for any reason other than a math or clerical error, you must attach a completed Form 8862 to your next tax return to claim the EIC. You must also qualify to claim the EIC by meeting all the rules described in this chapter.

However, if your EIC was denied or reduced as a result of a math or clerical error, don't attach Form 8862 to your next tax return. For example, if your arithmetic is incorrect, the IRS can correct it. If you don't provide a correct social security number, the IRS can deny the EIC. These kinds of errors are called math or clerical errors.

If your EIC for any year after 1996 was denied and it was determined that your error was due to reckless or intentional disregard of the EIC rules, then you can't claim the EIC for the next 2 years. If your error was due to fraud, then you can't claim the EIC for the next 10 years.

More information. See chapter 5 in Pub. 596 for more detailed information about the disallowance period and Form 8862.

Part A. Rules for Everyone

This part of the chapter discusses Rules 1 through 7. You must meet all seven rules to qualify for the EIC. If you don't meet all seven rules, you can't get the credit and you don't need to read the rest of the chapter.

If you meet all seven rules in this part, then read either *Part B* or *Part C* (whichever applies) for more rules you must meet.

Rule 1. Your AGI Must Be Less Than:

- $49,194 ($54,884 for married filing jointly) if you have three or more qualifying children,

- $45,802 ($51,492 for married filing jointly) if you have two qualifying children,

- $40,320 ($46,010 for married filing jointly) if you have one qualifying child, or

Table 35-1. **Earned Income Credit in a Nutshell**

First, you must meet all the rules in this column.		Second, you must meet all the rules in *one* of these columns, whichever applies.		Third, you must meet the rule in this column.
Part A. **Rules for Everyone**		**Part B.** **Rules if You Have a Qualifying Child**	**Part C.** **Rules if You Don't Have a Qualifying Child**	**Part D.** **Figuring and Claiming the EIC**
1. Your adjusted gross income (AGI) must be less than: • $49,194 ($54,884 for married filing jointly) if you have three or more qualifying children, • $45,802 ($51,492 for married filing jointly) if you have two qualifying children, •$40,320 ($46,010 for married filing jointly) if you have one qualifying child, or • $15,270 ($20,950 for married filing jointly) if you don't have a qualifying child.	**2.** You must have a valid social security number (SSN) by the due date of your 2018 return (including extensions). **3.** Your filing status can't be "Married filing separately." **4.** You must be a U.S. citizen or resident alien all year. **5.** You can't file Form 2555 or Form 2555-EZ (relating to foreign earned income). **6.** Your investment income must be $3,500 or less. **7.** You must have earned income.	**8.** Your child must meet the relationship, age, residency, and joint return tests. **9.** Your qualifying child can't be used by more than one person to claim the EIC. **10.** You can't be a qualifying child of another person.	**11.** You must be at least age 25 but under age 65. **12.** You can't be the dependent of another person. **13.** You can't be a qualifying child of another person. **14.** You must have lived in the United States more than half of the year.	**15.** Your earned income must be less than: • $49,194 ($54,884 for married filing jointly) if you have three or more qualifying children, • $45,802 ($51,492 for married filing jointly) if you have two qualifying children, • $40,320 ($46,010 for married filing jointly) if you have one qualifying child, or • $15,270 ($20,950 for married filing jointly) if you don't have a qualifying child.

- $15,270 ($20,950 for married filing jointly) if you don't have a qualifying child.

Adjusted gross income (AGI). AGI is the amount on line 7 of Form 1040. If your AGI is equal to or more than the applicable limit listed above, you can't claim the EIC.

Example. Your AGI is $40,550, you are single, and you have one qualifying child. You can't claim the EIC because your AGI isn't less than $40,320. However, if your filing status was married filing jointly, you might be able to claim the EIC because your AGI is less than $46,010.

Community property. If you are married, but qualify to file as head of household under special rules for married taxpayers living apart (see *Rule 3*, later), and live in a state that has community property laws, your AGI includes that portion of both your and your spouse's wages that you are required to include in gross income. This is different from the community property rules that apply under *Rule 7*, later.

Rule 2. You Must Have a Valid Social Security Number (SSN)

To claim the EIC, you (and your spouse, if filing a joint return) must have a valid SSN issued by the Social Security Administration (SSA) by the due date of your 2018 return (including extensions). Any qualifying child listed on Schedule EIC also must have a valid SSN by the due date of your 2018 return (including extensions). (See *Rule 8*, later, if you have a qualifying child.)

If your social security card (or your spouse's, if filing a joint return) says "Not valid for employment" and your SSN was issued so that you (or your spouse) could get a federally funded benefit, you can't get the EIC. An example of a federally funded benefit is Medicaid.

If you have a card with the legend "Not valid for employment" and your immigration status has changed so that you are now a U.S. citizen or permanent resident, ask the SSA for a new social security card without the legend.

U.S. citizen. If you were a U.S. citizen when you received your SSN, you have a valid SSN.

Valid for work only with INS or DHS authorization. If your social security card reads "Valid for work only with INS authorization" or "Valid for work only with DHS authorization," you have a valid SSN, but only if that authorization is still valid.

SSN missing or incorrect. If an SSN for you or your spouse is missing from your tax return or is incorrect, you may not get the EIC. If an SSN for you or your spouse is missing from your return because either you or your spouse didn't have a valid SSN on or before the due date of your 2018 return (including extensions), and you later get a valid SSN, you can't file an amended return to claim the EIC.

Other taxpayer identification number. You can't get the EIC if, instead of an SSN, you (or your spouse, if filing a joint return) have an individual taxpayer identification number (ITIN). ITINs are issued by the IRS to noncitizens who can't get an SSN.

No SSN. If you don't have a valid SSN by the due date of your 2018 return (including exten-

sions), enter "No" in the space to the left of line 17 (Form 1040). You can't claim the EIC on either your original or an amended 2018 return.

Getting an SSN. If you (or your spouse, if filing a joint return) don't have an SSN, you can apply for one by filing Form SS-5, Application for a Social Security Card, with the SSA. You can get Form SS-5 online at *SSA.gov*, from your local SSA office, or by calling the SSA at 1-800-772-1213.

Filing deadline approaching and still no SSN. If the filing deadline is approaching and you still don't have an SSN, you can request an automatic 6-month extension of time to file your return. You can get this extension by filing Form 4868, Application for Automatic Extension of Time to File U.S. Individual Income Tax Return. For more information, see chapter 1.

Rule 3. Your Filing Status Can't Be Married Filing Separately

If you are married, you usually must file a joint return to claim the EIC. Your filing status can't be "Married filing separately."

Spouse didn't live with you. If you are married and your spouse didn't live in your home at any time during the last 6 months of the year, you may be able to file as head of household, instead of married filing separately. In that case, you may be able to claim the EIC. For detailed information about filing as head of household, see chapter 2.

Rule 4. You Must Be a U.S. Citizen or Resident Alien All Year

If you (or your spouse, if married) were a nonresident alien for any part of the year, you can't claim the EIC unless your filing status is married filing jointly. You can use that filing status only if one spouse is a U.S. citizen or resident alien and you choose to treat the nonresident spouse as a U.S. resident. If you make this choice, you and your spouse are taxed on your worldwide income. If you (or your spouse, if married) were a nonresident alien for any part of the year and your filing status isn't married filing jointly, enter "No" on the line next to line 17 (Form 1040). If you need more information on making this choice, get Pub. 519, U.S. Tax Guide for Aliens.

Rule 5. You Can't File Form 2555 or Form 2555-EZ

You can't claim the EIC if you file Form 2555, Foreign Earned Income, or Form 2555-EZ, Foreign Earned Income Exclusion. You file these forms to exclude income earned in foreign countries from your gross income, or to deduct or exclude a foreign housing amount. U.S. possessions aren't foreign countries. See Pub. 54, Tax Guide for U.S. Citizens and Resident Aliens Abroad, for more detailed information.

Rule 6. Your Investment Income Must Be $3,500 or Less

You can't claim the EIC unless your investment income is $3,500 or less. If your investment income is more than $3,500, you can't claim the credit. For most people, investment income is the total of the following amounts.

- Taxable interest (line 2b of Form 1040).
- Tax-exempt interest (line 2a of Form 1040).
- Dividend income (line 3b of Form 1040).
- Capital gain net income (Schedule 1 (Form 1040), line 13, if more than zero).

See *Rule 6* in chapter 1 of Pub. 596 if:

- You are filing Schedule E (Form 1040), Form 4797, or Form 8814;
- You are reporting income from the rental of personal property on Schedule 1 (Form 1040), line 21; or
- You have income or loss from a passive activity.

Rule 7. You Must Have Earned Income

This credit is called the "earned income" credit because, to qualify, you must work and have earned income. If you are married and file a joint return, you meet this rule if at least one spouse works and has earned income. If you are an employee, earned income includes all

the taxable income you get from your employer. If you are self-employed or a statutory employee, you will figure your earned income on EIC Worksheet B in the instructions for Form 1040.

Earned Income

Earned income includes all of the following types of income.

1. Wages, salaries, tips, and other taxable employee pay. Employee pay is earned income only if it is taxable. Nontaxable employee pay, such as certain dependent care benefits and adoption benefits, isn't earned income. But there is an exception for nontaxable combat pay, which you can choose to include in earned income, as explained below.

2. Net earnings from self-employment.

3. Gross income received as a statutory employee.

Wages, salaries, and tips. Wages, salaries, and tips you receive for working are reported to you on Form W-2, in box 1. You should report these on Form 1040, line 1.

Nontaxable combat pay election. You can elect to include your nontaxable combat pay in earned income for the EIC. Electing to include nontaxable combat pay in earned income may increase or decrease your EIC. Figure the credit with and without your nontaxable combat pay before making the election.

If you make the election, you must include in earned income all nontaxable combat pay you received. If you are filing a joint return and both you and your spouse received nontaxable combat pay, you can each make your own election. In other words, if one of you makes the election, the other one can also make it but does not have to.

The amount of your nontaxable combat pay should be shown in box 12 of your Form W-2 with code "Q."

Self-employed persons and statutory employees. If you are self-employed or received income as a statutory employee, you must use the Form 1040 instructions to see if you qualify to get the EIC.

Approved Form 4361 or Form 4029

This section is for persons who have an approved:

- Form 4361, Application for Exemption From Self-Employment Tax for Use by Ministers, Members of Religious Orders and Christian Science Practitioners; or
- Form 4029, Application for Exemption From Social Security and Medicare Taxes and Waiver of Benefits.

Each approved form exempts certain income from social security taxes. Each form is discussed here in terms of what is or isn't earned income for the EIC.

Form 4361. Whether or not you have an approved Form 4361, amounts you received for performing ministerial duties as an employee count as earned income. This includes wages,

salaries, tips, and other taxable employee compensation.

If you have an approved Form 4361, a nontaxable housing allowance or the nontaxable rental value of a home isn't earned income. Also, amounts you received for performing ministerial duties, but not as an employee, don't count as earned income. Examples include fees for performing marriages and honoraria for delivering speeches.

Form 4029. Whether or not you have an approved Form 4029, all wages, salaries, tips, and other taxable employee compensation count as earned income. However, amounts you received as a self-employed individual don't count as earned income. Also, in figuring earned income, don't subtract losses on Schedule C, C-EZ, or F from wages on line 1 of Form 1040.

Disability Benefits

If you retired on disability, taxable benefits you receive under your employer's disability retirement plan are considered earned income until you reach minimum retirement age. Minimum retirement age generally is the earliest age at which you could have received a pension or annuity if you weren't disabled. You must report your taxable disability payments on Form 1040, line 1 until you reach minimum retirement age.

Beginning on the day after you reach minimum retirement age, payments you receive are taxable as a pension and aren't considered earned income. Report taxable pension payments on Form 1040, lines 4a and 4b.

Disability insurance payments. Payments you received from a disability insurance policy that you paid the premiums for aren't earned income. It doesn't matter whether you have reached minimum retirement age. If this policy is through your employer, the amount may be shown in box 12 of your Form W-2 with code "J."

Income That Is Not Earned Income

Examples of items that aren't earned income include interest and dividends, pensions and annuities, social security and railroad retirement benefits (including disability benefits), alimony and child support, welfare benefits, workers' compensation benefits, unemployment compensation (insurance), nontaxable foster care payments, and veterans' benefits, including VA rehabilitation payments. **Don't** include any of these items in your earned income.

Earnings while an inmate. Amounts received for work performed while an inmate in a penal institution aren't earned income when figuring the EIC. This includes amounts for work performed while in a work release program or while in a halfway house.

Workfare payments. Nontaxable workfare payments aren't earned income for the EIC. These are cash payments certain people receive from a state or local agency that administers public assistance programs funded under the federal Temporary Assistance for Needy Families (TANF) program in return for certain work activities such as (1) work experience activities (including remodeling or repairing public housing) if private sector employment isn't available, or (2) community service program activities.

Community property. If you are married, but qualify to file as head of household under special rules for married taxpayers living apart (see *Rule 3*, earlier), and live in a state that has community property laws, your earned income for the EIC doesn't include any amount earned by your spouse that is treated as belonging to you under those laws. That amount isn't earned income for the EIC, even though you must include it in your gross income on your income tax return. Your earned income includes the entire amount you earned, even if part of it is treated as belonging to your spouse under your state's community property laws.

Nevada, Washington, and California domestic partners. If you are a registered domestic partner in Nevada, Washington, or California, the same rules apply. Your earned income for the EIC doesn't include any amount earned by your partner. Your earned income includes the entire amount you earned. For details, see Pub. 555, Community Property.

Conservation Reserve Program (CRP) payments. If you were receiving social security retirement benefits or social security disability benefits at the time you received any CRP payments, your CRP payments aren't earned income for the EIC.

Nontaxable military pay. Nontaxable pay for members of the Armed Forces isn't considered earned income for the EIC. Examples of nontaxable military pay are combat pay, the Basic Allowance for Housing (BAH), and the Basic Allowance for Subsistence (BAS). See Pub. 3, Armed Forces' Tax Guide, for more information.

 Combat pay. You can elect to include your nontaxable combat pay in earned income for the EIC. See *Nontaxable combat pay election*, earlier.

Part B. Rules if You Have a Qualifying Child

If you have met all of the rules in *Part A*, read *Part B* to see if you have a qualifying child.

Part B discusses *Rules 8* through *10*. You must meet all three of these rules, in addition to the rules in *Parts A* and *D*, to qualify for the EIC with a qualifying child.

When you file Form 1040, you must attach Schedule EIC to your return to claim the EIC with a qualifying child. If you meet all the rules in *Part A* and this part, read *Part D* to find out what to do next.

 If you don't meet Rule 8, you don't have a qualifying child. Read Part C *to find out if you can get the EIC without a qualifying child.*

Rule 8. Your Child Must Meet the Relationship, Age, Residency, and Joint Return Tests

Your child is a qualifying child if your child meets four tests. The four tests are:

1. Relationship,
2. Age,
3. Residency, and
4. Joint return.

The four tests are illustrated in Figure 35-1. The paragraphs that follow contain more information about each test.

Relationship Test

To be your qualifying child, a child must be your:

- Son, daughter, stepchild, foster child, or a descendant of any of them (for example, your grandchild); or
- Brother, sister, half brother, half sister, stepbrother, stepsister, or a descendant of any of them (for example, your niece or nephew).

The following definitions clarify the relationship test.

Adopted child. An adopted child is always treated as your own child. The term "adopted child" includes a child who was lawfully placed with you for legal adoption.

Foster child. For the EIC, a person is your foster child if the child is placed with you by an authorized placement agency or by judgement, decree, or other order of any court of competent jurisdiction. An authorized placement agency includes:

- A state or local government agency,
- A tax-exempt organization licensed by a state, and
- An Indian tribal government or an organization authorized by an Indian tribal government to place Indian children.

Example. Debbie, who is 12 years old, was placed in your care 2 years ago by an authorized agency responsible for placing children in foster homes. Debbie is your foster child.

Age Test

Your child must be:

1. Under age 19 at the end of 2018 and younger than you (or your spouse, if filing jointly);
2. Under age 24 at the end of 2018, a student, and younger than you (or your spouse, if filing jointly); or
3. Permanently and totally disabled at any time during 2018, regardless of age.

The following examples and definitions clarify the age test.

Example 1—Child not under age 19. Your son turned 19 on December 10. Unless he was permanently and totally disabled or a student, he isn't a qualifying child because, at the end of the year, he wasn't **under** age 19.

Example 2—Child not younger than you or your spouse. Your 23-year-old brother, who is a full-time student and unmarried, lives with you and your spouse. He isn't disabled. Both you and your spouse are 21 years old and you file a joint return. Your brother isn't your qualifying child because he isn't younger than you or your spouse.

Example 3—Child younger than your spouse but not younger than you. The facts are the same as in *Example 2* except that your spouse is 25 years old. Because your brother is younger than your spouse, he is your qualifying child even though he isn't younger than you.

Student defined. To qualify as a student, your child must be, during some part of each of any 5 calendar months during the calendar year:

1. A full-time student at a school that has a regular teaching staff, course of study, and regular student body at the school; or
2. A student taking a full-time, on-farm training course given by a school described in (1), or a state, county, or local government.

The 5 calendar months need not be consecutive.

A full-time student is a student who is enrolled for the number of hours or courses the school considers to be full-time attendance.

School defined. A school can be an elementary school, junior or senior high school, college, university, or technical, trade, or mechanical school. However, on-the-job training courses, correspondence schools, and schools offering courses only through the Internet don't count as schools for the EIC.

Vocational high school students. Students who work in co-op jobs in private industry as a part of a school's regular course of classroom and practical training are considered full-time students.

Permanently and totally disabled. Your child is permanently and totally disabled if both of the following apply.

1. He or she can't engage in any substantial gainful activity because of a physical or mental condition.
2. A doctor determines the condition has lasted or can be expected to last continuously for at least a year or can lead to death.

Residency Test

Your child must have lived with you in the United States for more than half of 2018.

You can't claim the EIC for a child who didn't live with you for more than half of the year, even if you paid most of the child's living expenses. The IRS may ask you for documents to show you lived with each qualifying child. Documents you might want to keep for this purpose include school and child care records and other records that show your child's address.

The following paragraphs clarify the residency test.

United States. This means the 50 states and the District of Columbia. It doesn't include Puerto Rico or U.S. possessions such as Guam.

Homeless shelter. Your home can be any location where you regularly live. You don't need a traditional home. For example, if your child lived with you for more than half the year in one or more homeless shelters, your child meets the residency test.

Military personnel stationed outside the United States. U.S. military personnel stationed outside the United States on extended active duty are considered to live in the United States during that duty period for purposes of the EIC.

Extended active duty. Extended active duty means you are called or ordered to duty for an indefinite period or for a period of more than 90 days. Once you begin serving your extended active duty, you are still considered to have been on extended active duty even if you don't serve more than 90 days.

Birth or death of a child. A child who was born or died in 2018 is treated as having lived with you for more than half of 2018 if your home was the child's home for more than half the time he or she was alive in 2018.

Temporary absences. Count time that you or your child is away from home on a temporary absence due to a special circumstance as time the child lived with you. Examples of a special circumstance include illness, school attendance, business, vacation, military service, and detention in a juvenile facility.

Kidnapped child. A kidnapped child is treated as living with you for more than half of the year if the child lived with you for more than half the part of the year before the date of the kidnapping or following the date of the child's return. The child must be presumed by law enforcement authorities to have been kidnapped by someone who isn't a member of your family or your child's family. This treatment applies for all years until the child is returned. However, the last year this treatment can apply is the earlier of:

1. The year there is a determination that the child is dead, or

2. The year the child would have reached age 18.

If your qualifying child has been kidnapped and meets these requirements, enter "KC," instead of a number, on line 6 of Schedule EIC.

Joint Return Test

To meet this test, the child can't file a joint return for the year.

Exception. An exception to the joint return test applies if your child and his or her spouse file a joint return only to claim a refund of income tax withheld or estimated tax paid.

Example 1—Child files joint return. You supported your 18-year-old daughter, and she lived with you all year while her husband was in the Armed Forces. He earned $25,000 for the year. The couple files a joint return. Because your daughter and her husband filed a joint return, she isn't your qualifying child.

Example 2—Child files joint return only to claim a refund of withheld tax. Your 18-year-old son and his 17-year-old wife had $800 of wages from part-time jobs and no other income. They don't have a child. Neither is required to file a tax return. Taxes were taken out of their pay, so they filed a joint return only to get a refund of the withheld taxes. The exception to the joint return test applies, so your son may be your qualifying child if all the other tests are met.

Example 3—Child files joint return to claim American opportunity credit. The facts are the same as in *Example 2* except no taxes were taken out of your son's pay. He and his wife aren't required to file a tax return, but they file a joint return to claim an American opportunity credit of $124 and get a refund of that amount. Because claiming the American opportunity credit is their reason for filing the return, they aren't filing it only to get a refund of income tax withheld or estimated tax paid. The exception to the joint return test doesn't apply, so your son isn't your qualifying child.

Married child. Even if your child doesn't file a joint return, if your child was married at the end of the year, he or she can't be your qualifying child unless:

1. You can claim the child as a dependent, or

2. The reason you can't claim the child as a dependent is that you let the child's other parent claim the child as a dependent under the *Special rule for divorced or separated parents (or parents who live apart)*, later.

Social security number (SSN). The qualifying child must have a valid SSN by the due date of your 2018 return (including extensions) unless the child was born and died in 2018 and you attach to your return a copy of the child's birth certificate, death certificate, or hospital records showing a live birth. You can't claim the EIC on the basis of a qualifying child if:

1. The qualifying child's SSN is missing from your tax return or is incorrect;

2. The qualifying child's social security card says "Not valid for employment" and was issued for use in getting a federally funded benefit; or

3. Instead of an SSN, the qualifying child has:

a. An individual taxpayer identification number (ITIN), which is issued to a noncitizen who can't get an SSN; or

b. An adoption taxpayer identification number (ATIN), which is issued to adopting parents who can't get an SSN for the child being adopted until the adoption is final.

If you have more than one qualifying child and only one has a valid SSN, you can use only that child to claim the EIC. For more information about SSNs, see *Rule 2*.

Rule 9. Your Qualifying Child Can't Be Used by More Than One Person To Claim the EIC

Sometimes a child meets the tests to be a qualifying child of more than one person. However, only one of these persons can actually treat the child as a qualifying child. Only that person can use the child as a qualifying child to take all of the following tax benefits (provided the person is eligible for each benefit).

1. The child tax credit and credit for other dependents and additional child tax credit.

2. Head of household filing status.

3. The credit for child and dependent care expenses.

4. The exclusion for dependent care benefits.

5. The EIC.

The other person can't take any of these benefits based on this qualifying child. In other words, you and the other person can't agree to divide these tax benefits between you.

The tiebreaker rules explained next explain who, if anyone, can claim the EIC when more than one person has the same qualifying child. However, the tiebreaker rules don't apply if the other person is your spouse and you file a joint return.

Tiebreaker rules. To determine which person can treat the child as a qualifying child to claim the six tax benefits just listed, the following tiebreaker rules apply.

- If only one of the persons is the child's parent, the child is treated as the qualifying child of the parent.

- If the parents file a joint return together and can claim the child as a qualifying child, the child is treated as the qualifying child of the parents.

- If the parents don't file a joint return together but both parents claim the child as a qualifying child, the IRS will treat the child as the qualifying child of the parent with whom the child lived for the longer period of time during the year. If the child lived with each parent for the same amount of time, the IRS will treat the child as the qualifying child of the parent who had the higher adjusted gross income (AGI) for the year.

Figure 35-1. **Tests for Qualifying Child**

Caution: Figure 35-1 is an overview of the tests to claim a qualifying child. For details, see the rest of this chapter.

Relationship

A qualifying child is a child who is your . . .

Son, daughter, stepchild, foster child, or a descendant of any of them (for example, your grandchild)

OR

Brother, sister, half brother, half sister, stepbrother, stepsister, or a descendant of any of them (for example, your niece or nephew)

Age

was . . .

Under age 19 at the end of 2018 and younger than you (or your spouse, if filing jointly)

OR

Under age 24 at the end of 2018, a student, and younger than you (or your spouse, if filing jointly)

OR

Permanently and totally disabled at any time during the year, regardless of age

Joint Return

Who is not filing a joint return for 2018 (or is filing a joint return for 2018 only to claim a refund of income tax withheld or estimated tax paid)

Residency

Who lived with you in the United States for more than half of 2018.

 You can't claim the EIC for a child who didn't live with you for more than half of the year, even if you paid most of the child's living expenses. The IRS may ask you for documents to show you lived with each qualifying child. Documents you might want to keep for this purpose include school and child care records and other records that show your child's address.

 *If the child didn't live with you for more than half of the year because of a temporary absence, birth, death, or kidnapping, see Temporary absences, Birth or death of child, or Kidnapped child in this chapter.*

- If no parent can claim the child as a qualifying child, the child is treated as the qualifying child of the person who had the highest AGI for the year.

- If a parent can claim the child as a qualifying child but no parent does so claim the child, the child is treated as the qualifying child of the person who had the highest AGI for the year, but only if that person's AGI is higher than the highest AGI of any of the child's parents who can claim the child.

 If you have a qualifying child for the EIC who is claimed as a qualifying child by another taxpayer, you may be able to qualify for the EIC under the rules for taxpayers without a qualifying child. See Part C, later.

Subject to these tiebreaker rules, you and the other person may be able to choose which of you claims the child as a qualifying child. See Examples 1 through 12, later.

If you can't claim the EIC because your qualifying child is treated under the tiebreaker rules as the qualifying child of another person for 2018, you may be able to take the EIC using a different qualifying child, or take the EIC using the rules in Part C for people who don't have a qualifying child.

If the other person can't claim the EIC. If you and someone else have the same qualifying child but the other person can't claim the EIC because he or she isn't eligible or his or her earned income or AGI is too high, you may be able to treat the child as a qualifying child. See Examples 6 and 7, later. But you can't treat the child as a qualifying child to claim the EIC if the other person uses the child to claim any of the other five tax benefits listed earlier.

Examples. The following examples may help you in determining whether you can claim the EIC when you and someone else have the same qualifying child.

Example 1—Child lived with parent and grandparent. You and your 2-year-old son Jimmy lived with your mother all year. You are 25 years old, unmarried, and your AGI is $9,000. Your only income was $9,000 from a part-time job. Your mother's only income was $20,000 from her job, and her AGI is $20,000. Jimmy's father didn't live with you or Jimmy. The special rule explained later for divorced or separated parents (or parents who live apart) doesn't apply. Jimmy is a qualifying child of both you and your mother because he meets the relationship, age, residency, and joint return tests for both you and your mother. However, only one of you can treat him as a qualifying child to claim the EIC (and the other tax benefits listed earlier for which that person qualifies). He isn't a qualifying child of anyone else, including his father. If you don't claim Jimmy as a qualifying child for the EIC or any of the other tax benefits listed earlier, your mother can treat him as a qualifying child to claim the EIC (and any of the other tax benefits listed earlier for which she qualifies).

Example 2—Parent has higher AGI than grandparent. The facts are the same as in Example 1 except your AGI is $25,000. Because your mother's AGI isn't higher than yours, she can't claim Jimmy as a qualifying child. Only you can claim him.

Example 3—Two persons claim same child. The facts are the same as in Example 1 except that you and your mother both claim Jimmy as a qualifying child. In this case, you as the child's parent will be the only one allowed to claim Jimmy as a qualifying child for the EIC and the other tax benefits listed earlier for which you qualify. The IRS will disallow your mother's claim to the EIC with a qualifying child and any of the other tax benefits listed earlier based on Jimmy. Your mother can't take the EIC for a taxpayer without a qualifying child because her AGI is more than $15,270.

Example 4—Qualifying children split between two persons. The facts are the same as in Example 1 except that you also have two other young children who are qualifying children of both you and your mother. Only one of you can claim each child. However, if your mother's AGI is higher than yours, you can allow your mother to claim one or more of the children. For example, if you claim one child, your mother can claim the other two.

Example 5—Taxpayer who is a qualifying child. The facts are the same as in Example 1 except that you are only 18 years old. This means you are a qualifying child of your mother. Because of Rule 10, discussed next, you can't claim the EIC and can't claim Jimmy as a qualifying child. Only your mother may be able to treat Jimmy as a qualifying child to claim the EIC. If your mother meets all the other requirements for claiming the EIC and you don't claim Jimmy as a qualifying child for any of the other tax benefits listed earlier, your mother can claim both you and Jimmy as qualifying children for the EIC.

Example 6—Grandparent with too much earned income to claim EIC. The facts are the same as in Example 1 except that your mother earned $50,000 from her job. Because your mother's earned income is too high for her to claim the EIC, only you can claim the EIC using your son.

Example 7—Parent with too much earned income to claim EIC. The facts are the same as in Example 1 except that you earned $50,000 from your job and your AGI is $50,500. Your earned income is too high for you to claim the EIC. But your mother can't claim the EIC either, because her AGI isn't higher than yours.

Example 8—Separated parents. You, your husband, and your 10-year-old son Joey lived together until August 1, 2018, when your husband moved out of the household. In August and September, Joey lived with you. For the rest of the year, Joey lived with your husband, who is Joey's father. Joey is a qualifying child of both you and your husband because he lived with each of you for more than half the year and because he met the relationship, age, and joint return tests for both of you. At the end of the year, you and your husband still weren't divorced, legally separated, or separated under a written separation agreement, so the special

rule for divorced or separated parents (or parents who live apart) doesn't apply.

You and your husband will file separate returns. Your husband agrees to let you treat Joey as a qualifying child. This means, if your husband doesn't claim Joey as a qualifying child for any of the tax benefits listed earlier, you can claim him as a qualifying child for any tax benefit listed earlier for which you qualify. However, your filing status is married filing separately, so you can't claim the EIC or the credit for child and dependent care expenses. See Rule 3.

Example 9—Separated parents claim same child. The facts are the same as in Example 8 except that you and your husband both claim Joey as a qualifying child. In this case, only your husband will be allowed to treat Joey as a qualifying child. This is because, during 2018, the boy lived with him longer than with you. You can't claim the EIC (either with or without a qualifying child) because your filing status is married filing separately. Your husband's filing status is also married filing separately, so he can't claim the EIC or the credit for child and dependent care expenses. See Rule 3, earlier.

Example 10—Unmarried parents. You, your 5-year-old son, and your son's father lived together all year. You and your son's father aren't married. Your son is a qualifying child of both you and his father because he meets the relationship, age, residency, and joint return tests for both you and his father. Your earned income and AGI are $12,000, and your son's father's earned income and AGI are $14,000. Neither of you had any other income. Your son's father agrees to let you treat the child as a qualifying child. This means, if your son's father doesn't claim your son as a qualifying child for the EIC or any of the other tax benefits listed earlier, you can claim him as a qualifying child for the EIC and any of the other tax benefits listed earlier for which you qualify.

Example 11—Unmarried parents claim same child. The facts are the same as in Example 10 except that you and your son's father both claim your son as a qualifying child. In this case, only your son's father will be allowed to treat your son as a qualifying child. This is because his AGI, $14,000, is more than your AGI, $12,000. You can claim the EIC without a qualifying child.

Example 12—Child didn't live with a parent. You and your 7-year-old niece, your sister's child, lived with your mother all year. You are 25 years old, and your AGI is $9,300. Your only income was from a part-time job. Your mother's AGI is $15,000. Her only income was from her job. Your niece's parents file jointly, have an AGI of less than $9,000, and don't live with you or their child. Your niece is a qualifying child of both you and your mother because she meets the relationship, age, residency, and joint return tests for both you and your mother. However, only your mother can treat her as a qualifying child. This is because your mother's AGI, $15,000, is more than your AGI, $9,300.

Special rule for divorced or separated parents (or parents who live apart). A child will be treated as the qualifying child of his or her noncustodial parent (for purposes of claiming the child tax credit, but not for the EIC) if all of the following statements are true.

1. The parents:

    a. Are divorced or legally separated under a decree of divorce or separate maintenance;

    b. Are separated under a written separation agreement; or

    c. Lived apart at all times during the last 6 months of 2018, whether or not they are or were married.

2. The child received over half of his or her support for the year from the parents.

3. The child is in the custody of one or both parents for more than half of 2018.

4. Either of the following statements is true.

    a. The custodial parent signs Form 8332 or a substantially similar statement that he or she will not claim the child as a dependent for the year, and the noncustodial parent attaches the form or statement to his or her return. If the divorce decree or separation agreement went into effect after 1984 and before 2009, the noncustodial parent may be able to attach certain pages from the decree or agreement instead of Form 8332.

    b. A pre-1985 decree of divorce or separate maintenance or written separation agreement that applies to 2018 provides that the noncustodial parent can claim the child as a dependent, and the noncustodial parent provides at least $600 for support of the child during 2018.

For details, see chapter 3. If a child is treated as the qualifying child of the noncustodial parent under this special rule for children of divorced or separated parents (or parents who live apart), only the noncustodial parent can claim the child tax credit for the child. However, only the custodial parent, if eligible, or another eligible taxpayer can claim the child as a qualifying child for the EIC. For details and examples, see *Applying the tiebreaker rules to divorced or separated parents (or parents who live apart)* in chapter 3.

Rule 10. You Can't Be a Qualifying Child of Another Taxpayer

You are a qualifying child of another taxpayer (such as your parent, guardian, or foster parent) if all of the following statements are true.

1. You are that person's son, daughter, stepchild, foster child, or a descendant of any of them. Or, you are that person's brother, sister, half brother, half sister, stepbrother, or stepsister (or a descendant of any of them).

2. You were:

    a. Under age 19 at the end of the year and younger than that person (or that person's spouse, if the person files jointly);

    b. Under age 24 at the end of the year, a student, and younger than that person (or that person's spouse, if the person files jointly); or

    c. Permanently and totally disabled, regardless of age.

3. You lived with that person in the United States for more than half of the year.

4. You aren't filing a joint return for the year (or are filing a joint return only to claim a refund of withheld income tax or estimated tax paid).

For more details about the tests to be a qualifying child, see *Rule 8*, earlier.

If you are a qualifying child of another taxpayer, you can't claim the EIC. This is true even if the person for whom you are a qualifying child doesn't claim the EIC or meet all of the rules to claim the EIC. Enter "No" in the space to the left of line 17 (Form 1040).

Example. You and your daughter lived with your mother all year. You are 22 years old, unmarried, and attended a trade school full time. You had a part-time job and earned $5,700. You had no other income. Because you meet the relationship, age, residency, and joint return tests, you are a qualifying child of your mother. She can claim the EIC if she meets all the other requirements. Because you are your mother's qualifying child, you can't claim the EIC. This is so even if your mother can't or doesn't claim the EIC.

Child of person not required to file a return. You aren't the qualifying child of another taxpayer (and so may qualify to claim the EIC) if the person for whom you meet the relationship, age, residency, and joint return tests isn't required to file an income tax return and either:

• Doesn't file an income tax return, or

• Files a return only to get a refund of income tax withheld or estimated tax paid.

Example. The facts are the same as in the last example except your mother had no gross income, isn't required to file a 2018 tax return, and doesn't file a 2018 tax return. As a result, you aren't your mother's qualifying child. You can claim the EIC if you meet all the other requirements to do so.

See *Rule 10* in Pub. 596 for additional examples.

Part C. Rules if You Don't Have a Qualifying Child

Read this part if you:

1. Don't have a qualifying child, and

2. Have met all the rules in *Part A*.

Part C discusses *Rules 11* through *14*. You must meet all four of these rules, in addition to the rules in *Parts A* and *D*, to qualify for the EIC without a qualifying child.

 If you have a qualifying child, the rules in this part don't apply to you. You can claim the credit only if you meet all the rules in Parts A, B, and D. See Rule 8, earlier, to find out if you have a qualifying child.

Rule 11. You Must Be at Least Age 25 but Under Age 65

You must be at least age 25 but under age 65 at the end of 2018. If you are married filing a joint return, either you or your spouse must be at least age 25 but under age 65 at the end of 2018. It doesn't matter which spouse meets the age test, as long as one of the spouses does.

You meet the age test if you were born after December 31, 1953, and before January 2, 1994. If you are married filing a joint return, you meet the age test if either you or your spouse was born after December 31, 1953, and before January 2, 1994.

If neither you nor your spouse meets the age test, you can't claim the EIC. Enter "No" in the space to the left of line 17 (Form 1040).

Example 1. You are age 28 and unmarried. You meet the age test.

Example 2—Spouse meets age test. You are married and filing a joint return. You are age 23 and your spouse is age 27. You meet the age test because your spouse is at least age 25 but under age 65.

Death of spouse. If you are filing a joint return with your spouse who died in 2018, you meet the age test if your spouse was at least age 25 but under age 65 at the time of death.

Your spouse is considered to reach age 25 on the day before his or her 25th birthday. However, the rule for reaching age 65 is different; your spouse reaches age 65 on his or her 65th birthday.

Even if your spouse was born before January 2, 1994, he or she isn't considered at least age 25 at the end of 2018 unless he or she was at least age 25 at the time of death.

Example 1. You are married and filing a joint return with your spouse who died in August 2018. You are age 67. Your spouse would have become age 65 in November 2018. Because your spouse was under age 65 when she died, you meet the age test.

Example 2. Your spouse was born on February 14, 1993, and died on February 13, 2018. Your spouse is considered age 25 at the time of death. However, if your spouse died on February 12, 2018, your spouse isn't considered age 25 at the time of death and isn't at least age 25 at the end of 2018.

Death of taxpayer. If you are preparing a return for someone who died in 2018, see *Death of taxpayer* in Pub. 596 to determine whether the age test in Rule 11 is met.

Rule 12. You Can't Be the Dependent of Another Person

If you **aren't** filing a joint return, you meet this rule if you did **not** check the box under your name that says "Someone can claim you as a dependent."

If you **are** filing a joint return, you meet this rule if you did **not** check either box that says "Someone can claim you as a dependent" or "Someone can claim your spouse as a dependent."

If you aren't sure whether someone else can claim you (or your spouse, if filing a joint return) as a dependent, read the rules for claiming a dependent in chapter 3.

If someone else can claim you (or your spouse, if filing a joint return) as a dependent on his or her return, but doesn't, you still can't claim the credit.

Example 1. In 2018, you were age 25, single, and living at home with your parents. You worked and weren't a student. You earned $7,500. Your parents can't claim you as a dependent. When you file your return, you do not check the "Someone can claim you as a dependent" checkbox. You meet this rule. You can claim the EIC if you meet all the other requirements.

Example 2. The facts are the same as in Example 1 except that you earned $2,000. Your parents can claim you as a dependent but decide not to. You don't meet this rule. You can't claim the credit because your parents could have claimed you as a dependent.

Joint returns. You generally can't be claimed as a dependent by another person if you are married and file a joint return.

However, another person may be able to claim you as a dependent if you and your spouse file a joint return only to get a refund of income tax withheld or estimated tax paid. But neither you nor your spouse can be claimed as a dependent by another person if you claim the EIC on your joint return.

Example 1. You are 26 years old. You and your wife live with your parents and had $800 of wages from part-time jobs and no other income. Neither you nor your wife is required to file a tax return. You don't have a child. Taxes were taken out of your pay, so you file a joint return only to get a refund of the withheld taxes. Your parents aren't disqualified from claiming you as a dependent just because you filed a joint return.

Example 2. The facts are the same as in Example 1 except no taxes were taken out of your pay. Also, you and your wife aren't required to file a tax return, but you file a joint return to claim an EIC of $63 and get a refund of that amount. Because claiming the EIC is your reason for filing the return, you aren't filing it only to get a refund of income tax withheld or estimated tax paid. Your parents can't claim you or your wife as a dependent.

Rule 13. You Can't Be a Qualifying Child of Another Taxpayer

You are a qualifying child of another taxpayer (your parent, guardian, foster parent, etc.) if all of the following statements are true.

1. You are that person's son, daughter, stepchild, foster child, or a descendant of any of them. Or, you are that person's brother, sister, half brother, half sister, stepbrother, or stepsister (or a descendant of any of them).

2. You were:

    a. Under age 19 at the end of the year and younger than that person (or that person's spouse, if the person files jointly);

    b. Under age 24 at the end of the year, a student (as defined in Rule 8, earlier), and younger than that person (or that person's spouse, if the person files jointly); or

    c. Permanently and totally disabled, regardless of age.

3. You lived with that person in the United States for more than half of the year.

4. You aren't filing a joint return for the year (or are filing a joint return only to claim a refund of withheld income tax or estimated tax paid).

For more details about the tests to be a qualifying child, see Rule 8, earlier.

If you are a qualifying child of another taxpayer, you can't claim the EIC. This is true even if the person for whom you are a qualifying child doesn't claim the EIC or meet all of the rules to claim the EIC. Enter "No" in the space to the left of line 17 (Form 1040).

Example. You lived with your mother all year. You are age 26, unmarried, and permanently and totally disabled. Your only income was from a community center where you went three days a week to answer telephones. You earned $5,000 for the year and provided more than half of your own support. Because you meet the relationship, age, residency, and joint return tests, you are a qualifying child of your mother for the EIC. She can claim the EIC if she meets all the other requirements. Because you are a qualifying child of your mother, you can't claim the EIC. This is so even if your mother can't or doesn't claim the EIC.

Joint returns. You generally can't be a qualifying child of another taxpayer if you are married and file a joint return.

However, you may be a qualifying child of another taxpayer if you and your spouse file a joint return for the year only to get a refund of income tax withheld or estimated tax paid. But neither you nor your spouse can be a qualifying child of another taxpayer if you claim the EIC on your joint return.

Child of person not required to file a return. You aren't the qualifying child of another taxpayer (and so may qualify to claim the EIC) if the person for whom you meet the relationship, age, residency, and joint return tests isn't required to file an income tax return and either:

- Doesn't file an income tax return, or
- Files a return only to get a refund of income tax withheld or estimated tax paid.

Example. You lived all year with your father. You are 27 years old, unmarried, permanently and totally disabled, and earned $13,000. You have no other income, no children, and provided more than half of your own support. Your father had no gross income, isn't required to file a 2018 tax return, and doesn't file a 2018 tax return. As a result, you aren't your father's qualifying child. You can claim the EIC if you meet all the other requirements to do so.

See Rule 13 in Pub. 596 for additional examples.

Rule 14. You Must Have Lived in the United States More Than Half of the Year

Your home (and your spouse's, if filing a joint return) must have been in the United States for more than half the year.

If it wasn't, enter "No" in the space to the left of line 17 (Form 1040).

United States. This means the 50 states and the District of Columbia. It doesn't include Puerto Rico or U.S. possessions such as Guam.

Homeless shelter. Your home can be any location where you regularly live. You don't need a traditional home. If you lived in one or more homeless shelters in the United States for more than half the year, you meet this rule.

Military personnel stationed outside the United States. U.S. military personnel stationed outside the United States on extended active duty (defined in Rule 8, earlier) are considered to live in the United States during that duty period for purposes of the EIC.

Part D. Figuring and Claiming the EIC

Read this part if you have met all the rules in Parts A and B, or all the rules in Parts A and C.

Part D discusses Rule 15. You must meet this rule, in addition to the rules in Parts A and B, or Parts A and C, to qualify for the EIC.

This part of the chapter also explains how to figure the amount of your credit. You have two choices.

1. Have the IRS figure the EIC for you. If you want to do this, see The IRS Will Figure the EIC for You, later.

2. Figure the EIC yourself. If you want to do this, see How To Figure the EIC Yourself, later.

Rule 15. Your Earned Income Must Be Less Than:

- $49,194 ($54,884 for married filing jointly) if you have three or more qualifying children,

- $45,802 ($51,492 for married filing jointly) if you have two qualifying children,

- $40,320 ($46,010 for married filing jointly) if you have one qualifying child, or

- $15,270 ($20,950 for married filing jointly) if you don't have a qualifying child.

Earned income generally means wages, salaries, tips, other taxable employee pay, and net earnings from self-employment. Employee pay is earned income only if it is taxable. Nontaxable employee pay, such as certain dependent care benefits and adoption benefits, isn't earned income. But there is an exception for nontaxable combat pay, which you can choose to include in earned income. Earned income is explained in detail in *Rule 7*, earlier.

Figuring earned income. If you are self-employed, a statutory employee, or a member of the clergy or a church employee who files Schedule SE (Form 1040), you will figure your earned income when you fill out Part 4 of EIC Worksheet B in the Form 1040 instructions.

Otherwise, figure your earned income by using the worksheet in *Step 5* of the Form 1040 instructions for line 17a.

When using one of those worksheets to figure your earned income, you will start with the amount on Form 1040, line 1. You will then reduce that amount by any amount included on that line and described in the following list.

- Scholarship or fellowship grants not reported on a Form W-2.

- Inmate's income.

- Pension or annuity from deferred compensation plans.

- Certain Medicaid waiver payments.

Scholarship or fellowship grants not reported on a Form W-2. A scholarship or fellowship grant that wasn't reported to you on a Form W-2 isn't considered earned income for the EIC.

Inmate's income. Amounts received for work performed while an inmate in a penal institution aren't earned income for the EIC. This includes amounts received for work performed while in a work release program or while in a halfway house. If you received any amount for work done while an inmate in a penal institution and that amount is included in the total on Form 1040, line 1, put "PRI" and the amount on the dotted line next to Form 1040, line 1.

Pension or annuity from deferred compensation plans. A pension or annuity from a nonqualified deferred compensation plan or a nongovernmental section 457 plan isn't considered earned income for the EIC. If you received such an amount and it was included in the total on Form 1040, line 1, put "DFC" and the amount on the dotted line next to Form 1040, line 1. This amount may be reported in box 11 of your Form W-2. If you received such an amount but box 11

is blank, contact your employer for the amount received as a pension or annuity.

Medicaid waiver payments. Medicaid waiver payments you exclude from income aren't earned income for the EIC. These are payments received for providing nonmedical support services under a plan of care to someone in your home. If these payments were incorrectly reported to you in box 1 of Form(s) W-2 and you included them in the total on line 1 of Form 1040 because you could not get a corrected Form W-2, report them as described in the instructions for Schedule 1 (Form 1040), line 21. For more information about these payments, see chapter 12 or Pub. 525.

Clergy. If you are a member of the clergy who files Schedule SE and the amount on line 2 of that schedule includes an amount that was also reported on Form 1040, line 1, subtract that amount from the amount on Form 1040, line 1 and enter the result on line 1 of the worksheet in *Step 5* of the Form 1040 instructions for line 17a. Enter "Clergy" in the space to the left of line 17 (Form 1040).

Church employees. A church employee means an employee (other than a minister or member of a religious order) of a church or qualified church-controlled organization that is exempt from employer social security and Medicare taxes. If you received wages as a church employee and included any amount on both line 5a of Schedule SE and Form 1040, line 1, subtract that amount from the amount on Form 1040, line 1 and enter the result on line 1 of the worksheet in *Step 5* of the Form 1040 instructions for line 17a.

The IRS Will Figure the EIC for You

 If you want the IRS to figure the amount of your EIC, see chapter 29.

How To Figure the EIC Yourself

To figure the EIC yourself, use the EIC Worksheet in the instructions for Form 1040. If you have a qualifying child, complete Schedule EIC and attach it to your return.

Special Instructions–EIC Worksheets

You will need to decide whether to use EIC Worksheet A or EIC Worksheet B to figure the amount of your EIC. This section explains how to use these worksheets and how to report the EIC on your return.

EIC Worksheet A. Use EIC Worksheet A if you weren't self-employed at any time in 2018 and aren't a member of the clergy, a church employee who files Schedule SE, or a statutory employee filing Schedule C or C-EZ.

EIC Worksheet B. Use EIC Worksheet B if you were self-employed at any time in 2018 or are a member of the clergy, a church employee who files Schedule SE, or a statutory employee

filing Schedule C or C-EZ. If any of the following situations apply to you, read the paragraph and then complete EIC Worksheet B.

Net earnings from self-employment $400 or more. If your net earnings from self-employment are $400 or more, be sure to correctly fill out Schedule SE (Form 1040) and pay the proper amount of self-employment tax. If you don't, you may not get all the EIC you are entitled to.

 When figuring your net earnings from self-employment, you must claim all your allowable business expenses.

When to use the optional methods of figuring net earnings. Using the optional methods on Schedule SE to figure your net earnings from self-employment may qualify you for the EIC or give you a larger credit. If your net earnings (without using the optional methods) are less than $5,280, see the Instructions for Schedule SE (Form 1040) for details about the optional methods.

More information. If you and your spouse both have self-employment income or either of you is a statutory employee, see *How To Figure the EIC Yourself* in Pub. 596.

Example

The following comprehensive example (complete with filled-in forms) may be helpful.

Example—John and Janet Smith

John and Janet Smith are married and will file a joint return. They have one child, Amy, who is 3 years old. Amy lived with John and Janet for all of 2018. John worked and earned $9,500. Janet worked part of the year and earned $1,500. Their earned income and AGI are $11,000. John and Janet qualify for the EIC and fill out the EIC Worksheet and Schedule EIC. The Smiths will attach Schedule EIC to Form 1040 when they send their completed return to the IRS.

They took the following steps to complete Schedule EIC and the EIC Worksheet.

Completing Schedule EIC

The Smiths complete Schedule EIC because they have a qualifying child.

Completing the EIC Worksheet

Next, the Smiths will complete the EIC Worksheet to figure their EIC.

Line 1. The Smiths enter $11,000 (their earned income).

Line 2. The Smiths go to the Earned Income Credit Table in the Form 1040 instructions. The Smiths find their income of $11,000 within the range of $11,000 to $11,050. They follow this line across to the column that describes their filing status and number of children and find $3,461. They enter $3,461 on line 2.

Line 3. The Smiths enter their AGI of $11,000.

Line 4. The Smiths check the "Yes" box because lines 1 and 3 are the same ($11,000).

They skip line 5 and enter the amount from line 2 ($3,461) on line 6.

Line 6. The Smiths' EIC is $3,461.

SCHEDULE EIC
(Form 1040)

Department of the Treasury
Internal Revenue Service (99)

Earned Income Credit
Qualifying Child Information

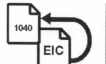

▶ Complete and attach to Form 1040 only if you have a qualifying child.
▶ Go to *www.irs.gov/ScheduleEIC* for the latest information.

OMB No. 1545-0074

2018

Attachment
Sequence No. **43**

Name(s) shown on return

John and Janet Smith

Your social security number

222-00-2222

Before you begin:
- See the instructions for Form 1040, line 17a, to make sure that (**a**) you can take the EIC, and (**b**) you have a qualifying child.
- Be sure the child's name on line 1 and social security number (SSN) on line 2 agree with the child's social security card. Otherwise, at the time we process your return, we may reduce or disallow your EIC. If the name or SSN on the child's social security card is not correct, call the Social Security Administration at 1-800-772-1213.

⚠ **CAUTION**
- *You can't claim the EIC for a child who didn't live with you for more than half of the year.*
- *If you take the EIC even though you are not eligible, you may not be allowed to take the credit for up to 10 years. See the instructions for details.*
- *It will take us longer to process your return and issue your refund if you do not fill in all lines that apply for each qualifying child.*

Qualifying Child Information

	Child 1	Child 2	Child 3
1 Child's name If you have more than three qualifying children, you have to list only three to get the maximum credit.	First name Last name Amy Smith	First name Last name	First name Last name
2 Child's SSN The child must have an SSN as defined in the instructions for Form 1040, line 17a, unless the child was born and died in 2018. If your child was born and died in 2018 and did not have an SSN, enter "Died" on this line and attach a copy of the child's birth certificate, death certificate, or hospital medical records showing a live birth.	000-00-2223		
3 Child's year of birth	Year 2 0 1 5 *If born after 1999 **and** the child is younger than you (or your spouse, if filing jointly), skip lines 4a and 4b; go to line 5.*	Year ____ *If born after 1999 **and** the child is younger than you (or your spouse, if filing jointly), skip lines 4a and 4b; go to line 5.*	Year ____ *If born after 1999 **and** the child is younger than you (or your spouse, if filing jointly), skip lines 4a and 4b; go to line 5.*
4 a Was the child under age 24 at the end of 2018, a student, and younger than you (or your spouse, if filing jointly)?	☐ **Yes.** ☐ **No.** *Go to line 5.* *Go to line 4b.*	☐ **Yes.** ☐ **No.** *Go to line 5.* *Go to line 4b.*	☐ **Yes.** ☐ **No.** *Go to line 5.* *Go to line 4b.*
b Was the child permanently and totally disabled during any part of 2018?	☐ **Yes.** ☐ **No.** *Go to line 5.* The child is not a qualifying child.	☐ **Yes.** ☐ **No.** *Go to line 5.* The child is not a qualifying child.	☐ **Yes.** ☐ **No.** *Go to line 5.* The child is not a qualifying child.
5 Child's relationship to you (for example, son, daughter, grandchild, niece, nephew, eligible foster child, etc.)	daughter		
6 Number of months child lived with you in the United States during 2018 • If the child lived with you for more than half of 2018 but less than 7 months, enter "7." • If the child was born or died in 2018 and your home was the child's home for more than half the time he or she was alive during 2018, enter "12."	12 months *Do not enter more than 12 months.*	____ months *Do not enter more than 12 months.*	____ months *Do not enter more than 12 months.*

For Paperwork Reduction Act Notice, see your tax return instructions.

Cat. No. 13339M

Schedule EIC (Form 1040) 2018

Filled-In EIC Worksheet—John and Janet Smith

Part 1

All Filers

1. Enter your earned income from Step 5.

   | 1 | $11,000 |

2. Look up the amount on line 1 in the EIC Table to find the credit. Be sure you use the correct column for your filing status and the number of children you have. Enter the credit here.

   | 2 | $3,461 |

   If line 2 is zero, (STOP) You can't take the credit. Enter "No EIC" to the left of the entry space for line 17a.

3. Enter the amount from Form 1040, line 7.

   | 3 | $11,000 |

4. Are the amounts on lines 3 and 1 the same?

   ☑ **Yes.** Skip line 5; enter the amount from line 2 on line 6.

   ☐ **No.** Go to line 5.

Part 2

Filers Who Answered "No" on Line 4

5. If you have:
   - No qualifying children, is the amount on line 3 less than $8,500 ($14,200 if married filing jointly)?
   - 1 or more qualifying children, is the amount on line 3 less than $18,700 ($24,350 if married filing jointly)?

   ☐ **Yes.** Leave line 5 blank; enter the amount from line 2 on line 6.

   ☐ **No.** Look up the amount on line 3 in the EIC Table to find the credit. Be sure you use the correct column for your filing status and the number of children you have. Enter the credit here.

   | 5 | |

   Look at the amounts on lines 5 and 2.
   Then, enter the smaller amount on line 6.

Part 3

Your Earned Income Credit

6. This is your earned income credit.

   | 6 | $3,461 |

   Enter this amount on Form 1040, line 17a.

   Reminder—

   √ If you have a qualifying child, complete and attach Schedule EIC.

   If your EIC for a year after 1996 was reduced or disallowed, see Form 8862, who must file, earlier to find out if you must file Form 8862 to take the credit for 2018.

EIC Eligibility Checklist

You may claim the EIC if you answer "Yes" to all the following questions.*	Yes	No

1. Is your AGI less than:
   - $15,270 ($20,950 for married filing jointly) if you don't have a qualifying child,
   - $40,320 ($46,010 for married filing jointly) if you have one qualifying child,
   - $45,802 ($51,492 for married filing jointly) if you have two qualifying children, or
   - $49,194 ($54,884 for married filing jointly) if you have more than two qualifying children?
   (See *Rule 1*.) ☐ ☐

2. Do you, your spouse, and your qualifying child each have a valid SSN that you got by the due date of your 2018 return (including extensions)? (See *Rule 2*.) ☐ ☐

3. Is your filing status married filing jointly, head of household, qualifying widow(er), or single?
   (See *Rule 3*.)
   Caution: If you or your spouse is a nonresident alien, answer "**Yes**" only if your filing status is married filing jointly. (See *Rule 4*.) ☐ ☐

4. Answer "**Yes**" if you aren't filing Form 2555 or Form 2555-EZ. Otherwise, answer "**No**."
   (See *Rule 5*.) ☐ ☐

5. Is your investment income $3,500 or less? (See *Rule 6*.) ☐ ☐

6. Is your total earned income at least $1 but less than: ☐ ☐
   - $15,270 ($20,950 for married filing jointly) if you don't have a qualifying child,
   - $40,320 ($46,010 for married filing jointly) if you have one qualifying child,
   - $45,802 ($51,492 for married filing jointly) if you have two qualifying children, or
   - $49,194 ($54,884 for married filing jointly) if you have more than two qualifying children?
   (See *Rules 7* and *15*.)

7. Answer "**Yes**" if (a) you aren't a qualifying child of another taxpayer or (b) you are filing a joint return. Otherwise, answer "**No**." (See *Rules 10* and *13*.) ☐ ☐

   STOP: If you have a qualifying child, answer questions 8 and 9 and skip 10–12. If you don't have a qualifying child, or if another person is entitled to treat your child as a qualifying child under the tiebreaker rules explained in Rule 9, skip questions 8 and 9 and answer 10–12.*

8. Does your child meet the relationship, age, residency, and joint return tests for a qualifying child and have a valid SSN that he or she got by the due date of your 2018 return (including extensions)?
   (See *Rule 8*.) ☐ ☐

9. Is your child a qualifying child only for you? Answer "**Yes**" if (a) your qualifying child doesn't meet the tests to be a qualifying child of any other person or (b) your qualifying child meets the tests to be a qualifying child of another person but you are the person entitled to treat the child as a qualifying child under the tiebreaker rules explained in *Rule 9*. ☐

10. Were you (or your spouse, if filing a joint return) at least age 25 but under 65 at the end of 2018? (See *Rule 11*.) ☐ ☐

11. Answer "**Yes**" if (a) you can't be claimed as a dependent on anyone else's return or (b) you are filing a joint return. Otherwise answer "**No**." (See *Rule 12*.) ☐ ☐

12. Was your main home (and your spouse's, if filing a joint return) in the United States for more than half the year? (See *Rule 14*.) ☐ ☐

---

* **PERSONS WITH A QUALIFYING CHILD:** If you answered "**Yes**" to questions 1 through 9, you can claim the EIC. Remember to fill out Schedule EIC and attach it to your Form 1040. If you answered "**Yes**" to questions 1 through 7 and "**No**" to question 8, answer questions 10 through 12 to see if you can claim the EIC without a qualifying child.

PERSONS WITHOUT A QUALIFYING CHILD: If you answered "**Yes**" to questions 1 through 7, and 10 through 12, you can claim the EIC.

If you answered "No" to any question that applies to you: You can't claim the EIC.

36.

Premium Tax Credit (PTC)

What's New

At the time this publication went to print, Congress was considering legislation that would do the following.

1. Provide additional tax relief for those affected by certain 2018 disasters.

2. Extend certain tax benefits that expired at the end of 2017 and that currently can't be claimed on your 2018 tax return.

3. Change certain other tax provisions.

To learn whether this legislation was enacted resulting in changes that affect your 2018 tax return, go to Recent Developments at _IRS.gov/ Pub17_.

Reminders

Qualified small employer health reimbursement arrangement (QSEHRA). Under a QSEHRA, an eligible employer can reimburse eligible employees for medical expenses, including premiums for Marketplace health insurance. If you were covered under a QSEHRA, your employer should have reported the annual permitted benefit in box 12 of your Form W-2 with code FF. See _Qualified Small Employer Health Reimbursement Arrangement_ in Pub. 974 for more information.

Report changes in circumstances when you re-enroll in coverage and during the year. If advance payments of the premium tax credit (APTC) are being paid for an individual in your tax family (described later) and you have had certain changes in circumstances (see the examples below), it is important that you promptly report them to the Marketplace where you enrolled in coverage. Reporting changes in circumstances promptly will allow the Marketplace to adjust your APTC to reflect the premium tax credit (PTC) you are estimated to be able to take on your tax return. Adjusting your APTC when you re-enroll in coverage and during the year can help you avoid owing tax when you file your tax return. Changes that you should report to the Marketplace include the following.

- Changes in household income.

- Moving to a different address.

- Gaining or losing eligibility for other health care coverage.

- Gaining, losing, or other changes to employment.

- Birth or adoption.

- Marriage or divorce.

- Other changes affecting the composition of your tax family.

For more information on how to report a change in circumstances to the Marketplace, see _HealthCare.gov_ or your State Marketplace website.

Health coverage tax credit (HCTC). The HCTC is a tax credit that pays a percentage of health insurance premiums for certain eligible taxpayers and their qualified family members. The HCTC and the PTC are different tax credits that have different eligibility rules. If you think you may be eligible for the HCTC, see Form 8885 and its instructions or visit _IRS.gov/HCTC_ before completing Form 8962.

Health insurance options. If you need health coverage, visit _HealthCare.gov_ to learn about health insurance options that are available for you and your family, how to purchase health insurance, and how you might qualify to get financial assistance with the cost of insurance.

Additional information. For additional information about the tax provisions of the Affordable Care Act (ACA), including the individual shared responsibility provisions, the PTC, and the employer shared responsibility provisions, see _IRS.gov/Affordable-Care-Act/Individuals-and-Families_ or call the IRS Healthcare Hotline for ACA questions (1-800-919-0452).

Introduction

You may be able to take the PTC only for health insurance coverage in a qualified health plan purchased through a Health Insurance Marketplace (also known as an Exchange). This includes a qualified health plan purchased on _HealthCare.gov_ or through a State Marketplace.

This chapter provides an overview of the following.

- What is the PTC.

- Who can take the PTC.

- Terms you may need to know.

- How to take the PTC.

Useful Items

You may want to see:

Publication

❏ **974** Premium Tax Credit (PTC)

Form (and Instructions)

❏ **1095-A** Health Insurance Marketplace Statement

❏ **8962** Premium Tax Credit (PTC)

For these and other useful items, go to _IRS.gov/ Forms_.

What is the Premium Tax Credit (PTC)?

Premium tax credit (PTC). The PTC is a tax credit for certain people who enroll, or whose family member enrolls, in a qualified health plan. The credit provides financial assistance to pay the premiums for the qualified health plan offered through a Marketplace by reducing the amount of tax you owe, giving you a refund, or increasing your refund amount. You must file Form 8962 to compute and take the PTC on your tax return.

Advance payment of the premium tax credit (APTC). APTC is a payment during the year to your insurance provider that pays for part or all of the premiums for a qualified health plan covering you or another individual in your tax family. Your APTC eligibility is based on the Marketplace's estimate of the PTC you will be able to take on your tax return. If APTC was paid for you or another individual in your tax family, you must file Form 8962 to reconcile (compare) this APTC with your PTC. If the APTC is _more_ than your PTC, you have excess APTC and you must repay the excess, subject to certain limitations. If the APTC is _less_ than the PTC, you can get a credit for the difference, which reduces your tax payment or increases your refund.

See _Alternative calculation for year of marriage_ below for a special rule that may reduce your excess APTC if you got married in 2018.

Changes in circumstances. The Marketplace determined your eligibility for and the amount of your 2018 APTC using projections of your income and the number of individuals you certified to the Marketplace would be in your tax family (yourself, spouse, and dependents) when you enrolled in a qualified health plan. If this information changed during 2018 and you did not promptly report it to the Marketplace, the amount of APTC paid may be substantially different from the amount of PTC you can take on your tax return. See _Report changes in circumstances when you re-enroll in coverage and during the year_, earlier, for changes that can affect the amount of your PTC.

Alternative calculation for year of marriage. If you got married during 2018 and APTC was paid for an individual in your tax family, you may want to use the alternative calculation for year of marriage, an optional calculation that may allow you to repay less excess APTC than you would under the general rules. You will determine your eligibility using the Instructions for Form 8962 and compute the alternative calculation using Pub. 974.

Who Can Take the PTC?

You can take the PTC for 2018 if you meet all the conditions under (1) **and** (2) below.

1. For at least 1 month of the year, all of the following were true.

   a. An individual in your tax family was enrolled in a qualified health plan offered through the Marketplace on the first day of the month.

   b. That individual was not eligible for minimum essential coverage (MEC) for the month, other than coverage in the individual market. An individual is considered eligible for MEC for the month only if he or she was eligible for every day of the month (see _Minimum essential coverage (MEC)_, later).

c. The portion of the enrollment premiums for the month for which you are responsible was paid by the due date of your tax return (**not** including extensions). However, if you became eligible for APTC because of a successful eligibility appeal and you retroactively enrolled in the plan, then the portion of the enrollment premium for which you are responsible must be paid on or before the 120th day following the date of the appeals decision.

2. You are an applicable taxpayer for 2018. To be an applicable taxpayer, you must meet all of the following requirements.

   a. Your household income for 2018 is at least 100% but no more than 400% of the federal poverty line for your family size (provided in Tables 1-1, 1-2, and 1-3 in the Instructions for Form 8962). See the Instructions for Form 8962 for exceptions when household income is below 100% of the federal poverty line.

   b. No one can claim you as a dependent on a tax return for 2018.

   c. If you were married at the end of 2018, generally you must file a joint return. However, filing a separate return from your spouse will not disqualify you from being an applicable taxpayer if you meet certain requirements described under *Married taxpayers* in the Instructions for Form 8962.

For more information on taking the PTC and the requirements to be an applicable taxpayer, see the Instructions for Form 8962.

Terms You May Need to Know

Tax family. For purposes of the PTC, your tax family consists of the following individuals.

- You, if you file a tax return for the year and you can't be claimed as a dependent on someone else's 2018 tax return.

- Your spouse if filing jointly and he or she can't be claimed as a dependent on someone else's 2018 tax return.

- Your dependents whom you claim on your 2018 tax return. If you are filing Form 1040NR, you should include your dependents in your tax family only if you are a U.S. national; a resident of Canada, Mexico, or South Korea; or a resident of India who was a student or business apprentice. See the Instructions for Form 8962 for more information on figuring your tax family size.

Note. Listing your dependents by name and SSN or individual taxpayer identification number (ITIN) on your tax return is the same as claiming them as dependents. If you have more than four dependents, see the Instructions for Form 1040 or Form 1040NR.

Household income. For purposes of the PTC, household income is the modified adjusted gross income (modified AGI) of you and your spouse (if filing a joint return) plus the modified AGI of each individual in your tax family whom you claim as a dependent and who is required to file a tax return because his or her income meets the income tax return filing threshold. Household income does not include the modified AGI for those individuals whom you claim as dependents and who are filing a 2018 return only to claim a refund of withheld income tax or estimated tax. See the Instructions for Form 8962 to determine your household income.

Modified AGI. For purposes of the PTC, modified AGI is the AGI on your tax return plus certain income that is not subject to tax (foreign earned income, tax-exempt interest, and the portion of social security benefits that is not taxable). Use Worksheet 1-1 and Worksheet 1-2 in the Form 8962 instructions to determine your modified AGI.

Qualified health plan. For purposes of the PTC, a qualified health plan is a health insurance plan or policy purchased through a Marketplace at the bronze, silver, gold, or platinum level. Catastrophic health plans and stand-alone dental plans purchased through the Marketplace, and all plans purchased through the Small Business Health Options Program (SHOP), aren't qualified health plans for purposes of the PTC. Therefore, they do not qualify a taxpayer to take the PTC.

Minimum essential coverage (MEC). A separate tax provision requires most individuals to have qualifying health coverage, qualify for a coverage exemption, or make a payment with their tax return. Health coverage that satisfies this requirement is called MEC. An individual in your tax family who is eligible for MEC (except coverage in the individual market) for a month is not in your coverage family for that month. Therefore, you cannot take the PTC for that individual's coverage for the months that individual is eligible for MEC. In addition to qualified health plans and other coverage in the individual market, MEC includes:

- Most coverage through government-sponsored programs (including Medicaid coverage, Medicare part A or C, the Children's Health Insurance Program (CHIP), certain benefits for veterans and their families, TRICARE, and health coverage for Peace Corps volunteers);

- Most types of employer-sponsored coverage; and

- Other health coverage the Department of Health and Human Services designates as MEC.

In most cases, you are eligible for MEC if the coverage is available to you whether or not you enroll in it. However, special rules apply to certain types of MEC as explained in the Form 8962 instructions.

While coverage purchased in the individual market outside the Marketplace is MEC, eligibility for this type of coverage does not prevent you from being eligible for the PTC for Marketplace coverage. Coverage purchased in the individual market outside the Marketplace does not qualify for the PTC.

For more details on MEC, see Pub. 974. You also can check *IRS.gov/Affordable-Care-Act/Individuals-and-Families/Individual-Shared-Responsibility-Provision* for future updates about types of coverage that are recognized as MEC.

Enrollment premiums. The enrollment premiums are the total amount of the premiums for the month, reduced by any premium amounts for that month that were refunded, for one or more qualified health plans in which any individual in your tax family enrolled. Form 1095-A, Part III, column A, reports the enrollment premiums.

You generally aren't allowed a monthly credit amount for the month if any part of the enrollment premiums for which you are responsible that month has not been paid by the due date of your tax return (not including extensions). However, if you became eligible for APTC because of a successful eligibility appeal and you retroactively enrolled in the plan, the portion of the enrollment premium for which you are responsible must be paid on or before the 120th day following the date of the appeals decision. Premiums another person pays on your behalf are treated as paid by you.

How To Take the PTC

You must file Form 8962 with your income tax return if any of the following apply to you.

- You are taking the PTC.

- APTC was paid for you or another individual in your tax family.

- APTC was paid for an individual you told the Marketplace would be in your tax family and neither you nor anyone else included that individual in a tax family. See *Individual you enrolled who is not included in a tax family* under *Lines 12 Through 23—Monthly Calculation* in the Instructions for Form 8962.

If any of the circumstances above apply to you, you must file an income tax return and attach Form 8962 even if you aren't otherwise required to file. You must file Form 1040.

Form 1095-A, Health Insurance Marketplace Statement. You will need Form 1095-A to complete Form 8962. The Marketplace uses Form 1095-A to report certain information to the IRS about individuals who enrolled in a qualified health plan through the Marketplace. The Marketplace sends copies to individuals to allow them to accurately file a tax return taking the PTC and reconciling APTC. For coverage in 2018, the Marketplace is required to provide or send Form 1095-A to the individual(s) identified in the Marketplace enrollment application by January 31, 2019. If you are expecting to receive Form 1095-A for a qualified health plan and you do not receive it by early February, contact the Marketplace.

Under certain circumstances (for example, where two spouses enroll in a qualified health plan and divorce during the year), the Marketplace will provide Form 1095-A to one taxpayer, but another taxpayer also will need the information from that form to complete Form 8962. The recipient of Form 1095-A should provide a copy to other taxpayers as needed.

Allocating policy amounts. You need to allocate policy amounts (enrollment premiums, second lowest cost silver plan (SLCSP) premiums, and/or APTC) on a Form 1095-A between your tax family and another tax family if:

1. The policy covered at least one individual in your tax family and at least one individual in another tax family; and

2. Either:

   a. You received a Form 1095-A for the policy that does not accurately represent the members of your tax family who were enrolled in the policy (meaning that it either lists someone who is not in your tax family or does not list a member of your tax family who was enrolled in the policy), or

   b. The other tax family received a Form 1095-A for the policy that includes a member of your tax family.

If both (1) and (2) above apply to you, check the "Yes" box on line 9 of Form 8962. For each policy to which (1) and (2) above apply, follow the instructions in Table 3. Allocation of Policy Amounts—Line 9, in the Form 8962 instructions, to determine which allocation rule applies for that qualified health plan.

A qualified health plan may have covered at least one individual in your tax family and one individual not in your tax family if:

- You got divorced during the year,

- You are married but filing a separate return from your spouse,

- You or an individual in your tax family was enrolled in a qualified health plan by someone who is not part of your tax family (for example, your ex-spouse enrolled a child whom you are claiming as a dependent), or

- You or an individual in your tax family enrolled someone not part of your tax family in a qualified health plan (for example, you enrolled a child whom your ex-spouse is claiming as a dependent).

37.

Other Credits

What's New

At the time this publication went to print, Congress was considering legislation that would do the following.

1. *Provide additional tax relief for those affected by certain 2018 disasters.*

2. *Extend certain tax benefits that expired at the end of 2017 and that currently can't be claimed on your 2018 tax return.*

3. *Change certain other tax provisions.*

To learn whether this legislation was enacted resulting in changes that affect your 2018 tax return, go to Recent Developments at IRS.gov/ Pub17.

Adoption credit. The maximum adoption credit is $13,810 for 2018. See *Adoption Credit*, later.

Excess withholding of social security and railroad retirement tax. Social security tax and tier 1 railroad retirement (RRTA) tax were both withheld during 2018 at a rate of 6.2% of wages up to $128,400. If you worked for more than one employer and had too much social security or RRTA tax withheld during 2018, you may be entitled to a credit for the excess withholding. See *Credit for Excess Social Security Tax or Railroad Retirement Tax Withheld*, later.

Alternative fuel vehicle refueling property credit. The credit for alternative fuel vehicle refueling property has expired for refueling property placed in service after 2017. However, some persons who received an alternative fuel vehicle refueling property credit from a fiscal year partnership or fiscal year S corporation may be able to claim the credit. See *Alternative Fuel Vehicle Refueling Property Credit*, later.

Alternative motor vehicle credit. The alternative motor vehicle credit expired for vehicles purchased after 2017. However, if you purchased the vehicle in 2017, but placed it in service during 2018, you may still be able to claim the credit for 2018. See *Alternative Motor Vehicle Credit*, later.

Residential energy credits. The nonbusiness energy property credit expired on December 31, 2017. See *Residential Energy Credit*, later.

Plug-in electric drive motor vehicle credit. The credit for qualified two-wheeled plug-in electric vehicles expired for vehicles acquired after 2017. However, you may be able to claim this credit if you acquired the qualified two-wheeled vehicle in 2017 and placed it in service during 2018. See *Plug-in Electric Drive Motor Vehicle Credit*, later.

Retirement savings contributions credit (saver's credit). Beginning in 2018, you can claim this credit for contributions you make to an ABLE account of which you are the designated beneficiary. See Pub. 907, Tax Highlights for Persons with Disabilities, for more information.

Introduction

This chapter discusses the following nonrefundable credits.

- Adoption credit.
- Alternative motor vehicle credit.
- Alternative fuel vehicle refueling property credit.
- Credit to holders of tax credit bonds.
- Foreign tax credit.
- Mortgage interest credit.
- Nonrefundable credit for prior year minimum tax.
- Plug-in electric drive motor vehicle credit.

- Residential energy credit.
- Retirement savings contributions credit.

This chapter also discusses the following refundable credits.

- Credit for tax on undistributed capital gain.
- Health coverage tax credit.
- Credit for excess social security tax or railroad retirement tax withheld.

Several other credits are discussed in other chapters in this publication.

- Child and dependent care credit (chapter 31).
- Credit for the elderly or the disabled (chapter 32).
- Child tax credit/Credit for other dependents (chapter 33).
- Education credits (chapter 34).
- Earned income credit (chapter 35).
- Premium tax credit (chapter 36).

Nonrefundable credits. The first part of this chapter, *Nonrefundable Credits*, covers 10 credits that you subtract from your tax. These credits may reduce your tax to zero. If these credits are more than your tax, the excess isn't refunded to you.

Refundable credits. The second part of this chapter, *Refundable Credits*, covers three credits that are treated as payments and are refundable to you. These credits are added to the federal income tax withheld and any estimated tax payments you made. If this total is more than your total tax, the excess may be refunded to you.

Useful Items

You may want to see:

Publication

❏ **502** Medical and Dental Expenses

❏ **514** Foreign Tax Credit for Individuals

❏ **530** Tax Information for Homeowners

❏ **590-A** Contributions to Individual Retirement Arrangements (IRAs)

❏ **590-B** Distributions from Individual Retirement Arrangements (IRAs)

Form (and Instructions)

❏ **1116** Foreign Tax Credit

❏ **2439** Notice to Shareholder of Undistributed Long-Term Capital Gains

❏ **5695** Residential Energy Credit

❏ **8396** Mortgage Interest Credit

❏ **8801** Credit for Prior Year Minimum Tax — Individuals, Estates, and Trusts

❏ **8828** Recapture of Federal Mortgage Subsidy

❏ **8839** Qualified Adoption Expenses

- ❑ **8880** Credit for Qualified Retirement Savings Contributions
- ❑ **8885** Health Coverage Tax Credit
- ❑ **8910** Alternative Motor Vehicle Credit
- ❑ **8911** Alternative Fuel Vehicle Refueling Property Credit
- ❑ **8912** Credit to Holders of Tax Credit Bonds
- ❑ **8936** Qualified Plug-in Electric Drive Motor Vehicle Credit

For these and other useful items, go to *IRS.gov/ Forms*.

Nonrefundable Credits

The credits discussed in this part of the chapter can reduce your tax. However, if the total of these credits is more than your tax, the excess isn't refunded to you.

Adoption Credit

You may be able to take a tax credit of up to $13,810 for qualified expenses paid to adopt an eligible child. The credit may be allowed for the adoption of a child with special needs even if you don't have any qualified expenses.

If your modified adjusted gross income (AGI) is more than $207,140, your credit is reduced. If your modified AGI is $247,140 or more, you can't take the credit.

Qualified adoption expenses. Qualified adoption expenses are reasonable and necessary expenses directly related to, and whose principal purpose is for, the legal adoption of an eligible child. These expenses include:

- Adoption fees,
- Court costs,
- Attorney fees,
- Travel expenses (including amounts spent for meals and lodging) while away from home, and
- Re-adoption expenses to adopt a foreign child.

Nonqualified expenses. Qualified adoption expenses don't include expenses:

- That violate state or federal law;
- For carrying out any surrogate parenting arrangement;
- For the adoption of your spouse's child;
- For which you received funds under any federal, state, or local program;
- Allowed as a credit or deduction under any other federal income tax rule; or
- Paid or reimbursed by your employer or any other person or organization.

Eligible child. The term "eligible child" means any individual:

- Under 18 years old, or
- Physically or mentally incapable of caring for himself or herself.

Child with special needs. An eligible child is a child with special needs if all three of the following apply.

1. The child was a citizen or resident of the United States (including U.S. possessions) at the time the adoption process began.
2. A state (including the District of Columbia) has determined that the child can't or shouldn't be returned to his or her parents' home.
3. The state has determined that the child won't be adopted unless assistance is provided to the adoptive parents. Factors used by states to make this determination include:
   a. The child's ethnic background;
   b. The child's age;
   c. Whether the child is a member of a minority or sibling group; and
   d. Whether the child has a medical condition or a physical, mental, or emotional handicap.

The state must make a determination that a child has special needs before the child is considered to be a child with special needs. A child having a specific factor or condition isn't enough to establish that the state has made a determination of special needs.

When to take the credit. Generally, until the adoption becomes final, you take the credit in the year after your qualified expenses were paid or incurred. If the adoption becomes final, you take the credit in the year your expenses were paid or incurred. See the Instructions for Form 8839 for more specific information on when to take the credit.

Foreign child. If the child isn't a U.S. citizen or resident at the time the adoption process began, you can't take the credit unless the adoption becomes final. You treat all adoption expenses paid or incurred in years before the adoption becomes final as paid or incurred in the year it becomes final.

How to take the credit. Figure your 2018 nonrefundable credit and any carryforward to 2019 on Form 8839 and attach it to your Form 1040. Include the credit in your total for Schedule 3 (Form 1040), line 54. Check box c and enter "8839" on the line next to that box.

More information. For more information, see the Instructions for Form 8839.

Alternative Motor Vehicle Credit

An alternative motor vehicle is a vehicle with at least four wheels that qualifies as a qualified fuel cell vehicle.

The alternative motor vehicle credit expired for vehicles purchased after 2017. However, if you purchased the vehicle in 2017, but placed it in service during 2018, you may still be able to claim the credit for 2018.

 At the time this publication went to print, Congress had not enacted legislation on expired provisions. To find out if legislation has been enacted, go to Recent Developments at IRS.gov/Pub17.

Qualified fuel cell vehicle. A qualified fuel cell vehicle is a new vehicle propelled by power derived from one or more cells that convert chemical energy directly into electricity by combining oxygen with hydrogen fuel, and that meets certain additional requirements.

Amount of credit. Generally, you can rely on the manufacturer's certification to the IRS that a specific make, model, and model year vehicle qualifies for the credit and the amount of the credit for which it qualifies. In the case of a foreign manufacturer, you generally can rely on its domestic distributor's certification to the IRS.

Ordinarily, the amount of the credit is 100% of the manufacturer's (or domestic distributor's) certification to the IRS of the maximum credit allowable.

How to take the credit. To take the credit, you must complete Form 8910 and attach it to your Form 1040. Include the credit in your total for Schedule 3 (Form 1040), line 54. Check box c and enter "8910" on the line next to that box.

Don't report vehicles purchased after 2017 on Form 8910 unless the credit is extended.

More information. For more information on the credit, see the Instructions for Form 8910.

Alternative Fuel Vehicle Refueling Property Credit

The credit for alternative fuel vehicle refueling property has expired for refueling property placed in service after 2017.

However, if you are a partner in a fiscal year partnership or a shareholder of a fiscal year S corporation, you may receive an alternative fuel vehicle refueling property credit for 2018. See the instructions for your Schedule K-1 for details on how to claim the credit.

⚠️ *At the time this publication went to print, Congress had not enacted legislation on expired provisions. To find out if legislation has been enacted, go to Recent Developments at IRS.gov/Pub17.*

More information. For more information on the credit, see the Instructions for Form 8911.

Credit to Holders of Tax Credit Bonds

Tax credit bonds are bonds in which the holder receives a tax credit in lieu of some or all of the interest on the bond.

You may be able to take a credit if you are a holder of one of the following bonds.

- Clean renewable energy bonds (issued before 2010).
- New clean renewable energy bonds.
- Qualified energy conservation bonds.
- Qualified school construction bonds.
- Qualified zone academy bonds.
- Build America bonds.

In some instances, an issuer may elect to receive a credit for interest paid on the bond. If the issuer makes this election, you can't also claim a credit.

Interest income. The amount of any tax credit allowed (figured before applying tax liability limits) must be included as interest income on your tax return.

How to take the credit. Complete Form 8912 and attach it to your Form 1040. Include the credit in your total for Schedule 3 (Form 1040), line 54. Check box c and enter "8912" on the line next to that box.

More information. For more information, see the Instructions for Form 8912.

Foreign Tax Credit

You generally can choose to take income taxes you paid or accrued during the year to a foreign country or U.S. possession as a credit against your U.S. income tax. Or you can deduct them as an itemized deduction (see chapter 23).

You can't take a credit (or deduction) for foreign income taxes paid on income that you exclude from U.S. tax under any of the following.

1. Foreign earned income exclusion.

2. Foreign housing exclusion.

3. Income from Puerto Rico exempt from U.S. tax.

4. Possession exclusion.

Limit on the credit. Unless you can elect not to file Form 1116 (see *Exception*, later), your foreign tax credit can't be more than your U.S. tax liability (the total of Form 1040, line 11a, and Schedule 2 (Form 1040), line 46, multiplied by a fraction. The numerator of the fraction is your taxable income from sources outside the United States. The denominator is your total taxable income from U.S. and foreign sources. See Pub. 514 for more information.

How to take the credit. Complete Form 1116 and attach it to your Form 1040. Enter the credit on Schedule 3 (Form 1040), line 48.

Exception. You don't have to complete Form 1116 to take the credit if all of the following apply.

1. All of your foreign source gross income was "passive category income" (which includes most interest and dividends) and all of that income and the foreign tax paid on it were reported to you on qualified payee statements such as Form 1099-INT and Form 1099-DIV (or substitute statements).

2. You held the stock or bonds on which the dividends and interest were paid for at least 16 days and weren't obligated to pay these amounts to someone else.

3. You aren't filing Form 4563 or excluding income from sources within Puerto Rico.

4. The total of your foreign taxes wasn't more than $300 (not more than $600 if married filing jointly).

5. All of your foreign taxes were:

    a. Legally owed and not eligible for a refund or reduced tax rate under a tax treaty, and

    b. Paid to countries that are recognized by the United States and don't support terrorism.

More information. For more information on the credit and these requirements, see the Instructions for Form 1116.

Mortgage Interest Credit

The mortgage interest credit is intended to help lower-income individuals own a home. If you qualify, you can take the credit each year for part of the home mortgage interest you pay.

Who qualifies. You may be eligible for the credit if you were issued a qualified Mortgage Credit Certificate (MCC) from your state or local government. Generally, an MCC is issued only in connection with a new mortgage for the purchase of your main home.

Amount of credit. Figure your credit on Form 8396. If your mortgage loan amount is equal to (or smaller than) the certified indebtedness (loan) amount shown on your MCC, enter on Form 8396, line 1, all the interest you paid on your mortgage during the year.

If your mortgage loan amount is larger than the certified indebtedness amount shown on your MCC, you can figure the credit on only part of the interest you paid. To find the amount to enter on line 1, multiply the total interest you paid during the year on your mortgage by the following fraction.

$$\frac{\text{Certified indebtedness amount on your MCC}}{\text{Original amount of your mortgage}}$$

Limit based on credit rate. If the certificate credit rate is more than 20%, the credit you are allowed can't be more than $2,000. If two or more persons (other than a married couple filing a joint return) hold an interest in the home to which the MCC relates, this $2,000 limit must be divided based on the interest held by each person. See Pub. 530 for more information.

Carryforward. Your credit (after applying the limit based on the credit rate) is also subject to a limit based on your tax that is figured using Form 8396. If your allowable credit is reduced because of this tax liability limit, you can carry forward the unused portion of the credit to the next 3 years or until used, whichever comes first.

If you are subject to the $2,000 limit because your certificate credit rate is more than 20%, you can't carry forward any amount more than $2,000 (or your share of the $2,000 if you must divide the credit).

How to take the credit. Figure your 2018 credit and any carryforward to 2019 on Form 8396, and attach it to your Form 1040. Be sure to include any credit carryforward from 2015, 2016, and 2017.

Include the credit in your total for Schedule 3 (Form 1040), line 54. Check box c and enter "8396" on the line next to that box.

Reduced home mortgage interest deduction. If you itemize your deductions on Schedule A (Form 1040), you must reduce your home mortgage interest deduction by the amount of the mortgage interest credit shown on Form 8396, line 3. You must do this even if part of that amount is to be carried forward to 2019. For more information about the home mortgage interest deduction, see chapter 24.

Recapture of federal mortgage subsidy. If you received an MCC with your mortgage loan, you may have to recapture (pay back) all or part of the benefit you received from that program. The recapture may be required if you sell or dispose of your home at a gain during the first 9 years after the date you closed your mortgage loan. See the Instructions for Form 8828 and chapter 15 for more information.

More information. For more information on the credit, see the Form 8396 instructions.

Nonrefundable Credit for Prior Year Minimum Tax

The tax laws give special treatment to some kinds of income and allow special deductions and credits for some kinds of expenses. If you benefit from these laws, you may have to pay at least a minimum amount of tax in addition to any other tax on these items. This is called the alternative minimum tax.

The special treatment of some items of income and expenses only allows you to postpone paying tax until a later year. If in prior years you paid alternative minimum tax because of these tax postponement items, you may be able to take a credit for prior year minimum tax against your current year's regular tax.

You may be able to take a credit against your regular tax if for 2017 you had:

- An alternative minimum tax liability and adjustments or preferences other than exclusion items,

- A minimum tax credit that you are carrying forward to 2018, or

- An unallowed qualified electric vehicle credit.

How to take the credit. Figure your 2018 nonrefundable credit (if any), and any carryforward to 2019 on Form 8801, and attach it to your Form 1040. Include the credit in your total for Schedule 3 (Form 1040), line 54, and check box b. You can carry forward any unused credit for prior year minimum tax to later years until it is completely used.

More information. For more information on the credit, see the Instructions for Form 8801.

Plug-in Electric Drive Motor Vehicle Credit

You may be able to take this credit if you placed in service for business or personal use a qualified plug-in electric drive motor vehicle in 2018 and you meet some other requirements.

The credit for qualified two-wheeled plug-in electric vehicles expired for vehicles acquired after 2017. However, you may be able to take the credit if you acquired the vehicle in 2017 but placed it in service for business or personal use in 2018. See the Instructions for Form 8936 for more information.

 At the time this publication went to print, Congress had not enacted legislation on expired provisions. To find out if legislation has been enacted, go to Recent Developments at IRS.gov/Pub17.

Qualified plug-in electric drive motor vehicle. This is a new vehicle with at least four wheels that:

- Is propelled to a significant extent by an electric motor that draws electricity from a battery that has a capacity of not less than 4 kilowatt hours and is capable of being recharged from an external source of electricity, and

- Has a gross vehicle weight of less than 14,000 pounds.

Qualified two-wheeled plug-in electric vehicle. This is a new vehicle with two wheels that:

- Is capable of achieving a speed of 45 miles per hour or greater,

- Is propelled to a significant extent by an electric motor that draws electricity from a battery that has a capacity of not less than 2.5 kilowatt hours and is capable of being recharged from an external source of electricity, and

- Has a gross vehicle weight of less than 14,000 pounds.

Certification and other requirements. Generally, you can rely on the manufacturer's (or, in the case of a foreign manufacturer, its domestic distributor's) certification to the IRS that a specific make, model, and model year vehicle qualifies for the credit and, if applicable, the amount of the credit for which it qualifies. However, if the IRS publishes an announcement that the certification for any specific make, model, and model year vehicle has been withdrawn, you can't rely on the certification for such a vehicle purchased after the date of publication of the withdrawal announcement.

The following requirements must also be met to qualify for the credit.

- You are the owner of the vehicle. If the vehicle is leased, only the lessor, and not the lessee, is entitled to the credit.

- You placed the vehicle in service during 2018.

- The vehicle is manufactured primarily for use on public streets, roads, and highways.

- The original use of the vehicle began with you.

- You acquired the vehicle for your use or to lease to others, and not for resale.

- You use the vehicle primarily in the United States.

How to take the credit. To take the credit, you must complete Form 8936 and attach it to your Form 1040. Include the credit in your total for Schedule 3 (Form 1040), line 54. Check box c and enter "8936" on the line next to that box.

Don't report two-wheeled vehicles acquired after 2017 on Form 8936 unless the credit is extended.

More information. For more information on the credit, see the Instructions for Form 8936.

Residential Energy Credit

You may be able to claim the residential energy efficient property credit if you made energy saving improvements to your home located in the United States in 2018.

Note. If you are a member of a condominium management association for a condominium you own or a tenant-stockholder in a cooperative housing corporation, you are treated as having paid your proportionate share of any costs of the association or corporation.

 The nonbusiness energy property credit has expired. At the time this publication went to print, Congress had not enacted legislation on expired provisions. To find out if legislation has been enacted, go to Recent Developments at IRS.gov/Pub17.

Residential energy efficient property credit. You may be able to take a credit of 30% of your costs of qualified solar electric property, qualified solar water heating property, small wind energy property, geothermal heat pump property, and fuel cell property. Include any labor costs properly allocable to the onsite preparation, assembly, or original installation of the residential energy efficient property and for piping or wiring to interconnect such property to the home.

Basis reduction. You must reduce the basis of your home by the amount of any credit allowed.

How to take the credit. Complete Form 5695 and attach it to your Form 1040. Enter the credit on Schedule 3 (Form 1040), line 53.

More information. For more information on the credit, see the Instructions for Form 5695.

Retirement Savings Contributions Credit (Saver's Credit)

You may be able to take this credit if you, or your spouse if filing jointly, made:

- Contributions (other than rollover contributions) to a traditional or Roth IRA;

- Elective deferrals to a 401(k) or 403(b) plan (including designated Roth contributions) or to a governmental 457, SEP, or SIMPLE plan;

- Voluntary employee contributions to a qualified retirement plan (including the federal Thrift Savings Plan);

- Contributions to a 501(c)(18)(D) plan; or

- Contributions to an ABLE account by the designated beneficiary.

However, you can't take the credit if either of the following applies.

1. The amount on Form 1040, line 7, is more than $31,500 ($47,250 if head of

household; $63,000 if married filing jointly).

2. The person(s) who made the qualified contribution or elective deferral: (a) was born after January 1, 2001, (b) is claimed as a dependent on someone else's 2018 tax return, or (c) was a student (defined next).

Student. You were a student if during any part of 5 calendar months of 2018 you:

- Were enrolled as a full-time student at a school; or

- Took a full-time, on-farm training course given by a school or a state, county, or local government agency.

School. A school includes a technical, trade, or mechanical school. It doesn't include an on-the-job training course, correspondence school, or school offering courses only through the Internet.

How to take the credit. Figure the credit on Form 8880. Enter the credit on your Schedule 3 (Form 1040), line 51, and attach Form 8880 to your return.

More information. For more information on the credit, see the Form 8880 instructions.

Refundable Credits

The credits discussed in this part of the chapter are treated as payments of tax. If the total of these credits, withheld federal income tax, and estimated tax payments is more than your total tax, the excess can be refunded to you.

Credit for Tax on Undistributed Capital Gain

You must include in your income any amounts that regulated investment companies (commonly called mutual funds) or real estate investment trusts (REITs) allocated to you as capital gain distributions, even if you didn't actually receive them. If the mutual fund or REIT paid a tax on the capital gain, you are allowed a credit for the tax since it is considered paid by you. The mutual fund or REIT will send you Form 2439 showing your share of the undistributed capital gains and the tax paid, if any.

How to take the credit. To take the credit, attach Copy B of Form 2439 to your Form 1040. Include the amount from box 2 of your Form 2439 in the total for Schedule 5 (Form 1040), line 74, and check box a.

More information. See *Capital Gain Distributions* in chapter 8 for more information on undistributed capital gains.

Health Coverage Tax Credit

 Relatively few people are eligible for the Health Coverage Tax Credit (HCTC). See the Instructions for Form 8885, Health Coverage Tax Credit, to determine whether you can claim the credit.

You can elect to take the health coverage tax credit only if (a) you were an eligible trade adjustment assistance (TAA) recipient, alternative TAA (ATAA) recipient, reemployment TAA (RTAA) recipient, or Pension Benefit Guaranty Corporation (PBGC) payee (defined later); or you were a qualifying family member of one of these individuals who passed away or finalized a divorce with you; (b) you can't be claimed as a dependent on someone else's 2018 tax return; and (c) you have met all of the conditions listed on line 1 of Form 8885. If you can't be claimed as a dependent on someone else's 2018 tax return, complete Form 8885, Part I, to see if you are eligible to take this credit.

 Even if you can't claim the HCTC on your income tax return, you must still file Form 8885 to elect the HCTC for any months you participated in the advance monthly payment program.

TAA recipient. You were an eligible TAA recipient as of the first day of the month if, for any day in that month or the prior month, you:

- Received a trade readjustment allowance, or

- Would have been entitled to receive such an allowance except that you had not exhausted all rights to any unemployment insurance (except additional compensation that is funded by a state and isn't reimbursed from any federal funds) to which you were entitled (or would be entitled if you applied).

Example. You received a trade readjustment allowance for January 2018. You were an eligible TAA recipient as of the first day of January and February.

ATAA recipient. You were an eligible ATAA recipient as of the first day of the month if, for that month or the prior month, you received benefits under an ATAA program for older workers established by the Department of Labor.

Example. You received benefits under an ATAA program for older workers for October 2018. The program was established by the Department of Labor. You were an eligible ATAA recipient as of the first day of October and November.

RTAA recipient. You were an eligible RTAA recipient as of the first day of the month if, for that month or the prior month, you received benefits under an RTAA program for older workers established by the Department of Labor.

PBGC payee. You were an eligible PBGC payee as of the first day of the month, if both of the following apply.

1. You were age 55 to 65 and not enrolled in Medicare as of the first day of the month.

2. You received a benefit for that month paid by the PBGC under title IV of the Employee Retirement Income Security Act of 1974 (ERISA).

If you received a lump-sum payment from the PBGC after August 5, 2002, you meet item

(2) above for any month that you would have received a PBGC benefit if you had not received the lump-sum payment.

How to take the credit. The HCTC is an election. If you are eligible for the credit, you must elect the HCTC to receive the benefit of the HCTC. You make your election by checking the box on line 1 of Form 8885 for the first eligible coverage month you are electing to take the HCTC and all boxes on line 1 for each eligible coverage month after the election month. Once you elect to take the HCTC for a month in 2018, the election to take the HCTC applies to all subsequent eligible coverage months in 2018. The election doesn't apply to any month for which you aren't eligible to take the HCTC.

For 2018, the election must be made not later than the due date (including extensions) of your tax return.

More information. For definitions and special rules, including those relating to qualified health insurance plans, qualifying family members, the effect of certain life events, and employer-sponsored health insurance plans, see Pub. 502 and the Instructions for Form 8885.

Credit for Excess Social Security Tax or Railroad Retirement Tax Withheld

Most employers must withhold social security tax from your wages. If you work for a railroad employer, that employer must withhold tier 1 railroad retirement (RRTA) tax and tier 2 RRTA tax.

If you worked for two or more employers in 2018, you may have had too much social security tax withheld from your pay. If one or more of those employers was a railroad employer, too much tier 1 RRTA tax may also have been withheld at the 6.2% rate. You can claim the excess social security or tier 1 RRTA tax as a credit against your income tax when you file your return. For the tier 1 RRTA tax, only use the portion of the tier 1 RRTA tax that was taxed at the 6.2% rate when figuring if excess tier 1 RRTA tax was withheld; don't include any portion of the tier 1 RRTA tax that was withheld at the Medicare tax rate (1.45%) or the Additional Medicare Tax rate (0.9%). The following table shows the maximum amount of wages subject to tax and the maximum amount of tax that should have been withheld for 2018.

Type of tax	Maximum wages subject to tax	Maximum tax that should have been withheld
Social security or RRTA tier 1	$128,400	$7,960.80
RRTA tier 2	$ 95,400	$4,674.60

 All wages are subject to Medicare tax withholding.

 Use Form 843, Claim for Refund and Request for Abatement, to claim a refund of excess tier 2 RRTA tax. Be sure to attach a copy of all of your W-2 forms.

Employer's error. If any one employer withheld too much social security or tier 1 RRTA tax, you can't take the excess as a credit against your income tax. The employer should adjust the tax for you. If the employer doesn't adjust the overcollection, you can file a claim for refund using Form 843.

Joint return. If you are filing a joint return, you can't add the social security or tier 1 RRTA tax withheld from your spouse's wages to the amount withheld from your wages. Figure the withholding separately for you and your spouse to determine if either of you has excess withholding.

How to figure the credit if you didn't work for a railroad. If you didn't work for a railroad during 2018, figure the credit as follows:

1. Add all social security tax withheld (but not more than $7,961 for each employer). Enter the total here . . . . _____

2. Enter any uncollected social security tax on tips or group-term life insurance included in the total on Schedule 4 (Form 1040), line 62, identified by "UT" . . . . _____

3. Add lines 1 and 2. If $7,961 or less, stop here. You can't take the credit . . . . _____

4. Social security tax limit 7,961

5. Credit. Subtract line 4 from line 3. Enter the result here and on Schedule 5 (Form 1040), line 72 . . . . $ _____

Example. You are married and file a joint return with your spouse who had no gross income in 2018. During 2018, you worked for the Brown Technology Company and earned $76,400 in wages. Social security tax of $4,737 was withheld. You also worked for another employer in 2018 and earned $55,000 in wages. $3,410 of social security tax was withheld from these wages. Because you worked for more than one employer and your total wages were more than $128,400, you can take a credit of $186 (($4,737 + $3,410) - $7,961) for the excess social security tax withheld.

1. Add all social security tax withheld (but not more than $7,961 for each employer). Enter the total here $8,147

2. Enter any uncollected social security tax on tips or group-term life insurance included in the total on Schedule 4 (Form 1040), line 62, identified by "UT" . . . . . -0-

3. Add lines 1 and 2. If $7,961 or less, stop here. You can't take the credit 8,147

4. Social security tax limit 7,961

5. Credit. Subtract line 4 from line 3. Enter the result here and on Schedule 5 (Form 1040), line 72 . . . . $186

How to figure the credit if you worked for a railroad. If you were a railroad employee at any time during 2018, figure the credit as follows:

1. Add all social security and tier 1 RRTA tax withheld at the 6.2% rate (but not more than $7,961 for each employer). Enter the total here . . . . _____

2. Enter any uncollected social security and tier 1 RRTA tax on tips or group-term life insurance included in the total on Schedule 4 (Form 1040), line 62, identified by "UT" . . . . _____

3. Add lines 1 and 2. If $7,961 or less, stop here. You can't take the credit . . . . _____

4. Social security and tier 1 RRTA tax limit 7,961

5. Credit. Subtract line 4 from line 3. Enter the result here and on Schedule 5 (Form 1040), line 72 . . . . $ _____

How to take the credit. Enter the credit on Schedule 5 (Form 1040), line 72.

More information. For more information on the credit, see Pub. 505.

2018 Tax Table

 CAUTION

See the instructions for line 11a in the Instructions for Form 1040 to see if you must use the Tax Table below to figure your tax.

Example. Mr. and Mrs. Brown are filing a joint return. Their taxable income on Form 1040, line 10, is $25,300. First, they find the $25,300-25,350 taxable income line. Next, they find the column for married filing jointly and read down the column. The amount shown where the taxable income line and filing status column meet is $2,658. This is the tax amount they should enter on Form 1040, line 11a.

Sample Table

At least	But less than	Single	Married filing jointly*	Married filing separately	Head of a household
			Your tax is—		
25,200	25,250	2,837	2,646	2,837	2,755
25,250	25,300	2,843	2,652	2,843	2,761
25,300	25,350	2,849	(2,658)	2,849	2,767
25,350	25,400	2,855	2,664	2,855	2,773

If line 10 (taxable income) is— At least	But less than	Single	Married filing jointly*	Married filing separately	Head of a household
			Your tax is—		
0	5	0	0	0	0
5	15	1	1	1	1
15	25	2	2	2	2
25	50	4	4	4	4
50	75	6	6	6	6
75	100	9	9	9	9
100	125	11	11	11	11
125	150	14	14	14	14
150	175	16	16	16	16
175	200	19	19	19	19
200	225	21	21	21	21
225	250	24	24	24	24
250	275	26	26	26	26
275	300	29	29	29	29
300	325	31	31	31	31
325	350	34	34	34	34
350	375	36	36	36	36
375	400	39	39	39	39
400	425	41	41	41	41
425	450	44	44	44	44
450	475	46	46	46	46
475	500	49	49	49	49
500	525	51	51	51	51
525	550	54	54	54	54
550	575	56	56	56	56
575	600	59	59	59	59
600	625	61	61	61	61
625	650	64	64	64	64
650	675	66	66	66	66
675	700	69	69	69	69
700	725	71	71	71	71
725	750	74	74	74	74
750	775	76	76	76	76
775	800	79	79	79	79
800	825	81	81	81	81
825	850	84	84	84	84
850	875	86	86	86	86
875	900	89	89	89	89
900	925	91	91	91	91
925	950	94	94	94	94
950	975	96	96	96	96
975	1,000	99	99	99	99

1,000

At least	But less than	Single	Married filing jointly*	Married filing separately	Head of a household
			Your tax is—		
1,000	1,025	101	101	101	101
1,025	1,050	104	104	104	104
1,050	1,075	106	106	106	106
1,075	1,100	109	109	109	109
1,100	1,125	111	111	111	111
1,125	1,150	114	114	114	114
1,150	1,175	116	116	116	116
1,175	1,200	119	119	119	119
1,200	1,225	121	121	121	121
1,225	1,250	124	124	124	124
1,250	1,275	126	126	126	126
1,275	1,300	129	129	129	129
1,300	1,325	131	131	131	131
1,325	1,350	134	134	134	134
1,350	1,375	136	136	136	136
1,375	1,400	139	139	139	139
1,400	1,425	141	141	141	141
1,425	1,450	144	144	144	144
1,450	1,475	146	146	146	146
1,475	1,500	149	149	149	149
1,500	1,525	151	151	151	151
1,525	1,550	154	154	154	154
1,550	1,575	156	156	156	156
1,575	1,600	159	159	159	159
1,600	1,625	161	161	161	161
1,625	1,650	164	164	164	164
1,650	1,675	166	166	166	166
1,675	1,700	169	169	169	169
1,700	1,725	171	171	171	171
1,725	1,750	174	174	174	174
1,750	1,775	176	176	176	176
1,775	1,800	179	179	179	179
1,800	1,825	181	181	181	181
1,825	1,850	184	184	184	184
1,850	1,875	186	186	186	186
1,875	1,900	189	189	189	189
1,900	1,925	191	191	191	191
1,925	1,950	194	194	194	194
1,950	1,975	196	196	196	196
1,975	2,000	199	199	199	199

2,000

At least	But less than	Single	Married filing jointly*	Married filing separately	Head of a household
			Your tax is—		
2,000	2,025	201	201	201	201
2,025	2,050	204	204	204	204
2,050	2,075	206	206	206	206
2,075	2,100	209	209	209	209
2,100	2,125	211	211	211	211
2,125	2,150	214	214	214	214
2,150	2,175	216	216	216	216
2,175	2,200	219	219	219	219
2,200	2,225	221	221	221	221
2,225	2,250	224	224	224	224
2,250	2,275	226	226	226	226
2,275	2,300	229	229	229	229
2,300	2,325	231	231	231	231
2,325	2,350	234	234	234	234
2,350	2,375	236	236	236	236
2,375	2,400	239	239	239	239
2,400	2,425	241	241	241	241
2,425	2,450	244	244	244	244
2,450	2,475	246	246	246	246
2,475	2,500	249	249	249	249
2,500	2,525	251	251	251	251
2,525	2,550	254	254	254	254
2,550	2,575	256	256	256	256
2,575	2,600	259	259	259	259
2,600	2,625	261	261	261	261
2,625	2,650	264	264	264	264
2,650	2,675	266	266	266	266
2,675	2,700	269	269	269	269
2,700	2,725	271	271	271	271
2,725	2,750	274	274	274	274
2,750	2,775	276	276	276	276
2,775	2,800	279	279	279	279
2,800	2,825	281	281	281	281
2,825	2,850	284	284	284	284
2,850	2,875	286	286	286	286
2,875	2,900	289	289	289	289
2,900	2,925	291	291	291	291
2,925	2,950	294	294	294	294
2,950	2,975	296	296	296	296
2,975	3,000	299	299	299	299

(Continued)

* This column must also be used by a qualifying widow(er).

If line 10 (taxable income) is—		And you are—			
At least	But less than	Single	Married filing jointly *	Married filing separately	Head of a household
		Your tax is—			

3,000

At least	But less than	Single	Married filing jointly *	Married filing separately	Head of a household
3,000	3,050	303	303	303	303
3,050	3,100	308	308	308	308
3,100	3,150	313	313	313	313
3,150	3,200	318	318	318	318
3,200	3,250	323	323	323	323
3,250	3,300	328	328	328	328
3,300	3,350	333	333	333	333
3,350	3,400	338	338	338	338
3,400	3,450	343	343	343	343
3,450	3,500	348	348	348	348
3,500	3,550	353	353	353	353
3,550	3,600	358	358	358	358
3,600	3,650	363	363	363	363
3,650	3,700	368	368	368	368
3,700	3,750	373	373	373	373
3,750	3,800	378	378	378	378
3,800	3,850	383	383	383	383
3,850	3,900	388	388	388	388
3,900	3,950	393	393	393	393
3,950	4,000	398	398	398	398

4,000

At least	But less than	Single	Married filing jointly *	Married filing separately	Head of a household
4,000	4,050	403	403	403	403
4,050	4,100	408	408	408	408
4,100	4,150	413	413	413	413
4,150	4,200	418	418	418	418
4,200	4,250	423	423	423	423
4,250	4,300	428	428	428	428
4,300	4,350	433	433	433	433
4,350	4,400	438	438	438	438
4,400	4,450	443	443	443	443
4,450	4,500	448	448	448	448
4,500	4,550	453	453	453	453
4,550	4,600	458	458	458	458
4,600	4,650	463	463	463	463
4,650	4,700	468	468	468	468
4,700	4,750	473	473	473	473
4,750	4,800	478	478	478	478
4,800	4,850	483	483	483	483
4,850	4,900	488	488	488	488
4,900	4,950	493	493	493	493
4,950	5,000	498	498	498	498

5,000

At least	But less than	Single	Married filing jointly *	Married filing separately	Head of a household
5,000	5,050	503	503	503	503
5,050	5,100	508	508	508	508
5,100	5,150	513	513	513	513
5,150	5,200	518	518	518	518
5,200	5,250	523	523	523	523
5,250	5,300	528	528	528	528
5,300	5,350	533	533	533	533
5,350	5,400	538	538	538	538
5,400	5,450	543	543	543	543
5,450	5,500	548	548	548	548
5,500	5,550	553	553	553	553
5,550	5,600	558	558	558	558
5,600	5,650	563	563	563	563
5,650	5,700	568	568	568	568
5,700	5,750	573	573	573	573
5,750	5,800	578	578	578	578
5,800	5,850	583	583	583	583
5,850	5,900	588	588	588	588
5,900	5,950	593	593	593	593
5,950	6,000	598	598	598	598

6,000

At least	But less than	Single	Married filing jointly *	Married filing separately	Head of a household
6,000	6,050	603	603	603	603
6,050	6,100	608	608	608	608
6,100	6,150	613	613	613	613
6,150	6,200	618	618	618	618
6,200	6,250	623	623	623	623
6,250	6,300	628	628	628	628
6,300	6,350	633	633	633	633
6,350	6,400	638	638	638	638
6,400	6,450	643	643	643	643
6,450	6,500	648	648	648	648
6,500	6,550	653	653	653	653
6,550	6,600	658	658	658	658
6,600	6,650	663	663	663	663
6,650	6,700	668	668	668	668
6,700	6,750	673	673	673	673
6,750	6,800	678	678	678	678
6,800	6,850	683	683	683	683
6,850	6,900	688	688	688	688
6,900	6,950	693	693	693	693
6,950	7,000	698	698	698	698

7,000

At least	But less than	Single	Married filing jointly *	Married filing separately	Head of a household
7,000	7,050	703	703	703	703
7,050	7,100	708	708	708	708
7,100	7,150	713	713	713	713
7,150	7,200	718	718	718	718
7,200	7,250	723	723	723	723
7,250	7,300	728	728	728	728
7,300	7,350	733	733	733	733
7,350	7,400	738	738	738	738
7,400	7,450	743	743	743	743
7,450	7,500	748	748	748	748
7,500	7,550	753	753	753	753
7,550	7,600	758	758	758	758
7,600	7,650	763	763	763	763
7,650	7,700	768	768	768	768
7,700	7,750	773	773	773	773
7,750	7,800	778	778	778	778
7,800	7,850	783	783	783	783
7,850	7,900	788	788	788	788
7,900	7,950	793	793	793	793
7,950	8,000	798	798	798	798

8,000

At least	But less than	Single	Married filing jointly *	Married filing separately	Head of a household
8,000	8,050	803	803	803	803
8,050	8,100	808	808	808	808
8,100	8,150	813	813	813	813
8,150	8,200	818	818	818	818
8,200	8,250	823	823	823	823
8,250	8,300	828	828	828	828
8,300	8,350	833	833	833	833
8,350	8,400	838	838	838	838
8,400	8,450	843	843	843	843
8,450	8,500	848	848	848	848
8,500	8,550	853	853	853	853
8,550	8,600	858	858	858	858
8,600	8,650	863	863	863	863
8,650	8,700	868	868	868	868
8,700	8,750	873	873	873	873
8,750	8,800	878	878	878	878
8,800	8,850	883	883	883	883
8,850	8,900	888	888	888	888
8,900	8,950	893	893	893	893
8,950	9,000	898	898	898	898

9,000

At least	But less than	Single	Married filing jointly *	Married filing separately	Head of a household
9,000	9,050	903	903	903	903
9,050	9,100	908	908	908	908
9,100	9,150	913	913	913	913
9,150	9,200	918	918	918	918
9,200	9,250	923	923	923	923
9,250	9,300	928	928	928	928
9,300	9,350	933	933	933	933
9,350	9,400	938	938	938	938
9,400	9,450	943	943	943	943
9,450	9,500	948	948	948	948
9,500	9,550	953	953	953	953
9,550	9,600	959	958	959	958
9,600	9,650	965	963	965	963
9,650	9,700	971	968	971	968
9,700	9,750	977	973	977	973
9,750	9,800	983	978	983	978
9,800	9,850	989	983	989	983
9,850	9,900	995	988	995	988
9,900	9,950	1,001	993	1,001	993
9,950	10,000	1,007	998	1,007	998

10,000

At least	But less than	Single	Married filing jointly *	Married filing separately	Head of a household
10,000	10,050	1,013	1,003	1,013	1,003
10,050	10,100	1,019	1,008	1,019	1,008
10,100	10,150	1,025	1,013	1,025	1,013
10,150	10,200	1,031	1,018	1,031	1,018
10,200	10,250	1,037	1,023	1,037	1,023
10,250	10,300	1,043	1,028	1,043	1,028
10,300	10,350	1,049	1,033	1,049	1,033
10,350	10,400	1,055	1,038	1,055	1,038
10,400	10,450	1,061	1,043	1,061	1,043
10,450	10,500	1,067	1,048	1,067	1,048
10,500	10,550	1,073	1,053	1,073	1,053
10,550	10,600	1,079	1,058	1,079	1,058
10,600	10,650	1,085	1,063	1,085	1,063
10,650	10,700	1,091	1,068	1,091	1,068
10,700	10,750	1,097	1,073	1,097	1,073
10,750	10,800	1,103	1,078	1,103	1,078
10,800	10,850	1,109	1,083	1,109	1,083
10,850	10,900	1,115	1,088	1,115	1,088
10,900	10,950	1,121	1,093	1,121	1,093
10,950	11,000	1,127	1,098	1,127	1,098

11,000

At least	But less than	Single	Married filing jointly *	Married filing separately	Head of a household
11,000	11,050	1,133	1,103	1,133	1,103
11,050	11,100	1,139	1,108	1,139	1,108
11,100	11,150	1,145	1,113	1,145	1,113
11,150	11,200	1,151	1,118	1,151	1,118
11,200	11,250	1,157	1,123	1,157	1,123
11,250	11,300	1,163	1,128	1,163	1,128
11,300	11,350	1,169	1,133	1,169	1,133
11,350	11,400	1,175	1,138	1,175	1,138
11,400	11,450	1,181	1,143	1,181	1,143
11,450	11,500	1,187	1,148	1,187	1,148
11,500	11,550	1,193	1,153	1,193	1,153
11,550	11,600	1,199	1,158	1,199	1,158
11,600	11,650	1,205	1,163	1,205	1,163
11,650	11,700	1,211	1,168	1,211	1,168
11,700	11,750	1,217	1,173	1,217	1,173
11,750	11,800	1,223	1,178	1,223	1,178
11,800	11,850	1,229	1,183	1,229	1,183
11,850	11,900	1,235	1,188	1,235	1,188
11,900	11,950	1,241	1,193	1,241	1,193
11,950	12,000	1,247	1,198	1,247	1,198

(Continued)

* This column must also be used by a qualifying widow(er).

If line 10 (taxable income) is— At least	But less than	And you are— Single	Married filing jointly*	Married filing separately	Head of a household
					Your tax is—

12,000

At least	But less than	Single	Married filing jointly*	Married filing separately	Head of a household
12,000	12,050	1,253	1,203	1,253	1,203
12,050	12,100	1,259	1,208	1,259	1,208
12,100	12,150	1,265	1,213	1,265	1,213
12,150	12,200	1,271	1,218	1,271	1,218
12,200	12,250	1,277	1,223	1,277	1,223
12,250	12,300	1,283	1,228	1,283	1,228
12,300	12,350	1,289	1,233	1,289	1,233
12,350	12,400	1,295	1,238	1,295	1,238
12,400	12,450	1,301	1,243	1,301	1,243
12,450	12,500	1,307	1,248	1,307	1,248
12,500	12,550	1,313	1,253	1,313	1,253
12,550	12,600	1,319	1,258	1,319	1,258
12,600	12,650	1,325	1,263	1,325	1,263
12,650	12,700	1,331	1,268	1,331	1,268
12,700	12,750	1,337	1,273	1,337	1,273
12,750	12,800	1,343	1,278	1,343	1,278
12,800	12,850	1,349	1,283	1,349	1,283
12,850	12,900	1,355	1,288	1,355	1,288
12,900	12,950	1,361	1,293	1,361	1,293
12,950	13,000	1,367	1,298	1,367	1,298

13,000

At least	But less than	Single	Married filing jointly*	Married filing separately	Head of a household
13,000	13,050	1,373	1,303	1,373	1,303
13,050	13,100	1,379	1,308	1,379	1,308
13,100	13,150	1,385	1,313	1,385	1,313
13,150	13,200	1,391	1,318	1,391	1,318
13,200	13,250	1,397	1,323	1,397	1,323
13,250	13,300	1,403	1,328	1,403	1,328
13,300	13,350	1,409	1,333	1,409	1,333
13,350	13,400	1,415	1,338	1,415	1,338
13,400	13,450	1,421	1,343	1,421	1,343
13,450	13,500	1,427	1,348	1,427	1,348
13,500	13,550	1,433	1,353	1,433	1,353
13,550	13,600	1,439	1,358	1,439	1,358
13,600	13,650	1,445	1,363	1,445	1,363
13,650	13,700	1,451	1,368	1,451	1,369
13,700	13,750	1,457	1,373	1,457	1,375
13,750	13,800	1,463	1,378	1,463	1,381
13,800	13,850	1,469	1,383	1,469	1,387
13,850	13,900	1,475	1,388	1,475	1,393
13,900	13,950	1,481	1,393	1,481	1,399
13,950	14,000	1,487	1,398	1,487	1,405

14,000

At least	But less than	Single	Married filing jointly*	Married filing separately	Head of a household
14,000	14,050	1,493	1,403	1,493	1,411
14,050	14,100	1,499	1,408	1,499	1,417
14,100	14,150	1,505	1,413	1,505	1,423
14,150	14,200	1,511	1,418	1,511	1,429
14,200	14,250	1,517	1,423	1,517	1,435
14,250	14,300	1,523	1,428	1,523	1,441
14,300	14,350	1,529	1,433	1,529	1,447
14,350	14,400	1,535	1,438	1,535	1,453
14,400	14,450	1,541	1,443	1,541	1,459
14,450	14,500	1,547	1,448	1,547	1,465
14,500	14,550	1,553	1,453	1,553	1,471
14,550	14,600	1,559	1,458	1,559	1,477
14,600	14,650	1,565	1,463	1,565	1,483
14,650	14,700	1,571	1,468	1,571	1,489
14,700	14,750	1,577	1,473	1,577	1,495
14,750	14,800	1,583	1,478	1,583	1,501
14,800	14,850	1,589	1,483	1,589	1,507
14,850	14,900	1,595	1,488	1,595	1,513
14,900	14,950	1,601	1,493	1,601	1,519
14,950	15,000	1,607	1,498	1,607	1,525

15,000

At least	But less than	Single	Married filing jointly*	Married filing separately	Head of a household
15,000	15,050	1,613	1,503	1,613	1,531
15,050	15,100	1,619	1,508	1,619	1,537
15,100	15,150	1,625	1,513	1,625	1,543
15,150	15,200	1,631	1,518	1,631	1,549
15,200	15,250	1,637	1,523	1,637	1,555
15,250	15,300	1,643	1,528	1,643	1,561
15,300	15,350	1,649	1,533	1,649	1,567
15,350	15,400	1,655	1,538	1,655	1,573
15,400	15,450	1,661	1,543	1,661	1,579
15,450	15,500	1,667	1,548	1,667	1,585
15,500	15,550	1,673	1,553	1,673	1,591
15,550	15,600	1,679	1,558	1,679	1,597
15,600	15,650	1,685	1,563	1,685	1,603
15,650	15,700	1,691	1,568	1,691	1,609
15,700	15,750	1,697	1,573	1,697	1,615
15,750	15,800	1,703	1,578	1,703	1,621
15,800	15,850	1,709	1,583	1,709	1,627
15,850	15,900	1,715	1,588	1,715	1,633
15,900	15,950	1,721	1,593	1,721	1,639
15,950	16,000	1,727	1,598	1,727	1,645

16,000

At least	But less than	Single	Married filing jointly*	Married filing separately	Head of a household
16,000	16,050	1,733	1,603	1,733	1,651
16,050	16,100	1,739	1,608	1,739	1,657
16,100	16,150	1,745	1,613	1,745	1,663
16,150	16,200	1,751	1,618	1,751	1,669
16,200	16,250	1,757	1,623	1,757	1,675
16,250	16,300	1,763	1,628	1,763	1,681
16,300	16,350	1,769	1,633	1,769	1,687
16,350	16,400	1,775	1,638	1,775	1,693
16,400	16,450	1,781	1,643	1,781	1,699
16,450	16,500	1,787	1,648	1,787	1,705
16,500	16,550	1,793	1,653	1,793	1,711
16,550	16,600	1,799	1,658	1,799	1,717
16,600	16,650	1,805	1,663	1,805	1,723
16,650	16,700	1,811	1,668	1,811	1,729
16,700	16,750	1,817	1,673	1,817	1,735
16,750	16,800	1,823	1,678	1,823	1,741
16,800	16,850	1,829	1,683	1,829	1,747
16,850	16,900	1,835	1,688	1,835	1,753
16,900	16,950	1,841	1,693	1,841	1,759
16,950	17,000	1,847	1,698	1,847	1,765

17,000

At least	But less than	Single	Married filing jointly*	Married filing separately	Head of a household
17,000	17,050	1,853	1,703	1,853	1,771
17,050	17,100	1,859	1,708	1,859	1,777
17,100	17,150	1,865	1,713	1,865	1,783
17,150	17,200	1,871	1,718	1,871	1,789
17,200	17,250	1,877	1,723	1,877	1,795
17,250	17,300	1,883	1,728	1,883	1,801
17,300	17,350	1,889	1,733	1,889	1,807
17,350	17,400	1,895	1,738	1,895	1,813
17,400	17,450	1,901	1,743	1,901	1,819
17,450	17,500	1,907	1,748	1,907	1,825
17,500	17,550	1,913	1,753	1,913	1,831
17,550	17,600	1,919	1,758	1,919	1,837
17,600	17,650	1,925	1,763	1,925	1,843
17,650	17,700	1,931	1,768	1,931	1,849
17,700	17,750	1,937	1,773	1,937	1,855
17,750	17,800	1,943	1,778	1,943	1,861
17,800	17,850	1,949	1,783	1,949	1,867
17,850	17,900	1,955	1,788	1,955	1,873
17,900	17,950	1,961	1,793	1,961	1,879
17,950	18,000	1,967	1,798	1,967	1,885

18,000

At least	But less than	Single	Married filing jointly*	Married filing separately	Head of a household
18,000	18,050	1,973	1,803	1,973	1,891
18,050	18,100	1,979	1,808	1,979	1,897
18,100	18,150	1,985	1,813	1,985	1,903
18,150	18,200	1,991	1,818	1,991	1,909
18,200	18,250	1,997	1,823	1,997	1,915
18,250	18,300	2,003	1,828	2,003	1,921
18,300	18,350	2,009	1,833	2,009	1,927
18,350	18,400	2,015	1,838	2,015	1,933
18,400	18,450	2,021	1,843	2,021	1,939
18,450	18,500	2,027	1,848	2,027	1,945
18,500	18,550	2,033	1,853	2,033	1,951
18,550	18,600	2,039	1,858	2,039	1,957
18,600	18,650	2,045	1,863	2,045	1,963
18,650	18,700	2,051	1,868	2,051	1,969
18,700	18,750	2,057	1,873	2,057	1,975
18,750	18,800	2,063	1,878	2,063	1,981
18,800	18,850	2,069	1,883	2,069	1,987
18,850	18,900	2,075	1,888	2,075	1,993
18,900	18,950	2,081	1,893	2,081	1,999
18,950	19,000	2,087	1,898	2,087	2,005

19,000

At least	But less than	Single	Married filing jointly*	Married filing separately	Head of a household
19,000	19,050	2,093	1,903	2,093	2,011
19,050	19,100	2,099	1,908	2,099	2,017
19,100	19,150	2,105	1,914	2,105	2,023
19,150	19,200	2,111	1,920	2,111	2,029
19,200	19,250	2,117	1,926	2,117	2,035
19,250	19,300	2,123	1,932	2,123	2,041
19,300	19,350	2,129	1,938	2,129	2,047
19,350	19,400	2,135	1,944	2,135	2,053
19,400	19,450	2,141	1,950	2,141	2,059
19,450	19,500	2,147	1,956	2,147	2,065
19,500	19,550	2,153	1,962	2,153	2,071
19,550	19,600	2,159	1,968	2,159	2,077
19,600	19,650	2,165	1,974	2,165	2,083
19,650	19,700	2,171	1,980	2,171	2,089
19,700	19,750	2,177	1,986	2,177	2,095
19,750	19,800	2,183	1,992	2,183	2,101
19,800	19,850	2,189	1,998	2,189	2,107
19,850	19,900	2,195	2,004	2,195	2,113
19,900	19,950	2,201	2,010	2,201	2,119
19,950	20,000	2,207	2,016	2,207	2,125

20,000

At least	But less than	Single	Married filing jointly*	Married filing separately	Head of a household
20,000	20,050	2,213	2,022	2,213	2,131
20,050	20,100	2,219	2,028	2,219	2,137
20,100	20,150	2,225	2,034	2,225	2,143
20,150	20,200	2,231	2,040	2,231	2,149
20,200	20,250	2,237	2,046	2,237	2,155
20,250	20,300	2,243	2,052	2,243	2,161
20,300	20,350	2,249	2,058	2,249	2,167
20,350	20,400	2,255	2,064	2,255	2,173
20,400	20,450	2,261	2,070	2,261	2,179
20,450	20,500	2,267	2,076	2,267	2,185
20,500	20,550	2,273	2,082	2,273	2,191
20,550	20,600	2,279	2,088	2,279	2,197
20,600	20,650	2,285	2,094	2,285	2,203
20,650	20,700	2,291	2,100	2,291	2,209
20,700	20,750	2,297	2,106	2,297	2,215
20,750	20,800	2,303	2,112	2,303	2,221
20,800	20,850	2,309	2,118	2,309	2,227
20,850	20,900	2,315	2,124	2,315	2,233
20,900	20,950	2,321	2,130	2,321	2,239
20,950	21,000	2,327	2,136	2,327	2,245

(Continued)

* This column must also be used by a qualifying widow(er).

21,000

If line 10 (taxable income) is—		And you are—			
At least	But less than	Single	Married filing jointly *	Married filing separately	Head of a household
		Your tax is—			
21,000	21,050	2,333	2,142	2,333	2,251
21,050	21,100	2,339	2,148	2,339	2,257
21,100	21,150	2,345	2,154	2,345	2,263
21,150	21,200	2,351	2,160	2,351	2,269
21,200	21,250	2,357	2,166	2,357	2,275
21,250	21,300	2,363	2,172	2,363	2,281
21,300	21,350	2,369	2,178	2,369	2,287
21,350	21,400	2,375	2,184	2,375	2,293
21,400	21,450	2,381	2,190	2,381	2,299
21,450	21,500	2,387	2,196	2,387	2,305
21,500	21,550	2,393	2,202	2,393	2,311
21,550	21,600	2,399	2,208	2,399	2,317
21,600	21,650	2,405	2,214	2,405	2,323
21,650	21,700	2,411	2,220	2,411	2,329
21,700	21,750	2,417	2,226	2,417	2,335
21,750	21,800	2,423	2,232	2,423	2,341
21,800	21,850	2,429	2,238	2,429	2,347
21,850	21,900	2,435	2,244	2,435	2,353
21,900	21,950	2,441	2,250	2,441	2,359
21,950	22,000	2,447	2,256	2,447	2,365

22,000

At least	But less than	Single	Married filing jointly *	Married filing separately	Head of a household
22,000	22,050	2,453	2,262	2,453	2,371
22,050	22,100	2,459	2,268	2,459	2,377
22,100	22,150	2,465	2,274	2,465	2,383
22,150	22,200	2,471	2,280	2,471	2,389
22,200	22,250	2,477	2,286	2,477	2,395
22,250	22,300	2,483	2,292	2,483	2,401
22,300	22,350	2,489	2,298	2,489	2,407
22,350	22,400	2,495	2,304	2,495	2,413
22,400	22,450	2,501	2,310	2,501	2,419
22,450	22,500	2,507	2,316	2,507	2,425
22,500	22,550	2,513	2,322	2,513	2,431
22,550	22,600	2,519	2,328	2,519	2,437
22,600	22,650	2,525	2,334	2,525	2,443
22,650	22,700	2,531	2,340	2,531	2,449
22,700	22,750	2,537	2,346	2,537	2,455
22,750	22,800	2,543	2,352	2,543	2,461
22,800	22,850	2,549	2,358	2,549	2,467
22,850	22,900	2,555	2,364	2,555	2,473
22,900	22,950	2,561	2,370	2,561	2,479
22,950	23,000	2,567	2,376	2,567	2,485

23,000

At least	But less than	Single	Married filing jointly *	Married filing separately	Head of a household
23,000	23,050	2,573	2,382	2,573	2,491
23,050	23,100	2,579	2,388	2,579	2,497
23,100	23,150	2,585	2,394	2,585	2,503
23,150	23,200	2,591	2,400	2,591	2,509
23,200	23,250	2,597	2,406	2,597	2,515
23,250	23,300	2,603	2,412	2,603	2,521
23,300	23,350	2,609	2,418	2,609	2,527
23,350	23,400	2,615	2,424	2,615	2,533
23,400	23,450	2,621	2,430	2,621	2,539
23,450	23,500	2,627	2,436	2,627	2,545
23,500	23,550	2,633	2,442	2,633	2,551
23,550	23,600	2,639	2,448	2,639	2,557
23,600	23,650	2,645	2,454	2,645	2,563
23,650	23,700	2,651	2,460	2,651	2,569
23,700	23,750	2,657	2,466	2,657	2,575
23,750	23,800	2,663	2,472	2,663	2,581
23,800	23,850	2,669	2,478	2,669	2,587
23,850	23,900	2,675	2,484	2,675	2,593
23,900	23,950	2,681	2,490	2,681	2,599
23,950	24,000	2,687	2,496	2,687	2,605

24,000

At least	But less than	Single	Married filing jointly *	Married filing separately	Head of a household
24,000	24,050	2,693	2,502	2,693	2,611
24,050	24,100	2,699	2,508	2,699	2,617
24,100	24,150	2,705	2,514	2,705	2,623
24,150	24,200	2,711	2,520	2,711	2,629
24,200	24,250	2,717	2,526	2,717	2,635
24,250	24,300	2,723	2,532	2,723	2,641
24,300	24,350	2,729	2,538	2,729	2,647
24,350	24,400	2,735	2,544	2,735	2,653
24,400	24,450	2,741	2,550	2,741	2,659
24,450	24,500	2,747	2,556	2,747	2,665
24,500	24,550	2,753	2,562	2,753	2,671
24,550	24,600	2,759	2,568	2,759	2,677
24,600	24,650	2,765	2,574	2,765	2,683
24,650	24,700	2,771	2,580	2,771	2,689
24,700	24,750	2,777	2,586	2,777	2,695
24,750	24,800	2,783	2,592	2,783	2,701
24,800	24,850	2,789	2,598	2,789	2,707
24,850	24,900	2,795	2,604	2,795	2,713
24,900	24,950	2,801	2,610	2,801	2,719
24,950	25,000	2,807	2,616	2,807	2,725

25,000

At least	But less than	Single	Married filing jointly *	Married filing separately	Head of a household
25,000	25,050	2,813	2,622	2,813	2,731
25,050	25,100	2,819	2,628	2,819	2,737
25,100	25,150	2,825	2,634	2,825	2,743
25,150	25,200	2,831	2,640	2,831	2,749
25,200	25,250	2,837	2,646	2,837	2,755
25,250	25,300	2,843	2,652	2,843	2,761
25,300	25,350	2,849	2,658	2,849	2,767
25,350	25,400	2,855	2,664	2,855	2,773
25,400	25,450	2,861	2,670	2,861	2,779
25,450	25,500	2,867	2,676	2,867	2,785
25,500	25,550	2,873	2,682	2,873	2,791
25,550	25,600	2,879	2,688	2,879	2,797
25,600	25,650	2,885	2,694	2,885	2,803
25,650	25,700	2,891	2,700	2,891	2,809
25,700	25,750	2,897	2,706	2,897	2,815
25,750	25,800	2,903	2,712	2,903	2,821
25,800	25,850	2,909	2,718	2,909	2,827
25,850	25,900	2,915	2,724	2,915	2,833
25,900	25,950	2,921	2,730	2,921	2,839
25,950	26,000	2,927	2,736	2,927	2,845

26,000

At least	But less than	Single	Married filing jointly *	Married filing separately	Head of a household
26,000	26,050	2,933	2,742	2,933	2,851
26,050	26,100	2,939	2,748	2,939	2,857
26,100	26,150	2,945	2,754	2,945	2,863
26,150	26,200	2,951	2,760	2,951	2,869
26,200	26,250	2,957	2,766	2,957	2,875
26,250	26,300	2,963	2,772	2,963	2,881
26,300	26,350	2,969	2,778	2,969	2,887
26,350	26,400	2,975	2,784	2,975	2,893
26,400	26,450	2,981	2,790	2,981	2,899
26,450	26,500	2,987	2,796	2,987	2,905
26,500	26,550	2,993	2,802	2,993	2,911
26,550	26,600	2,999	2,808	2,999	2,917
26,600	26,650	3,005	2,814	3,005	2,923
26,650	26,700	3,011	2,820	3,011	2,929
26,700	26,750	3,017	2,826	3,017	2,935
26,750	26,800	3,023	2,832	3,023	2,941
26,800	26,850	3,029	2,838	3,029	2,947
26,850	26,900	3,035	2,844	3,035	2,953
26,900	26,950	3,041	2,850	3,041	2,959
26,950	27,000	3,047	2,856	3,047	2,965

27,000

At least	But less than	Single	Married filing jointly *	Married filing separately	Head of a household
27,000	27,050	3,053	2,862	3,053	2,971
27,050	27,100	3,059	2,868	3,059	2,977
27,100	27,150	3,065	2,874	3,065	2,983
27,150	27,200	3,071	2,880	3,071	2,989
27,200	27,250	3,077	2,886	3,077	2,995
27,250	27,300	3,083	2,892	3,083	3,001
27,300	27,350	3,089	2,898	3,089	3,007
27,350	27,400	3,095	2,904	3,095	3,013
27,400	27,450	3,101	2,910	3,101	3,019
27,450	27,500	3,107	2,916	3,107	3,025
27,500	27,550	3,113	2,922	3,113	3,031
27,550	27,600	3,119	2,928	3,119	3,037
27,600	27,650	3,125	2,934	3,125	3,043
27,650	27,700	3,131	2,940	3,131	3,049
27,700	27,750	3,137	2,946	3,137	3,055
27,750	27,800	3,143	2,952	3,143	3,061
27,800	27,850	3,149	2,958	3,149	3,067
27,850	27,900	3,155	2,964	3,155	3,073
27,900	27,950	3,161	2,970	3,161	3,079
27,950	28,000	3,167	2,976	3,167	3,085

28,000

At least	But less than	Single	Married filing jointly *	Married filing separately	Head of a household
28,000	28,050	3,173	2,982	3,173	3,091
28,050	28,100	3,179	2,988	3,179	3,097
28,100	28,150	3,185	2,994	3,185	3,103
28,150	28,200	3,191	3,000	3,191	3,109
28,200	28,250	3,197	3,006	3,197	3,115
28,250	28,300	3,203	3,012	3,203	3,121
28,300	28,350	3,209	3,018	3,209	3,127
28,350	28,400	3,215	3,024	3,215	3,133
28,400	28,450	3,221	3,030	3,221	3,139
28,450	28,500	3,227	3,036	3,227	3,145
28,500	28,550	3,233	3,042	3,233	3,151
28,550	28,600	3,239	3,048	3,239	3,157
28,600	28,650	3,245	3,054	3,245	3,163
28,650	28,700	3,251	3,060	3,251	3,169
28,700	28,750	3,257	3,066	3,257	3,175
28,750	28,800	3,263	3,072	3,263	3,181
28,800	28,850	3,269	3,078	3,269	3,187
28,850	28,900	3,275	3,084	3,275	3,193
28,900	28,950	3,281	3,090	3,281	3,199
28,950	29,000	3,287	3,096	3,287	3,205

29,000

At least	But less than	Single	Married filing jointly *	Married filing separately	Head of a household
29,000	29,050	3,293	3,102	3,293	3,211
29,050	29,100	3,299	3,108	3,299	3,217
29,100	29,150	3,305	3,114	3,305	3,223
29,150	29,200	3,311	3,120	3,311	3,229
29,200	29,250	3,317	3,126	3,317	3,235
29,250	29,300	3,323	3,132	3,323	3,241
29,300	29,350	3,329	3,138	3,329	3,247
29,350	29,400	3,335	3,144	3,335	3,253
29,400	29,450	3,341	3,150	3,341	3,259
29,450	29,500	3,347	3,156	3,347	3,265
29,500	29,550	3,353	3,162	3,353	3,271
29,550	29,600	3,359	3,168	3,359	3,277
29,600	29,650	3,365	3,174	3,365	3,283
29,650	29,700	3,371	3,180	3,371	3,289
29,700	29,750	3,377	3,186	3,377	3,295
29,750	29,800	3,383	3,192	3,383	3,301
29,800	29,850	3,389	3,198	3,389	3,307
29,850	29,900	3,395	3,204	3,395	3,313
29,900	29,950	3,401	3,210	3,401	3,319
29,950	30,000	3,407	3,216	3,407	3,325

(Continued)

* This column must also be used by a qualifying widow(er).

30,000

If line 10 (taxable income) is—		Single	Married filing jointly *	Married filing separately	Head of a household
At least	But less than				
30,000	30,050	3,413	3,222	3,413	3,331
30,050	30,100	3,419	3,228	3,419	3,337
30,100	30,150	3,425	3,234	3,425	3,343
30,150	30,200	3,431	3,240	3,431	3,349
30,200	30,250	3,437	3,246	3,437	3,355
30,250	30,300	3,443	3,252	3,443	3,361
30,300	30,350	3,449	3,258	3,449	3,367
30,350	30,400	3,455	3,264	3,455	3,373
30,400	30,450	3,461	3,270	3,461	3,379
30,450	30,500	3,467	3,276	3,467	3,385
30,500	30,550	3,473	3,282	3,473	3,391
30,550	30,600	3,479	3,288	3,479	3,397
30,600	30,650	3,485	3,294	3,485	3,403
30,650	30,700	3,491	3,300	3,491	3,409
30,700	30,750	3,497	3,306	3,497	3,415
30,750	30,800	3,503	3,312	3,503	3,421
30,800	30,850	3,509	3,318	3,509	3,427
30,850	30,900	3,515	3,324	3,515	3,433
30,900	30,950	3,521	3,330	3,521	3,439
30,950	31,000	3,527	3,336	3,527	3,445

31,000

At least	But less than	Single	Married filing jointly *	Married filing separately	Head of a household
31,000	31,050	3,533	3,342	3,533	3,451
31,050	31,100	3,539	3,348	3,539	3,457
31,100	31,150	3,545	3,354	3,545	3,463
31,150	31,200	3,551	3,360	3,551	3,469
31,200	31,250	3,557	3,366	3,557	3,475
31,250	31,300	3,563	3,372	3,563	3,481
31,300	31,350	3,569	3,378	3,569	3,487
31,350	31,400	3,575	3,384	3,575	3,493
31,400	31,450	3,581	3,390	3,581	3,499
31,450	31,500	3,587	3,396	3,587	3,505
31,500	31,550	3,593	3,402	3,593	3,511
31,550	31,600	3,599	3,408	3,599	3,517
31,600	31,650	3,605	3,414	3,605	3,523
31,650	31,700	3,611	3,420	3,611	3,529
31,700	31,750	3,617	3,426	3,617	3,535
31,750	31,800	3,623	3,432	3,623	3,541
31,800	31,850	3,629	3,438	3,629	3,547
31,850	31,900	3,635	3,444	3,635	3,553
31,900	31,950	3,641	3,450	3,641	3,559
31,950	32,000	3,647	3,456	3,647	3,565

32,000

At least	But less than	Single	Married filing jointly *	Married filing separately	Head of a household
32,000	32,050	3,653	3,462	3,653	3,571
32,050	32,100	3,659	3,468	3,659	3,577
32,100	32,150	3,665	3,474	3,665	3,583
32,150	32,200	3,671	3,480	3,671	3,589
32,200	32,250	3,677	3,486	3,677	3,595
32,250	32,300	3,683	3,492	3,683	3,601
32,300	32,350	3,689	3,498	3,689	3,607
32,350	32,400	3,695	3,504	3,695	3,613
32,400	32,450	3,701	3,510	3,701	3,619
32,450	32,500	3,707	3,516	3,707	3,625
32,500	32,550	3,713	3,522	3,713	3,631
32,550	32,600	3,719	3,528	3,719	3,637
32,600	32,650	3,725	3,534	3,725	3,643
32,650	32,700	3,731	3,540	3,731	3,649
32,700	32,750	3,737	3,546	3,737	3,655
32,750	32,800	3,743	3,552	3,743	3,661
32,800	32,850	3,749	3,558	3,749	3,667
32,850	32,900	3,755	3,564	3,755	3,673
32,900	32,950	3,761	3,570	3,761	3,679
32,950	33,000	3,767	3,576	3,767	3,685

33,000

At least	But less than	Single	Married filing jointly *	Married filing separately	Head of a household
33,000	33,050	3,773	3,582	3,773	3,691
33,050	33,100	3,779	3,588	3,779	3,697
33,100	33,150	3,785	3,594	3,785	3,703
33,150	33,200	3,791	3,600	3,791	3,709
33,200	33,250	3,797	3,606	3,797	3,715
33,250	33,300	3,803	3,612	3,803	3,721
33,300	33,350	3,809	3,618	3,809	3,727
33,350	33,400	3,815	3,624	3,815	3,733
33,400	33,450	3,821	3,630	3,821	3,739
33,450	33,500	3,827	3,636	3,827	3,745
33,500	33,550	3,833	3,642	3,833	3,751
33,550	33,600	3,839	3,648	3,839	3,757
33,600	33,650	3,845	3,654	3,845	3,763
33,650	33,700	3,851	3,660	3,851	3,769
33,700	33,750	3,857	3,666	3,857	3,775
33,750	33,800	3,863	3,672	3,863	3,781
33,800	33,850	3,869	3,678	3,869	3,787
33,850	33,900	3,875	3,684	3,875	3,793
33,900	33,950	3,881	3,690	3,881	3,799
33,950	34,000	3,887	3,696	3,887	3,805

34,000

At least	But less than	Single	Married filing jointly *	Married filing separately	Head of a household
34,000	34,050	3,893	3,702	3,893	3,811
34,050	34,100	3,899	3,708	3,899	3,817
34,100	34,150	3,905	3,714	3,905	3,823
34,150	34,200	3,911	3,720	3,911	3,829
34,200	34,250	3,917	3,726	3,917	3,835
34,250	34,300	3,923	3,732	3,923	3,841
34,300	34,350	3,929	3,738	3,929	3,847
34,350	34,400	3,935	3,744	3,935	3,853
34,400	34,450	3,941	3,750	3,941	3,859
34,450	34,500	3,947	3,756	3,947	3,865
34,500	34,550	3,953	3,762	3,953	3,871
34,550	34,600	3,959	3,768	3,959	3,877
34,600	34,650	3,965	3,774	3,965	3,883
34,650	34,700	3,971	3,780	3,971	3,889
34,700	34,750	3,977	3,786	3,977	3,895
34,750	34,800	3,983	3,792	3,983	3,901
34,800	34,850	3,989	3,798	3,989	3,907
34,850	34,900	3,995	3,804	3,995	3,913
34,900	34,950	4,001	3,810	4,001	3,919
34,950	35,000	4,007	3,816	4,007	3,925

35,000

At least	But less than	Single	Married filing jointly *	Married filing separately	Head of a household
35,000	35,050	4,013	3,822	4,013	3,931
35,050	35,100	4,019	3,828	4,019	3,937
35,100	35,150	4,025	3,834	4,025	3,943
35,150	35,200	4,031	3,840	4,031	3,949
35,200	35,250	4,037	3,846	4,037	3,955
35,250	35,300	4,043	3,852	4,043	3,961
35,300	35,350	4,049	3,858	4,049	3,967
35,350	35,400	4,055	3,864	4,055	3,973
35,400	35,450	4,061	3,870	4,061	3,979
35,450	35,500	4,067	3,876	4,067	3,985
35,500	35,550	4,073	3,882	4,073	3,991
35,550	35,600	4,079	3,888	4,079	3,997
35,600	35,650	4,085	3,894	4,085	4,003
35,650	35,700	4,091	3,900	4,091	4,009
35,700	35,750	4,097	3,906	4,097	4,015
35,750	35,800	4,103	3,912	4,103	4,021
35,800	35,850	4,109	3,918	4,109	4,027
35,850	35,900	4,115	3,924	4,115	4,033
35,900	35,950	4,121	3,930	4,121	4,039
35,950	36,000	4,127	3,936	4,127	4,045

36,000

At least	But less than	Single	Married filing jointly *	Married filing separately	Head of a household
36,000	36,050	4,133	3,942	4,133	4,051
36,050	36,100	4,139	3,948	4,139	4,057
36,100	36,150	4,145	3,954	4,145	4,063
36,150	36,200	4,151	3,960	4,151	4,069
36,200	36,250	4,157	3,966	4,157	4,075
36,250	36,300	4,163	3,972	4,163	4,081
36,300	36,350	4,169	3,978	4,169	4,087
36,350	36,400	4,175	3,984	4,175	4,093
36,400	36,450	4,181	3,990	4,181	4,099
36,450	36,500	4,187	3,996	4,187	4,105
36,500	36,550	4,193	4,002	4,193	4,111
36,550	36,600	4,199	4,008	4,199	4,117
36,600	36,650	4,205	4,014	4,205	4,123
36,650	36,700	4,211	4,020	4,211	4,129
36,700	36,750	4,217	4,026	4,217	4,135
36,750	36,800	4,223	4,032	4,223	4,141
36,800	36,850	4,229	4,038	4,229	4,147
36,850	36,900	4,235	4,044	4,235	4,153
36,900	36,950	4,241	4,050	4,241	4,159
36,950	37,000	4,247	4,056	4,247	4,165

37,000

At least	But less than	Single	Married filing jointly *	Married filing separately	Head of a household
37,000	37,050	4,253	4,062	4,253	4,171
37,050	37,100	4,259	4,068	4,259	4,177
37,100	37,150	4,265	4,074	4,265	4,183
37,150	37,200	4,271	4,080	4,271	4,189
37,200	37,250	4,277	4,086	4,277	4,195
37,250	37,300	4,283	4,092	4,283	4,201
37,300	37,350	4,289	4,098	4,289	4,207
37,350	37,400	4,295	4,104	4,295	4,213
37,400	37,450	4,301	4,110	4,301	4,219
37,450	37,500	4,307	4,116	4,307	4,225
37,500	37,550	4,313	4,122	4,313	4,231
37,550	37,600	4,319	4,128	4,319	4,237
37,600	37,650	4,325	4,134	4,325	4,243
37,650	37,700	4,331	4,140	4,331	4,249
37,700	37,750	4,337	4,146	4,337	4,255
37,750	37,800	4,343	4,152	4,343	4,261
37,800	37,850	4,349	4,158	4,349	4,267
37,850	37,900	4,355	4,164	4,355	4,273
37,900	37,950	4,361	4,170	4,361	4,279
37,950	38,000	4,367	4,176	4,367	4,285

38,000

At least	But less than	Single	Married filing jointly *	Married filing separately	Head of a household
38,000	38,050	4,373	4,182	4,373	4,291
38,050	38,100	4,379	4,188	4,379	4,297
38,100	38,150	4,385	4,194	4,385	4,303
38,150	38,200	4,391	4,200	4,391	4,309
38,200	38,250	4,397	4,206	4,397	4,315
38,250	38,300	4,403	4,212	4,403	4,321
38,300	38,350	4,409	4,218	4,409	4,327
38,350	38,400	4,415	4,224	4,415	4,333
38,400	38,450	4,421	4,230	4,421	4,339
38,450	38,500	4,427	4,236	4,427	4,345
38,500	38,550	4,433	4,242	4,433	4,351
38,550	38,600	4,439	4,248	4,439	4,357
38,600	38,650	4,445	4,254	4,445	4,363
38,650	38,700	4,451	4,260	4,451	4,369
38,700	38,750	4,459	4,266	4,459	4,375
38,750	38,800	4,470	4,272	4,470	4,381
38,800	38,850	4,481	4,278	4,481	4,387
38,850	38,900	4,492	4,284	4,492	4,393
38,900	38,950	4,503	4,290	4,503	4,399
38,950	39,000	4,514	4,296	4,514	4,405

(Continued)

* This column must also be used by a qualifying widow(er).

If line 10 (taxable income) is—		And you are—			
At least	But less than	Single	Married filing jointly *	Married filing separately	Head of a household
		Your tax is—			

39,000

At least	But less than	Single	Married filing jointly *	Married filing separately	Head of a household
39,000	39,050	4,525	4,302	4,525	4,411
39,050	39,100	4,536	4,308	4,536	4,417
39,100	39,150	4,547	4,314	4,547	4,423
39,150	39,200	4,558	4,320	4,558	4,429
39,200	39,250	4,569	4,326	4,569	4,435
39,250	39,300	4,580	4,332	4,580	4,441
39,300	39,350	4,591	4,338	4,591	4,447
39,350	39,400	4,602	4,344	4,602	4,453
39,400	39,450	4,613	4,350	4,613	4,459
39,450	39,500	4,624	4,356	4,624	4,465
39,500	39,550	4,635	4,362	4,635	4,471
39,550	39,600	4,646	4,368	4,646	4,477
39,600	39,650	4,657	4,374	4,657	4,483
39,650	39,700	4,668	4,380	4,668	4,489
39,700	39,750	4,679	4,386	4,679	4,495
39,750	39,800	4,690	4,392	4,690	4,501
39,800	39,850	4,701	4,398	4,701	4,507
39,850	39,900	4,712	4,404	4,712	4,513
39,900	39,950	4,723	4,410	4,723	4,519
39,950	40,000	4,734	4,416	4,734	4,525

40,000

At least	But less than	Single	Married filing jointly *	Married filing separately	Head of a household
40,000	40,050	4,745	4,422	4,745	4,531
40,050	40,100	4,756	4,428	4,756	4,537
40,100	40,150	4,767	4,434	4,767	4,543
40,150	40,200	4,778	4,440	4,778	4,549
40,200	40,250	4,789	4,446	4,789	4,555
40,250	40,300	4,800	4,452	4,800	4,561
40,300	40,350	4,811	4,458	4,811	4,567
40,350	40,400	4,822	4,464	4,822	4,573
40,400	40,450	4,833	4,470	4,833	4,579
40,450	40,500	4,844	4,476	4,844	4,585
40,500	40,550	4,855	4,482	4,855	4,591
40,550	40,600	4,866	4,488	4,866	4,597
40,600	40,650	4,877	4,494	4,877	4,603
40,650	40,700	4,888	4,500	4,888	4,609
40,700	40,750	4,899	4,506	4,899	4,615
40,750	40,800	4,910	4,512	4,910	4,621
40,800	40,850	4,921	4,518	4,921	4,627
40,850	40,900	4,932	4,524	4,932	4,633
40,900	40,950	4,943	4,530	4,943	4,639
40,950	41,000	4,954	4,536	4,954	4,645

41,000

At least	But less than	Single	Married filing jointly *	Married filing separately	Head of a household
41,000	41,050	4,965	4,542	4,965	4,651
41,050	41,100	4,976	4,548	4,976	4,657
41,100	41,150	4,987	4,554	4,987	4,663
41,150	41,200	4,998	4,560	4,998	4,669
41,200	41,250	5,009	4,566	5,009	4,675
41,250	41,300	5,020	4,572	5,020	4,681
41,300	41,350	5,031	4,578	5,031	4,687
41,350	41,400	5,042	4,584	5,042	4,693
41,400	41,450	5,053	4,590	5,053	4,699
41,450	41,500	5,064	4,596	5,064	4,705
41,500	41,550	5,075	4,602	5,075	4,711
41,550	41,600	5,086	4,608	5,086	4,717
41,600	41,650	5,097	4,614	5,097	4,723
41,650	41,700	5,108	4,620	5,108	4,729
41,700	41,750	5,119	4,626	5,119	4,735
41,750	41,800	5,130	4,632	5,130	4,741
41,800	41,850	5,141	4,638	5,141	4,747
41,850	41,900	5,152	4,644	5,152	4,753
41,900	41,950	5,163	4,650	5,163	4,759
41,950	42,000	5,174	4,656	5,174	4,765

42,000

At least	But less than	Single	Married filing jointly *	Married filing separately	Head of a household
42,000	42,050	5,185	4,662	5,185	4,771
42,050	42,100	5,196	4,668	5,196	4,777
42,100	42,150	5,207	4,674	5,207	4,783
42,150	42,200	5,218	4,680	5,218	4,789
42,200	42,250	5,229	4,686	5,229	4,795
42,250	42,300	5,240	4,692	5,240	4,801
42,300	42,350	5,251	4,698	5,251	4,807
42,350	42,400	5,262	4,704	5,262	4,813
42,400	42,450	5,273	4,710	5,273	4,819
42,450	42,500	5,284	4,716	5,284	4,825
42,500	42,550	5,295	4,722	5,295	4,831
42,550	42,600	5,306	4,728	5,306	4,837
42,600	42,650	5,317	4,734	5,317	4,843
42,650	42,700	5,328	4,740	5,328	4,849
42,700	42,750	5,339	4,746	5,339	4,855
42,750	42,800	5,350	4,752	5,350	4,861
42,800	42,850	5,361	4,758	5,361	4,867
42,850	42,900	5,372	4,764	5,372	4,873
42,900	42,950	5,383	4,770	5,383	4,879
42,950	43,000	5,394	4,776	5,394	4,885

43,000

At least	But less than	Single	Married filing jointly *	Married filing separately	Head of a household
43,000	43,050	5,405	4,782	5,405	4,891
43,050	43,100	5,416	4,788	5,416	4,897
43,100	43,150	5,427	4,794	5,427	4,903
43,150	43,200	5,438	4,800	5,438	4,909
43,200	43,250	5,449	4,806	5,449	4,915
43,250	43,300	5,460	4,812	5,460	4,921
43,300	43,350	5,471	4,818	5,471	4,927
43,350	43,400	5,482	4,824	5,482	4,933
43,400	43,450	5,493	4,830	5,493	4,939
43,450	43,500	5,504	4,836	5,504	4,945
43,500	43,550	5,515	4,842	5,515	4,951
43,550	43,600	5,526	4,848	5,526	4,957
43,600	43,650	5,537	4,854	5,537	4,963
43,650	43,700	5,548	4,860	5,548	4,969
43,700	43,750	5,559	4,866	5,559	4,975
43,750	43,800	5,570	4,872	5,570	4,981
43,800	43,850	5,581	4,878	5,581	4,987
43,850	43,900	5,592	4,884	5,592	4,993
43,900	43,950	5,603	4,890	5,603	4,999
43,950	44,000	5,614	4,896	5,614	5,005

44,000

At least	But less than	Single	Married filing jointly *	Married filing separately	Head of a household
44,000	44,050	5,625	4,902	5,625	5,011
44,050	44,100	5,636	4,908	5,636	5,017
44,100	44,150	5,647	4,914	5,647	5,023
44,150	44,200	5,658	4,920	5,658	5,029
44,200	44,250	5,669	4,926	5,669	5,035
44,250	44,300	5,680	4,932	5,680	5,041
44,300	44,350	5,691	4,938	5,691	5,047
44,350	44,400	5,702	4,944	5,702	5,053
44,400	44,450	5,713	4,950	5,713	5,059
44,450	44,500	5,724	4,956	5,724	5,065
44,500	44,550	5,735	4,962	5,735	5,071
44,550	44,600	5,746	4,968	5,746	5,077
44,600	44,650	5,757	4,974	5,757	5,083
44,650	44,700	5,768	4,980	5,768	5,089
44,700	44,750	5,779	4,986	5,779	5,095
44,750	44,800	5,790	4,992	5,790	5,101
44,800	44,850	5,801	4,998	5,801	5,107
44,850	44,900	5,812	5,004	5,812	5,113
44,900	44,950	5,823	5,010	5,823	5,119
44,950	45,000	5,834	5,016	5,834	5,125

45,000

At least	But less than	Single	Married filing jointly *	Married filing separately	Head of a household
45,000	45,050	5,845	5,022	5,845	5,131
45,050	45,100	5,856	5,028	5,856	5,137
45,100	45,150	5,867	5,034	5,867	5,143
45,150	45,200	5,878	5,040	5,878	5,149
45,200	45,250	5,889	5,046	5,889	5,155
45,250	45,300	5,900	5,052	5,900	5,161
45,300	45,350	5,911	5,058	5,911	5,167
45,350	45,400	5,922	5,064	5,922	5,173
45,400	45,450	5,933	5,070	5,933	5,179
45,450	45,500	5,944	5,076	5,944	5,185
45,500	45,550	5,955	5,082	5,955	5,191
45,550	45,600	5,966	5,088	5,966	5,197
45,600	45,650	5,977	5,094	5,977	5,203
45,650	45,700	5,988	5,100	5,988	5,209
45,700	45,750	5,999	5,106	5,999	5,215
45,750	45,800	6,010	5,112	6,010	5,221
45,800	45,850	6,021	5,118	6,021	5,227
45,850	45,900	6,032	5,124	6,032	5,233
45,900	45,950	6,043	5,130	6,043	5,239
45,950	46,000	6,054	5,136	6,054	5,245

46,000

At least	But less than	Single	Married filing jointly *	Married filing separately	Head of a household
46,000	46,050	6,065	5,142	6,065	5,251
46,050	46,100	6,076	5,148	6,076	5,257
46,100	46,150	6,087	5,154	6,087	5,263
46,150	46,200	6,098	5,160	6,098	5,269
46,200	46,250	6,109	5,166	6,109	5,275
46,250	46,300	6,120	5,172	6,120	5,281
46,300	46,350	6,131	5,178	6,131	5,287
46,350	46,400	6,142	5,184	6,142	5,293
46,400	46,450	6,153	5,190	6,153	5,299
46,450	46,500	6,164	5,196	6,164	5,305
46,500	46,550	6,175	5,202	6,175	5,311
46,550	46,600	6,186	5,208	6,186	5,317
46,600	46,650	6,197	5,214	6,197	5,323
46,650	46,700	6,208	5,220	6,208	5,329
46,700	46,750	6,219	5,226	6,219	5,335
46,750	46,800	6,230	5,232	6,230	5,341
46,800	46,850	6,241	5,238	6,241	5,347
46,850	46,900	6,252	5,244	6,252	5,353
46,900	46,950	6,263	5,250	6,263	5,359
46,950	47,000	6,274	5,256	6,274	5,365

47,000

At least	But less than	Single	Married filing jointly *	Married filing separately	Head of a household
47,000	47,050	6,285	5,262	6,285	5,371
47,050	47,100	6,296	5,268	6,296	5,377
47,100	47,150	6,307	5,274	6,307	5,383
47,150	47,200	6,318	5,280	6,318	5,389
47,200	47,250	6,329	5,286	6,329	5,395
47,250	47,300	6,340	5,292	6,340	5,401
47,300	47,350	6,351	5,298	6,351	5,407
47,350	47,400	6,362	5,304	6,362	5,413
47,400	47,450	6,373	5,310	6,373	5,419
47,450	47,500	6,384	5,316	6,384	5,425
47,500	47,550	6,395	5,322	6,395	5,431
47,550	47,600	6,406	5,328	6,406	5,437
47,600	47,650	6,417	5,334	6,417	5,443
47,650	47,700	6,428	5,340	6,428	5,449
47,700	47,750	6,439	5,346	6,439	5,455
47,750	47,800	6,450	5,352	6,450	5,461
47,800	47,850	6,461	5,358	6,461	5,467
47,850	47,900	6,472	5,364	6,472	5,473
47,900	47,950	6,483	5,370	6,483	5,479
47,950	48,000	6,494	5,376	6,494	5,485

(Continued)

* This column must also be used by a qualifying widow(er).

48,000

At least	But less than	Single	Married filing jointly *	Married filing separately	Head of a household
48,000	48,050	6,505	5,382	6,505	5,491
48,050	48,100	6,516	5,388	6,516	5,497
48,100	48,150	6,527	5,394	6,527	5,503
48,150	48,200	6,538	5,400	6,538	5,509
48,200	48,250	6,549	5,406	6,549	5,515
48,250	48,300	6,560	5,412	6,560	5,521
48,300	48,350	6,571	5,418	6,571	5,527
48,350	48,400	6,582	5,424	6,582	5,533
48,400	48,450	6,593	5,430	6,593	5,539
48,450	48,500	6,604	5,436	6,604	5,545
48,500	48,550	6,615	5,442	6,615	5,551
48,550	48,600	6,626	5,448	6,626	5,557
48,600	48,650	6,637	5,454	6,637	5,563
48,650	48,700	6,648	5,460	6,648	5,569
48,700	48,750	6,659	5,466	6,659	5,575
48,750	48,800	6,670	5,472	6,670	5,581
48,800	48,850	6,681	5,478	6,681	5,587
48,850	48,900	6,692	5,484	6,692	5,593
48,900	48,950	6,703	5,490	6,703	5,599
48,950	49,000	6,714	5,496	6,714	5,605

49,000

At least	But less than	Single	Married filing jointly *	Married filing separately	Head of a household
49,000	49,050	6,725	5,502	6,725	5,611
49,050	49,100	6,736	5,508	6,736	5,617
49,100	49,150	6,747	5,514	6,747	5,623
49,150	49,200	6,758	5,520	6,758	5,629
49,200	49,250	6,769	5,526	6,769	5,635
49,250	49,300	6,780	5,532	6,780	5,641
49,300	49,350	6,791	5,538	6,791	5,647
49,350	49,400	6,802	5,544	6,802	5,653
49,400	49,450	6,813	5,550	6,813	5,659
49,450	49,500	6,824	5,556	6,824	5,665
49,500	49,550	6,835	5,562	6,835	5,671
49,550	49,600	6,846	5,568	6,846	5,677
49,600	49,650	6,857	5,574	6,857	5,683
49,650	49,700	6,868	5,580	6,868	5,689
49,700	49,750	6,879	5,586	6,879	5,695
49,750	49,800	6,890	5,592	6,890	5,701
49,800	49,850	6,901	5,598	6,901	5,707
49,850	49,900	6,912	5,604	6,912	5,713
49,900	49,950	6,923	5,610	6,923	5,719
49,950	50,000	6,934	5,616	6,934	5,725

50,000

At least	But less than	Single	Married filing jointly *	Married filing separately	Head of a household
50,000	50,050	6,945	5,622	6,945	5,731
50,050	50,100	6,956	5,628	6,955	5,737
50,100	50,150	6,967	5,634	6,967	5,743
50,150	50,200	6,978	5,640	6,978	5,749
50,200	50,250	6,989	5,646	6,989	5,755
50,250	50,300	7,000	5,652	7,000	5,761
50,300	50,350	7,011	5,658	7,011	5,767
50,350	50,400	7,022	5,664	7,022	5,773
50,400	50,450	7,033	5,670	7,033	5,779
50,450	50,500	7,044	5,676	7,044	5,785
50,500	50,550	7,055	5,682	7,055	5,791
50,550	50,600	7,066	5,688	7,066	5,797
50,600	50,650	7,077	5,694	7,077	5,803
50,650	50,700	7,088	5,700	7,088	5,809
50,700	50,750	7,099	5,706	7,099	5,815
50,750	50,800	7,110	5,712	7,110	5,821
50,800	50,850	7,121	5,718	7,121	5,827
50,850	50,900	7,132	5,724	7,132	5,833
50,900	50,950	7,143	5,730	7,143	5,839
50,950	51,000	7,154	5,736	7,154	5,845

51,000

At least	But less than	Single	Married filing jointly *	Married filing separately	Head of a household
51,000	51,050	7,165	5,742	7,165	5,851
51,050	51,100	7,176	5,748	7,176	5,857
51,100	51,150	7,187	5,754	7,187	5,863
51,150	51,200	7,198	5,760	7,198	5,869
51,200	51,250	7,209	5,766	7,209	5,875
51,250	51,300	7,220	5,772	7,220	5,881
51,300	51,350	7,231	5,778	7,231	5,887
51,350	51,400	7,242	5,784	7,242	5,893
51,400	51,450	7,253	5,790	7,253	5,899
51,450	51,500	7,264	5,796	7,264	5,905
51,500	51,550	7,275	5,802	7,275	5,911
51,550	51,600	7,286	5,808	7,286	5,917
51,600	51,650	7,297	5,814	7,297	5,923
51,650	51,700	7,308	5,820	7,308	5,929
51,700	51,750	7,319	5,826	7,319	5,935
51,750	51,800	7,330	5,832	7,330	5,941
51,800	51,850	7,341	5,838	7,341	5,950
51,850	51,900	7,352	5,844	7,352	5,961
51,900	51,950	7,363	5,850	7,363	5,972
51,950	52,000	7,374	5,856	7,374	5,983

52,000

At least	But less than	Single	Married filing jointly *	Married filing separately	Head of a household
52,000	52,050	7,385	5,862	7,385	5,994
52,050	52,100	7,396	5,868	7,396	6,005
52,100	52,150	7,407	5,874	7,407	6,016
52,150	52,200	7,418	5,880	7,418	6,027
52,200	52,250	7,429	5,886	7,429	6,038
52,250	52,300	7,440	5,892	7,440	6,049
52,300	52,350	7,451	5,898	7,451	6,060
52,350	52,400	7,462	5,904	7,462	6,071
52,400	52,450	7,473	5,910	7,473	6,082
52,450	52,500	7,484	5,916	7,484	6,093
52,500	52,550	7,495	5,922	7,495	6,104
52,550	52,600	7,506	5,928	7,506	6,115
52,600	52,650	7,517	5,934	7,517	6,126
52,650	52,700	7,528	5,940	7,528	6,137
52,700	52,750	7,539	5,946	7,539	6,148
52,750	52,800	7,550	5,952	7,550	6,159
52,800	52,850	7,561	5,958	7,561	6,170
52,850	52,900	7,572	5,964	7,572	6,181
52,900	52,950	7,583	5,970	7,583	6,192
52,950	53,000	7,594	5,976	7,594	6,203

53,000

At least	But less than	Single	Married filing jointly *	Married filing separately	Head of a household
53,000	53,050	7,605	5,982	7,605	6,214
53,050	53,100	7,616	5,988	7,616	6,225
53,100	53,150	7,627	5,994	7,627	6,236
53,150	53,200	7,638	6,000	7,638	6,247
53,200	53,250	7,649	6,006	7,649	6,258
53,250	53,300	7,660	6,012	7,660	6,269
53,300	53,350	7,671	6,018	7,671	6,280
53,350	53,400	7,682	6,024	7,682	6,291
53,400	53,450	7,693	6,030	7,693	6,302
53,450	53,500	7,704	6,036	7,704	6,313
53,500	53,550	7,715	6,042	7,715	6,324
53,550	53,600	7,726	6,048	7,726	6,335
53,600	53,650	7,737	6,054	7,737	6,346
53,650	53,700	7,748	6,060	7,748	6,357
53,700	53,750	7,759	6,066	7,759	6,368
53,750	53,800	7,770	6,072	7,770	6,379
53,800	53,850	7,781	6,078	7,781	6,390
53,850	53,900	7,792	6,084	7,792	6,401
53,900	53,950	7,803	6,090	7,803	6,412
53,950	54,000	7,814	6,096	7,814	6,423

54,000

At least	But less than	Single	Married filing jointly *	Married filing separately	Head of a household
54,000	54,050	7,825	6,102	7,825	6,434
54,050	54,100	7,836	6,108	7,836	6,445
54,100	54,150	7,847	6,114	7,847	6,456
54,150	54,200	7,858	6,120	7,858	6,467
54,200	54,250	7,869	6,126	7,869	6,478
54,250	54,300	7,880	6,132	7,880	6,489
54,300	54,350	7,891	6,138	7,891	6,500
54,350	54,400	7,902	6,144	7,902	6,511
54,400	54,450	7,913	6,150	7,913	6,522
54,450	54,500	7,924	6,156	7,924	6,533
54,500	54,550	7,935	6,162	7,935	6,544
54,550	54,600	7,946	6,168	7,946	6,555
54,600	54,650	7,957	6,174	7,957	6,566
54,650	54,700	7,968	6,180	7,968	6,577
54,700	54,750	7,979	6,186	7,979	6,588
54,750	54,800	7,990	6,192	7,990	6,599
54,800	54,850	8,001	6,198	8,001	6,610
54,850	54,900	8,012	6,204	8,012	6,621
54,900	54,950	8,023	6,210	8,023	6,632
54,950	55,000	8,034	6,216	8,034	6,643

55,000

At least	But less than	Single	Married filing jointly *	Married filing separately	Head of a household
55,000	55,050	8,045	6,222	8,045	6,654
55,050	55,100	8,056	6,228	8,056	6,665
55,100	55,150	8,067	6,234	8,067	6,676
55,150	55,200	8,078	6,240	8,078	6,687
55,200	55,250	8,089	6,246	8,089	6,698
55,250	55,300	8,100	6,252	8,100	6,709
55,300	55,350	8,111	6,258	8,111	6,720
55,350	55,400	8,122	6,264	8,122	6,731
55,400	55,450	8,133	6,270	8,133	6,742
55,450	55,500	8,144	6,276	8,144	6,753
55,500	55,550	8,155	6,282	8,155	6,764
55,550	55,600	8,166	6,288	8,166	6,775
55,600	55,650	8,177	6,294	8,177	6,786
55,650	55,700	8,188	6,300	8,188	6,797
55,700	55,750	8,199	6,306	8,199	6,808
55,750	55,800	8,210	6,312	8,210	6,819
55,800	55,850	8,221	6,318	8,221	6,830
55,850	55,900	8,232	6,324	8,232	6,841
55,900	55,950	8,243	6,330	8,243	6,852
55,950	56,000	8,254	6,336	8,254	6,863

56,000

At least	But less than	Single	Married filing jointly *	Married filing separately	Head of a household
56,000	56,050	8,265	6,342	8,265	6,874
56,050	56,100	8,276	6,348	8,276	6,885
56,100	56,150	8,287	6,354	8,287	6,896
56,150	56,200	8,298	6,360	8,298	6,907
56,200	56,250	8,309	6,366	8,309	6,918
56,250	56,300	8,320	6,372	8,320	6,929
56,300	56,350	8,331	6,378	8,331	6,940
56,350	56,400	8,342	6,384	8,342	6,951
56,400	56,450	8,353	6,390	8,353	6,962
56,450	56,500	8,364	6,396	8,364	6,973
56,500	56,550	8,375	6,402	8,375	6,984
56,550	56,600	8,386	6,408	8,386	6,995
56,600	56,650	8,397	6,414	8,397	7,006
56,650	56,700	8,408	6,420	8,408	7,017
56,700	56,750	8,419	6,426	8,419	7,028
56,750	56,800	8,430	6,432	8,430	7,039
56,800	56,850	8,441	6,438	8,441	7,050
56,850	56,900	8,452	6,444	8,452	7,061
56,900	56,950	8,463	6,450	8,463	7,072
56,950	57,000	8,474	6,456	8,474	7,083

* This column must also be used by a qualifying widow(er).

(Continued)

If line 10 (taxable income) is—		And you are—			
At least	But less than	Single	Married filing jointly *	Married filing separately	Head of a household
		Your tax is—			

57,000

At least	But less than	Single	MFJ *	MFS	HoH
57,000	57,050	8,485	6,462	8,485	7,094
57,050	57,100	8,496	6,468	8,496	7,105
57,100	57,150	8,507	6,474	8,507	7,116
57,150	57,200	8,518	6,480	8,518	7,127
57,200	57,250	8,529	6,486	8,529	7,138
57,250	57,300	8,540	6,492	8,540	7,149
57,300	57,350	8,551	6,498	8,551	7,160
57,350	57,400	8,562	6,504	8,562	7,171
57,400	57,450	8,573	6,510	8,573	7,182
57,450	57,500	8,584	6,516	8,584	7,193
57,500	57,550	8,595	6,522	8,595	7,204
57,550	57,600	8,606	6,528	8,606	7,215
57,600	57,650	8,617	6,534	8,617	7,226
57,650	57,700	8,628	6,540	8,628	7,237
57,700	57,750	8,639	6,546	8,639	7,248
57,750	57,800	8,650	6,552	8,650	7,259
57,800	57,850	8,661	6,558	8,661	7,270
57,850	57,900	8,672	6,564	8,672	7,281
57,900	57,950	8,683	6,570	8,683	7,292
57,950	58,000	8,694	6,576	8,694	7,303

58,000

At least	But less than	Single	MFJ *	MFS	HoH
58,000	58,050	8,705	6,582	8,705	7,314
58,050	58,100	8,716	6,588	8,716	7,325
58,100	58,150	8,727	6,594	8,727	7,336
58,150	58,200	8,738	6,600	8,738	7,347
58,200	58,250	8,749	6,606	8,749	7,358
58,250	58,300	8,760	6,612	8,760	7,369
58,300	58,350	8,771	6,618	8,771	7,380
58,350	58,400	8,782	6,624	8,782	7,391
58,400	58,450	8,793	6,630	8,793	7,402
58,450	58,500	8,804	6,636	8,804	7,413
58,500	58,550	8,815	6,642	8,815	7,424
58,550	58,600	8,826	6,648	8,826	7,435
58,600	58,650	8,837	6,654	8,837	7,446
58,650	58,700	8,848	6,660	8,848	7,457
58,700	58,750	8,859	6,666	8,859	7,468
58,750	58,800	8,870	6,672	8,870	7,479
58,800	58,850	8,881	6,678	8,881	7,490
58,850	58,900	8,892	6,684	8,892	7,501
58,900	58,950	8,903	6,690	8,903	7,512
58,950	59,000	8,914	6,696	8,914	7,523

59,000

At least	But less than	Single	MFJ *	MFS	HoH
59,000	59,050	8,925	6,702	8,925	7,534
59,050	59,100	8,936	6,708	8,936	7,545
59,100	59,150	8,947	6,714	8,947	7,556
59,150	59,200	8,958	6,720	8,958	7,567
59,200	59,250	8,969	6,726	8,969	7,578
59,250	59,300	8,980	6,732	8,980	7,589
59,300	59,350	8,991	6,738	8,991	7,600
59,350	59,400	9,002	6,744	9,002	7,611
59,400	59,450	9,013	6,750	9,013	7,622
59,450	59,500	9,024	6,756	9,024	7,633
59,500	59,550	9,035	6,762	9,035	7,644
59,550	59,600	9,046	6,768	9,046	7,655
59,600	59,650	9,057	6,774	9,057	7,666
59,650	59,700	9,068	6,780	9,068	7,677
59,700	59,750	9,079	6,786	9,079	7,688
59,750	59,800	9,090	6,792	9,090	7,699
59,800	59,850	9,101	6,798	9,101	7,710
59,850	59,900	9,112	6,804	9,112	7,721
59,900	59,950	9,123	6,810	9,123	7,732
59,950	60,000	9,134	6,816	9,134	7,743

60,000

At least	But less than	Single	MFJ *	MFS	HoH
60,000	60,050	9,145	6,822	9,145	7,754
60,050	60,100	9,156	6,828	9,156	7,765
60,100	60,150	9,167	6,834	9,167	7,776
60,150	60,200	9,178	6,840	9,178	7,787
60,200	60,250	9,189	6,846	9,189	7,798
60,250	60,300	9,200	6,852	9,200	7,809
60,300	60,350	9,211	6,858	9,211	7,820
60,350	60,400	9,222	6,864	9,222	7,831
60,400	60,450	9,233	6,870	9,233	7,842
60,450	60,500	9,244	6,876	9,244	7,853
60,500	60,550	9,255	6,882	9,255	7,864
60,550	60,600	9,266	6,888	9,266	7,875
60,600	60,650	9,277	6,894	9,277	7,886
60,650	60,700	9,288	6,900	9,288	7,897
60,700	60,750	9,299	6,906	9,299	7,908
60,750	60,800	9,310	6,912	9,310	7,919
60,800	60,850	9,321	6,918	9,321	7,930
60,850	60,900	9,332	6,924	9,332	7,941
60,900	60,950	9,343	6,930	9,343	7,952
60,950	61,000	9,354	6,936	9,354	7,963

61,000

At least	But less than	Single	MFJ *	MFS	HoH
61,000	61,050	9,365	6,942	9,365	7,974
61,050	61,100	9,376	6,948	9,376	7,985
61,100	61,150	9,387	6,954	9,387	7,996
61,150	61,200	9,398	6,960	9,398	8,007
61,200	61,250	9,409	6,966	9,409	8,018
61,250	61,300	9,420	6,972	9,420	8,029
61,300	61,350	9,431	6,978	9,431	8,040
61,350	61,400	9,442	6,984	9,442	8,051
61,400	61,450	9,453	6,990	9,453	8,062
61,450	61,500	9,464	6,996	9,464	8,073
61,500	61,550	9,475	7,002	9,475	8,084
61,550	61,600	9,486	7,008	9,486	8,095
61,600	61,650	9,497	7,014	9,497	8,106
61,650	61,700	9,508	7,020	9,508	8,117
61,700	61,750	9,519	7,026	9,519	8,128
61,750	61,800	9,530	7,032	9,530	8,139
61,800	61,850	9,541	7,038	9,541	8,150
61,850	61,900	9,552	7,044	9,552	8,161
61,900	61,950	9,563	7,050	9,563	8,172
61,950	62,000	9,574	7,056	9,574	8,183

62,000

At least	But less than	Single	MFJ *	MFS	HoH
62,000	62,050	9,585	7,062	9,585	8,194
62,050	62,100	9,596	7,068	9,596	8,205
62,100	62,150	9,607	7,074	9,607	8,216
62,150	62,200	9,618	7,080	9,618	8,227
62,200	62,250	9,629	7,086	9,629	8,238
62,250	62,300	9,640	7,092	9,640	8,249
62,300	62,350	9,651	7,098	9,651	8,260
62,350	62,400	9,662	7,104	9,662	8,271
62,400	62,450	9,673	7,110	9,673	8,282
62,450	62,500	9,684	7,116	9,684	8,293
62,500	62,550	9,695	7,122	9,695	8,304
62,550	62,600	9,706	7,128	9,706	8,315
62,600	62,650	9,717	7,134	9,717	8,326
62,650	62,700	9,728	7,140	9,728	8,337
62,700	62,750	9,739	7,146	9,739	8,348
62,750	62,800	9,750	7,152	9,750	8,359
62,800	62,850	9,761	7,158	9,761	8,370
62,850	62,900	9,772	7,164	9,772	8,381
62,900	62,950	9,783	7,170	9,783	8,392
62,950	63,000	9,794	7,176	9,794	8,403

63,000

At least	But less than	Single	MFJ *	MFS	HoH
63,000	63,050	9,805	7,182	9,805	8,414
63,050	63,100	9,816	7,188	9,816	8,425
63,100	63,150	9,827	7,194	9,827	8,436
63,150	63,200	9,838	7,200	9,838	8,447
63,200	63,250	9,849	7,206	9,849	8,458
63,250	63,300	9,860	7,212	9,860	8,469
63,300	63,350	9,871	7,218	9,871	8,480
63,350	63,400	9,882	7,224	9,882	8,491
63,400	63,450	9,893	7,230	9,893	8,502
63,450	63,500	9,904	7,236	9,904	8,513
63,500	63,550	9,915	7,242	9,915	8,524
63,550	63,600	9,926	7,248	9,926	8,535
63,600	63,650	9,937	7,254	9,937	8,546
63,650	63,700	9,948	7,260	9,948	8,557
63,700	63,750	9,959	7,266	9,959	8,568
63,750	63,800	9,970	7,272	9,970	8,579
63,800	63,850	9,981	7,278	9,981	8,590
63,850	63,900	9,992	7,284	9,992	8,601
63,900	63,950	10,003	7,290	10,003	8,612
63,950	64,000	10,014	7,296	10,014	8,623

64,000

At least	But less than	Single	MFJ *	MFS	HoH
64,000	64,050	10,025	7,302	10,025	8,634
64,050	64,100	10,036	7,308	10,036	8,645
64,100	64,150	10,047	7,314	10,047	8,656
64,150	64,200	10,058	7,320	10,058	8,667
64,200	64,250	10,069	7,326	10,069	8,678
64,250	64,300	10,080	7,332	10,080	8,689
64,300	64,350	10,091	7,338	10,091	8,700
64,350	64,400	10,102	7,344	10,102	8,711
64,400	64,450	10,113	7,350	10,113	8,722
64,450	64,500	10,124	7,356	10,124	8,733
64,500	64,550	10,135	7,362	10,135	8,744
64,550	64,600	10,146	7,368	10,146	8,755
64,600	64,650	10,157	7,374	10,157	8,766
64,650	64,700	10,168	7,380	10,168	8,777
64,700	64,750	10,179	7,386	10,179	8,788
64,750	64,800	10,190	7,392	10,190	8,799
64,800	64,850	10,201	7,398	10,201	8,810
64,850	64,900	10,212	7,404	10,212	8,821
64,900	64,950	10,223	7,410	10,223	8,832
64,950	65,000	10,234	7,416	10,234	8,843

65,000

At least	But less than	Single	MFJ *	MFS	HoH
65,000	65,050	10,245	7,422	10,245	8,854
65,050	65,100	10,256	7,428	10,256	8,865
65,100	65,150	10,267	7,434	10,267	8,876
65,150	65,200	10,278	7,440	10,278	8,887
65,200	65,250	10,289	7,446	10,289	8,898
65,250	65,300	10,300	7,452	10,300	8,909
65,300	65,350	10,311	7,458	10,311	8,920
65,350	65,400	10,322	7,464	10,322	8,931
65,400	65,450	10,333	7,470	10,333	8,942
65,450	65,500	10,344	7,476	10,344	8,953
65,500	65,550	10,355	7,482	10,355	8,964
65,550	65,600	10,366	7,488	10,366	8,975
65,600	65,650	10,377	7,494	10,377	8,986
65,650	65,700	10,388	7,500	10,388	8,997
65,700	65,750	10,399	7,506	10,399	9,008
65,750	65,800	10,410	7,512	10,410	9,019
65,800	65,850	10,421	7,518	10,421	9,030
65,850	65,900	10,432	7,524	10,432	9,041
65,900	65,950	10,443	7,530	10,443	9,052
65,950	66,000	10,454	7,536	10,454	9,063

(Continued)

* This column must also be used by a qualifying widow(er).

If line 10 (taxable income) is—		And you are—				If line 10 (taxable income) is—		And you are—				If line 10 (taxable income) is—		And you are—			
At least	But less than	Single	Married filing jointly*	Married filing separately	Head of a household	At least	But less than	Single	Married filing jointly*	Married filing separately	Head of a household	At least	But less than	Single	Married filing jointly*	Married filing separately	Head of a household
		Your tax is—						Your tax is—						Your tax is—			
66,000						**69,000**						**72,000**					
66,000	66,050	10,465	7,542	10,465	9,074	69,000	69,050	11,125	7,902	11,125	9,734	72,000	72,050	11,785	8,262	11,785	10,394
66,050	66,100	10,476	7,548	10,476	9,085	69,050	69,100	11,136	7,908	11,136	9,745	72,050	72,100	11,796	8,268	11,796	10,405
66,100	66,150	10,487	7,554	10,487	9,096	69,100	69,150	11,147	7,914	11,147	9,756	72,100	72,150	11,807	8,274	11,807	10,416
66,150	66,200	10,498	7,560	10,498	9,107	69,150	69,200	11,158	7,920	11,158	9,767	72,150	72,200	11,818	8,280	11,818	10,427
66,200	66,250	10,509	7,566	10,509	9,118	69,200	69,250	11,169	7,926	11,169	9,778	72,200	72,250	11,829	8,286	11,829	10,438
66,250	66,300	10,520	7,572	10,520	9,129	69,250	69,300	11,180	7,932	11,180	9,789	72,250	72,300	11,840	8,292	11,840	10,449
66,300	66,350	10,531	7,578	10,531	9,140	69,300	69,350	11,191	7,938	11,191	9,800	72,300	72,350	11,851	8,298	11,851	10,460
66,350	66,400	10,542	7,584	10,542	9,151	69,350	69,400	11,202	7,944	11,202	9,811	72,350	72,400	11,862	8,304	11,862	10,471
66,400	66,450	10,553	7,590	10,553	9,162	69,400	69,450	11,213	7,950	11,213	9,822	72,400	72,450	11,873	8,310	11,873	10,482
66,450	66,500	10,564	7,596	10,564	9,173	69,450	69,500	11,224	7,956	11,224	9,833	72,450	72,500	11,884	8,316	11,884	10,493
66,500	66,550	10,575	7,602	10,575	9,184	69,500	69,550	11,235	7,962	11,235	9,844	72,500	72,550	11,895	8,322	11,895	10,504
66,550	66,600	10,586	7,608	10,586	9,195	69,550	69,600	11,246	7,968	11,246	9,855	72,550	72,600	11,906	8,328	11,906	10,515
66,600	66,650	10,597	7,614	10,597	9,206	69,600	69,650	11,257	7,974	11,257	9,866	72,600	72,650	11,917	8,334	11,917	10,526
66,650	66,700	10,608	7,620	10,608	9,217	69,650	69,700	11,268	7,980	11,268	9,877	72,650	72,700	11,928	8,340	11,928	10,537
66,700	66,750	10,619	7,626	10,619	9,228	69,700	69,750	11,279	7,986	11,279	9,888	72,700	72,750	11,939	8,346	11,939	10,548
66,750	66,800	10,630	7,632	10,630	9,239	69,750	69,800	11,290	7,992	11,290	9,899	72,750	72,800	11,950	8,352	11,950	10,559
66,800	66,850	10,641	7,638	10,641	9,250	69,800	69,850	11,301	7,998	11,301	9,910	72,800	72,850	11,961	8,358	11,961	10,570
66,850	66,900	10,652	7,644	10,652	9,261	69,850	69,900	11,312	8,004	11,312	9,921	72,850	72,900	11,972	8,364	11,972	10,581
66,900	66,950	10,663	7,650	10,663	9,272	69,900	69,950	11,323	8,010	11,323	9,932	72,900	72,950	11,983	8,370	11,983	10,592
66,950	67,000	10,674	7,656	10,674	9,283	69,950	70,000	11,334	8,016	11,334	9,943	72,950	73,000	11,994	8,376	11,994	10,603
67,000						**70,000**						**73,000**					
67,000	67,050	10,685	7,662	10,685	9,294	70,000	70,050	11,345	8,022	11,345	9,954	73,000	73,050	12,005	8,382	12,005	10,614
67,050	67,100	10,696	7,668	10,696	9,305	70,050	70,100	11,356	8,028	11,356	9,965	73,050	73,100	12,016	8,388	12,016	10,625
67,100	67,150	10,707	7,674	10,707	9,316	70,100	70,150	11,367	8,034	11,367	9,976	73,100	73,150	12,027	8,394	12,027	10,636
67,150	67,200	10,718	7,680	10,718	9,327	70,150	70,200	11,378	8,040	11,378	9,987	73,150	73,200	12,038	8,400	12,038	10,647
67,200	67,250	10,729	7,686	10,729	9,338	70,200	70,250	11,389	8,046	11,389	9,998	73,200	73,250	12,049	8,406	12,049	10,658
67,250	67,300	10,740	7,692	10,740	9,349	70,250	70,300	11,400	8,052	11,400	10,009	73,250	73,300	12,060	8,412	12,060	10,669
67,300	67,350	10,751	7,698	10,751	9,360	70,300	70,350	11,411	8,058	11,411	10,020	73,300	73,350	12,071	8,418	12,071	10,680
67,350	67,400	10,762	7,704	10,762	9,371	70,350	70,400	11,422	8,064	11,422	10,031	73,350	73,400	12,082	8,424	12,082	10,691
67,400	67,450	10,773	7,710	10,773	9,382	70,400	70,450	11,433	8,070	11,433	10,042	73,400	73,450	12,093	8,430	12,093	10,702
67,450	67,500	10,784	7,716	10,784	9,393	70,450	70,500	11,444	8,076	11,444	10,053	73,450	73,500	12,104	8,436	12,104	10,713
67,500	67,550	10,795	7,722	10,795	9,404	70,500	70,550	11,455	8,082	11,455	10,064	73,500	73,550	12,115	8,442	12,115	10,724
67,550	67,600	10,806	7,728	10,806	9,415	70,550	70,600	11,466	8,088	11,466	10,075	73,550	73,600	12,126	8,448	12,126	10,735
67,600	67,650	10,817	7,734	10,817	9,426	70,600	70,650	11,477	8,094	11,477	10,086	73,600	73,650	12,137	8,454	12,137	10,746
67,650	67,700	10,828	7,740	10,828	9,437	70,650	70,700	11,488	8,100	11,488	10,097	73,650	73,700	12,148	8,460	12,148	10,757
67,700	67,750	10,839	7,746	10,839	9,448	70,700	70,750	11,499	8,106	11,499	10,108	73,700	73,750	12,159	8,466	12,159	10,768
67,750	67,800	10,850	7,752	10,850	9,459	70,750	70,800	11,510	8,112	11,510	10,119	73,750	73,800	12,170	8,472	12,170	10,779
67,800	67,850	10,861	7,758	10,861	9,470	70,800	70,850	11,521	8,118	11,521	10,130	73,800	73,850	12,181	8,478	12,181	10,790
67,850	67,900	10,872	7,764	10,872	9,481	70,850	70,900	11,532	8,124	11,532	10,141	73,850	73,900	12,192	8,484	12,192	10,801
67,900	67,950	10,883	7,770	10,883	9,492	70,900	70,950	11,543	8,130	11,543	10,152	73,900	73,950	12,203	8,490	12,203	10,812
67,950	68,000	10,894	7,776	10,894	9,503	70,950	71,000	11,554	8,136	11,554	10,163	73,950	74,000	12,214	8,496	12,214	10,823
68,000						**71,000**						**74,000**					
68,000	68,050	10,905	7,782	10,905	9,514	71,000	71,050	11,565	8,142	11,565	10,174	74,000	74,050	12,225	8,502	12,225	10,834
68,050	68,100	10,916	7,788	10,916	9,525	71,050	71,100	11,576	8,148	11,576	10,185	74,050	74,100	12,236	8,508	12,236	10,845
68,100	68,150	10,927	7,794	10,927	9,536	71,100	71,150	11,587	8,154	11,587	10,196	74,100	74,150	12,247	8,514	12,247	10,856
68,150	68,200	10,938	7,800	10,938	9,547	71,150	71,200	11,598	8,160	11,598	10,207	74,150	74,200	12,258	8,520	12,258	10,867
68,200	68,250	10,949	7,806	10,949	9,558	71,200	71,250	11,609	8,166	11,609	10,218	74,200	74,250	12,269	8,526	12,269	10,878
68,250	68,300	10,960	7,812	10,960	9,569	71,250	71,300	11,620	8,172	11,620	10,229	74,250	74,300	12,280	8,532	12,280	10,889
68,300	68,350	10,971	7,818	10,971	9,580	71,300	71,350	11,631	8,178	11,631	10,240	74,300	74,350	12,291	8,538	12,291	10,900
68,350	68,400	10,982	7,824	10,982	9,591	71,350	71,400	11,642	8,184	11,642	10,251	74,350	74,400	12,302	8,544	12,302	10,911
68,400	68,450	10,993	7,830	10,993	9,602	71,400	71,450	11,653	8,190	11,653	10,262	74,400	74,450	12,313	8,550	12,313	10,922
68,450	68,500	11,004	7,836	11,004	9,613	71,450	71,500	11,664	8,196	11,664	10,273	74,450	74,500	12,324	8,556	12,324	10,933
68,500	68,550	11,015	7,842	11,015	9,624	71,500	71,550	11,675	8,202	11,675	10,284	74,500	74,550	12,335	8,562	12,335	10,944
68,550	68,600	11,026	7,848	11,026	9,635	71,550	71,600	11,686	8,208	11,686	10,295	74,550	74,600	12,346	8,568	12,346	10,955
68,600	68,650	11,037	7,854	11,037	9,646	71,600	71,650	11,697	8,214	11,697	10,306	74,600	74,650	12,357	8,574	12,357	10,966
68,650	68,700	11,048	7,860	11,048	9,657	71,650	71,700	11,708	8,220	11,708	10,317	74,650	74,700	12,368	8,580	12,368	10,977
68,700	68,750	11,059	7,866	11,059	9,668	71,700	71,750	11,719	8,226	11,719	10,328	74,700	74,750	12,379	8,586	12,379	10,988
68,750	68,800	11,070	7,872	11,070	9,679	71,750	71,800	11,730	8,232	11,730	10,339	74,750	74,800	12,390	8,592	12,390	10,999
68,800	68,850	11,081	7,878	11,081	9,690	71,800	71,850	11,741	8,238	11,741	10,350	74,800	74,850	12,401	8,598	12,401	11,010
68,850	68,900	11,092	7,884	11,092	9,701	71,850	71,900	11,752	8,244	11,752	10,361	74,850	74,900	12,412	8,604	12,412	11,021
68,900	68,950	11,103	7,890	11,103	9,712	71,900	71,950	11,763	8,250	11,763	10,372	74,900	74,950	12,423	8,610	12,423	11,032
68,950	69,000	11,114	7,896	11,114	9,723	71,950	72,000	11,774	8,256	11,774	10,383	74,950	75,000	12,434	8,616	12,434	11,043

(Continued)

* This column must also be used by a qualifying widow(er).

| If line 10 (taxable income) is— | | And you are— | | | |
At least	But less than	Single	Married filing jointly *	Married filing separately	Head of a household
		Your tax is—			

75,000

At least	But less than	Single	Married filing jointly *	Married filing separately	Head of a household
75,000	75,050	12,445	8,622	12,445	11,054
75,050	75,100	12,456	8,628	12,456	11,065
75,100	75,150	12,467	8,634	12,467	11,076
75,150	75,200	12,478	8,640	12,478	11,087
75,200	75,250	12,489	8,646	12,489	11,098
75,250	75,300	12,500	8,652	12,500	11,109
75,300	75,350	12,511	8,658	12,511	11,120
75,350	75,400	12,522	8,664	12,522	11,131
75,400	75,450	12,533	8,670	12,533	11,142
75,450	75,500	12,544	8,676	12,544	11,153
75,500	75,550	12,555	8,682	12,555	11,164
75,550	75,600	12,566	8,688	12,566	11,175
75,600	75,650	12,577	8,694	12,577	11,186
75,650	75,700	12,588	8,700	12,588	11,197
75,700	75,750	12,599	8,706	12,599	11,208
75,750	75,800	12,610	8,712	12,610	11,219
75,800	75,850	12,621	8,718	12,621	11,230
75,850	75,900	12,632	8,724	12,632	11,241
75,900	75,950	12,643	8,730	12,643	11,252
75,950	76,000	12,654	8,736	12,654	11,263

76,000

At least	But less than	Single	Married filing jointly *	Married filing separately	Head of a household
76,000	76,050	12,665	8,742	12,665	11,274
76,050	76,100	12,676	8,748	12,676	11,285
76,100	76,150	12,687	8,754	12,687	11,296
76,150	76,200	12,698	8,760	12,698	11,307
76,200	76,250	12,709	8,766	12,709	11,318
76,250	76,300	12,720	8,772	12,720	11,329
76,300	76,350	12,731	8,778	12,731	11,340
76,350	76,400	12,742	8,784	12,742	11,351
76,400	76,450	12,753	8,790	12,753	11,362
76,450	76,500	12,764	8,796	12,764	11,373
76,500	76,550	12,775	8,802	12,775	11,384
76,550	76,600	12,786	8,808	12,786	11,395
76,600	76,650	12,797	8,814	12,797	11,406
76,650	76,700	12,808	8,820	12,808	11,417
76,700	76,750	12,819	8,826	12,819	11,428
76,750	76,800	12,830	8,832	12,830	11,439
76,800	76,850	12,841	8,838	12,841	11,450
76,850	76,900	12,852	8,844	12,852	11,461
76,900	76,950	12,863	8,850	12,863	11,472
76,950	77,000	12,874	8,856	12,874	11,483

77,000

At least	But less than	Single	Married filing jointly *	Married filing separately	Head of a household
77,000	77,050	12,885	8,862	12,885	11,494
77,050	77,100	12,896	8,868	12,896	11,505
77,100	77,150	12,907	8,874	12,907	11,516
77,150	77,200	12,918	8,880	12,918	11,527
77,200	77,250	12,929	8,886	12,929	11,538
77,250	77,300	12,940	8,892	12,940	11,549
77,300	77,350	12,951	8,898	12,951	11,560
77,350	77,400	12,962	8,904	12,962	11,571
77,400	77,450	12,973	8,913	12,973	11,582
77,450	77,500	12,984	8,924	12,984	11,593
77,500	77,550	12,995	8,935	12,995	11,604
77,550	77,600	13,006	8,946	13,006	11,615
77,600	77,650	13,017	8,957	13,017	11,626
77,650	77,700	13,028	8,968	13,028	11,637
77,700	77,750	13,039	8,979	13,039	11,648
77,750	77,800	13,050	8,990	13,050	11,659
77,800	77,850	13,061	9,001	13,061	11,670
77,850	77,900	13,072	9,012	13,072	11,681
77,900	77,950	13,083	9,023	13,083	11,692
77,950	78,000	13,094	9,034	13,094	11,703

78,000

At least	But less than	Single	Married filing jointly *	Married filing separately	Head of a household
78,000	78,050	13,105	9,045	13,105	11,714
78,050	78,100	13,116	9,056	13,116	11,725
78,100	78,150	13,127	9,067	13,127	11,736
78,150	78,200	13,138	9,078	13,138	11,747
78,200	78,250	13,149	9,089	13,149	11,758
78,250	78,300	13,160	9,100	13,160	11,769
78,300	78,350	13,171	9,111	13,171	11,780
78,350	78,400	13,182	9,122	13,182	11,791
78,400	78,450	13,193	9,133	13,193	11,802
78,450	78,500	13,204	9,144	13,204	11,813
78,500	78,550	13,215	9,155	13,215	11,824
78,550	78,600	13,226	9,166	13,226	11,835
78,600	78,650	13,237	9,177	13,237	11,846
78,650	78,700	13,248	9,188	13,248	11,857
78,700	78,750	13,259	9,199	13,259	11,868
78,750	78,800	13,270	9,210	13,270	11,879
78,800	78,850	13,281	9,221	13,281	11,890
78,850	78,900	13,292	9,232	13,292	11,901
78,900	78,950	13,303	9,243	13,303	11,912
78,950	79,000	13,314	9,254	13,314	11,923

79,000

At least	But less than	Single	Married filing jointly *	Married filing separately	Head of a household
79,000	79,050	13,325	9,265	13,325	11,934
79,050	79,100	13,336	9,276	13,336	11,945
79,100	79,150	13,347	9,287	13,347	11,956
79,150	79,200	13,358	9,298	13,358	11,967
79,200	79,250	13,369	9,309	13,369	11,978
79,250	79,300	13,380	9,320	13,380	11,989
79,300	79,350	13,391	9,331	13,391	12,000
79,350	79,400	13,402	9,342	13,402	12,011
79,400	79,450	13,413	9,353	13,413	12,022
79,450	79,500	13,424	9,364	13,424	12,033
79,500	79,550	13,435	9,375	13,435	12,044
79,550	79,600	13,446	9,386	13,446	12,055
79,600	79,650	13,457	9,397	13,457	12,066
79,650	79,700	13,468	9,408	13,468	12,077
79,700	79,750	13,479	9,419	13,479	12,088
79,750	79,800	13,490	9,430	13,490	12,099
79,800	79,850	13,501	9,441	13,501	12,110
79,850	79,900	13,512	9,452	13,512	12,121
79,900	79,950	13,523	9,463	13,523	12,132
79,950	80,000	13,534	9,474	13,534	12,143

80,000

At least	But less than	Single	Married filing jointly *	Married filing separately	Head of a household
80,000	80,050	13,545	9,485	13,545	12,154
80,050	80,100	13,556	9,496	13,556	12,165
80,100	80,150	13,567	9,507	13,567	12,176
80,150	80,200	13,578	9,518	13,578	12,187
80,200	80,250	13,589	9,529	13,589	12,198
80,250	80,300	13,600	9,540	13,600	12,209
80,300	80,350	13,611	9,551	13,611	12,220
80,350	80,400	13,622	9,562	13,622	12,231
80,400	80,450	13,633	9,573	13,633	12,242
80,450	80,500	13,644	9,584	13,644	12,253
80,500	80,550	13,655	9,595	13,655	12,264
80,550	80,600	13,666	9,606	13,666	12,275
80,600	80,650	13,677	9,617	13,677	12,286
80,650	80,700	13,688	9,628	13,688	12,297
80,700	80,750	13,699	9,639	13,699	12,308
80,750	80,800	13,710	9,650	13,710	12,319
80,800	80,850	13,721	9,661	13,721	12,330
80,850	80,900	13,732	9,672	13,732	12,341
80,900	80,950	13,743	9,683	13,743	12,352
80,950	81,000	13,754	9,694	13,754	12,363

81,000

At least	But less than	Single	Married filing jointly *	Married filing separately	Head of a household
81,000	81,050	13,765	9,705	13,765	12,374
81,050	81,100	13,776	9,716	13,776	12,385
81,100	81,150	13,787	9,727	13,787	12,396
81,150	81,200	13,798	9,738	13,798	12,407
81,200	81,250	13,809	9,749	13,809	12,418
81,250	81,300	13,820	9,760	13,820	12,429
81,300	81,350	13,831	9,771	13,831	12,440
81,350	81,400	13,842	9,782	13,842	12,451
81,400	81,450	13,853	9,793	13,853	12,462
81,450	81,500	13,864	9,804	13,864	12,473
81,500	81,550	13,875	9,815	13,875	12,484
81,550	81,600	13,886	9,826	13,886	12,495
81,600	81,650	13,897	9,837	13,897	12,506
81,650	81,700	13,908	9,848	13,908	12,517
81,700	81,750	13,919	9,859	13,919	12,528
81,750	81,800	13,930	9,870	13,930	12,539
81,800	81,850	13,941	9,881	13,941	12,550
81,850	81,900	13,952	9,892	13,952	12,561
81,900	81,950	13,963	9,903	13,963	12,572
81,950	82,000	13,974	9,914	13,974	12,583

82,000

At least	But less than	Single	Married filing jointly *	Married filing separately	Head of a household
82,000	82,050	13,985	9,925	13,985	12,594
82,050	82,100	13,996	9,936	13,996	12,605
82,100	82,150	14,007	9,947	14,007	12,616
82,150	82,200	14,018	9,958	14,018	12,627
82,200	82,250	14,029	9,969	14,029	12,638
82,250	82,300	14,040	9,980	14,040	12,649
82,300	82,350	14,051	9,991	14,051	12,660
82,350	82,400	14,062	10,002	14,062	12,671
82,400	82,450	14,073	10,013	14,073	12,682
82,450	82,500	14,084	10,024	14,084	12,693
82,500	82,550	14,096	10,035	14,096	12,704
82,550	82,600	14,108	10,046	14,108	12,716
82,600	82,650	14,120	10,057	14,120	12,728
82,650	82,700	14,132	10,068	14,132	12,740
82,700	82,750	14,144	10,079	14,144	12,752
82,750	82,800	14,156	10,090	14,156	12,764
82,800	82,850	14,168	10,101	14,168	12,776
82,850	82,900	14,180	10,112	14,180	12,788
82,900	82,950	14,192	10,123	14,192	12,800
82,950	83,000	14,204	10,134	14,204	12,812

83,000

At least	But less than	Single	Married filing jointly *	Married filing separately	Head of a household
83,000	83,050	14,216	10,145	14,216	12,824
83,050	83,100	14,228	10,156	14,228	12,836
83,100	83,150	14,240	10,167	14,240	12,848
83,150	83,200	14,252	10,178	14,252	12,860
83,200	83,250	14,264	10,189	14,264	12,872
83,250	83,300	14,276	10,200	14,276	12,884
83,300	83,350	14,288	10,211	14,288	12,896
83,350	83,400	14,300	10,222	14,300	12,908
83,400	83,450	14,312	10,233	14,312	12,920
83,450	83,500	14,324	10,244	14,324	12,932
83,500	83,550	14,336	10,255	14,336	12,944
83,550	83,600	14,348	10,266	14,348	12,956
83,600	83,650	14,360	10,277	14,360	12,968
83,650	83,700	14,372	10,288	14,372	12,980
83,700	83,750	14,384	10,299	14,384	12,992
83,750	83,800	14,396	10,310	14,396	13,004
83,800	83,850	14,408	10,321	14,408	13,016
83,850	83,900	14,420	10,332	14,420	13,028
83,900	83,950	14,432	10,343	14,432	13,040
83,950	84,000	14,444	10,354	14,444	13,052

* This column must also be used by a qualifying widow(er).

(Continued)

84,000

At least	But less than	Single	Married filing jointly*	Married filing separately	Head of a household
84,000	84,050	14,456	10,365	14,456	13,064
84,050	84,100	14,468	10,376	14,468	13,076
84,100	84,150	14,480	10,387	14,480	13,088
84,150	84,200	14,492	10,398	14,492	13,100
84,200	84,250	14,504	10,409	14,504	13,112
84,250	84,300	14,516	10,420	14,516	13,124
84,300	84,350	14,528	10,431	14,528	13,136
84,350	84,400	14,540	10,442	14,540	13,148
84,400	84,450	14,552	10,453	14,552	13,160
84,450	84,500	14,564	10,464	14,564	13,172
84,500	84,550	14,576	10,475	14,576	13,184
84,550	84,600	14,588	10,486	14,588	13,196
84,600	84,650	14,600	10,497	14,600	13,208
84,650	84,700	14,612	10,508	14,612	13,220
84,700	84,750	14,624	10,519	14,624	13,232
84,750	84,800	14,636	10,530	14,636	13,244
84,800	84,850	14,648	10,541	14,648	13,256
84,850	84,900	14,660	10,552	14,660	13,268
84,900	84,950	14,672	10,563	14,672	13,280
84,950	85,000	14,684	10,574	14,684	13,292

85,000

At least	But less than	Single	Married filing jointly*	Married filing separately	Head of a household
85,000	85,050	14,696	10,585	14,696	13,304
85,050	85,100	14,708	10,596	14,708	13,316
85,100	85,150	14,720	10,607	14,720	13,328
85,150	85,200	14,732	10,618	14,732	13,340
85,200	85,250	14,744	10,629	14,744	13,352
85,250	85,300	14,756	10,640	14,756	13,364
85,300	85,350	14,768	10,651	14,768	13,376
85,350	85,400	14,780	10,662	14,780	13,388
85,400	85,450	14,792	10,673	14,792	13,400
85,450	85,500	14,804	10,684	14,804	13,412
85,500	85,550	14,816	10,695	14,816	13,424
85,550	85,600	14,828	10,706	14,828	13,436
85,600	85,650	14,840	10,717	14,840	13,448
85,650	85,700	14,852	10,728	14,852	13,460
85,700	85,750	14,864	10,739	14,864	13,472
85,750	85,800	14,876	10,750	14,876	13,484
85,800	85,850	14,888	10,761	14,888	13,496
85,850	85,900	14,900	10,772	14,900	13,508
85,900	85,950	14,912	10,783	14,912	13,520
85,950	86,000	14,924	10,794	14,924	13,532

86,000

At least	But less than	Single	Married filing jointly*	Married filing separately	Head of a household
86,000	86,050	14,936	10,805	14,936	13,544
86,050	86,100	14,948	10,816	14,948	13,556
86,100	86,150	14,960	10,827	14,960	13,568
86,150	86,200	14,972	10,838	14,972	13,580
86,200	86,250	14,984	10,849	14,984	13,592
86,250	86,300	14,996	10,860	14,996	13,604
86,300	86,350	15,008	10,871	15,008	13,616
86,350	86,400	15,020	10,882	15,020	13,628
86,400	86,450	15,032	10,893	15,032	13,640
86,450	86,500	15,044	10,904	15,044	13,652
86,500	86,550	15,056	10,915	15,056	13,664
86,550	86,600	15,068	10,926	15,068	13,676
86,600	86,650	15,080	10,937	15,080	13,688
86,650	86,700	15,092	10,948	15,092	13,700
86,700	86,750	15,104	10,959	15,104	13,712
86,750	86,800	15,116	10,970	15,116	13,724
86,800	86,850	15,128	10,981	15,128	13,736
86,850	86,900	15,140	10,992	15,140	13,748
86,900	86,950	15,152	11,003	15,152	13,760
86,950	87,000	15,164	11,014	15,164	13,772

87,000

At least	But less than	Single	Married filing jointly*	Married filing separately	Head of a household
87,000	87,050	15,176	11,025	15,176	13,784
87,050	87,100	15,188	11,036	15,188	13,796
87,100	87,150	15,200	11,047	15,200	13,808
87,150	87,200	15,212	11,058	15,212	13,820
87,200	87,250	15,224	11,069	15,224	13,832
87,250	87,300	15,236	11,080	15,236	13,844
87,300	87,350	15,248	11,091	15,248	13,856
87,350	87,400	15,260	11,102	15,260	13,868
87,400	87,450	15,272	11,113	15,272	13,880
87,450	87,500	15,284	11,124	15,284	13,892
87,500	87,550	15,296	11,135	15,296	13,904
87,550	87,600	15,308	11,146	15,308	13,916
87,600	87,650	15,320	11,157	15,320	13,928
87,650	87,700	15,332	11,168	15,332	13,940
87,700	87,750	15,344	11,179	15,344	13,952
87,750	87,800	15,356	11,190	15,356	13,964
87,800	87,850	15,368	11,201	15,368	13,976
87,850	87,900	15,380	11,212	15,380	13,988
87,900	87,950	15,392	11,223	15,392	14,000
87,950	88,000	15,404	11,234	15,404	14,012

88,000

At least	But less than	Single	Married filing jointly*	Married filing separately	Head of a household
88,000	88,050	15,416	11,245	15,416	14,024
88,050	88,100	15,428	11,256	15,428	14,036
88,100	88,150	15,440	11,267	15,440	14,048
88,150	88,200	15,452	11,278	15,452	14,060
88,200	88,250	15,464	11,289	15,464	14,072
88,250	88,300	15,476	11,300	15,476	14,084
88,300	88,350	15,488	11,311	15,488	14,096
88,350	88,400	15,500	11,322	15,500	14,108
88,400	88,450	15,512	11,333	15,512	14,120
88,450	88,500	15,524	11,344	15,524	14,132
88,500	88,550	15,536	11,355	15,536	14,144
88,550	88,600	15,548	11,366	15,548	14,156
88,600	88,650	15,560	11,377	15,560	14,168
88,650	88,700	15,572	11,388	15,572	14,180
88,700	88,750	15,584	11,399	15,584	14,192
88,750	88,800	15,596	11,410	15,596	14,204
88,800	88,850	15,608	11,421	15,608	14,216
88,850	88,900	15,620	11,432	15,620	14,228
88,900	88,950	15,632	11,443	15,632	14,240
88,950	89,000	15,644	11,454	15,644	14,252

89,000

At least	But less than	Single	Married filing jointly*	Married filing separately	Head of a household
89,000	89,050	15,656	11,465	15,656	14,264
89,050	89,100	15,668	11,476	15,668	14,276
89,100	89,150	15,680	11,487	15,680	14,288
89,150	89,200	15,692	11,498	15,692	14,300
89,200	89,250	15,704	11,509	15,704	14,312
89,250	89,300	15,716	11,520	15,716	14,324
89,300	89,350	15,728	11,531	15,728	14,336
89,350	89,400	15,740	11,542	15,740	14,348
89,400	89,450	15,752	11,553	15,752	14,360
89,450	89,500	15,764	11,564	15,764	14,372
89,500	89,550	15,776	11,575	15,776	14,384
89,550	89,600	15,788	11,586	15,788	14,396
89,600	89,650	15,800	11,597	15,800	14,408
89,650	89,700	15,812	11,608	15,812	14,420
89,700	89,750	15,824	11,619	15,824	14,432
89,750	89,800	15,836	11,630	15,836	14,444
89,800	89,850	15,848	11,641	15,848	14,456
89,850	89,900	15,860	11,652	15,860	14,468
89,900	89,950	15,872	11,663	15,872	14,480
89,950	90,000	15,884	11,674	15,884	14,492

90,000

At least	But less than	Single	Married filing jointly*	Married filing separately	Head of a household
90,000	90,050	15,896	11,685	15,896	14,504
90,050	90,100	15,908	11,696	15,908	14,516
90,100	90,150	15,920	11,707	15,920	14,528
90,150	90,200	15,932	11,718	15,932	14,540
90,200	90,250	15,944	11,729	15,944	14,552
90,250	90,300	15,956	11,740	15,956	14,564
90,300	90,350	15,968	11,751	15,968	14,576
90,350	90,400	15,980	11,762	15,980	14,588
90,400	90,450	15,992	11,773	15,992	14,600
90,450	90,500	16,004	11,784	16,004	14,612
90,500	90,550	16,016	11,795	16,016	14,624
90,550	90,600	16,028	11,806	16,028	14,636
90,600	90,650	16,040	11,817	16,040	14,648
90,650	90,700	16,052	11,828	16,052	14,660
90,700	90,750	16,064	11,839	16,064	14,672
90,750	90,800	16,076	11,850	16,076	14,684
90,800	90,850	16,088	11,861	16,088	14,696
90,850	90,900	16,100	11,872	16,100	14,708
90,900	90,950	16,112	11,883	16,112	14,720
90,950	91,000	16,124	11,894	16,124	14,732

91,000

At least	But less than	Single	Married filing jointly*	Married filing separately	Head of a household
91,000	91,050	16,136	11,905	16,136	14,744
91,050	91,100	16,148	11,916	16,148	14,756
91,100	91,150	16,160	11,927	16,160	14,768
91,150	91,200	16,172	11,938	16,172	14,780
91,200	91,250	16,184	11,949	16,184	14,792
91,250	91,300	16,196	11,960	16,196	14,804
91,300	91,350	16,208	11,971	16,208	14,816
91,350	91,400	16,220	11,982	16,220	14,828
91,400	91,450	16,232	11,993	16,232	14,840
91,450	91,500	16,244	12,004	16,244	14,852
91,500	91,550	16,256	12,015	16,256	14,864
91,550	91,600	16,268	12,026	16,268	14,876
91,600	91,650	16,280	12,037	16,280	14,888
91,650	91,700	16,292	12,048	16,292	14,900
91,700	91,750	16,304	12,059	16,304	14,912
91,750	91,800	16,316	12,070	16,316	14,924
91,800	91,850	16,328	12,081	16,328	14,936
91,850	91,900	16,340	12,092	16,340	14,948
91,900	91,950	16,352	12,103	16,352	14,960
91,950	92,000	16,364	12,114	16,364	14,972

92,000

At least	But less than	Single	Married filing jointly*	Married filing separately	Head of a household
92,000	92,050	16,376	12,125	16,376	14,984
92,050	92,100	16,388	12,136	16,388	14,996
92,100	92,150	16,400	12,147	16,400	15,008
92,150	92,200	16,412	12,158	16,412	15,020
92,200	92,250	16,424	12,169	16,424	15,032
92,250	92,300	16,436	12,180	16,436	15,044
92,300	92,350	16,448	12,191	16,448	15,056
92,350	92,400	16,460	12,202	16,460	15,068
92,400	92,450	16,472	12,213	16,472	15,080
92,450	92,500	16,484	12,224	16,484	15,092
92,500	92,550	16,496	12,235	16,496	15,104
92,550	92,600	16,508	12,246	16,508	15,116
92,600	92,650	16,520	12,257	16,520	15,128
92,650	92,700	16,532	12,268	16,532	15,140
92,700	92,750	16,544	12,279	16,544	15,152
92,750	92,800	16,556	12,290	16,556	15,164
92,800	92,850	16,568	12,301	16,568	15,176
92,850	92,900	16,580	12,312	16,580	15,188
92,900	92,950	16,592	12,323	16,592	15,200
92,950	93,000	16,604	12,334	16,604	15,212

(Continued)

* This column must also be used by a qualifying widow(er).

If line 10 (taxable income) is—		And you are—			
At least	But less than	Single	Married filing jointly *	Married filing separately	Head of a household
			Your tax is—		

93,000

At least	But less than	Single	Married filing jointly *	Married filing separately	Head of a household
93,000	93,050	16,616	12,345	16,616	15,224
93,050	93,100	16,628	12,356	16,628	15,236
93,100	93,150	16,640	12,367	16,640	15,248
93,150	93,200	16,652	12,378	16,652	15,260
93,200	93,250	16,664	12,389	16,664	15,272
93,250	93,300	16,676	12,400	16,676	15,284
93,300	93,350	16,688	12,411	16,688	15,296
93,350	93,400	16,700	12,422	16,700	15,308
93,400	93,450	16,712	12,433	16,712	15,320
93,450	93,500	16,724	12,444	16,724	15,332
93,500	93,550	16,736	12,455	16,736	15,344
93,550	93,600	16,748	12,466	16,748	15,356
93,600	93,650	16,760	12,477	16,760	15,368
93,650	93,700	16,772	12,488	16,772	15,380
93,700	93,750	16,784	12,499	16,784	15,392
93,750	93,800	16,796	12,510	16,796	15,404
93,800	93,850	16,808	12,521	16,808	15,416
93,850	93,900	16,820	12,532	16,820	15,428
93,900	93,950	16,832	12,543	16,832	15,440
93,950	94,000	16,844	12,554	16,844	15,452

94,000

At least	But less than	Single	Married filing jointly *	Married filing separately	Head of a household
94,000	94,050	16,856	12,565	16,856	15,464
94,050	94,100	16,868	12,576	16,868	15,476
94,100	94,150	16,880	12,587	16,880	15,488
94,150	94,200	16,892	12,598	16,892	15,500
94,200	94,250	16,904	12,609	16,904	15,512
94,250	94,300	16,916	12,620	16,916	15,524
94,300	94,350	16,928	12,631	16,928	15,536
94,350	94,400	16,940	12,642	16,940	15,548
94,400	94,450	16,952	12,653	16,952	15,560
94,450	94,500	16,964	12,664	16,964	15,572
94,500	94,550	16,976	12,675	16,976	15,584
94,550	94,600	16,988	12,686	16,988	15,596
94,600	94,650	17,000	12,697	17,000	15,608
94,650	94,700	17,012	12,708	17,012	15,620
94,700	94,750	17,024	12,719	17,024	15,632
94,750	94,800	17,036	12,730	17,036	15,644
94,800	94,850	17,048	12,741	17,048	15,656
94,850	94,900	17,060	12,752	17,060	15,668
94,900	94,950	17,072	12,763	17,072	15,680
94,950	95,000	17,084	12,774	17,084	15,692

95,000

At least	But less than	Single	Married filing jointly *	Married filing separately	Head of a household
95,000	95,050	17,096	12,785	17,096	15,704
95,050	95,100	17,108	12,796	17,108	15,716
95,100	95,150	17,120	12,807	17,120	15,728
95,150	95,200	17,132	12,818	17,132	15,740
95,200	95,250	17,144	12,829	17,144	15,752
95,250	95,300	17,156	12,840	17,156	15,764
95,300	95,350	17,168	12,851	17,168	15,776
95,350	95,400	17,180	12,862	17,180	15,788
95,400	95,450	17,192	12,873	17,192	15,800
95,450	95,500	17,204	12,884	17,204	15,812
95,500	95,550	17,216	12,895	17,216	15,824
95,550	95,600	17,228	12,906	17,228	15,836
95,600	95,650	17,240	12,917	17,240	15,848
95,650	95,700	17,252	12,928	17,252	15,860
95,700	95,750	17,264	12,939	17,264	15,872
95,750	95,800	17,276	12,950	17,276	15,884
95,800	95,850	17,288	12,961	17,288	15,896
95,850	95,900	17,300	12,972	17,300	15,908
95,900	95,950	17,312	12,983	17,312	15,920
95,950	96,000	17,324	12,994	17,324	15,932

96,000

At least	But less than	Single	Married filing jointly *	Married filing separately	Head of a household
96,000	96,050	17,336	13,005	17,336	15,944
96,050	96,100	17,348	13,016	17,348	15,956
96,100	96,150	17,360	13,027	17,360	15,968
96,150	96,200	17,372	13,038	17,372	15,980
96,200	96,250	17,384	13,049	17,384	15,992
96,250	96,300	17,396	13,060	17,396	16,004
96,300	96,350	17,408	13,071	17,408	16,016
96,350	96,400	17,420	13,082	17,420	16,028
96,400	96,450	17,432	13,093	17,432	16,040
96,450	96,500	17,444	13,104	17,444	16,052
96,500	96,550	17,456	13,115	17,456	16,064
96,550	96,600	17,468	13,126	17,468	16,076
96,600	96,650	17,480	13,137	17,480	16,088
96,650	96,700	17,492	13,148	17,492	16,100
96,700	96,750	17,504	13,159	17,504	16,112
96,750	96,800	17,516	13,170	17,516	16,124
96,800	96,850	17,528	13,181	17,528	16,136
96,850	96,900	17,540	13,192	17,540	16,148
96,900	96,950	17,552	13,203	17,552	16,160
96,950	97,000	17,564	13,214	17,564	16,172

97,000

At least	But less than	Single	Married filing jointly *	Married filing separately	Head of a household
97,000	97,050	17,576	13,225	17,576	16,184
97,050	97,100	17,588	13,236	17,588	16,196
97,100	97,150	17,600	13,247	17,600	16,208
97,150	97,200	17,612	13,258	17,612	16,220
97,200	97,250	17,624	13,269	17,624	16,232
97,250	97,300	17,636	13,280	17,636	16,244
97,300	97,350	17,648	13,291	17,648	16,256
97,350	97,400	17,660	13,302	17,660	16,268
97,400	97,450	17,672	13,313	17,672	16,280
97,450	97,500	17,684	13,324	17,684	16,292
97,500	97,550	17,696	13,335	17,696	16,304
97,550	97,600	17,708	13,346	17,708	16,316
97,600	97,650	17,720	13,357	17,720	16,328
97,650	97,700	17,732	13,368	17,732	16,340
97,700	97,750	17,744	13,379	17,744	16,352
97,750	97,800	17,756	13,390	17,756	16,364
97,800	97,850	17,768	13,401	17,768	16,376
97,850	97,900	17,780	13,412	17,780	16,388
97,900	97,950	17,792	13,423	17,792	16,400
97,950	98,000	17,804	13,434	17,804	16,412

98,000

At least	But less than	Single	Married filing jointly *	Married filing separately	Head of a household
98,000	98,050	17,816	13,445	17,816	16,424
98,050	98,100	17,828	13,456	17,828	16,436
98,100	98,150	17,840	13,467	17,840	16,448
98,150	98,200	17,852	13,478	17,852	16,460
98,200	98,250	17,864	13,489	17,864	16,472
98,250	98,300	17,876	13,500	17,876	16,484
98,300	98,350	17,888	13,511	17,888	16,496
98,350	98,400	17,900	13,522	17,900	16,508
98,400	98,450	17,912	13,533	17,912	16,520
98,450	98,500	17,924	13,544	17,924	16,532
98,500	98,550	17,936	13,555	17,936	16,544
98,550	98,600	17,948	13,566	17,948	16,556
98,600	98,650	17,960	13,577	17,960	16,568
98,650	98,700	17,972	13,588	17,972	16,580
98,700	98,750	17,984	13,599	17,984	16,592
98,750	98,800	17,996	13,610	17,996	16,604
98,800	98,850	18,008	13,621	18,008	16,616
98,850	98,900	18,020	13,632	18,020	16,628
98,900	98,950	18,032	13,643	18,032	16,640
98,950	99,000	18,044	13,654	18,044	16,652

99,000

At least	But less than	Single	Married filing jointly *	Married filing separately	Head of a household
99,000	99,050	18,056	13,665	18,056	16,664
99,050	99,100	18,068	13,676	18,068	16,676
99,100	99,150	18,080	13,687	18,080	16,688
99,150	99,200	18,092	13,698	18,092	16,700
99,200	99,250	18,104	13,709	18,104	16,712
99,250	99,300	18,116	13,720	18,116	16,724
99,300	99,350	18,128	13,731	18,128	16,736
99,350	99,400	18,140	13,742	18,140	16,748
99,400	99,450	18,152	13,753	18,152	16,760
99,450	99,500	18,164	13,764	18,164	16,772
99,500	99,550	18,176	13,775	18,176	16,784
99,550	99,600	18,188	13,786	18,188	16,796
99,600	99,650	18,200	13,797	18,200	16,808
99,650	99,700	18,212	13,808	18,212	16,820
99,700	99,750	18,224	13,819	18,224	16,832
99,750	99,800	18,236	13,830	18,236	16,844
99,800	99,850	18,248	13,841	18,248	16,856
99,850	99,900	18,260	13,852	18,260	16,868
99,900	99,950	18,272	13,863	18,272	16,880
99,950	100,000	18,284	13,874	18,284	16,892

$100,000
or over
use the Tax
Computation
Worksheet

* This column must also be used by a qualifying widow(er).

2018 Tax Computation Worksheet—Line 11a

See the instructions for line 11a in the Instructions for Form 1040 to see if you must use the worksheet below to figure your tax.

Note. If you're required to use this worksheet to figure the tax on an amount from another form or worksheet, such as the Qualified Dividends and Capital Gain Tax Worksheet, the Schedule D Tax Worksheet, Schedule J, Form 8615, or the Foreign Earned Income Tax Worksheet, enter the amount from that form or worksheet in column (a) of the row that applies to the amount you're looking up. Enter the result on the appropriate line of the form or worksheet that you're completing.

Section A—Use if your filing status is **Single**. Complete the row below that applies to you.

Taxable income. If line 10 is—	(a) Enter the amount from line 10	(b) Multiplication amount	(c) Multiply (a) by (b)	(d) Subtraction amount	Tax. Subtract (d) from (c). Enter the result here and on Form 1040, line 11a
At least $100,000 but not over $157,500	$	× 24% (0.24)	$	$ 5,710.50	$
Over $157,500 but not over $200,000	$	× 32% (0.32)	$	$ 18,310.50	$
Over $200,000 but not over $500,000	$	× 35% (0.35)	$	$ 24,310.50	$
Over $500,000	$	× 37% (0.37)	$	$ 34,310.50	$

Section B—Use if your filing status is **Married filing jointly** or **Qualifying widow(er)**. Complete the row below that applies to you.

Taxable income. If line 10 is—	(a) Enter the amount from line 10	(b) Multiplication amount	(c) Multiply (a) by (b)	(d) Subtraction amount	Tax. Subtract (d) from (c). Enter the result here and on Form 1040, line 11a
At least $100,000 but not over $165,000	$	× 22% (0.22)	$	$ 8,121.00	$
Over $165,000 but not over $315,000	$	× 24% (0.24)	$	$ 11,421.00	$
Over $315,000 but not over $400,000	$	× 32% (0.32)	$	$ 36,621.00	$
Over $400,000 but not over $600,000	$	× 35% (0.35)	$	$ 48,621.00	$
Over $600,000	$	× 37% (0.37)	$	$ 60,621.00	$

Section C—Use if your filing status is **Married filing separately**. Complete the row below that applies to you.

Taxable income. If line 10 is—	(a) Enter the amount from line 10	(b) Multiplication amount	(c) Multiply (a) by (b)	(d) Subtraction amount	Tax. Subtract (d) from (c). Enter the result here and on Form 1040, line 11a
At least $100,000 but not over $157,500	$	× 24% (0.24)	$	$ 5,710.50	$
Over $157,500 but not over $200,000	$	× 32% (0.32)	$	$ 18,310.50	$
Over $200,000 but not over $300,000	$	× 35% (0.35)	$	$ 24,310.50	$
Over $300,000	$	× 37% (0.37)	$	$ 30,310.50	$

Section D—Use if your filing status is **Head of household**. Complete the row below that applies to you.

Taxable income. If line 10 is—	(a) Enter the amount from line 10	(b) Multiplication amount	(c) Multiply (a) by (b)	(d) Subtraction amount	Tax. Subtract (d) from (c). Enter the result here and on Form 1040, line 11a
At least $100,000 but not over $157,500	$	× 24% (0.24)	$	$ 7,102.00	$
Over $157,500 but not over $200,000	$	× 32% (0.32)	$	$ 19,702.00	$
Over $200,000 but not over $500,000	$	× 35% (0.35)	$	$ 25,702.00	$
Over $500,000	$	× 37% (0.37)	$	$ 35,702.00	$

2018 Tax Rate Schedules

The Tax Rate Schedules are shown so you can see the tax rate that applies to all levels of taxable income. Don't use them to figure your tax. Instead, see chapter 29.

Schedule X—If your filing status is **Single**

If your taxable income is: Over—	But not over—	The tax is:	of the amount over—
$0	$9,525	.... 10%	$0
9,525	38,700	$952.50 + 12%	9,525
38,700	82,500	4,453.50 + 22%	38,700
82,500	157,500	14,089.50 + 24%	82,500
157,500	200,000	32,089.50 + 32%	157,500
200,000	500,000	45,689.50 + 35%	200,000
500,000	....	150,689.50 + 37%	500,000

Schedule Y-1—If your filing status is **Married filing jointly** or **Qualifying widow(er)**

If your taxable income is: Over—	But not over—	The tax is:	of the amount over—
$0	$19,050	.... 10%	$0
19,050	77,400	$1,905.00 + 12%	19,050
77,400	165,000	8,907.00 + 22%	77,400
165,000	315,000	28,179.00 + 24%	165,000
315,000	400,000	64,179.00 + 32%	315,000
400,000	600,000	91,379.00 + 35%	400,000
600,000	....	161,379.00 + 37%	600,000

Schedule Y-2—If your filing status is **Married filing separately**

If your taxable income is: Over—	But not over—	The tax is:	of the amount over—
$0	$9,525	.... 10%	$0
9,525	38,700	$952.50 + 12%	9,525
38,700	82,500	4,453.50 + 22%	38,700
82,500	157,500	14,089.50 + 24%	82,500
157,500	200,000	32,089.50 + 32%	157,500
200,000	300,000	45,689.50 + 35%	200,000
300,000	....	80,689.50 + 37%	300,000

Schedule Z—If your filing status is **Head of household**

If your taxable income is: Over—	But not over—	The tax is:	of the amount over—
$0	$13,600	.... 10%	$0
13,600	51,800	$1,360.00 + 12%	13,600
51,800	82,500	5,944.00 + 22%	51,800
82,500	157,500	12,698.00 + 24%	82,500
157,500	200,000	30,698.00 + 32%	157,500
200,000	500,000	44,298.00 + 35%	200,000
500,000	....	149,298.00 + 37%	500,000

Your Rights as a Taxpayer

This section explains your rights as a taxpayer and the processes for examination, appeal, collection, and refunds.

The Taxpayer Bill of Rights

1. The Right to Be Informed. Taxpayers have the right to know what they need to do to comply with the tax laws. They are entitled to clear explanations of the laws and IRS procedures in all tax forms, instructions, publications, notices, and correspondence. They have the right to be informed of IRS decisions about their tax accounts and to receive clear explanations of the outcomes.

2. The Right to Quality Service. Taxpayers have the right to receive prompt, courteous, and professional assistance in their dealings with the IRS, to be spoken to in a way they can easily understand, to receive clear and easily understandable communications from the IRS, and to speak to a supervisor about inadequate service.

3. The Right to Pay No More than the Correct Amount of Tax. Taxpayers have the right to pay only the amount of tax legally due, including interest and penalties, and to have the IRS apply all tax payments properly.

4. The Right to Challenge the IRS's Position and Be Heard. Taxpayers have the right to raise objections and provide additional documentation in response to formal IRS actions or proposed actions, to expect that the IRS will consider their timely objections and documentation promptly and fairly, and to receive a response if the IRS does not agree with their position.

5. The Right to Appeal an IRS Decision in an Independent Forum. Taxpayers are entitled to a fair and impartial administrative appeal of most IRS decisions, including many penalties, and have the right to receive a written response regarding the Office of Appeals' decision. Taxpayers generally have the right to take their cases to court.

6. The Right to Finality. Taxpayers have the right to know the maximum amount of time they have to challenge the IRS's position as well as the maximum amount of time the IRS has to audit a particular tax year or collect a tax debt. Taxpay-ers have the right to know when the IRS has finished an audit.

7. The Right to Privacy. Taxpay-ers have the right to expect that any IRS inquiry, examination, or enforcement action will comply with the law and be no more intrusive than necessary, and will respect all due process rights, including search and seizure protections and will provide, where applicable, a collection due process hearing.

8. The Right to Confidentiality. Taxpayers have the right to expect that any information they provide to the IRS will not be disclosed unless authorized by the taxpayer or by law. Taxpayers have the right to expect appropriate action will be taken against employees, return preparers, and others who wrong-fully use or disclose taxpayer return information.

9. The Right to Retain Representation. Taxpayers have the right to retain an authorized representative of their choice to represent them in their dealings with the IRS. Taxpayers have the right to seek assistance from a Low Income Taxpayer Clinic if they cannot afford representation.

10. The Right to a Fair and Just Tax System. Taxpayers have the right to expect the tax system to consider facts and circumstances that might affect their underlying liabilities, ability to pay, or ability to provide information timely. Taxpay-ers have the right to receive assistance from the Taxpayer Advocate Service if they are experiencing financial difficulty or if the IRS has not resolved their tax issues properly and timely through its normal channels.

Examinations (Audits)

We accept most taxpayers' returns as filed. If we inquire about your return or select it for examination, it does not suggest that you are dishonest. The inquiry or examination may or may not result in more tax. We may close your case without change; or, you may receive a refund.

The process of selecting a return for examination usually begins in one of two ways. First, we use computer programs to identify returns that may have incorrect amounts. These programs may be based on information returns, such as Forms 1099 and W-2, on studies of past examinations, or on certain issues identified by compliance projects. Second, we use information from outside sources that indicates that a return may have incorrect amounts. These sources may include newspapers, public records, and individuals. If we determine that the information is accurate and reliable, we may use it to select a return for examination.

Publication 556, Examination of Returns, Appeal Rights, and Claims for Refund, explains the rules and procedures that we follow in examinations. The following sections give an overview of how we conduct examinations.

By mail. We handle many examinations and inquiries by mail. We will send you a letter with either a request for more information or a reason why we believe a change to your return may be needed. You can respond by mail or you can request a personal interview with an examiner. If you mail us the requested information or provide an explanation, we may or may not agree with you, and we will explain the reasons for any changes. Please do not hesitate to write to us about anything you do not understand.

By interview. If we notify you that we will conduct your examination through a personal interview, or you request such an interview, you have the right to ask that the examination take place at a reasonable time and place that is convenient for both you and the IRS. If our examiner proposes any changes to your return, he or she will explain the reasons for the changes. If you do not agree with these changes, you can meet with the examiner's supervisor.

Repeat examinations. If we examined your return for the same items in either of the 2 previous years and proposed no change to your tax liability, please contact us as soon as possible so we can see if we should discontinue the examination.

Appeals

If you do not agree with the examiner's proposed changes, you can appeal them to the Appeals Office of the IRS. Most differences can be settled without expensive and time-consuming court trials. Your appeal rights are explained in detail in both Publication 5, Your Appeal Rights and How To Prepare a Protest If You Don't Agree, and Publication 556, Examination of Returns, Appeal Rights, and Claims for Refund.

If you do not wish to use the Appeals Office or disagree with its findings, you may be able to take your case to the U.S. Tax Court, U.S. Court of Federal Claims, or the U.S. District Court where you live. If you take your case to court, the IRS will have the burden of proving certain facts if you kept adequate records to show your tax liability, cooperated with the IRS, and meet certain other conditions. If the court agrees with you on most issues in your case and finds that our position was largely unjustified, you may be able to recover some of your administrative and litigation costs. You will not be eligible to recover these costs unless you tried to resolve your case administratively, including going through the appeals system, and you gave us the information necessary to resolve the case.

Collections

Publication 594, The IRS Collection Process, explains your rights and responsibilities regarding payment of federal taxes. It describes:

- What to do when you owe taxes. It describes what to do if you get a tax bill and what to do if you think your bill is wrong. It also covers making installment payments, delaying collection action, and submitting an offer in compromise.

- IRS collection actions. It covers liens, releasing a lien, levies, releasing a levy, seizures and sales, and release of property.

- IRS certification to the State Department of a seriously delinquent tax debt, which will generally result in denial of a passport application and may lead to revocation of a passport.

Your collection appeal rights are explained in detail in Publication 1660, Collection Appeal Rights.

Innocent spouse relief. Generally, both you and your spouse are each responsible for paying the full amount of tax, interest, and penalties due on your joint return. However, if you qualify for innocent spouse relief, you may be relieved of part or all of the joint liability. To request relief, you must file Form 8857, Request for Innocent Spouse Relief. For more information on innocent spouse relief, see Publication 971, Innocent Spouse Relief, and Form 8857.

Potential third party contacts. Generally, the IRS will deal directly with you or your duly authorized representative. However, we sometimes talk with other persons if we need information that you have been unable to provide, or to verify information we have received. If we do contact other persons, such as a neighbor, bank, employer, or employees, we will generally need to tell them limited information, such as your name. The law prohibits us from disclosing any more information than is necessary to obtain or verify the information we are seeking. Our need to contact other persons may continue as long as there is activity in your case. If we do contact other persons, you have a right to request a list of those contacted. Your request can be made by telephone, in writing, or during a personal interview.

Refunds

You may file a claim for refund if you think you paid too much tax. You must generally file the claim within 3 years from the date you filed your original return or 2 years from the date you paid the tax, whichever is later. The law generally provides for interest on your refund if it is not paid within 45 days of the date you filed your return or claim for refund. Publication 556, Examination of Returns, Appeal Rights, and Claims for Refund, has more information on refunds.

If you were due a refund but you did not file a return, you generally must file your return within 3 years from the date the return was due (including extensions) to get that refund.

Taxpayer Advocate Service

TAS is an *independent* organization within the IRS that can help protect your taxpayer rights. We can offer you help if your tax problem is causing a hardship, or you've tried but haven't been able to resolve your problem with the IRS. If you qualify for our assistance, which is always free, we will do everything possible to help you. Visit *TaxpayerAdvocate.irs.gov* or call 1-877-777-4778.

Tax Information

The IRS provides the following sources for forms, publications, and additional information.

- *Internet*: IRS.gov.
- *Tax Questions*: *IRS.gov/help/tax-law-questions* and *How To Get Tax Help*.
- *Forms and Publications*: *IRS.gov/Forms* and *IRS.gov/OrderForms*.
- *Small Business Ombudsman*: A small business entity can participate in the regulatory process and comment on enforcement actions of the IRS by calling 1-888-REG-FAIR.
- *Treasury Inspector General for Tax Administration*: You can confidentially report misconduct, waste, fraud, or abuse by an IRS employee by calling 1-800-366-4484. People who are deaf, hard of hearing, or have a speech disability and who have access to TTY/TDD equipment can call 1-800-877-8339. You can remain anonymous.

How To Get Tax Help

If you have questions about a tax issue, need help preparing your tax return, or want to download free publications, forms, or instructions, go to IRS.gov and find resources that can help you right away.

Tax reform. Major tax reform legislation impacting individuals, businesses, and tax-exempt entities was approved by Congress in the Tax Cuts and Jobs Act on December 22, 2017. Go to *IRS.gov/ TaxReform* for information and updates on how this legislation affects your taxes.

Preparing and filing your tax return. Find free options to prepare and file your return on IRS.gov or in your local community if you qualify.

The Volunteer Income Tax Assistance (VITA) program offers free tax help to people who generally make $55,000 or less, persons with disabilities, and limited-English-speaking taxpayers who need help preparing their own tax returns. The Tax Counseling for the Elderly (TCE) program offers free tax help for all taxpayers, particularly those who are 60 years of age and older. TCE volunteers specialize in answering questions about pensions and retirement-related issues unique to seniors.

You can go to IRS.gov to see your options for preparing and filing your return which include the following.

- **Free File.** Go to *IRS.gov/ FreeFile* to see if you qualify to use brand-name software to prepare and *e-file* your federal tax return for free.

- **VITA.** Go to *IRS.gov/VITA*, download the free IRS2Go app, or call 800-906-9887 to find the nearest VITA location for free tax return preparation.

- **TCE.** Go to *IRS.gov/TCE*, download the free IRS2Go app, or call 888-227-7669 to find the nearest TCE location for free tax return preparation.

Getting answers to your tax questions. On IRS.gov, get answers to your tax questions anytime, anywhere.

- Go to *IRS.gov/Help* for a variety of tools that will help you get answers to some of the most common tax questions.

- Go to *IRS.gov/ITA* for the Interactive Tax Assistant, a tool that will ask you questions on a number of tax law topics

and provide answers. You can print the entire interview and the final response for your records.

- You may also be able to access tax law information in your electronic filing software.

Getting tax forms and publications. Go to *IRS.gov/Forms* to view, download, or print all of the forms and publications you may need. You can also download and view popular tax publications and instructions (including the 1040 instructions) on mobile devices as an eBook at no charge. Or you can go to *IRS.gov/OrderForms* to place an order and have forms mailed to you within 10 business days.

Access your online account (individual taxpayers only). Go to *IRS.gov/Account* to securely access information about your federal tax account.

- View the amount you owe, pay online, or set up an online payment agreement.

- Access your tax records online.

- Review the past 24 months of your payment history.

- Go to *IRS.gov/SecureAccess* to review the required identity authentication process.

Using direct deposit. The fastest way to receive a tax refund is to combine direct deposit and IRS *e-file*. Direct deposit securely and electronically transfers your refund directly into your financial account. Eight in 10 taxpayers use direct deposit to receive their refund. The IRS issues more than 90% of refunds in less than 21 days.

Refund timing for returns claiming certain credits. The IRS can't issue refunds before mid-February 2019 for returns that claimed the earned income credit (EIC) or the additional child tax credit (ACTC). This applies to the entire refund, not just the portion associated with these credits.

Getting a transcript or copy of a return. The quickest way to get a copy of your tax transcript is to go to *IRS.gov/Transcripts*. Click on either "Get Transcript Online" or "Get Transcript by Mail" to order a copy of your transcript. If you prefer, you can:

- Order your transcript by calling 800-908-9946, or

- Mail Form 4506-T or Form 4506T-EZ (both available on IRS.gov).

Using online tools to help prepare your return. Go to *IRS.gov/ Tools* for the following.

- The *Earned Income Tax Credit Assistant* (*IRS.gov/ EITCAssistant*) determines if you're eligible for the EIC.

- The *Online EIN Application* (*IRS.gov/EIN*) helps you get an employer identification number.

- The *IRS Withholding Calculator* (*IRS.gov/W4App*) estimates the amount you should have withheld from your paycheck for federal income tax purposes and can help you perform a "paycheck checkup."

- The *First Time Homebuyer Credit Account Look-up* (*IRS.gov/HomeBuyer*) tool provides information on your repayments and account balance.

- The *Sales Tax Deduction Calculator* (*IRS.gov/SalesTax*) figures the amount you can claim if you itemize deductions on Schedule A (Form 1040), choose not to claim state and local income taxes, and you didn't save your receipts showing the sales tax you paid.

Resolving tax-related identity theft issues.

- The IRS doesn't initiate contact with taxpayers by email or telephone to request personal or financial information. This includes any type of electronic communication, such as text messages and social media channels.

- Go to *IRS.gov/IDProtection* for information.

- If your SSN has been lost or stolen or you suspect you're a victim of tax-related identity theft, visit *IRS.gov/ IdentityTheft* to learn what steps you should take.

Checking on the status of your refund.

- Go to *IRS.gov/Refunds*.

- The IRS can't issue refunds before mid-February 2019, for returns that claimed the EIC or the ACTC. This applies to the entire refund, not just the por-

tion associated with these credits.

- Download the official IRS2Go app to your mobile device to check your refund status.

- Call the automated refund hotline at 800-829-1954.

Making a tax payment. The IRS uses the latest encryption technology to ensure your electronic payments are safe and secure. You can make electronic payments online, by phone, and from a mobile device using the IRS2Go app. Paying electronically is quick, easy, and faster than mailing in a check or money order. Go to *IRS.gov/ Payments* to make a payment using any of the following options.

- *IRS Direct Pay*: Pay your individual tax bill or estimated tax payment directly from your checking or savings account at no cost to you.

- **Debit or credit card:** Choose an approved payment processor to pay online, by phone, and by mobile device.

- **Electronic Funds Withdrawal:** Offered only when filing your federal taxes using tax return preparation software or through a tax professional.

- **Electronic Federal Tax Payment System:** Best option for businesses. Enrollment is required.

- **Check or money order:** Mail your payment to the address listed on the notice or instructions.

- **Cash:** You may be able to pay your taxes with cash at a participating retail store.

What if I can't pay now? Go to *IRS.gov/Payments* for more information about your options.

- Apply for an *online payment agreement* (*IRS.gov/OPA*) to meet your tax obligation in monthly installments if you can't pay your taxes in full today. Once you complete the online process, you will receive immediate notification of whether your agreement has been approved.

- Use the *Offer in Compromise Pre-Qualifier* (*IRS.gov/OIC*) to see if you can settle your tax debt for less than the full amount you owe.

Checking the status of an amended return. Go to *IRS.gov/WMAR* to track the status of Form 1040X amended returns. Please note that it can take up to 3 weeks from the date you mailed your amended return for it to show up in our system and processing it can take up to 16 weeks.

Understanding an IRS notice or letter. Go to *IRS.gov/Notices* to find additional information about responding to an IRS notice or letter.

Contacting your local IRS office. Keep in mind, many questions can be answered on IRS.gov without visiting an IRS Tax Assistance Center (TAC). Go to *IRS.gov/LetUsHelp* for the topics people ask about most. If you still need help, IRS TACs provide tax help when a tax issue can't be handled online or by phone. All TACs now provide service by appointment so you'll know in advance that you can get the service you need without long wait times. Before you visit, go to *IRS.gov/TACLocator* to find the nearest TAC, check hours, available services, and appointment options. Or, on the IRS2Go app, under the Stay Connected tab, choose the Contact Us option and click on "Local Offices."

Watching IRS videos. The IRS Video portal (*IRSVideos.gov*) contains video and audio presentations for individuals, small businesses, and tax professionals.

Getting tax information in other languages. For taxpayers whose native language isn't English, we have the following resources available. Taxpayers can find information on IRS.gov in the following languages:

- *Spanish* (*IRS.gov/Spanish*).
- *Chinese* (*IRS.gov/Chinese*).
- *Vietnamese* (*IRS.gov/Vietnamese*).
- *Korean* (*IRS.gov/Korean*).
- *Russian* (*IRS.gov/Russian*).

The IRS TACs provide over-the-phone interpreter service in over 170 languages, and the service is available free to taxpayers.

The Taxpayer Advocate Service (TAS) Is Here To Help You

What is TAS?

TAS is an *independent* organization within the IRS that helps taxpayers and protects taxpayer rights. Their job is to ensure that every taxpayer is treated fairly and that you know and understand your rights under the *Taxpayer Bill of Rights*.

How Can You Learn About Your Taxpayer Rights?

The Taxpayer Bill of Rights describes 10 basic rights that all taxpayers have when dealing with the IRS. Go to *TaxpayerAdvocate.IRS.gov* to help you understand *what these rights mean to you* and how they apply. These are **your** rights. Know them. Use them.

What Can TAS Do For You?

TAS can help you resolve problems that you can't resolve with the IRS. And their service is free. If you qualify for their assistance, you will be assigned to one advocate who will work with you throughout the process and will do everything possible to resolve your issue. TAS can help you if:

- Your problem is causing financial difficulty for you, your family, or your business;
- You face (or your business is facing) an immediate threat of adverse action; or
- You've tried repeatedly to contact the IRS but no one has responded, or the IRS hasn't responded by the date promised.

How Can You Reach TAS?

TAS has offices *in every state, the District of Columbia, and Puerto Rico*. Your local advocate's number is in your local directory and at *TaxpayerAdvocate.IRS.gov/Contact-Us*. You can also call them at 877-777-4778.

How Else Does TAS Help Taxpayers?

TAS works to resolve large-scale problems that affect many taxpayers. If you know of one of these broad issues, please report it to them at *IRS.gov/SAMS*.

TAS also has a website, *Tax Reform Changes*, which shows you how the new tax law may change your future tax filings and helps you plan for these changes. The information is categorized by tax topic in the order of the IRS Form 1040. Go to *TaxChanges.us* for more information

Low Income Taxpayer Clinics (LITCs)

LITCs are independent from the IRS. LITCs represent individuals whose income is below a certain level and need to resolve tax problems with the IRS, such as audits, appeals, and tax collection disputes. In addition, clinics can provide information about taxpayer rights and responsibilities in different languages for individuals who speak English as a second language. Services are offered for free or a small fee. To find a clinic near you, visit *TaxpayerAdvocate.IRS.gov/LITCmap* or see IRS Pub. 4134, *Low Income Taxpayer Clinic List*.

Index

To help us develop a more useful index, please let us know if you have ideas for index entries. See "Comments and Suggestions" in the "Introduction" for the ways you can reach us.

Real estate taxes *(Cont.)*

Where To File

Mail your return to the address shown below that applies to you. If you want to use a private delivery service, see *Private delivery services* in chapter 1.

TIP

Envelopes without enough postage will be returned to you by the post office. Your envelope may need additional postage if it contains more than five pages or is oversized (for example, it is over 1/4 inch thick). Also, include your complete return address.

IF you live in...	THEN send your return to the address below if you are requesting a refund or are NOT enclosing a payment...	OR send your return to the address below if you ARE enclosing a payment (check or money order)...
Florida, Louisiana, Mississippi, Texas	Department of the Treasury Internal Revenue Service Austin, TX 73301-0002	Internal Revenue Service P.O. Box 1214 Charlotte, NC 28201-1214
Alaska, Arizona, California, Colorado, Hawaii, Idaho, Nevada, New Mexico, Oregon, Utah, Washington, Wyoming	Department of the Treasury Internal Revenue Service Fresno, CA 93888-0002	Internal Revenue Service P.O. Box 7704 San Francisco, CA 94120-7704
Arkansas, Illinois, Indiana, Iowa, Kansas, Michigan, Minnesota, Montana, Nebraska, North Dakota, Ohio, Oklahoma, South Dakota, Wisconsin	Department of the Treasury Internal Revenue Service Fresno, CA 93888-0002	Internal Revenue Service P.O. Box 802501 Cincinnati, OH 45280-2501
Alabama, Georgia, Kentucky, New Jersey, North Carolina, South Carolina, Tennessee, Virginia	Department of the Treasury Internal Revenue Service Kansas City, MO 64999-0002	Internal Revenue Service P.O. Box 931000 Louisville, KY 40293-1000
Delaware, Maine, Massachusetts, Missouri, New Hampshire, New York, Vermont	Department of the Treasury Internal Revenue Service Kansas City, MO 64999-0002	Internal Revenue Service P.O. Box 37008 Hartford, CT 06176-7008
Connecticut, District of Columbia, Maryland, Pennsylvania, Rhode Island, West Virginia	Department of the Treasury Internal Revenue Service Ogden, UT 84201-0002	Internal Revenue Service P.O. Box 37910 Hartford, CT 06176-7910
A foreign country, U.S. possession or territory*, or use an APO or FPO address, or file Form 2555, 2555-EZ, or 4563, or are a dual-status alien	Department of the Treasury Internal Revenue Service Austin, TX 73301-0215	Internal Revenue Service P.O. Box 1303 Charlotte, NC 28201-1303

* If you live in American Samoa, Puerto Rico, Guam, the U.S. Virgin Islands, or the Northern Mariana Islands, see Pub. 570.

Order Form
for Forms and
Publications

You can view and download the tax forms and publications you need at IRS.gov/Forms. *You also can place an order for forms at* IRS.gov/OrderForms *to avoid having to complete and mail the order form.*

The most frequently ordered forms and publications are listed on the order form below. You will receive two copies of each form, one copy of the instructions, and one copy of each publication you order. To help reduce waste, please order only the items you need to prepare your return.

How To Use the Order Form

Circle the items you need on the order form. Use the blank spaces to order items not listed. If you need more space, attach a separate sheet of paper.

Print or type your name and address accurately in the space provided on the order form to ensure delivery of your order. Enclose the order form in an envelope and mail it to the IRS address shown next. You should receive your order within 10 business days after we receive your request.

Don't send your tax return to the address shown here. Instead, see *Where To File.*
Mail Your Order Form To:
Internal Revenue Service
1201 N. Mitsubishi Motorway
Bloomington, IL 61705-6613

▲ *Cut here* ▲

Save Money and Time by Going Online!
Download or order these and other forms and publications at IRS.gov/Forms

Order Form

Please print.

Name

Postal mailing address | Apt./Suite/Room

City | State | ZIP code

Foreign country | International postal code

Daytime phone number
(   )

Circle the forms and publications you need. The instructions for any form you order will be included.

Use the **blank** spaces to order items not listed.

Use your QR Reader app on your smartphone to scan this code and get connected to the IRS Forms and Publications homepage.

1040*	Schedule F (1040)	2106	8606	Pub. 1	Pub. 527	Pub. 587	
Schedule A (1040)	Schedule H (1040)	2441	8822	Pub. 334	Pub. 529	Pub. 590-A	
Schedule B (1040)	Schedule J (1040)	3903	8829	Pub. 463	Pub. 535	Pub. 590-B	
Schedule C (1040)	Schedule R (1040)	4562	8863	Pub. 501	Pub. 547	Pub. 596	
Schedule C-EZ (1040)	Schedule SE (1040)	4684	8917	Pub. 502	Pub. 550	Pub. 915	
Schedule D (1040)	Schedule 8812 (1040)	4868	8959	Pub. 505	Pub. 551	Pub. 946	
Form 8949	1040-ES (2019)	5405	8960	Pub. 523	Pub. 554	Pub. 970	
Schedule E (1040)	1040-V	6251	8962	Pub. 525	Pub. 575	Pub. 972	
Schedule EIC (1040)	1040X	8283	8965	Pub. 526	Pub. 583	Pub. 4681	

* If you order Form 1040, you also will receive Schedules 1 through 6.

Made in the USA
Lexington, KY
19 July 2019